Questioning Capital Punishment

The death penalty has inspired controversy for centuries. Raising questions regarding capital punishment rather than answering them, *Questioning Capital Punishment* offers the footing needed to allow for more informed consideration and analysis of these controversies. Acker edits judicial decisions that have addressed constitutional challenges to capital punishment and its administration in the United States and uses complementary materials to offer historical, empirical, and normative perspectives about death penalty policies and practices. This book is ideal for upper-level undergraduate and graduate classes in criminal justice.

James R. Acker is a Distinguished Teaching Professor in the School of Criminal Justice at the University at Albany. He received his JD at Duke University and his PhD in criminal justice at the University at Albany. He has edited several books and authored numerous scholarly articles that focus on legal and empirical aspects of capital punishment. In 2005, Acker helped establish the National Death Penalty Archive at the University at Albany, a repository that houses one of the largest and most significant collections of historical materials relating to the death penalty in the United States. His other academic interests include the integration of social science into law, legal doctrine relating to criminal procedure, criminal law, and juvenile justice, and issues pertaining to miscarriages of justice.

Criminology and Justice Studies Series
Edited by Shaun L. Gabbidon, *Penn State Harrisburg*

Criminology and Justice Studies offers works that make both intellectual and stylistic innovations in the study of crime and criminal justice. The goal of the series is to publish works that model the best scholarship and thinking in the criminology and criminal justice field today, but in a style that connects that scholarship to a wider audience including advanced undergraduates, graduate students, and the general public. The works in this series help fill the gap between academic monographs and encyclopedic textbooks by making innovative scholarship accessible to a large audience without the superficiality of many texts.

Books in the Series

Published:

Biosocial Criminology: New Directions in Theory and Research
Edited by Anthony Walsh and Kevin M. Beaver

Community Policing in America
Jeremy M. Wilson

Criminal Justice Theory: Explaining the Nature and Behavior of Criminal Justice
Edited by David E. Duffee and Edward R. Maguire

Lifers: Seeking Redemption in Prison
John Irwin

Race, Law and American Society: 1607 to Present
Gloria J. Browne-Marshall

Today's White Collar Crime
Hank J. Brightman

White Collar Crime: Opportunity Perspectives
Michael Benson and Sally Simpson

The New Criminal Justice: American Communities and the Changing World of Crime Control
John Klofas, Natalie Hipple, and Edmund McGarrell

The Policing of Terrorism: Organizational and Global Perspectives
Mathieu Deflem

Criminological Perspectives in Race and Crime, 2/e
Shaun Gabbidon

Corrections
Jeanne Stinchcomb

Community Policing
Michael Palmiotto

A Theory of African American Offending
James Unnever and Shaun Gabbidon

When Crime Appears: The Role of Emergence
Jean McGloin, Christopher Sullivan, and Leslie Kennedy

Voices from Criminal Justice
Edited by Heith Copes and Mark Pogrebin

Crime and the Life Course, 2/e
Michael Benson

Wrongful Convictions and Miscarriages of Justice
Edited by C. Ron Huff and Martin Killias

Human Trafficking: Interdisciplinary Perspectives
Edited by Mary C. Burke

Race, Law and American Society, 2/e: 1607 to Present
Gloria J. Browne-Marshall

Research Methods in Crime and Justice
Brian Withrow

Crime and Networks
Edited by Carlo Morselli

Wrongful Conviction and Criminal Justice Reform
Edited by Marvin Zalman and Julia Carrano

Questioning Capital Punishment: Law, Policy, and Practice
James R. Acker

Titles of Related Interest

Due Process Denied: Detentions and Deportations in the United States
Tanya Golash-Boza

Torture: A Sociology of Violence and Human Rights
Lisa Hajjar

Beyond the Prison Industrial Complex: Crime and Incarceration in the 21st Century
Kevin Wehr and Elyshia Aseltine

From Trafficking to Terror: Constructing a Global Social Problem
Pardis Mahdavi

The Pains of Mass Imprisonment
Benjamin Fleury-Steiner and Jamie Longazel

Reviews for *Questioning Capital Punishment*:

"This is a remarkable book by a renowned teacher and scholar. It tells about America's return to capital punishment after it was outlawed in 1972. The story is keyed to the twists and turns in the thinking and writing of Supreme Court Justices whose decisions have determined the fate of thousands of convicted murderers. And it is timely because the future of the death penalty appears to be moving from the hands of the High Court to those of the people like you and me. In the past dozen years six states have abandoned the death penalty and the pace appears to be picking up."
—**William Bowers**, Director of the Capital Jury Project

"*Questioning Capital Punishment* offers an outstanding, comprehensive overview of one of our most enduring legal controversies, the death penalty. In clear and engaging prose, Acker first delineates the justifications for and against this most extreme punishment, then illustrates the many challenges in its application, including its legal complexity and the threats it poses to justice and fairness in its administration. This is an essential text for students and others interested in learning more about the contemporary American capital punishment system."
—**Mona Lynch**, School of Social Ecology, University of California, Irvine

"Balanced, thoughtful and thought-provoking, this fine text is a well-written and highly engaging tour of the main ways we should examine capital punishment when we think carefully about our ultimate penal sanction."
—**Robert Johnson**, Justice, Law, and Criminology, American University, author of *Condemned to Die* and *Death Work*.

"Questioning Capital Punishment offers a thoughtful and well-edited compendium of materials and commentary that introduce the difficult moral and policy issues surrounding capital punishment and explain the complex constitutional doctrines and legal institutions that shape the imposition of the death penalty in the United States today. In the rapidly changing political and legal landscape around capital punishment, this volume offers up-to-the-minute materials and fair-minded questions to counter the partisan bromides that often dominate the conversation. A terrific introduction to a timely and important issue."
—**Carol Steiker**, Harvard Law School

"Full of fascinating details, this book raises important, thought provoking questions about the ultimate penalty. It is an eloquent, well documented exploration of a wide range of issues interspersing the author's own cogent discussion with quotes from landmark court cases and recognized social scientists and legal philosophers."
—**Wanda D. Foglia**, Law and Justice Studies, Rowan University

Questioning Capital Punishment

Law, Policy, and Practice

James R. Acker

Routledge
Taylor & Francis Group

NEW YORK AND LONDON

First published 2014
by Routledge
711 Third Avenue, New York, NY 10017

and by Routledge
2 Park Square, Milton Park, Abingdon, Oxon, OX14 4RN

Routledge is an imprint of the Taylor & Francis Group, an informa business

Library of Congress Cataloging-in-Publication Data

Acker, James R., 1951– author.
Questioning capital punishment : law, policy, and practice / by James R. Acker.
    pages cm. — (Criminology and justice studies series)
  Includes bibliographical references and index.
  1. Capital punishment—United States. I. Title.
KF9227.C2A97   2014
364.660973—dc23   2013049185

ISBN: 978-0-415-63943-9 (hbk)
ISBN: 978-0-415-63944-6 (pbk)
ISBN: 978-1-315-77605-7 (ebk)

Typeset in Adobe Caslon Pro
by Apex CoVantage, LLC

Printed and bound in the United States of America by Sheridan Books, Inc. (a Sheridan Group Company).

To Jenny, Elizabeth, Anna, and Ethan.

And, to students—past, present, and future—who have been and remain willing to grapple with the many fundamental questions of justice embedded in the laws, policies, and principles that envelop capital punishment.

Contents

Preface

The Death Penalty in America: A Brief Introduction and Overview

However else it might be described—and the choices are many, covering the full spectrum that includes the ultimate form of justice and the ultimate injustice—the death penalty is controversial. It has been since the country's beginning days. Capital punishment was authorized and practiced in all of the original states and under federal law. It has never been without both supporters and detractors. Several of the nation's Founding Fathers were familiar with the recently translated treatise, *On Crimes and Punishments,* written in 1764 by the Italian philosopher and jurist, Cesare Beccaria. The first sentence in the chapter devoted to the death penalty in this provocative work left little doubt about where Beccaria stood on the issue: "This useless prodigality of torments, which has never made men better, has prompted me to examine whether death is really useful and just in a well-organized government."[1] His resounding repudiation of capital punishment in favor of life imprisonment, which at least some of his contemporaries found persuasive, contains kernels of many of the essential arguments made against the death penalty today.[2]

This is not to say that Beccaria's arguments, or those advanced by other opponents of capital punishment, have carried the day in this country. In an October 2013 Gallup Poll, a declining yet still decisive majority (60%) of respondents replied affirmatively to the question, "Are you in favor of the death penalty for a person convicted of murder?"[3] At the end of 2013, 32 states, the federal government, and the United States Military authorized the death penalty for aggravated murder[4] and, less regularly, for treason or other crimes threatening sovereign authority.[5] Well in excess of 3,000 prisoners were under sentence of death nationwide.[6] More than 1,350 executions had been carried out since 1977,[7] when they resumed after the Supreme Court affirmed the constitutionality of the "guided discretion" capital sentencing legislation[8] enacted in the wake of *Furman v. Georgia* (1972).[9] In that landmark case, a bare majority of the justices, each offering a different rationale, relied on the Eighth Amendment's prohibition against cruel and unusual punishments to invalidate all death sentences then in effect throughout the country.

Notwithstanding this showing of support for the death penalty, there is evidence that many Americans are ambivalent about capital punishment, if not opposed to it. As recently as 1994, four out of five (80%) Gallup Poll respondents reported favoring the death penalty for murder, a considerably higher rate than the 60% measure obtained in 2013.[10] When asked to choose whether death or life imprisonment without parole (LWOP) "is the better penalty for murder," respondents in 2010 were almost evenly divided: 49% favored capital punishment, 46% favored LWOP, and 6% had no opinion.[11]

The past decade has seen six states dispense with their capital-punishment laws. New Jersey lawmakers repealed the state death penalty statute in 2007 and legislative repeal soon followed in four additional states (New Mexico, in 2009; Illinois, in 2011; Connecticut, in 2012; and Maryland, in 2013).[12] In New York, the legislature declined to revive its capital punishment law after the state's highest court declared it unconstitutional in 2004.[13]

Newly imposed death sentences have dropped dramatically since the mid-1990s. In 1995, 311 offenders were sentenced to death across the country. By 2000, the number of new death sentences had fallen to 224. Annual totals dropped to 140 in 2005; 109 in 2010; and 77 in 2012.[14] Executions also have been in decline. From a modern-era high of 98 in 1999, 60 or fewer executions have been carried out annually since 2004, with 43 occurring in both 2011 and 2012.[15]

My Purpose for Writing this Book, Disciplinary Perspectives, and the Intended Audience

As even these basic facts and developments suggest, controversy surrounding the death penalty has long endured and it continues unabated. The materials in the following pages identify the principal fault lines and explore the dominant issues that help account for the widely divergent and often passionately held views about capital punishment. They are not presented to persuade or to promote the merits of different positions that might be taken, but rather to help stimulate more critical thought and discussion about them. The aim is to raise questions rather than purport to answer them, and to offer the footing needed to allow for more informed consideration and analysis of the key premises and points of disputation along the way.

The readings draw on diverse disciplines and methodologies, as is necessary to do justice to the rich mix of issues that nestle at the core of the death penalty and its several dimensions. Capital punishment is an instrument of law. It is imposed pursuant to procedures that have been shaped in significant part by the constitutional rulings of the United States Supreme Court. Accordingly, a number of prominent Supreme Court decisions pertaining to the death penalty are presented in the pages that follow. The decisions have been edited substantially because of their length, although I have tried my best to preserve the essential arguments and reasoning employed by the justices. Occasional excerpts from oral arguments before the Supreme Court also are included, as are provisions from select death-penalty statutes and the views of legal scholars as expressed in law review articles and legal treatises.

Also included are discussions of research studies that have addressed important empirical dimensions of capital punishment—for example, its effectiveness as a deterrent to murder, its financial costs relative to life imprisonment, evidence of racial disparities or other arbitrariness in charging and sentencing decisions, the relationship between "death qualifying" capital trial juries and trial outcomes, and many others. Additional readings focus on the ethics and morality of the death penalty, on its history, and on the politics of capital punishment. The variety and complexity of the foundational questions and issues pertaining to the death penalty invite and make relevant a broad array of disciplinary perspectives.

This volume is intended for anyone who is interested in exploring the history and current status of capital punishment in this country, including its legal foundations, its justifications, and its empirical and policy dimensions. It is suitable for use in academic classes in criminal justice, political science, history, sociology, and related disciplines that either focus specifically on the death penalty, or else devote attention to issues of punishment and the administration of justice more generally. The readings are appropriate for undergraduate students and can serve as well in graduate seminars. The materials are designed to stimulate critical thinking and analysis and, hopefully, correspondingly lively discussion.

The book is divided into three parts. The initial part examines the primary justifications offered in support of capital punishment as well as the principal objections raised against them. The focus then shifts to substantive (threshold eligibility) and procedural (selection) aspects of capital sentencing, including the performance of key actors who figure into punishment decisions. The last section covers post-conviction issues, including appeals, life under sentence of death, clemency, and executions. Entire volumes could easily be devoted to any and all of the individual topics addressed within the book's main sections. What can be presented here nevertheless is intended to help illuminate the undercurrents of the many important controversies surrounding the death penalty and, hopefully, also help inspire further reflection about them.

Endnotes

1. Cesare Beccaria, *On Crimes and Punishments* 45, trans. Henry Paolucci (Indianapolis: Bobbs-Merrill Co., orig. 1764/1963).
2. John D. Bessler, *Cruel & Unusual: The American Death Penalty and the Founders' Eighth Amendment* (Boston: Northeastern University Press 2012).
3. Gallup, "Death Penalty," retrieved November 15, 2013 from www.gallup.com/poll/1606/death-penalty.aspx.
4. Death Penalty Information Center, "States With and Without the Death Penalty," retrieved November 15, 2013 from www.deathpenaltyinfo.org/states-and-without-death-penalty.
5. U.S. Dept. of Justice, Bureau of Justice Statistics, *Capital Punishment, 2011—Statistical Tables* 5, Table 1 (July 2013), retrieved August 15, 2013 from www.deathpenaltyinfo.org/documents/cp11st.pdf.

6. Death Penalty Information Center, "Death Row Inmates by State," retrieved November 15, 2013 from www.deathpenaltyinfo.org/death-row-inmates-state-and-size-death-row-year#state.

7. Death Penalty Information Center, "Executions by Year," retrieved December 6, 2013 from http://www.deathpenaltyinfo.org/executions-year.

8. *Gregg v. Georgia,* 428 U.S. 153 (1976); *Proffitt v. Florida,* 428 U.S. 242 (1976); *Jurek v. Texas,* 428 U.S. 262 (1976).

9. 408 U.S. 238 (1972).

10. Gallup, *supra* note 3.

11. Frank Newport, "In U.S., 64% Support Death Penalty in Cases of Murder," (Nov. 8, 2010), retrieved August 15, 2013 from www.gallup.com/poll/144284/support-death-penalty-cases-murder.aspx.

12. Death Penalty Information Center, *supra* note 4; Rob Warden, "How and Why Illinois Abolished the Death Penalty," 30 *Law & Inequality* 245, 284–285 (2012).

13. *People v. LaValle,* 817 N.E.2d 341 (N.Y. 2004); *People v. Taylor,* 878 N.E.2d 969 (N.Y. 2007); James R. Acker, "Be Careful What You Ask For: Lessons From New York's Recent Experiment With Capital Punishment," 32 *Vermont Law Review* 683 (2008).

14. U.S. Dept. of Justice, *supra* note 5, at 19 (Table 16); Death Penalty Information Center, *The Death Penalty in 2012: Year End Report* 1 (Dec. 2012), retrieved November 15, 2013 from http://deathpenaltyinfo.org/documents/2012YearEnd.pdf.

15. Death Penalty Information Center, "Executions by Year," *supra* note 7.

Acknowledgments

It has been my good fortune to work with the thoughtful guidance and helpful support offered by Routledge and the Taylor & Francis Group, and in particular with Stephen Rutter and Margaret Moore. I also very much appreciate the feedback offered by those individuals who reviewed and commented on the initial draft of this volume:

Margaret Vandiver	University of Memphis
Robert Bohm	University of Central Florida
Simon Cole	University of California, Irvine
Cindy Carvelis Hughes	Western Carolina University
Gordon Waldo	Florida State University

The book has benefited greatly by my being able to take advantage of their insights and suggestions. Of course, I assume sole responsibility for shortcomings that remain.

I

THE DEATH PENALTY'S JUSTIFICATIONS

PRO AND CON

1

RETRIBUTION (JUST DESERTS)

The Death Penalty as Retributive Justice: A Case in Point?

United States v. McVeigh, 153 F.3d 1166 (10th Cir. 1998), *cert. den.*, 526 U.S. 1007 (1999)

Defendant-appellant Timothy J. McVeigh ("McVeigh") was tried, convicted, and sentenced to death on eleven counts stemming from the bombing of the Alfred P. Murrah Federal Building ("Murrah Building") in Oklahoma City, Oklahoma, that resulted in the deaths of 168 people. . . .

BACKGROUND

At 9:02 in the morning of April 19, 1995, a massive explosion tore apart the Murrah Building in Oklahoma City, Oklahoma, killing a total of 168 people and injuring hundreds more. On August 10, 1995, a federal grand jury returned an eleven-count indictment against McVeigh and Terry Lynn Nichols ("Nichols") charging: one count of conspiracy to use a weapon of mass destruction . . .; one count of use of a weapon of mass destruction . . .; one count of destruction by explosives . . .; and eight counts of first-degree murder. . . .

. . . The destruction of the Murrah Building killed 163 people in the building and five people outside. Fifteen children in the Murrah Building day care center, visible from the front of the building, and four children visiting the building were included among the victims. Eight federal law enforcement officials also lost their lives. The explosion, felt and heard six

miles away, tore a gaping hole into the front of the Murrah Building and covered the streets with glass, debris, rocks, and chunks of concrete. Emergency workers who reported to the scene made heroic efforts to rescue people still trapped in the building.

The Murrah Building was destroyed by a 3,000–6,000 pound bomb comprised of an ammonium nitrate-based explosive carried inside a rented Ryder truck. In the fall of 1994, McVeigh and Nichols sought, bought, and stole all the materials needed to construct the bomb. . . . Using various aliases, McVeigh and Nichols rented a number of storage lockers in Kansas where they stored the bomb components. In order to fund their conspiracy, McVeigh and Nichols robbed a gun dealer in Arkansas in November of 1994.

In a letter to Michael and Lori Fortier written around September of 1994, McVeigh disclosed that he and Terry Nichols had decided to take some type of positive offensive action against the federal government in response to the government's siege of the Branch Davidians in Waco, Texas, in 1993. On a subsequent visit to their home, McVeigh told the Fortiers that he planned to blow up a federal building. McVeigh later informed the Fortiers that he wanted to cause a general uprising in America and that the bombing would occur on the anniversary of the end of the Waco siege. McVeigh rationalized the inevitable loss of life by concluding that anyone who worked in the federal building was guilty by association with those responsible for Waco.

McVeigh stated that he had figured out how to make a truck into a bomb using fifty-five-gallon drums filled with ammonium nitrate combined with explosives stolen from the quarry. McVeigh demonstrated the shaped charge he intended to use for the bomb by arranging soup cans on the floor in the same triangle shape in which he was going to place fifty-five-gallon barrels filled with ammonium nitrate combined with nitromethane in the truck. McVeigh also diagramed the truck, barrels, and fusing system on a piece of paper, and stated that he intended to use a Ryder truck. McVeigh told the Fortiers that he chose the Murrah Building as the target because he believed that (1) the orders for the attack at Waco emanated from the building, (2) the building housed people involved in the Waco raid, and (3) the building's U-shape and glass front made it an easy target. . . .

Also, towards the end of 1994, McVeigh typed a number of letters discussing the justified use of violence against federal agents as retaliation for the events in Waco. McVeigh told his sister and one of his friends that he had moved from the propaganda stage to the action stage in his dispute with the federal government. McVeigh then warned his sister that "something big" was going to happen in April, and asked her to extend her April 1995 Florida vacation. He also instructed her not to write to him any more lest she incriminate herself. The manner in which the bombing was carried out closely tracked several books bought by McVeigh, which he often encouraged his friends to read,

describing how to make a powerful bomb mixing ammonium nitrate with nitromethane and romanticizing self-declared patriots who blow up federal buildings. McVeigh was familiar with explosives and had detonated a pipe bomb prior to the attack on the Murrah Building.

From April 14 to 18, 1995, McVeigh stayed at the Dreamland Motel located in Junction City, Kansas. On April 14, 1995, McVeigh purchased a 1977 yellow Mercury Marquis from Junction City Firestone in Junction City, Kansas. While waiting to take possession of the car from the dealer, McVeigh made a phone call using the Bridges calling card to Elliott's Body Shop ("Elliott's") in Junction City, Kansas, seeking a twenty-foot Ryder truck for a one-way rental to Omaha. McVeigh also called Nichols.

During the search of the blast site, the FBI located the rear axle of the Ryder truck used to carry the bomb. The vehicle identification number from the axle matched that of the Ryder truck rented to McVeigh by Elliott's on April 15, 1995, and picked up by McVeigh two days prior to the blast. McVeigh rented the truck under the name "Robert King" using a phony South Dakota drivers license that Lori Fortier had helped McVeigh create.

McVeigh drove to Oklahoma City in the rented Ryder truck, which he had made into a bomb, parking the vehicle in front of the Murrah Building and running to the yellow Mercury that he and Nichols had stashed as a getaway car in a nearby alley a couple of days before the bombing. A Ford key fitting the Ryder truck was found in an alley near where McVeigh had told Michael Fortier that the getaway car would be parked. McVeigh hand-printed a sign inside the yellow Mercury, "Not Abandoned; Please do not tow; will move by April 23 (Needs Battery & Cable)." McVeigh deliberately parked the car so that a building would stand between the car and the blast, shielding McVeigh from the explosion. The bomb then exploded.

Just 77 minutes after the blast, Oklahoma State Trooper Charles Hanger ("Hanger") stopped the yellow Mercury driven by McVeigh because the car had no license tags. The stop occurred between mile markers 202 and 203 on Interstate 35, just before the exit for Billings, Oklahoma, precisely 77.9 miles north of the Murrah Building. Before he was stopped by Hanger, McVeigh was headed northbound away from Oklahoma City towards Kansas. A person driving the posted speed limit would have reached the point of the stop 75 minutes after leaving the Murrah Building. If McVeigh had left the Murrah Building right after the bombing, he would have arrived at the Billings exit around 10:17 a.m., the approximate time of the stop.

Hanger arrested McVeigh upon discovering that he was carrying a concealed, loaded gun. Hanger transported McVeigh to Noble County Jail in Perry, Oklahoma, where McVeigh was booked and incarcerated for unlawfully carrying a weapon and transporting a loaded firearm. Noble County authorities took custody of McVeigh's clothing and property, including earplugs, and issued him prison garb. Two days later, on April 21, 1995, the federal government filed a Complaint against McVeigh for unlawful destruction by explosives. Oklahoma then transferred McVeigh to federal custody on the federal bombing charges. An FBI test performed later found that McVeigh's clothing and the earplugs contained explosives residue, including PETN, EGDN, and nitroglycerine—chemicals associated with the materials used in the construction of the bomb.

A subsequent inventory search of the yellow Mercury uncovered a sealed envelope containing documents arguing that the federal government had commenced open warfare on the liberty of the American people and justifying the killing of government officials in the defense of liberty. Finally, three days after the arrest, Hanger found a Paulsen's Military Supply business card on the floor of his cruiser bearing McVeigh's fingerprints. McVeigh had written on the back of the card, "TNT @ $5/ stick Need more" and "Call After 01, May, See if I can get some more."

... On June 2, 1997, after four days of deliberations, the jury returned guilty verdicts on all eleven counts charged in the Indictment. The penalty phase of trial commenced on June 4, 1997, and concluded with summations and jury instructions on June 12, 1997. The jury deliberated for two days before returning special findings recommending that McVeigh be sentenced to death. After denying McVeigh's motion for a new trial, the district court accepted the jury recommendation on August 14, 1997, sentencing McVeigh to death on all eleven counts.

Timothy McVeigh was executed by lethal injection in the Federal Correctional Institute in Terre Haute, Indiana, on June 11, 2001. Ten survivors of the blast and family members of victims killed in the explosion of the Alfred P. Murrah Federal Building witnessed his execution in person, and 232 survivors and victims' relatives viewed it from Oklahoma City via a closed-circuit broadcast. McVeigh offered no final words from the execution chamber. He had previously arranged to have written copies of William Ernest Henley's poem "Invictus" distributed to media representatives.[1] The verses suggest no hint of remorse.

> Out of the night that covers me,
> Black as the Pit from pole to pole,
> I thank whatever gods may be
> For my unconquerable soul.
>
> In the fell clutch of circumstance
> I have not winced nor cried aloud.
> Under the bludgeonings of chance
> My head is bloody, but unbowed.
>
> Beyond this place of wrath and tears
> Looms but the Horror of the shade,
> And yet the menace of the years
> Finds, and shall find, me unafraid.
>
> It matters not how strait the gate,
> How charged with punishments the scroll.
> I am the master of my fate:
> I am the captain of my soul.

Is retribution, or just deserts, a legitimate objective of punishment? Does the death penalty represent just deserts for Timothy McVeigh? Would a lesser sanction, such as life imprisonment without the possibility of parole, be adequate to fulfill the retributive function of punishment in response to his crimes? How should the sentiments of the survivors of the explosion and the family members of those slain figure in answering these questions?

Retribution and Capital Punishment

Retributive Justice and the Principle of Proportionality

Some objectives of punishment, such as deterrence and incapacitation, are primarily instrumental or utilitarian in nature. They aim to modify or regulate future behavior. Not so retribution. Retributive justice presumes that offenders deserve to be punished for their blameworthy acts and that no additional justification is needed. Punishment is a just response to criminal conduct, imposed on offenders for violating rules of law that others willingly abide by as a condition of ordered social living. Retribution is normative rather than instrumental in character, and it is backward-looking. It focuses on the harm caused and the offender's culpable mental state at the time the crime was committed. In this context, retribution is synonymous with just deserts.[2]

Implicit within the concept of retributive justice is the principle of proportionality: that the amount or severity of punishment should have some fair correspondence to the seriousness of the crime. Although its true meaning is much debated, particularly whether it is a limiting principle or instead an affirmative prescription, the biblical passage, "[T]hou shalt give life for life, eye for eye, tooth for tooth . . .,"[3] is frequently cited in support of the proportionality precept. Justice Lewis Powell elaborated on the constitutional dimension of proportionate punishment in a case in which a thrice-convicted property offender, whose crimes involved roughly $230 in total economic value, was sentenced to life imprisonment under a Texas habitual felon statute.

> The scope of the [Eighth Amendment's] Cruel and Unusual Punishments Clause extends not only to barbarous methods of punishment, but also to punishments that are grossly disproportionate. Disproportionality analysis measures the relationship between the nature and number of offenses committed and the severity of the punishment inflicted upon the offender. The inquiry focuses on whether a person deserves such punishment, not simply on whether punishment would serve a utilitarian goal. A statute that levied a mandatory life sentence for overtime parking might well deter vehicular lawlessness, but it would offend our felt sense of justice.[4]

In theory, the offender's punishment could precisely mirror the offense. In Iran, for example, a woman blinded by a spurned suitor who threw acid in her eyes recently was afforded the prerogative, pursuant to Sharia law and the Islamic Penal Code, of having her assailant punished by being blinded with acid. She ultimately declined to exercise that option.[5] Proportionality does not necessarily demand literal "eye for an eye" correspondence between crime and punishment. An alternative approach presumes relative scaling, meaning that the most serious crimes receive the most serious punishment authorized by law, whatever that might be, while lesser crimes are punished less severely.

Is Capital Punishment Retributive Justice?

Outside of the death-penalty context, American systems of justice unambiguously repudiate reliance on a literal symmetry between crime and punishment. There is little evident enthusiasm for responding to offenders in kind. We thus do not inflict bodily injury on individuals found guilty of assault nor burn down the houses of those convicted of arson. Even with respect to murder and capital punishment, the apparent literal correspondence between crime and punishment is imperfect. A murderer who claims multiple victims, such as Timothy McVeigh, cannot be caused to suffer multiple deaths. Moreover, few would have the stomach for subjecting a torture-murderer to endure prolonged, excruciating pain before executing him. For those who would choose to inflict such punishment, the Constitution stands as a barrier. In one of its earliest death-penalty cases, rejecting an Eighth Amendment challenge to execution by firing squad, the Supreme Court explained:

> Difficulty would attend the effort to define with exactness the extent of the constitutional provision which provides that cruel and unusual punishments shall not be inflicted; but it is safe to affirm that punishments of torture, . . . and all others in the same line of unnecessary cruelty, are forbidden by that amendment to the Constitution.[6]

Putting to one side the issue of "'torture' and other 'barbarous' methods"[7] of execution, can capital punishment be justified on the ground that it represents just deserts, or appropriate retributive justice, for a convicted murderer? In *Gregg v. Georgia*, the Supreme Court was asked to rule that the death penalty inherently violates the Eighth Amendment because it serves no constitutionally permissible purposes. Consider the following excerpt from the plurality opinion, jointly authored by Justices Stewart, Powell, and Stevens, in this case.

Gregg v. Georgia, 428 U.S. 153, 96 S.Ct. 2909, 49 L.Ed.2d 859 (1976)

[T]he Eighth Amendment demands more than that a challenged punishment be acceptable to contemporary society. The Court also must ask whether it comports with the basic concept of human dignity at the core of the Amendment. Trop v. Dulles, 356 U.S. [86], 100 [(1958)] (plurality opinion). Although we cannot "invalidate a category of penalties because we deem less severe penalties adequate to serve the ends of penology," Furman v. Georgia, 408 U.S. [238], 451 [(1972)] (Powell, J., dissenting), the sanction imposed cannot be so totally without penological justification that it results in the gratuitous infliction of suffering.

The death penalty is said to serve two principal social purposes: retribution and deterrence of capital crimes by prospective offenders.[FN28]

FN28. Another purpose that has been discussed is the incapacitation of dangerous criminals and the consequent prevention of crimes that they may otherwise commit in the future.

In part, capital punishment is an expression of society's moral outrage at particularly offensive conduct. This function may be unappealing to many, but it is essential in an ordered society that asks its citizens to rely on legal processes rather than self-help to vindicate their wrongs.

"The instinct for retribution is part of the nature of man, and channeling that instinct in the administration of criminal justice serves an important purpose in promoting the stability of a society governed by law. When people begin to believe that organized society is unwilling or unable to impose upon criminal offenders the punishment they 'deserve,' then there are sown the seeds of anarchy of self-help, vigilante justice, and lynch law." Furman v. Georgia, supra, 408 U.S., at 308, (Stewart, J., concurring).

"Retribution is no longer the dominant objective of the criminal law," Williams v. New York, 337 U.S. 241, 248 (1949), but neither is it a forbidden objective nor one inconsistent with our respect for the dignity of men. Indeed, the decision that capital punishment may be the appropriate sanction in extreme cases is an expression of the community's belief that certain crimes are themselves so grievous an affront to humanity that the only adequate response may be the penalty of death.[FN30]

FN30. Lord Justice Denning, Master of the Rolls of the Court of Appeal in England, spoke to this effect before the British Royal Commission on Capital Punishment:

> "Punishment is the way in which society expresses its denunciation of wrong doing: and, in order to maintain respect for law, it is essential that the punishment inflicted for grave crimes should adequately reflect the revulsion felt by the great majority of citizens for them. It is a mistake to consider the objects of punishment as being deterrent or reformative or preventive and nothing else. . . . The truth is that some crimes are so outrageous that society insists on adequate punishment, because the wrongdoer deserves it, irrespective of whether it is a deterrent or not." Royal Commission on Capital Punishment, Minutes of Evidence, Dec. 1, 1949, p. 207 (1950).

A contemporary writer has noted more recently that opposition to capital punishment "has much more appeal when the discussion is merely academic than when the community is confronted with a crime, or a series of crimes, so gross, so heinous, so cold-blooded that anything short of death seems an inadequate response." Raspberry, Death sentence, The Washington Post, Mar. 12, 1976, p. A27, cols. 5–6.

. . . [W]e cannot say that the judgment of the Georgia Legislature that capital punishment may be necessary in some cases is clearly wrong. Considerations of federalism, as well as respect for the ability of a legislature to evaluate, in terms of its particular State, the moral consensus concerning the death penalty and its social utility as a sanction, require us to conclude, in the absence of more convincing evidence, that the infliction of death as a punishment for murder is not without justification and thus is not unconstitutionally severe.

Finally, we must consider whether the punishment of death is disproportionate in relation to the crime for which it is imposed. There is no question that death as a punishment is unique in its severity and irrevocability. When a defendant's life is at stake, the Court has been particularly sensitive to insure that every safeguard is observed. But we are concerned here only with the imposition of capital punishment for the crime of murder, and when a life has been taken deliberately by the offender,[FN35] we cannot say that the punishment is invariably disproportionate to the crime. It is an extreme sanction, suitable to the most extreme of crimes.

FN35. We do not address here the question whether the taking of the criminal's life is a proportionate sanction where no victim has been deprived of life for example, when capital punishment is imposed for rape, kidnaping, or armed robbery that does not result in the death of any human being.

We hold that the death penalty is not a form of punishment that may never be imposed, regardless of the circumstances of the offense, regardless of the character of the offender, and regardless of the procedure followed in reaching the decision to impose it.

Do you agree with the assertion that there is an "instinct for retribution," which is "part of the nature of man"?

When the opinion argues that "channeling that instinct in the administration of criminal justice serves an important purpose in promoting the stability of a society governed by law," does it suggest that retribution has utilitarian or instrumental functions in addition to its expressive purpose?

Even accepting these premises, is capital punishment the exclusive way of harnessing the posited retributive instinct, to help ensure that "citizens [will] rely on legal processes rather than self-help to vindicate their wrongs"? Might alternative sanctions be capable of doing so? Is there any evidence that "self-help, vigilante justice, and lynch law" flourish in jurisdictions that make no use of the death penalty?

Are "certain crimes . . . so grievous an affront to humanity that the only adequate response may be the penalty of death"? Might Timothy McVeigh's crimes fall into that category? Would the crimes of Troy Gregg—the man whose death sentence was under consideration by the justices in *Gregg v. Georgia*—so qualify?

On Wednesday morning, November 21, 1973, the appellant Gregg (age 25) and a traveling companion Floyd Ralford ('Sam') Allen (age 16) were hitchhiking north in Florida. They had only $8 between them when they were given a ride by the . . . victims [Fred Edward Simmons and Bob Durwood ('Tex') Moore]. About two hundred forty miles north of Miami on the Florida Turnpike, their automobile broke down. A Florida State Highway Patrolman accompanied Simmons and Moore to an automobile dealer where Simmons purchased a 1960 red and white Pontiac. Thereafter, they again picked up Gregg and Allen and resumed their journey northward. En route, both Simmons and Moore were seen in possession of large sums of money.

At the intersection of I-10 and I-75 in north Florida, another hitchhiker, Dennis Weaver, was picked up. He rode with the group until he got out at the intersection of I-85 and Highway 23 (North Druid Hills Road) in Atlanta, Georgia, at approximately 11:00 p.m. that evening. Gregg drove during the time Weaver was in the car while Simmons and Moore did

considerable drinking. No fighting words were exchanged by any of the men while he was present.

Allen stated to a police detective in the appellant's presence as follows: that at the intersection of Georgia Highway 20 and I-85 in Gwinnett County, Georgia, they stopped for a rest stop and Simmons and Moore got out; that Gregg turned around and told Allen to get out, 'we're going to rob them'; that Gregg lay up on the car with a gun in his hand to get good aim and as Simmons and Moore were coming back up the bank he fired three shots; that one of the men fell and the other staggered; that Gregg then circled around the back of the car and approached the two men, both of whom were then lying in a drainage ditch; that Gregg placed the gun to one's head and pulled the trigger, then went quickly to the other one and placed the gun at his head and pulled the trigger again; that he took their money and whatever contents were in their pockets; and that he then told Allen to get in the car and they drove away.

The bodies of Simmons and Moore were found in the drainage ditch. A State Crime

Laboratory medical examiner stated that death was caused by gunshot wounds, that Simmons had been shot in the right corner of the right eye in the region of the temple and Moore had been shot once in the right cheek of the face and once in the rear of his head.

On Friday morning, November 23, 1973, the hitchhiker, Dennis Weaver, went to an Atlanta restaurant for breakfast. While there he noticed an article on the front page of an Atlanta newspaper that led him to call the Gwinnett County Police Department. He told them he thought Gregg and Allen were going to Asheville, North Carolina. In response to a bulletin from Gwinnett County authorities, the Asheville Police apprehended Gregg driving Simmons' 1960 Pontiac at about 3:00 p.m. November 24, 1973. With him in the car were

Allen and three other persons. A .25-caliber automatic pistol was found in Gregg's pocket. He also had approximately $107 in cash. Ballistics tests subsequently established that bullets from the gun in Gregg's pocket caused the death of Simmons and Moore.

Weaver accompanied police officers to Asheville where he identified the automobile in which he had ridden with Gregg and the two victims, and headbands worn by Gregg and Allen.

At the scene of the crimes, when confronted with a narration of the crimes by Allen, Gregg made no protest. When asked if that was how it happened, he responded, 'Yes, it was.'

In rebuttal of defense evidence the state established that when asked by an Asheville detective why he did it, Gregg replied: 'By God, I wanted them dead.'[8]

Would you want any additional information about the commission of the murders, or about Troy Gregg, before deciding whether death is appropriate retributive justice for the crimes? If so, what would you want to know, and why?

The retributive justification for capital punishment has many adherents. When asked in Gallup Poll surveys, "Why do you favor the death penalty for persons convicted of murder?" the top answer volunteered by supporters of the death penalty over the past several years overwhelmingly has been: "Eye for an eye/They took a life/Fits the crime."[9] At the turn of the 21st century, scholars reviewing the last 25 years of public debate about capital punishment observed: "[W]e have witnessed the ascendancy of what has become the most important contemporary pro-death penalty argument: retribution. . . . Those who commit the most premeditated or heinous murders should be executed simply on the grounds that they deserve it."[10]

Professor Robert Blecker has passionately defended the retributive basis for capital punishment.

Retribution—literally "pay back"—persists as punishment's essential measure, justification, and limit. Naturally grateful, we reward those who bring us pleasure. Instinctively resentful, we punish those who cause us pain. Retributively, society intentionally inflicts pain and suffering on criminals because and to the extent they deserve it. But only to the extent they deserve it.

. . . But retribution should not be confused with vengeance or revenge. The two are very different although they stem from a common desire to inflict pain on the source of

pain. Revenge may be limitless and misdirected at the undeserving, as with collective punishment. Retribution, however, must be limited and proportional—no more (or less) than
what's deserved.[11]

In Professor Blecker's view, retribution is grounded in more than "an abstract sense
of duty"; it springs fundamentally from deep-seated and morally compelling emotion.

> Emotive retributivists' urge to punish . . . stems directly from a projected empathy with the
> victim's suffering. . . . Haunted by the victim's suffering, retributive death penalty supporters
> cannot forget or forgive the victim's fate.[12]

Because retribution demands punishment proportionate to the crime, it simultaneously serves as a limiting principle. "Thus, we retributivists are as concerned with
ensuring that criminals do *not* get punished beyond what they deserve as we are that
they affirmatively get what they deserve."[13]

In his book defending the principled foundations of the death penalty, *For Capital
Punishment: Crime and the Morality of the Death Penalty,* Walter Berns maintains:

> Capital punishment . . . serves to remind us of the majesty of the moral order that is
> embodied in our law and of the terrible consequences of its breach. . . . The criminal law
> must possess a dignity far beyond that possessed by mere statutory enactment or utilitar-
> ian and self-interested calculations; the powerful means we have to give it that dignity is
> to authorize it to impose the ultimate penalty. The criminal law must be made awful, by
> which I mean, awe-inspiring, or commanding "profound respect or reverential fear." It must
> remind us of the moral order by which alone we can live as *human* beings, and in our day
> the only punishment that can do this is capital punishment.[14]

Another prominent death-penalty proponent, Ernest van den Haag, concurs: "The paramount moral purpose of punishment is retributive justice."[15] According to van den Haag,

> Capital punishment, a deliberate expulsion from human society, is meant to add deserved
> moral ignominy to death. This irks some abolitionists, who feel that nobody should be
> blamed for whatever he does. But murder deserves blame. Death may well be less punish-
> ment than what some criminals deserve.[16]

He elaborated:

> Some writers insist that the suffering the death penalty imposes on murderers exceeds the
> suffering of their victims. This is hard to determine, but probably true in some cases and
> not in other cases. However, the comparison is irrelevant. Murderers are punished, as are
> all offenders, not just for the suffering they caused their victims, but for the harm they do
> to society by making life insecure, by threatening everyone, and by requiring protective
> measures. Punishment, ultimately, is a vindication of the moral and legal order of society
> and not limited by the *Lex Talionis,* meant to limit private retaliation for harms originally
> regarded as private.[17]

Objections to a Retributive Justification for the Death Penalty

Of course, not everyone agrees that retribution can justify punishment by death or that it is a constitutionally legitimate basis for the death penalty. Hugo Adam Bedau, a prominent foe of capital punishment, has raised difficult specific questions in response to Ernest van den Haag's retributivist arguments.

> [van den Haag] makes it clear in passing that murderers *deserve* to die, and that the principal justification of the death penalty is *justice*. He seems to believe that *desert* tells us *whom* to punish (guilty criminals), *what* they deserve as their punishment (murderers deserve death), and *why* this is what they deserve (justice). Yet his position on these issues is incomplete and unsatisfactory, for at least two reasons. First, he does not defend a mandatory death penalty. . . .
>
> Second, what are we to make of his fundamental proposition that *murderers deserve the death penalty?* Is it supposed to be a necessary moral truth that anyone can see to be true simply by understanding the concepts used to express it, an analytic *a priori* proposition? . . . [T]his proposition must be somehow established by derivation from more fundamental norms. What are they? Since he has rejected *lex talionis*—the obvious if unsatisfactory answer—and supplied no alternative, we are left to guess.[18]

Justice Thurgood Marshall repudiated retribution as a constitutionally adequate justification for the death penalty and explained why in his opinion in *Furman v. Georgia*, 408 U.S. 238, 342–345 (1972) (concurring in the judgment).

In order to assess whether or not death is an excessive or unnecessary penalty, it is necessary to consider the reasons why a legislature might select it as punishment for one or more offenses, and examine whether less severe penalties would satisfy the legitimate legislative wants as well as capital punishment. If they would, then the death penalty is unnecessary cruelty, and, therefore, unconstitutional. There are six purposes conceivably served by capital punishment: retribution, deterrence, prevention of repetitive criminal acts, encouragement of guilty pleas and confessions, eugenics, and economy. . . .

A. The concept of retribution is one of the most misunderstood in all of our criminal jurisprudence. The principal source of confusion derives from the fact that, in dealing with

the concept, most people confuse the question 'why do men in fact punish?' with the question 'what justifies men in punishing?' Men may punish for any number of reasons, but the one reason that punishment is morally good or morally justifiable is that someone has broken the law. Thus, it can correctly be said that breaking the law is the sine qua non of punishment, or, in other words, that we only tolerate punishment as it is imposed on one who deviates from the norm established by the criminal law.

The fact that the State may seek retribution against those who have broken its laws does not mean that retribution may then become the State's sole end in punishing. Our jurisprudence has always accepted deterrence in general, deterrence of individual recidivism, isolation of dangerous persons, and rehabilitation as proper goals of punishment. Retaliation, vengeance, and retribution have been roundly condemned as intolerable aspirations for a government in a free society.

Punishment as retribution has been condemned by scholars for centuries, and the Eighth Amendment itself was adopted to prevent punishment from becoming synonymous with vengeance.

In Weems v. United States, 217 U.S. [349,] 381 [(1910)], the Court in the course of holding that Weems' punishment violated the Eighth Amendment, contrasted it with penalties provided for other offenses and concluded:

'[T]his contrast shows more than different exercises of legislative judgment. It is greater than that. It condemns the sentence in this case as cruel and unusual. It exhibits a difference between unrestrained power and that which is exercised under the spirit of constitutional limitations formed to establish justice. The State thereby suffers nothing and loses no power. The purpose of punishment is fulfilled, crime is repressed by penalties of just, not tormenting, severity, its repetition is prevented, and hope is given for the reformation of the criminal.'

It is plain that the view of the Weems Court was that punishment for the sake of retribution was not permissible under the Eighth Amendment. This is the only view that the Court could have taken if the 'cruel and unusual' language were to be given any meaning. Retribution surely underlies the imposition of some punishment on one who commits a criminal act. But, the fact that some punishment may be imposed does not mean that any punishment is permissible. If retribution alone could serve as a justification for any particular penalty, then all penalties selected by the legislature would be definition be acceptable means for designating society's moral approbation of a particular act. The 'cruel and unusual' language would thus be read out of the Constitution. . . .

To preserve the integrity of the Eighth Amendment, the Court has consistently denigrated retribution as a permissible goal of punishment. It is undoubtedly correct that there is a demand for vengeance on the part of many persons in a community against one who is convicted of a particularly offensive act. At times a cry is heard that morality requires vengeance to evidence society's abhorrence of the act. But the Eighth Amendment is our insulation from our baser selves. The 'cruel and unusual' language limits the avenues through which vengeance can be channeled. Were this not so, the language would be empty and a return to the rack and other tortures would be possible in a given case.

Mr. Justice Story wrote that the Eighth Amendment's limitation on punishment 'would seem to be wholly unnecessary in a free government, since it is scarcely possible that any department of such a government should authorize or justify such atrocious conduct.'[FN88]

FN88. 2 J. Story, On the Constitution § 1903, p. 650 (5th ed. 1891).

I would reach an opposite conclusion—that only in a free society would men recognize their inherent weaknesses and seek to compensate for them by means of a Constitution.

The history of the Eighth Amendment supports only the conclusion that retribution for its own sake is improper.

Justice Marshall asserts that "the Eighth Amendment is our insulation from our baser selves." What do you understand that assertion to mean? What does it have to do with retributive justice? And what does it have to do with capital punishment?

Professor Anthony Amsterdam was the chief architect of the series of constitutional challenges to capital punishment initiated by the NAACP Legal Defense Fund (LDF) in the mid-1960s. The LDF largely commanded the legal battle waged against the death penalty over the next several years. His responses to questions during oral argument before the Supreme Court in *Furman v. Georgia* foreshadowed the position he and the LDF would take in later cases.

Justice Potter Stewart: Before you sit down Mr. Amsterdam, I just want to be sure that I understand your ultimate argument.

Is it this that even if assuming that retribution as a—is a permissible ingredient of punishment, even assuming that rational people could conclude that the death sentence is the maximum deterrent with the minimum unnecessary cruelty, death in electric chair.

Even assuming we are dealing with somebody who is not capable of being rehabilitated, an incorrigible person.

Even assuming that rational people can conclude that this punishment under these circumstances is the most efficient and the most inexpensive and the most—and that it assures the most complete isolation of a convicted man from ever getting back in the society.

Even assuming all of those things which are the basic arguments made by your brothers and sisters on the other side, you say it is still violative of the Eighth Amendment, am I right in my understanding of that?

Mr. Amsterdam: That is correct, Your Honor.

The Eighth Amendment we see is a limitation. . . .

It is a limitation on means that says that the legislature may not use cruel penalties, cruel and unusual penalties, even though they may serve [a] legitimate cause . . .

. . . [O]n this record it is our submission that accepting each and every one of those propositions, the death is a cruel and unusual punishment.

Justice Potter Stewart: That is what I understood to be your argument.[19]

Four years later, in his appearance before the Supreme Court in *Woodson v. North Carolina*, Professor Amsterdam again argued that capital punishment violates the Eighth Amendment's prohibition against cruel and unusual punishments. He stood fast in maintaining that retribution cannot serve as a constitutional justification for the death penalty.

Unidentified Justice: Before you go on . . ., can you conceive of any crime as to which you would consider the death penalty an appropriate response by society?

Mr. Anthony G. Amsterdam: No.

Unidentified Justice: Let me put a case to you, you read about Buchenwald one of the camps in Germany in which thousands of Jewish citizens were exterminated, it is unthinkable that that could happen again but who would have thought it would happened in the 20th century in a country as civilized that Germany was supposed to be.

If we [would] have had jurisdiction over the commandant of Buchenwald, would you have thought capital punishment was appropriate in response to what that man or woman was responsible for?

Mr. Anthony G. Amsterdam: . . . I think I probably would respond the same way all . . . human beings [would] to the kind of atrocities that Your Honor is raising.

We all have an instinctive reaction that says you know "kill [him]", but I think the answer to the question that Your Honor is raising, with that crime or any other crime, being consistent with the Eighth Amendment to the Constitution [of the] United States against the history in which this Court must now apply that Amendment.

At this point in time, my answer would be no.

That is the second of our two arguments, not the first, but it is the second and the answer is categorically no.

Justice Lewis F. Powell: So if . . . some fanatic set off a hydrogen bomb, [that, say,] destroyed New York City. Do you still . . . think the appropriate remedy for that would be . . . to put him in prison to have [him released on] parole in seven years?

Mr. Anthony G. Amsterdam: Mr. Justice Powell, there is no question in my mind that the state must have and that it does have ample remedies against people who are going to set off hydrogen bombs.

There is no-

Justice Lewis F. Powell: For example? . . .

Unidentified Justice: Putting him in prison in a solitary confinement for life with no parole, solitary confinement.

Mr. Anthony G. Amsterdam: . . . I think that under certain limited circumstances, it may be permissible to incarcerate somebody . . . I see no constitutional objection at all. For life imprisonment without a parole. . . .

Unidentified Justice: You are foreclosing altogether the use of capital punishment under any and all circumstance and society must have some effective alternative to protect people and I am asking you what do you think it could be?

Mr. Anthony G. Amsterdam: Life imprisonment without . . . possibility of parole. . . .

Unidentified Justice: Plus solitary confinement.

(Inaudible) would kill anyone else in the prison [?]. . . .

Mr. Anthony G. Amsterdam: Well I just—this seems to me to be a manner [sic] of a prison management.

The way you prevent children from hurting themselves [with] sharp objects, you put the sharp objects out of their reach, you do not punish them and do not rely exclusively on punishment for picking up sharp object[s], you manage the prisons better, you get them in securities.[20]

In his answer to whether the death penalty would be appropriate for the "commandant of Buchenwald," Amsterdam drew a distinction between "an instinctive reaction that says . . . 'kill him'" and the more measured constraints imposed by the Constitution. His response was reminiscent of Justice Marshall's assertion, in the above-quoted portion of his concurring opinion in *Furman v. Georgia*, that "[t]he 'cruel and unusual' language limits the avenues through which vengeance can be channeled."[21] We earlier considered Professor Robert Blecker's insistence that "retribution" as justification for punishment differs importantly from the impulse of "revenge" or "vengeance." Voicing similar sentiments, Professor Steven Gey has argued:

Revenge draws on a darker part of the human psyche, which most societies take care not to enshrine in law. Revenge tends to deny the imposition of a rational limit or structure to punishment. At the enforcement level, a punishment system premised on revenge tells the sentencer to depend on the viscera instead of the intellect to assess the level of punishment necessary in each case: one feels revenge, one does not think it. . . . [T]he revenge justification seems to trade the morally upstanding desideratum of jus talionis (just deserts) for the amoral and bloodthirsty lex talionis (an eye for an eye). To put it a slightly different way, punishment becomes justified by power rather than morality. . . .

The retributivist Robert Nozick has offered one of the most thorough and systematic attempts to distinguish revenge theories from retributive theories. Nozick suggests five characteristics that distinguish revenge from retribution. . . .

(1) "Retribution is done for a wrong, while revenge may be done for an injury or harm or slight and need not be for a wrong." This is another way of saying that revenge may be disproportionate to the moral gravity of the crime. . . .

(2) "Retribution sets an internal limit to the amount of punishment, according to the seriousness of the wrong, whereas revenge internally need set no limits." This is another reference to the proportionality requirement of retribution, under which punishment is just only if it matches the moral culpability of the offender. . . .

(3) Revenge is personal and inflicted because of what the defendant did to the punisher's own person, relative, or group. "On the other hand, the dispenser of retributive punishment need not have any such personal tie with the victim of the wrongful conduct." . . . Reducing the distance between the sentencer and the victim introduces the emotions of revenge. . . . To the extent that the victim has interests in excess of those necessary to serve society's more general retributive or utilitarian interests in punishment, those interests can only be characterized as premised on instincts of personal revenge. . . .

(4) "Revenge involves a particular emotional tone, pleasure in the suffering of another," which is missing in retribution. . . . [C]oncern for the victim's personal pain is different in kind from the retributive concern with maintaining an abstract correspondence between the defendant's moral guilt and his or her just deserts.

(5) It is not necessary that revenge be general and the revenger need not avenge again in similar circumstances.[22]

Even if we accept that retribution and revenge are different, are their distinguishing characteristics useful in helping us decide whether capital punishment is justifiable on retributive grounds?

The Worst of the Worst

For now, we will confine our discussion of retribution and the death penalty to just one crime, murder, and to adult offenders who suffer no glaring mental disabilities. We later will consider whether capital punishment can or should be imposed for other offenses (such as rape) and on other offenders (such as juveniles and intellectually disabled or mentally retarded individuals).

All grades of criminal homicide involve the same harm: the death of a human being. The punishment prescribed for the different categories of killings nevertheless varies dramatically, ranging from the possibility of probation (*e.g.*, for involuntary manslaughter and vehicular homicide) through possible death (for capital murder). The proportionality principle that is integral to retributive justice must clearly be sensitive to considerations in addition to the harm occasioned by a crime.

If retribution does not demand (or even tolerate) death for all who commit criminal homicide, we must ask what factors in addition to harm define the seriousness of crimes and thus help inform their punishment. Our task is more complicated still, for the Supreme Court has ruled that the law cannot automatically exact capital punishment even for first-degree murder,[23] including narrower subcategories of that crime, such as the slaying of a police officer[24] or a new killing committed by a prisoner already serving a sentence of life imprisonment imposed for a prior murder.[25] Relevant characteristics of the crime and the offender also must be considered before a capital sentencing decision is made.

What sorting principles are available to identify those murders and murderers for whom capital punishment uniquely represents retributive justice, or just deserts?

Retributivism adherent Robert Blecker does not support capital punishment for all or even most murderers, but only for "the 'worst of the worst,'" as calibrated by "the extreme harm [such murderers] cause (rape-murder, mass-murder, child-murder, torture-murder) along with the attitude with which they cause it—sadistically or with a depraved callousness."[26] He would include among the worst of the worst, "red collar killers"—that is,

> corporate safety directors and other decision makers . . . who, with depraved indifference to human life, run deadly workplaces or manufacture lethal products, which can poison a community's streams or soil, or knowingly and recklessly expose unsuspecting employees, consumers, or local residents to a grave risk of death which kills them, all from that "purest" of motives—the profit motive.[27]

If we assume, for now, that not all murders and murderers should be punished by death, and that capital punishment should be reserved exclusively for the worst of the worst of them, we face the difficult task of explaining more precisely what characterizes that nebulous grouping. The Supreme Court has waffled concerning the minimal constitutional expectations governing the death-penalty-eligible category of killings and killers.

When the justices decided *McGautha v. California*[28] in 1971, Justice Harlan's majority opinion considered the challenge of defining the specific attributes of "deathworthiness"[29] (for want of a better term) to be beyond daunting; he deemed it impossible. While rejecting a due process challenge to laws entrusting juries to make life-and-death decisions on their own, without concrete legal standards or guidance, the Court in *McGautha* found no better solution than to defer to the considered judgment of the jurors.

> To identify before the fact those characteristics of criminal homicides and their perpetrators which call for the death penalty, and to express these characteristics in language which can be fairly understood and applied by the sentencing authority, appear to be tasks which are beyond present human ability. . . .
>
> The States are entitled to assume that jurors confronted with the truly awesome responsibility of decreeing death for a fellow human will act with due regard for the consequences of their decision and will consider a variety of factors, many of which will have been suggested by the evidence or by the arguments of defense counsel. For a court to attempt to catalog the appropriate factors in this elusive area could inhibit rather than expand the scope of consideration, for no list of circumstances would ever be really complete. The infinite variety of cases and facets to each case would make general standards either meaningless 'boiler-plate' or a statement of the obvious that no jury would need.[30]

Whatever their merits, those premises did not survive the justices' fragmented views in *Furman v. Georgia*[31] regarding standardless capital sentencing decisions when measured against the Eighth Amendment's prohibition against cruel and unusual punishments. In that seminal decision, decided just one year after *McGautha*, five members of the Court concluded that the death penalty, as then administered, violated the Eighth Amendment. Although Justices Brennan and Marshall reasoned that capital punishment is *per se* (inherently) unconstitutional, regardless of the sentencing criteria used,[32] Justices Douglas,[33] Stewart,[34] and White[35] focused on infirmities in the sentencing procedures and the resulting unacceptable outcomes. The latter three justices concluded, respectively, that death-penalty decisions made at the unfettered discretion of juries were tainted by invidious discrimination, were wantonly freakish or arbitrary, and failed to advance retributive or other legitimate goals of punishment. We will consider the justices' opinions in *Furman* in greater detail in chapter 4.

In its next significant death-penalty decisions, issued July 2, 1976, the Supreme Court invalidated mandatory capital punishment laws but approved "guided discretion" sentencing legislation as remedying the constitutional defects identified by various of the justices in *Furman*. The plurality opinion of Justices Stewart, Powell, and Stevens in *Gregg v. Georgia* noted approvingly that a murder conviction, standing alone, was insufficient to expose an offender to death-penalty eligibility under the state's revamped statute. Instead, the legislature had acted "to narrow the class of murderers subject to capital punishment by specifying 10 statutory aggravating circumstances, one of which must be found by the jury to exist beyond a reasonable doubt before a death sentence can ever be imposed."[36]

In later cases the justices made clear that narrowing the class of death-eligible crimes to ensure that capital punishment is available for only a subcategory of especially "aggravated" murders is a constitutional requirement. Subsequent rulings also highlighted the distinction between the "eligibility" and "selection" stages of the capital sentencing process, and explained the different rules governing the corresponding decisions. Justice Kennedy's majority opinion in *Tuilaepa v. California*[37] offered the following summary.

Our capital punishment cases under the Eighth Amendment address two different aspects of the capital decisionmaking process: the eligibility decision and the selection decision. To be eligible for the death penalty, the defendant must be convicted of a crime for which the death penalty is a proportionate punishment. To render a defendant eligible for the death penalty in a homicide case, we have indicated that the trier of fact must convict the defendant of murder and find one "aggravating circumstance" (or its equivalent) at either the guilt or penalty phase. The aggravating circumstance may be contained in the definition of the crime or in a separate sentencing factor (or in both). As we have explained, the aggravating circumstance must meet two requirements. First, the circumstance may not apply to every defendant convicted of a murder; it must apply only to a subclass of defendants convicted of murder. See *Arave v. Creech*, 507 U.S. 463, 474 (1993) ("If the sentencer fairly could conclude that an aggravating circumstance applies to *every* defendant eligible for the death penalty, the circumstance is constitutionally infirm"). Second, the aggravating circumstance may not be unconstitutionally vague.

We have imposed a separate requirement for the selection decision, where the sentencer determines whether a defendant eligible for the death penalty should in fact receive that sentence. "What is important at the selection stage is an *individualized* determination on the basis of the character of the individual and the circumstances of the crime." *Zant* [*v. Stephens*, 462 U.S. 862], 879 [(1983)]. That requirement is met when the jury can consider relevant mitigating evidence of the character and record of the defendant and the circumstances of the crime.

The eligibility decision fits the crime within a defined classification. Eligibility factors almost of necessity require an answer to a question with a factual nexus to the crime or the defendant so as to "make rationally reviewable the process for imposing a sentence of death." *Arave*, 507 U.S., at 471. The selection decision, on the other hand, requires individualized sentencing and must be expansive enough to accommodate relevant mitigating evidence so as to assure an assessment of the defendant's culpability. The objectives of these two inquiries can be in some tension, at least when the inquiries occur at the same time. There is one principle common to both decisions, however: The State must ensure that the process is neutral and principled so as to guard against bias or caprice in the sentencing decision.

Death-penalty *eligibility* requirements are sometimes described as representing a threshold that separates the relatively narrow band of crimes that qualify for capital punishment consideration from the considerably larger body of crimes that do not. Case-specific *selection* factors, which help determine whether offenders who qualify for capital punishment consideration in fact should be sentenced to death, begin to operate (in principle) if and only if the eligibility threshold is crossed. In *Zant v. Stephens*,[38] Georgia's capital sentencing framework, which includes distinctive eligibility and selection stages, was analogized to a pyramid intersected by horizontal planes.

The [Georgia Supreme] Court . . . explained the state-law premises for its treatment of aggravating circumstances by analogizing the entire body of Georgia law governing homicides to a pyramid. It explained:

"All cases of homicide of every category are contained within the pyramid. The consequences flowing to the perpetrator increase in severity as the cases proceed from the base to the apex, with the death penalty applying only to those few cases which are contained in the space just beneath the apex. To reach that category a case must pass through three planes of division between the base and the apex.

"The first plane of division above the base separates from all homicide cases those which fall into the category of murder. This plane is established by the legislature in statutes defining terms such as murder, voluntary manslaughter, involuntary manslaughter, and justifiable homicide. In deciding whether a given case falls above or below this plane, the function of the trier of facts is limited to finding facts. The plane remains fixed unless moved by legislative act.

"The second plane separates from all murder cases those in which the penalty of death is a possible punishment. This plane is established by statutory definitions of aggravating circumstances. The function of the factfinder is again limited to making a determination of whether certain facts have been established. . . .

[A] given case [of murder] may not move above this second plane unless at least one statutory aggravating circumstance exists.

"The third plane separates, from all cases in which a penalty of death may be imposed, those cases in which it shall be imposed. There is an absolute discretion in the factfinder to place any given case below the plane and not impose death. The plane itself is established by the factfinder. In establishing the plane, the factfinder considers all evidence in extenuation, mitigation and aggravation of punishment. There is a final limitation on the imposition of the death penalty resting in the automatic appeal procedure: This court determines whether the penalty of death was imposed under the influence of passion, prejudice, or any other arbitrary factor; whether the statutory aggravating circumstances are supported by the evidence; and Performance of this function may cause this court to remove a case from the death penalty category but can never have the opposite result.

"The purpose of the statutory aggravating circumstances is to limit to a large degree, but not completely, the factfinder's discretion. Unless at least one of the ten statutory aggravating circumstances exists, the death penalty may not be imposed in any event. If there exists at least one statutory aggravating circumstance, the death penalty may be imposed but the factfinder has a discretion to decline to do so without giving any reason. In making the decision as to the penalty, the factfinder takes into consideration all circumstances before it from both the guilt-innocence and the sentence phases of the trial. These circumstances relate both to the offense and the defendant.

"A case may not pass the second plane into that area in which the death penalty is authorized unless at least one statutory aggravating circumstance is found. However, this plane is passed regardless of the number of statutory aggravating circumstances found, so long as there is at least one. Once beyond this plane, the case enters the area of the factfinder's discretion, in which all the facts and circumstances of the case determine, in terms of our metaphor, whether or not the case passes the third plane and into the area in which the death penalty is imposed."

We will consider these matters in considerably more detail in chapter 4. We now return to the challenge presented by that fundamental tenet of retributivism: that the most severe punishment authorized by law should be reserved for the most serious crimes and the most highly culpable offenders. Our quest, in other words, is to define the subcategory of criminal homicides that uniquely merit consideration for capital punishment—to decide which killings qualify as the worst of the worst—and to describe them with enough precision to provide meaningful guidance to the decision makers charged with applying the defining criteria.

How would you begin?

Most state legislatures (Texas is a notable exception) and Congress (for the federal death penalty) have adopted some variation of the model chosen by Georgia, as generally described in the above excerpts from *Gregg v. Georgia* and *Zant v. Stephens*. Initially, death-penalty-eligible murders are defined by "aggravating factors" that distinguish certain killings as especially serious or heinous, or identify certain killers as being especially culpable. This approach, in turn, has roots in the Model Penal Code (MPC), as approved by the American Law Institute in 1962. The plurality opinion in *Gregg* referenced the aggravating factors included in the MPC to refute the suggestion "that standards to guide a capital jury's sentencing deliberations are impossible to formulate."[39] The "aggravating circumstances" identified in the MPC were:

(a) The murder was committed by a convict under sentence of imprisonment.
(b) The defendant was previously convicted of another murder or of a felony involving the use or threat of violence to the person.
(c) At the time the murder was committed the defendant also committed another murder.
(d) The defendant knowingly created a great risk of death to many persons.
(e) The murder was committed while the defendant was engaged or was an accomplice in the commission of, or an attempt to commit, or flight after committing or attempting to commit robbery, rape or deviate sexual intercourse by force or threat of force, arson, burglary or kidnapping.

(f) The murder was committed for the purpose of avoiding or preventing a lawful arrest or effecting an escape from lawful custody.

(g) The murder was committed for pecuniary gain.

(h) The murder was especially heinous, atrocious or cruel, manifesting exceptional depravity.[40]

Do those considerations succeed in helping to provide a "'meaningful basis for distinguishing the few cases in which [the death penalty] is imposed from the many cases in which it is not'"?[41] Are there additional factors relating to how or why the offense was committed, or that concern the victim or the offender, that ought to be included? Should any of the identified factors be eliminated? Are the factors sufficiently clear to offer meaningful guidance?

After an aggravating circumstance has been proven to accompany a murder and the threshold of death-penalty eligibility crossed, what additional factors should be considered to decide which offenders should receive and which should be spared punishment by death?

In *Gregg*, the justices again invoked the Model Penal Code's provisions as a defensible capital sentencing approach. The MPC included a list of "mitigating circumstances" which, as the Court later explained, represent relevant aspects "of a defendant's character or record and any of the circumstances of the offense that the defendant proffers as a basis for a sentence less than death."[42] The Code's drafters had recommended that "the main circumstances of aggravation and of mitigation . . . should be weighed *and* weighed against each other when they are presented in a concrete case."[43] More specifically, the MPC stated that the sentencing authority

shall take into account the aggravating and mitigating circumstances enumerated in [the Code] and any other facts that it deems relevant, but it shall not impose or recommend sentence of death unless it finds one of the aggravating circumstances enumerated in [the Code] and further finds that there are no mitigating circumstances sufficiently substantial to call for leniency.[44]

The "mitigating factors" enumerated in the Model Penal Code were as follows:

(a) The defendant has no significant history of prior criminal activity.

(b) The murder was committed while the defendant was under the influence of extreme mental or emotional disturbance.

(c) The victim was a participant in the defendant's homicidal conduct or consented to the homicidal act.

(d) The murder was committed under circumstances which the defendant believed to provide a moral justification or extenuation for his conduct.

(e) The defendant was an accomplice in a murder committed by another person and his participation in the homicidal act was relatively minor.

(f) The defendant acted under duress or under the domination of another person.

(g) At the time of the murder, the capacity of the defendant to appreciate the criminality (wrongfulness) of his conduct or to conform his conduct to the requirements of law was impaired as a result of mental disease or defect or intoxication.

(h) The youth of the defendant at the time of the crime.[45]

Note that "mitigating factors" do not excuse or justify a crime. They are offered to somehow diminish the offender's moral culpability and thus support a punishment less severe than death. The Supreme Court has ruled that in capital cases the sentencing authority cannot be limited to consider only those mitigating factors detailed in a statute, but must be allowed to give "effect to [any] evidence relevant to a defendant's background or character or the circumstances of the offense that mitigates against the death penalty."[46]

What is the relationship between the mitigating factors enumerated in the Model Penal Code and a murderer's "deathworthiness"?

If that listing or any other statutory attempt to identify mitigating circumstances relevant to a capital sentencing decision cannot be considered exhaustive, what additional factors might help militate against a sentence of death?

Is the process of allowing the sentencer to take mitigating factors into account, and then weighing or balancing them against aggravating factors before making a death-penalty decision, a satisfactory way of defining the "worst of the worst" murders and murderers?

Perhaps ironically, in 2009 the American Law Institute voted to rescind the provisions of the Model Penal Code pertaining to capital sentencing. This decision was based on concerns shared by many members about

> the administration of death-penalty laws derived from § 210.6. . . . Unless we are confident we can recommend procedures that would meet the most important of the concerns, the Institute should not play a further role in legitimating capital punishment, no matter how unintentionally, by retaining the section in the Model Penal Code.[47]

Other jurisdictions have enacted capital sentencing statutes that differ somewhat from the original MPC model. California, for example, has adopted a "trifurcated" process. Offenders convicted of first-degree murder are eligible for the death penalty if the prosecution alleges and proves one or more statutory "special circumstances," which function essentially as aggravating factors.[48] In cases where a special circumstance has been established and defendants are found death-eligible, the jury considers additional statutorily enumerated "factors," the presence or absence of which can help support a sentence of either death or life imprisonment without parole, as appropriate.[49] One of those factors, consistent with the Supreme Court's admonition that a vehicle be provided to allow all relevant mitigation evidence offered by a defendant in a capital case to be considered, invites evidence of "[a]ny other circumstance which extenuates the gravity of the crime even though it is not a legal excuse for the crime."[50] The sentencing authority is instructed to sentence the offender to death if it "concludes that the aggravating circumstances outweigh the mitigating circumstances."[51]

Texas's capital sentencing framework is different still. A defendant becomes eligible for the death penalty in Texas if convicted of capital murder (defined as murder accompanied by one or more specified aggravating elements)[52] and then, during the trial's penalty phase, the jurors unanimously agree that "there is a probability that the defendant would commit criminal acts of violence that would constitute a continuing threat to society."[53] Death-eligible offenders then are sentenced according to jurors' response to the question:

> Whether, taking into consideration all of the evidence, including the circumstances of the offense, the defendant's character and background, and the personal moral culpability of the defendant, there is a sufficient mitigating circumstance or circumstances to warrant that a sentence of life imprisonment without parole rather than a death sentence be imposed.[54]

From a retributive perspective, do the capital sentencing schemes adopted in California and Texas appear to be any more or less satisfactory than the framework originally proposed in the Model Penal Code?

In light of the Supreme Court mandate that the sentencing authority must be allowed to give effect to any evidence presented in a case that is "relevant to the defendant's background or character or the circumstances of the offense that mitigates against the death penalty,"[55] is it even possible for legislation to define the "worst of the worst" killings and killers, or must this judgment inevitably be rendered after the fact, on a case-by-case basis?

Was Justice Harlan right when he concluded in *McGautha v. California* that "[t]o identify before the fact those characteristics of criminal homicides and their perpetrators which call for the death penalty, and to express these characteristics in language which can be fairly understood and applied by the sentencing authority, appear to be tasks which are beyond present human ability"?[56] What, if anything, does the answer to this question have to do with whether capital punishment can be justified on retributive grounds in response to murder?

Conclusion

The dominant reasons offered in support of capital punishment have waxed and waned over time. Currently, retribution is far and away the leading justification cited by proponents of the death penalty. A recent Gallup poll revealed that supporters of capital punishment volunteered reasons including "an eye for an eye," and it "fits the crime," or a close variant roughly three times as often as the next leading factor.[57] Adherents of this perspective have argued that some crimes are so heinous that death, and death alone is adequate retribution. Opponents tend to counter that although retribution may help explain why we punish criminal offenders, it does not dictate what the precise form or amount of punishment should be. They argue that the "eye for an eye" formula is inadequate to justify the death penalty, pointing out that all grades of criminal homicide involve the loss of life yet punishment other than death is deemed fitting for the overwhelming majority of them.

Most retributivists agree that not all criminal homicides, and not even all murders, should automatically be punished by death. The Supreme Court has ruled that mandatory capital punishment, which precludes consideration of individual offense circumstances and offender characteristics, is unconstitutional for even the most highly aggravated killings. The challenge thus arises to find agreement about which murders and murderers represent the "worst of the worst," and consequently command the strongest retributive justification for the ultimate punishment known to law.

We have considered the solutions to this challenge that have been incorporated into different death penalty statutes and that have gained the approval of the United States Supreme Court. The most common approach involves requiring proof of one or more statutorily enumerated "aggravating factors," involving some aspect of how, why, or against whom the murder was committed, and relevant characteristics of the offender (such as prior criminal record) as a prerequisite to establishing the offender's eligibility for the death penalty. Then, the offender must be given the opportunity to offer evidence of relevant "mitigating factors" that arguably diminish his or her culpability or moral responsibility. The relative weight given to the aggravating and mitigating factors by the sentencing authority determines whether the offender should be included among the worst of the worst and hence sentenced to death.

We will consider many additional issues suggested by these essential attributes of modern death-penalty laws in subsequent chapters.

Endnotes

1. Jody Lynee Madeira, *Killing McVeigh: The Death Penalty and the Myth of Closure* 221–258 (New York: New York University Press 2012).
2. *See* Andrew von Hirsch, *Doing Justice: The Choice of Punishments* 45–55 (New York: Hill and Wang 1976).
3. *Exodus* 21:23–24.
4. *Rummel v. Estelle*, 445 U.S. 263, 288 (1980) (Powell, J., dissenting). *See also Ewing v. California*, 538 U.S. 11, 21 (2003).
5. Stephanie Hegarty, "Iran Acid Attack: Ameneh Bahrami's Quest for Justice," *BBC News Middle East* (June 1, 2011), retrieved October 2, 2012 from www.bbc.co.uk/news/world-middle-east-13578731; "Iranian Man Who Blinded Student Saved From 'Eye for an Eye' Justice," *Telegraph* (July 31, 2011), retrieved October 2, 2012 from www.telegraph.co.uk/news/worldnews/middleeast/iran/8673476/Iranian-man-who-blinded-student-saved-from-eye-for-an-eye-justice.html.
6. *Wilkerson v. Utah*, 99 U.S. 130, 135–136 (1879). *See also Baze v. Rees*, 553 U.S. 35 (2008).
7. *Gregg v. Georgia*, 428 U.S. 153, 170 (1976) (plurality opinion).
8. *Gregg v. State*, 210 S.E.2d 659, 662–663 (Ga. 1974).
9. Gallup.com, *Death Penalty*, retrieved October 2, 2012 from www.gallup.com/poll/1606/death-penalty.aspx.
10. Michael L. Radelet & Marian J. Borg, "The Changing Nature of Death Penalty Debates," 26 *Annual Review of Sociology* 43, 52 (2000).

11. Professor Robert Blecker's Statement to Accompany Testimony Before the New Jersey Death Penalty Study Commission 10/11/06 (Supplemented), retrieved October 6, 2012 from www.google.com/url?sa=t&rct=j&q=&esrc=s&source=web&cd=2&ved=0CCs QFjAB&url=http%3A%2F%2Fwww.cjlf.org%2Ffiles%2FNJDP_BleckerStatement. doc&ei=kohwUIKQJvSH0QHcwIGAAg&usg=AFQjCNH4h6kXpEIobDSkQ-m2ityh O8Vt7g.

12. Robert Blecker, "But Did They Listen? The New Jersey Death Penalty Commission's Exercise in Abolitionism: A Reply," 5 *Rutgers Journal of Law & Public Policy* 9 (2007).

13. Professor Robert Blecker's Statement, *supra* note 11.

14. Walter Berns, *For Capital Punishment: Crime and the Morality of the Death Penalty* 172–173 (Lanham, MD: University Press of America 1991).

15. Ernest van den Haag, "Justice, Deterrence and the Death Penalty," in James R. Acker, Robert M. Bohm & Charles S. Lanier (eds.), *America's Experiment With Capital Punishment: Reflections on the Past, Present, and Future of the Ultimate Penal Sanction* 233, 238 (Durham, NC: Carolina Academic Press, 2d ed. 2003).

16. *Id.,* at 237.

17. Ernest van den Haag, "The Death Penalty Once More," in Hugo Adam Bedau (ed.), *The Death Penalty in America: Current Controversies* 445, 453 (New York: Oxford University Press 1997).

18. Hugo Adam Bedau, "A Reply to van den Haag," in Hugo Adam Bedau (ed.), *The Death Penalty in America: Current Controversies* 457, 466 (New York: Oxford University Press 1997).

19. Transcript of oral argument, *Furman v. Georgia,* 408 U.S. 238 (1972), retrieved October 8, 2012 from www.oyez.org/cases/1970-1979/1971/1971_69_5003.

20. Transcript of oral argument, *Woodson v. North Carolina,* 428 U.S. 280 (1976), retrieved October 8, 2012 from www.oyez.org/cases/1970-1979/1975/1975_75_5491.

21. *Furman v. Georgia,* 408 U.S. 238, 345 (1972) (Marshall, J., concurring in the judgment). A few months before the U.S. Supreme Court issued its decision in *Furman,* the California Supreme Court ruled in *People v. Anderson,* 493 P.2d 880 (Cal. 1972), that the death penalty violated the California Constitution's prohibition against "cruel or unusual punishments." Chief Justice Wright's majority opinion included an expression similar to Justice Marshall's. "Our conclusion that the death penalty may no longer be exacted in California consistently with [the state constitution] is not grounded in sympathy for those who would commit crimes of violence, but in concern for the society that diminishes itself whenever it takes the life of one of its members. Lord Chancellor Gardiner reminded the House of Lords, debating abolition of capital punishment in England: 'When we abolished the punishment for treason that you should be hanged, and then cut down while still alive, and then disemboweled while still alive, and then quartered, we did not abolish that punishment because we sympathized with traitors, but because we took the view that it was a punishment no longer consistent with our self respect.' (268 Hansard, Parliamentary Debates (5th Series) (Lords, 43d Parl., First Sess., 1964–1965) (1965) p. 703.)" *People v. Anderson,* 493 P.2d, at 899. California voters subsequently approved a state constitutional amendment that negated the court's ruling in *Anderson.*

22. Steven G. Gey, "Justice Scalia's Death Penalty," 20 *Florida State University Law Review* 67, 125–129 (1992), *quoting* Robert Nozick, *Philosophical Explanations* 366–368 (Cambridge, MA: Harvard University Press 1981).

23. *Woodson v. North Carolina,* 428 U.S. 280 (1976); *Roberts (Stanislaus) v. Louisiana,* 428 U.S. 325 (1976).

24. *Roberts (Harry) v. North Carolina,* 431 U.S. 633 (1977).

25. *Sumner v. Shuman,* 483 U.S. 66 (1987).

26. Blecker, "But Did They Listen?," *supra* note 12. *See also* Robert Blecker, "The Road Not Considered: Revising New Jersey's Death Penalty Statute," 32 *Seton Hall Legislative Journal*

241 (2008); Robert Blecker, "Roots," in James R. Acker, Robert M. Bohm & Charles S. Lanier (eds.), *America's Experiment With Capital Punishment: Reflections on the Past, Present, and Future of the Ultimate Penal Sanction* 169 (Durham, NC: Carolina Academic Press, 2d ed. 2003).

27. Blecker, "The Road Not Considered," *supra* note 26, at 248.
28. 402 U.S. 183 (1971).
29. *See generally, Lackey v. State*, 819 S.W.2d 111, 132 (Tex. Crim. App 1989), *abrogated, Tennard v. Dretke*, 542 U.S. 274 (2004); Phyllis L. Crocker, "Concepts of Culpability and Deathworthiness: Differentiating Between Guilt and Punishment in Death Penalty Cases," 66 *Fordham Law Review* 21 (1997).
30. *McGautha v. California*, 408 U.S. 183, 204, 207–208 (1971).
31. 408 U.S. 238 (1972).
32. *Id.*, 408 U.S., at 257–306 (Brennan, J., concurring in the judgment); 408 U.S., at 314–374 (Marshall, J., concurring in the judgment).
33. *Id.*, 408 U.S., at 240–257 (Douglas, J., concurring in the judgment).
34. *Id.*, 408 U.S., at 306–310 (Stewart, J., concurring in the judgment).
35. *Id.*, 408 U.S., at 310–314 (White, J., concurring in the judgment).
36. *Gregg v. Georgia*, 428 U.S. 153, 196–197 (1976) (plurality opinion) (footnote omitted).
37. 512 U.S. 967, 971–973 (1994).
38. 462 U.S. 862, 870–872 (1983), *quoting Zant v. Stephens*, 297 S.E.2d 1, 3–4 (Ga. 1982).
39. *Gregg v. Georgia*, 428 U.S. 153, 193 (1976) (plurality opinion) (footnote omitted).
40. *Id.*, 428 U.S., at 193 n. 44, *quoting* American Law Institute, Model Penal Code § 210.6 (3) (Proposed Official Draft 1962).
41. *Id.*, 428 U.S., at 188, *quoting Furman v. Georgia*, 408 U.S. 238, 313 (1972) (White, J., concurring in the judgment).
42. *Lockett v. Ohio*, 438 U.S. 586, 604 (1978) (plurality opinion) (footnote omitted).
43. *Gregg v. Georgia*, 428 U.S. 153, 193 (1976) (plurality opinion), *quoting* American Law Institute, Model Penal Code § 210.6, Comment 3, p. 71 (Tent. Draft No. 9, 1959) (emphasis in original).
44. American Law Institute, Model Penal Code § 210.6 (2) (Proposed Official Draft 1962).
45. *Gregg v. Georgia*, 428 U.S. 153, 193 n. 44 (1976) (plurality opinion), *quoting* American Law Institute, Model Penal Code § 210.6 (4) (Proposed Official Draft 1962).
46. *Abdul-Kabir v. Quarterman*, 550 U.S. 233, 252 (2007), *quoting Franklin v. Lynaugh*, 487 U.S. 164, 184–185 (1988) (O'Connor, J., concurring in the judgment). This basic principle derives from *Lockett v. Ohio*, 438 U.S. 586, 604 (1978), where Chief Justice Burger's plurality opinion concluded that "the Eighth and Fourteenth Amendments require that the sentencer . . . not be precluded from considering, *as a mitigating factor*, any aspect of a defendant's character or record and any of the circumstances of the offense that the defendant proffers as a basis for a sentence less than death" (emphasis in original) (footnote omitted). *See also Hitchcock v. Dugger*, 481 U.S. 393 (1987). See note 42 and accompanying text, *supra*.
47. American Law Institute, *Report of the Council to the Membership of The American Law Institute on the Matter of the Death Penalty* 4 (2009), retrieved January 14, 2013 from www.ali.org/doc/Capital%20Punishment_web.pdf. *See also* Carol S. Steiker & Jordan M. Steiker, "No More Tinkering: The American Law Institute and the Death Penalty Provisions of the Model Penal Code," 89 *Texas Law Review* 353 (2010).
48. Cal. Penal Code § 190.2.
49. *Id.*, § 190.3.
50. *Id.*, § 190.3 (k).
51. *Id.*, § 190.3.
52. Tex. Penal Code § 19.03.
53. Tex. Code Criminal Procedure Art. 37.071 (2)(b)(1).

54. Tex. Code Criminal Procedure Art. 37.071 (2)(e)(1).

55. *See* note 46 and accompanying text, *supra*.

56. *See* note 30 and accompanying text, *supra*.

57. Gallup.com, *Death Penalty* (based on polling results from May 2003), retrieved January 12, 2013 from www.gallup.com/poll/1606/death-penalty.aspx. *See* note 9 and accompanying text, *supra; see generally* Radelet & Borg, *supra* note 10.

2

DETERRENCE

Introduction

The threat of punishment functions in part to discourage people from violating rules. We see this principle at work throughout numerous walks of life. It surfaces, for example, when parents give advance warning to their children of the unpleasant consequences of engaging in forbidden behavior. It almost certainly helps explain why most motorists dutifully deposit coins in a parking meter when they leave their car next to one, and adhere reasonably close to the speed limit while driving. It undergirds and is a prime justification for enforcing the criminal law. Potential sanctions obviously do not dissuade all who are tempted to break rules; if they did, there would be no crime. However, when violators are caught and held accountable, their punishment serves as an example for others that a similar fate awaits them in the event they are so bold as to follow suit. When the prospect of punishment, particularly as realized through its application to a known offender, discourages individuals who have not violated the law from doing so, it has functioned as a general deterrent to crime.

At first blush, it may seem self-evident that the threat of capital punishment should deter murder. After all, who would commit a murder knowing that doing so risks coming at the expense of his or her own life? On the other hand, how likely is it that prospective murderers think along these lines, contemplating the penal sanctions that attach to a killing and deciding whether or not to take a potential victim's life depending on the odds of being caught, convicted, and executed? Moreover, could capital punishment plausibly be counterproductive? Could state-sponsored executions desensitize citizens to killing, send a message that lethal violence is acceptable and, contrary to expectations, actually help stimulate criminal homicide? If it is unclear whether applying the death penalty might either discourage or incite future killings, can we simply compare the murder rates in jurisdictions that do and do not enforce capital punishment to find the answers? And if no definitive answers emerge and uncertainty reigns, what legal and policy implications concerning the death penalty and its use should follow? We explore these and related issues in this chapter.

Deterrence and the Death Penalty: Law, Assumptions, and Logic

The Constitutional Perspective

In *Gregg v. Georgia*,[1] the Supreme Court was asked to rule that the death penalty is inherently unconstitutional. Addressing this claim, the plurality opinion of Justices Stewart, Powell, and Stevens acknowledged that

> [a]lthough we cannot "invalidate a category of penalties because we deem less severe penalties adequate to serve the ends of penology," *Furman v. Georgia*, 408 U.S. [238], 451 [(1972)] (Powell, J., dissenting), the sanction imposed cannot be so totally without penological justification that it results in the gratuitous infliction of suffering.[2]

In chapter 1 we saw that the justices rejected the *per se* challenge to capital punishment. The Court concluded that retribution represents one constitutionally permissible justification for the death penalty. Although noting its controversial nature, the justices accepted general deterrence as another.[3]

The death penalty is said to serve two principal social purposes: retribution and deterrence of capital crimes by prospective offenders. . . .

Statistical attempts to evaluate the worth of the death penalty as a deterrent to crimes by potential offenders have occasioned a great deal of debate.[FN31] The results simply have been inconclusive. As one opponent of capital punishment has said:

FN31. *See, e.g.*, Peck, The Deterrent Effect of Capital Punishment: Ehrlich and His Critics, 85 Yale L.J. 359 (1976); Baldus & Cole, A Comparison of the Work of Thorsten Sellin and Isaac Ehrlich on the Deterrent Effect of Capital Punishment, 85 Yale L.J. 170 (1975); Bowers & Pierce, The Illusion of Deterrence in Isaac Ehrlich's Research on Capital Punishment, 85 Yale L.J. 187 (1975); Ehrlich, The Deterrent Effect of Capital Punishment: A Question of Life and Death, 65 Am. Econ. Rev. 397 (June 1975); Hook, The Death Sentence, in The Death Penalty in America 146 (H. Bedau ed. 1967); T. Sellin, The Death Penalty,

A Report for the Model Penal Code Project of the American Law Institute (1959).

"[A]fter all possible inquiry, including the probing of all possible methods of inquiry, we do not know, and for systematic and easily visible reasons cannot know, what the truth about this 'deterrent' effect may be. . . .

"The inescapable flaw is . . . that social conditions in any state are not constant through time, and that social conditions are not the same in any two states. If an effect were observed (and the observed effects, one way or another, are not large) then one could not at all tell whether any of this effect is attributable to the presence or absence of capital punishment. A 'scientific' that is to say, a soundly based conclusion is simply impossible, and no methodological path out of this tangle suggests itself." C. Black, Capital Punishment: The Inevitability of Caprice and Mistake 25–26 (1974).

Although some of the studies suggest that the death penalty may not function as a significantly greater deterrent than lesser penalties,[FN32] there is no convincing empirical evidence either supporting or refuting this view. We may nevertheless assume safely that there are murderers, such as those who act in passion, for whom the threat of death has little or no deterrent effect. But for many others, the death penalty undoubtedly is a significant deterrent. There are carefully contemplated murders, such as murder for hire, where the possible penalty of death may well enter into the cold calculus that precedes the decision to act.[FN33] And there are some categories of murder, such as murder by a life prisoner, where other sanctions may not be adequate.[FN34]

FN32. *See, e.g.,* The Death Penalty in America, *supra,* at 258–332; Report of the Royal Commission on Capital Punishment, 1949–1953, Cmd. 8932.

FN33. Other types of calculated murders, apparently occurring with increasing frequency, include the use of bombs or other means of indiscriminate killings, the extortion murder of hostages or kidnap victims, and the execution-style killing of witnesses to a crime.

FN34. We have been shown no statistics breaking down the total number of murders into the categories described above. The overall trend in the number of murders committed in the nation, however, has been upward for some time. In 1964, reported murders totaled an estimated 9,250. During the ensuing decade, the number reported increased 123%, until it totaled approximately 20,600 in 1974. In 1972, the year *Furman* was announced, the total estimated was 18,520. Despite a fractional decrease in 1975 as compared with 1974, the number of murders increased in the three years immediately following *Furman* to approximately 20,400, an increase of almost 10%. *See* FBI, Uniform Crime Reports, for 1964, 1972, 1974, and 1975, Preliminary Annual Release.

The value of capital punishment as a deterrent of crime is a complex factual issue the resolution of which properly rests with the legislatures, which can evaluate the results of statistical studies in terms of their own local conditions and with a flexibility of approach that is not available to the courts. *Furman v. Georgia,* 408 U.S. [238], 403–405 [(1972)] (Burger, C.J., dissenting). Indeed, many of the post-*Furman* statutes reflect just such a responsible effort to define those crimes and those criminals for which capital punishment is most probably an effective deterrent.

In sum, we cannot say that the judgment of the Georgia Legislature that capital punishment may be necessary in some cases is clearly wrong. Considerations of federalism, as well as respect for the ability of a legislature to evaluate, in terms of its particular State, the moral consensus concerning the death penalty and its social utility as a sanction, require us to conclude, in the absence of more convincing evidence, that the infliction of death as a punishment for murder is not without justification and thus is not unconstitutionally severe.

To have value as a general deterrent, the death penalty need not, and realistically could not be expected to discourage *all* future murders and prospective murderers. It should suffice to identify a subcategory of murders or potential offenders that would be discouraged by the threat of capital punishment but not by alternative sanctions. In this regard, the plurality opinion in *Gregg* ventures that the risk of being punished with death "undoubtedly is a significant deterrent" for "many," including murderers for hire and others who "carefully contemplate[]" killing. It nevertheless might be fair to ask whether those who do "carefully contemplate" killings in advance would be discouraged from carrying out their plans not only by the prospect of being executed, but also by the thought of spending the rest of their lives in prison.

On the other hand, perhaps the death penalty might be necessary and effective to serve as a deterrent for some potential murderers. For example, what if the punishment for kidnapping or rape is life imprisonment and, having committed such a crime, the offender is contemplating whether he should leave his victim alive knowing that she could serve as a witness in the event he is captured and brought to trial. If the death penalty is not available in the jurisdiction, what incentive does the kidnapper or rapist have not to murder his victim? Or consider an offender who already is serving a sentence of life imprisonment. Absent the risk of the death penalty, is a life term prisoner essentially immune from punishment if he commits a murder?

The *Gregg* plurality opinion characterizes scientific attempts to evaluate the death penalty's general deterrent value as "inconclusive" and laments that "there is no convincing empirical evidence either supporting or refuting" the deterrence hypothesis. The justices ultimately appear to disclaim their own competence to resolve such "a complex factual issue" and instead defer to the presumed legislative judgment that the death penalty is a superior deterrent to murder than alternative sanctions; a judgment that "we cannot say . . . is clearly wrong." These assertions hardly represent a ringing endorsement of the death penalty's value as a general deterrent to murder.

If capital punishment's contribution to general deterrence is a question of fact, as it seems to be—the availability and use of the death penalty either does or does not affect a jurisdiction's murder rate—is the legislative branch or the judiciary better suited to answer it? On the one hand, a legislature can hold hearings at which testimony and evidence can be offered and evaluated, and it can do so free of any constraints that might be associated with a specific case in which the issue arises. On the other hand, the politically supercharged nature of debates about capital punishment and the potential that elected officials' judgment will be affected by matters removed from the facts might suggest that the courts should be entrusted to resolve the empirical issues important to their constitutional rulings.[4]

Notwithstanding the justices' reasoning in *Gregg,* the Court has not always been willing to defer to presumed legislative findings that capital punishment advances the goal of general deterrence. A measure of judicial independence was registered in *Enmund v. Florida,* 458 U.S. 782 (1982), where the Court invalidated the death sentence imposed on an offender convicted of felony murder who had served as the getaway car driver in a robbery that resulted in the death of the elderly victims. There was no evidence that Enmund (as opposed to his accomplices) personally killed or attempted to kill the victims, or intended that lethal force would be used in the robbery's commission. With respect to deterrence, Justice White's majority opinion explained:[5]

We are quite unconvinced . . . that the threat that the death penalty will be imposed for murder will measurably deter one who does not kill and has no intention or purpose that life will be taken. Instead, it seems likely that "capital punishment can serve as a deterrent only when murder is the result of premeditation and deliberation," *Fisher v. United States*, 328 U.S. 463, 484 (1946) (Frankfurter, J., dissenting), for if a person does not intend that life be taken or contemplate that lethal force will be employed by others, the possibility that the death penalty will be imposed for vicarious felony murder will not "enter into the cold calculus that precedes the decision to act." *Gregg v. Georgia*, 428 U.S., at 186 (footnote omitted).

It would be very different if the likelihood of a killing in the course of a robbery were so substantial that one should share the blame for the killing if he somehow participated in the felony. But competent observers have concluded that there is no basis in experience for the notion that death so frequently occurs in the course of a felony for which killing is not an essential ingredient that the death penalty should be considered as a justifiable deterrent to the felony itself. Model Penal Code § 210.2, Comment, p. 38,

and n. 96. This conclusion was based on three comparisons of robbery statistics, each of which showed that only about one-half of one percent of robberies resulted in homicide. The most recent national crime statistics strongly support this conclusion.[FN24] In addition to the evidence that killings only rarely occur during robberies is the fact . . . that however often death occurs in the course of a felony such as robbery, the death penalty is rarely imposed on one only vicariously guilty of the murder, a fact which further attenuates its possible utility as an effective deterrence.

FN24. An estimated total of 548,809 robberies occurred in the United States in 1980. U.S. Dept. of Justice, Federal Bureau of Investigation, Uniform Crime Reports 17 (1981). Approximately 2,361 persons were murdered in the United States in 1980 in connection with robberies, *id.*, at 13, and thus only about 0.43% of robberies in the United States in 1980 resulted in homicide. See also Cook, The Effect of Gun Availability on Robbery and Robbery Murder, in 3 R. Haveman & B. Zellner, Policy Studies Review Annual 743, 747 (1980) (0.48% of all robberies result in murder).

Are there other kinds of murders or murderers, in addition to the circumstances described in *Enmund v. Florida*, for which it would be difficult to justify using the death penalty to promote general deterrence? For example, might there be reasons to doubt that mentally retarded offenders, or juveniles, would be dissuaded from killing by the possibility that they might receive a death sentence if caught and convicted? Regarding mentally retarded individuals, consider the respective views of Justice Stevens (for the majority) and Justice Scalia (in dissent) in *Atkins v. Virginia*, 536 U.S. 304 (2002). Justice Stevens reasoned as follows:[6]

With respect to deterrence—the interest in preventing capital crimes by prospective offenders—"it seems likely that 'capital punishment can serve as a deterrent only when

murder is the result of premeditation and deliberation,'" *Enmund*, 458 U.S., at 799. Exempting the mentally retarded from that punishment will not affect the "cold calculus that precedes the decision" of other potential murderers. *Gregg*, 428 U.S., at 186. Indeed, that sort of calculus is at the opposite end of the spectrum from behavior of mentally retarded offenders. The theory of deterrence in capital sentencing is predicated upon the notion that the increased severity of the punishment will inhibit criminal actors from carrying out murderous conduct. Yet it is the same cognitive and behavioral impairments that make these defendants less morally culpable—for example, the diminished ability to understand and process information, to learn from experience, to engage in logical reasoning, or to control impulses—that also make it less likely that they can process the information of the possibility of execution as a penalty and, as a result, control their conduct based upon that information. Nor will exempting the mentally retarded from execution lessen the deterrent effect of the death penalty with respect to offenders who are not mentally retarded. Such individuals are unprotected by the exemption and will continue to face the threat of execution. Thus, executing the mentally retarded will not measurably further the goal of deterrence.

Justice Scalia took exception with this argument for the following reasons[7]:

[Deterrence] is not advanced, the Court tells us, because the mentally retarded are "less likely" than their non-retarded counterparts to "process the information of the possibility of execution as a penalty and . . . control their conduct based upon that information." Of course this leads to the . . . conclusion . . . that the mentally retarded (because they are less deterred) are more likely to kill—which neither I nor the society at large believes. In any event, even the Court does not say that *all* mentally retarded individuals cannot "process the information of the possibility of execution as a penalty and . . . control their conduct based upon that information"; it merely asserts that they are "less likely" to be able to do so. But surely the deterrent effect of a penalty is adequately vindicated if it successfully deters many, but not all, of the target class. Virginia's death penalty, for example, does not fail of its deterrent effect simply because *some* criminals are unaware that Virginia *has* the death penalty. In other words, the supposed fact that *some* retarded criminals cannot fully appreciate the death penalty has nothing to do with the deterrence rationale.

An analogous debate took place in *Roper v. Simmons*, 543 U.S. 551 (2005), where the Court considered whether the Eighth Amendment forbids the execution of offenders younger than age 18 who commit murder. Justice Kennedy's majority opinion concluded, in part, that the death penalty cannot be justified on deterrence grounds for juveniles.[8]

As for deterrence, it is unclear whether the death penalty has a significant or even measurable deterrent effect on juveniles. . . . In general we leave to legislatures the assessment of the efficacy of various criminal penalty schemes. Here, however, the absence of evidence of deterrent effect is of special concern because the same characteristics that render juveniles less culpable than adults suggest as well that juveniles will be less susceptible to deterrence. In particular, as the plurality observed in *Thompson* [*v. Oklahoma*, 487 U.S. 815, 837 (1988)], "[t]he likelihood that the teenage offender has made the kind of cost-benefit analysis that attaches any weight to

the possibility of execution is so remote as to be virtually nonexistent." To the extent the juvenile death penalty might have residual deterrent effect, it is worth noting that the punishment of life imprisonment without the possibility of parole is itself a severe sanction, in particular for a young person.

Justice Scalia's rejoinder followed.[9]

The Court claims that "juveniles will be less susceptible to deterrence," because "[t]he likelihood that the teenage offender has made the kind of cost-benefit analysis that attaches any weight to the possibility of execution is so remote as to be virtually nonexistent,'" (quoting *Thompson,* 487 U.S., at 837). The Court unsurprisingly finds no support for this astounding proposition, save its own case law. The facts of this very case show the proposition to be

false. Before committing the crime, Simmons encouraged his friends to join him by assuring them that they could "get away with it" because they were minors. This fact may have influenced the jury's decision to impose capital punishment despite Simmons' age. Because the Court refuses to entertain the possibility that its own unsubstantiated generalization about juveniles could be wrong, it ignores this evidence entirely.

If the Court is willing to make more critical examination of the premises of the deterrence argument in the above contexts—involving the death penalty's defensibility for (some) participants in a felony murder as well as for mentally retarded and juvenile murderers—is the deference displayed to legislative bodies on the more general issue in *Gregg v. Georgia* nevertheless appropriate, or is it somewhat perplexing? Should judicial deference to implicit legislative fact-finding be variable, depending on what issues or class of individuals are implicated by a ruling? On further reflection, is it conceivable that resolving whether capital punishment is a general deterrent to murder is a secondary consideration, subservient to the truly decisive question of whether the death penalty can be justified on retributive grounds?

Recall Justice Powell's observation in *Rummel v. Estelle,* which we considered in chapter 1: "A statute that levied a mandatory life sentence for overtime parking might well deter vehicular lawlessness, but it would offend our felt sense of justice."[10] What are the implications of this assertion for determining whether, when all is said and done, the question of deterrence is (or should be) of central concern to the Court's acceptance of capital punishment? Should the death penalty's effectiveness as a deterrent be either a necessary or a sufficient condition of its constitutionality?

The Court embraced general deterrence as a permissible objective of capital punishment, and one that plausibly could be promoted, in 1976, early in its post-*Furman*
death penalty jurisprudence. Justice Stevens joined the plurality opinion in *Gregg v.
Georgia*, in which the deterrence rationale was endorsed. More than three decades
later he rescinded his views, not only about deterrence but, more fundamentally, about
whether administering the death penalty could be squared with the Constitution. He
did so in a concurring opinion issued in *Baze v. Rees*, 553 U.S. 35 (2008), a case that
directly involved whether Kentucky's use of lethal injection to carry out executions
violated the Eighth Amendment. In relevant part, Justice Stevens reasoned:[11]

The legitimacy of deterrence as an acceptable justification for the death penalty is . . .
questionable, at best. Despite 30 years of
empirical research in the area, there remains
no reliable statistical evidence that capital punishment in fact deters potential offenders.[FN13]
In the absence of such evidence, deterrence
cannot serve as a sufficient penological justification for this uniquely severe and irrevocable
punishment. . . .

FN13. Admittedly, there has been a recent
surge in scholarship asserting the deterrent effect of the death penalty, see, *e.g.*,
Mocan & Gittings, Getting off Death Row:
Commuted Sentences and the Deterrent
Effect of Capital Punishment, 46 J. Law &
Econ. 453 (2003); Adler & Summers, Capital Punishment Works, Wall Street Journal,
Nov. 2, 2007, p. A13, but there has been
an equal, if not greater, amount of scholarship criticizing the methodologies of those

studies and questioning the results, see,
e.g., Fagan, Death and Deterrence Redux:
Science, Law and Causal Reasoning on
Capital Punishment, 4 Ohio St. J.Crim. L.
255 (2006); Donohue & Wolfers, Uses and
Abuses of Empirical Evidence in the Death
Penalty Debate, 58 Stan. L.Rev. 791 (2005).

. . . [J]ust as Justice White ultimately based
his conclusion in *Furman* on his extensive
exposure to countless cases for which death
is the authorized penalty, I have relied on my
own experience in reaching the conclusion
that the imposition of the death penalty represents "the pointless and needless extinction
of life with only marginal contributions to any
discernible social or public purposes. A penalty with such negligible returns to the State
[is] patently excessive and cruel and unusual
punishment violative of the Eighth Amendment." *Furman*, 408 U.S., at 312 (White, J.,
concurring).

As in the other cases we have considered, Justice Scalia did not allow the arguments
advanced to undermine the deterrence rationale to go unanswered.[12]

According to Justice STEVENS, the death
penalty promotes none of the purposes of
criminal punishment because it neither prevents more crimes than alternative measures
nor serves a retributive purpose. He argues that
"the recent rise in statutes providing for life

imprisonment without the possibility of parole"
means that States have a ready alternative to
the death penalty. Moreover, "[d]espite 30 years
of empirical research in the area, there remains
no reliable statistical evidence that capital punishment in fact deters potential offenders."

Taking the points together, Justice STEVENS concludes that the availability of alternatives, and what he describes as the unavailability of "reliable statistical evidence," renders capital punishment unconstitutional. In his view, the benefits of capital punishment—as compared to other forms of punishment such as life imprisonment—are outweighed by the costs.

These conclusions are not supported by the available data. Justice STEVENS' analysis barely acknowledges the "significant body of recent evidence that capital punishment may well have a deterrent effect, possibly a quite powerful one." Sunstein & Vermeule, Is Capital Punishment Morally Required? Acts, Omissions, and Life–Life Tradeoffs, 58 Stan. L.Rev. 703, 706 (2005); see also id., at 706, n. 9 (listing the approximately half a dozen studies supporting this conclusion). According to a "leading national study," "each execution prevents some eighteen murders, on average." Id., at 706. "If the current evidence is even roughly correct . . . then a refusal to impose capital punishment will effectively condemn numerous innocent people to death." Ibid.

Of course, it may well be that the empirical studies establishing that the death penalty has a powerful deterrent effect are incorrect, and some scholars have disputed its deterrent value. See [Justice Stevens' opinion at] n. 13. But that is not the point. It is simply not our place to choose one set of responsible empirical studies over another in interpreting the Constitution. Nor is it our place to demand that state legislatures support their criminal sanctions with foolproof empirical studies, rather than commonsense predictions about human behavior. "The value of capital punishment as a deterrent of crime is a complex factual issue the resolution of which properly rests with the legislatures, which can evaluate the results of statistical studies in terms of their own local conditions and with a flexibility of approach that is not available to the courts." Gregg, supra, at 186 (joint opinion of Stewart, Powell, and STEVENS, JJ.). Were Justice STEVENS' current view the constitutional test, even his own preferred criminal sanction—life imprisonment without the possibility of parole—may fail constitutional scrutiny, because it is entirely unclear that enough empirical evidence supports that sanction as compared to alternatives such as life with the possibility of parole.

Why do you suppose such controversy surrounds the general deterrence question? Before turning to what the justices in the *Gregg* plurality identified as "[s]tatistical attempts to evaluate the worth of the death penalty as a deterrent to crimes by potential offenders,"[13] let us pause to examine the logical underpinnings of the competing perspectives.

The Logic (or Illogic) of Capital Punishment as a General Deterrent

Consider Ernest van den Haag's straightforward reasoning regarding the logical argument supporting the death penalty's effectiveness as a general deterrent.

> Our penal system rests on the proposition that more severe penalties are more deterrent than less severe penalties. We assume, rightly, I believe, that a $5 fine deters rape less than a $500 fine, and that the threat of five years in prison will deter more than either fine.

This assumption rests on the common experience that, once aware of them, people learn to avoid natural dangers the more likely these are to be injurious and the more severe the likely injuries. People endowed with ordinary common sense (a class which includes some sociologists) have found no reason why behavior with respect to legal dangers should differ from behavior with respect to natural dangers. Indeed, it does not. Hence, the legal system proportions threatened penalties to the gravity of crimes, both to do justice and to achieve deterrence in proportion to that gravity.

Thus, if it is true that the more severe the penalty the greater the deterrent effect, then the most severe penalty—the death penalty—would have the greatest deterrent effect. Arguments to the contrary assume either that capital crimes never are deterrable (sometimes merely because not all capital crimes have been deterred), or that, beyond some point, the deterrent effect of added severity is necessarily zero. Perhaps. But the burden of proof must be borne by those who presume to have located the point of zero marginal returns before the death penalty.[14]

Many will agree with the premise that capital punishment is "the most severe penalty" imposed by law. Many also will agree that both "common experience" and "common sense" support "the proposition that more severe penalties are more deterrent than less severe" ones. Does the conclusion thus follow that, as a logical matter, the death penalty should operate as the most effective general deterrent to murder?

Classical criminologists consider more to be important to the posited relationship between punishment and deterrence than the *severity* of the threatened sanction for offending. Cesare Beccaria, the Italian political philosopher whose early treatise *On Crimes and Punishment* was read widely by this country's founders,[15] and British philosopher Jeremy Bentham, regarded as the progenitor of modern utilitarianism, both argued that additional factors critically influence prospective offenders' decision making.[16] Most prominent are the perceived *certainty* that punishment will be imposed for offending, and its *celerity*, or how quickly it follows the offense's commission.[17] Capital punishment does not fare so well when measured against the latter criteria.

With respect to the certainty that murder will result in punishment by death, consider the following figures:[18]

Table 2.1   Criminal Homicides, Death Sentences, and Executions in the United States

YEAR	NUMBER OF CRIMINAL HOMICIDES	NUMBER OF DEATH SENTENCES	NUMBER OF EXECUTIONS
1980	23,040	173	0
1985	18,976	262	18
1990	23,438	251	23
1995	21,606	326	56
2000	15,586	235	85
2005	16,692	138	60
2010	15,094	104	46

The picture presented by these figures is not perfect. Many forms of criminal homicide do not qualify as capital murder and consequently are not punishable by death. The number of criminal homicides committed annually applies to the entire country, including those states (and the District of Columbia) without the death penalty. Lags exist between the years in which a murder is committed, when a death sentence is imposed and, especially, when an execution is carried out. Even allowing for adjustments to take such considerations into account, it would be strained, at best, to argue that the connection between committing a murder and being sentenced to death and executed is at all close to certain.[19]

As for celerity, or as Bentham put it, the "*propinquity* or *remoteness*"[20] of punishment and offense, the death penalty again does not receive high marks. Offenders executed in 2010 had spent, on average, 178 months on death row, or nearly 15 years, awaiting their fate.[21] Delays of three decades or more between sentence and execution are not unheard of. For example, Manuel Valle was executed in Florida in 2011 following 33 years of death row incarceration.[22]

But perhaps these details are beside the point. It would not be surprising to learn that few who contemplate or commit murder are such sophisticated students of capital punishment that they are conversant with the specific probabilities of being convicted and executed or how much time could be expected to lapse in the process. Subjective beliefs or perceptions, even if wildly inaccurate, are likely to be more important than objective facts.[23] Bentham thus observed:

> It is the idea only of the punishment (or, in other words, the *apparent* punishment) that really acts upon the mind; the punishment itself (the *real* punishment) acts not any farther than as giving rise to that idea. It is the apparent punishment, therefore, that does all the service.[24]

If deterrence theory hinges on the presumed linkages between prospective offenders' subjective beliefs (about the consequences of their actions), their motivations, and their future behavior—specifically, in this context, whether the threat of capital punishment dampens the propensity to commit murder—we should attempt to flesh out the particular assumptions that are at work.

> Deterrence theory finds parallel roots in classical criminology and in assumptions about human nature in economic theory. In particular, economic theory posits that an individual of any moral level, criminal or law-abiding, wants to maximize gains of material satisfaction and to minimize painful losses or risks associated with punishment in general and execution in particular. Homicidal benefits might include such things as material acquisition and/or psychological satisfaction. If the rationally calculating potential murderer sees the risk of these costs exceeding the likelihood of these benefits, her choice would be to abandon the homicidal course of conduct.[25]

Bentham declared "the principle of utility" to be "the foundation" of his work and the essential explanatory premise regarding the relationship between punishment and deterrence.

By the principle of utility is meant that principle which approves or disapproves of every action whatsoever, according to the tendency which it appears to have to augment or diminish the happiness of the party whose interest is in question: or, what is the same thing in other words, to promote or to oppose that happiness. . . .

By utility is meant that property in any object, whereby it tends to produce benefit, advantage, pleasure, good, or happiness, . . . or (what comes again to the same thing) to prevent the happening of mischief, pain, evil, or unhappiness to the party whose interest is considered.[26]

Applying this principle, it follows that: "*The value of the punishment must not be less in any case than what is sufficient to outweigh that of the profit of the offence.*"[27] Beccaria embraced a similar premise: "For a punishment to attain its end, the evil which it inflicts has only to exceed the advantage derivable from the crime. . . ."[28]

Is this how people really make decisions about their future conduct and, in particular, about whether they will commit murder?

Does it seem plausible that individuals who are contemplating murder pause before acting, weigh the benefits and costs of going forward, and then act or refrain from acting based on the result of those calculations?

And, of crucial importance, if capital punishment is to be justified on general deterrence grounds, its value is only as great as the *marginal* or *incremental* contribution made beyond alternative punishments that are available, such as life imprisonment without the possibility of parole. In other words, if people do engage in a benefit-cost analysis before deciding whether to commit murder, how many would willingly accept the "cost" of spending the rest of their life in prison, but would be discouraged from acting only by the prospect of being punished by death? Consider Justice Brennan's skeptical appraisal of these assumptions in his concurring opinion in *Furman v. Georgia.*[29]

It is important to focus upon the precise import of this argument [concerning the general deterrence value of capital punishment]. It is not denied that many, and probably most, capital crimes cannot be deterred by the threat of punishment. Thus the argument can apply only to those who think rationally about the commission of capital crimes. Particularly is that true when the potential criminal, under this argument, must not only consider the risk of punishment, but also distinguish between two possible punishments. The concern, then, is with a particular type of potential criminal, the rational person who will commit a capital crime knowing that the punishment is long-term imprisonment, which may well be for the rest of his life, but will not commit the crime knowing that the punishment is death. On the face of it, the assumption that such persons exist is implausible.

If the argument in support of capital punishment as a general deterrent to murder is premised on the assumptions that: (a) prospective murderers (or at least a fair number of them) are rational actors who (b) calculate the benefits and costs of killing before deciding whether to go forward, and (c) they will proceed to kill if they risk being punished "only" by life imprisonment without parole, but (d) they will be discouraged from killing exclusively by the perceived risk of being executed, then it may be difficult to defend on logical grounds.

Yet deterrence may operate more subtly. Most people almost certainly refrain from committing murder for reasons other than a fear of being caught and punished. Their conduct instead is likely to be governed by internalized notions of right and wrong. The incorporated norms and values, in turn, arguably are reinforced and made meaningful, in part, by social cues, including the official condemnation and punishment that attaches to wrongdoing. This sentiment was captured forcefully by 19th-century British jurist Sir James Fitzjames Stephen, who wrote:

> Some men, probably, abstain from murder because they fear that if they committed murder they would be hanged. Hundreds of thousands abstain from murder because they regard it with horror. One great reason why they regard murder with horror is that murderers are hanged with the hearty approbation of all reasonable men.[30]

Alternatively stated, punishment may help prevent crime not simply (or primarily) because it inspires fear, but because its existence and infliction in response to crime helps validate and strengthen social norms. This essential idea has roots in Emile Durkheim's classic writings regarding the role of punishment in expressing and legitimating values considered important to social solidarity.

> [The role of punishment] is not the one commonly perceived. It does not serve, or serves only very incidentally, to correct the guilty person or to scare off any possible imitators. . . . Its real function is to maintain inviolate the cohesion of society by sustaining the common consciousness in all its vigour. If that consciousness were thwarted so categorically, it would necessarily lose some of its power, were an emotional reaction from the community not forthcoming to make good that loss. Thus there would result a relaxation in the bonds of social solidarity. . . . This is why it is right to maintain that the criminal should suffer in proportion to his crime, and why theories that deny to punishment any expiatory character appear, in the minds of many, to subvert the social order. . . . Thus, without being paradoxical, we may state that punishment is above all intended to have its effect upon honest people. Since it serves to heal the wounds inflicted upon the collective sentiments, it can only fulfil this role where such sentiments exist, and in so far as they are active.[31]

Jack Gibbs has identified "normative validation" as one important mechanism through which punishment helps prevent crime. This construct is conceptually distinct from general deterrence, which operates through instilling fear of threatened sanctions.

> [L]egal punishment may give rise to or at least reinforce social condemnations of an act. Stated more abstractly, one possible consequence of legal punishment is normative validation, and the indirect consequence is greater conformity to laws in a manner *independent of deterrence*. Individuals refrain from illegal acts not because they fear punishment but because they evaluate the acts negatively, and legal punishments maintain or intensify those

negative evaluations. Stated another way, individuals have internalized the norm that the law expresses, and legal punishments contribute to that internalization.[32]

As thought-provoking and even plausible as these sociological notions may be, do they make a persuasive case that the death penalty in particular, as opposed to some form of meaningful punishment such as life imprisonment, is essential to reinforce and help inculcate norms against murder? If capital punishment is uniquely capable of fulfilling such a role, how do residents within states and countries that have no death penalty come to share the sentiment that murder is so horribly wrong? Moreover, is there some risk that the norms and values transmitted by executions are sufficiently ambiguous that they could be counterproductive? Might the officially sanctioned use of lethal force in the form of capital punishment convey the message to some that life is expendable, or that the state has tacitly expressed approval for killing in other contexts? These latter suggestions are at the core of the so-called "brutalization" hypothesis, which we consider next.

Might the Death Penalty Have a Brutalizing Effect?

It has been theorized that executions might increase murder, not deter them, and that the brutalization effect is the consequence of the beastly example that executions present. Executions devalue human life and "demonstrate that it is correct and appropriate to kill those who have gravely offended us." Thus, the lesson taught by capital punishment may be "the legitimacy of lethal vengeance, not of deterrence."[33]

Speculation that executions inspire rather than discourage murder is not new. In 1846, Robert Rantoul, Jr., then a Massachusetts legislator and later a United States Senator, offered statistical evidence supporting his contention that "after every instance in which the law violates the sanctity of human life, that life is held less sacred by the community among whom the outrage is perpetrated."[34] Decades earlier, Cesare Beccaria advanced a related argument.

The death penalty cannot be useful, because of the example of barbarity it gives men. If the passions or the necessities of war have taught the shedding of human blood, the laws, moderators of the conduct of men, should not extend the beastly example, which becomes more pernicious since the inflicting of legal death is attended with much study and formality. It seems to me absurd that the laws, which are an expression of the public will, which detest and punish homicide, should themselves commit it, and that to deter citizens from murder, they order a public one.[35]

Justices Brennan echoed these essential themes in his opinion in *Furman v. Georgia.*

If capital crimes require the punishment of death in order to provide moral reinforcement for the basic values of the community, those values can only be undermined when death is so rarely inflicted upon the criminals who commit the crimes. Furthermore, it is certainly doubtful that the infliction of death by the State does in fact strengthen the community's moral code; if the deliberate extinguishment of human life has any effect at all, it more likely tends to lower our respect for life and brutalize our values. That, after all, is why we no longer carry out public executions.[36]

Justice Marshall cited the potential brutalizing effect of capital punishment in his *Furman* opinion, as well, noting that "there is some evidence that imposition of capital punishment may actually encourage crime, rather than deter it."[37] He maintained that even if occasional cases purporting to illustrate the deterrent value of the death penalty were credited, they "may be more than counterbalanced by the tendency of capital punishment to incite certain crimes."[38]

Professor Anthony Amsterdam, the architect of the constitutional challenges in the NAACP Legal Defense Fund's campaign against the death penalty, maintained that "the plain message of capital punishment . . . is that life ceases to be sacred whenever someone with the power to take it away decides that there is a sufficiently compelling pragmatic reason to do so."[39] He invited consideration of

the well documented cases of persons who kill *because* there is a death penalty. One of these was Pamela Watkins, a baby-sitter in San Jose who had made several unsuccessful suicide attempts and was frightened to try again. She finally strangled two children so that the state of California would execute her. In various bizarre forms, this "suicide-murder" syndrome is reported by psychiatrists again and again.[40]

One of the psychiatrists to whom Professor Amsterdam may have been referring was Dr. Bernard Diamond, a professor of psychiatry and law at the University of California, Berkeley. Diamond wrote that

[a] number of psychiatrists who have examined persons who have committed homicides have told me informally that they are convinced that, in certain instances, the threat of imposition of the death penalty has acted as an instigator rather than as a deterrant [sic] to the commission of the crime. It seems to be common knowledge among such experts that a killer's expectation of execution is one method of suicide.[41]

Diamond himself interviewed a multiple murderer evidencing such tendencies, whom he identified as "Martin," shortly before the man's execution in California. Diamond asked Martin "what he would have done if California had had no capital punishment. He answered, 'I would have had to go to another state where they did have capital punishment and do it all there.'"[42] Diamond concluded:

Capital punishment, with its dramatic rituals and ceremonies, is an essential component of such games with fate. There may be fantasies of welcoming execution as a form of glorified crucifixion, to be followed by resurrection. It surely is no deterrent. The perpetrator of the terminal act does not fear death, he longs for death. What he fears is life, with its miseries and desperate conflicts. To such a one, prison is to be feared above all else, for it promises a continuation of the old miseries. Hence, the consistently expressed preference for death over prison by such offenders.[43]

Of course, theories, anecdotes, and case studies are a far cry from solid evidence in support of capital punishment's purported brutalization effect. Counterexamples and case histories contraindicating brutalization and supporting deterrence can just as readily be offered. We next turn to research studies that have attempted to systematically investigate the relationship, if any, that exists between the death penalty and the commission of murder.

The Death Penalty, Deterrence, and Brutalization: What Does the Research Evidence Suggest?

Imagine designing a study to determine whether the death penalty influences the murder rate and, if so, the circumstances under which it has such an effect. Where would you begin?

It is tempting simply to compare the murder rate in states that do and do not have the death penalty, or in death-penalty states that carry out executions with comparatively high or low frequency.[44] A moment's reflection would diminish our confidence in this strategy. How much would it help us to know, for example, that in 2011 the murder rate in South Dakota, which has the death penalty, was 2.5 per 100,000, whereas the murder rate in New York, without capital punishment, was 4.0 per 100,000? Or that in Texas (which has conducted more than four times as many executions as any other state since 1977) the murder rate for that same year was 4.4 per 100,000?[45] Much more certainly accounts for the different homicide rates in these states than whether they have the death penalty and how often murderers are executed.

It similarly would be risky to focus on a single state and examine its murder rate during years when it did and did not have or make use of the death penalty. For example, Iowa repealed its death penalty statute in 1872, reenacted capital punishment legislation in 1878, and maintained its law on the books until 1965, when it again became an abolition jurisdiction.[46] Although we could compare the murder rates in Iowa during intervals when capital punishment was and was not available, we should be reluctant to attribute any observed fluctuations to the changed status of the death penalty law. Too many other changes might have occurred and too many other circumstances might have influenced the varying murder rates in the pre- and post-abolition periods.

A comparison of homicide rates between states that do and do not have death penalty laws might nevertheless be of some interest, particularly if we choose contiguous states that appear to be generally similar in terms of demographic, economic, and other relevant characteristics. The same might be said for examining murder rates within the same state during pre- and post-abolition eras of capital punishment. If we confine our attention to the years straddling the changed status of the law and observe corresponding annual homicide rates, any trends or patterns, while not definitive, might at least be suggestive. The early deterrence and brutalization studies tended to adopt these strategies.

Thorsten Sellin reported the homicide rates for several contiguous abolition and retention states during each of the years between 1920 and 1963. He examined the following state groupings (abolition jurisdictions are marked by an asterisk [*]): (a) Maine,* New Hampshire, and Vermont; (b) Rhode Island,* Connecticut, and Massachusetts; (c) Minnesota,* Wisconsin,* and Iowa; (d) Michigan,* Indiana, and Ohio; (e) Kansas (until 1935),* Colorado, and Missouri; (f) North Dakota* and South Dakota (until 1939)*. No distinctive patterns emerged. Instead, he reported, "within each group of contiguous states it would be impossible to identify the abolitionist state." He argued that "[t]he conclusion is inevitable that the presence of the death penalty—in law or practice—does not influence homicide death rates."[47] In a later study employing a similar strategy, Peterson and Bailey examined the murder rates in contiguous death penalty and abolition jurisdictions between 1980 and 2000. Acknowledging the limitations of this methodology, they echoed Sellin in reporting that "[t]hese comparisons . . . yielded negligible results for the deterrence hypothesis."[48]

Sellin also compared murder rates in 11 states that had "experimented with abolition" at various points in their history through the early 1960s. After examining the homicide data at his disposal, which were of "admittedly poor" quality, he reported that "[i]f any conclusion can be drawn . . . it is that there is no evidence that the abolition of the death penalty generally causes an increase in criminal homicides or that its re-introduction is followed by a decline. The explanation of changes in homicide rates must be sought elsewhere."[49] Other researchers of this era reported similar findings, generally concurring that "abolition and/or reintroduction of capital punishment [within the observed states] was sometimes followed by an increase in murders and sometimes not."[50]

Increasingly sophisticated statistical methods allowed researchers to attempt to isolate the death penalty penalty's unique influence on homicide rates by "controlling" for other factors that also might affect the incidence of murder. Professor Isaac Ehrlich published his study of the deterrent value of capital punishment, which employed such techniques, shortly before *Gregg v. Georgia* and its companion cases were argued in the Supreme Court. The study figured prominently in briefs supporting deterrence as a legitimate objective of capital punishment[51] and was cited in the plurality opinion of Justices Stewart, Powell, and Stevens.[52] It examined executions and homicides within the United States occurring in the years 1933–1969, while simultaneously considering such additional factors as the probability of offenders' apprehension, conviction, and execution for murder; unemployment rates; estimates of per capita income; and the percentage of the population between 14 and 24 years of age. Ehrlich interpreted the results as indicating "the existence of a pure deterrent effect of capital punishment. In fact, the empirical analysis suggests that on average the tradeoff between the execution of an offender and the lives of potential victims it might have saved was of the order of magnitude of 1 for 8 for the period 1933–1967 in the United States."[53]

Justice Marshall disputed the study's validity in his dissenting opinion in *Gregg*.[54]

In *Furman*, I canvassed the relevant data on the deterrent effect of capital punishment. 408 U.S., at 347–354.[FN2] The state of knowledge at that point, after literally centuries of debate, was summarized as follows by a United Nations Committee:

FN2. *See e.g.*, T. Sellin, The Death Penalty, A Report for the Model Penal Code Project of the American Law Institute (1959).

"It is generally agreed between the retentionists and abolitionists, whatever their opinions about the validity of comparative studies of deterrence, that the data which now exist show no correlation between the existence of capital punishment and lower rates of capital crime."[FN3]

FN3. United Nations, Department of Economic and Social Affairs, Capital Punishment, pt. II, P 159, p. 123 (1968).

The available evidence, I concluded in *Furman*, was convincing that "capital punishment is not necessary as a deterrent to crime in our society." *Id.*, at 353.

The Solicitor General in his amicus brief in these cases relies heavily on a study by Isaac Ehrlich,[FN4] reported a year after *Furman*, to support the contention that the death penalty does deter murder. Since the Ehrlich study was not available at the time of *Furman* and since it is the first scientific study to suggest that the death penalty may have a deterrent effect, I will briefly consider its import.

FN4. I. Ehrlich, The Deterrent Effect of Capital Punishment: A Question of Life and Death (Working Paper No. 18, National Bureau of Economic Research, Nov. 1973);

Ehrlich, The Deterrent Effect of Capital Punishment: A Question of Life and Death, 65 Am.Econ.Rev. 397 (June 1975).

The Ehrlich study focused on the relationship in the Nation as a whole between the homicide rate and "execution risk" the fraction of persons convicted of murder who were actually executed. Comparing the differences in homicide rate and execution risk for the years 1933 to 1969, Ehrlich found that increases in execution risk were associated with increases in the homicide rate. But when he employed the statistical technique of multiple regression analysis to control for the influence of other variables posited to have an impact on the homicide rate,[FN6] Ehrlich found a negative correlation between changes in the homicide rate and changes in execution risk. His tentative conclusion was that for the period from 1933 to 1967 each additional execution in the United States might have saved eight lives.

FN6. The variables other than execution risk included probability of arrest, probability of conviction given arrest, national aggregate measures of the percentage of the population between age 14 and 24, the unemployment rate, the labor force participation rate, and estimated per capita income.

The methods and conclusions of the Ehrlich study have been severely criticized on a number of grounds.[FN8] It has been suggested, for example, that the study is defective because it compares execution and homicide rates on a nationwide, rather than a state-by-state, basis. The aggregation of data from all States including those that have been [*sic*] abolished the death penalty obscures the relationship between murder and execution rates. Under Ehrlich's methodology, a decrease in the execution risk in one State combined with an increase in the murder rate in another State would, all other things being equal, suggest a deterrent effect that quite obviously would not exist. Indeed, a deterrent effect would be suggested if, once again all other things being equal, one State abolished the death penalty and experienced no change in the murder rate, while another State experienced an increase in the murder rate.

FN8. *See* Passell & Taylor, The Deterrent Effect of Capital Punishment: Another View (unpublished Columbia University Discussion Paper 74–7509, Mar. 1975), reproduced in Brief for Petitioner App. E in *Jurek v. Texas*, O.T. 1975, No. 75–5844; Passell, The Deterrent Effect of the Death Penalty: A Statistical Test, 28 Stan.L.Rev. 61 (1975); Baldus & Cole, A Comparison of the Work of Thorsten Sellin & Isaac Ehrlich on the Deterrent Effect of Capital Punishment, 85 Yale L.J. 170 (1975); Bowers & Pierce, The Illusion of Deterrence in Isaac Ehrlich's Research on Capital Punishment, 85 Yale L.J. 187 (1975); Peck, The Deterrent Effect of Capital Punishment: Ehrlich and His Critics, 85 Yale L.J. 359 (1976). *See also* Ehrlich, Deterrence: Evidence and Inference, 85 Yale L.J. 209 (1975); Ehrlich, Rejoinder, 85 Yale L.J. 368 (1976). In addition to the items discussed in text, criticism has been directed at the quality of Ehrlich's data, his choice of explanatory variables, his failure to account for the interdependence of those variables, and his assumptions as to the mathematical form of the relationship between the homicide rate and the explanatory variables.

The most compelling criticism of the Ehrlich study is that its conclusions are extremely sensitive to the choice of the time period included in the regression analysis. Analysis of Ehrlich's data reveals that all empirical support for the deterrent effect of capital punishment disappears when the five most recent years are removed from his time series, that is to say, whether a decrease in the execution risk corresponds to an increase or a decrease in the murder rate depends on the ending point of the sample period.[FN10] This finding has cast severe doubts on the reliability of Ehrlich's tentative conclusions. Indeed, a recent regression study, based on Ehrlich's theoretical model but using cross-section state data for the years 1950 and 1960 found no support for the conclusion that executions act as a deterrent.[FN12]

FN10. Bowers & Pierce, *supra*, n. 8, at 197–198. *See also* Passell & Taylor, *supra*, n. 8, at 2–66 2–68.

FN12. Pass--ell, *supra*, n. 8.

The Ehrlich study, in short, is of little, if any, assistance in assessing the deterrent impact of the death penalty. The evidence I reviewed in *Furman*[FN13] remains convincing, in my view that "capital punishment is not necessary as a deterrent to crime in our society." 408 U.S., at 353. The justification for the death penalty must be found elsewhere.

FN13. *See also* Bailey, Murder and Capital Punishment: Some Further Evidence, 45 Am.J.Orthopsychiatry 669 (1975); W. Bowers, Executions in America 121–163 (1974).

A review published in 1978 under the auspices of the National Research Council of the National Academy of Sciences largely concurred with Justice Marshall's analysis, citing a list of reasons explaining why "Ehrlich's results cannot be used at this time to pass judgment on the use of the death penalty. . . . [Para.] . . . The deterrent effect of capital punishment is definitely not a settled matter, and this is the strongest social scientific conclusion that can be reached at the present time."[55]

During this same era, other researchers were investigating the brutalization hypothesis in an effort to learn whether, in direct contradiction to the deterrence theory, the execution of murderers might actually spark a rise in the homicide rate by stimulating new killings that otherwise would not have been committed. William Bowers and Glenn Pierce made note of every execution that occurred in New York during each of the 692 months between January 1906 and August 1963, when the state last used its electric chair. Imposing a one-year time lag, they also noted the number of criminal homicides committed in New York between January 1907 and August 1964. After taking account of seasonal trends for both executions and homicides, they found modest support for a short-term brutalization effect. In particular:

> [O]n the average, the presence of one or more executions in a given month adds two homicides to the number committed in the next month.
>
> A similar but weaker effect appears for the presence of executions two months earlier. . . . [Analysis] suggests that, on the average, executions imposed in a given month add one homicide to the number committed two months later. We say "suggest" here because the observed pattern in the data is not sufficiently strong . . . to be statistically significant at the .05 probability level.[56]

To complicate matters further, other researchers have presented some evidence suggesting that executions deter certain types of murders but have a brutalizing effect with respect to others, stimulating their commission. These scholars have argued that it is overly simplistic and potentially misleading to focus on the overall homicide rate when investigating deterrence and brutalization because doing so masks the important differential effects of the death penalty on different kinds of killings. Studies have suggested, for example, that executions, and especially those receiving extensive publicity, might inspire the commission of murders involving arguments between offenders and victims who are strangers. On the other hand, executions might deter felony murders from being committed when non-strangers are victims.[57]

Studying the execution and homicide rates within individual states between 1977 and 1996, Joanna Shepherd similarly reported mixed findings regarding capital punishment, deterrence, and brutalization. Focusing on effects within the specific jurisdictions, she found evidence of deterrence in six states, of brutalization in 13 states, and that there was no relationship between executions and murder in eight states. She explained the differential effects by suggesting a "threshold effect" concerning the regularity of executions. "In states with fewer than a threshold of approximately nine

executions during the sample period, each execution increases the number of murders. In states that exceed the threshold, executions deter murder."[58] She made some
"back-of-the-envelope calculations" that produced "very imprecise"[59] estimates of the
net effect of executions on murder when the deterrent and brutalization effects she
found were combined.

> There were 192 executions between 1977 and 1996 in deterrent states, fifty-four in no effect
> states, and 112 in brutalization states. I multiplied the median number of murders deterred
> or incited in each state by the total number of executions in each state to compute the net
> lives saved or lost. In deterrent states over the twenty-year sample period, executions saved
> approximately 6,918 lives.
>
> Subtracting the 192 executions yields a net lives saved of 6,726, or approximately 336 per
> year. In no-effect states, fifty-four lives were lost, all executions.
>
> In brutalization states, the 112 executions caused approximately 5,246 murders—again,
> this estimate is very rough. Adding the 112 executions yields the total lives lost of 5,358.
> This was 268 per year. . . .
>
> Considering the lives only of innocent people—ignoring the deaths of the convicts
> whom executions kill directly—capital punishment saves lives. Subtracting the murders
> caused in the brutalization states (very roughly 5,246) from those saved in the deterrence
> states (6,918) shows that net lives saved nationwide from executions is 1,672, or eighty-four
> per year.[60]

Shepherd drew three policy implications from the results of her study:

> First, if deterrence is the objective, then capital punishment generally succeeds in the few
> states with many executions. Second, the many states with numbers of executions below
> the threshold may be executing people needlessly. Indeed, instead of deterring crime, the
> executions may be inducing additional murders: a rough total estimate is that, in the many
> states where executions induce murders rather than deter them, executions cause an addi-
> tional 250 murders per year. Third, to achieve deterrence, states must generally execute many
> people. If a state is unwilling to establish such a large execution program, it should consider
> abandoning capital punishment.[61]

The numerous assumptions required concerning the factors that influence murder
rates (including variations within individual states and within discrete subcategories of
murder), the complexity of the mathematical models used to investigate the possible
deterrence and brutalization effects of capital punishment, and the sensitivity of the
models to the underlying assumptions, time frames, and measurement issues, continue
to produce controversy about whether scientific research evidence has contributed
meaningfully to this debate.[62] A 2008 survey solicited the views of distinguished criminologists (past presidents, fellows, and Sutherland Award recipients of the American
Society of Criminology) on various death penalty issues related to deterrence. To the
question, "Do you feel that the death penalty acts as a deterrent to the commitment to

[sic] murder—that it lowers the murder rate, or not?," 88% of the respondents answered "No," while 5% said "Yes," and 7% expressed no opinion.[63]

A 1978 review completed in connection with a National Research Council (NRC) panel report on the deterrent and incapacitative effects of punishment considered the methodology and results of research that had investigated the deterrent effects of capital punishment. Focusing principally on the work of Thorsten Sellin and Isaac Ehrlich, the review concluded that "[t]he deterrent effect of capital punishment is definitely not a settled matter, and this is the strongest social scientific conclusion that can be reached at the present time."[64] A generation later, a 2012 committee of the NRC analyzed the numerous studies published subsequent to the Supreme Court's decision in *Gregg v. Georgia* that had examined the death penalty's possible influence on criminal homicide. The committee's cornerstone conclusion suggested that little had changed.

> The committee concludes that research to date on the effect of capital punishment on homicide is not informative about whether capital punishment decreases, increases, or has no effect on homicide rates. Therefore, the committee recommends that these studies not be used to inform deliberations requiring judgments about the effect of the death penalty on homicide. Consequently, claims that research demonstrates that capital punishment decreases or increases the homicide rate by a specified amount or has no effect on the homicide rate should not influence policy judgments about capital punishment.[65]

Two principal shortcomings in the new research accounted for the committee's inability to draw more definitive conclusions.

> One major deficiency in all the existing studies is that none specify the noncapital sanction components of the sanction regime for the punishment of homicide. Another major deficiency is the use of incomplete or implausible models of potential murderers' perceptions of and response to the capital punishment component of a sanction regime. Without this basic information, it is impossible to draw credible findings about the effect of the death penalty on homicide.[66]

While acknowledging the difficulty in designing and carrying out studies that would produce firmer conclusions about the relationship between the death penalty and criminal homicide, the 2012 NRC committee expressed some confidence that the challenge was not insurmountable.[67] To that end, it made a number of specific recommendations for securing more reliable information.[68] It remains to be seen whether future generations of researchers will succeed in overcoming the obstacles that have confronted scholars and policymakers for centuries in gaining more definitive answers about the unique deterrent or brutalization effects that capital punishment may or may not have on the commission of murder.

A Note on the Burden of Persuasion and Related Policy Issues

If the jury arguably is still out, logically and empirically, about whether capital punishment laws and/or executions help deter future murders (putting to one side, for now, the death penalty's possible brutalizing or murder-inducing effects), what policy implications follow from this uncertainty? Consider the views of Ernest van den Haag, who below makes reference to the controversial conclusion reached by Isaac Ehrlich that approximately eight murders were deterred by each execution carried out in this country between 1933 and 1967.

[W]ith respect to deterrence, we must now choose:

(1) To trade the certain shortening of the life of a convicted murderer against the survival of between seven and eight innocent victims whose future murder by others becomes more probable, unless the convicted murderer is executed;

(2) To trade the certain survival of the convicted murderer against the loss of the lives of between seven and eight innocent victims, who are more likely to be murdered by others if the convicted murderer is allowed to survive.

Prudence as well as morality command us to choose the first alternative. . . .

. . . I should now regard it as irresponsible not to shorten the lives of convicted murderers simply because we cannot be altogether sure that their execution will lengthen the lives of innocent victims: It seems immoral to let convicted murderers survive at the probable—or even at the merely possible—expense of the lives of innocent victims who might have been spared had the murderers been executed.[69]

In a variation of this argument, Cass Sunstein and Adrian Vermeule ask indulgence of the assumption, rooted in a few recent research findings, that executions deter future murders, perhaps on the order of 18 innocent lives being spared for each convicted murderer whose death sentence is carried out. Reminiscent of van den Haag's thesis, they maintain:

If the current evidence is even roughly correct . . . then a refusal to impose capital punishment will effectively condemn numerous innocent people to death. States that choose life imprisonment, when they might choose capital punishment, are ensuring the deaths of a large number of innocent people. On moral grounds, a choice that effectively condemns large numbers of people to death seems objectionable to say the least.[70]

They intimate that such reasoning is persuasive even absent their stipulation that the death penalty's deterrent effects should be presumed.

But let us suppose, plausibly, that the evidence of deterrence remains inconclusive. . . . A degree of doubt . . . need not be taken to suggest that existing evidence is irrelevant for purposes of policy and law. In regulation as a whole, it is common to embrace some version of the precautionary principle—the idea that steps should be taken to prevent significant harm even if cause-and-effect relationships remain unclear and even if the risk is not likely to come to fruition. Even if we reject strong versions of the precautionary principle, it hardly seems sensible that governments should ignore evidence demonstrating a significant possibility that a certain step will save large numbers of innocent lives.[71]

Carol Steiker's attempted refutation of Sunstein and Vermeule's central arguments draws attention to the significance of the differences between *acts* and *omissions* (as in the government's carrying out executions, and its failure to carry out executions) that result in harms, and between *intending* to cause a result (such as the death of a convicted murderer by government execution) and *knowing* or *risking* that a result will occur (as in deaths caused by future murderers that may be attributable to the government's failure to execute).

The central insight on which Sunstein and Vermeule stake their argument is that the government is a distinctive moral actor that is equally responsible for things it lets happen as for things it does. . . .

But while the point may go very far in the regulatory context . . . it does not go nearly as far as they suggest in the capital punishment context. . . . In the regulatory context, when the government makes life-life tradeoffs, its treatment of lives on either side of the tradeoff is identical; it is risking lives whether it acts or fails to act, but in neither case is its purpose to take life. In the capital punishment context, this moral equivalence in the treatment of lives does not obtain; the government knowingly or recklessly loses or "takes" lives by not executing (assuming that it knows or thinks there is a good chance that executions deter), but it purposefully takes lives by executing. Sunstein and Vermeule wish to say that knowing or risking that others will act purposefully is the moral equivalent of acting purposefully oneself, or that even if it is not equivalent for individuals, it somehow becomes equivalent for the government (hence, their dramatic assertion that private murders should be viewed as the moral equivalent of government "executions"). But we do not recognize this moral equivalence for individual actors, and there is no good reason to do so for the government as actor, either. . . .

. . . One can agree that the government is "acting" when (if) it fails to provide optimal deterrence for private murders and that, therefore, it bears some moral responsibility for those deaths and has a moral obligation to try to prevent them. But this acknowledgement does not entail that the government is required to take any action that would prevent such murders, no matter how morally problematic that action might be. Sunstein and Vermeule's insistence that the government is morally obligated to retain capital punishment depends on collapsing a further distinction—the distinction between purposeful and nonpurposeful killing. . . . The evasion of this further distinction is necessary to equilibrate the government's accountability for deaths it commands and for murders it forbids but fails to adequately deter, and thus to permit the choice to retain or abolish capital punishment to be portrayed as a "life-life tradeoff." . . .

Of course, Sunstein and Vermeule could (and do, briefly) claim that the government's purposeful killings are independently morally justified because the lives that it takes by executions are (usually) those of guilty murderers, while the lives that it knowingly or recklessly cedes to private murder are by definition those of innocents. But when they switch to this kind of moral justification for the state's purposeful killing, Sunstein and Vermeule have switched to the language of deontological moral theory (retributivism) and thus acknowledge the nonequivalence of the state's actions in taking life through execution and through suboptimal deterrence of private murder: they are no longer on the terrain of life-life tradeoffs at all.[72]

Legal and policy decisions frequently must be made in the face of uncertainty about the consequences of alternative courses of action. In light of the arguments and available evidence pertaining to capital punishment's potential to deter (or stimulate) future murders, does a clearly correct choice emerge concerning whether the death penalty should or should not be utilized? As noted earlier in this chapter, the plurality opinion in *Gregg v. Georgia* relied on insights offered by Professor Charles Black to help make the case that the uncertainties surrounding capital punishment and its deterrent effect on murder were inevitable and essentially defied resolution.

> [A]fter all possible inquiry, including the probing of all possible methods of inquiry, we do not know, and for systematic and easily visible reasons cannot know, what the truth about this "deterrent" effect may be. . . .
>
> The inescapable flaw is . . . that social conditions in any state are not constant through time, and that social conditions are not the same in any two states. If an effect were observed (and the observed effects, one way or another, are not large) then one could not at all tell whether any of this effect is attributable to the presence or absence of capital punishment. A "scientific" that is to say, a soundly based conclusion is simply impossible, and no methodological path out of this tangle suggests itself. C. Black, *Capital Punishment: The Inevitability of Caprice and Mistake* 25–26 (1974).[73]

Professor Black's continuing observations, not quoted by the justices in *Gregg*, followed:

> When I last sampled this enormous literature, I found two scholars were arguing over where the "burden of proof" lay—whether, that is to say, the man who asserts that capital punishment deters has to prove this proposition or lose out, or whether the man who asserts that it does *not* deter has to prove this proposition or lose out. When you observe that an argument is in that posture, you can be very sure that neither side has a convincing case.[74]

Conclusion

We may be little closer now than we were at the beginning of this chapter to having firm conclusions about whether, how, and under what circumstances having and enforcing a capital punishment law influences a jurisdiction's murder rate. Whatever the relationship may be, the challenge is to try to identify the death penalty's unique contribution to deterrence (or brutalization)—its marginal or incremental effects— above and beyond that associated with alternative threatened sanctions such as life imprisonment without the possibility of parole. The Supreme Court has accepted that a legislature could rationally conclude that the threat of capital punishment deters at least some future murders more effectively than does the threat of life imprisonment.

Logically, it is possible to envision some prospective murderers who would not be deterred by the threat of life imprisonment and would only be prevented from killing by the prospect of being executed—perhaps a prisoner who already is serving a life term sentence, or a rapist or kidnapper who already faces life imprisonment for committing that crime and contemplates whether to leave his victim alive to possibly testify against him. On the other hand, it also is logically possible that government-sponsored executions have a brutalizing effect and occasionally encourage misguided citizens to commit murder by debasing the value of life and serving as an example that killing can be condoned in response to serious transgressions.

Research evidence has lent support to both such hypotheses. The required assumptions and complex mathematical modeling that undergird research on the deterrent and brutalizing effects of capital punishment inject such uncertainty into the analyses that, after investigating numerous studies conducted over an extensive period of time and in multiple jurisdictions, a distinguished panel of experts commissioned by the National Research Council came to the essential conclusion in 2012 that the studies remain inconclusive. If we accept that assessment, the best research to date has "not [been] informative about whether capital punishment decreases, increases, or has no effect on homicide rates."[75]

The implications of the logical stand-offs and the conflicting and uncertain empirical evidence concerning the death penalty's utility in deterring future murders may be just as elusive as answers to the many other questions involving deterrence, brutalization, and capital punishment. The centuries-old debates surrounding these issues appear destined to continue for the foreseeable future.

Endnotes

1. 428 U.S. 153 (1976).
2. *Gregg v. Georgia*, 428 U.S. 153, 182–183 (1976) (plurality opinion).
3. *Id.*, 428 U.S., at 183–187.
4. *See generally* Caitlin E. Borgmann, "Rethinking Judicial Deference to Legislative Fact-Finding," 84 *Indiana Law Journal* 1 (2009); James R. Acker, "A Different Agenda: The Supreme Court, Empirical Research Evidence, and Capital Punishment Decisions, 1986–1989," 27 *Law & Society Review* 65 (1993).
5. *Enmund v. Florida*, 458 U.S. 782, 798–800 (1982) (footnote omitted). As discussed in Chapter 5, the Supreme Court modified its ruling in *Enmund* regarding death penalty-eligibility for defendants convicted of felony murder in *Tison v. Arizona*, 481 U.S. 137 (1987).
6. *Atkins v. Virginia*, 536 U.S. 304, 319–320 (2002).
7. *Id.*, 536 U.S., at 351–352 (dissenting opinion).
8. *Roper v. Simmons*, 543 U.S. 551, 571–572 (2005).
9. *Id.*, 543 U.S., at 621–622 (dissenting opinion).
10. 445 U.S. 263, 280 (1980) (dissenting opinion).
11. *Baze v. Rees*, 553 U.S. 35, 79, 86 (2008) (concurring in the judgment).

12. *Id.*, 553 U.S., at 89–90 (concurring in the judgment).

13. *Gregg v. Georgia*, 428 U.S. 153, 184 (1976) (plurality opinion).

14. Ernest van den Haag, "In Defense of the Death Penalty: A Legal-Practical-Moral Analysis," 14 *Criminal Law Bulletin* 51, 59–60 (1978) (footnote omitted).

15. Cesare Beccaria, *On Crimes and Punishment*, trans. Henry Paolucci (Indianapolis: Bobbs-Merrill Co., orig. 1764/1963). *See generally* John D. Bessler, *Cruel & Unusual: The American Death Penalty and the Founders' Eighth Amendment* (Boston: Northeastern University Press 2012).

16. Jeremy Bentham, *An Introduction to the Principles of Morals and Legislation* (New York: Hafner Publishing Co., orig. 1789/1948). *See generally* Hugo Adam Bedau, "Bentham's Utilitarian Critique of the Death Penalty," 74 *Journal of Criminal Law & Criminology* 1033 (1983).

17. *See generally* Raymond Paternoster, "How Much Do We Really Know About Criminal Deterrence?" 100 *Journal of Criminal Law & Criminology* 765, 783–784 (2010); Jeffrey Fagan, "Death and Deterrence Redux: Science, Law and Causal Reasoning on Capital Punishment," 4 *Ohio State Journal of Criminal Law* 255, 300 (2006); Rudolph J. Gerber, "Economic and Historical Implications for Capital Punishment Deterrence," 18 *Notre Dame Journal of Law, Ethics, & Public Policy* 437, 440 (2004).

18. The information presented in Table 2.1 is derived from the following sources: U.S. Dept. of Justice, Bureau of Justice Statistics, *Homicide Trends in the United States, 1980–2008* (Nov. 2011), retrieved January 25, 2013 from http://bjs.ojp.usdoj.gov/content/pub/pdf/htus8008.pdf; U.S. Dept. of Justice, Bureau of Justice Statistics, *Homicide Trends in the United States,* "Long Term Trends" (2010), retrieved January 25, 2013 from http://bjs.ojp.usdoj.gov/content/pub/pdf/htius.pdf; James R. Acker, "The Flow and Ebb of American Capital Punishment," in Marvin D. Krohn, Alan J. Lizotte & Gina Penly Hall (eds.), *Handbook on Crime and Deviance* 297, 310 (New York: Springer 2009); Death Penalty Information Center, "Death Sentences in the United States From 1977 by State and by Year," retrieved January 25, 2013 from www.deathpenaltyinfo.org/death-sentences-united-states-1977-2008; Death Penalty Information Center, "Executions by Year Since 1976," retrieved January 25, 2013 from www.deathpenaltyinfo.org/executions-year.

19. *See* Fagan, *supra* note 17, at 300: "[N]o more than one homicide in four is capital-eligible, few of these are selected for prosecution, and the percentage of death row cases that proceed to execution for states other than Texas remains very low." (Footnotes omitted.)

20. Bentham, *supra* note 16, at 29; *see id.*, at 187.

21. U.S. Dept. of Justice, Bureau of Justice Statistics, *Capital Punishment, 2010—Statistical Tables* 12, Table 8 (Dec. 2011), retrieved January 26, 2013 from http://bjs.ojp.usdoj.gov/content/pub/pdf/cp10st.pdf.

22. *See Valle v. Florida*, 132 S.Ct. 1 (2011) (Breyer, J., dissenting from denial of certiorari); Death Penalty Information Center, "Time on Death Row," retrieved January 26, 2013 from www.deathpenaltyinfo.org/time-death-row.

23. *Cf.*, Greg Pogarsky, Alex R. Piquero & Ray Paternoster, "Modeling Change in Perceptions About Sanction Threats: The Neglected Linkage in Deterrence Theory," 20 *Journal of Quantitative Criminology* 343 (2004); Greg Pogarsky, "Identifying 'Deterrable' Offenders: Implications for Research on Deterrence," 19 *Justice Quarterly* 431 (2002).

24. Bentham, *supra* note 16, at 193 (emphasis in original).

25. Gerber, *supra* note 17, at 440 (footnotes omitted).

26. Bentham, *supra* note 16, at 2.

27. *Id.*, at 179 (emphasis in original) (footnotes omitted).

28. Beccaria, *supra* note 15, at 43.

29. 408 U.S. 238, 301 (1972) (Brennan, J., concurring in the judgment).

30. Sir James Fitzjames Stephen, *A General View of the Criminal Law of England* 99 (1863), *quoted in* Dan M. Kahan & Martha C. Nussbaum, "Two Conceptions of Emotion in Criminal Law," 96 *Columbia Law Review* 269, 374 n. 396 (1996).

31. Emile Durkheim, *The Division of Labor in Society*, trans. W. D. Hall (New York: Free Press, orig. 1893/1984).

32. Jack P. Gibbs, *Crime, Punishment, and Deterrence* 80 (New York: Elsevier Scientific Publishing Co. 1975) (emphasis in original) (citation and footnote omitted). *See also* Jack P. Gibbs, "Preventive Effects of Capital Punishment Other Than Deterrence," 14 *Criminal Law Bulletin* 34, 40–43 (1976).

33. Joanna M. Shepherd, "Deterrence Versus Brutalization: Capital Punishment's Differing Impacts Among States," 104 *Michigan Law Review* 203, 240 (2005) (footnotes and citations omitted).

34. Luther Hamilton, ed., *Memoirs, Speeches, and Writings of Robert Rantoul, Jr.* 494 (Boston: John P. Jewett 1854), *quoted in* William J. Bowers & Glenn L. Pierce, "Deterrence or Brutalization: What Is the Effect of Executions?" 26 *Crime & Delinquency* 453, 456 (1980).

35. Beccaria, *supra* note 15, at 50. *See* Bowers & Pierce, *supra* note 34, at 456.

36. *Furman v. Georgia*, 408 U.S. 238, 303 (1972) (Brennan, J., concurring in the judgment).

37. *Id.*, 408 U.S., at 351 (Marshall, J., concurring in the judgment) (footnote omitted).

38. *Id.*, 408 U.S., at 353 (footnote omitted).

39. Anthony Amsterdam, "Capital Punishment," in Hugo Adam Bedau, ed., *The Death Penalty in America* 346, 352–353 (New York: Oxford University Press, 3d ed. 1982).

40. *Id.*, at 357 (emphasis in original).

41. Bernard L. Diamond, "Murder and the Death Penalty: A Case Report," 45 *American Journal of Orthopsychiatry* 712, 712 (1975).

42. *Id.*, at 720.

43. *Id.*, at 721.

44. *See* Death Penalty Information Center, "Deterrence: States Without the Death Penalty Have Consistently Lower Murder Rates," retrieved February 8, 2013 from www.deathpenaltyinfo.org/deterrence-states-without-death-penalty-have-had-consistently-lower-murder-rates#stateswithvwithout.

45. Death Penalty Information Center, "Murder Rates Nationally and by State," retrieved February 8, 2013 from www.deathpenaltyinfo.org/murder-rates-nationally-and-state#MRalpha.

46. Stuart Banner, *The Death Penalty: An American History* 220–221 (Cambridge, MA: Harvard University Press 2002).

47. Thorsten Sellin, "Homicide in Retentionist and Abolitionist States," in Thorsten Sellin (ed.), *Capital Punishment* 135, 138 (New York: Harper & Row 1967). *See also* Thorsten Sellin, "Death and Imprisonment as Deterrents to Murder," in Hugo Adam Bedau (ed.), *The Death Penalty in America* 274 (Garden City, NY: Anchor Books, rev. ed. 1967).

48. Ruth D. Peterson & William C. Bailey, "Is Capital Punishment an Effective Deterrent for Murder? An Examination of Social Science Research," in James R. Acker, Robert M. Bohm & Charles S. Lanier (eds.), *America's Experiment With Capital Punishment: Reflections on the Past, Present, and Future of the Ultimate Penal Sanction* 251, 255 (Durham, NC: Carolina Academic Press, 2d ed. 2003).

49. Thorsten Sellin, "Experiments With Abolition," in *Capital Punishment, supra* note 47, at 122, 124.

50. Peterson & Bailey, *supra* note 48, at 253.

51. *See., e.g.*, Brief for the United States as Amici Curiae, *Gregg v. Georgia et al.* at 38 ("A recent study has tentatively concluded that when capital punishment was *actually used* a significant number of lives were saved: over the period studied, and after controlling for the effects of other variables, using the death penalty instead of imprisonment may have deterred eight murders for each execution actually carried out. See Ehrlich, *The Deterrent Effect of Capital Punishment*, 65 Am. Econ. Rev. 397 (1975).") (Emphasis in original, footnote omitted).

52. *Gregg v. Georgia*, 428 U.S. 153, 184 n. 31 (1976) (*see* chapter text following note 3, *supra*).

53. Isaac Ehrlich, "The Deterrent Effect of Capital Punishment: A Question of Life and Death," 65 *American Economic Review* 397, 398 (1975).

54. *Gregg v. Georgia*, 428 U.S. 153, 233–236 (1976) (Marshall, J., dissenting).

55. Lawrence R. Klein, Brian Forst & Victor Filatov, "The Deterrent Effect of Capital Punishment: An Assessment of the Estimates," in Alfred Blumstein, Jacqueline Cohen & Daniel Nagin (eds.), *Deterrence and Incapacitation: Estimating the Effects of Criminal Sanctions on Crime Rates* 336, 358–359 (Washington, D.C.: National Academy of Sciences 1978).

56. William J. Bowers & Glenn L. Pierce, "Deterrence or Brutalization: What Is the Effect of Executions?," 26 *Crime & Delinquency* 453, 473 (1980).

57. *See* John K. Cochran & Mitchell B. Chamlin, "Deterrence and Brutalization: The Dual Effects of Executions," 17 *Justice Quarterly* 685 (2000); William C. Bailey, "Deterrence, Brutalization, and the Death Penalty: Another Examination of Oklahoma's Return to Capital Punishment," 36 *Criminology* 711 (1998); John K. Cochran, Mitchell B. Chamlin & Mark Seith, "Deterrence or Brutalization? An Impact Assessment of Oklahoma's Return to Capital Punishment," 32 *Criminology* 107 (1994).

58. Shepherd, *supra* note 33, at 233–234.

59. *Id.*, at 231.

60. *Id.*, at 232.

61. *Id.*, at 248.

62. *See, e.g.,* Hasham Dezhbakhsh, Paul H. Rubin & Joanna M. Shepherd, "Does Capital Punishment Have a Deterrent Effect? New Evidence From Postmoratorium Panel Data," 5 *American Law and Economics Review* 344 (2003); Hashem Dezhbakhsh & Joanna M. Shepherd, "The Deterrent Effect of Capital Punishment: Evidence From a 'Judicial Experiment,'" 44 *Economic Inquiry* 512 (2006); Jeffrey Fagan, "Death and Deterrence Redux: Science, Law and Causal Reasoning on Capital Punishment," 4 *Ohio State Journal of Criminal Law* 255 (2006); John J. Donohue & Justin Wolfers, "Uses and Abuses of Empirical Evidence in the Death Penalty Debate," 58 *Stanford Law Review* 791 (2006); Tomislav V. Kovandzic, Lynne M. Vieraitis & Denise Paquette Boots, "Does the Death Penalty Save Lives? New Evidence From State Panel Data, 1977 to 2006," 8 *Criminology & Public Policy* 803 (2009); Kenneth C. Land, Raymond H.C. Teske, Jr. & Hui Zheng, "The Short-Term Effects of Executions on Homicides: Deterrence, Displacement, or Both?," 47 *Criminology* 1009 (2009).

63. Michael L. Radelet & Traci L. Lacock, "Do Executions Lower Homicide Rates?: The Views of Leading Criminologists," 99 *Journal of Criminal Law & Criminology* 489, 505 (2009). *See also* Michael L. Radelet & Ronald L. Akers, "Deterrence and the Death Penalty: The Views of the Experts," 87 *Journal of Criminal Law & Criminology* 1 (1996) (reporting results of a 1995 survey of past presidents of the American Society of Criminology, the Academy of Criminal Justice Sciences, and the Law and Society Association, in which 84% responded "No" to the question, "Do you feel that the death penalty acts as a deterrent to the commitment [sic] of murder—that it lowers the murder rate, or what?"; 12% responded "Yes"; and 4.5% had no opinion).

64. Klein, Forst & Filatov, *supra* note 55, at 359.

65. National Research Council of the National Academies, Committee on Deterrence and the Death Penalty, *Deterrence and the Death Penalty* 2 (Washington, D.C. The National Academies Press 2012).

66. *Id.*, at 3.

67. *Id.*, at 7.

68. *Id.*, at 7–8, 101–123.

69. Ernest van den Haag, "In Defense of the Death Penalty: A Legal-Practical-Moral Analysis," 14 *Criminal Law Bulletin* 51, 58–59 (1978).

70. Cass R. Sunstein & Adrian Vermeule, "Is Capital Punishment Morally Required? Acts, Omissions, and Life-Life Tradeoffs," 58 *Stanford Law Review* 703, 706 (2005) (footnote omitted).

71. *Id.* at 715 (footnotes omitted).

72. Carol S. Steiker, "No, Capital Punishment Is Not Morally Required: Deterrence, Deontology, and the Death Penalty," 58 *Stanford Law Review* 751, 756–763 (2005) (footnotes omitted). Reproduced with permission of School of Law, Stanford University via Copyright Clearance Center.

73. *Gregg v. Georgia*, 428 U.S. 153, 185 (1976) (plurality opinion), *quoting* Charles L. Black, Jr., *Capital Punishment: The Inevitability of Caprice and Mistake* 25–26 (New York: W.W. Norton & Co. 1974).

74. Black, *supra* note 73, at 26.

75. See text accompanying note 65, *supra*.

3

INCAPACITATION, COST, AND CONSIDERATION FOR VICTIMS

Introduction

We have considered the two principal justifications offered in support of capital punishment: retribution and deterrence. We now consider three additional purposes that often are advanced. The first is incapacitation, or protecting society from the risk that individuals convicted of a capital crime will reoffend. The second concerns the relative financial costs of capital punishment and long-term imprisonment, with the question being whether executing offenders is cheaper than incarcerating them for life. The third is that victims' survivors—their spouses, parents, children, and intimate others—are owed the offender's execution in the name of justice and to provide a sense of closure as they struggle to cope with the devastating emotional consequences of losing a loved one to murder.

Incapacitation

When the Supreme Court rejected the argument advanced in *Gregg v. Georgia* that the death penalty is *per se* unconstitutional, the plurality opinion of Justices Stewart, Powell, and Stevens observed that: "The death penalty is said to serve two principal social purposes: retribution and deterrence of capital crimes by prospective offenders."[1] An accompanying footnote acknowledged that: "Another purpose that has been discussed is the incapacitation of dangerous criminals and the consequent prevention of crimes that they may otherwise commit in the future."[2] This function requires little elaboration. As Justice Marshall put it in *Furman v. Georgia*: "Much of what must be said about the death penalty as a device to prevent recidivism is obvious—if a murderer is executed, he cannot possibly commit another offense."[3]

Nevertheless, the plurality opinion's relegation of incapacitation to a footnote in *Gregg* and its muted endorsement of this objective suggested that the justices did not consider it to be on equal footing with retribution and deterrence as a justification for the death penalty. This much was made explicit a few years later in *Spaziano v. Florida*, where Justice Blackmun's majority opinion explained: "Although incapacitation has never been embraced as a sufficient justification for the death penalty, it is a legitimate consideration in a capital sentencing proceeding."[4] In that same case, Justice Stevens, a member of the *Gregg* plurality, elaborated:[5]

In general, punishment may rationally be imposed for four reasons: (1) to rehabilitate the offender; (2) to incapacitate him from committing offenses in the future; (3) to deter others from committing offenses; or (4) to assuage the victim's or the community's desire for revenge or retribution. The first of these purposes is obviously inapplicable to the death sentence. The second would be served by execution, but in view of the availability of imprisonment as an alternative means of preventing the defendant from violating the law in the future, the death sentence would clearly be an excessive response to this concern.[FN19] We are thus left with deterrence and retribution as the justifications for capital punishment.

> FN19. Although incapacitation was identified as one rationale that had been advanced for the death penalty in *Gregg*, 428 U.S., at 183, n. 28 (opinion of STEWART, POWELL, and STEVENS, JJ.), we placed no reliance upon this rationale in upholding the imposition of capital punishment under the Eighth Amendment, and this ground was not mentioned at all by four of the seven Justices who voted to uphold the death penalty in *Gregg* and its companion cases. In any event, incapacitation alone could not justify the imposition of capital punishment, for if it did mandatory death penalty statutes would be constitutional, and, as we have held, they are not.

In 2008, two years before he retired from the Court, Justice Stevens repudiated the position he had taken on incapacitation in *Gregg*: "While incapacitation may have been a legitimate rationale in 1976, the recent rise in statutes providing for life imprisonment without the possibility of parole demonstrates that incapacitation is neither a necessary nor a sufficient justification for the death penalty."[6]

Texas's death-penalty statute was among those reviewed by the Court in 1976. This law elevated incapacitation to a primary consideration and its sentencing criteria and procedures differed significantly from the guided discretion statutes adopted in Georgia and Florida, which also were being challenged. Jerry Lane Jurek had been convicted of capital murder while kidnapping and raping a 10-year-old girl. He was sentenced to death under Texas's newly enacted post-*Furman* statute, as described below in the Supreme Court decision upholding the law.

Jurek v. Texas, 428 U.S. 262, 96 S.Ct. 2959, 49 L.Ed.2d 929 (1976)

Judgment of the Court, and opinion of Mr. Justice STEWART, Mr. Justice POWELL, and Mr. Justice STEVENS, announced by Mr. Justice STEVENS. . . .

III

A

After this Court held Texas' system for imposing capital punishment unconstitutional in Branch v. Texas, decided with Furman v. Georgia, 408 U.S. 238 (1972), the Texas Legislature narrowed the scope of its laws relating to capital punishment. The new Texas Penal Code limits capital homicides to intentional and knowing murders committed in five situations: murder of a peace officer or fireman; murder committed in the course of kidnaping, burglary, robbery, forcible rape, or arson; murder committed for remuneration; murder committed while escaping or attempting to escape from a penal institution; and murder committed by a prison inmate when the victim is a prison employee. See Tex. Penal Code § 19.03 (1974).

In addition, Texas adopted a new capital-sentencing procedure. See Tex. Code Crim. Proc., Art. 37.071 (Supp. 1975–1976). That procedure requires the jury to answer three questions in a proceeding that takes place subsequent to the return of a verdict finding a person guilty of one of the above categories of murder. The questions the jury must answer are these:

"(1) whether the conduct of the defendant that caused the death of the deceased was committed deliberately and with the reasonable expectation that the death of the deceased or another would result;

"(2) whether there is a probability that the defendant would commit criminal acts of violence that would constitute a continuing threat to society; and

"(3) if raised by the evidence, whether the conduct of the defendant in killing the deceased was unreasonable in response to the provocation, if any, by the deceased." Art. 37.071(b) (Supp. 1975–1976).

If the jury finds that the State has proved beyond a reasonable doubt that the answer to each of the three questions is yes, then the death sentence is imposed. If the jury finds that the answer to any question is no, then a sentence of life imprisonment results.[FN5] The law also provides for an expedited review by the Texas Court of Criminal Appeals. . . .

FN5. The jury can answer "yes" only if all members agree; it can answer "no" if 10 of 12 members agree. . . .

While Texas has not adopted a list of statutory aggravating circumstances the existence of which can justify the imposition of the death penalty as have Georgia and Florida, its action in narrowing the categories of murders for which a death sentence may ever be imposed serves much the same purpose. . . . Thus, in essence, the Texas statute requires that the jury find the existence of a statutory aggravating circumstance before the death penalty may be imposed. . . .

But a sentencing system that allowed the jury to consider only aggravating circumstances would almost certainly fall short of providing the individualized sentencing determination that we today have held in Woodson v. North Carolina, 428 U.S. 280 [(1976)] to be required by the Eighth and Fourteenth Amendments. . . . A jury must be allowed to consider on the basis of all relevant evidence not only why a death sentence should be imposed, but also why it should not be imposed.

. . . The Texas statute does not explicitly speak of mitigating circumstances; it directs only that the jury answer three questions. Thus, the constitutionality of the Texas procedures turns on whether the enumerated questions allow consideration of particularized mitigating factors.

The second Texas statutory question asks the jury to determine "whether there is a probability that the defendant would commit criminal acts of violence that would constitute a continuing threat to society" if he were not sentenced to death. The Texas Court of Criminal Appeals has yet to define precisely the meanings of such terms as "criminal acts of violence" or "continuing threat to society." In the present case, however, it indicated that it will interpret this second question so as to allow a defendant to bring to the jury's attention whatever mitigating circumstances he may be able to show:

"In determining the likelihood that the defendant would be a continuing threat to society, the jury could consider whether the defendant had a significant criminal record. It could consider the range and severity of his prior criminal conduct. It could further look to the age of the defendant and whether or not at the time of the commission of the offense he was acting under duress or under the domination of another. It could also consider whether the defendant was under an extreme form of mental or emotional pressure, something less, perhaps, than insanity, but more than the emotions of the average man, however inflamed, could withstand." 522 S.W.2d, at 939–940. . . .

Thus, Texas law essentially requires that one of five aggravating circumstances be found before a defendant can be found guilty of capital murder, and that in considering whether to impose a death sentence the jury may be asked to consider whatever evidence of mitigating circumstances the defense can bring before it. It thus appears that, as in Georgia and Florida, the Texas capital-sentencing procedure guides and focuses the jury's objective consideration of the particularized circumstances of the individual offense and the individual offender before it can impose a sentence of death.

B

As in the Georgia and Florida cases, however, the petitioner contends that the substantial legislative changes that Texas made in response to this Court's Furman decision are no more than cosmetic in nature and have in fact not eliminated the arbitrariness and caprice of the system held in Furman to violate the Eighth and Fourteenth Amendments. . . .

Focusing on the second statutory question that Texas requires a jury to answer in considering whether to impose a death sentence, the petitioner argues that it is impossible to predict future behavior and that the question is so vague as to be meaningless. It is, of course, not easy to predict future behavior. The fact that such a determination is difficult, however, does not mean that it cannot be made. Indeed, prediction of future criminal conduct is an essential element in many of the decisions rendered throughout our criminal justice system. The decision whether to admit a defendant to bail, for instance, must often turn on a judge's prediction of the defendant's future conduct. And any sentencing authority must predict a convicted person's probable future conduct when it engages in the process of determining what punishment to impose. For those sentenced to prison, these same predictions must be made by parole authorities. The task that a Texas jury must perform in answering the statutory question in issue is thus basically no different from the task performed countless times each day throughout the American system of criminal justice. What is essential is that the jury have before it all possible relevant information about the individual defendant whose fate it must determine. Texas law clearly assures that all such evidence will be adduced.

IV

We conclude that Texas' capital-sentencing procedures, like those of Georgia and Florida, do not violate the Eighth and Fourteenth Amendments. . . .

[Chief Justice Burger and Justices White, Rehnquist, and Blackmun concurred in the judgment. Justices Brennan and Marshall dissented.]

The second special issue considered by Texas juries, which is at the heart of the state's capital sentencing scheme, brings incapacitation to the fore by focusing on the offender's likely future dangerousness. Before a death sentence can be imposed, the jury must conclude unanimously, and beyond a reasonable doubt, that the answer is "yes" to "whether there is a probability that the defendant would commit criminal acts of violence that would constitute a continuing threat to society."

Conceptually, does it seem odd that, under this law, whether an offender will live or die does not depend exclusively on his past murderous conduct but rather hinges on what he might do in the future? Or instead, as the plurality opinion maintains, is "[t]he task that a Texas jury must perform in answering the statutory question . . . basically no different from the task performed countless times each day throughout the American system of criminal justice"? If, by definition, incapacitation has a future orientation, and if someone who already has committed a capital offense might engage in additional "criminal acts of violence," are there any reasons not to embrace this traditional sentencing objective in the death penalty context?

Embedded in the special issue are several terms that are cryptic if not obscure. In combination, they almost have an Alice-in-Wonderland-like quality. At the outset, jurors are instructed that before they answer "Yes" to the question, they must be convinced beyond a reasonable doubt not that the defendant *will* commit future acts of criminal violence, but rather that "there is a *probability*" he would do so. Such a finding has been likened to a requirement for responding with "a definite maybe."[7] A conscientious, literal-minded juror almost certainly would be hard pressed not to believe that there is *some* "probability" that a convicted capital murderer would pose a risk of future violence.[8]

And what, precisely, are "criminal acts of violence"? Presumably, something less than a repeat murder would qualify, perhaps even a misdemeanor assault, but the text of the statute offers no clarification. Nor is it clear what "a continuing threat" connotes, or what is meant by the "society"—the one within prison walls or the world outside of those walls—that will be threatened.[9] The Texas courts have consistently declined to order that jurors be instructed about the specific meaning of the words in the special issue. The Texas Court of Criminal Appeals has explained that: "Where terms used are words simple in themselves, and are used in their ordinary meaning, jurors are supposed to know such common meaning and terms and under such circumstances such common words are not necessarily to be defined in the charge to the jury."[10]

Texas's capital sentencing statute was revised following the Supreme Court's 1989 ruling in *Penry v. Lynaugh*,[11] a case in which Johnny Paul Penry, an intellectually disabled offender, had been convicted of murder and sentenced to death. The justices ruled that the three questions put to the jury during the penalty phase were inadequate to allow the jurors to give effect to mitigation evidence associated with Penry's impaired intellectual functioning. In fact, the Court reasoned, a jury might be especially likely to return a death sentence under the special issues framework if it concluded that Penry's impaired learning ability and poor impulse control would elevate the risk of his engaging in future violent conduct. Mental retardation would not serve as a mitigating factor but, almost perversely, would operate to Penry's detriment. The Texas legislature consequently rewrote the law, but future dangerousness remains a central consideration. The revised sentencing framework still requires the jury to respond affirmatively to "whether there is a probability that the defendant would commit criminal acts of violence that would constitute a continuing threat to society."[12] On making such a finding, the jury then must answer:

> Whether, taking into consideration all of the evidence, including the circumstances of the offense, the defendant's character and background, and the personal moral culpability of the defendant, there is a sufficient mitigating circumstance or circumstances to warrant that a sentence of life imprisonment without parole rather than a death sentence be imposed.[13]

Oregon, which has a capital sentencing statute that closely resembles Texas's law, is the only other jurisdiction that uses the special issue framework and makes predictions about an offender's future dangerousness such a central concern.[14] In Virginia, however, convicted murderers are ineligible for the death penalty unless the jury concludes that they present a risk of future dangerousness or, in the alternative, that their offense was particularly heinous.[15] The offender's predicted future dangerousness is a sentencing consideration (recognized either by statute or as a non-statutory factor) in numerous other death-penalty jurisdictions.[16] Interviews conducted with former jurors in capital cases as well as mock studies suggest that whether or not they are invited or authorized by law to do so, jurors discuss and their sentencing decisions are heavily influenced by the risk that an offender will be dangerous to others if he is not executed.[17] In short, future dangerousness predictions can and often do determine whether a capital offender will live or die.

We thus should be interested in the accuracy of such predictions. If they are not to be trusted, then the legitimacy of sentencing statutes predicated on future dangerousness findings as well as the reliability of sentences imposed in individual cases are called into serious question. These issues arose in the following case, in which the Supreme Court considered whether expert psychiatric testimony about the defendant's future dangerousness was properly admitted for the jury's consideration in a Texas capital sentencing proceeding. Thomas A. Barefoot was convicted of murdering a Texas law enforcement officer who had stopped him for questioning about a suspected arson. Barefoot had escaped from a New Mexico jail several months earlier, where he had been awaiting trial on statutory rape and kidnapping charges. Two psychiatrists, Dr. John Holbrook and Dr. James Grigson, testified for the prosecution at the penalty phase of Barefoot's capital murder trial. Neither had interviewed Barefoot. In response to assumptions set forth in the form of a lengthy hypothetical question, each opined that Barefoot would likely engage in future acts of criminal violence and represent a continuing threat to society. The jury responded affirmatively to the "future dangerousness" sentencing issue and Barefoot was sentenced to death. His conviction and death sentence were upheld in the lower courts.[18]

Barefoot v. Estelle, 463 U.S. 880, 103 S.Ct. 3383, 77 L.Ed.2d 1090 (1983)

Justice WHITE delivered the opinion of the Court. . . .

III

[Petitioner argues] that his death sentence must be set aside because the Constitution of the United States barred the testimony of the two psychiatrists who testified against him at the punishment hearing. . . . First, it is urged that psychiatrists, individually and as a group, are incompetent to predict with an acceptable degree of reliability that a particular criminal will commit other crimes in the future and so represent a danger to the community. Second, it is said that in any event, psychiatrists should not be permitted to testify about future dangerousness in response to hypothetical questions and without having examined the defendant personally. . . . [W]e reject each of these arguments.

A

The suggestion that no psychiatrist's testimony may be presented with respect to a defendant's future dangerousness is somewhat like asking us to disinvent the wheel. In the first place, it is contrary to our cases. If the likelihood of a defendant committing further crimes is a constitutionally acceptable criterion for imposing the death penalty, which it is, *Jurek v. Texas*, 428 U.S. 262 (1976), and if it is not impossible for even a lay person sensibly to arrive at that conclusion, it makes little sense, if any, to submit that psychiatrists, out of the entire universe of persons who might have an opinion on the issue, would know so little about the subject that they should not be permitted to testify. . . . Acceptance of petitioner's position that expert testimony about future dangerousness

is far too unreliable to be admissible would immediately call into question [several] other contexts in which predictions of future behavior are constantly made. . . .

In the second place, the rules of evidence generally extant at the federal and state levels anticipate that relevant, unprivileged evidence should be admitted and its weight left to the fact finder, who would have the benefit of cross examination and contrary evidence by the opposing party. Psychiatric testimony predicting dangerousness may be countered not only as erroneous in a particular case but as generally so unreliable that it should be ignored. If the jury may make up its mind about future dangerousness unaided by psychiatric testimony, jurors should not be barred from hearing the views of the State's psychiatrists along with opposing views of the defendant's doctors.

Third, petitioner's view mirrors the position expressed in the amicus brief of the American Psychiatric Association (APA). . . . We are not persuaded that [expert psychiatric] testimony is almost entirely unreliable and that the fact-finder and the adversary system will not be competent to uncover, recognize, and take due account of its shortcomings.

The *amicus* does not suggest that there are not other views held by members of the Association or of the profession generally. Indeed, as this case and others indicate, there are those doctors who are quite willing to testify at the sentencing hearing, who think, and will say, that they know what they are talking about, and who expressly disagree with the Association's point of view. . . . If they are so obviously wrong and should be discredited, there should be no insuperable problem in doing so by calling members of the Association who are of that view. . . . Neither petitioner nor the Association suggests that psychiatrists are always wrong with respect to future dangerousness, only most of the time. Yet the submission is that this category of testimony should be excised entirely from all trials. We are unconvinced, however, at least as of now, that the adversary process cannot be trusted to sort out the reliable from the unreliable evidence and opinion about future dangerousness, particularly when the convicted felon has the opportunity to present his own side of the case. . . .

B

Whatever the decision may be about the use of psychiatric testimony, in general, on the issue of future dangerousness, petitioner urges that such testimony must be based on personal examination of the defendant and may not be given in response to hypothetical questions. We disagree. Expert testimony, whether in the form of an opinion based on hypothetical questions or otherwise, is commonly admitted as evidence where it might help the factfinder do its assigned job. . . .

. . . Although cases such as this involve the death penalty, we perceive no constitutional barrier to applying the ordinary rules of evidence governing the use of expert testimony. . . .

IV

. . . There is no doubt that the psychiatric testimony increased the likelihood that petitioner would be sentenced to death, but this fact does not make that evidence inadmissible, any more than it would with respect to other relevant evidence against any defendant in a criminal case. At bottom, to agree with petitioner's basic position would seriously undermine and in effect overrule *Jurek v. Texas.* . . . We are not inclined, however, to overturn the decision in that case.

The judgment of the District Court is *Affirmed.*

Justice BLACKMUN, with whom Justice BRENNAN and Justice MARSHALL join in Parts I-IV, dissenting.

. . . The Court holds that psychiatric testimony about a defendant's future dangerousness is admissible, despite the fact that such testimony is wrong two times out of three. The Court reaches this result—even in a capital case—because, it is said, the testimony is subject to cross-examination and impeachment. In the present state of psychiatric knowledge, this is too much for me. One may accept this in a routine lawsuit for money damages, but when a person's life is at stake—no matter how heinous his offense—a requirement of greater reliability should prevail. In a capital case, the specious testimony of a psychiatrist, colored in the eyes of an impressionable jury by the inevitable untouchability of a medical specialist's words, equates with death itself.

I

. . . At the sentencing hearing, the State established that Barefoot had two prior convictions for drug offenses and two prior convictions for unlawful possession of firearms. None of these convictions involved acts of violence. At the guilt stage of the trial, for the limited purpose of establishing that the crime was committed in order to evade police custody, the State had presented evidence that Barefoot had escaped from jail in New Mexico where he was being held on charges of statutory rape and unlawful restraint of a minor child with intent to commit sexual penetration against the child's will. The prosecution also called several character witnesses at the sentencing hearing, from towns in five States. Without mentioning particular examples of Barefoot's conduct, these witnesses testified that Barefoot's reputation for being a peaceable and law abiding citizen was bad in their respective communities.

Last, the prosecution called Doctors Holbrook and Grigson, whose testimony extended over more than half the hearing. Neither had examined Barefoot or requested the opportunity to examine him. . . .

Each psychiatrist . . . was given an extended hypothetical question asking him to assume as true about Barefoot the four prior convictions for nonviolent offenses, the bad reputation for being law abiding in various communities, the New Mexico escape, the events surrounding the murder for which he was on trial and, in Doctor Grigson's case, the New Mexico arrest. On the basis of the hypothetical question, Doctor Holbrook diagnosed Barefoot "within a reasonable psychiatr[ic] certainty," as a "criminal sociopath." He testified that he knew of no treatment that could change this condition, and that the condition would not change for the better but "may become accelerated" in the next few years. Finally, Doctor Holbrook testified that, "within reasonable psychiatric certainty," there was "a probability that the Thomas A. Barefoot in that hypothetical will commit criminal acts of violence in the future that would constitute a continuing threat to society," and that his opinion would not change if the "society" at issue was that within Texas prisons rather than society outside prison.

Doctor Grigson then testified that, on the basis of the hypothetical question, he could diagnose Barefoot "within reasonable psychiatric certainty" as an individual with "a fairly classical, typical, sociopathic personality disorder." He placed Barefoot in the "most severe category" of sociopaths (on a scale of one to ten, Barefoot was "above ten"), and stated that there was no known cure for the condition. Finally, Doctor Grigson testified that whether Barefoot was in society at large or in a prison society there was a "*one hundred percent and absolute*" chance that Barefoot would commit future acts of criminal violence that would constitute a continuing threat to society. . . .

After an hour of deliberation, the jury answered "yes" to the two statutory questions, and Thomas Barefoot was sentenced to death.

II

A

The American Psychiatric Association (APA), participating in this case as *amicus curiae*, informs us that "[t]he unreliability of psychiatric predictions of long-term future dangerousness is by now an established fact within the profession." Brief for American Psychiatric Association, as *Amicus Curiae*, 12 (APA Brief). The APA's best estimate is that *two out of three* predictions of long-term future violence made by psychiatrists are wrong. . . . Neither the Court nor the State of Texas has cited a single reputable scientific source contradicting the unanimous conclusion of professionals in this field that psychiatric predictions of long-term future violence are wrong more often than they are right.

The APA also concludes, as do researchers that have studied the issue, that psychiatrists simply have no expertise in predicting long-term future dangerousness. A layman with access to relevant statistics can do at least as well and possibly better; psychiatric training is not relevant to the factors that validly can be employed to make such predictions, and psychiatrists consistently err on the side of overpredicting violence. Thus, while Doctors Grigson and Holbrook were presented by the State and by self-proclamation as experts at predicting future dangerousness, the scientific literature makes crystal clear that they had no expertise whatever. . . .

B

It is impossible to square admission of this purportedly scientific but actually baseless testimony with the Constitution's paramount concern for reliability in capital sentencing. . . .

The danger of an unreliable death sentence created by this testimony cannot be brushed aside on the ground that the "'jury [must] have before it all possible relevant information about the individual defendant whose fate it must determine.'" . . .

Indeed, unreliable scientific evidence is widely acknowledged to be prejudicial. The reasons for this are manifest. "The major danger of scientific evidence is its potential to mislead the jury; an aura of scientific infallibility may shroud the evidence and thus lead the jury to accept it without critical scrutiny." Giannelli, The Admissibility of Novel Scientific Evidence: *Frye v. United States*, a Half-Century Later, 80 Colum.L.Rev. 1197, 1237 (1980). . . .

. . . [T]he Court's remarkable observation that "[n]either petitioner nor the [APA] suggests that psychiatrists are *always wrong* with respect to future dangerousness, *only most of the time*," (emphasis supplied), misses the point completely, and its claim that this testimony was no more problematic than "other relevant evidence against any defendant in a criminal case," is simply incredible. Surely, this Court's commitment to ensuring that death sentences are imposed reliably and reasonably requires that nonprobative and highly prejudicial testimony on the ultimate question of life or death be excluded from a capital sentencing hearing.

III

A

Despite its recognition that the testimony at issue was probably wrong and certainly prejudicial, the Court holds this testimony admissible because the Court is "unconvinced . . . that the adversary process cannot be trusted to sort out the reliable from the unreliable evidence and opinion about future dangerousness." One can only wonder how juries are to separate valid from invalid expert opinions when the "experts" themselves are so obviously unable to do so. . . .

. . . [T]he Court relies on the proposition that the rules of evidence generally "anticipate that relevant, unprivileged evidence should be admitted and its weight left to the factfinder, who would have the benefit of cross-examination and contrary evidence by the opposing party." But the Court simply ignores hornbook law that, despite the availability of cross-examination and rebuttal witnesses, "opinion evidence is not admissible if the court believes that the state of the pertinent art or scientific knowledge does not permit a reasonable opinion to be asserted." McCormick, Evidence 31 (1972). . . . In no area is purportedly "expert" testimony admitted for the jury's consideration where it cannot be demonstrated that it is correct more often than not. . . . The risk that a jury will be incapable of separating "scientific" myth from reality is deemed unacceptably high.

B

The Constitution's mandate of reliability, with the stakes at life or death, precludes reliance on cross-examination and the opportunity to present rebuttal witnesses as an antidote for this distortion of the truth-finding process. Cross examination is unlikely to reveal the fatuousness of psychiatric predictions because such predictions often rest, as was the case here, on psychiatric categories and intuitive clinical judgments not susceptible to cross-examination and rebuttal. . . .

Nor is the presentation of psychiatric witnesses on behalf of the defense likely to remove the prejudicial taint of misleading testimony by prosecution psychiatrists. No reputable expert would be able to predict with confidence that the defendant will *not* be violent; at best, the witness will be able to give his opinion that all predictions of dangerousness are unreliable. . . .

IV

The Court is simply wrong in claiming that psychiatric testimony respecting future dangerousness is necessarily admissible in light of *Jurek v. Texas,* 428 U.S. 262 (1976). . . . *Jurek* involved "only lay testimony." . . .

Jurek merely upheld Texas' substantive decision to condition the death sentence upon proof of a probability that the defendant will commit criminal acts of violence in the future. Whether the evidence offered by the prosecution to prove that probability is so unreliable as to violate a capital defendant's rights to due process is an entirely different matter, one raising only questions of fair procedure. . . .

Our constitutional duty is to ensure that the State proves future dangerousness, if at all, in a reliable manner. . . . Texas' choice of substantive factors does not justify loading the factfinding process against the defendant through the presentation of what is, at bottom, false testimony. . . .

V

I would vacate petitioner's death sentence, and remand for further proceedings consistent with these views.

As noted in the Court's opinion, the psychiatrists who diagnosed Barefoot as a "sociopath" and so confidently predicted that he would "commit criminal acts of violence that would constitute a continuing threat to society" had never spoken with Barefoot nor even laid eyes on him until they delivered their testimony in court. Their opinions were offered in response to lengthy hypothetical questions that were based on evidence introduced at Barefoot's trial. The Supreme Court had ruled in another Texas case involving Dr. James Grigson, who testified at Barefoot's trial and who was commonly referred to as "Dr. Death" because of the persuasive nature of his future dangerousness testimony,[19] that capital defendants who have not put their own mental state at issue need not speak with the prosecution's mental health experts.[20]

If the statistics cited by the American Psychiatric Association are close to being accurate—"that *two out of three* predictions of long-term future violence made by psychiatrists are wrong"—should such predictions be admissible in capital sentencing

hearings? Could we do as well by flipping a coin? Can cross-examination and counter-
vailing testimony by defense experts, as the majority opinion concludes, "be trusted to sort
out the reliable from the unreliable evidence and opinion about future dangerousness"?

A considerable body of research suggests that predictions of future behavior based
on objective facts that describe an individual and his or her relevant life history—
resembling the actuarial techniques used by insurance companies to estimate individual life expectancies—are significantly more reliable than predictions stemming from
the largely subjective, clinical assessments that inform psychiatric diagnoses.[21] Relying
on actuarial methods, we might make note of a defendant's age, education, marital status, prior criminal record, history of drug or alcohol abuse, and a number of other variables, ascertain how others sharing those same characteristics have tended to behave,
and thereby estimate the likelihood that the individual in whom we are interested will
engage in future violence. But what if one of the correlates of criminal violence is race
or ethnicity; would reliance on such a constitutionally suspect characteristic undermine
the integrity of the scientific calculation?

This issue arose when Victor Saldano was sentenced to death in Texas in 1996 following a prosecution expert's reliance on Saldano's Hispanic ethnicity as a risk factor
for likely future dangerousness. After the state courts upheld his death sentence, the
U.S. Supreme Court agreed to consider whether factoring Saldano's ethnicity into the
future dangerousness prediction violated his equal protection rights. Before the case
was argued in the Supreme Court, the Texas Attorney General confessed error, conceding that "[b]ecause the use of race [sic] in Saldano's sentencing seriously undermined
the fairness, integrity or public reputation of the judicial process, Texas . . . agrees that
Saldano is entitled to a new sentencing hearing."[22] Following that new hearing, Saldano once again was sentenced to death.[23] What if it is true, statistically, that males
are more likely than females to engage in violence? If weight were attached to the fact
that Saldano is a man at his sentencing hearing, would his equal protection rights have
been violated?

If predictions of future violence are of uncertain reliability in individual cases, is
it at least a fair assumption that convicted murderers are dangerous as a class? In his
concurring opinion in *Furman v. Georgia*, Justice Marshall asserted: "The fact is . . . that
murderers are extremely unlikely to commit other crimes either in prison or upon their
release. For the most part, they are first offenders, and when released from prison they
are known to become model citizens."[24] Professor Anthony Amsterdam similarly has
noted that: "Warden Lawes of Sing Sing and Governor Wallace of Alabama, among
others, regularly employed murder convicts as house servants because they were among
the very safest of prisoners. There are exceptions, of course; but these can be handled by
adequate prison security."[25] Nevertheless, how might most people be expected to react
on learning that a convicted murderer is living next door?

The Court's decision in *Furman* resulted in the hundreds of offenders then under
sentence of death being spared execution. The condemned inmates were resentenced

to life imprisonment and almost all were integrated into the general prison population after being removed from death row. Many of them eventually were paroled. Taking advantage of this natural experiment, James Marquart and Jon Sorensen examined the subsequent criminal histories and prison disciplinary records of 558 *Furman*-commuted offenders from 29 states and the District of Columbia (including 474 murderers, 81 rapists, and four armed robbers). They followed the behavior of the former death row inmates between 1972 (starting in mid-year, after *Furman* was decided) and 1987. They summarized their findings:

> We tracked these 558 prisoners' institutional and release behavior for nearly fifteen years. In the prison setting, these prisoners committed six murders—killing four prisoners and two correctional officers. However, the majority of the former death row prisoners served out their sentences with few instances of serious institutional misconduct. A minority were responsible for the bulk of disciplinary infractions.
>
> Over the course of the fifteen years, 239 *Furman*-commuted prisoners were released to the free community. These parolees have spent an average of five years in society. Twenty-one percent recidivated and were returned to prison, 12% committing new felonies. Only one parolee from Texas committed a second homicide. On the other hand, nearly 80% of those released to free society have not, at least officially, committed additional crimes.[26]

Marquart and Sorensen noted that the seven individuals who committed murder following the commutation of their death sentences represented 1.3% of the 558 prisoners whose behavior they followed. Conversely stated, 98.7% of that group did not commit a new murder during the 15 years following their release from death row. Other research suggested that four among the *Furman*-commuted population were innocent and had been wrongfully convicted and sentenced to death. Marquart and Sorensen concluded by observing that:

> Certainly, execution of all 558 prisoners would have prevented [the seven new murders that were committed]. However, such a 'preemptive strike' would not have greatly protected society. . . . The question becomes whether saving the lives of the seven victims was worth the execution of four innocent inmates.[27]

A related question is whether executing all 558 prisoners in service of the death penalty's incapacitation function would represent literal "overkill" in light of their findings that the overwhelming majority of the death-sentenced inmates did not commit murder and did not disproportionately engage in prison violence during the 15-year period studied.

While informative, these findings could not hope to be definitive about the magnitude of the threat posed by capital offenders who are not executed. In the first place, official records of criminal convictions and prison infractions are imperfect measures of the inmates' dangerousness. Violent acts that may have been committed by the *Furman*-commuted prisoners but were not detected obviously could not be included.

In addition, the study followed the commuted prisoners only through 1987. It thus could not capture later acts of violence. One famous, although exceptional case illustrating this shortcoming involved Kenneth Allen McDuff, who had been sentenced to death for committing three murders in Texas in 1966 and was later spared execution as a result of *Furman*. McDuff was paroled in 1989. He then embarked on a violent crime spree, murdering as many as nine women. He was apprehended in 1992, convicted of capital murder, and ultimately was executed in 1998.[28]

Marquart and Sorensen's above-described research focused on prisoners who had been sentenced to death before *Furman* was decided. Under modern statutes, only aggravated forms of murder can be punished by death. Moreover, in Texas, most prominently, and occasionally elsewhere, juries in capital cases now are tasked with specifically distinguishing between murderers who are and are not likely to engage in future criminal violence. The *Furman*-commuted prisoners thus might not be representative of today's death penalty-eligible offenders.

Studies investigating the future dangerousness of capital murderers in the post-*Furman* era have tried to account for these changes. In general, they have reaffirmed Marquart and Sorensen's essential findings. A small number of modern era death-sentenced offenders have killed again following reversal of their capital sentences and their return to the general prison population to serve a life sentence and/or their being paroled. The overwhelming majority have not, nor is their institutional or post-release behavior demonstrably more violent (frequently, it is less so) than murderers who were not sentenced to death or in comparison to maximum security prisoners in general. Accurately predicting which offenders will engage in future acts of violence remains elusive, at best.[29]

What conclusions should be drawn about whether incapacitation is a defensible justification for capital punishment, either generally or in individual cases? What mix of empirical and normative considerations is best used to resolve the underlying critical issues?

If a death sentence is grounded on the "probability" that the offender will "commit criminal acts of violence" in the future, should the sentencing decision be revisited if circumstances suggest that the prediction was wrong or no longer is credible? For example, what if, owing to age or infirmity, an offender's changed physical condition negates his likely dangerousness? This is far from a hypothetical possibility. With death row confinement sometimes exceeding two and even three decades, prisoners age 70 and older, sometimes wheelchair-bound, have recently been executed.[30] Andre Thomas, a mentally ill Texas murderer, gouged out (and ate) his one good eye while under sentence of death (he had gouged out his other eye while awaiting trial). Was he thereafter likely to commit criminal acts of violence, even if he posed such a risk when sentenced?[31] Or what if a convicted murderer undergoes a genuine spiritual conversion while awaiting execution, becoming a "different person" than at the time of sentencing?

Karla Faye Tucker, who was convicted of capital murder in Texas and sentenced to death in 1984 for killing a man by delivering repeated blows to his body with a pickax, has been cited as an example of an individual whose character underwent such a complete transformation that the future dangerousness prediction made when she was sentenced arguably no longer remained defensible. Tucker reportedly became a devout Christian following the murder and genuinely renounced her prior lifestyle while on death row. Several prominent religious figures, including Pat Robertson and Sister Helen Prejean, called for her life to be spared, as did prison guards who watched over her, and even prosecutors from the office that secured her conviction and death sentence. Neither the courts nor then-Governor George W. Bush intervened. She was executed in 1998.[32]

Should evidence of an offender's changed character following a crime or penalty hearing matter, particularly when a prediction of future dangerousness helps support a capital sentencing decision? Consider Justice Marshall's dissent from the Supreme Court's denial of certiorari and denial of a stay of execution in the following case.

Evans v. Muncy, 498 U.S. 927, 111 S.Ct. 309, 112 L.Ed.2d 295 (1990)

Justice MARSHALL, dissenting. . . .

I

[Wilbert] Evans was convicted of capital murder and sentenced to death. At the sentencing phase, the jury's verdict was predicated on a *single* aggravating circumstance: that if allowed to live Evans would pose a serious threat of future danger to society. See Va. Code § 19.2–264.4(C) (1990). Without this finding, Evans could not have been sentenced to death.

While Evans was on death row at the Mecklenberg Correctional Facility, an event occurred that casts grave doubt on the jury's prediction of Evans' future dangerousness. On May 31, 1984, six death row inmates at Mecklenberg attempted to engineer an escape. Armed with makeshift knives, these inmates took hostage 12 prison guards and 2 female nurses. The guards were stripped of their clothes and weapons, bound, and blindfolded. The nurses

also were stripped of their clothes, and one was bound to an inmate's bed.

According to uncontested affidavits presented by guards taken hostage during the uprising, Evans took decisive steps to calm the riot, saving the lives of several hostages, and preventing the rape of one of the nurses. For instance, Officer Ricardo Holmes, who was bound by the escaping inmates and forced into a closet with other hostages, states that he heard Evans imploring to the escaping inmates, "'Don't hurt anybody and everything will be allright.'" Officer Holmes continues:

"It was very clear to me that [Evans] was trying to keep [the escaping inmates] calm and prevent them from getting out of control. . . . Based upon what I saw and heard, it is my firm opinion that if any of the escaping inmates had tried to harm us, Evans would have come to our aid. It is my belief that had it not been for Evans, I might not be here today."

Other guards taken hostage during the uprising verify Officer Holmes' judgment that

Evans protected them and the other hostages from danger. According to Officer Prince Thomas, Evans interceded to prevent the rape of Nurse Ethyl Barksdale by one of the escaping inmates. Officer Harold Crutchfield affirms that Evans' appeals to the escapees not to harm anyone may have meant the difference between life and death for the hostages. . . . According to Officer Crutchfield, after the escapees had left the area in which they were holding the guards hostage, Evans tried to force open the closet door and free the guards—albeit unsuccessfully. Officers Holmes, Thomas, and Crutchfield, and five other prison officials all attest that Evans' conduct during the May 31, 1984, uprising was consistent with his exemplary behavior during his close to 10 years on death row.

Evans filed a writ of habeas corpus and application for a stay of his execution before the United States District Court for the Eastern District of Virginia. He urged that the jury's prediction of his future dangerousness be reexamined in light of his conduct during the Mecklenberg uprising. Evans proffered that these events would prove that the jury's prediction was unsound and thereby invalidate the sole aggravating circumstance on which the jury based its death sentence. For this reason, Evans argued that his death sentence must be vacated. The District Court stayed the execution and ordered a hearing. The Court of Appeals reversed and vacated the stay.

II

Remarkably, the State of Virginia's opposition to Evans' application to stay the execution barely contests either Evans' depiction of the relevant events or Evans' conclusion that these events reveal the clear error of the jury's prediction of Evans' future dangerousness.

In other words, the State concedes that the sole basis for Evans' death sentence—future dangerousness—in fact *does not exist*.

The only ground asserted by the State for permitting Evans' execution to go forward is its interest in procedural finality. According to the State, permitting a death row inmate to challenge a finding of future dangerousness by reference to facts occurring after the sentence will unleash an endless stream of litigation. . . .

In my view, the Court's decision to let Wilbert Evans be put to death is a compelling statement of the failure of this Court's capital jurisprudence. This Court's approach since *Gregg v. Georgia* has blithely assumed that strict procedures will satisfy the dictates of the Eighth Amendment's ban on cruel and unusual punishment. As Wilbert Evans' claim makes crystal clear, even the most exacting procedures are fallible. Just as the jury occasionally "gets it wrong" about whether a defendant charged with murder is innocent or guilty, so, too, can the jury "get it wrong" about whether a defendant convicted of murder is deserving of death, notwithstanding the exacting procedures imposed by the Eighth Amendment. . . .

The State's interest in "finality" is no answer to this flaw in the capital sentencing system. It may indeed be the case that a State cannot realistically accommodate postsentencing evidence casting doubt on a jury's finding of future dangerousness; but it hardly follows from this that it is *Wilbert Evans* who should bear the burden of this procedural limitation. In other words, if it is impossible to construct a system capable of accommodating *all* evidence relevant to a man's entitlement to be spared death—no matter when that evidence is disclosed—then it is the *system*, not the life of the man sentenced to death, that should be dispatched.

The indifferent shrug of the shoulders with which the Court answers the failure of its procedures in this case reveals the utter bankruptcy of its notion that a system of capital punishment can coexist with the Eighth Amendment. A death sentence that is *dead wrong* is no less so simply because its deficiency is not uncovered until the eleventh hour. A system of capital punishment that would permit Wilbert Evans' execution notwithstanding as-to-now unrefuted evidence showing that death is an improper sentence is a system that cannot stand.

I would stay Wilbert Evans' execution.

Cost

In February 2013, a few weeks before the Maryland Legislature voted on a bill to repeal the state's death penalty, a Hagerstown newspaper invited residents to register their views about the issue. One respondent, who supported retaining the death penalty, "pointed to the cost of life in prison. . . ." Another capital punishment supporter also expressed concern about "the expense of somebody sitting in jail for life."[33] The Legislature ultimately approved abolishing the death penalty. Governor Martin O'Malley hailed the repeal effort, citing several reasons in support of it. Financial savings was among them. "Capital punishment is expensive," he asserted. "[R]ather than continuing to throw taxpayers' money at an ineffective death penalty, our state has chosen . . . to replace capital punishment with a more effective and cost efficient public policy: life without parole."[34]

Whose assessment of the relative expense of capital punishment and life imprisonment is more reliable: the Maryland citizens who expressed their views, or the governor? The United States Bureau of Justice Statistics reported that the average cost in 2001 of incarcerating a state prisoner for one year was $22,650, although there was considerable variation among the states (Maine spent the most, at $44,379 per prisoner, while Alabama spent the least, $8,128; Maryland's annual expenditures were slightly above the national average, at $26,398).[35] Using the national average annual expenditures, and assuming that a life prison sentence for a murderer convicted in his 20s is roughly 50 years, the incarceration costs alone (*i.e.*, not figuring in expenses associated with the trial and appeals), unadjusted for inflation, would be approximately $1.13 million. How could keeping a murderer in prison for the rest of his life possibly be less expensive than executing him?

A 2008 study completed by the Urban Institute decisively backed the governor's financial views. After analyzing a sample of the 1,136 death penalty-eligible murder cases in Maryland between 1978 and 1999, the researchers concluded that:

[A]n average capital-eligible case in which prosecutors did not seek the death penalty will cost approximately $1.1 million over the lifetime of the case. A capital-eligible case in which prosecutors unsuccessfully sought the death penalty will cost $1.8 million and a capital-eligible case resulting in a death sentence will cost approximately $3 million. In total, we forecast that the lifetime costs to Maryland taxpayers of these capitally-prosecuted cases will be $186 million.[36]

These findings are not out of line with studies completed in other states that have focused on the cost of the death penalty. In North Carolina, it has been estimated that taxpayers "would have spent almost $11 million less each year [2005 and 2006] on criminal justice activities (including imprisonment) without the death penalty."[37] The additional annual costs associated with the death penalty in California, where more than 700 offenders were stockpiled on death row in 2013, are considerably higher, estimated to be $137 million in 2008[38] and $184 million in 2009.[39] Senior Judge Arthur Alarcon of the Ninth Circuit Court of Appeals and Professor Paula Mitchell concluded that California had spent in excess of $4 billion to administer its death penalty between 1978 and 2010. During that time, the State executed 13 offenders.[40] A 2009 review of relevant research evidence reported:

> Fourteen studies have estimated the costs of capital punishment, including one study of the federal death penalty and 13 state- or county-level studies. . . . Each study concludes that the presence of capital punishment results in additional costs. However, there is substantial variation in the cost estimates. Among the five studies that compare the cost of a death sentence with the cost of a capital-eligible case in which no death notice is filed, the average (additional) cost per case is $650,000, but the estimates range from about $100,000 to more than $1.7 million.[41]

What accounts for the consistent finding, in jurisdiction after jurisdiction, that it is actually cheaper to prosecute, convict, sentence, and keep murderers in prison for life than to seek and carry out their capital punishment?

The high stakes in capital cases, where life and death are at issue, tend to motivate both the prosecution and defense to leave no stone unturned in investigating the charges, filing and litigating motions, invoking expert witnesses, and conducting the trial. Trials are longer and considerably more complex. Jury selection can consume days or weeks. The parties must prepare not only for a guilt trial but, in the event of a conviction, for a subsequent penalty hearing which requires a separate investigation and is likely to involve a new round of expert and other witnesses. If a death sentence is secured, the offender will be consigned to the heightened security of death row, which is more expensive than confinement in the general prison population. Appeals and post-conviction review are protracted, typically extending for well over a decade. The costs of the lethal drugs, corrections staff, and the facilities required to carry out an execution may not be substantial, but they add to what represents a considerably more sizeable investment than is required for murder prosecutions that seek and result in the defendant's life imprisonment.[42]

Importantly, the cumulative costs of maintaining a system of capital punishment greatly exceed the costs incurred in cases that culminate in an execution. Heightened pre-trial and trial expenditures will be made in all cases prosecuted capitally, whether or not a conviction and death sentence result. Considerable variation exists among jurisdictions, but it is not uncommon for juries to impose life sentences, rather than death, in half or more of the capital murder cases that proceed to a penalty hearing.[43] In addition, there is an unusually high reversal rate in capital cases, requiring frequent retrials and/or substitution of a life sentence for the original sentence of death. Slightly more than two-thirds (68%) of cases nationwide in which a death sentence was imposed between 1973 and 1995 resulted in the conviction or sentence being overturned on appeal or at a later stage of judicial review.[44] As with trials that do not produce a death sentence, when a new trial is ordered or a capital sentence is vacated on appeal and a life sentence is then imposed,[45] the substantial monetary costs supporting a capital prosecution represent a wasted investment.

On the other hand, some have argued that without the prospect of a death sentence to use as leverage, prosecutors are severely hampered in plea bargaining in first-degree murder cases because defendants who otherwise would plead guilty in exchange for a life sentence will have nothing to lose by proceeding to trial. The resulting increase in jury trials thus could negate cost savings that might accompany capital punishment's elimination.[46] A study investigating this possibility focused on guilty pleas in aggravated murder cases in New York prior to and following the state's enactment of its 1995 death penalty statute.[47] It produced somewhat mixed findings: defendants pled guilty at the same rate during both periods, but they more frequently pled guilty to the original charge when the death penalty law was in effect instead of bargaining for a reduced charge and receiving a commensurately lower sentence. The study concluded:

> [T]he death penalty makes defendants more likely to plead guilty to their original charge, yet no more likely to plead guilty in general—suggesting that the threat of capital punishment encourages defendants to accept deals that they otherwise would have rejected. . . .
>
> These results are potentially relevant in at least two areas of criminal justice policy. First, since the death penalty affects only the *terms* of the deals defendants make but does not seem to increase defendants' propensity to plea bargain in general, the threat of the death penalty does not seem to reduce the total number of cases that proceed to trial. Thus, the well-documented costs of capital trials do not appear to be offset by reducing total trial costs through plea bargains. Second, while the death penalty does not discourage defendants from going to trial, it does increase the bargaining position of DAs. Opponents of capital punishment might argue that, based on this finding, the threat of the death penalty is powerful enough to compel an innocent person to accept a plea bargain.[48]

A second study, based on death-eligible murder cases in Georgia between 1993 and 2000, came to a different conclusion. It found that having death available as a sentencing option significantly influenced defendants to plead guilty when they otherwise would have proceeded to trial, increasing the odds of a guilty plea by as much as 20 to 25 percentage points. Despite that finding, the study also concluded that "the magnitude of the effect [of a potential death sentence in helping to induce guilty pleas] is clearly insufficient to offset the substantial administrative and financial costs" occasioned in the capital cases that proceed to trial.[49] The study offered a conservative estimate that:

> [T]he threat of the death penalty increases the likelihood of reaching a plea agreement [in Georgia murder cases] by approximately 20 percentage points. In practical terms, the death penalty increases the plea-bargaining rate from approximately 40% to 60%. In other words, the threat of capital punishment deters roughly two out of every ten death-noticed defendants from pursuing a trial . . . Based on the high costs associated with litigating a single capital trial and the rather modest ability of the death penalty to deter defendants from pursuing trial, capital punishment does not appear to be a cost-justified bargaining chip.[50]

Cost issues may be dwarfed by the ethical questions presented by prosecutors leveraging guilty pleas by promising to pursue a capital sentence if the defendant pleads not guilty and proceeds to trial. Although some prosecutors dismiss the notion that they would use the death penalty as a bargaining tool, many defense attorneys believe otherwise.[51] Lawmakers occasionally have cited the production of guilty pleas as a reason supporting death penalty legislation.[52] But critics maintain that invoking the threat of a capital sentence to induce a defendant to plead guilty is illegitimate and unduly coercive.

For instance, Justice Marshall argued in *Furman v. Georgia* that "[i]f the death penalty is used to encourage guilty pleas and thus to deter suspects from exercising their rights under the Sixth Amendment to jury trials, it is unconstitutional."[53] A majority of the justices have nevertheless declined to find that guilty pleas motivated by a desire to avoid a death sentence are inherently coerced or involuntary.[54] Even if the threat of execution is not coercive as a matter of law, it undeniably represents enormous pressure. Innocent defendants confronted with this dilemma have been known to falsely confess and plead guilty to avoid risking a capital sentence.[55] Commentators have disputed the propriety of prosecutors using a possible death sentence as a plea bargaining tool for diverse reasons.[56] Professor Albert Alschuler has argued:

> Plea bargaining undermines the most common rationale for the death penalty. Proponents of this penalty maintain that some crimes are so horrible that they simply require it. They insist that no lesser punishment can adequately express the community's condemnation. But the actions of American prosecutors convey an entirely different message: No lesser punishment can adequately express the community's condemnation unless the accused pleads guilty. For defendants who agree to save the government the costs of a trial, lesser punishments are just fine. These defendants' horrible crimes do not demand death after all. In the immortal words of Gilda Radner, "Never mind." Plea bargaining devalues the death penalty. It changes what the death penalty is about.[57]

Discussion centering on the cost of capital punishment must at some point turn to alternative uses for the invested resources and their value in comparison to maintaining the death penalty. Efforts to repeal death penalty legislation sometimes are couched in these terms. For example, California voters confronted a ballot initiative in 2012 asking them to make life imprisonment without parole, rather than death, the maximum punishment for murder. The measure, defeated by a margin of 52% to 48%, was designed in part "[t]o save the taxpayers $1 billion in five years so those dollars can be invested in local law enforcement, our children's schools, and services for the elderly and disabled," and "[t]o use some of the savings from replacing the death penalty to create the SAFE California Fund, to provide funding for local law enforcement, specifically police departments, Sheriffs, and District Attorney Offices, to increase the rate at which homicide and rape cases are solved."[58] A narrowly defeated bill to repeal Colorado's capital punishment law in 2009 would have used "any savings resulting from the abolition of the death penalty to increase funding for the Cold Case Homicide Team of the Colorado Bureau of Investigation. . . ."[59] The recent successful abolition efforts in New Jersey, New Mexico, Illinois, and Maryland specifically tied cost savings resulting from the repeal of capital punishment laws to investments to support victims and/or law enforcement.[60]

In addition to disputing that the death penalty is or has to be more expensive than sentencing murderers to life imprisonment, supporters of capital punishment often counter cost-based arguments by asking, "How do you put a price on justice?"[61] One commentator has argued that cost considerations should have no bearing on debates about capital punishment.

> For life to hang in the balance and be weighed against dollars and cents seems quite inappropriate. . . . The burden capital punishment imposes on the wallets of the taxpayers is surely trivial in comparison to the burden this punishment should place on the lives of those affected and on the collective conscience of all Americans. . . .
>
> . . . [M]oney should not determine whether a man lives or dies.[62]

David Garland recounts a rather vivid demonstration of the principle that, for many devotees of capital punishment, financial considerations are no match for their sentiments about what justice demands.

> Consider . . . the enthusiasm with which hundreds of Californians donated money to ensure that the serial killer Gerald Gallego would be put to death rather than languish on death row. Gallego had been convicted of murder and sentenced to death in California, but, given that state's postconviction processes, it was thought unlikely that he would ever be executed. In 1984, California's governor agreed to extradite Gallego to face murder charges in Nevada, since he would be more likely to be executed if tried and convicted in that state. When it emerged that the Nevada county where the murders had occurred could not afford the $60,000 cost of a capital trial, the journalist Stan Gillian of the *Sacramento Bee* wrote a column urging Californians to send money to the county treasurer: "There must be 59,999 other Californians besides me happy enough to see Gallego in the clutches of no-nonsense Nevada to send a dollar to help the cause. My buck's on the way." In the weeks that followed,

almost 1,800 donations were sent, totaling more than $26,000. . . . Gallego was sentenced to death by a Nevada court, but no execution had occurred by the time of his death from cancer in 2002.[63]

Murder Victims and Their Survivors

In his agonized dissenting opinion in *Furman v. Georgia,* Justice Harry Blackmun voted to uphold the constitutionality of the capital punishment laws under review, while at the same time confessing that: "I yield to no one in the depth of my distaste, antipathy, and, indeed, abhorrence, for the death penalty, with all its aspects of physical distress and fear and of moral judgment exercised by finite minds."[64] While explaining why his personal views about capital punishment must be kept separate from his obligations as a jurist, he observed:

> It is not without interest . . . to note that, although the several concurring opinions acknowledge the heinous and atrocious character of the offenses committed by the petitioners, none of those opinions makes reference to the misery the petitioners' crimes occasioned to the victims, to the families of the victims, and to the communities where the offenses took place. The arguments for the respective petitioners, particularly the oral arguments, were similarly and curiously devoid of reference to the victims. . . . [T]hese cases are here because offenses to innocent victims were perpetrated. This fact, and the terror that occasioned it, and the fear that stalks the streets of many of our cities today perhaps deserve not to be entirely overlooked.[65]

Victim-based justifications are frequently offered in support of capital punishment, either to promote justice or under the guise of offering closure, or some measure of relief, to grieving family members and loved ones. The harsh impact of murder cannot be overstated. In addition to the lost life of the victim, the ensuing waves of pain and sorrow wash expansively over families, friends, and acquaintances, and spill over considerably broader communities. On average, murder victims are survived by between seven and ten family members.[66] A 1991 study estimated that more than 16 million Americans had lost an immediate family member, a more distant relative, or a close friend to criminal homicide, including those caused by drunk drivers.[67] A 2009 estimate put that figure even higher, projecting that roughly 15% of young adults are survivors of criminal homicide victims.[68] Whether the death penalty can help salve the wounds caused by murder is far less settled. Some maintain that capital punishment is so infrequently imposed for murder that it is but a hollow promise of justice for overwhelming numbers of murder victims' survivors, and that in the rare cases when it is pursued it is as likely to impede healing as to promote it. Some go even further and intimate that coupling support for the death penalty with a concern for victims is little more than political exploitation.

At a minimum, it is disputable whether capital punishment can represent justice for victims and their families when that option is denied them in nearly all murder cases.

[O]nly a tiny percentage of murders culminate in an execution. In 2009, for example, a reported 12,418 arrests were made for murder and non-negligent manslaughter. In contrast, only 112 offenders were added to the nation's death rows, and 52 were executed. . . . [These] figures would suggest that less than 1 percent (0.90 percent) of arrests for intentional criminal homicide result in a sentence of death, and that executions are even rarer, representing less than one half of one percent (0.42 percent) of the annual arrests. Alternatively stated, more than 99 percent of murder victims' survivors will never see the murderer of their loved one sentenced to death, let alone executed.[69]

In addition, it is fallacious to assume that all victims' family members will seek or support capital punishment for their loved one's murderer. Murder victims' survivors are not a monolithic group who hold uniform attitudes about punishment. Many had scarcely thought about the death penalty before involuntarily assuming their status as a co-victim or survivor. Once in that position, some strongly believe in the death penalty and others strongly oppose it.[70] Whether to support a capital prosecution can be a divisive issue among already-grieving family members who are not of the same mind. A further complication arises in intra-familial murders, involving spouses, or parents and children, where survivors include relatives of both the offender and the victim.[71]

The other benefit that capital punishment sometimes is heralded as offering is providing murder victims' survivors with a sense of "closure." The precise meaning of this term is elusive, but it typically is used to connote some sense of finality, if not healing, that results from an offender's death sentence and execution.[72] Media accounts often attribute references to closure to victims' family members in connection with capital murder cases.[73] Other survivors passionately dismiss the notion that an execution will bring the promised relief. For example, a couple whose son and daughter-in-law were murdered in Virginia remarked, "Does anyone know or care to know that the favored term 'closure' is so wrong and offensive . . .? There is no closure, nor can there ever be."[74] Following Timothy McVeigh's execution, a woman whose daughter was a victim of McVeigh's 1995 bombing of the Alfred P. Murrah Building in Oklahoma City wrote, "I will live with the pain of the loss of my daughter for the rest of my life. When the lid of my casket is closed only then will I have closure."[75]

Indeed, in contrast to their asserted palliative benefits, capital prosecutions have a heightened potential to inflict additional trauma on murder victims' survivors and inhibit the grief resolution process. Death penalty trials tend to be more highly publicized and considerably more time-consuming than trials where the death penalty is not sought, exposing survivors to elongated proceedings under the glare of intense media scrutiny. If a conviction results but the jury imposes a sentence of life imprisonment, "[f]amilies [may] feel affronted by the idea that somehow their loved one was not important enough for the death penalty."[76] Frequent reversals and retrials mean that a death sentence originally imposed may never be carried out. When an execution does occur the tumultuous passage of years—sometimes 30 or more—following the trial can cause emotions to remain raw and roil when they otherwise might have begun to stabilize and subside over time.[77] And in the rare case where an offender is executed, there is no guarantee that the expected relief will ensue. Murder victims' survivors have reported feeling their loved one's loss just as acutely following the offender's execution.[78]

The considerable gap between what is promised murder victims' survivors and what is delivered has led some to conclude that branding the death penalty as a victims' rights issue is little more than political rhetoric designed to curry public support for capital punishment.[79] Professor Franklin Zimring has written:

> [The] symbolic transformation of execution into a victim-service program provides three powerful functions for the death penalty in the United States. First, it gives the horrifying process of human execution a positive impact that many citizens can identify with: closure, not vengeance. Second, this degovernmentalization of the rationale of the death penalty means that citizens do not have to worry about executions as an excessive use of power by and for the government. When "closure" is the major aim of lethal injections, the execution of criminals becomes another public service, like street cleaning or garbage removal, where the government is the servant of the community rather than its master.
>
> The third function of the transformation of execution into a victim service gesture is that it links the symbolism of execution to a long American history of community control of punishment. The United States is not far removed from its age of vigilante punishment, and the nostalgia for many of the symbols and sentiments of punishment as a community rather than a government enterprise is quite powerful in many parts of the modern United States.[80]

Another vexing issue is whether voices memorializing victims and reciting the devastating consequences of their murder should be heard at capital sentencing hearings. Some firmly believe that they should, while others are concerned that such emotionally laden testimony threatens to overwhelm the "reasoned moral response"[81] that is expected in a jury's punishment decision. The Supreme Court has gone pillar to post regarding the admissibility of victim impact evidence in capital trials. The justices first considered this issue in 1987 in *Booth v. Maryland,*[82] ruling in a 5–4 decision that testimony about the personal characteristics of murder victims and the trauma suffered by their survivors "creates an impermissible risk that the capital sentencing decision will be made in an arbitrary manner." Justice Powell's majority opinion identified several reasons supporting the conclusion that victim impact statements (VIS) are constitutionally inadmissible in capital cases.

While the full range of foreseeable consequences of a defendant's actions may be relevant in other criminal and civil contexts, we cannot agree that it is relevant in the unique circumstance of a capital sentencing hearing. In such a case, it is the function of the sentencing jury to "express the conscience of the community on the ultimate question of life or death." *Witherspoon v. Illinois,* 391 U.S. 510, 519 (1968). When carrying out this task the jury is required to focus on the defendant as a "uniquely individual human bein[g]." *Woodson v.*

North Carolina, 428 U.S. 280, 304 (1976). The focus of a VIS, however, is not on the defendant, but on the character and reputation of the victim and the effect on his family. These factors may be wholly unrelated to the blameworthiness of a particular defendant. . . . [T]he defendant often will not know the victim, and therefore will have no knowledge about the existence or characteristics of the victim's family. Moreover, defendants rarely select their victims based on whether the murder will have an effect on anyone other than the person murdered. Allowing the jury to rely on a VIS therefore could result in imposing the death sentence because of factors about which the defendant was unaware, and that were irrelevant to the decision to kill. This evidence thus could divert the jury's attention away from the defendant's background and record, and the circumstances of the crime. . . .

As evidenced by the full text of the VIS in this case, . . . the family members were articulate and persuasive in expressing their grief and the extent of their loss. But in some cases the victim will not leave behind a family, or the family members may be less articulate in describing their feelings even though their sense of loss is equally severe. The fact that the imposition of the death sentence may turn on such distinctions illustrates the danger of allowing juries to consider this information. Certainly the degree to which a family is willing and able to express its grief is irrelevant to the decision whether a defendant, who may merit the death penalty, should live or die.

Nor is there any justification for permitting such a decision to turn on the perception that the victim was a sterling member of the community rather than someone of questionable character.[FN8] This type of information does not provide a "principled way to distinguish [cases] in which the death penalty was imposed, from the many cases in which it was not." *Godfrey v. Georgia*, 446 U.S. 420, 433 (1980) (opinion of Stewart, J.).

FN8. We are troubled by the implication that defendants whose victims were assets to their community are more deserving of punishment than those whose victims are perceived to be less worthy. Of course, our system of justice does not tolerate such distinctions.

We also note that it would be difficult—if not impossible—to provide a fair opportunity to rebut such evidence without shifting the focus of the sentencing hearing away from the defendant. A threshold problem is that victim impact information is not easily susceptible to rebuttal. Presumably the defendant would have the right to cross-examine the declarants, but he rarely would be able to show that the family members have exaggerated the degree of sleeplessness, depression, or emotional trauma suffered. Moreover, if the state is permitted to introduce evidence of the victim's personal qualities, it cannot be doubted that the defendant also must be given the chance to rebut this evidence. Putting aside the strategic risks of attacking the victim's character before the jury, in appropriate cases the defendant presumably would be permitted to put on evidence that the victim was of dubious moral character, was unpopular, or was ostracized from his family. The prospect of a "mini-trial" on the victim's character is more than simply unappealing; it could well distract the sentencing jury from its constitutionally required task—determining whether the death penalty is appropriate in light of the background and record of the accused and the particular circumstances of the crime. We thus reject the contention that the presence or absence of emotional distress of the victim's family, or the victim's personal characteristics, are proper sentencing considerations in a capital case.

The second type of information presented to the jury in the VIS was the family members' opinions and characterizations of the crimes. The [victims'] son, for example, stated that his parents were "butchered like animals," and that he "doesn't think anyone should be able to do something like that and get away with it." The VIS also noted that the [victims'] daughter

"could never forgive anyone for killing [her parents] that way. She can't believe that any-body could do that to someone. The victims' daughter states that animals wouldn't do this. [The perpetrators] didn't have to kill because there was no one to stop them from looting. . . . The murders show the vicious-ness of the killers' anger. She doesn't feel

that the people who did this could ever be rehabilitated and she doesn't want them to be able to do this again or put another fam-ily through this."

One can understand the grief and anger of the family caused by the brutal murders in this case, and there is no doubt that jurors gener-ally are aware of these feelings. But the formal presentation of this information by the State can serve no other purpose than to inflame the jury and divert it from deciding the case on the relevant evidence concerning the crime and the defendant. As we have noted, any decision to impose the death sentence must "be, and appear to be, based on reason rather than caprice or emotion." *Gardner v. Florida*, [430 U.S. 349, 358 (1977)] (opinion of STEVENS, J.). The admission of these emotionally charged opinions as to what conclusions the jury should draw from the evidence clearly is inconsistent with the reasoned decisionmaking we require in capital cases.

Just four years later, following the retirement of Justice Powell, who authored the majority opinion in *Booth*, and Justice Brennan, who joined that opinion, *Booth v. Maryland* was overruled. Justices Kennedy and Souter, the replacements for the former members of the Court, joined Chief Justice Rehnquist's 6–3 majority opinion that repudiated *Booth* in *Payne v. Tennessee*.[83] Justice Marshall charged in his angry dissent that "[n]either the law nor the facts supporting *Booth* . . . underwent any change in the last four years. Only the personnel of this Court did." The Chief Justice's opinion explained the basis of the majority's disagreement with *Booth*.

The State presented the testimony of Cha-risse's [one of Payne's victims] mother, Mary Zvolanek. When asked how Nicholas had been affected by the murders of his mother and sis-ter, she responded:

"He cries for his mom. He doesn't seem to understand why she doesn't come home.

And he cries for his sister Lacie. He comes to me many times during the week and asks me, Grandmama, do you miss my Lacie. And I tell him yes. He says, I'm worried about my Lacie."

In arguing for the death penalty during closing argument, the prosecutor commented on the continuing effects of Nicholas' experience, stating:

"But we do know that Nicholas was alive. And Nicholas was in the same room. Nicholas was still conscious. His eyes were open. He responded to the paramedics. He was able to follow their directions. He was able to hold his intestines in as he was carried to the ambulance. So he knew what happened to his mother and baby sister."

"There is nothing you can do to ease the pain of any of the families involved in this case. There is nothing you can do to ease the pain of Bernice or Carl Payne, and that's a tragedy. There is nothing you can do basically to ease the pain of Mr. and Mrs. Zvolanek, and that's a tragedy. They will have to live with it the rest of their lives. There is obviously nothing you can do for Charisse and Lacie Jo. But there is something that you can do for Nicholas.

"Somewhere down the road Nicholas is going to grow up, hopefully. He's going to want to know what happened. And he is going to know what happened to his baby sister and his mother. He is going to want to know what type of justice was done. He is going to want to know what happened. With your verdict, you will provide the answer."

In the rebuttal to Payne's closing argument, the prosecutor stated:

"You saw the videotape this morning. You saw what Nicholas Christopher will carry in his mind forever. When you talk about cruel, when you talk about atrocious, and when you talk about heinous, that picture will always come into your mind, probably throughout the rest of your lives. . . .

" . . . No one will ever know about Lacie Jo because she never had the chance to grow up. Her life was taken from her at the age of two years old. So, no there won't be a high school

principal to talk about Lacie Jo Christopher, and there won't be anybody to take her to her high school prom. And there won't be anybody there—there won't be her mother there or Nicholas' mother there to kiss him at night. His mother will never kiss him good night or pat him as he goes off to bed, or hold him and sing him a lullaby. . . .

"[Petitioner's attorney] wants you to think about a good reputation, people who love the defendant and things about him. He doesn't want you to think about the people who love Charisse Christopher, her mother and daddy who loved her. The people who loved little Lacie Jo, the grandparents who are still here. The brother who mourns for her every single day and wants to know where his best little playmate is. He doesn't have anybody to watch cartoons with him, a little one. These are the things that go into why it is especially cruel, heinous, and atrocious, the burden that that child will carry forever."

The jury sentenced Payne to death on each of the murder counts. . . .

We granted certiorari, to reconsider our holdings in *Booth* and [*South Carolina v. Gathers*, 490 U.S. 805 (1989)] that the Eighth Amendment prohibits a capital sentencing jury from considering "victim impact" evidence relating to the personal characteristics of the victim and the emotional impact of the crimes on the victim's family. . . .

Booth and *Gathers* were based on two premises: that evidence relating to a particular victim or to the harm that a capital defendant causes a victim's family do not in general reflect on the defendant's "blameworthiness," and that only evidence relating to "blameworthiness" is relevant to the capital sentencing decision. However, the assessment of harm caused by the defendant as a result of the crime charged has understandably been an important concern of the criminal law, both in determining the elements of the offense and in determining the appropriate punishment. Thus, two equally blameworthy criminal defendants may be guilty of different offenses solely because their acts cause differing amounts of harm. "If a bank robber aims his gun at a guard, pulls the trigger, and kills his target, he may be put to death. If the gun unexpectedly misfires, he may not. His moral guilt in both cases is identical, but his responsibility in the former is greater." *Booth*, 482 U.S., at 519 (SCALIA, J., dissenting). . . .

We have held that a State cannot preclude the sentencer from considering "any relevant mitigating evidence" that the defendant proffers in support of a sentence less than death. *Eddings v. Oklahoma*, 455 U.S. 104, 114 (1982). . . . [The] misreading of precedent in *Booth* has, we think, unfairly weighted the scales in a capital trial; while virtually no limits are placed on the relevant mitigating evidence a capital defendant may introduce concerning his own circumstances, the State is barred from either offering "a quick glimpse of the life" which a defendant "chose to extinguish," *Mills v. Maryland*, 486 U.S., 367, 397 (1988) (REHNQUIST, C.J., dissenting), or demonstrating the loss to the victim's family and to society which has resulted from the defendant's homicide.

The *Booth* Court reasoned that victim impact evidence must be excluded because it would be difficult, if not impossible, for the defendant to rebut such evidence without shifting the focus of the sentencing hearing away from the defendant, thus creating a "'mini-trial' on the victim's character." In many cases the evidence relating to the victim is already before the jury at least in part because of its relevance at the guilt phase of the trial. But even as to additional

evidence admitted at the sentencing phase, the mere fact that for tactical reasons it might not be prudent for the defense to rebut victim impact evidence makes the case no different than others in which a party is faced with this sort of a dilemma. . . .

Payne echoes the concern voiced in *Booth's* case that the admission of victim impact evidence permits a jury to find that defendants whose victims were assets to their community are more deserving of punishment than those whose victims are perceived to be less worthy. As a general matter, however, victim impact evidence is not offered to encourage comparative judgments of this kind—for instance, that the killer of a hardworking, devoted parent deserves the death penalty, but that the murderer of a reprobate does not. It is designed to show instead *each* victim's "uniqueness as an individual human being," whatever the jury might think the loss to the community resulting from his death might be. The facts of *Gathers* are an excellent illustration of this: The evidence showed that the victim was an out of work, mentally handicapped individual, perhaps not, in the eyes of most, a significant contributor to society, but nonetheless a murdered human being. . . .

We are now of the view that a State may properly conclude that for the jury to assess meaningfully the defendant's moral culpability and blameworthiness, it should have before it at the sentencing phase evidence of the specific harm caused by the defendant. "[T]he State has a legitimate interest in counteracting the mitigating evidence which the defendant is entitled to put in, by reminding the sentencer that just as the murderer should be considered as an individual, so too the victim is an individual whose death represents a unique loss to society and in particular to his family." *Booth*, 482 U.S., at 517 (WHITE, J., dissenting) (citation omitted). By turning the victim into a "faceless stranger at the penalty phase of a capital trial," *Gathers,* 490 U.S., at 821 (O'CONNOR, J., dissenting), *Booth* deprives the State of the full moral force of its evidence and may prevent the jury from having before it all the information necessary to determine the proper punishment for a first-degree murder. . . .

We thus hold that if the State chooses to permit the admission of victim impact evidence and prosecutorial argument on that subject, the Eighth Amendment erects no *per se* bar. A State may legitimately conclude that evidence about the victim and about the impact of the murder on the victim's family is relevant to the jury's decision as to whether or not the death penalty should be imposed. There is no reason to treat such evidence differently than other relevant evidence is treated. . . . [FN2] . . .

FN2. Our holding today is limited to the holdings of *Booth* . . . and . . . *Gathers,* that evidence and argument relating to the victim and the impact of the victim's death on the victim's family are inadmissible at a capital sentencing hearing. *Booth* also held that the admission of a victim's family members' characterizations and opinions about the crime, the defendant, and the appropriate sentence violates the Eighth Amendment. No evidence of the latter sort was presented at the trial in this case.

Which are the better arguments regarding the admissibility of victim impact evidence in capital sentencing hearings: those offered in Justice Powell's opinion in *Booth,* or those advanced in Chief Justice Rehnquist's opinion in *Payne?*

The victim impact evidence in *Booth* was introduced through a probation officer, who read statements provided by the victims' family members. In *Payne,* the victim impact evidence was presented through the direct testimony of a surviving family member. In more recent cases, courts have allowed videos portraying snippets of the victim's life, accompanied by music and narration, to be introduced before juries at capital sentencing hearings.[84] Do such presentations risk being so emotionally powerful that jurors will be unfairly swayed by passion or sentiment in making their sentencing decisions, or are they simply another way of depicting the measure of harm caused by a murder and thus appropriately admitted as victim impact evidence?

Conclusion

In this chapter we have considered three policy objectives that have been offered in support of capital punishment: the incapacitation of dangerous offenders, cost considerations, and responding to the suffering of murder victims and their survivors. While important, these ends are generally considered subsidiary to the dominant constitutionally accepted justifications for capital punishment of retribution and deterrence. Issues of incapacitation, cost, and consideration for murder victims' survivors nevertheless often arise in debates about the death penalty and its application in individual cases. Each of these sentencing functions has empirical (or factual) as well as normative (or ideological) dimensions.

For example, before we reach a conclusion about whether the death penalty can be justified as a guard against murderers offending again in the future, we should inquire about convicted murderers' general propensity to engage in repeat criminal violence, our ability to make accurate predictions in individual cases, and whether alternatives to execution, such as secure long-term confinement, can be similarly effective. With respect to financial considerations, we must assess not only the comparative costs associated with the death penalty and life imprisonment, but also whether a price tag can or should be put on issues so deeply imbued with justice and morality. Regarding victims and their survivors, we should consider not only how many survivors can expect the offender who claimed the life of their loved one to be executed, but also how many would want that outcome, and whether the relief sought in the form of a capital prosecution and execution will likely be delivered.

These questions are important. The answers are complicated. Discussions about the death penalty and its justifications, including incapacitation, its expense relative to lengthy incarceration, and the sense of justice and measure of relief it may or may not provide for murder victims' survivors, will certainly continue.

Endnotes

1. 428 U.S. 153, 183 (1976) (footnote omitted).
2. *Id.*, at 183 n. 28.
3. 408 U.S. 238, 355 (1972) (Marshall, J., concurring in the judgment).
4. 468 U.S. 447, 461–462 (1984).
5. *Spaziano v. Florida,* 468 U.S. 447, 477–478 & n. 19 (1984) (Stevens, J., concurring in part and dissenting in part).
6. *Baze v. Rees,* 553 U.S. 35, 78 (2008) (footnote omitted) (Stevens, J., concurring in the judgment).
7. *Cf.,* John Monahan & David Wexler, "A Definite Maybe: Proof and Probability in Civil Commitment," 2 *Law & Human Behavior* 37 (1978).
8. Prior to the Supreme Court's ruling in *Jurek v. Texas,* 428 U.S. 262 (1976), Judge Odom of the Texas Court of Criminal Appeals "complained [that] the Legislature declined to specify any particular level of probability in this special issue:

    > What did the Legislature mean when it provided that a man's life or death shall rest upon whether there exists a 'probability' that he will perform certain acts in the future? Did it mean, as the words read, is there *a* probability, some probability, any probability? We may say there is a twenty percent probability that it will rain tomorrow, or a ten or five percent probability. Though this be a small probability, yet it is some probability, *a* probability, and no one would say it is no probability or not a probability. It has been written: 'It is probable that many things will happen contrary to probability,' and 'A thousand probabilities do not make one fact.' The statute does not require a particular degree of probability but only directs that *some* probability need be found. The absence of a specification as to what degree of probability is required is itself a vagueness inherent in the term as used in this issue. Our common sense understanding of the term leaves the statute too vague to pass constitutional muster.

    "[*Jurek v. State,* 522 S.W.2d 934, 945 (Tex. Crim. App. 1975) (Odom, J., concurring and dissenting)] (footnote omitted). But the Supreme Court disagreed with Judge Odom's constitutional concerns about the vague nature of 'a probability' in the special issue." *Coble v. State*, 330 S.W.3d 253, 268 n. 18 (Tex. Crim. App. 2010), *cert. denied*, 131 S.Ct. 3030 (2011).

See also Murphy v. State, 112 S.W.3d 592, 607–608 (Tex. Crim. App. 2003) (Johnson, J., concurring), *cert. denied*, 541 U.S. 940 (2004).

> In a capital murder trial in which the state seeks the death penalty, Texas law requires jurors to determine whether "there is a probability that the defendant would commit criminal acts of violence that would constitute a continuing threat to society. . . ." . . . Thus, it is imperative that jurors understand the difference between "probable" and "possible."
>
> While it is possible that I will win the lottery, it is not probable; indeed, it is highly improbable. . . .
>
> If a juror confuses "probable" and "possible" and also believes that there is a small chance that the defendant might commit violent acts in the future, even if that juror also believes that another violent act is unlikely, that juror may feel compelled to find that the defendant is a future danger. If that juror is also the twelfth vote, the cost of that confusion is the defendant's life.

9. *See Druery v. State*, 225 S.W.3d 491, 506–507 (Tex. Crim. App.), *cert. denied*, 552 U.S. 1028 (2007) ("[T]he State has the burden of proving beyond a reasonable doubt that there is a probability that [the defendant] would commit criminal acts of violence in the future, so as to constitute a continuing threat, whether in or out of prison.") (footnote omitted); *Coble v. State*, 330 S.W.3d 253, 269 (Tex. Crim. App. 2010) (footnote omitted), *cert. denied*, 131 S.Ct. 3030 (2011) ("[J]uries appropriately focus upon the defendant's individual character for violence and the probability that he would commit acts of violence in whatever society he found himself. Obviously, the likelihood that a defendant does not or will not pose a heightened risk of violence in the structured prison community is a relevant, indeed important, criterion, but it is not the exclusive focus of the 'future dangerousness' issue.")

10. *King v. State*, 553 S.W.2d 105, 107 (Tex. Crim. App. 1977), *cert. denied*, 434 U.S. 1088 (1978), *quoting Joubert v. State*, 124 S.W.2d 368, 369 (Tex. Crim. App. 1938). *See also Estrada v. State*, 313 S.W.3d 274, 281–282 (Tex. Crim. App. 2010), *cert. denied*, 131 S.Ct. 905 (2011).

11. *Penry v. Lynaugh*, 492 U.S. 302, 109 S.Ct. 2934, 106 L.Ed.2d 256 (1989).

12. Tex. Code Crim. Proc. Art. 37.071 (2)(b)(1) (Vernon 2004). In pertinent cases, the jury also must answer affirmatively to "whether the defendant actually caused the death of the deceased or did not actually cause the death of the deceased but intended to kill the deceased or another or anticipated that a human life would be taken." *Id.*, Art. 37.071 (2)(b)(2). Unlike the original statute, the revised law also provides that the alternative sentence to death is life imprisonment without parole. *Id.*, Art. 37.071 (2)(a)(1).

13. *Id.*, Art. 37.071 (2)(e)(1).

14. Ore. Rev. Stat. § 163.150 (2005).

15. Va. Code Ann. § 19.2–264.2 ("In assessing the penalty of any person convicted of an offense for which the death penalty may be imposed, a sentence of death shall not be imposed unless the court or jury shall (1) after consideration of the past criminal record of convictions of the defendant, find that there is a probability that the defendant would commit criminal acts of violence that would constitute a continuing serious threat to society or that his conduct in committing the offense for which he stands charged was outrageously or wantonly vile, horrible or inhuman in that it involved torture, depravity of mind or an aggravated battery to the victim; and (2) recommend that the penalty of death be imposed.").

16. *See* William W. Berry III, "Ending Death by Dangerousness: A Path to the De Facto Abolition of the Death Penalty," 52 *Arizona Law Review* 889, 897–900 (2010) (discussing jurisdictions in which future dangerousness is a statutory or non-statutory capital sentencing factor).

17. Mark D. Cunningham, Jon R. Sorensen & Thomas J. Reidy, "Capital Jury Decision-Making: The Limitations of Predictions of Future Violence," 15 *Psychology, Public Policy, and Law* 223, 225–226 (2009); Jon Sorensen & James Marquart, "Future Dangerousness and Incapacitation," in James R. Acker, Robert M. Bohm & Charles S. Lanier (eds.), *America's Experiment With Capital Punishment: Reflections on the Past, Present, and Future of the Ultimate Penal Sanction* 283, 284–287 (Durham, NC: Carolina Academic Press, 2d ed. 2003); John H. Blume, Stephen P. Garvey & Sheri Lynn Johnson, "Future Dangerousness in Capital Cases: Always 'At Issue'," 86 *Cornell Law Review* 397 (2001).

18. The facts resulting in Barefoot's murder conviction and death sentence are set forth in *Barefoot v. State*, 596 S.W.2d 875 (Tex. Crim. App. 1980) and in the Supreme Court's opinion, *Barefoot v. Estelle*, 463 U.S. 880 (1983).

19. *See* Ron Rosenbaum, "Travels With Dr. Death," *Vanity Fair* 141 (May 1990).

20. *Estelle v. Smith*, 451 U.S. 454, 101 S.Ct. 1866, 68 L.Ed.2d 359 (1981).

21. *See* John Monahan, "A Jurisprudence of Risk Assessment: Forecasting Harm Among Prisoners, Predators, and Patients," 92 *Virginia Law Review* 391, 405–426 (2006); Jonathan R. Sorensen & Rocky L. Pilgrim, "An Actuarial Risk Assessment of Violence Posed by Capital Murder Defendants," 90 *Journal of Criminal Law & Criminology* 1251 (2000).

22. Monahan, *supra* note 21, at 392 (*quoting* Steve Lash, "Texas Death Case Set Aside," *Houston Chronicle* 1A (June 6, 2000). *See Saldano v. Texas*, 530 U.S. 1212, 120 S.Ct. 2214, 147 L.Ed.2d 246 (2000).

23. *Saldano v. State*, 232 S.W.3d 77 (Tex. Crim. App. 2007).

24. 408 U.S. 238, 355 (1972) (Marshall, J., concurring in the judgment) (footnotes omitted).

25. Anthony Amsterdam, "Capital Punishment," in Hugo Adam Bedau (ed.), *The Death Penalty in America* 346, 354 (New York: Oxford University Press, 3d ed. 1982).

26. James W. Marquart & Jonathan R. Sorensen, "A National Study of the *Furman*-Commuted Inmates: Assessing the Threat to Society From Capital Offenders," 23 *Loyola of Los Angeles Law Review* 5, 27 (1989) (footnotes omitted).

27. *Id.*, at 27–28.

28. *See* Paul Cassell, "In Defense of the Death Penalty," 42 *Prosecutor* 10 (Dec. 2008); Guy Goldberg & Gena Bunn, "Balancing Fairness and Finality: A Comprehensive Review of the Texas Death Penalty," 5 *Texas Review of Law and Politics* 49, 130 (2000); Danya W. Blair, "A Matter of Life and Death: Why Life Without Parole Should Be a Sentencing Option in Texas," 22 *American Journal of Criminal Law* 191, 191–193 (1994); *McDuff v. State*, 939 S.W.2d 607 (Tex. Crim. App.), *cert. denied*, 522 U.S. 944 (1997).

29. *See, e.g.,* James W. Marquart, Sheldon Ekland-Olson & Jonathan R. Sorensen, "Gazing Into the Crystal Ball: Can Jurors Accurately Predict Dangerousness in Capital Cases?," 23 *Law & Society Review* 449 (1989); Jonathan R. Sorensen & Rocky L. Pilgrim, "An Actuarial Risk Assessment of Violence Posed by Capital Murder Defendants," 90 *Journal of Criminal Law & Criminology* 1251 (2000); Mitzi Dorland & Daniel Krauss, "The Danger of Dangerousness in Capital Sentencing: Exacerbating the Problem of Arbitrary and Capricious Decision-Making," 29 *Law & Psychology Review* 63, 92–100 (2005); Mark Douglas Cunningham & Jon R. Sorensen, "Capital Offenders in Texas Prisons: Rates, Correlates, and an Actuarial Analysis of Violent Misconduct," 31 *Law & Human Behavior* 553 (2007); Jon Sorensen, "Researching Future Dangerousness," in Charles S. Lanier, William J. Bowers & James R. Acker, eds., *The Future of America's Death Penalty: An Agenda for the Next Generation of Capital Punishment Research* 359 (Durham, NC: Carolina Academic Press 2009).

30. *See Allen v. Ornoski*, 435 F.3d 946 (9th Cir.), *cert. den.*, 546 U.S. 1136 (2006). *See also* Meghan Shapiro, "An Overdose of Dangerousness: How 'Future Dangerousness' Catches the Least Culpable Capital Defendants and Undermines the Rationale for the Executions It Supports," 35 *American Journal of Criminal Law* 145, 181 n. 188 (2008). *See generally* Elizabeth Rapaport, "A Modest Proposal: The Aged of Death Row Should Be Deemed Too Old to Execute," 77 *Brooklyn Law Review* 1089 (2012).

31. *See Thomas v. State*, 2008 WL 4531976 (Tex. Crim. App. 2008); *Ex parte Thomas*, 2009 WL 693606 (Tex. Crim. App. 2009); *Ex parte Thomas*, 2010 WL 1795738 (Tex. Crim. App. 2010).
32. *See* Mary Sigler, "Mercy, Clemency, and the Case of Karla Faye Tucker," 4 *Ohio State Journal of Criminal Law* 455 (2007); Melynda J. Price, "Litigating Salvation: Race, Religion and Innocence in the Karla Faye Tucker and Gary Graham Cases," 15 *Southern California Review of Law & Social Justice* 267 (2006); Walter C. Long, "Karla Faye Tucker: A Case for Restorative Justice," 27 *American Journal of Criminal Law* 117, 121–123 (1999).
33. Caleb Calhoun, "Local Residents Share Thoughts on Md. Death Penalty," *Herald-Mail.com* (Feb. 15, 2013), retrieved March 22, 2013 from http://articles.herald-mail.com/2013-02-15/news/37125225_1_death-penalty-capital-punishment-innocent-person.
34. Martin O'Malley, "Repealing Maryland's Death Penalty," *Politico* (March 18, 2013), retrieved March 22, 2013 from www.politico.com/story/2013/03/martin-omalley-repealing-marylands-death-penalty-88972.html.
35. James J. Stephan, *State Prison Expenditures, 2001*, at 1–3 (Washington, D.C.: U.S. Dept. of Justice, Bureau of Justice Statistics 2004), retrieved March 30, 2013 from http://bjs.gov/content/pub/pdf/spe01.pdf.
36. John Roman, Aaron Chalfin, Aaron Sundquist, Carly Knight & Askar Darmenov, *The Cost of the Death Penalty in Maryland*, Abstract (Urban Institute 2008), retrieved March 23, 2013 from www.urban.org/publications/411625.html.
37. Philip J. Cook, "Potential Savings From Abolition of the Death Penalty in North Carolina," 11 *American Law and Economics Review* 498, 499 (2009).
38. California Commission on the Fair Administration of Justice, *Final Report* 117 (2008), retrieved March 23, 2013 from www.ccfaj.org/documents/CCFAJFinalReport.pdf.
39. Arthur L. Alarcon & Paula M. Mitchell, "Executing the Will of the Voters?: A Roadmap to Mend or End the California Legislature's Multi-Billion Dollar Death Penalty Debacle," 44 *Loyola of Los Angeles Law Review* S41, S109 (2011).
40. *Id.*
41. John K. Roman, Aaron J. Chalfin & Carly L. Knight, "Reassessing the Cost of the Death Penalty Using Quasi-Experimental Methods: Evidence From Maryland," 11 *American Law and Economics Review* 530, 533 (2009) (footnote omitted); *see id.* at 534–536 (discussing the studies involved).
42. *See* Robert M. Bohm, "The Economic Costs of Capital Punishment: Past, Present, and Future," in James R. Acker, Robert M. Bohm & Charles S. Lanier, eds., *America's Experiment With Capital Punishment: Reflections on the Past, Present, and Future of the Ultimate Penal Sanction* 573 (Durham, NC: Carolina Academic Press, 2d ed. 2003); Robert L. Spangenberg & Elizabeth R. Walsh, "Capital Punishment or Life Imprisonment? Some Cost Considerations," 23 *Loyola of Los Angeles Law Review* 45 (1989); Margot Garey, "The Cost of Taking a Life: Dollars and Sense of the Death Penalty," 18 *U.C. Davis Law Review* 1221 (1985).
43. Between 1988 and 2012, 140 of the 212 federal death penalty trials in which juries returned sentencing verdicts (66%) resulted in life sentences and 72 (34%) resulted in death sentences. Death Penalty Information Center, "Federal Death Penalty," retrieved March 30, 2013 from www.deathpenaltyinfo.org/federal-death-penalty#statutes; David C. Baldus, George G. Woodworth & Charles S. Pulaski, Jr., *Equal Justice and the Death Penalty: A Legal and Empirical Analysis* 233 (Boston: Northeastern University Press 1990) ("The available information about post-*Furman* death-sentencing rates is . . . incomplete, but it does suggest slightly higher jury death sentencing rates [compared to pre-*Furman* rates] in some (but clearly not all) jurisdictions: .55 in Georgia, .48 in California, .36 in Colorado, .64 in Cook County, Illinois, 1.0 in Dallas, .25 in Delaware, .74 in Florida, .49 in Louisiana, .42 in Maryland, .50 in North Carolina, .36 in New Jersey, and .60 in Mississippi." (footnotes omitted)).

44. James S. Liebman, Jeffrey Fagan & Valerie West, "A Broken System: Error Rates in Capital Cases, 1973–1995," at 3–6 (2000), retrieved March 30, 2013 from www2.law.columbia.edu/ instructionalservices/liebman/liebman_final.pdf.

45. Liebman *et al.* report that among the cases in their sample where the conviction or death sentence was vacated on state post-conviction review, "*82%* (247 out of 301) of the capital judgments . . . were replaced on retrial with a sentence *less* than death, or *no* sentence at all. In the latter regard, 7% (22/301) of the reversals for serious error resulted in a determination on retrial that the defendant was *not guilty* of the capital offense." *Id.,* at 27 (emphasis in original) (footnotes omitted).

46. *See* Aliza B. Kaplan, "Oregon's Death Penalty: The Practical Reality," 17 *Lewis & Clark Law Review* 1, 45–46 n. 330 (2013); James R. Acker, "Be Careful What You Ask For: Lessons From New York's Recent Experience With Capital Punishment," 32 *Vermont Law Review* 683, 714–715 (2008) (quoting testimony of Professor Robert Blecker in a 2005 public hearing before standing committees of the New York Assembly); Kent S. Scheidegger, "The Death Penalty and Plea Bargaining to Life Sentences," Working Paper 09–01 (2009) (Sacramento, CA: Criminal Justice Legal Foundation), retrieved March 30, 2013 from www. cjlf.org/publications/papers/wpaper09-01.pdf. *See also* George H. Brauchler, "Death Penalty Is a Tool of Justice," *Denver Post* (March 31, 2013) ("Currently, defense attorneys initiate contact with prosecutors on murder cases for which the death penalty is a potential outcome and request to plead guilty to life in prison instead of facing death. Without the death penalty, dozens of additional lengthy jury trials will be necessary with the predictable, numerous and lengthy appeals lasting many years. That cost is never considered in an evaluation of the death penalty's fiscal impact."), retrieved April 12, 2013 from www.denverpost.com/ opinion/ci_22895409/death-penalty-is-tool-justice. Mr. Brauchler, the District Attorney for Colorado's 18th Judicial District, announced his intention to seek the death penalty in the prosecution of James Holmes, who allegedly shot and killed 12 individuals and wounded 58 others in an Aurora, Colorado, movie theater in July 2012.

47. New York's 1995 death penalty statute was ruled unconstitutional in 2004 and replacement legislation was not enacted, leaving the state without capital punishment. *See People v. LaValle,* 817 N.E.2d 341 (N.Y. 2004); *People v. Taylor,* 878 N.E.2d 969 (N.Y. 2007).

48. Ilyana Kuziemko, "Does the Threat of the Death Penalty Affect Plea Bargaining in Murder Cases? Evidence From New York's 1995 Reinstatement of Capital Punishment," 8 *American Law and Economics Review* 116, 140–141 (2006).

49. Sherod Thaxton, "Leveraging Death," 103 *Journal of Criminal Law & Criminology* 475, 549 (2013).

50. *Id.,* at 483–484.

51. *See* Susan Ehrhard, "Plea Bargaining and the Death Penalty: An Exploratory Study," 29 *Justice System Journal* 313 (2008).

52. *See* Josh Bolinger, "Smigiel: Death Penalty Bill Was 'One of the Hardest Votes,'" *Cecil Daily* (March 18, 2013) (Mike Smigiel, a member of the Maryland House of Delegates, argued during the debate over a bill to repeal Maryland's death penalty that capital punishment "is used as a plea bargaining technique to keep the worst of the worst, those who kill others, off the streets and in jail to serve a sentence of life without the possibility of parole. 'Why should we take that tool from the box?' Smigiel said. 'When you remove it, then they will face life without parole and life with parole, and they'll end up with parole. They'll have the ability to walk among us one day.'"), retrieved March 30, 2013 from www.cecildaily.com/ news/local_news/article_af2bd1f4-8f72-11e2-8c8c-001a4bcf887a.html.

53. 408 U.S. 238, 355 (1972) (Marshall, J., concurring in the judgment).

54. *See Brady v. United States,* 397 U.S. 742 (1970); *North Carolina v. Alford,* 400 U.S. 25 (1970).

55. *See* Daina Borteck, "Pleas for DNA Testing: Why Lawmakers Should Amend State Post-Conviction DNA Testing Statutes to Apply to Prisoners Who Pled Guilty," 25 *Cardozo Law Review* 1429, 1442–45 (2004) (discussing cases of Christopher Ochoa, in Texas,

and Jerry Frank Townsend, in Florida, each of whom falsely confessed to one or more murder charges and pled guilty to avoid a potential death sentence, and each of whom subsequently was exonerated); Welsh S. White, "Confessions in Capital Cases," 2003 *Illinois Law Review* 979, 1009–1012 (2003) (discussing cases of Christopher Ochoa, in Texas, and Anthony Gray, in Maryland, who also falsely confessed and pled guilty to murder to avoid a possible death sentence, and who later was exonerated based in part on DNA evidence).

56. *See, e.g.,* Lucian E. Dervan, "Bargained Justice: Plea-Bargaining's Innocence Problem and the *Brady* Safety-Valve," 2012 *Utah Law Review* 51 (2012); Jonathan E. Gradess & Andrew L.B. Davies, "The Cost of the Death Penalty in America: Directions for Future Research," in Charles S. Lanier, William J. Bowers & James R. Acker, eds., *The Future of America's Death Penalty: An Agenda for the Next Generation of Capital Punishment Research* 397, 408–409 (Durham, NC: Carolina Academic Press 2009); Russell D. Covey, "Fixed Justice: Reforming Plea Bargaining With Plea-Based Ceilings," 82 *Tulane Law Review* 1237, 1282–84 (2008).

57. Albert W. Alschuler, "Plea Bargaining and the Death Penalty," 58 *DePaul Law Review* 671, 674 (2009).

58. Proposition 34, Proposed Law, The SAFE California Act, § 3 (2), (3) (2012), retrieved April 13, 2013 from http://vig.cdn.sos.ca.gov/2012/general/pdf/text-proposed-laws-v2.pdf#nameddest=prop34. *See generally* James R. Acker, "Your Money and Your Life: How Cost Nearly Killed California's Death Penalty," 24 *Correctional Law Reporter* 69 (2013).

59. Colorado HB09–1274 (2009), Summary of Legislation, retrieved April 13, 2013 from www.leg.state.co.us/clics/clics2009a/csl.nsf/fsbillcont3/3D3051B266D2F5CA8725753 7001A3D75?Open&file=HB1274_00.pdf. *See also* Jessica Fender & Lynn Bartels, "Bid to Repeal Death Penalty Fails in Senate," *Denver Post* (May 6, 2009), retrieved April 13, 2013 from www.denverpost.com/politics/ci_12307296; Michael L. Radelet & Dawn Stanley, "Learning From Homicide Co-Victims: A University-Based Project," in James R. Acker & David R. Karp, eds., *Wounds That Do Not Bind: Victim-Based Perspectives on the Death Penalty* 397 (Durham, NC: Carolina Academic Press 2006).

60. *See* Lyn Suzanne Entzeroth, "The End of the Beginning: The Politics of Death and the American Death Penalty Regime in the Twenty-First Century," 90 *Oregon Law Review* 797, 816–832 (2012). For similar comparative cost-based arguments in New York, where legislative committees conducted hearings while considering whether to attempt to revise the death penalty law that had been declared unconstitutional in 2004 by the New York Court of Appeals, *see* Acker, *supra* note 46, at 711–720.

61. Howard Mintz, "The Cost of California's Death Penalty," *San Jose Mercury News* (May 16, 2012) (*quoting* McGregor Scott, former U.S. Attorney in Sacramento), retrieved April 13, 2013 from www.mercurynews.com/crime-courts/ci_20497754/cost-californias-death-pen alty?. *See also* Robert Blecker, "But Did They Listen? The New Jersey Death Penalty Commission's Exercise in Abolitionism: A Reply," 5 *Rutgers Journal of Law & Public Policy* 9 (2007).

62. Dawinder S. Sidhu, "On Appeal: Reviewing the Case Against the Death Penalty," 111 *West Virginia Law Review* 453, 468 (2009).

63. David Garland, *Peculiar Institution: America's Death Penalty in an Age of Abolition* 304–305 (Cambridge, MA: Belknap Press of Harvard University Press 2010) (footnote omitted).

64. 408 U.S. 238, 405 (1972) (Blackmun, J., dissenting).

65. *Id.,* 408 U.S., at 413–414.

66. Margaret Vandiver, "The Impact of the Death Penalty on the Families of Homicide Victims and of Condemned Prisoners," in James R. Acker, Robert M. Bohm & Charles S. Lanier (eds.), *America's Experiment With Capital Punishment: Reflections on the Past, Present, and Future of the Ultimate Penal Sanction* 613, 615 (Durham, NC: Carolina Academic Press, 2d ed. 2003), *citing* L.M. Redmond, *Surviving: When Someone You Love Was Murdered* 5 (Clearwater, FL: Psychological Consultation and Educational Services, Inc. 1989).

67. Vandiver, *supra* note 66, *citing* A. Amick-McMullan, D.G. Kilpatrick & H.S. Resnick, "Homicide as a Risk Factor for PTSD Among Surviving Family Members," 15 *Behavior Modification* 545, 551–552 (1991).

68. Marilyn Peterson Armour & Mark S. Umbreit, "Assessing the Impact of the Ultimate Penal Sanction on Homicide Survivors: A Two State Comparison," 96 *Marquette Law Review* 1, 4 (2012), *citing* Heide M. Zinzow *et al.*, "Losing a Loved One to Homicide: Prevalence and Mental Health Correlates in a National Sample of Young Adults," 22 *Journal of Traumatic Stress* 20, 24 (2009).

69. James R. Acker, "The Myth of Closure and Capital Punishment," in Robert M. Bohm & Jeffery T. Walker (eds.), *Demystifying Crime and Criminal Justice* 254, 257 (New York: Oxford University Press, 2d ed. 2013) (citations omitted).

70. Rachel King, *Don't Kill in Our Names: Families of Murder Victims Speak Out Against the Death Penalty* (Newark, NJ: Rutgers University Press 2003); Renny R. Cushing & Susannah Sheffer, *Dignity Denied: The Experience of Murder Victims' Family Members Who Oppose the Death Penalty* (Cambridge, MA: Murder Victims' Families for Reconciliation 2002).

71. Vandiver, *supra* note 66, at 243–244.

72. *See* Susan A. Bandes, "Victims, 'Closure,' and the Sociology of Emotion," 72 *Law & Contemporary Problems* 1, 1–3 (Spring 2009).

73. Samuel R. Gross & Daniel J. Matheson, "What They Say at the End: Capital Victims' Families and the Press," 88 *Cornell Law Review* 486, 490–494 (2003).

74. Stanley Rosenbluth & Phyllis Rosenbluth, "Accidental Death Is Fate, Murder Is Pure Evil," in James R. Acker & David R. Karp (eds.), *Wounds That Do Not Bind: Victim-Based Perspectives on the Death Penalty* 103, 107 (Durham, NC: Carolina Academic Press 2006).

75. Marsha Kimble, "My Journey and the Riddle," in Acker & Karp, *Wounds That Do Not Bind, supra* note 74, at 127, 138. *See generally* Jody Lynee Madeira, *Killing McVeigh: The Death Penalty and the Myth of Closure* (New York: New York University Press 2012).

76. Tammy Krause, "Reaching Out to the Other Side: Defense-Based Victim Outreach in Capital Cases," in Acker & Karp, *Wounds That Do Not Bind, supra* note 74, at 379, 394.

77. *See* Mark D. Reed & Brenda Simms Blackwell, "Secondary Victimization Among Families of Homicide Victims: The Impact of the Justice Process on Co-Victims' Psychological Adjustment and Service Utilization," in Acker & Karp, *Wounds That Do Not Bind, supra* note 74, at 253.

78. Lynne Henderson, "Co-opting Compassion: The Federal Victim's Rights Amendment," 10 *St. Thomas Law Review* 579, 601–602 (1998).

79. *See, e.g.,* Austin Sarat, *When the State Kills: Capital Punishment and the American Condition* 33–59 (Princeton, NJ: Princeton University Press 2001). *See generally* Bandes, *supra* note 72, at 26; Marie Gottschalk, "Dismantling the Carceral State: The Future of Penal Policy Reform," 84 *Texas Law Review* 1693, 1727–28 (2006); Wayne A. Logan, "Casting New Light on an Old Subject: Death Penalty Abolitionism for a New Millennium," 100 *Michigan Law Review* 1336, 1346–53 (2002).

80. Franklin E. Zimring, *The Contradictions of American Capital Punishment* 62 (New York: Oxford University Press 2003).

81. *California v. Brown*, 538 U.S. 545 (1987) (O'Connor, J., concurring).

82. 482 U.S. 496 (1987).

83. 501 U.S. 808 (1991).

84. *See Kelly v. California*, 555 U.S. 1020 (2008) (Stevens, J., dissenting from denial of certiorari). *See also* Jerome Deise & Raymond Paternoster, "More Than a 'Quick Glimpse of the Life': The Relationship Between Victim Impact Evidence and Death Sentencing," 40 *Hastings Constitutional Law Quarterly* 611 (2013); Emily Holland, "Moving Pictures . . . Maintaining Justice? Clarifying the Right Role for Victim Impact Videos in the Capital Context," 17 *Berkeley Journal of Criminal Law* 147 (2012); Alicia N. Harden, "Drawing the Line at Pushing 'Play': Barring Video Montages as Victim Impact Evidence at Capital Sentencing Trials," 99 *Kentucky Law Journal* 845 (2010–2011).

II

DECIDING WHO DIES

LAW AND PRACTICE

4

CAPITAL PUNISHMENT FOR MURDER
SENTENCING CRITERIA AND PROCEDURES

Introduction

In *Gregg v. Georgia*[1] and its four companion cases,[2] all decided on July 2, 1976, the Supreme Court announced the broad constitutional principles that govern modern death penalty jurisprudence. These decisions established the following propositions. Capital punishment for the crime of aggravated murder is not inherently (or *per se*) cruel and unusual, in violation of the Eighth Amendment. Yet death, in its severity and finality, is qualitatively different from other criminal sanctions. Death sentences consequently must satisfy a heightened standard of reliability. To minimize the risk of arbitrary capital sentencing decisions, legislation must define a relatively narrow range of death penalty–eligible crimes, the sentencing authority must give individualized consideration to relevant offense and offender circumstances and have discretion to impose a sentence less than death, and appellate court review of cases resulting in a death sentence must be available.

The Supreme Court's 1972 decision in *Furman v. Georgia*[3] brought an end to one death-penalty era. The Court's 1976 decisions marked the beginning of a new and tumultuous one, in which the justices became immersed in a sea of litigation that resulted in a series of doctrinal starts and stops as they found themselves policing numerous details of capital punishment administration. This chapter briefly traces the historical roots of the modern era requirements governing capital sentencing decisions, starting with the country's formative years and culminating in the Court's landmark decision in *Furman*. It next considers the constitutional framework for capital punishment decisions that the Court constructed in the post-*Furman* death-penalty era. This discussion begins with *Gregg* and its companion cases and then touches on several of the Court's subsequent significant pronouncements. The primary focus remains on the criteria and procedures that are designed to channel capital sentencing decisions and that distinguish the modern-era laws, and on the attendant uncertainties and tensions grounded in the reforms that comprise a part of the Court's constitutional handiwork.

We limit our consideration in this chapter to the capital sentencing decisions made in cases of aggravated murder. In chapter 5 we examine whether crimes in addition to murder can (and should) be punished by death. We further will inquire whether some offenders, even if convicted of aggravated murder, are (and should be) constitutionally ineligible to receive a death sentence.

Capital Sentencing Decisions: From Early Statehood to *Furman v. Georgia*

Capital sentencing decisions were not complicated when the American colonies declared their independence from England. The death penalty followed automatically on conviction for capital crimes—and there were several—in all of the original states. Mandatory capital punishment upon conviction, for which neither judge nor jury had the discretion to impose a lesser sentence, was a carry-over practice from colonial and British law.[4]

Various mechanisms nevertheless allowed some softening of the inflexible mandatory sentencing policy. First-time offenders could be spared execution through a judge's conferral of the "benefit of clergy." This doctrine originally was fashioned to shield priests and clerics from the jurisdiction of royal courts and ensure their trial in the ecclesiastical courts, where capital punishment was not available. Over time, the benefit of clergy was stretched well beyond its original purpose and was used by secular criminal court judges to avoid imposing automatic death sentences in cases involving lay defendants. Instead of being punished by death, offenders given the benefit of clergy originally were branded on the thumb with a hot iron (a marking which prohibited their claiming the benefit a second time) and then were permitted to return to the community. Later practice allowed offenders receiving the benefit of clergy to be fined, incarcerated, or "transported" (banished) to another jurisdiction.[5]

Other practices made mandatory capital sentencing laws less rigid in their application. Juries frequently rebelled against sending offenders to the gallows and thus "nullified" mandatory capital punishment laws by refusing to convict defendants subject to them, despite clear evidence of guilt.[6] The liberal use of executive clemency also spared many defendants who had been convicted and automatically sentenced to death from execution.[7]

Although mandatory capital sentencing upon conviction was the uniform practice during the country's early history, it gradually gave way, owing to the twin concerns that automatic death sentences worked frequent injustices and also proved to be unenforceable.[8] State legislatures responded initially by limiting the reach of the death penalty to fewer crimes. A leading example was Pennsylvania's 1794 statutory innovation that created degrees of murder and restricted capital punishment to murder in the first-degree.[9] As the 19th century progressed, states began authorizing juries to recommend that offenders be sentenced either to death or to the penitentiary. Maryland introduced discretionary sentencing for some capital crimes (but not murder) in 1809. Tennessee was the first state to take that step for murder, doing so in 1838. By 1963, mandatory capital sentencing had given way in all jurisdictions save for the rarest of crimes.[10]

Ironically, investing juries with discretion to sentence defendants convicted of capital crimes either to death or a term of imprisonment raised a new set of troubling issues. By the mid-1960s, most states required juries to make their guilt and sentencing decisions during the same deliberations, based exclusively on the trial evidence pertaining to the charged crime. A few states relied on bifurcated capital proceedings, which consisted of a guilt-innocence trial followed, in the event of conviction, by a separate penalty phase at which additional evidence could be introduced and arguments made that focused specifically on the sentencing decision. Under neither system were juries offered guidance regarding how or why they should consider recommending mercy or a sentence of death.[11] The instructions given the jury during the penalty phase of a bifurcated capital murder trial in California—in a case reviewed by the U.S. Supreme Court in *McGautha v. California* (1971)—are illustrative:[12]

> [I]n this part of the trial the law does not forbid you from being influenced by pity for the defendants and you may be governed by mere sentiment and sympathy for the defendants in arriving at a proper penalty in this case; however, the law does forbid you from being governed by mere conjecture, prejudice, public opinion or public feeling. . . .
>
> . . . Notwithstanding facts, if any, proved in mitigation or aggravation, in determining which punishment [death or life imprisonment] shall be inflicted, you are entirely free to act according to your own judgment, conscience, and absolute discretion. . . .
>
> Now, beyond prescribing the two alternative penalties, the law itself provides no standard for the guidance of the jury in the selection of the penalty, but, rather, commits the whole matter of determining which of the two penalties shall be fixed to the judgment, conscience, and absolute discretion of the jury.[13]

The jury sentenced Dennis McGautha to death. He argued, as did James Crampton, the defendant in the companion case before the Supreme Court, who had been sentenced to death pursuant to Ohio's unitary trial procedure, that giving juries the unfettered discretion to make a decision as momentous as sparing or taking human life, absent legal standards or criteria, violated his Fourteenth Amendment due process rights. The Supreme Court disagreed, by vote of 6–3. Justice Harlan's majority opinion reasoned:

> Those who have come to grips with the hard task of actually attempting to draft means of channeling capital sentencing discretion have confirmed the lesson taught by . . . history. . . . To identify before the fact those characteristics of criminal homicides and their perpetrators which call for the death penalty, and to express these characteristics in language which can be fairly understood and applied by the sentencing authority, appear to be tasks which are beyond present human ability. . . .
>
> . . . In light of history, experience, and the present limitations of human knowledge, we find it quite impossible to say that committing to the untrammeled discretion of the jury the power to pronounce life or death in capital cases is offensive to anything in the Constitution. The States are entitled to assume that jurors confronted with the truly awesome responsibility of decreeing death for a fellow human will act with due regard for the consequences of their decision and will consider a variety of factors, many of which will have been

suggested by the evidence or by the arguments of defense counsel. For a court to attempt to catalog the appropriate factors in this elusive area could inhibit rather than expand the scope of consideration, for no list of circumstances would ever be really complete. The infinite variety of cases and facets to each case would make general standards either meaningless 'boiler-plate' or a statement of the obvious that no jury would need.

Just one year later, the Court made an abrupt about-face. In a fractured decision spilling over nearly 250 pages in the *United States Reports*, in which each of the justices in the 5–4 "majority" wrote separately because they found insufficient common ground to join the others' opinions, the Court ruled in *Furman v. Georgia*[14] that death sentences imposed at the unbridled discretion of juries and judges violate the Eighth Amendment's prohibition against cruel and unusual punishments. *Furman's* limited holding was expressed in a one-paragraph *per curiam* opinion that encompassed the three capital cases that had been joined for decision.

PER CURIAM

Petitioner in [*Furman v. Georgia*] was convicted of murder in Georgia and was sentenced to death. . . . Petitioner in [*Jackson v. Georgia*] was convicted of rape in Georgia and was sentenced to death. . . . Petitioner in [*Branch v. Texas*] was convicted of rape in Texas and was sentenced to death. . . . Certiorari was granted limited to the following question: 'Does the imposition and carrying out of the death penalty in [these cases] constitute cruel and unusual punishment in violation of the Eighth and Fourteenth Amendments?' The Court holds that the imposition and carrying out of the death penalty in these cases constitute cruel and unusual punishment in violation of the Eighth and Fourteenth Amendments. The judgment in each case is therefore reversed insofar as it leaves undisturbed the death sentence imposed, and the cases are remanded for further proceedings. So ordered.

In its effect, the Court's holding was anything but limited. This landmark decision invalidated virtually all death-penalty laws then on the books and cleared the nation's death rows of the more than 600 offenders awaiting execution, causing all of them to be resentenced to terms of imprisonment.[15] Among the five members of the *Furman* Court who found the death sentences at issue to be unconstitutional, Justices Brennan[16] and Marshall[17] alone held the view that the Eighth Amendment flatly prohibits the death penalty under all circumstances. The others focused on various problems associated with wholly discretionary and standardless capital sentencing decisions.

Justice Douglas was concerned that the unregulated decision-making process resulted in capital sentences being applied in an invidiously discriminatory manner, particularly against unpopular and politically powerless classes of defendants.

The generality of a law inflicting capital punishment is one thing. What may be said of the validity of a law on the books and what may be done with the law in its application do, or may, lead to quite different conclusions.

It would seem to be incontestable that the death penalty inflicted on one defendant is 'unusual' if it discriminates against him by reason of his race, religion, wealth, social position, or class, or if it is imposed under a procedure that gives room for the play of such prejudices. . . .

We cannot say from facts disclosed in these records that these defendants were sentenced to death because they were black. Yet our task is not restricted to an effort to divine what motives impelled these death penalties. Rather, we deal with a system of law and of justice that leaves to the uncontrolled discretion of judges or juries the determination whether defendants committing these crimes should die or be imprisoned. Under these laws no standards govern the selection of the penalty. People live or die, dependent on the whim of one man or of 12. . . .

Those who wrote the Eighth Amendment knew what price their forebears had paid for a system based, not on equal justice, but on discrimination. In those days the target was not the blacks or the poor, but the dissenters, those who opposed absolutism in government, who struggled for a parliamentary regime, and who opposed governments' recurring efforts to foist a particular religion on the people. But the tool of capital punishment was used with vengeance against the opposition and those unpopular with the regime. One cannot read this history without realizing that the desire for equality was reflected in the ban against 'cruel and unusual punishments' contained in the Eighth Amendment.

In a Nation committed to equal protection of the laws there is no permissible 'caste' aspect of law enforcement. Yet we know that the discretion of judges and juries in imposing the death penalty enables the penalty to be selectively applied, feeding prejudices against the accused if he is poor and despised, and lacking political clout, or if he is a member of a suspect or unpopular minority, and saving those who by social position may be in a more protected position. . . .

A law that stated that anyone making more than $50,000 would be exempt from the death penalty would plainly fall, as would a law that in terms said that blacks, those who never went beyond the fifth grade in school, those who made less than $3,000 a year, or those who were unpopular or unstable should be the only people executed. A law which in the overall view reaches that result in practice has no more sanctity than a law which in terms provides the same.

Thus, these discretionary statutes are unconstitutional in their operation. They are pregnant with discrimination and discrimination is an ingredient not compatible with the idea of equal protection of the laws that is implicit in the ban on 'cruel and unusual' punishments.

Any law which is nondiscriminatory on its face may be applied in such a way as to violate the Equal Protection Clause of the Fourteenth Amendment. Such conceivably might be the fate of a mandatory death penalty, where equal or lesser sentences were imposed on the elite, a harsher one on the minorities or members of the lower castes. Whether a mandatory death penalty would otherwise be constitutional is a question I do not reach.

Justice Stewart's concerns were different. His central focus was the wholesale lack of rhyme or reason—the utter unpredictability and irrationality—that he discerned as characterizing capital punishment decisions.

The penalty of death differs from all other forms of criminal punishment, not in degree but in kind. It is unique in its total irrevocability. It is unique in its rejection of rehabilitation of the convict as a basic purpose of criminal justice. And it is unique, finally, in its absolute renunciation of all that is embodied in our concept of humanity. . . .

Legislatures—state and federal—have sometimes specified that the penalty of death shall be the mandatory punishment for every person convicted of engaging in certain designated criminal conduct. . . .

If we were reviewing death sentences imposed under these or similar laws, we would be faced with the need to decide whether capital punishment is unconstitutional for all crimes and under all circumstances. We would need to decide whether a legislature—state or federal—could constitutionally determine that certain criminal conduct is so atrocious that society's interest in deterrence and retribution wholly outweighs any considerations of reform or rehabilitation of the perpetrator, and that, despite the inconclusive empirical evidence, only the automatic penalty of death will provide maximum deterrence. . . .

The constitutionality of capital punishment in the abstract is not, however, before us in these cases. . . .

Instead, the death sentences now before us are the product of a legal system that brings them, I believe, within the very core of the Eighth Amendment's guarantee against cruel and unusual punishments. . . . In the first place, it is clear that these sentences are 'cruel' in the sense that they excessively go beyond, not in degree but in kind, the punishments that the state legislatures have determined to be necessary. In the second place, it is equally clear that these sentences are 'unusual' in the sense that the penalty of death is infrequently imposed for murder, and that its imposition for rape is extraordinarily rare. But I do not rest by conclusion upon these two propositions alone.

These death sentences are cruel and unusual in the same way that being struck by lightning is cruel and unusual. For, of all the people convicted of rapes and murders in 1967 and 1968, many just as reprehensible as these, the petitioners are among a capriciously selected random handful upon whom the sentence of death has in fact been imposed. My concurring Brothers have demonstrated that, if any basis can be discerned for the selection of these few to be sentenced to die, it is the constitutionally impermissible basis of race. But racial discrimination has not been proved, and I put it to one side. I simply conclude that the Eighth and Fourteenth Amendments cannot tolerate the infliction of a sentence of death under legal systems that permit this unique penalty to be so wantonly and so freakishly imposed.

Justice White's reasons for invalidating the death sentences on Eighth Amendment grounds were different still. In his view, capital punishment was so rarely applied that it had ceased to be a credible form of retribution or deterrence. As administered, it was "cruel and unusual" because it exacted human life without discernible social benefits.

The facial constitutionality of statutes requiring the imposition of the death penalty for first-degree murder, for more narrowly defined categories of murder, or for rape would present quite different issues under the Eighth Amendment than are posed by the cases before us. . . . I do not at all intimate that the death penalty is unconstitutional per se or that there is no system of capital punishment that would comport with the Eighth Amendment. That question . . . is not presented by these cases and need not be decided.

The narrower question to which I address myself concerns the constitutionality of capital punishment statutes under which (1) the legislature authorizes the imposition of the death penalty for murder or rape; (2) the legislature does not itself mandate the penalty in any particular class or kind of case (that is, legislative will is not frustrated if the penalty is never imposed), but delegates to judges or juries the decisions as to those cases, if any, in which the penalty will be utilized; and (3) judges and juries have ordered the death penalty with such infrequency that the odds are now very much against imposition and execution of the penalty with respect to any convicted murderer or rapist. . . .

I begin with what I consider a near truism: that the death penalty could so seldom be imposed that it would cease to be a credible deterrent or measurably to contribute to any other end of punishment in the criminal justice system. It is perhaps true that no matter how infrequently those convicted of rape or murder are executed, the penalty so imposed is not disproportionate to the crime and those executed may deserve exactly what they received. It would also be clear that executed defendants are finally and completely incapacitated from again committing rape or murder or any other crime. But when imposition of the penalty reaches a certain degree of infrequency, it would be very doubtful that any existing general need for retribution would be measurably satisfied. Nor could it be said with confidence that society's need for specific deterrence justifies death for so few when for so many in like circumstances life imprisonment or shorter prison terms are judged sufficient, or that community values are measurably reinforced by authorizing a penalty so rarely invoked.

Most important, a major goal of the criminal law—to deter others by punishing the convicted criminal—would not be substantially served where the penalty is so seldom invoked that it ceases to be the credible threat essential to influence the conduct of others. For present purposes I accept the morality and utility of punishing one person to influence another. I accept also the effectiveness of punishment generally and need not reject the death penalty as a more effective deterrent than a lesser punishment. But common sense and experience tell us that seldom-enforced laws become ineffective measures for controlling human conduct and that the death penalty, unless imposed with sufficient frequency, will make little contribution to deterring those crimes for which it may be exacted.

The imposition and execution of the death penalty are obviously cruel in the dictionary sense. But the penalty has not been considered cruel and unusual punishment in the constitutional sense because it was thought justified by the social ends it was deemed to serve. At the moment that it ceases realistically to further these purposes, however, the emerging question is whether its imposition in such circumstances would violate the Eighth Amendment. It is my view that it would, for its imposition would then be the pointless and needless extinction of life with only marginal contributions to any discernible social or public purposes. A penalty with such negligible returns to the State would be patently excessive and cruel and unusual punishment violative of the Eighth Amendment.

It is also my judgment that this point has been reached with respect to capital punishment as it is presently administered under the statutes involved in these cases. Concededly, it is difficult to prove as a general proposition that capital punishment, however administered, more effectively serves the ends of the criminal law than does imprisonment. But however that may be, I cannot avoid the conclusion that as the statutes before us are now administered, the penalty is so infrequently imposed that the threat of execution is too attenuated to be of substantial service to criminal justice. . . .

. . . I must arrive at judgment; and I can do no more than state a conclusion based on 10 years of almost daily exposure to the facts and circumstances of hundreds and hundreds of federal and state criminal cases involving crimes for which death is the authorized penalty. That conclusion . . . is that the death penalty is exacted with great infrequency even for the most atrocious crimes and that there

is no meaningful basis for distinguishing the few cases in which it is imposed from the many cases in which it is not. The short of it is that the policy of vesting sentencing authority primarily in juries—a decision largely motivated by the desire to mitigate the harshness of the law and to bring community judgment to bear on the sentence as well as guilt or innocence—has so effectively achieved its aims that capital punishment within the confines of the statutes now before us has for all practical purposes run its course. . . .

. . . [P]ast and present legislative judgment with respect to the death penalty loses much of its force when viewed in light of the recurring practice of delegating sentencing authority to the jury and the fact that a jury, in its own discretion and without violating its trust or any statutory policy, may refuse to impose the death penalty no matter what the circumstances of the crime. Legislative 'policy' is thus necessarily defined not by what is legislatively authorized but by what juries and judges do in exercising the discretion so regularly conferred upon them. In my judgment what was done in these cases violated the Eighth Amendment.

Four members of the Court—Chief Justice Burger and Justices Blackmun, Powell, and Rehnquist—issued dissenting opinions. Individually or collectively, they questioned how capital punishment could be considered "cruel and unusual" when it was a customary practice at the time the Eighth Amendment was ratified.[18] They argued that the Fifth Amendment, which was ratified at the same time as the Eighth Amendment, makes explicit reference to capital punishment in its Grand Jury, Double Jeopardy, and Due Process Clauses,[19] thus making it implausible that the Framers doubted the government's authority to punish crimes with death.[20] They emphasized the Court's departure from *stare decisis*, noting the unbroken history of prior cases recognizing the constitutionality of capital punishment, including the very recent decision in *McGautha v. California*.[21] They suggested that no sentencing system could achieve complete consistency and disputed assertions that the death sentences imposed by

juries under current laws necessarily smacked of arbitrariness or invidious discrimination, as opposed to principled selectivity.[22] They identified federalism and the states'
autonomy in matters of criminal law as casualties of the decision.[23] And they insisted
that legislative bodies and not the Court, and certainly not the justices' personal predi-
lections, should determine death-penalty policies.[24]

Reaction to the Court's ruling in *Furman* was immediate and intense. Some hailed
the decision as long overdue. Some predicted that the death penalty had forever come
to an end in America.[25] Others accused the justices of flagrantly overstepping their
bounds, and in the process crippling the states in their ability to protect citizens from
violence and administer their criminal laws. They vowed to resuscitate capital punishment, by constitutional amendment if necessary.[26] Legislative bodies began trying to
make sense of the lengthy and complicated opinions in *Furman* with hopes of designing new death-penalty statutes that would respond to the justices' diverse concerns.
A new crop of capital punishment statutes took shape and a new wave of murderers
was consigned to death rows pursuant to them. Four years passed before the Court
would consider whether the revised sentencing procedures had solved the constitutional deficiencies that had doomed the laws in effect when *Furman* was decided.

The 1976 Decisions and the Dawning of the Modern Era of Capital Punishment

The states that reenacted death-penalty laws in response to *Furman* adopted one of
two basic strategies. Some returned to mandatory death sentencing. Others enacted
"guided discretion" sentencing legislation—laws which incorporated provisions
designed to infuse greater rationality and consistency in capital sentencing decisions
and still allowed juries or judges to choose whether convicted offenders should be punished by death or by life imprisonment. In 1976, four years after their epochal decision
in *Furman,* the justices evaluated the different approaches while deciding cases that
had originated in five separate states.

At least ten states reverted to mandatory capital punishment laws in the wake of
Furman, in apparent response to the problems associated with discretionary sentencing that had been identified by Justices Douglas, Stewart, and White in their *Furman*
opinions. If discretionary sentencing allowed for invidious discrimination (Douglas),
randomness and arbitrariness (Stewart), and such infrequent use of the death penalty
that the goals of retribution and deterrence were not served (White), the automatic
use of capital punishment upon conviction—the antithesis of unbridled discretion—
seemed to offer a logical solution. Yet, in two of the cases considered by the justices in
the quintet of 1976 decisions, *Woodson v. North Carolina*[27] and *Roberts v. Louisiana*,[28]
the Court, by vote of 5–4, disagreed.

Justices Stewart, Powell, and Stevens issued the plurality opinions in *Woodson* and
Roberts that found the mandatory death-penalty laws unconstitutional. Justices Brennan and Marshall concurred in the judgment, adhering to their views, as expressed in

Furman, that capital punishment under all circumstances violates the Eighth Amendment. The reasons for invalidating the mandatory death penalty laws were explained at greatest length by the plurality in *Woodson.*

In this case, James Tyrone Woodson, Luby Waxton, Leonard Tucker, and Johnnie Lee Carroll were alleged to have participated in the robbery of a Dunn, North Carolina, convenience store, during which the store's cashier was shot and killed. Woodson and Waxton were tried for first-degree murder, which under North Carolina's post-*Furman* law carried a mandatory death penalty. Tucker and Carroll were allowed to plead guilty to lesser charges and testified as prosecution witnesses. The prosecution's evidence indicated that Waxton and Tucker entered the store while Woodson and Carroll remained outside in the getaway car. Tucker testified that Waxton fired the shot that killed the cashier. Testifying in his own defense, Waxton admitted going into the store, but claimed that Tucker had fired the fatal shot. Woodson testified that he had been drinking heavily prior to the robbery and that he accompanied the other men to the store under duress, after being threatened at gunpoint by Waxton. The jury found Woodson and Waxton guilty as charged, resulting in the automatic death sentences that ultimately were invalidated by the Supreme Court.

The Eighth Amendment stands to assure that the State's power to punish is "exercised within the limits of civilized standards." *Trop v. Dulles,* 356 U.S. 86, 100 (1958) (plurality opinion). Central to the application of the Amendment is a determination of contemporary standards regarding the infliction of punishment. . . . [I]ndicia of societal values identified in prior opinions include history and traditional usage, legislative enactments, and jury determinations.

. . . The history of mandatory death penalty statutes in the United States . . . reveals that the practice of sentencing to death all persons convicted of a particular offense has been rejected as unduly harsh and unworkably rigid. The two crucial indicators of evolving standards of decency respecting the imposition of punishment in our society jury determinations and legislative enactments both point conclusively to the repudiation of automatic death sentences. At least since the Revolution, American jurors have, with some regularity, disregarded

their oaths and refused to convict defendants where a death sentence was the automatic consequence of a guilty verdict. . . . [C]ontinuing evidence of jury reluctance to convict persons of capital offenses in mandatory death penalty jurisdictions resulted in legislative authorization of discretionary jury sentencing. . . .

. . . [L]egislative measures adopted by the people's chosen representatives weigh heavily in ascertaining contemporary standards of decency. The consistent course charted by the state legislatures and by Congress since the middle of the past century demonstrates that the aversion of jurors to mandatory death penalty statutes is shared by society at large. . . .

Although it seems beyond dispute that, at the time of the *Furman* decision in 1972, mandatory death penalty statutes had been renounced by American juries and legislatures, there remains the question whether the mandatory statutes adopted by North Carolina and a number of other States following *Furman* evince a sudden reversal of societal values regarding the imposition of capital punishment. In view of the persistent and unswerving legislative rejection of mandatory death penalty statutes beginning in 1838 and continuing for more than 130 years until *Furman*, it seems evident that the post-*Furman* enactments reflect attempts by the States to retain the death penalty in a form consistent with the Constitution, rather than a renewed societal acceptance of mandatory death sentencing. The fact that some States have adopted mandatory measures following *Furman* while others have legislated standards to guide jury discretion appears attributable to diverse readings of this Court's multi-opinioned decision in that case. . . .

It is now well established that the Eighth Amendment draws much of its meaning from "the evolving standards of decency that mark the progress of a maturing society." *Trop v. Dulles*, 356 U.S., at 101 (plurality opinion). . . . North Carolina's mandatory death penalty statute for first-degree murder departs markedly from contemporary standards respecting the imposition of the punishment of death and thus cannot be applied consistently with the Eighth and Fourteenth Amendments' requirement that the State's power to punish "be exercised within the limits of civilized standards." *Id.*, at 100.

A separate deficiency of North Carolina's mandatory death sentence statute is its failure to provide a constitutionally tolerable response to *Furman's* rejection of unbridled jury discretion in the imposition of capital sentences. Central to the limited holding in *Furman* was the conviction that the vesting of standardless sentencing power in the jury violated the Eighth and Fourteenth Amendments. It is argued that North Carolina has remedied the inadequacies of the death penalty statutes held

unconstitutional in *Furman* by withdrawing all sentencing discretion from juries in capital cases. But when one considers the long and consistent American experience with the death penalty in first-degree murder cases, it becomes evident that mandatory statutes enacted in response to *Furman* have simply papered over the problem of unguided and unchecked jury discretion.

. . . In view of the historic record, it is only reasonable to assume that many juries under mandatory statutes will continue to consider the grave consequences of a conviction in reaching a verdict. North Carolina's mandatory death penalty statute provides no standards to guide the jury in its inevitable exercise of the power to determine which first-degree murderers shall live and which shall die. And there is no way under the North Carolina law for the judiciary to check arbitrary and capricious exercise of that power through a review of death sentences. Instead of rationalizing the sentencing process, a mandatory scheme may well exacerbate the problem identified in *Furman* by resting the penalty determination on the particular jury's willingness to act lawlessly. While a mandatory death penalty statute may reasonably be expected to increase the number of persons sentenced to death, it does not fulfill *Furman's* basic requirement by replacing arbitrary and wanton jury discretion with objective standards to guide, regularize, and make rationally reviewable the process for imposing a sentence of death.

A third constitutional shortcoming of the North Carolina statute is its failure to allow the particularized consideration of relevant aspects of the character and record of each convicted defendant before the imposition upon him of a sentence of death. In *Furman*, members of the Court acknowledge what cannot fairly be denied that death is a punishment different from all other sanctions in kind rather than degree. A process that accords no significance to relevant facets of the character and record of the individual offender or the circumstances of the particular offense excludes from consideration in fixing the ultimate punishment of death the possibility of compassionate or mitigating factors stemming from the diverse frailties of humankind. It treats all persons convicted of a designated offense not as uniquely individual human beings, but as members of a faceless, undifferentiated mass to be subjected to the blind infliction of the penalty of death. . . .

This conclusion rests squarely on the predicate that the penalty of death is qualitatively different from a sentence of imprisonment, however long. Death, in its finality, differs more from life imprisonment than a 100-year prison term differs from one of only a year or two. Because of that qualitative difference, there is a corresponding difference in the need for reliability in the determination that death is the appropriate punishment in a specific case.

For the reasons stated, we conclude that the death sentences imposed upon the petitioners under North Carolina's mandatory death sentence statute violated the Eighth and Fourteenth Amendments and therefore must be set aside.

Chief Justice Burger and Justices White, Blackmun, and Rehnquist dissented, as they did in *Roberts v. Louisiana,* the other 1976 decision striking a mandatory capital sentence. In later cases, the Court invalidated more narrowly focused mandatory death-penalty provisions—for the murder of a police officer,[29] and for murder committed by a prisoner who already was serving a life-term sentence without the possibility of parole[30]—suggesting that individualized consideration of offense and offender circumstances is a constitutional requirement in all capital sentencing decisions.

Most states that reworked their death-penalty laws following the Court's ruling in *Furman* enacted some form of "guided discretion" capital sentencing legislation. These statutes varied in their particulars, but all preserved the sentencing authority's prerogative of imposing either death or a prison sentence on offenders convicted of capital crimes, while structuring the decision-making process in an attempt to guard against the unprincipled and irregular punishment decisions that Justices Douglas, Stewart, and White had identified as problems in their *Furman* opinions. The new, post-*Furman* capital-sentencing laws enacted in Georgia, Florida, and Texas were upheld in the other three cases comprising the Court's 1976 decisions, with Justices Brennan and Marshall the lone dissenters. Justices Stewart, Powell, and Stevens again joined to issue the lead plurality opinion in each of the cases. Their reasons for approving the guided discretion capital-sentencing statutes—principles that form the core of the Court's modern death-penalty jurisprudence—were developed at greatest length in *Gregg v. Georgia.*

In November 1973, Troy Gregg and a companion, Floyd Allen, were picked up while hitchhiking by Fred Simmons and Bob Moore. When the car pulled into a rest stop outside of Atlanta late at night, Gregg used a .25 caliber pistol to shoot Simmons and Moore at a distance, and then fired another bullet into each man's head at close range, killing them. He took their money and other valuables, and he and Allen drove away in Simmons' car. They later were apprehended and Gregg was tried on two counts of murder and two counts of armed robbery. Murder was defined broadly in Georgia to include unlawful killings committed with malice aforethought or during the commission of a felony. The crime was punishable by death or life imprisonment.[31] Gregg was convicted of murder and sentenced to death pursuant to the revised capital-sentencing legislation Georgia had enacted in 1972, shortly after *Furman* was decided. The statute included several new provisions.

Under the revised law, defendants convicted of murder were eligible to be considered for the death penalty if and only if the prosecution alleged and proved beyond a reasonable doubt, at a separate penalty hearing conducted following the guilt phase of the trial, the existence of one or more statutory "aggravating factors." The class of death-penalty eligible crimes thus was narrowed according to legislatively approved criteria. The penalty hearing was conducted before the same jury that heard the guilt-phase evidence. In addition to offering proof of the alleged statutory aggravating factor(s) during the trial's penalty phase, the prosecution was allowed to introduce other evidence supporting a sentence of death. The defendant, correspondingly, could offer "evidence in extenuation [or] mitigation . . . of punishment"[32] at the penalty hearing. "Upon the conclusion of the evidence and arguments, the judge shall give the jury appropriate instructions and the jury shall retire to determine the punishment to be imposed."[33] The jury's sentencing verdict could be death, if the jury unanimously agreed and identified the statutory aggravating factors on which it relied, or life imprisonment. Cases resulting in a death sentence were appealed to the Georgia Supreme Court, "which is directed to consider 'the punishment as well as any errors enumerated by way of appeal,' and to determine":

(1) Whether the sentence of death was imposed under the influence of passion, prejudice, or any[] arbitrary factor, and

(2) Whether . . . the evidence supports the jury's . . . finding of a statutory aggravating circumstance . . ., and

(3) Whether the sentence of death is excessive or disproportionate to the penalty imposed in similar cases, considering both the crime and the defendant.[34]

The Georgia statute enumerated ten aggravating circumstances, any of which sufficed to establish a murder defendant's death-penalty eligibility if proven beyond a reasonable doubt at the trial's penalty phase:

(1) The offense of murder, rape, armed robbery, or kidnapping was committed by a person with a prior record of conviction for a capital felony, or the offense of murder was committed by a person who has a substantial history of serious assaultive criminal convictions.

(2) The offense of murder, rape, armed robbery, or kidnapping was committed while the offender was engaged in the commission of another capital felony, or aggravated battery, or the offense of murder was committed while the offender was engaged in the commission of burglary or arson in the first degree.

(3) The offender by his act of murder, armed robbery, or kidnapping knowingly created a great risk of death to more than one person in a public place by means of a weapon or device which would normally be hazardous to the lives of more than one person.

(4) The offender committed the offense of murder for himself or another, for the purpose of receiving money or any other thing of monetary value.

(5) The murder of a judicial officer, former judicial officer, district attorney or solicitor or former district attorney or solicitor during or because of the exercise of his official duty.

(6) The offender caused or directed another to commit murder or committed murder as an agent or employee of another person.

(7) The offense of murder, rape, armed robbery, or kidnapping was outrageously or wantonly vile, horrible or inhuman in that it involved torture, depravity of mind, or an aggravated battery to the victim.

(8) The offense of murder was committed against any peace officer, corrections employee or fireman while engaged in the performance of his official duties.

(9) The offense of murder was committed by a person in, or who has escaped from, the lawful custody of a peace officer or place of lawful confinement.

(10) The murder was committed for the purpose of avoiding, interfering with, or preventing a lawful arrest or custody in a place of lawful confinement, of himself or another.[35]

In seeking the death penalty for Troy Gregg, the prosecution had alleged three statutory aggravating factors: that the murders were committed while Gregg was engaged in the commission of another capital felony (at the time, armed robbery qualified as a capital felony under Georgia law); that Gregg committed the murders for the purpose of receiving money or other things of monetary value (Simmons' car and the victims' valuables); and that the murders were "outrageously and wantonly vile, horrible or inhuman in that [they] involved torture [or] depravity of mind. . . ." In support of its death sentences, the jury found that the first two aggravating factors had been established for each of the murder counts. The Georgia Supreme Court affirmed Gregg's murder convictions and death sentences on appeal. The U.S. Supreme Court granted certiorari to consider whether "the imposition of the death sentences in this case [represents] 'cruel and unusual' punishment in violation of the Eighth and Fourteenth Amendments."[36] The plurality opinion of Justices Stewart, Powell, and Stevens first considered, and rejected, the claim that capital punishment for aggravated murder *per se* violates the Eighth Amendment. It then examined whether the revised statutory procedures under which Gregg was sentenced to death were constitutionally adequate.

IV

...

A

While *Furman* did not hold that the infliction of the death penalty *per se* violates the Constitution's ban on cruel and unusual punishments, it did recognize that the penalty of death is different in kind from any other punishment imposed under our system of criminal justice. Because of the uniqueness of the death penalty, *Furman* held that it could not be imposed under sentencing procedures that created a substantial risk that it would be inflicted in an arbitrary and capricious manner. . . .

Furman mandates that where discretion is afforded a sentencing body on a matter so grave as the determination of whether a human life should be taken or spared, that discretion must be suitably directed and limited so as to minimize the risk of wholly arbitrary and capricious action. . . .

It is certainly not a novel proposition that discretion in the area of sentencing be exercised in an informed manner. . . .

. . . If an experienced trial judge, who daily faces the difficult task of imposing sentences, has a vital need for accurate information about a defendant and the crime he committed in order to be able to impose a rational sentence in the typical criminal case, then accurate sentencing information is an indispensable prerequisite to a reasoned determination of whether a defendant shall live or die by a jury of people who may never before have made a sentencing decision.

Jury sentencing has been considered desirable in capital cases in order "to maintain a link between contemporary community values and the penal system[,] a link without which the determination of punishment could hardly reflect 'the evolving standards of decency that

mark the progress of a maturing society.'"[FN39] But it creates special problems. Much of the information that is relevant to the sentencing decision may have no relevance to the question of guilt, or may even be extremely prejudicial to a fair determination of that question. This problem, however, is scarcely insurmountable. Those who have studied the question suggest that a bifurcated procedure one in which the question of sentence is not considered until the determination of guilt has been made is the best answer. . . .

FN39. *Witherspoon v. Illinois*, 391 U.S. [510, 519 n. 15 (1968)], quoting *Trop v. Dulles*, 356 U.S. [86, 101 (1958)] (plurality opinion).

But the provision of relevant information under fair procedural rules is not alone sufficient to guarantee that the information will be properly used in the imposition of punishment, especially if sentencing is performed by a jury. Since the members of a jury will have had little, if any, previous experience in sentencing, they are unlikely to be skilled in dealing with the information they are given. To the extent that this problem is inherent in jury sentencing, it may not be totally correctible. It seems clear, however, that the problem will be alleviated if the jury is given guidance regarding the factors about the crime and the defendant that the State, representing organized society, deems particularly relevant to the sentencing decision. . . .

While some have suggested that standards to guide a capital jury's sentencing deliberations are impossible to formulate,[FN43] the fact is that such standards have been developed. When the drafters of the Model Penal Code faced this problem, they concluded "that it is within the realm of possibility to point to the main circumstances of aggravation and of mitigation that should be weighed *and* weighed against each other when they are presented in a concrete case." ALI, Model Penal Code § 201.6, Comment 3, p. 71 (Tent. Draft No. 9, 1959) (emphasis in original). While such standards are by necessity somewhat general, they do provide guidance to the sentencing authority and thereby reduce the likelihood that it will impose a sentence that fairly can be called capricious or arbitrary. Where the sentencing authority is required to specify the factors it relied upon in reaching its decision, the further safeguard of meaningful appellate review is available to ensure that death sentences are not imposed capriciously or in a freakish manner. . . .

FN43. See *McGautha v. California*, 402 U.S. [183, 204–207 (1971)]. . . .

B

. . . In the wake of *Furman*, Georgia amended its capital punishment statute, but chose not to narrow the scope of its murder provisions. . . .

Georgia did act, however, to narrow the class of murderers subject to capital punishment by specifying 10 statutory aggravating circumstances, one of which must be found by the jury to exist beyond a reasonable doubt before a death sentence can ever be imposed. In addition, the jury is authorized to consider any other appropriate aggravating or mitigating circumstances. The jury is not required to find any mitigating circumstance in order to make a recommendation of mercy that is binding on the trial court, but it must find a *statutory* aggravating circumstance before recommending a sentence of death.

These procedures require the jury to consider the circumstances of the crime and the criminal before it recommends sentence. No longer can a Georgia jury do as Furman's jury did: reach a finding of the defendant's guilt and then, without guidance or direction, decide whether he should live or die. Instead, the jury's attention is directed to the specific circumstances of the crime: Was it committed in the course of another capital felony? Was it committed for money? Was it committed upon a peace officer or judicial officer? Was it committed in a particularly heinous way or in a manner that endangered the lives of many persons? In addition, the jury's attention is focused on the characteristics of the person who committed the crime: Does he have a record of prior convictions for capital offenses? Are there any special facts about this defendant that mitigate against imposing capital punishment (*e.g.*, his youth, the extent of his cooperation with the police, his emotional state at the time of the crime). As a result, while some jury discretion still exists, "the discretion to be exercised is controlled by clear and objective standards so as to produce non-discriminatory application." *Coley v. State*, 204 S.E.2d 612, 615 (Ga. 1974).

As an important additional safeguard against arbitrariness and caprice, the Georgia statutory scheme provides for automatic appeal of all death sentences to the State's Supreme Court. That court is required by statute to review each sentence of death and determine whether it was imposed under the influence of passion or prejudice, whether the evidence supports the jury's finding of a statutory aggravating circumstance, and whether the sentence is disproportionate compared to those sentences imposed in similar cases.

. . . On their face these procedures seem to satisfy the concerns of *Furman*. No longer should there be "no meaningful basis for distinguishing the few cases in which (the death penalty) is imposed from the many cases in which it is not." 408 U.S., at 313 (White, J., concurring).

The petitioner contends, however, that the changes in the Georgia sentencing procedures are only cosmetic, that the arbitrariness and capriciousness condemned by *Furman* continue to exist in Georgia both in traditional practices that still remain and in the new sentencing procedures adopted in response to *Furman*.

1

First, the petitioner focuses on the opportunities for discretionary action that are inherent in the processing of any murder case under Georgia law. He notes that the state prosecutor has unfettered authority to select those persons whom he wishes to prosecute for a capital offense and to plea bargain with them. Further, at the trial the jury may choose to convict a defendant of a lesser included offense rather than find him guilty of a crime punishable by death, even if the evidence would support a capital verdict. And finally, a defendant who is convicted and sentenced to die may have his sentence commuted by the Governor of the State and the Georgia Board of Pardons and Paroles.

The existence of these discretionary stages is not determinative of the issues before us. At each of these stages an actor in the criminal justice system makes a decision which may remove a defendant from consideration as a candidate for the death penalty. *Furman*, in contrast, dealt with the decision to impose the death sentence on a specific individual who had been convicted of a capital offense. Nothing in any of our cases suggests that the decision to afford an individual defendant mercy violates the Constitution. *Furman* held only that, in order to minimize the risk that the death penalty would be imposed on a capriciously selected group

of offenders, the decision to impose it had to be guided by standards so that the sentencing authority would focus on the particularized circumstances of the crime and the defendant.

2

The petitioner further contends that the capital-sentencing procedures adopted by Georgia in response to *Furman* do not eliminate the dangers of arbitrariness and caprice in jury sentencing that were held in *Furman* to be violative of the Eighth and Fourteenth Amendments. He claims that the statute is so broad and vague as to leave juries free to act as arbitrarily and capriciously as they wish in deciding whether to impose the death penalty. . . . Specifically, Gregg urges that the statutory aggravating circumstances are too broad and too vague, that the sentencing procedure allows for arbitrary grants of mercy, and that the scope of the evidence and argument that can be considered at the presentence hearing is too wide. . . . [After reviewing the Georgia Supreme Court's action in several appealed cases resulting in death sentences, the justices rejected these claims.]

The petitioner next argues that the requirements of *Furman* are not met here because the jury has the power to decline to impose the death penalty even if it finds that one or more statutory aggravating circumstances are present in the case. This contention misinterprets *Furman*. Moreover, it ignores the role of the Supreme Court of Georgia which reviews each death sentence to determine whether it is proportional to other sentences imposed for similar crimes. Since the proportionality requirement on review is intended to prevent caprice in the decision to inflict the penalty, the isolated decision of a jury to afford mercy does not render unconstitutional death sentences imposed on defendants who were sentenced under a system that does not create a substantial risk of arbitrariness or caprice. . . .

3

Finally, the Georgia statute has an additional provision designed to assure that the death penalty will not be imposed on a capriciously selected group of convicted defendants. The new sentencing procedures require that the State Supreme Court review every death sentence to determine whether it was imposed under the influence of passion, prejudice, or any other arbitrary factor, whether the evidence supports the findings of a statutory aggravating circumstance, and "[w]hether the sentence of death is excessive or disproportionate to the penalty imposed in similar cases, considering both the crime and the defendant." . . .

V

The basic concern of *Furman* centered on those defendants who were being condemned to death capriciously and arbitrarily. Under the procedures before the Court in that case, sentencing authorities were not directed to give attention to the nature or circumstances of the crime committed or to the character or record of the defendant. Left unguided, juries imposed the death sentence in a way that could only be called freakish. The new Georgia sentencing procedures, by contrast, focus the jury's attention on the particularized nature of the crime and the particularized characteristics of the individual defendant. While the jury is permitted to consider any aggravating or mitigating circumstances, it must find and identify at least one statutory aggravating factor before it may impose a penalty of death. In this way the jury's discretion is channeled. No longer can a jury wantonly and freakishly impose the death sentence; it is always circumscribed by the legislative guidelines. In addition, the review function of the Supreme Court of Georgia affords additional assurance that the concerns that prompted our decision in *Furman* are not present to any significant degree in the Georgia procedure applied here.

For the reasons expressed in this opinion, we hold that the statutory system under which Gregg was sentenced to death does not violate the Constitution.

While approving Georgia's capital-sentencing statute, the *Gregg* plurality emphasized: "We do not intend to suggest that only the above-described procedures would be permissible under *Furman* or that any sentencing system constructed along these general lines would inevitably satisfy the concerns of *Furman*, for each distinct system must be examined on an individual basis."[37] And indeed, the revised death-penalty laws enacted in Florida and Texas that were reviewed and approved in *Gregg's* companion cases, *Proffitt v. Florida*[38] and *Jurek v. Texas*,[39] differed in important respects from Georgia's post-*Furman* statute.

Florida law made first-degree murder (defined as unlawfully killing another with a premeditated design, or in the perpetration of designated felonies, or by use of a bomb or destructive device, or through the unlawful distribution of heroin[40]) punishable by death or life imprisonment. As in Georgia, capital trials in Florida were bifurcated: a separate penalty hearing, held before the same jury that had determined guilt, followed the defendant's conviction for first-degree murder. At this hearing, the prosecution was allowed to introduce evidence corresponding to any of the eight aggravating circumstances enumerated in the sentencing statute. The statute also listed seven mitigating factors. "At the conclusion of the hearing the jury is directed to consider '[w]hether sufficient mitigating circumstances exist . . . which outweigh the aggravating circumstances found to exist; and . . . [b]ased on these considerations, whether the defendant should be sentenced to life [imprisonment] or death.'"[41] The jury's sentencing verdict did not have to be unanimous (a 7–5 vote sufficed), and it was advisory only. The trial judge retained the ultimate sentencing authority after considering the jury's recommendation.[42]

> The trial judge is also directed to weigh the statutory aggravating and mitigating circumstances when he determines the sentence to be imposed on a defendant. The statute requires that if the trial court imposes a sentence of death, "it shall set forth in writing its findings upon which the sentence of death is based as to the facts: (a) [t]hat sufficient [statutory] aggravating circumstances exist . . . and (b) [t]hat there are insufficient [statutory] mitigating circumstances . . . to outweigh the aggravating circumstances."[43]

Appeals in cases resulting in a death sentence were heard by the Florida Supreme Court. Although not required by statute, the state supreme court examined the sentences imposed in similar murder cases to determine whether the death sentence under review on appeal appeared to be comparatively excessive.[44]

The plurality opinion in *Proffitt* identified the fact that trial judges determine sentences in capital cases, rather than juries, as "[t]he basic difference"[45] between Florida's procedures and the Georgia provisions approved in *Gregg*. But there were other differences of note. In Florida, aggravating and mitigating circumstances were to be weighed against one another (rather than simply "considered") to determine whether a life or death sentence should be imposed. The Florida statute also itemized mitigating factors (Georgia's did not), resulting in some uncertainty about whether judges and juries could consider nonstatutory mitigating circumstances as well.[46] The justices did not find any of the differences between Florida's and Georgia's laws to be constitutionally significant and they upheld Florida's revised statute. The plurality opinion concluded that:

> Under Florida's capital-sentencing procedures, in sum, trial judges are given specific and detailed guidance to assist them in deciding whether to impose a death penalty or imprisonment for life. Moreover, their decisions are reviewed to ensure that they are consistent with other sentences imposed in similar circumstances. Thus, in Florida, as in Georgia, it is no longer true that there is "'no meaningful basis for distinguishing the few cases in which (the death penalty) is imposed from the many cases in which it is not.'" *Gregg v. Georgia,*

428 U.S., at 188, *quoting Furman v. Georgia*, 408 U.S., at 313 (White, J, concurring). On its face the Florida system thus satisfies the constitutional deficiencies identified in *Furman*.[47]

The third guided discretion capital-sentencing statute that the Court approved in 1976 was Texas's, a law that differed markedly from Georgia's and Florida's. Rather than directing that the sentencing authority consider or balance aggravating and mitigating factors to determine punishment, the post-*Furman* Texas statute—as we saw in chapter 3—specified that following a defendant's conviction for capital murder[48] and the presentation of evidence at the ensuing penalty-phase hearing, the jury must answer three questions:

(1) whether the conduct of the defendant that caused the death of the deceased was committed deliberately and with the reasonable expectation that the death of the deceased or another would result;

(2) whether there is a probability that the defendant would commit criminal acts of violence that would constitute a continuing threat to society; and

(3) if raised by the evidence, whether the conduct of the defendant in killing the deceased was unreasonable in response to the provocation, if any, by the deceased.[49]

An affirmative answer to all three questions (based on proof beyond a reasonable doubt) resulted in a death sentence; a negative answer to any of the questions required a sentence of life imprisonment.[50] The Texas Court of Criminal Appeals provided expedited review of death-penalty cases on appeal.[51] The U.S. Supreme Court concluded that the revised capital sentencing statute satisfied constitutional standards. Justices Stewart, Powell, and Stevens again joined to issue the plurality opinion in *Jurek v. Texas*.

While Texas has not adopted a list of statutory aggravating circumstances the existence of which can justify the imposition of the death penalty as have Georgia and Florida, its action in narrowing the categories of murders for which a death sentence may ever be imposed serves much the same purpose. In fact, each of the five classes of murders made capital by the Texas statute is encompassed in Georgia and Florida by one or more of their statutory aggravating circumstances. For example, the Texas statute requires the jury at the guilt-determining stage to consider whether the crime was committed in the course of a particular felony, whether it was committed for hire, or whether the defendant was an inmate of a penal institution at the time of its commission. Thus, in essence, the Texas statute requires that the jury find the existence of a statutory aggravating circumstance before the death penalty may be imposed. So far as consideration of aggravating circumstances is concerned, therefore, the principal difference between Texas and the other two States is that the death penalty is an available sentencing option even potentially for a smaller class of murders in Texas. Otherwise the statutes are similar. Each requires the sentencing authority to focus on the particularized nature of the crime.

But a sentencing system that allowed the jury to consider only aggravating circumstances would almost certainly fall short of providing the individualized sentencing determination that we today have held in *Woodson v. North Carolina*, 428 U.S. 280, 303–305 [(1976)] to be required by the Eighth and Fourteenth Amendments. For such a system would approach the mandatory laws that we today hold unconstitutional in *Woodson* and *Roberts v. Louisiana*, 428 U.S. 325 [(1976)]. A jury must be allowed to consider on the basis of all relevant evidence not only why a death sentence should be imposed, but also why it should not be imposed.

Thus, in order to meet the requirement of the Eighth and Fourteenth Amendments, a capital-sentencing system must allow the sentencing authority to consider mitigating circumstances. In *Gregg v. Georgia*, we today hold constitutionally valid a capital-sentencing system that directs the jury to consider any mitigating factors, and in *Proffitt v. Florida* we likewise hold constitutional a system that directs the judge and advisory jury to consider certain enumerated mitigating circumstances. The Texas statute does not explicitly speak of mitigating circumstances; it directs only that the jury answer three questions. Thus, the constitutionality of the Texas procedures turns on whether the enumerated questions allow consideration of particularized mitigating factors.

The second Texas statutory question asks the jury to determine "whether there is a probability that the defendant would commit criminal acts of violence that would constitute a continuing threat to society" if he were not sentenced to death. The Texas Court of Criminal Appeals has yet to define precisely the meanings of such terms as "criminal acts of violence" or "continuing threat to society." In the present case, however, it indicated that it will interpret this second question so as to allow a defendant to bring to the jury's attention whatever mitigating circumstances he may be able to show:

"In determining the likelihood that the defendant would be a continuing threat to society, the jury could consider whether the defendant had a significant criminal record. It could consider the range and severity of his prior criminal conduct. It could further look to the age of the defendant and whether or not at the time of the commission of the offense he was acting under duress or under the domination of another. It could also consider whether the defendant was under an extreme form of mental or emotional pressure, something less, perhaps, than insanity, but more than the emotions of the average man, however inflamed, could withstand." 522 S.W.2d, at 939–940. . . .

Thus, Texas law essentially requires that one of five aggravating circumstances be found before a defendant can be found guilty of capital murder, and that in considering whether to impose a death sentence the jury may be asked to consider whatever evidence of mitigating circumstances the defense can bring before it. It thus appears that, as in Georgia and Florida, the Texas capital-sentencing procedure guides and focuses the jury's objective consideration of the particularized circumstances of the individual offense and the individual offender before it can impose a sentence of death.

The Court's decisions in the 1976 cases thus identified the hallmarks of constitutionally acceptable capital sentencing procedures. In striking mandatory death-penalty laws, *Woodson* and *Roberts* demanded that the sentencing authority give individualized consideration to relevant offense and offender circumstances before deciding whether death—a unique sanction in fact and in law because of its severity, finality, and irrevocability—is an appropriate punishment. In upholding the guided discretion statutes at issue in *Gregg, Proffitt,* and *Jurek,* the justices identified apparently critical commonalities. Relying on legislative criteria, the new enactments narrowed the range of offenses and the class of offenders punishable by death. They did so in their definition of capital murder and/or by requiring proof of "aggravating factors" or responses to "special issues" (as in Texas) during the trial's sentencing phase. The statutes also provided for appellate court review of capital convictions and sentences. More than a decade later, in *McCleskey v. Kemp,* 481 U.S. 279, 302–306 (1987), the Court summarized the core requirements for capital sentencing procedures to survive Eighth Amendment scrutiny, as envisioned in the 1976 decisions.

[In *Gregg v. Georgia,* we] explained the fundamental principle of *Furman,* that "where discretion is afforded a sentencing body on a matter so grave as the determination of whether a human life should be taken or spared, that discretion must be suitably directed and limited so as to minimize the risk of wholly arbitrary and capricious action." 428 U.S. [153, 189 (1976)].

. . . In *Woodson v. North Carolina,* 428 U.S. 280 (1976), we invalidated a mandatory capital sentencing system, finding that the "respect for humanity underlying the Eighth Amendment requires consideration of the character and record of the individual offender and the circumstances of the particular offense as a constitutionally indispensable part of the process of inflicting the penalty of death." *Id.,* at 304 (plurality opinion of STEWART, POWELL, and STEVENS, JJ.). Similarly, a State must "narrow the class of murderers subject to capital punishment," *Gregg v. Georgia,* 428 U.S., at 196, by providing "specific and detailed guidance" to the sentencer. *Proffitt v. Florida,* 428 U.S. 242, 253 (1976) (joint opinion of STEWART, POWELL, and STEVENS, JJ.).

In contrast to the carefully defined standards that must narrow a sentencer's discretion

to *impose* the death sentence, the Constitution limits a State's ability to narrow a sentencer's discretion to consider relevant evidence that might cause it to *decline to impose* the death sentence. . . . Any exclusion of the "compassionate or mitigating factors stemming from the diverse frailties of humankind" that are relevant to the sentencer's decision would fail to treat all persons as "uniquely individual human beings." *Woodson v. North Carolina, supra,* 428 U.S., at 304. . . .

In sum, our decisions since *Furman* have identified a constitutionally permissible range of discretion in imposing the death penalty. First, there is a required threshold below which the death penalty cannot be imposed. In this context, the State must establish rational criteria that narrow the decisionmaker's judgment as to whether the circumstances of a particular defendant's case meet the threshold. . . . Second, States cannot limit the sentencer's consideration of any relevant circumstance that could cause it to decline to impose the penalty. In this respect, the State cannot channel the sentencer's discretion, but must allow it to consider any relevant information offered by the defendant.

Does critical examination of the post-*Furman* "guided discretion" death-penalty statutes instill confidence in the justices' conclusions that the new laws succeeded in minimizing the risk of arbitrariness in capital sentencing decisions? Consider the validity of the arguments raised by the petitioner in *Gregg* that, notwithstanding the revised procedures, discretion incapable of being harnessed by the new laws continued to run rampant in different guises, including:

- "[T]he . . . prosecutor has unfettered authority to select those persons whom he wishes to prosecute for a capital offense and to plea bargain with them."
- "[T]he jury may choose to convict a defendant of a lesser included offense rather than find him guilty of a crime punishable by death, even if the evidence would support a capital verdict."
- "[A] defendant who is convicted and sentenced to die may have his sentence commuted. . . ."
- "[The capital sentencing] statute is so broad and vague as to leave juries free to act as arbitrarily and capriciously as they wish in deciding whether to impose the death penalty."
- "[T]he jury has the power to decline to impose the death penalty even if it finds that one or more statutory aggravating circumstances are present. . . ."

Perhaps surprisingly, one critic of the blueprint for approved capital-sentencing procedures that emerged from the 1976 decisions was Justice Rehnquist, who concurred that the guided-discretion statutes were constitutionally acceptable but found no reason to invalidate the mandatory laws under review. He voiced his skepticism about the guided discretion laws in his dissenting opinion in *Woodson v. North Carolina*.

Mr. Justice REHNQUIST, dissenting. . . .

[One] constitutional flaw which the plurality finds in North Carolina's mandatory system is that it has simply "papered over" the problem of unchecked jury discretion. . . . The basic factual assumption of the plurality seems to be that for any given number of first-degree murder defendants subject to capital punishment, there will be a certain number of jurors who will be unwilling to impose the death penalty even though they are entirely satisfied that the necessary elements of the substantive offense are made out. . . .

For purposes of argument, I accept the plurality's hypothesis; but it seems to me impossible to conclude from it that a mandatory death sentence statute such as North Carolina enacted is any less sound constitutionally than are the systems enacted by Georgia, Florida, and Texas which the Court upholds.

In Georgia juries are entitled to return a sentence of life, rather than death, for no reason whatever, simply based upon their own subjective notions of what is right and what is wrong. In Florida the judge and jury are required to weigh legislatively enacted aggravating factors against legislatively enacted mitigating factors, and then base their choice between life or death on an estimate of the result of that weighing. Substantial discretion exists here, too, though it is somewhat more canalized than it is in Georgia. Why these types of discretion are regarded by the plurality as constitutionally permissible, while that which may occur in the North Carolina system is not, is not readily apparent. The freakish and arbitrary nature of the death penalty described in the separate concurring opinions of Justices Stewart, and White in *Furman* arose not from the perception that so *many* capital sentences were being imposed but from the perception that so *few* were bring imposed. To conclude that the North Carolina system is bad because juror nullification may permit jury discretion while concluding that the Georgia and Florida systems are sound because they *require* this same discretion, is, as the plurality opinion demonstrates, inexplicable.

The Texas system much more closely approximates the mandatory North Carolina system which is struck down today. The jury is required to answer three statutory questions. If the questions are unanimously answered in the affirmative, the death penalty *must* be imposed. It is extremely difficult to see how this system can be any less subject to the infirmities caused by juror nullification which the plurality concludes are fatal to North Carolina's statute. . . .

The plurality seems to believe that provision for appellate review will afford a check upon the instances of juror arbitrariness in a discretionary system. But it is not at all apparent that appellate review of death sentences, through a process of comparing the facts of one case in which a death sentence was imposed with the facts of another in which such a sentence was imposed, will afford any meaningful protection against whatever arbitrariness results from jury discretion. All that such review of death sentences can provide is a comparison of fact situations which must in their nature

be highly particularized if not unique, and the only relief which it can afford is to single out the occasional death sentence which in the view of the reviewing court does not conform to the standards established by the legislature. . . .

Appellate review affords no correction whatever with respect to those fortunate few who are the beneficiaries of random discretion exercised by juries, whether under an admittedly discretionary system or under a purportedly mandatory system. It may make corrections at one end of the spectrum, but cannot at the other. . . .

The plurality's insistence on "standards" to "guide the jury in its inevitable exercise of the power to determine which . . . murderers shall live and which shall die" is squarely contrary to the Court's opinion in *McGautha v. California*, 402 U.S. 183 (1971). . . . Its abandonment of *stare decisis* in this repudiation of *McGautha* is a far lesser mistake than its substitution of a superficial and contrived constitutional doctrine for the genuine wisdom contained in *McGautha*. . . .

The plurality opinion's insistence . . . that if the death penalty is to be imposed there must be "particularized consideration of relevant aspects of the character and record of each convicted defendant" is buttressed by neither case authority nor reason. . . .

The plurality . . . relies upon the indisputable proposition that "death is different" for the result which it reaches. . . . But the respects in which death is "different" from other punishment which may be imposed upon convicted criminals do not seem to me to establish the proposition that the Constitution requires individualized sentencing.

Although the Court's 1976 decisions ushered in the new era of capital punishment in the United States by resolving many fundamental questions, they simultaneously left many questions unanswered and generated a host of important subsidiary issues. The next several years would find the justices contending with these matters and persuade some of them that the capital sentencing framework derived from the 1976 cases was fatally flawed.

Beyond the 1976 Decisions: Doctrinal Refinements and Tensions

Nonarbitrariness and Individualization: Considering Mitigation Evidence

Furman's core imperative, gleaned from the individual opinions of the justices who agreed that the capital-sentencing procedures then in effect violated the Eighth Amendment, is to ensure that capital-sentencing "discretion must be suitably directed and limited so as to minimize the risk of wholly arbitrary and capricious action." *Gregg v. Georgia,* 428 U.S. 153, 189 (1976) (plurality opinion). A corollary mandate, announced in *Woodson v. North Carolina,* 428 U.S. 280, 304 (1976) (plurality opinion) and central to the Court's invalidation of mandatory capital-sentencing laws, is that "the fundamental respect for humanity underlying the Eighth Amendment requires consideration of the character and record of the individual offender and the circumstances of the particular offense as a constitutionally indispensable part of the process of inflicting the penalty of death." *Furman* thus has been interpreted to require "nonarbitrariness" (or consistency) in capital sentencing, and *Woodson* to require "individualization."

Can a death-penalty statute produce predictable, regular sentencing outcomes consistent with legislatively defined criteria (nonarbitrariness), and simultaneously demand attention to idiosyncratic offender characteristics and offense circumstances (individualization)?

This dilemma was made more dramatically apparent just two years after *Gregg, Woodson,* and their companion cases solidified the twin principles. In *Lockett v. Ohio,* 438 U.S. 586 (1978), the justices reviewed the 1975 death sentence imposed on Sandra Lockett pursuant to Ohio's post-*Furman* capital punishment statute. Lockett was convicted of aggravated murder as an accomplice to an armed robbery that resulted in the shooting death of the proprietor of a pawnshop. The evidence suggested that she helped plan the robbery and was the getaway car driver, although she was not inside the pawnshop when the gun brandished by one of her three companions discharged and killed the pawnbroker as he struggled to resist the robbery. Ohio's death-penalty statute, enacted in 1974, imposed significant constraints on sentencing discretion in an apparent response to the concerns expressed in *Furman* about arbitrariness. Chief Justice Burger's opinion explained the essential features of the revised Ohio law and its application to Lockett.

Once a verdict of aggravated murder with specifications had been returned, the Ohio death penalty statute required the trial judge to impose a death sentence unless, after "considering the nature and circumstances of the offense" and Lockett's "history, character, and condition," he found by a preponderance of the evidence that (1) the victim had induced or facilitated the offense, (2) it was unlikely that Lockett would have committed the offense but for the fact that she "was under duress, coercion, or strong provocation," or (3) the offense was "primarily the product of [Lockett's] psychosis or mental deficiency." Ohio Rev. Code §§ 2929.03–2929.04(B) (1975).

In accord with the Ohio statute, the trial judge requested a presentence report as well as psychiatric and psychological reports. The reports contained detailed information about Lockett's intelligence, character, and background. The psychiatric and psychological reports described her as a 21-year-old with low-average or average intelligence, and not suffering from a mental deficiency. One of the psychologists reported that "her prognosis for rehabilitation" if returned to society was favorable. The presentence report showed that Lockett had committed no major offenses although she had a record of several minor ones as a juvenile and two minor offenses as an adult. It also showed that she had once used heroin but was receiving treatment at a drug abuse clinic and seemed to be "on the road to success" as far as her drug problem was concerned. It concluded that Lockett suffered no psychosis and was not mentally deficient.

After considering the reports and hearing argument on the penalty issue, the trial judge concluded that the offense had not been primarily the product of psychosis or mental deficiency. Without specifically addressing the other two statutory mitigating factors, the judge said that he had "no alternative, whether [he] like[d] the law or not" but to impose the death penalty. He then sentenced Lockett to death.

The statutory limitations on the introduction of mitigation evidence clearly could have affected the sentencing outcome in Lockett's case. In addition to Lockett's contention that she was not present in the pawnshop at the time of the killing and that she also lacked the intent to kill (made irrelevant to her conviction for aggravated murder pursuant to Ohio's aiding and abetting statute), she was relatively young (age 21), she did not have a substantial criminal record, and a presentence report and mental health evaluations indicated that she was a good candidate for rehabilitation.

In his plurality opinion, the Chief Justice explained why Ohio's capital sentencing statute violated the Eighth Amendment.

[Lockett] contends that the Eighth and Fourteenth Amendments require that the sentencer be given a full opportunity to consider mitigating circumstances in capital cases and that the Ohio statute does not comply with that requirement. . . .

Although legislatures remain free to decide how much discretion in sentencing should be reposed in the judge or jury in noncapital cases, the plurality opinion in *Woodson*, after reviewing the historical repudiation of mandatory sentencing in capital cases, 428 U.S. [280, 289–298 (1976)], concluded that

"in capital cases the fundamental respect for humanity underlying the Eighth Amendment . . . requires consideration of the character and record of the individual offender and the circumstances of the particular offense as a constitutionally indispensable part of the process of inflicting the penalty of death." *Id.*, at 304.

That declaration rested "on the predicate that the penalty of death is qualitatively different" from any other sentence. *Id.*, at 305. We are satisfied that this qualitative difference between death and other penalties calls for a greater degree of reliability when the death sentence is imposed. The mandatory death penalty statute in *Woodson* was held invalid because it permitted *no* consideration of "relevant facets of the character and record of the individual offender or the circumstances of the particular offense." *Id.*, at 304. The plurality did not attempt to indicate, however, which facets of an offender or his offense it deemed "relevant" in capital sentencing or what degree of consideration of "relevant facets" it would require.

We are now faced with those questions and we conclude that the Eighth and Fourteenth Amendments require that the sentencer, in all but the rarest kind of capital case,[FN11] not be precluded from considering, *as a mitigating factor*, any aspect of a defendant's character or record and any of the circumstances of the offense that the defendant proffers as a basis for a sentence less than death.[FN12] . . . Given that the imposition of death by public authority is so profoundly different from all other penalties, we cannot avoid the conclusion that an individualized decision is essential in capital cases. The need for treating each defendant in a capital case with that degree of respect due the uniqueness of the individual is far more important than in noncapital cases. A variety of flexible techniques—probation, parole, work furloughs, to name a few—and various post-conviction remedies may be available to modify an initial sentence of confinement in noncapital cases. The nonavailability of corrective or modifying mechanisms with respect to an executed capital sentence underscores the need for individualized consideration as a constitutional requirement in imposing the death sentence.

FN11. We express no opinion as to whether the need to deter certain kinds of homicide would justify a mandatory death sentence as, for example, when a prisoner—or escapee—under a life sentence is found guilty of murder. See *Roberts (Harry) v. Louisiana*, 431 U.S. 633, 637 n. 5 (1977).

FN12. Nothing in this opinion limits the traditional authority of a court to exclude, as irrelevant, evidence not bearing on the defendant's character, prior record, or the circumstances of his offense.

There is no perfect procedure for deciding in which cases governmental authority should be used to impose death. But a statute that prevents the sentencer in all capital cases from giving independent mitigating weight to aspects of the defendant's character and record and to circumstances of the offense proffered in mitigation creates the risk that the death penalty will be imposed in spite of factors which may call for a less severe penalty. When the choice is between life and death, that risk is unacceptable and incompatible with the commands of the Eighth and Fourteenth Amendments.

The Ohio death penalty statute does not permit the type of individualized consideration of mitigating factors we now hold to be required by the Eighth and Fourteenth Amendments in capital cases. . . .

. . . [O]nce it is determined that the victim did not induce or facilitate the offense, that the defendant did not act under duress or coercion, and that the offense was not primarily the product of the defendant's mental deficiency, the Ohio statute mandates the sentence of death. The absence of direct proof that the defendant intended to cause the death of the victim is relevant for mitigating purposes only if it is determined that it sheds some light on one of the three statutory mitigating factors. Similarly, consideration of a defendant's comparatively minor role in the offense, or age, would generally not be permitted, as such, to affect the sentencing decision.

The limited range of mitigating circumstances which may be considered by the sentencer under the Ohio statute is incompatible with the Eighth and Fourteenth Amendments. To meet constitutional requirements, a death penalty statute must not preclude consideration of relevant mitigating factors.

Justices White and Rehnquist disagreed with the requirement for the open-ended consideration of mitigation evidence. Each maintained that the holding in *Lockett* invited, if it did not compel, a return to the very problems associated with unregulated sentencing discretion that *Furman* had condemned. Justice White argued:

The Court has now completed its about-face since *Furman v. Georgia,* 408 U.S. 238 (1972). *Furman* held that as a result of permitting the sentencer to exercise unfettered discretion to impose or not to impose the death penalty for murder, the penalty was then being imposed discriminatorily, wantonly and freakishly, and so infrequently that any given death sentence was cruel and unusual. . . . Today it is held . . . that the sentencer may constitutionally impose the death penalty only as an exercise of his unguided discretion after being presented with all circumstances which the defendant might believe to be conceivably relevant to the appropriateness of the penalty for the individual offender.

With all due respect, I dissent. . . . I greatly fear that the effect of the Court's decision today will be to compel constitutionally a restoration of the state of affairs at the time *Furman* was decided, where the death penalty is imposed so erratically and the threat of execution is so attenuated for even the most atrocious murders that "its imposition would then be the pointless and needless extinction of life with only marginal contributions to any discernible social or public purposes." *Furman v. Georgia,* 408 U.S., at 312 (WHITE, J., concurring). By requiring as a matter of constitutional law that sentencing authorities be permitted to consider and in their discretion to act upon any and all mitigating circumstances, the Court permits them to refuse to impose the death penalty no matter what the circumstances of the crime. This invites a return to the pre-*Furman* days when the death penalty was generally reserved for those very few for whom society has least consideration. I decline to extend *Woodson* and *Roberts* in this respect.

Justice Rehnquist accused the Court of having "gone from pillar to post" in its death-penalty rulings in his dissenting opinion in *Lockett*.

It seems to me indisputably clear from today's opinion that, while we may not be writing on a clean slate, the Court is scarcely faithful to what has been written before. Rather, it makes a third distinct effort to address the same question, an effort which derives little support from any of the various opinions in *Furman* or from the prevailing opinions in the *Woodson* cases. . . . [T]he theme of today's opinion, far from supporting those views expressed in *Furman* which did appear to be carried over to the *Woodson* cases, tends to undercut those views. If a defendant as a matter of constitutional law is to be permitted to offer as evidence in the sentencing hearing any fact, however bizarre, which he wishes, even though the most sympathetically disposed trial judge could conceive of no basis upon which the jury might take it into account in imposing a sentence, the new constitutional doctrine will not eliminate arbitrariness or freakishness in the imposition of sentences, but will codify and institutionalize it. By encouraging defendants in capital cases, and presumably sentencing judges and juries, to take into consideration anything under the sun as a "mitigating circumstance,"

it will not guide sentencing discretion but will totally unleash it. It thus appears that the evil described by the *Woodson* plurality—that mandatory capital sentencing "papered over the problem of unguided and unchecked jury discretion," 428 U.S., at 302—was in truth not the unchecked discretion, but a system which "papered over" its exercise rather than spreading it on the record. . . .

. . . I am frank to say that I am uncertain whether today's opinion represents the seminal case in the exposition by this Court of the Eighth and Fourteenth Amendments as they apply to capital punishment, or whether instead it represents the third false start in this direction within the past six years. . . .

I continue to view *McGautha* as a correct exposition of the limits of our authority to revise state criminal procedures in capital cases under the Eighth and Fourteenth Amendments. Sandra Lockett was fairly tried, and was found guilty of aggravated murder. I do not think Ohio was required to receive any sort of mitigating evidence which an accused or his lawyer wishes to offer, and therefore I disagree with [this aspect] of the plurality's opinion.

These criticisms were mild in comparison to Justice Scalia's characterization of the clash between the "nonarbitrariness" and "individualization" strands of the Court's capital-punishment jurisprudence years later, in his concurring opinion in *Walton v. Arizona*, 497 U.S. 639, 656–674 (1990).

Since the 1976 cases, we have routinely read *Furman* as standing for the proposition that "channelling and limiting . . . the sentencer's discretion in imposing the death penalty" is a "fundamental constitutional requirement," *Maynard v. Cartwright*, 486 U.S. 356, 362 (1988), and

have insisted that States furnish the sentencer with "'clear and objective standards' that provide 'specific and detailed guidance,' and that 'make rationally reviewable the process for imposing a sentence of death,'" *Godfrey v. Georgia*, 446 U.S. [420, 428 (1980)] (footnotes omitted). . . .

Shortly after introducing our doctrine *requiring* constraints on the sentencer's discretion to "impose" the death penalty, the Court began developing a doctrine *forbidding* constraints on the sentencer's discretion to "*decline* to impose" it. *McCleskey v. Kemp,* [481 U.S. 279, 304 (1987)] (emphasis deleted). This second doctrine—counterdoctrine would be a better word—has completely exploded whatever coherence the notion of "guided discretion" once had. . . .

. . . [I]n *Woodson* and *Lockett,* it emerged that uniform treatment of offenders guilty of the same capital crime was not only not *required* by the Eighth Amendment, but was all but *prohibited.* . . . [T]he pluralities in those cases determined that a defendant could not be sentenced to death unless the sentencer was convinced, by an unconstrained and unguided evaluation of offender and offense, that death was the appropriate punishment. In short, the practice which in *Furman* had been described as the discretion to sentence to death and pronounced constitutionally prohibited, was in *Woodson* and *Lockett* renamed the discretion not to sentence to death and pronounced constitutionally required.

. . . [T]he *Woodson-Lockett* principle has prevented States from imposing all but the most minimal constraints on the sentencer's discretion to decide that an offender eligible for the death penalty should nonetheless not receive it. We have, in the first place, repeatedly rebuffed States' efforts to channel that discretion by specifying objective factors on which its exercise should rest. It would misdescribe the sweep of this principle to say that "all mitigating evidence" must be considered by the sentencer. That would assume some objective criterion of what is mitigating, which is precisely what we have forbidden. Our cases proudly announce

that the Constitution effectively prohibits the States from excluding from the sentencing decision *any* aspect of a defendant's character or record, or *any* circumstance surrounding the crime: that the defendant had a poor and deprived childhood, or that he had a rich and spoiled childhood; that he had a great love for the victim's race, or that he had a pathological hatred for the victim's race; that he has limited mental capacity, or that he has a brilliant mind which can make a great contribution to society; that he was kind to his mother, or that he despised his mother. *Whatever* evidence bearing on the crime or the criminal the defense wishes to introduce as rendering the defendant less deserving of the death penalty must be admitted into evidence and considered by the sentencer. *See, e.g., Lockett,* at 597 ("character, prior record, age, lack of specific intent to cause death, and . . . relatively minor part in the crime"); *Eddings v. Oklahoma,* 455 U.S. [104, 107 (1982)] (*inter alia,* that the defendant's "parents were divorced when he was 5 years old, and until he was 14 [he] lived with his mother without rules or supervision"); *Hitchcock v. Dugger,* 481 U.S. 393, 397 (1987) (*inter alia,* that "petitioner had been one of seven children in a poor family that earned its living by picking cotton; that his father had died of cancer and that petitioner had been a fond and affectionate uncle"); *Skipper v. South Carolina,* 476 U.S. [1, 4 (1986)] (that "petitioner had been a well-behaved and well-adjusted prisoner" while awaiting trial). Nor may States channel the sentencer's consideration of this evidence by defining the weight or significance it is to receive. . . . Rather, they must let the sentencer "give effect," *McKoy v. North Carolina,* 494 U.S. 433, 442–443 (1990), to mitigating evidence in whatever manner it pleases. Nor, when a jury is assigned the sentencing task, may the State attempt to impose structural rationality on the sentencing decision by requiring that mitigating circumstances be found unanimously, see *id.*, at 443; each juror must be allowed to determine and "give effect" to his perception of what evidence favors leniency, regardless of whether those perceptions command the assent of (or are even comprehensible to) other jurors.

To acknowledge that "there perhaps is an inherent tension" between this line of cases and the line stemming from *Furman, McCleskey v. Kemp,* 481 U.S., at 363 (BLACKMUN, J., dissenting), is rather like saying that there was perhaps an inherent tension between the Allies and the Axis Powers in World War II. And to refer to the two lines as pursuing "twin objectives," *Spaziano v. Florida,* 468 U.S. [447, 459 (1984)] is rather like referring to the twin objectives of good and evil. They cannot be reconciled. Pursuant to *Furman,* and in order "to achieve a more rational and equitable administration of the death penalty," *Franklin v. Lynaugh,* 487 U.S. 164, 181 (1988), we require that States "channel the sentencer's discretion by 'clear and objective standards' that provide 'specific and detailed guidance,'" *Godfrey v. Georgia,* 446 U.S., at 428. In the next breath, however, we say that "the State *cannot* channel the sentencer's discretion . . . to consider any relevant [mitigating] information

offered by the defendant," *McCleskey v. Kemp,* 481 U.S., at 306 (emphasis added), and that the sentencer must enjoy unconstrained discretion to decide whether any sympathetic factors bearing on the defendant or the crime indicate that he does not "deserve to be sentenced to death," *Penry v. Lynaugh,* 492 U.S. [302, 326 (1989)]. The latter requirement quite obviously destroys whatever rationality and predictability the former requirement was designed to achieve. . . .

. . . In fact, randomness and "freakishness" are even more evident in a system that requires aggravating factors to be found in great detail, since it permits sentencers to accord different treatment, for whatever mitigating reasons they wish, not only to two different murderers, but to two murderers whose crimes have been found to be of similar gravity. It is difficult enough to justify the *Furman* requirement so long as the States are *permitted* to allow random mitigation; but to impose it while simultaneously *requiring* random mitigation is absurd. . . .

. . . I cannot adhere to a principle so lacking in support in constitutional text and so plainly unworthy of respect under *stare decisis.* Accordingly, I will not, in this case or in the future, vote to uphold an Eighth Amendment claim that the sentencer's discretion has been unlawfully restricted.

Although Justice Scalia announced that he would no longer pay allegiance to "the *Woodson-Lockett* principle," a majority of the Supreme Court continues to do so, while still holding fast to *Furman's* requirement for "nonarbitrary" capital sentencing. Attempts have been made to reconcile the two doctrines, sometimes with the explanation that they apply at different stages of the sentencing decision. The demand for clear, consistent, objective standards (the "nonarbitrariness" principle) applies to the threshold requirement for defining a relatively narrow class of "death-eligible" offenders. Thereafter, the "individualization" principle—or the requirement that the sentencing authority be allowed to consider all relevant mitigation evidence—is used at the selection stage, *i.e.*, in determining which among the class of death-eligible offenders should be punished by death. Sufficiently compelling mitigating circumstances thus can be used in exercising the discretion to be merciful, or to better promote justice in individual cases, after an offender has crossed the threshold of death-penalty eligibility. In this way, the twin principles arguably complement one another by helping to guard against the risk of "overinclusiveness," or allowing offenders who are not truly deserving of capital punishment to suffer execution. Justice Stevens described this perspective in his dissenting opinion in *Walton v. Arizona*, in response to Justice Scalia's arguments.

Justice SCALIA announces . . . that henceforth he will not regard *Woodson v. North Carolina*, 428 U.S. 280 (1976), . . . *Lockett v. Ohio*, 438 U.S. 586 (1978), . . . and other cases adopting their reasoning as binding precedent. The major premise for this rejection of our capital sentencing jurisprudence is his professed inability to reconcile those cases with the central holding in *Furman v. Georgia*, 408 U.S. 238 (1972). Although there are other flaws in Justice SCALIA's opinion, it is at least appropriate to explain why his major premise is simply wrong.

The cases that Justice SCALIA categorically rejects today rest on the theory that the risk of arbitrariness condemned in *Furman* is a function of the size of the class of convicted persons who are eligible for the death penalty. When *Furman* was decided, Georgia included virtually all defendants convicted of forcible rape, armed robbery, kidnaping, and first-degree murder in that class. As the opinions in *Furman* observed, in that large class of cases race and other irrelevant factors unquestionably played an unacceptable role in determining which defendants would die and which would live. However, the size of the class may be narrowed to reduce sufficiently that risk of arbitrariness, even if a jury is then given complete discretion to show mercy when evaluating the individual characteristics of the few individuals who have been found death eligible. . . .

The Georgia Supreme Court itself understood the concept that Justice SCALIA apparently has missed. In *Zant v. Stephens*, 462 U.S. 862 (1983), we quoted the following excerpt from its opinion analogizing the law governing homicides in Georgia to a pyramid:

"'All cases of homicide of every category are contained within the pyramid. The consequences flowing to the perpetrator increase in severity as the cases proceed from the base of the apex, with the death penalty applying only to those few cases which are contained in the space just beneath the apex. To reach that category a case must pass through three planes of division between the base and the apex.

"'The first plane of division above the base separates from all homicide cases those which fall into the category of murder. This plane is established by the legislature in statutes defining terms such as murder, voluntary manslaughter, involuntary manslaughter, and justifiable homicide. In deciding whether a given case falls above or below this plane, the function of the trier of facts is limited to finding facts. The plane remains fixed unless moved by legislative act.

"'The second plane separates from all murder cases those in which the penalty of death is a possible punishment. This plane is established by statutory definitions of aggravating circumstances. The function of the factfinder is again limited to making a determination of whether certain facts have been established. . . . [A] given case may not move above this second plane unless at least one statutory aggravating circumstance exists.

"'The third plane separates, from all cases in which a penalty of death may be imposed, those cases in which it shall be imposed. There is an absolute discretion in the factfinder to place any given case below the plane and not impose death. The plane itself is established by the factfinder. In establishing the plane, the factfinder considers all evidence in extenuation, mitigation and aggravation of punishment. . . .

"'The purpose of the statutory aggravating circumstances is to limit to a large degree, but not completely, the factfinder's discretion. Unless at least one of the ten statutory aggravating circumstances exists, the death penalty may not be imposed in any event. If there exists at least one statutory aggravating circumstance, the death penalty may be imposed but the factfinder has a discretion to decline to do so without giving any reason. . . .

"'A case may not pass the second plane into that area in which the death penalty is authorized unless at least one statutory aggravating circumstance is found. However, this plane is passed regardless of the number of statutory aggravating circumstances found, so long as there is at least one. Once beyond this plane, the case enters the area of the factfinder's discretion, in which all the facts and circumstances of the case determine, in terms of our metaphor, whether or not the case passes the third plane

and into the area in which the death penalty is imposed.' 297 S.E.2d 1, 3–4 (Ga. 1982)." *Id.*, at 870–872.

Justice SCALIA ignores the difference between the base of the pyramid and its apex. A rule that forbids unguided discretion at the base is completely consistent with one that requires discretion at the apex. After narrowing the class of cases to those at the tip of the pyramid, it is then appropriate to allow the sentencer discretion to show mercy based on individual mitigating circumstances in the cases that remain.

Perhaps a rule that allows the specific facts of particular cases to make the difference between life and death—a rule that is consistent with the common-law tradition of case-by-case adjudication—provides less certainty than legislative guidelines that mandate the death penalty whenever specified conditions are met. Such guidelines would fit nicely in a Napoleonic Code drafted in accord with the continental approach to the formulation of legal rules. However, this Nation's long experience with mandatory death sentences—a history recounted at length in our opinion in *Woodson* and entirely ignored by Justice SCALIA today—has led us to reject such rules. I remain convinced that the approach . . . followed by Justice Stewart, Justice Powell, and myself in 1976, and thereafter repeatedly endorsed by this Court, is not only wiser, but far more just, than the reactionary position espoused by Justice SCALIA today.

Does the pyramid analogy—in which progressively narrower bands of criminal homicides and offenders are identified, with the highly discretionary consideration and use of mitigation evidence applying only at the apex to a class already determined to be death-penalty eligible through adherence to largely objective, statutorily defined criteria—help reconcile the "nonarbitrariness" and "individualization" principles? Or, as Justice Scalia maintained in *Walton*, 497 U.S., at 666–667, does it cut in the other direction because "randomness and 'freakishness' are even more evident in a system that requires aggravating factors to be found in great detail, since it permits sentencers to accord different treatment, for whatever mitigating reasons they wish, not only to two different murderers, but to two murderers whose crimes have been found to be of similar gravity"?

Do the examples cited in Justice Scalia's opinion in *Walton* of mitigation evidence that the Court has considered constitutionally relevant, and thus worthy of consideration in capital sentencing decisions—*e.g.*, parental divorce while the offender was young and subsequent lack of supervision; being from a poor family that earned its living picking cotton and having a father who died from cancer—seem to bear on the decision of whether a defendant convicted of committing an aggravated murder should live or die? What sort of evidence did the *Lockett* plurality opinion have in mind when it cautioned, 438 U.S., at 604 n. 12, that, "Nothing in this opinion limits the traditional authority of a court to exclude, as irrelevant, evidence not bearing on the defendant's character, prior record, or the circumstances of his offense"?

Is it helpful to categorize mitigation evidence as bearing on different qualities— such as an offender's culpability at the time of the crime, his or her general character, or his or her likely future dangerousness—and to consider the potential relevancy of evidence to a capital sentencing decision with those different purposes in mind?[52]

In *Penry v. Lynaugh*, 492 U.S. 302 (1989), the Court ruled that Texas's special issues framework for guiding capital-sentencing discretion, which the justices had upheld in 1976 in *Jurek v. Texas*, was unconstitutional as applied because it limited the jury's ability to give effect to potentially relevant mitigation evidence. Evidence in the case suggested that the offender, Johnny Paul Penry, had been abused as a child and that he was mentally retarded. (In chapter 5, we will see that the Court's conclusion in *Penry* that the Eighth Amendment does not forbid the execution of mentally retarded offenders subsequently was rejected, and that this aspect of *Penry* was overruled in *Atkins v. Virginia*.[53]) As described in *Jurek*, Texas's statute required that a death sentence be imposed if the jury responded affirmatively to the three special issues, including whether the offender posed a risk of future dangerousness. Justice O'Connor's majority opinion explained that the statute did not provide an effective vehicle for the jury's consideration of Penry's mitigation evidence.

Eddings [*v. Oklahoma*, 455 U.S. 104 (1982)] makes clear that it is not enough simply to allow the defendant to present mitigating evidence to the sentencer. The sentencer must also be able to consider and give effect to that evidence in imposing sentence. Only then can we be sure that the sentencer has treated the defendant as a "uniquely individual human bein[g]" and has made a reliable determination that death is the appropriate sentence. *Woodson* [*v. North Carolina*, 428 U.S. 280, 304 (1976)]. "Thus, the sentence imposed at the penalty stage should reflect a reasoned *moral* response to the defendant's background, character, and crime." *California v. Brown*, 479 U.S. [538, 545 (1987)] (O'CONNOR, J., concurring) (emphasis in original).

Although Penry offered mitigating evidence of his mental retardation and abused childhood as the basis for a sentence of life imprisonment rather than death, the jury that sentenced him was only able to express its views on the appropriate sentence by answering three questions: Did Penry act deliberately when he murdered Pamela Carpenter? Is there a probability that he will be dangerous in the future? Did he act unreasonably in response to provocation? The jury was never instructed that it could consider the evidence offered by Penry as *mitigating* evidence and that it could give mitigating effect to that evidence in imposing sentence. . . .

Penry argues that his mitigating evidence of mental retardation and childhood abuse has relevance to his moral culpability beyond the scope of the special issues, and that the jury was unable to express its "reasoned moral response" to that evidence in determining whether death was the appropriate punishment. We agree. . . .

The second special issue asks "whether there is a probability that the defendant would commit criminal acts of violence that would constitute a continuing threat to society." The mitigating evidence concerning Penry's mental retardation indicated that one effect of his retardation is his inability to learn from his mistakes. Although this evidence is relevant to the second issue, it is relevant only as an *aggravating* factor because it suggests a "yes" answer to the question of future dangerousness. The prosecutor argued at the penalty hearing

that there was "a very strong probability, based on the history of this defendant, his previous criminal record, and the psychiatric testimony that we've had in this case, that the defendant will continue to commit acts of this nature." Even in a prison setting, the prosecutor argued, Penry could hurt doctors, nurses, librarians, or teachers who worked in the prison.

Penry's mental retardation and history of abuse is thus a two-edged sword: it may diminish his blameworthiness for his crime even as it indicates that there is a probability that he will be dangerous in the future. . . .

The State contends, however, that to instruct the jury that it could render a discretionary grant of mercy, or say "no" to the death penalty, based on Penry's mitigating evidence, would be to return to the sort of unbridled discretion that led to *Furman v. Georgia*, 408 U.S. 238 (1972). We disagree.

To be sure, *Furman* held that "in order to minimize the risk that the death penalty would be imposed on a capriciously selected group of offenders, the decision to impose it had to be guided by standards so that the sentencing authority would focus on the particularized circumstances of the crime and the defendant." *Gregg v. Georgia*, 428 U.S. 153, 199 (1976) (joint opinion of STEWART, POWELL, and STEVENS, JJ.). But as we made clear in *Gregg*, so long as the class of murderers subject to capital punishment is narrowed, there is no constitutional infirmity in a procedure that allows a jury to recommend mercy based on the mitigating evidence introduced by a defendant. . . .

In this case, in the absence of instructions informing the jury that it could consider and give effect to the mitigating evidence of Penry's mental retardation and abused background by declining to impose the death penalty, we conclude that the jury was not provided with a vehicle for expressing its "reasoned moral response" to that evidence in rendering its sentencing decision. Our reasoning in *Lockett* and *Eddings* thus compels a remand for resentencing so that we do not "risk that the death penalty will be imposed in spite of factors which may call for a less severe penalty." *Lockett,* 438 U.S., at 605.

Texas revised its capital sentencing statute in response to the Court's ruling in *Penry*. Among other changes, the law now provides that in cases where the jurors have answered "yes" to the special sentencing issues, they must then address an additional question:

> Whether, taking into consideration all of the evidence, including the circumstances of the offense, the defendant's character and background, and the personal moral culpability of the defendant, there is a sufficient mitigating circumstance or circumstances to warrant that a sentence of life imprisonment without parole rather than a death sentence be imposed.[54]

In *Mills v. Maryland,* 486 U.S. 367 (1988), the jury that had convicted Ralph Mills of capital murder was instructed at the conclusion of the trial's penalty phase to identify on a provided form the aggravating and mitigating factors that they had found in connection with their sentencing decision. Mills argued that the form and the trial judge's accompanying instructions suggested that the jury had to agree unanimously that one or more mitigating circumstances existed before such factors could be considered for sentencing purposes. He maintained that requiring jury unanimity on mitigating factors in order to credit them violated *Lockett* and corresponding Eighth Amendment principles.

The Supreme Court agreed, in a 5–4 decision. Justice Blackmun's majority opinion explained that a unanimity requirement could allow a lone juror to nullify evidence found persuasive by the remaining 11, permitting the holdout to arbitrarily deprive the defendant of the import of that evidence. "Under our cases, the sentencer must be permitted to consider all mitigating evidence. The possibility that a single juror could block such consideration, and consequently require the jury to impose the death sentence [based on the absence of mitigating circumstances], is one we dare not risk." 486 U.S., at 367. Pursuant to this ruling, any individual juror who believes that a relevant mitigating circumstance exists must be allowed to give effect to that evidence in his or her sentencing decision, whether or not other members of the jury agree.[55]

Do rulings in decisions such as *Penry* and *Mills* add further strain to the imperative of simultaneously promoting an acceptable measure of consistency and regularity ("nonarbitrariness") in capital-sentencing decisions, and requiring consideration of all relevant case-specific mitigation evidence offered by death-eligible offenders ("individualization")?

Aggravating Factors: Form and Function

We earlier saw that Georgia's post-*Furman* capital punishment statute itemized 10 aggravating factors. The law required proof of at least one of them at the trial's penalty phase to render a defendant convicted of murder eligible for the death penalty. The jury then considered whether a death sentence should be imposed after taking account of statutory and non-statutory aggravating factors as well as mitigating factors. Florida's revised statute enumerated eight aggravating factors. Like Georgia's statute, it required proof of at least one of them to establish the offender's death-eligibility. Unlike Georgia's law, only statutory aggravating factors were allowed to be considered in the sentencing decision. Florida's statute also provided that the aggravating factors that had been found to exist were to be weighed, or balanced, against mitigating factors to produce a life or death decision. Texas's post-*Furman* law was different still, in that it narrowed the range of death-eligible crimes and offenders by requiring proof during the trial's guilt phase that the offender committed one of five specific forms of capital murder. Following conviction, at the trial's penalty hearing, the jury's answers to special sentencing issues determined whether the offender would be sentenced to death.

Texas's "special issues" approach to capital sentencing is unorthodox. As we saw in chapter 3, only one other state (Oregon) relies on it, while Virginia uses a related variation. Texas is not alone in incorporating "aggravating factors" into its definition of capital murder to narrow the class of death-eligible crimes,[56] although the more common practice is to delay the jury's consideration of aggravating circumstances until a capital trial's penalty phase.[57] Statutory aggravating factors serve two constitutionally required functions. They "must genuinely narrow the class of persons eligible for the death penalty and must reasonably justify the imposition of a more severe sentence on the defendant compared to others found guilty of murder."[58]

The ten aggravating circumstances enumerated in Georgia's capital sentencing statute, presented earlier in this chapter, are fairly typical of those used in other jurisdictions. They can be grouped according to their focus on: (a) *offense* circumstances, including motive and manner of committing the murder (*e.g.,* in perpetration of a felony such as rape, robbery, kidnapping, or burglary; exposing others to a risk of death by using a special weapon or device; killing for the purpose of receiving money or something of monetary value; directing or causing another to kill as an agent or employee; the offense was "outrageously or wantonly vile, horrible or inhuman in that it involved torture, depravity of mind, or an aggravated battery to the victim"; or the killing was committed to avoid or prevent arrest or lawful confinement); (b) *offender* characteristics (*e.g.,* record of prior serious felony convictions; status as prisoner, jail inmate, or escapee); or (c) *victim* characteristics (*e.g.,* a judge or a prosecutor; a peace officer, corrections employee, or firefighter). Additional aggravating circumstances found in some other jurisdictions include killing young children, the elderly, or other vulnerable victims; killing multiple victims, either serially or in one or more closely related transactions; killings to prevent a witness from testifying or in retaliation for testimony; and killings committed as acts of terrorism.[59]

Individually and collectively, do these aggravating circumstances do a good job of identifying the "worst of the worst" murders and murderers, thus "reasonably justify[ing] a more severe sentence . . . compared to others found guilty of murder"? Are they sufficiently restrictive to "genuinely narrow the class of persons eligible for the death penalty"? Do they appear to coincide with or help promote the death penalty's primary objectives of retribution, general deterrence, and/or incapacitation?

Many of the aggravating circumstances found in contemporary capital punishment statutes are derived from the provisions first set forth in the Model Penal Code (MPC), which was promulgated by the American Law Institute (ALI) in 1962.[60] (In 2009 the ALI voted to rescind the death penalty sections of the MPC "in light of the current intractable institutional and structural obstacles to ensuring a minimally adequate system for administering capital punishment."[61]) One of the aggravating factors that appeared in the MPC addressed "the special case of a style of killing so indicative of utter depravity that imposition of the ultimate sanction should be considered."[62] The language used to capture this concept was: "The murder was especially heinous, atrocious or cruel, manifesting exceptional depravity"[63]—a circumstance commonly known as a "HAC" ("heinous, atrocious or cruel") factor. HAC factors are widely utilized; in some jurisdictions they have been found to be present in a majority of the cases in which death sentences are imposed.[64]

If the functions of statutory aggravating factors are to "genuinely narrow the class of persons eligible for the death penalty," and to distinguish some murders as deserving "a more severe sentence . . . compared to others," do HAC factors present any special problems? The Supreme Court considered the application of Georgia's version of a HAC factor in its 1980 decision in *Godfrey v. Georgia*.[65]

Robert Godfrey was convicted of murder and sentenced to death after the jury in his case placed exclusive reliance on Georgia's variation of the HAC factor: "The offense of murder . . . was outrageously or wantonly vile, horrible or inhuman in that it involved torture, depravity of mind, or an aggravated battery to the victim."[66] Following a heated argument with his wife, who had recently left him and moved into her mother's trailer, Godfrey grabbed his shotgun and walked to the trailer.

Peering through a window, he observed his wife, his mother-in-law, and his 11-year-old daughter playing a card game. He pointed the shotgun at his wife through the window and pulled the trigger. The charge from the gun struck his wife in the forehead and killed her instantly. He proceeded into the trailer, striking and injuring his fleeing daughter with the barrel of the gun. He then fired the gun at his mother-in-law, striking her in the head and killing her instantly.

The petitioner then called the local sheriff's office, identified himself, said where he was, explained that he had just killed his wife and mother-in-law, and asked that the sheriff come and pick him up. Upon arriving at the trailer, the law enforcement officers found the petitioner seated on a chair in open view near the driveway. He told one of the officers that "they're dead, I killed them" and directed the officer to the place where he had put the murder weapon. Later the petitioner told a police officer: "I've done a hideous crime, . . . but I have been thinking about it for eight years . . . I'd do it again."

A jury convicted Godfrey of murdering his wife and his mother-in-law. The prosecution alleged that each of the murders was "outrageously or wantonly vile, horrible or inhuman in that it involved . . . depravity of mind," the aggravating circumstance codified as Ga. Rev. Code § 27–2534.1 (b)(7) (Supp. 1975). The judge recited that language without further elaboration in his instructions to the jury at the trial's penalty phase, and the jury sentenced Godfrey to death for each of the murders in reliance on the (b)(7) aggravating circumstance. The Supreme Court invalidated the death sentence. Justice Stewart's plurality opinion explained that, as applied to Godfrey's case, the (b)(7) aggravating circumstance was unconstitutionally vague.

In *Furman v. Georgia*, 408 U.S. 238 [(1972)], the Court held that the penalty of death may not be imposed under sentencing procedures that create a substantial risk that the punishment will be inflicted in an arbitrary and capricious manner. *Gregg v. Georgia*, [428 U.S. 153, 189 (1976) (opinion of STEWART, POWELL, and STEVENS, JJ.)] reaffirmed this holding:

> "[W]here discretion is afforded a sentencing body on a matter so grave as the determination of whether a human life should be taken or spared, that discretion must be suitably directed and limited so as to minimize the risk of wholly arbitrary and capricious action."

A capital sentencing scheme must, in short, provide a "'meaningful basis for distinguishing the few cases in which [the penalty] is imposed from the many cases in which it is not.'" *Id.*, at 188, *Furman v. Georgia*, at 313 (WHITE, J., concurring).

This means that if a State wishes to authorize capital punishment it has a constitutional responsibility to tailor and apply its law in a manner that avoids the arbitrary and capricious infliction of the death penalty. Part of a State's responsibility in this regard is to define the crimes for which death may be the sentence in a way that obviates "standardless [sentencing] discretion." *Gregg v. Georgia*, at 196, n. 47. It must channel the sentencer's discretion by "clear and objective standards" that provide "specific and detailed guidance," and that "make rationally reviewable the process for imposing a sentence of death." As was made clear in *Gregg*, a death penalty "system could have standards so vague that they would fail adequately to channel the sentencing decision patterns of juries with the result that a pattern of arbitrary and capricious sentencing like that found unconstitutional in *Furman* could occur." 428 U.S., at 195.

In the case before us the Georgia Supreme Court has affirmed a sentence of death based upon no more than a finding that the offense was "outrageously or wantonly vile, horrible and inhuman." There is nothing in these few words, standing alone, that implies any inherent restraint on the arbitrary and capricious infliction of the death sentence. A person of ordinary sensibility could fairly characterize almost every murder as "outrageously or wantonly vile, horrible and inhuman." Such a view may, in fact, have been one to which the members of the jury in this case subscribed. If so, their preconceptions were not dispelled by the trial judge's sentencing instructions. These gave the jury no guidance concerning the meaning of any of § (b)(7)'s terms. In fact, the jury's interpretation of § (b)(7) can only be the subject of sheer speculation.

Justices Marshall and Brennan concurred in the judgment, and Chief Justice Burger and Justices White and Rehnquist dissented.

Godfrey does not imply that HAC factors inevitably are incapable of harnessing capital sentencing discretion. The jury that sentenced Godfrey to death was not given an instruction on the meaning of the (b)(7) circumstance that might have provided the guidance that was lacking in the statutory language. The U.S. Supreme Court has approved the use of HAC factors for capital sentencing purposes when their otherwise vague meaning has been clarified by judicial interpretation and communicated to the sentencing authority.[67]

Can statutory aggravating circumstances be used not only to establish death-eligibility for general classes of cases, but also to determine that individual offenders who are death-penalty eligible should be sentenced to death? Can a law require that offenders must be sentenced to death in cases where aggravating factors outweigh mitigating factors, or must the judge or jury be given the option of sentencing an offender to life imprisonment, even if it determines that the aggravating factors established in a case outweigh mitigating circumstances? The Supreme Court confronted these issues in *Blystone v. Pennsylvania*, 494 U.S. 299 (1990).

Pennsylvania law required that a death sentence be imposed "if the jury unanimously finds at least one aggravating circumstance . . . and no mitigating circumstances or if the jury unanimously finds one or more aggravating circumstances which outweigh any mitigating circumstances."[68] Scott Wayne Blystone was convicted of murder during the course of a robbery. His case, consequently, was death-penalty eligible under the statutory aggravating circumstance pertaining to killings committed in the perpetration of a contemporaneous felony. Contrary to the advice of counsel, he insisted that no mitigation evidence be presented on his behalf during the sentencing hearing.[69] The judge instructed the jury at the trial's penalty phase: "Your verdict must be a sentence of death if you unanimously find at least one aggravating circumstance and no mitigating circumstances."[70] Finding that the murder had taken place when Blystone robbed his victim of $13, and that no mitigating circumstances existed, the jury sentenced him to death. Blystone argued on appeal that the Pennsylvania law violated the Eighth Amendment because it was "mandatory"—offering the jury no choice but to sentence him to death under the circumstances. He maintained that the jury should have been allowed to make an independent assessment of whether the death penalty was appropriate in light of the specific facts of his case.

The Supreme Court rejected his argument in a 5–4 decision. Chief Justice Rehnquist's majority opinion explained:

We think that the Pennsylvania death penalty statute satisfies the requirement that a capital sentencing jury be allowed to consider and give effect to all relevant mitigating evidence. Section 9711 does not limit the types of mitigating evidence which may be considered, and subsection (e) provides a jury with a non-exclusive list of mitigating factors which may be taken into account—including a "catchall" category providing for the consideration of "[a]ny other evidence of mitigation concerning the character and record of the defendant and the circumstances of his offense." See 42 Pa. Cons. Stat. § 9711(e)(8) (1988). Nor is the statute impermissibly "mandatory" as that term was understood in *Woodson* or *Roberts*. Death is not automatically imposed upon conviction for certain types of murder. It is imposed only after a determination that the aggravating circumstances outweigh the mitigating circumstances present in the particular crime committed by the particular defendant, or that there are no such mitigating circumstances. This is sufficient under *Lockett* and *Penry*. . . .

. . . [P]etitioner asserts that the mandatory feature of his jury instructions—derived, of course, from the statute—precluded the jury from evaluating the weight of the particular aggravating circumstance found in his case. . . .

. . . We reject this argument. The presence of aggravating circumstances serves the purpose of limiting the class of death-eligible defendants, and the Eighth Amendment does not require that these aggravating circumstances be further refined or weighed by a jury. The requirement of individualized sentencing in capital cases is satisfied by allowing the jury to consider all relevant mitigating evidence. In petitioner's case the jury was specifically instructed to consider, as mitigating evidence, any "matter concerning the character or record of the defendant, or the circumstances of his offense." This was sufficient to satisfy the dictates of the Eighth Amendment.

Justice Brennan's dissent (joined in relevant part by Justices Marshall, Blackmun, and Stevens) took sharp exception with the majority opinion's reasoning and conclusions.

The hallmark of our Eighth Amendment jurisprudence is that because the "penalty of death is qualitatively different from a sentence of imprisonment," *Woodson v. North Carolina,* 428 U.S. 280, 305 (1976) (plurality opinion), capital punishment may not be imposed unless the sentencer makes an individualized determination that death is the appropriate sentence for a particular defendant. . . . Today, for the first time, the Court upholds a statute containing a mandatory provision that gives the legislature rather than the jury the ultimate decision whether the death penalty is appropriate in a particular set of circumstances. Such a statute deprives the defendant of the type of individualized sentencing hearing required by the Eighth Amendment. . . .

The statute . . . deprives the jury of any sentencing discretion once it has found one aggravating circumstance but no mitigating circumstances; the jury may not consider whether the aggravating circumstance, by itself, justifies the imposition of the most extreme sanction available to society. . . .

... The nature of the individualized determination required by *Woodson* is derived from this Court's recognition that the decision to impose the death penalty must reflect a reasoned moral judgment about the defendant's actions and character in light of all the circumstances of the offense and the defendant's background. Just as a jury must be free to consider and weigh mitigating circumstances as independently relevant to the defendant's moral culpability, a jury must also be able to consider and weigh the severity of each aggravating circumstance. The weight of an aggravating circumstance depends on the seriousness of the crime—a significant aspect of the defendant's moral culpability. Thus, a reasoned moral response to the defendant's conduct requires the consideration of the significance of both aggravating and mitigating factors. . . .

This Court has never held that a legislature may mandate the death sentence for any category of murderers. Instead, a legislature's role must be limited to the definition of the class of death-*eligible* defendants. A legislature does not, and indeed cannot, consider every possible fact pattern that technically will fall within an aggravating circumstance. Hence, the definition of an aggravating circumstance provides a basis for distinguishing crimes only on a *general* level; it does not embody the type of reasoned moral judgment required to justify the imposition of the death penalty. The Pennsylvania statute provides a stark example of this constitutional flaw. It permits the jury to find an aggravating circumstance if the killing was committed in the course of a felony. A variety of murders fit under this aggravating circumstance. Since the Pennsylvania Supreme Court has interpreted this aggravating circumstance to include *nonviolent* felonies, the aggravating circumstance covers a very wide range of cases. A jury, however, likely would draw a different inference about the culpability of the defendant—and therefore the propriety of the death sentence—if the murder were committed during a rape rather than (as here) during a $13 robbery. The majority today allows the legislature to preclude a jury from considering such factors in deciding whether to impose death. . . .

The mandatory language in the Pennsylvania statute . . . deprive[s] the jury of any power to make such an independent judgment. The jury's determination that an aggravating circumstance exists ends the decisionmaking process. In addition, whether an aggravating circumstance exists is generally a question of fact relating to either the circumstances of the offense, the status of the victim, or the defendant's criminal record. In many cases, the existence of the aggravating factor is not disputed. Finding an aggravating circumstance does not entail any moral judgment about the nature of the act or the actor, and therefore it does not give the jury an opportunity to decide whether it believes the defendant's particular offense warrants the death penalty. . . .

. . . [T]he majority summarily concludes that the Eighth Amendment is "satisfied" because the jury may consider mitigating evidence. Although our cases clearly hold that the ability to consider mitigating evidence is a constitutional requirement, it does not follow that this ability satisfies the constitutional demand for an individualized sentencing hearing. The "weight" of an aggravating circumstance is just as relevant to the propriety of the death penalty as the "weight" of any mitigating circumstances. The Court's unarticulated assumption that the legislature may define a group of crimes for which the death penalty is required in certain situations represents a marked departure from our previous cases.

In contrast to Pennsylvania's statute, in many "weighing" jurisdictions the balancing of aggravating and mitigating circumstances does not alone determine the sentence to be imposed in capital cases. Instead, a "life option" exists. After the sentencing authority concludes that the aggravating factors outweigh the mitigating factors, it must still consider whether the defendant *should* be sentenced to death. It need not do so.[71] New Hampshire's capital-sentencing law offers an example. It provides, in relevant part:

> [I]f the jury concludes that the aggravating factors outweigh the mitigating factors or that the aggravating factors, in the absence of any mitigating factors, are themselves sufficient to justify a death sentence, the jury, by unanimous vote only, may recommend that a sentence of death be imposed rather than a sentence of life imprisonment without possibility of parole. The jury, regardless of its findings with respect to aggravating and mitigating factors, is never required to impose a death sentence and the jury shall be so instructed.[72]

Is providing the sentencer with a "life option" even if aggravating factors outweigh mitigating factors more in keeping with Justice Brennan's position in *Blystone*? Is this approach preferable to the less flexible one reflected in Pennsylvania's statute? Are the different models reminiscent of the tension between "nonarbitrariness" and "individualization" in capital sentencing schemes?

Which party should have the burden of persuasion in jurisdictions that rely on a balancing of aggravating and mitigating circumstances as a part of the capital sentencing process? Should the prosecution be required to establish that aggravating factors outweigh mitigating factors to secure a death sentence, or should the defendant be expected to prove that sufficient mitigating circumstances exist to avoid one? At the guilt phase of criminal trials, as well as in civil commitment proceedings, where individual liberty is at stake, due process requires the government to bear the burden of persuasion.[73] Paradoxically, perhaps, that is not the constitutional rule when life is on the line: defendants can be required to prove that mitigating circumstances outweigh aggravating factors in order to avoid a death sentence.[74] Many jurisdictions follow this approach, while in others the government must prove that aggravating factors outweigh mitigating circumstances to justify a capital sentence.[75] Which policy is preferable?

Conclusion

We have seen that when the Supreme Court approved Georgia's post-*Furman* "guided discretion" capital-sentencing legislation in *Gregg v. Georgia,* the plurality opinion emphasized: "We do not intend to suggest that only [these statutory] procedures would be permissible under *Furman* or that any sentencing system constructed along these general lines would inevitably satisfy the concerns of *Furman,* for each distinct system must be examined on an individual basis."[76] Subsequent decisions confirmed the truth of this pledge.[77] Indeed, from a procedural standpoint, it is misleading to refer to "the death penalty" as if a uniform set of rules exist for structuring capital-sentencing decisions. It now is crystal clear, if it was not obvious when *Gregg* and its companion cases were decided, that markedly different criteria and procedures can be—and in fact are—used to regulate life-and-death sentencing decisions in the wake of *Furman v. Georgia*. Justice Kennedy summarized the governing constitutional principles regarding guided discretion capital-sentencing laws in his majority opinion in *Tuilaepa v. California*, 512 U.S. 967, 972–973 (1994).

Our capital punishment cases under the Eighth Amendment address two different aspects of the capital decisionmaking process: the eligibility decision and the selection decision. To be eligible for the death penalty, the defendant must be convicted of a crime for which the death penalty is a proportionate punishment. To render a defendant eligible for the death penalty in a homicide case, we have indicated that the trier of fact must convict the defendant of murder and find one "aggravating circumstance" (or its equivalent) at either the guilt or penalty phase. The aggravating circumstance may be contained in the definition of the crime or in a separate sentencing factor (or in both). As we have explained, the aggravating circumstance must meet two requirements. First, the circumstance may not apply to every defendant convicted of a murder; it must apply only to a subclass of defendants convicted of murder. Second, the aggravating circumstance may not be unconstitutionally vague.

We have imposed a separate requirement for the selection decision, where the sentencer determines whether a defendant eligible for the death penalty should in fact receive that sentence. "What is important at the selection stage is an *individualized* determination on the basis of the character of the individual and the circumstances of the crime." *Zant* [*v. Stephens*, 462 U.S. 862, 879 (1983)]. That requirement is met when the jury can consider relevant mitigating evidence of the character and record of the defendant and the circumstances of the crime.

The eligibility decision fits the crime within a defined classification. Eligibility factors almost of necessity require an answer to a question with a factual nexus to the crime or the defendant so as to "make rationally reviewable the process for imposing a sentence of death." *Arave* [*v. Creech*, 507 U.S. 463, 471 (1993)]. The selection decision, on the other hand, requires individualized sentencing and must be expansive enough to accommodate relevant mitigating evidence so as to assure an assessment of the defendant's culpability. The objectives of these two inquiries can be in some tension, at least when the inquiries occur at the same time. There is one principle common to both decisions, however: The State must ensure that the process is neutral and principled so as to guard against bias or caprice in the sentencing decision.

Justice Kennedy's concession in *Tuilaepa* that the objectives of "mak[ing] rationally reviewable the process for imposing a sentence of death" and the requirement for "individualized sentencing . . . expansive enough to accommodate relevant mitigating evidence" can be "in some tension" is a modest one. A majority of the Court not only has endorsed but has mandated this uneasy equilibrium between the "nonarbitrariness" and "individualization" requirements for capital sentencing. We nevertheless have seen Justice Scalia's unwillingness to subscribe to these doctrinal requirements, based on his argument that—"rather like . . . good and evil"—these twin objectives cannot be reconciled.[78] Justice Blackmun later arrived at this same conclusion. While Justice Scalia's solution was to abandon fidelity to the *Woodson-Lockett* line of cases, Justice Blackmun's resolution was more definitive. In *Callins v. Collins,* 510 U.S. 1141, 1143–1159 (1994) (dissenting from denial of certiorari), in one of his last opinions before retiring, Justice Blackmun declared, "From this day forward, I shall no longer tinker with the machinery of death." He thereupon renounced his allegiance to the Court's entire capital punishment jurisprudence.

Experience has taught us that the constitutional goal of eliminating arbitrariness and discrimination from the administration of death, see *Furman v. Georgia,* [408 U.S. 238 (1972)], can never be achieved without compromising an equally essential component of fundamental fairness—individualized sentencing. See *Lockett v. Ohio,* 438 U.S. 586 (1978).

It is tempting, when faced with conflicting constitutional commands, to sacrifice one for the other or to assume that an acceptable balance between them already has been struck. In the context of the death penalty, however, such jurisprudential maneuvers are wholly inappropriate. The death penalty must be imposed "fairly, and with reasonable consistency, or not at all." *Eddings v. Oklahoma,* 455 U.S. 104, 112 (1982).

To be fair, a capital sentencing scheme must treat each person convicted of a capital offense with that "degree of respect due the uniqueness of the individual." *Lockett v. Ohio,* 438 U.S., at 605 (plurality opinion). That means affording the sentencer the power and discretion to grant mercy in a particular case, and providing avenues for the consideration of any and all relevant mitigating evidence that would justify a sentence less than death. Reasonable consistency, on the other hand, requires that

the death penalty be inflicted evenhandedly, in accordance with reason and objective standards, rather than by whim, caprice, or prejudice. . . .

The theory . . . is that an appropriate balance can be struck between the *Furman* promise of consistency and the *Lockett* requirement of individualized sentencing if the death penalty is conceptualized as consisting of two distinct stages. In the first stage of capital sentencing, the demands of *Furman* are met by "narrowing" the class of death-eligible offenders according to objective, fact-bound characteristics of the defendant or the circumstances of the offense. Once the pool of death-eligible defendants has been reduced, the sentencer retains the discretion to consider whatever relevant mitigating evidence the defendant chooses to offer.

Over time, I have come to conclude that even this approach is unacceptable: It simply reduces, rather than eliminates, the number of people subject to arbitrary sentencing. It is the decision to sentence a defendant to death—not merely the decision to make a defendant eligible for death—that may not be arbitrary. While one might hope that providing the sentencer with as much relevant mitigating evidence as possible will lead to more rational and consistent sentences, experience has taught otherwise. It seems that the decision whether a human being should live or die is so inherently subjective—rife with all of life's understandings, experiences, prejudices, and passions—that it inevitably defies the rationality and consistency required by the Constitution. . . .

. . . [T]he consistency promised in *Furman* and the fairness to the individual demanded in *Lockett* are not only inversely related, but irreconcilable in the context of capital punishment. Any statute or procedure that could effectively eliminate arbitrariness from the administration of death would also restrict the sentencer's discretion to such an extent that the sentencer would be unable to give full consideration to the unique characteristics of each defendant and the circumstances of the offense. By the same token, any statute or procedure that would provide the sentencer with sufficient discretion to consider fully and act upon the unique circumstances of each defendant would "thro[w] open the back door to arbitrary and irrational

sentencing." *Graham v. Collins*, 506 U.S. [461, 494 (1993)] (THOMAS, J., concurring). All efforts to strike an appropriate balance between these conflicting constitutional commands are futile because there is a heightened need for both in the administration of death.

Perhaps one day this Court will develop procedural rules or verbal formulas that actually will provide consistency, fairness, and reliability in a capital sentencing scheme. I am not optimistic that such a day will come. I am more optimistic, though, that this Court eventually will conclude that the effort to eliminate arbitrariness while preserving fairness "in the infliction of [death] is so plainly doomed to failure that it—and the death penalty—must be abandoned altogether." *Godfrey v. Georgia*, 446 U.S. 420, 442 (1980) (Marshall, J., concurring in judgment). I may not live to see that day, but I have faith that eventually it will arrive. The path the Court has chosen lessens us all. I dissent.

Which of these approaches is the most palatable? To stay the course and accept the evident "tension" between *Furman's* "nonarbitrariness" principle and the *Woodson-Lockett* "individualization" requirement? To abandon the simultaneous pursuit of those goals, and invest in just one, as Justice Scalia did? To conclude, as Justice Blackmun did, that not only is it impossible to reconcile those sentencing objectives, but that the capital-sentencing process has proven to be altogether incapable of equitable administration? Or, can other, better ways be envisioned of fairly deciding how to identify the worst of the worst offenders and whether they should be punished by death?

Endnotes

1. 428 U.S. 153 (1976).
2. *Proffitt v. Florida*, 428 U.S. 242 (1976); *Jurek v. Texas*, 428 U.S. 262 (1976); *Woodson v. North Carolina*, 428 U.S. 280 (1976); *Roberts v. Louisiana*, 428 U.S. 325 (1976).
3. 408 U.S. 238 (1972).
4. *Woodson v. North Carolina*, 428 U.S. 280, 289–290 (1976) (plurality opinion); John W. Poulos, "The Supreme Court, Capital Punishment, and the Substantive Criminal Law: The Rise and Fall of Mandatory Capital Punishment," 28 *Arizona Law Review* 143, 146–147 (1986).

5. *See* Ruthann Robson, "Beyond Sumptuary: Constitutionalism, Clothes, and Bodies in Anglo-American Law," 2 *British Journal of American Legal Studies* 477, 499–500 (2013); George C. Thomas III, "Colonial Criminal Law and Procedure: The Royal Colony of New Jersey 1449–57," 1 *N.Y.U. Journal of Law & Liberty* 671, 697–698 (2005); Phillip M. Spector, "The Sentencing Rule of Lenity," 33 *University of Toledo Law Review* 511, 514–517 (2002); John H. Langbein, "Shaping the Eighteenth-Century Criminal Trial: A View From the Ryder Sources," 50 *University of Chicago Law Review* 1, 37–41 (1983).

6. *Woodson v. North Carolina*, 428 U.S. 280, 291 (1976) (plurality opinion); Philip English Mackey, "The Inutility of Mandatory Capital Punishment: An Historical Note," 54 *Boston University Law Review* 32 (1974).

7. James R. Acker, Talia Harmon & Craig Rivera, "Merciful Justice: Lessons From 50 Years of New York Death Penalty Commutations," 35 *Criminal Justice Review* 183, 187 (2010); James R. Acker, "The Death Penalty: An American History," 6 *Contemporary Justice Review* 169, 176 (2003).

8. *Woodson v. North Carolina*, 428 U.S. 280, 289–292 (1976) (plurality opinion).

9. Edwin R. Keedy, "History of the Pennsylvania Statute Creating Degrees of Murder," 97 *University of Pennsylvania Law Review* 759 (1949).

10. Poulos, *supra* note 4, at 148–151; Louis D. Bilionis, "Moral Appropriateness, Capital Punishment, and the *Lockett* Doctrine," 82 *Journal of Criminal Law & Criminology* 283, 289 n. 15 (1991).

11. *See* James R. Acker & Charles S. Lanier, "Beyond Human Ability? The Rise and Fall of Death Penalty Legislation," in James R. Acker, Robert M. Bohm & Charles S. Lanier (eds.), *America's Experiment With Capital Punishment: Reflections on the Past, Present, and Future of the Ultimate Penal Sanction* 85, 86 (Durham, NC: Carolina Academic Press, 2d ed. 2003).

12. *See also* Robert Weisberg, "Deregulating Death," 1983 *Supreme Court Review* 305 (1983).

13. *McGautha v. California*, 402 U.S. 183, 189–190 (1971).

14. 408 U.S. 238 (1972).

15. *See* Michael Meltsner, *Cruel and Unusual: The Supreme Court and Capital Punishment* 289–299 (New York: Random House 1973); James R. Acker, "The Flow and Ebb of American Capital Punishment," in Marvin D. Krohn, Alan J. Lizotte & Gina Penly Hall (eds.), *Handbook on Crime and Deviance* 297, 299 (New York: Springer 2009).

16. *Furman v. Georgia*, 408 U.S. 238, 257–306 (1972) (Brennan, J., concurring in the judgment).

17. *Id.*, 408 U.S., at 314–374 (Marshall, J., concurring in the judgment).

18. *Id.*, 408 U.S., at 380 (Burger, C.J., dissenting); 408 U.S., at 408 (Blackmun, J., dissenting); 408 U.S., at 417 (Powell, J., dissenting).

19. In relevant part, the Fifth Amendment to the United States Constitution provides: "No person shall be held for a capital . . . crime, unless on a presentment or indictment of a Grand Jury . . . ; nor shall any person be subject for the same offence to be twice put in jeopardy of life or limb; . . . nor be deprived of life . . . without due process of law. . . ."

20. *Furman v. Georgia*, 408 U.S. 208, 380 (1972) (Burger, C.J., dissenting); 408 U.S., at 419 (Powell, J., dissenting).

21. *Id.*, 408 U.S., at 428 (Powell, J., dissenting).

22. *Id.*, 408 U.S., at 388–389 (Burger, C.J., dissenting).

23. *Id.*, 408 U.S., at 411 (Blackmun, J., dissenting); 408 U.S., at 438–439, 462 (Powell, J., dissenting).

24. *Id.*, 408 U.S., at 383–384, 404–405 (Burger, C.J., dissenting); 408 U.S., at 410–411 (Blackmun, J., dissenting); 408 U.S., at 418, 431–433 (Powell, J., dissenting); 408 U.S., at 465–470 (Rehnquist, J., dissenting).

25. Meltsner, *supra* note 15, at 290–291.

26. *See* Franklin E. Zimring & Gordon Hawkins, *Capital Punishment and the American Agenda* 38–45 (New York: Cambridge University Press 1986); Meltsner, *supra* note 15, at 290–291; 306–309.

27. 428 U.S. 280 (1976).

28. 428 U.S. 325 (1976).

29. *Roberts (Harry) v. Louisiana,* 431 U.S. 633 (1977). The Supreme Court's 1976 decision that invalidated mandatory capital punishment pursuant to another provision of Louisiana's first-degree murder statute involved a different petitioner named Roberts. *Roberts (Stanislaus) v. Louisiana,* 428 U.S. 325 (1976).

30. *Sumner v. Shuman,* 483 U.S. 66 (1987).

31. *Gregg v. Georgia,* 428 U.S. 153, 163 n. 4 (1976) (plurality opinion), *citing* Ga. Code Ann. § 26–1101 (1972).

32. *Id.,* 428 U.S., at 163, *quoting* Ga. Code Ann. § 27–2503 (Supp. 1975).

33. *Id.,* 428 U.S., at 208 n. 2 (White, J., concurring in the judgment), *quoting* Georgia Laws, 1973, Act No. 74, p. 162.

34. *Id.,* 428 U.S., at 166–167 (plurality opinion), *quoting* Ga. Code Ann. § 27–2537 (Supp. 1975).

35. *Id.,* 428 U.S., at 165 n. 9, *quoting* Ga. Code Ann. § 27–2534.1 (b) (Supp. 1975).

36. *Id.,* 428 U.S., at 162.

37. *Id.,* 428 U.S., at 195 (footnote omitted).

38. 428 U.S. 242 (1976).

39. 428 U.S. 262 (1976).

40. *Id.,* 428 U.S., at 248 n. 4 (plurality opinion), *quoting* Fla. Stat. Ann. § 782.04 (Supp. 1976–1977).

41. *Id.,* 428 U.S., at 248 n. 6, *quoting* Fla. Stat. Ann. §§ 921.141 (2)(b) and (c) (Supp. 1976–1977).

42. Pursuant to a Florida Supreme Court decision, trial judges were authorized to impose a death sentence in cases where a jury had recommended life only if "'the facts suggesting a sentence of death [are] so clear and convincing that virtually no reasonable person could differ.'" *Id.,* 428 U.S., at 249, *quoting Tedder v. State,* 322 So.2d 908, 910 (Fla. 1975).

43. *Id.,* 428 U.S., at 250, *quoting* Fla. Stat. Ann. § 921.141 (3) (Supp. 1976–1977).

44. *Id.,* 428 U.S., at 250–251.

45. *Id.,* 428 U.S., at 252.

46. The plurality opinion observed that the statute contained no "limiting language" suggesting that only the enumerated mitigating circumstances could be relied on. *Id.,* 428 U.S., at 250 n. 8. Eleven years later, in *Hitchcock v. Dugger,* 481 U.S. 393 (1987), the Supreme Court invalidated a death sentence imposed in a Florida case where the trial judge had refused to consider evidence regarding nonstatutory mitigating circumstances.

47. *Proffitt v. Florida,* 428 U.S. 242, 253 (1976) (plurality opinion).

48. At the time that Jerry Lane Jurek committed the crime in the case resulting in his death sentence in the case reviewed by the Supreme Court, *Jurek v. Texas,* 428 U.S. 262 (1976), Texas law defined murder broadly. *Id.,* 428 U.S., at 265 n. 1 (plurality opinion), *quoting* Tex. Penal Code, Art. 1256 (1973). A new murder statute took effect January 1, 1974, which defined the crime more narrowly. *Id., quoting* Tex. Penal Code § 19.02 (a) (1974). Five forms of "murder with malice" were made punishable by death or life imprisonment: where the victim was a peace officer or firefighter; intentional killings committed in the course of designated felonies; murders for hire; killings committed by persons escaping or attempting to escape from a penal institution; and the murder committed by an incarcerated offender of a person employed by a penal institution. *Id., quoting* Tex. Penal Code, Art. 1257 (b) (1973), *superseded by* Tex. Penal Code § 19.03 (1974). Jurek had kidnapped a 10-year-old child with the intent to rape her, and then strangled the child and threw her into a river, where she drowned. *Id.,* 428 U.S., at 266–267.

49. *Id.,* 428 U.S., at 269, *quoting* Tex. Code Crim. Proc., Art. 37.071 (b) (Supp. 1975–1976).

50. Affirmative answers required unanimity; a negative answer could be produced by a vote of 10–2. *Id.,* 428 U.S., at 269 n. 5.

51. *Id.,* 428 U.S., at 269, *citing* Tex. Code Crim. Proc., Art. 37.071 (f) (1975–1976).

52. *See* Carol S. Steiker & Jordan M. Steiker, "Review Essay: Let God Sort Them Out? Refining the Individualization Requirement in Capital Sentencing," 102 *Yale Law Journal* 835 (1992); Scott W. Howe, "Resolving the Conflict in the Capital Sentencing Cases: A Desert-Oriented Theory of Regulation," 26 *Georgia Law Review* 323 (1992).

53. 536 U.S. 304 (2002).

54. Tex. Code Crim. Proc. Art. 37.071 (2) (e) (1) (2006).

55. *See also McKoy v. North Carolina*, 494 U.S. 433 (1990).

56. The Supreme Court has approved of this practice. *See Lowenfield v. Phelps*, 484 U.S. 231 (1988).

57. *See* James R. Acker & C.S. Lanier, "Capital Murder From Benefit of Clergy to Bifurcated Trials: Narrowing the Class of Offenses Punishable by Death," 29 *Criminal Law Bulletin* 291 (1993).

58. *Zant v. Stephens*, 462 U.S. 862, 877 (1983) (footnote omitted).

59. *See* James R. Acker & C.S. Lanier, "'Parsing This Lexicon of Death': Aggravating Factors in Capital Sentencing Statutes," 30 *Criminal Law Bulletin* 107 (1994).

60. American Law Institute, Model Penal Code § 210.6 (3) (a)-(h) (1962).

61. Carol S. Steiker & Jordan M. Steiker, "No More Tinkering: The American Law Institute and the Death Penalty Provisions of the Model Penal Code," 89 *Texas Law Review* 353, 354 (2010), *quoting* "Message From ALI Director Lance Liebman," retrieved June 15, 2013 from www.ali.org/_news/10232009.htm. *See generally* American Law Institute, *Report of the Council to the Membership of The American Law Institute on the Matter of the Death Penalty* (Apr. 15, 2009), retrieved June 15, 2013 from www.ali.org/doc/Capital%20Punishment_web.pdf.

62. American Law Institute, *Model Penal Code and Commentaries* 137 (official draft & revised comments 1980).

63. American Law Institute, Model Penal Code § 210.6 (3) (h) (1962).

64. Acker & Lanier, *supra* note 59, at 125.

65. 446 U.S. 420 (1980).

66. Ga. Code Ann. § 17–10–30 (b) (7) (2012) (formerly § 27–2534.1 (b) (7) (Supp. 1975)).

67. *See Bell v. Cone*, 543 U.S. 447 (2005) (Tennessee Supreme Court affirmance of death sentence based on "especially heinous, atrocious, or cruel" aggravating circumstance was not contrary to clearly established U.S. Supreme Court precedent and hence was to be respected on challenge via federal habeas corpus); *Arave v. Creech*, 507 U.S. 463 (1993) (as construed, Idaho aggravating factor of displaying "utter disregard for human life" provides sufficient guidance to comply with Eighth and Fourteenth Amendment requirements); *Walton v. Arizona*, 497 U.S. 639 (1990), *overruled in part on other grounds, Ring v. Arizona*, 536 U.S. 584 (2002) (as construed by Arizona Supreme Court, the "especially heinous, cruel, or depraved" statutory aggravating factor was not unconstitutionally vague).

68. *Blystone v. Pennsylvania*, 494 U.S. 299, 302 (1990), *quoting* Pa. Cons. Stat. § 9711(c)(1)(iv) (1988).

69. *Id.*, 494 U.S., at 306 n. 4.

70. *Id.*, 494 U.S., at 312 (Brennan, J., dissenting) (emphasis removed).

71. *See* James R. Acker & Charles S. Lanier, "Matters of Life or Death: The Sentencing Provisions in Capital Punishment Statutes," 31 *Criminal Law Bulletin* 19, 30–33 (1995).

72. N.H. Rev. Stat. Ann. § 630:5(IV) (1990).

73. *In re Winship*, 397 U.S. 358 (1970) (government must prove guilt in criminal prosecutions and juvenile delinquency adjudication hearings beyond a reasonable doubt); *Addington v. Texas*, 441 U.S. 418 (1979) (government must prove by clear and convincing evidence the facts necessary to support involuntary civil commitment, *i.e.*, that the individual is mentally ill and dangerous to him- or herself or others).

74. *See Kansas v. Marsh*, 548 U.S. 163 (2006); *Walton v. Arizona*, 497 U.S. 639 (1990), *overruled in part on other grounds, Ring v. Arizona*, 536 U.S. 584 (2002).

75. Acker & Lanier, *supra* note 71, at 34–42.

76. *Gregg v. Georgia,* 428 U.S. 153, 195 (1976) (plurality opinion) (footnote omitted).

77. *See, e.g., Pulley v. Harris,* 465 U.S. 37, 45 (1984) ("We take statutes as we find them. . . . As we said in *Gregg,* '[w]e do not intend to suggest that only the above-described procedures would be permissible under *Furman.* . . .'"); *Zant v. Stephens,* 462 U.S. 862, 874 (1983) ("A fair statement of the consensus expressed by the Court in *Furman* is 'that where discretion is afforded a sentencing body on a matter so grave as the determination of whether a human life should be taken or spared, that discretion must be suitably directed and limited so as to minimize the risk of wholly arbitrary and capricious action." *Gregg v. Georgia,* 428 U.S. 153, 189 (1976) (opinion of Stewart, Powell, and Stevens, JJ.). After thus summarizing the central mandate of *Furman,* the joint opinion in *Gregg* set forth a general exposition of sentencing procedures that would satisfy the concerns of *Furman, id., at* 189–195. But it expressly stated: "We do not intend to suggest that only the above-described procedures would be permissible under *Furman.* . . .").

78. *Walton v. Arizona,* 497 U.S. 639, 664 (1990) (Scalia, J., concurring in part and concurring in the judgment), *overruled in part on other grounds, Ring v. Arizona,* 536 U.S. 584 (2002).

5

PROPORTIONALITY

OFFENSES AND OFFENDERS

Introduction

What crimes should be punishable by death? Should all who commit those crimes be eligible for the death penalty or do certain classes of offenders—for example, juveniles, the intellectually disabled, and perhaps others—share characteristics that should render them altogether exempt from consideration for capital punishment? Should decisions about capital punishment for offenses and offenders be left to legislatures, and to the sentencing authority in individual trials, or does the Eighth Amendment's ban on cruel and unusual punishments flatly prohibit the death penalty in some cases?

The answers to these questions are certainly debatable. They have varied over the course of this country's history and, indeed, may continue to evolve in the future. The issues we consider in this chapter are different from, and in some respects are more fundamental than, the ones we considered in chapter 4, where our focus was on the criteria and procedures used to define death-penalty eligibility in capital murder cases and select from the death-eligible offenders those who ultimately should be punished by death. Here we inquire whether certain crimes and offenders are (or should be) deemed categorically ineligible for consideration for the death penalty, regardless of individual case circumstances.

Crimes Punishable by Death

Prisons for the long-term incarceration of criminal offenders were unknown in colonial America. They first emerged in the late 18th century and then, fueled in part by reformers who sought to rehabilitate and correct the errant ways of miscreants, spread rapidly throughout the new country beginning in the early 19th century.[1] Lacking prisons to sanction criminals and safeguard the community from them, the colonists necessarily relied on other options, including fines, banishment, shaming (such as public display in the stocks or pillory), corporal punishments (including whipping and branding), as well as capital punishment. The roster of crimes punishable by death was correspondingly lengthy, numbering 10 or more in almost all of the colonies. In the earliest days of statehood, capital punishment commonly was provided for murder, arson, burglary, robbery, rape, buggery, counterfeiting, and treason, and occasionally for crimes including forgery, horse theft, stealing from a church, mayhem, and a few others.[2]

Led by Dr. Benjamin Rush, Attorney General (and later Pennsylvania Supreme Court Justice) William Bradford, and like-minded humanitarians, Pennsylvania enacted legislation in 1794 that created two forms of murder, first-degree and second-degree. This novel statute limited the death penalty to first-degree murder, involving a variety of willful, premeditated, and deliberate killings, as well as killings committed during the commission of other serious felonies.[3] Over time, other states reserved capital punishment for progressively fewer crimes, doing so by law or in practice. As the 20th century unfolded, a continuously dwindling array of crimes was made punishable by death. Between 1930 and 1967 (the year of the last execution prior to the Supreme Court's invalidation of death-penalty laws nationwide in *Furman v. Georgia* (1972)[4]), all but a handful of the 3,859 executions carried out in the United States were for murder (86.4%) or rape (11.8%).[5] Other potentially capital crimes remained on the books in a few jurisdictions, including kidnapping, robbery, burglary, arson, assault committed by a life term prisoner, and train wrecking, as well as treason and espionage.[6]

When the justices first scrutinized the states' post-*Furman* capital punishment laws, in *Gregg v. Georgia* and its companion cases,[7] all of the death sentences under review had been imposed in response to convictions for aggravated murder. While rejecting the claim that punishment by death is invariably "cruel and unusual" and hence *per se* violates the Eighth Amendment, the plurality opinion in *Gregg* (issued by Justices Stewart, Powell, and Stevens) considered a number of subsidiary issues, including "whether the punishment of death is disproportionate in relation to the crime for which it is imposed." Emphasizing that "we are concerned here only with the imposition of capital punishment for the crime of murder, and when a life has been taken deliberately by the offender," the justices rejected the notion "that the punishment is invariably disproportionate to the crime. It is an extreme sanction, suitable to the most extreme of crimes." The opinion nevertheless cautioned: "We do not address here the question whether the taking of the criminal's life is a proportionate sanction where no victim has been deprived of life, for example, when capital punishment is imposed for rape, kidnaping, or armed robbery that does not result in the death of any human being."[8]

Capital Punishment for Rape

The following year, the Court confronted one of the questions it had reserved in *Gregg*, regarding capital punishment for crimes other than aggravated murder. It did so in another case arising from Georgia, this one involving a death sentence imposed on an offender for raping an adult victim. Ehrlich Anthony Coker escaped from prison in September 1974, where he had been serving three life sentences and additional terms of years following convictions for murder, rape, kidnapping, and aggravated assault.

He entered the home of a married couple, tied up the man, and raped the woman at knifepoint. He thereupon abducted the woman, driving away with her in the couple's car. He later released his victim without further injury. Coker subsequently was apprehended, brought to trial, and convicted of rape. Georgia law allowed rape to be punished by death if the prosecution proved one or more aggravating circumstances at a separate penalty hearing and, after considering additional evidence in aggravation and mitigation of punishment, the jury decided that a capital sentence should be imposed. The jury determined that two statutory aggravating factors had been proven—that the rape had been committed during the commission of another capital felony (armed robbery), and that Coker had a prior conviction for a capital felony. It sentenced Coker to death. Coker's conviction and death sentence were affirmed on appeal to the Georgia Supreme Court. The U.S. Supreme Court granted certiorari to consider whether "the punishment of death for rape violates the Eighth Amendment, which proscribes 'cruel and unusual punishments'. . . ."

Coker v. Georgia, 433 U.S. 584, 97 S.Ct. 2861, 53 L.Ed.2d 982 (1977)

Mr. Justice WHITE announced the judgment of the Court and filed an opinion in which Mr. Justice STEWART, Mr. Justice BLACKMUN, and Mr. Justice STEVENS, joined. . . .

II

. . . It is now settled that the death penalty is not invariably cruel and unusual punishment within the meaning of the Eighth Amendment; it is not inherently barbaric or an unacceptable mode of punishment for crime; neither is it always disproportionate to the crime for which it is imposed. It is also established that imposing capital punishment, at least for murder, in accordance with the procedures provided under the Georgia statutes saves the sentence from the infirmities which led the Court to invalidate the prior Georgia capital punishment statute in *Furman v. Georgia,* [408 U.S. 238 (1972)].

In sustaining the imposition of the death penalty in *Gregg* [*v. Georgia,* 428 U.S. 153 (1976)], however, the Court firmly embraced the holdings and dicta from prior cases, to the effect that the Eighth Amendment bars not only those punishments that are 'barbaric' but also those that are 'excessive' in relation to the crime committed. Under *Gregg,* a punishment is "excessive" and unconstitutional if it (1) makes no measurable contribution to acceptable goals of punishment and hence is nothing more than the purposeless and needless imposition of pain and suffering; or (2) is grossly out of proportion to the severity of the crime. A punishment might fail the test on either ground. Furthermore, these Eighth Amendment judgments should not be, or appear to be, merely the subjective views of individual Justices; judgment should be informed by objective factors to the maximum possible extent. To this end, attention must be given to the public attitudes concerning a particular sentence history and precedent, legislative attitudes, and the response of juries reflected in their sentencing decisions are to be consulted. In *Gregg,* after giving due regard to such sources, the Court's judgment was that the death penalty for deliberate murder was neither the purposeless imposition of severe punishment nor a punishment grossly disproportionate to the crime. But the Court reserved the question of the constitutionality of the death penalty when imposed for other crimes.

III

That question, with respect to rape of an adult woman, is now before us. We have concluded that a sentence of death is grossly dispropor-tionate and excessive punishment for the crime of rape and is therefore forbidden by the Eighth Amendment as cruel and unusual punishment.

A

As advised by recent cases, we seek guidance in history and from the objective evidence of the country's present judgment concerning the acceptability of death as a penalty for rape of an adult woman. At no time in the last 50 years have a majority of the States authorized death as a punishment for rape. In 1925, 18 States, the District of Columbia, and the Federal Government authorized capital punishment for the rape of an adult female. By 1971 just prior to the decision in *Furman v. Georgia*, that number had declined, but not substantially, to 16 States plus the Federal Government.[FN6] *Furman* then invalidated most of the capital punishment statutes in this country, including the rape statutes. . . .

FN6. Ala. Code, Tit. 14, § 395 (1958); Ark. Stat. Ann. § 41–3403 (1964); Fla. Stat. Ann. § 794.01 (1965); Ga. Code § 26–2001 (1970); Ky. Rev. Stat. Ann. §§ 435.080–435.090 (1962); La. Rev. Stat. Ann. § 14:42 (1950); Md. Ann. Code, Art. 27, § 461 (1957); Miss. Code Ann. § 2358 (1957);

Mo. Rev. Stat. § 559.260 (1969); Nev. Rev. Stat. § 200.360 (1963) (rape with substan-tial bodily harm); N.C. Gen. Stat. § 14–21 (1969); Okla. Stat. Ann., Tit. 21, § 1115 (1958); S.C. Code Ann. §§ 16–72, 16–80 (1962); Tenn. Code Ann. § 39–3702 (1955); Tex. Penal Code § 1189 (1961); Va. Code Ann. § 18.1–44 (1960); 18 U.S.C. § 2031.

. . . Thirty-five States immediately rein-stituted the death penalty for at least limited kinds of crime. . . .

But if the "most marked indication of soci-ety's endorsement of the death penalty for mur-der is the legislative response to *Furman*," *Gregg v. Georgia*, it should also be a telling datum that the public judgment with respect to rape, as reflected in the statutes providing the punish-ment for that crime, has been dramatically dif-ferent. In reviving death penalty laws to satisfy *Furman's* mandate, none of the States that had not previously authorized death for rape chose to include rape among capital felonies. Of the 16 States in which rape had been a capital offense, only three provided the death penalty for rape of an adult woman in their revised stat-utes Georgia, North Carolina, and Louisiana. In the latter two States, the death penalty was mandatory for those found guilty, and those laws were invalidated by *Woodson* and *Roberts*. When Louisiana and North Carolina, respond-ing to those decisions, again revised their cap-ital punishment laws, they reenacted the death penalty for murder but not for rape . . .

. . . The upshot is that Georgia is the sole jurisdiction in the United States at the present time that authorizes a sentence of death when the rape victim is an adult woman, and only two other jurisdictions provide capital punish-ment when the victim is a child.

The current judgment with respect to the death penalty for rape is not wholly unanimous among state legislatures, but it obviously weighs very heavily on the side of rejecting capital punishment as a suitable penalty for raping an adult woman.

B

It was also observed in *Gregg* that "[t]he jury . . . is a significant and reliable objective index of contemporary values because it is so directly involved," and that it is thus important to look to the sentencing decisions that juries have made in the course of assessing whether capital punishment is an appropriate penalty for the crime being tried. . . .

According to the factual submissions in this Court, out of all rape convictions in Georgia since 1973—and that total number has not been tendered—63 cases had been reviewed by the Georgia Supreme Court as of the time of oral argument; and of these, 6 involved a death sentence. . . . Georgia juries have thus sentenced rapists to death six times since 1973. This obviously is not a negligible number; and the State argues that as a practical matter juries simply reserve the extreme sanction for extreme cases of rape and that recent experience surely does not prove that jurors consider the death penalty to be a disproportionate punishment for every conceivable instance of rape, no matter how aggravated. Nevertheless, it is true that in the vast majority of cases, at least 9 out of 10, juries have not imposed the death sentence.

IV

These recent events evidencing the attitude of state legislatures and sentencing juries do not wholly determine this controversy, for the Constitution contemplates that in the end our own judgment will be brought to bear on the question of the acceptability of the death penalty under the Eighth Amendment. Nevertheless, the legislative rejection of capital punishment for rape strongly confirms our own judgment, which is that death is indeed a disproportionate penalty for the crime of raping an adult woman.

We do not discount the seriousness of rape as a crime. It is highly reprehensible, both in a moral sense and in its almost total contempt for the personal integrity and autonomy of the female victim and for the latter's privilege of choosing those with whom intimate relationships are to be established. Short of homicide, it is the "ultimate violation of self." It is also a violent crime because it normally involves force, or the threat of force or intimidation, to overcome the will and the capacity of the victim to resist. Rape is very often accompanied by physical injury to the female and can also inflict mental and psychological damage. Because it undermines the community's sense of security, there is public injury as well.

Rape is without doubt deserving of serious punishment; but in terms of moral depravity and of the injury to the person and to the public, it does not compare with murder, which does involve the unjustified taking of human life. Although it may be accompanied by another crime, rape by definition does not include the death of or even the serious injury to another person. The murderer kills; the rapist, if no more than that, does not. Life is over for the victim of the murderer; for the rape victim, life may not be nearly so happy as it was, but it is not over and normally is not beyond repair. We have the abiding conviction that the death penalty, which "is unique in its severity and irrevocability," *Gregg v. Georgia*, 428 U.S., at 187, is an excessive penalty for the rapist who, as such, does not take human life.

This does not end the matter; for under Georgia law, death may not be imposed for any capital offense, including rape, unless the jury or judge finds one of the statutory aggravating circumstances and then elects to impose that sentence. . . .

[Requiring proof of aggravating circumstances does not] change our conclusion that the death sentence imposed on Coker is a disproportionate punishment for rape. Coker had prior convictions for capital felonies rape, murder, and kidnaping but these prior convictions do not change the fact that the instant crime being punished is a rape not involving the taking of life.

It is also true that the present rape occurred while Coker was committing armed robbery, a felony for which the Georgia statutes authorize the death penalty. But Coker was tried for the robbery offense as well as for rape and received a separate life sentence for this crime. . . .

We note finally that in Georgia a person commits murder when he unlawfully and with malice aforethought, either express or implied, causes the death of another human being. He also commits that crime when in the commission of a felony he causes the death of another human being, irrespective of malice. But even where the killing is deliberate, it is not punishable by death absent proof of aggravating circumstances. It is difficult to accept the notion, and we do not, that the rapist, with or without aggravating circumstances, should be punished more heavily than the deliberate killer as long as the rapist does not himself take the life of his victim. The judgment of the Georgia Supreme Court upholding the death sentence

is reversed, and the case is remanded to that court for further proceedings not inconsistent with this opinion. . . .

[The opinions of Justices Brennan and Marshall, both of whom concurred in the judgment, are omitted.]

Mr. Justice POWELL, concurring in the judgment in part and dissenting in part.

I concur in the judgment of the Court on the facts of this case, and also in the plurality's reasoning supporting the view that ordinarily death is disproportionate punishment for the crime of raping an adult woman. . . .

[However, it] is . . . quite unnecessary for the plurality to write in terms so sweeping as to foreclose each of the 50 state legislatures from creating a narrowly defined substantive crime of aggravated rape punishable by death. [FN1] . . .

FN1. It is not this Court's function to formulate the relevant criteria that might distinguish aggravated rape from the more usual case, but perhaps a workable test would embrace the factors identified by Georgia: the cruelty or viciousness of the offender, the circumstances and manner in which the offense was committed, and the consequences suffered by the victim. . . .

As noted in *Snider v. Peyton*, 356 F.2d 626, 627 (CA4 1966), "[t]here is extreme variation in the degree of culpability of rapists." The deliberate viciousness of the rapist may be greater than that of the murderer. . . . There also is wide variation in the effect on the victim. . . . Some victims are so grievously injured physically or psychologically that life is beyond repair.

Thus, it may be that the death penalty is not disproportionate punishment for the crime of aggravated rape. . . . In a proper case a more discriminating inquiry than the plurality undertakes well might discover that both juries and legislatures have reserved the ultimate penalty for the case of an outrageous rape resulting in serious, lasting harm to the victim. I would not prejudge the issue. To this extent, I respectfully dissent.

Mr. Chief Justice BURGER, with whom Mr. Justice REHNQUIST joins, dissenting.

. . . Our task is not to give effect to our individual views on capital punishment; rather, we must determine what the Constitution permits a State to do under its reserved powers. In striking down the death penalty imposed upon the petitioner in this case, the Court has overstepped the bounds of proper constitutional adjudication by substituting its policy judgment for that of the state legislature. . . .

(1)

On December 5, 1971, the petitioner, Ehrlich Anthony Coker, raped and then stabbed to death a young woman. Less than eight months later Coker kidnaped and raped a second young woman. After twice raping this 16-year-old victim, he stripped her, severely beat her with a club, and dragged her into a wooded area where he left her for dead. He was apprehended and pleaded guilty to offenses stemming from these incidents. He was sentenced by three separate courts to three life terms, two 20-year terms, and one 8-year term of imprisonment. Each judgment specified that the sentences it imposed were to run consecutively rather than concurrently. Approximately 1½ years later, on September 2, 1974, petitioner escaped from the state prison where he was serving these sentences. He promptly raped another 16-year-old woman in the presence of her husband, abducted her from her home, and

threatened her with death and serious bodily harm. It is this crime for which the sentence now under review was imposed.

The Court today holds that the State of Georgia may not impose the death penalty on Coker. In so doing, it prevents the State from imposing any effective punishment upon Coker for his latest rape. The Court's holding, moreover, bars Georgia from guaranteeing its citizens that they will suffer no further attacks by this habitual rapist . . . as well as others in his position. . . . To what extent we have left States "elbowroom" to protect innocent persons from depraved human beings like Coker remains in doubt.

(2)

. . . Unlike the plurality, I would narrow the inquiry in this case to the question actually presented: Does the Eighth Amendment's ban against cruel and unusual punishment prohibit the State of Georgia from executing a person who has, within the space of three years, raped three separate women, killing one and attempting to kill another, who is serving prison terms exceeding his probable lifetime and who has not hesitated to escape confinement at the first available opportunity? Whatever one's view may be as to the State's constitutional power to impose the death penalty upon a rapist who stands before a court convicted for the first time, this case reveals a chronic rapist whose continuing danger to the community is abundantly clear. . . .

(3)

The plurality acknowledges the gross nature of the crime of rape. A rapist not only violates a victim's privacy and personal integrity, but inevitably causes serious psychological as well as physical harm in the process. The long-range effect upon the victim's life and health is likely to be irreparable; it is impossible to measure the harm which results. . . . Rape is not a mere physical attack[;] it is destructive of the human personality. The remainder of the victim's life may be gravely affected, and this in turn may have a serious detrimental effect upon her husband and any children she may have. . . . To speak blandly, as the plurality does, of rape victims who are "unharmed," or to classify the human outrage of rape, as does Mr. Justice POWELL, in terms of "excessively brutal," versus "moderately brutal," takes too little account of the profound suffering the crime imposes upon the victims and their loved ones.

Despite its strong condemnation of rape, the Court reaches the inexplicable conclusion that "the death penalty . . . is an excessive penalty" for the perpetrator of this heinous offense. . . .

(a)

The plurality opinion bases its analysis, in part, on the fact that "Georgia is the sole jurisdiction in the United States at the present time that authorizes a sentence of death when the rape victim is an adult woman." Surely, however, this statistic cannot be deemed determinative, or even particularly relevant. As the opinion concedes, two other States Louisiana and North Carolina have enacted death penalty statutes for adult rape since this Court's 1972 decision in *Furman v. Georgia*, 408 U.S. 238. If the Court is to rely on some "public opinion" process, does this not suggest the beginning of a "trend"?

More to the point, however, it is myopic to base sweeping constitutional principles upon the narrow experience of the past five years. Considerable uncertainty was introduced into this area of the law by this Court's *Furman*

decision. A large number of States found their death penalty statutes invalidated; legislatures were left in serious doubt by the expressions vacillating between discretionary and mandatory death penalties, as to whether this Court would sustain any statute imposing death as a criminal sanction. Failure of more States to enact statutes imposing death for rape of an adult woman may thus reflect hasty legislative compromise occasioned by time pressures following *Furman*, a desire to wait on the experience of those States which did enact such statutes, or simply an accurate forecast of today's holding.

In any case, when considered in light of the experience since the turn of this century, where more than one-third of American jurisdictions have consistently provided the death penalty for rape, the plurality's focus on the experience of the immediate past must be viewed as truly disingenuous. . . .

Our concern for human life must not be confined to the guilty; a state legislature is not to be thought insensitive to human values because it acts firmly to protect the lives and related values of the innocent. In this area the choices for legislatures are at best painful and difficult and deserve a high degree of deference. . . .

It is difficult to believe that Georgia would long remain alone in punishing rape by death if the next decade demonstrated a drastic reduction in its incidence of rape, an increased cooperation by rape victims in the apprehension and prosecution of rapists, and a greater confidence in the rule of law on the part of the populace. . . .

(b)

The subjective judgment that the death penalty is simply disproportionate to the crime of rape is even more disturbing than the "objective" analysis. . . . The plurality's conclusion on this point is based upon the bare fact that murder necessarily results in the physical death of the victim, while rape does not. However, no Member of the Court explains why this distinction has relevance, much less constitutional significance. It is, after all, not irrational nor constitutionally impermissible for a legislature to make the penalty more severe than the criminal act it punishes in the hope it would deter wrongdoing. . . .

Until now, the issue under the Eighth Amendment has not been the state of any particular victim after the crime, but rather whether the punishment imposed is grossly disproportionate to the evil committed by the perpetrator. As a matter of constitutional principle, that test cannot have the primitive simplicity of "life for life, eye for eye, tooth for tooth." Rather States must be permitted to engage in a more sophisticated weighing of values in dealing with criminal activity which consistently poses serious danger of death or grave bodily harm. . . .

The clear implication of today's holding appears to be that the death penalty may be properly imposed only as to crimes resulting in death of the victim. This casts serious doubt upon the constitutional validity of statutes imposing the death penalty for a variety of conduct which, though dangerous, may not necessarily result in any immediate death, *e.g.*, treason, airplane hijacking, and kidnaping. In that respect, today's holding does even more harm than is initially apparent. We cannot avoid taking judicial notice that crimes such as airplane hijacking, kidnaping, and mass terrorist activity constitute a serious and increasing danger to the safety of the public. It would be unfortunate indeed if the effect of today's holding were to inhibit States and the Federal Government from experimenting with various remedies including possibly imposition of the penalty of death to prevent and deter such crimes. . . .

Whatever our individual views as to the wisdom of capital punishment, I cannot agree that it is constitutionally impermissible for a state legislature to make the "solemn judgment" to impose such penalty for the crime of rape. Accordingly, I would leave to the States the task of legislating in this area of the law.

Whether capital punishment for the crime of raping an adult victim offends the Eighth Amendment's ban on cruel and unusual punishments requires constitutional interpretation. The issue thus falls to the Supreme Court for consideration. Yet how that question should be analyzed and answered is hardly straightforward. Justice White's plurality opinion in *Coker* explains that the cruel and unusual punishments clause prohibits sanctions that are "excessive"—or "grossly disproportionate"—in relation to the crime committed. The next step in the analysis is to identify a more concrete test for "excessiveness," resulting in the two-part inquiry requiring reference to (a) *objective* indicators of society's "evolving standards of decency" (including authorizing legislation and juries' sentencing decisions, which help illuminate how frequently the authorized punishment actually has been applied), and (b) the *justices' "own judgment"* (informed, in part, by the apparent fit between the punishment, the offender's culpability, and the harm caused by the crime, and by the penalty's contribution to the permissible objectives of retribution and deterrence).

In light of the confusion generated by the Court's decision in *Furman* (at which time no fewer than 16 states and the federal government authorized the death penalty for rape), and the recency of its approval of guided discretion capital sentencing legislation for the crime of murder in *Gregg*, just one year earlier, how much significance should be attributed to the fact that Georgia was the only jurisdiction with legislation authorizing the death penalty for the rape of an adult in 1977, when *Coker* was decided?

In the four years after Georgia's 1973 post-*Furman* death-penalty legislation was enacted, juries had sentenced offenders to death in six of the 63 rape cases (9.5%) reviewed on appeal by the Georgia Supreme Court. As Justice White notes, "[t]his obviously is not a negligible number; and the State argues that as a practical matter juries simply reserve the extreme sanction for extreme cases of rape. . . ." Why, then, does his opinion conclude that these sentencing practices supply further objective evidence that death is an excessive punishment for the crime of rape?

If the Court's consultation of objective indicators of societal standards of decency is a necessary part of its Eighth Amendment analysis, why isn't it also sufficient? Why do the justices engage in their own, independent analysis of whether the death penalty is excessive in relation to the crime of raping an adult victim? Does this aspect of the analysis enhance the legitimacy of the Court's conclusion, or does it threaten to undermine it by inviting the criticism that the justices' "personal preferences as to the wisdom of" the legislative policy, rather than neutral principles of adjudication, influenced the decision?

Coker already had been convicted of murder, two rapes, kidnapping, and aggravated assault, and was serving consecutive sentences of life imprisonment and 20 years for those crimes when he escaped from prison and committed the rape for which he was sentenced to death. If death is not available as punishment for rape under such circumstances, are any alternatives able to provide meaningful retribution, or serve as a deterrent for committing additional rapes? Chief Justice Burger's dissenting opinion raises the related concern of how society can be protected from someone such as Coker if capital punishment is not an option. These issues surfaced during the oral argument that preceded the Court's decision, in the following exchange between Justice Powell and David Kendall, Coker's attorney. Justice Stewart's comment at the conclusion of the exchange also is germane.

Justice Lewis F. Powell: Mr. Kendall, before you proceed, if we have a prison inmate who has been convicted of aggravated rape and sentenced to life, a mandatory life sentence under the statute that forbids parole and the inmate escapes and commits another aggravated rape, what punishment do you think would be appropriate?

Mr. Kendall: That, of course, is not the case presented here.

Justice Powell: I understand that.

Mr. Kendall: But it seems to me that in the circumstances of that case, imprisonment would be an appropriate punishment when judged by what society does to essentially all other people who are convicted of that crime.

Justice Powell: Would that be any punishment for that individual?

Mr. Kendall: Certainly, he would have the stigma of another rape conviction. Society would be protected since it would have kept him incarcerated.

Justice Powell: . . . [I]t would be protected to the same extent that it had been protected after his first conviction for rape.

Mr. Kendall: Yes, Mr. Justice Powell, that is—

Justice Powell: Yet he escaped.

Mr. Kendall: That is correct. Of course, petitioner Coker was incarcerated—

Justice Powell: I am not talking about Coker, I was asking your view as to whether or not there could ever be a situation where absent any other punishment, capital punishment would be appropriate for repetitive crimes of rape.

Mr. Kendall: Well, we think that the objective indicators that the Court pointed to in *Gregg* would indicate that society, where a life has not been taken, the death penalty is inappropriate to protect a value other than life.

Justice Powell: What deterrents would exist in the circumstances I described?

Mr. Kendall: I think that the deterrence connotes protection from society it seems to me in that case. I think that certainly if there is a life without parole statute, adding a sentence would not in and of itself impose more punishment. But insofar as deterrence is a question that relates to the general public, I think the usual safeguards that can be applied to prevent escapes would adequately protect the public. . . . [When Coker escaped, he was not] incarcerated in a maximum security facility. The state of Georgia can take more steps than it has taken . . . to protect society. Also, the state of Georgia can enact, as it has not yet enacted, some longer term of mandatory imprisonment for repeated crimes, whatever those crimes are. In Georgia, under Georgia Code Annotated 77–525, a prisoner comes up for parole in seven years, regardless of what his sentence is. Now, Georgia could extend that time, if it wished to do so.

Justice Potter Stewart: Of course, anybody who is serving a life sentence without a hope of pardon or parole who escapes can with practical impunity commit any offense, including whether it would be petty larceny or jaywalking or shoplifting, unless you decide that the only way to give him additional punishment is to put him to death for jaywalking or shoplifting or petty larceny.[9]

Related to this line of questioning, might there be a concern that if death were a possible punishment for rape, the rapist might have a diminished incentive to refrain from killing his victim and, indeed, might rationally be pushed to commit murder to avoid leaving a witness? Is such speculation better left to legislators or might such thinking appropriately find its way into the judiciary's constitutional analysis?

Justice White's opinion in *Coker* identifies the 16 states (in addition to the federal government) that made rape a capital offense as of 1971 (see footnote 6 above). Note the almost exclusively southern tenor of the states. Is this regional characteristic merely a coincidence or might it have some deeper sociological significance? Between 1930, when national statistics were first available, and 1964, when the country's last execution for rape was carried out, 455 offenders were punished by death for committing rape. Roughly nine out of ten (89.5%) of those executed for rape were Black.[10] Analysis of a large subset of those cases showed especially glaring disparities in cases involving Black defendants convicted of raping White women; approximately 36% of those convictions resulted in a death sentence, compared to 2% of the convictions involving other offender-victim racial combinations.[11] The opinions in *Coker* are silent regarding these historical patterns regarding race, rape, and capital punishment (Coker was White). Might this evidence suggest an important, albeit unarticulated subtext for the decision? We will explore racial disparities in the death penalty's administration in greater detail in chapter 6.

Although Coker's victim was only 16 years old, she was married and thus presumably was considered an emancipated minor. Justice White's opinion repeatedly defined the issue before the Court as whether the Eighth Amendment prohibits capital punishment for the "rape of an adult woman." What does the decision imply about the death penalty's availability for the rape of a child? Does an offender who rapes a young child evidence sufficiently heightened depravity and/or cause such aggravated harm that death should be a constitutionally acceptable punishment?

In 1998, Patrick Kennedy raped his 8-year-old stepdaughter in Jefferson Parish, Louisiana, inflicting such serious injuries that the child required emergency hospitalization and surgery. He was convicted of the aggravated rape of a child and a jury sentenced him to death pursuant to a Louisiana statute authorizing capital punishment for that crime. Testimony presented at the trial's penalty phase revealed that Kennedy previously had raped another 8-year-old girl. The Louisiana Supreme Court upheld his conviction and death sentence, concluding that *Coker* involved an adult victim and did not preclude capital punishment for the more serious crime of raping a child. The U.S. Supreme Court granted certiorari in *Kennedy v. Louisiana*, 554 U.S. 407, 128 S.Ct. 2641, 171 L.Ed.2d 525 (2008) to consider "whether the Constitution bars [Louisiana] from imposing the death penalty for the rape of a child. . . ."[12]

Using the two-part analysis outlined in *Coker*—one inquiry involving objective indicators of society's "evolving standards of decency," including the prevalence of authorizing legislation and juries' willingness to impose death sentences pursuant to those statutes, and the other depending on the justices' independent consideration of whether death is a proportional punishment for the crime—how should the issue presented in *Kennedy* be decided? What additional information would be useful to help inform such a decision?

Justice Kennedy's majority opinion in a 5–4 decision concluded that Louisiana's statute was unconstitutional. It held more broadly that, "As it relates to crimes against individuals, . . . the death penalty should not be expanded to instances where the victim's life was not taken."[13] This aspect of the ruling was specifically "limited to crimes against individual persons. We do not address, for example, crimes defining and punishing treason, espionage, terrorism, and drug kingpin activity, which are offenses against the State."[14]

In support of the conclusion that the Eighth Amendment forbids capital punishment for the crime of the aggravated rape of a child, Justice Kennedy first consulted the objective indicia of contemporary societal standards of decency, which most prominently involve legislation and sentencing practices.

The evidence of a national consensus with respect to the death penalty for child rapists . . . shows divided opinion but, on balance, an opinion against it. Thirty-seven jurisdictions—36 States plus the Federal Government—have the death penalty. . . . [O]nly six of those jurisdictions authorize the death penalty for rape of a child. Though our review of national consensus is not confined to tallying the number of States with applicable death penalty legislation, it is of significance that, in 45 jurisdictions, petitioner could not be executed for child rape of any kind. . . .

There are measures of consensus other than legislation. Statistics about the number of executions may inform the consideration whether capital punishment for the crime of child rape is regarded as unacceptable in our society. These statistics confirm our determination from our review of state statutes that there is a social consensus against the death penalty for the crime of child rape.

Nine States—Florida, Georgia, Louisiana, Mississippi, Montana, Oklahoma, South Carolina, Tennessee, and Texas—have permitted capital punishment for adult or child rape for some length of time between the Court's 1972 decision in *Furman* and today. Yet no individual has been executed for the rape of an adult or child since 1964, and no execution for any other nonhomicide offense has been conducted since 1963.

Louisiana is the only State since 1964 that has sentenced an individual to death for the crime of child rape; and petitioner and Richard Davis, who was convicted and sentenced to death for the aggravated rape of a 5-year-old child by a Louisiana jury in December 2007, are the only two individuals now on death row in the United States for a nonhomicide offense.

The justices' "own judgment" confirmed the conclusion that death is a constitutionally excessive punishment for raping a child.

Our decision is consistent with the justifications offered for the death penalty. *Gregg* instructs that capital punishment is excessive when it is grossly out of proportion to the crime or it does not fulfill the two distinct social purposes served by the death penalty: retribution and deterrence of capital crimes. . . .

The goal of retribution, which reflects society's and the victim's interests in seeing that the offender is repaid for the hurt he caused, does not justify the harshness of the death penalty here. In measuring retribution, as well as other objectives of criminal law, it is appropriate to distinguish between a particularly depraved murder that merits death as a form of retribution and the crime of child rape.

There is an additional reason for our conclusion that imposing the death penalty for child rape would not further retributive purposes. In considering whether retribution is served, among other factors we have looked to whether capital punishment "has the potential . . . to allow the community as a whole, including the surviving family and friends of the victim, to affirm its own judgment that the culpability of the prisoner is so serious that the ultimate penalty must be sought and imposed." *Panetti v. Quarterman,* 551 U.S. 930, 958 (2007). In considering the death penalty for nonhomicide offenses this inquiry necessarily also must include the question whether the death penalty balances the wrong to the victim.

It is not at all evident that the child rape victim's hurt is lessened when the law permits the death of the perpetrator. Capital cases require a long-term commitment by those who testify for the prosecution, especially when guilt and sentencing determinations are in multiple proceedings. In cases like this the key testimony is not just from the family but from the victim herself. During formative years of her adolescence, made all the more daunting for having to come to terms with the brutality of her experience, L.H. [the victim in this case] was required to discuss the case at length with law enforcement personnel. In a public trial she was required to recount once more all the details of the crime to a jury as the State pursued the death of her stepfather. And in the end the State made L.H. a central figure in its decision to seek the death penalty, telling the jury in closing statements: "[L.H.] is asking you, asking you to set up a time and place when he dies."

Society's desire to inflict the death penalty for child rape by enlisting the child victim to assist it over the course of years in asking for capital punishment forces a moral choice on the child, who is not of mature age to make that choice. . . .

There are, moreover, serious systemic concerns in prosecuting the crime of child rape that are relevant to the constitutionality of making it a capital offense. The problem of unreliable, induced, and even imagined child testimony means there is a "special risk of wrongful execution" in some child rape cases. *Atkins* [*v. Virginia,* 536 U.S. 304,] 321 [(2008)]. This undermines, at least to some degree, the meaningful contribution of the death penalty to legitimate goals of punishment. . . .

With respect to deterrence, if the death penalty adds to the risk of nonreporting, that, too, diminishes the penalty's objectives. Underreporting is a common problem with respect to child sexual abuse. . . . [O]ne of the most commonly cited reasons for nondisclosure is fear of negative consequences for the perpetrator, a concern that has special force where the abuser is a family member. . . . [W]hen the punishment is death, both the victim and the victim's family members may be more likely to shield the perpetrator from discovery, thus increasing underreporting. As a result, punishment by death may not result in more deterrence or more effective enforcement.

In addition, by in effect making the punishment for child rape and murder equivalent, a State that punishes child rape by death may remove a strong incentive for the rapist not to kill the victim. Assuming the offender behaves in a rational way, as one must to justify the penalty on grounds of deterrence, the penalty in some respects gives less protection, not more, to the victim, who is often the sole witness to the crime. It might be argued that, even if the death penalty results in a marginal increase in the incentive to kill, this is counterbalanced by a marginally increased deterrent to commit the crime at all. Whatever balance the legislature strikes, however, uncertainty on the point makes the argument for the penalty less compelling than for homicide crimes.

Each of these propositions, standing alone, might not establish the unconstitutionality of the death penalty for the crime of child rape. Taken in sum, however, they demonstrate the serious negative consequences of making child rape a capital offense. These considerations lead us to conclude, in our independent judgment, that the death penalty is not a proportional punishment for the rape of a child.

Justice Alito's dissent, which was joined by Chief Justice Roberts and Justices Scalia and Thomas, vigorously disputed the majority opinion's reasoning and conclusions.

I turn first to the Court's claim that there is "a national consensus" that it is never acceptable to impose the death penalty for the rape of a child. . . . In assessing current norms, the Court relies primarily on the fact that only 6 of the 50 States now have statutes that permit the death penalty for this offense. But this statistic is a highly unreliable indicator of the views of state lawmakers and their constituents. . . . [D]icta in this Court's decision in *Coker v. Georgia*, 433 U.S. 584 (1977), has stunted legislative consideration of the question whether the death penalty for the targeted offense of raping a young child is consistent with prevailing standards of decency. The *Coker* dicta gave state legislators and others good reason to fear that any law permitting the imposition of the death penalty for this crime would meet precisely the fate that has now befallen the Louisiana statute that is currently before us, and this threat strongly discouraged state legislators—regardless of their own values and those of their constituents—from supporting the enactment of such legislation. . . .

If anything can be inferred from state legislative developments, the message is very different from the one that the Court perceives. In just the past few years, despite the shadow cast by the *Coker* dicta, five States have enacted targeted capital child-rape laws. If, as the Court seems to think, our society is "evolving" toward ever higher "standards of decency," these enactments might represent the beginning of a new evolutionary line. . . .

. . . [T]he Court argues that statistics about the number of executions in rape cases support its perception of a "national consensus," but here too the statistics do not support the Court's position. The Court notes that the last execution for the rape of a child occurred in 1964, but the Court fails to mention that litigation regarding the constitutionality of the death penalty brought executions to a halt across the board in the late 1960's. . . . The Court also fails to mention that in Louisiana, since the state law was amended in 1995 to make child rape a capital offense, prosecutors have asked juries to return death verdicts in four cases. In two of those cases, Louisiana juries imposed the death penalty. This 50% record is hardly evidence that juries share the Court's view that the death penalty for the rape of a young child is unacceptable under even the most aggravated circumstances. . . .

I do not suggest that six new state laws necessarily establish a "national consensus" or even that they are sure evidence of an ineluctable trend. In terms of the Court's metaphor of moral evolution, these enactments might have turned out to be an evolutionary dead end. But they might also have been the beginning of a strong new evolutionary line. We will never know, because the Court today snuffs out the line in its incipient stage. . . .

A major theme of the Court's opinion is that permitting the death penalty in child-rape cases is not in the best interests of the victims of these crimes and society at large. In this vein, the Court suggests that it is more painful for child-rape victims to testify when the prosecution is seeking the death penalty. The Court also argues that "a State that punishes child rape by death may remove a strong incentive for the rapist not to kill the victim," and may discourage the reporting of child rape.

These policy arguments, whatever their merits, are simply not pertinent to the question whether the death penalty is "cruel and unusual" punishment. . . .

The Court's final—and, it appears, principal—justification for its holding is that murder, the only crime for which defendants have been executed since this Court's 1976 death penalty decisions, is unique in its moral depravity and in the severity of the injury that it inflicts on the victim and the public. . . .

With respect to the question of moral depravity, is it really true that every person who is convicted of capital murder and sentenced to death is more morally depraved than every child rapist? . . .

. . . I have little doubt that, in the eyes of ordinary Americans, the very worst child rapists—predators who seek out and inflict serious physical and emotional injury on defenseless young children—are the epitome of moral depravity.

With respect to the question of the harm caused by the rape of a child in relation to the harm caused by murder, it is certainly true that the loss of human life represents a unique harm, but that does not explain why other grievous harms are insufficient to permit a death sentence. And the Court does not take the position that no harm other than the loss of life is sufficient. The Court takes pains to limit its holding to "crimes against individual persons" and to exclude "offenses against the State," a category that the Court stretches—without explanation—to include "drug kingpin activity." But the Court makes no effort to explain why the harm caused by such crimes is necessarily greater than the harm caused by the rape of young children. . . .

The harm that is caused to the victims and to society at large by the worst child rapists is grave. It is the judgment of the Louisiana lawmakers and those in an increasing number of other States that these harms justify the death penalty. The Court provides no cogent explanation why this legislative judgment should be overridden. Conclusory references to "decency," "moderation," "restraint," "full progress," and "moral judgment" are not enough.

The Court's decision in *Kennedy v. Louisiana* was announced June 25, 2008. To the justices' chagrin, neither they nor the litigants had then made note of the fact that not only did six states authorize capital punishment for the rape of a child, but the Uniform Code of Military Justice did so, as well. On October 1, 2008, after this oversight was called to the justices' attention, the Court issued a brief decision modifying its original opinion and denying Louisiana's petition for rehearing.[15] Justice Scalia took advantage of these developments to issue a blistering statement, joined by Chief Justice Roberts, respecting the denial of the petition for rehearing.

Respondent has moved for rehearing of this case because there has come to light a federal statute enacted in 2006 permitting the death sentence under the Uniform Code of Military Justice for rape of a minor. See Pub. L. 109–163, § 552(b)(1), 119 Stat. 3263. This provision was not cited by either party, nor by any of the numerous *amici* in the case; it was first brought to the Court's attention after the opinion had issued, in a letter signed by 85 Members of Congress. Respondent asserts that rehearing is justified because this statute calls into question the majority opinion's conclusion that there is a national consensus against capital punishment for rape of a child.

I am voting against the petition for rehearing because the views of the American people on the death penalty for child rape were, to tell the truth, irrelevant to the majority's decision in this case. The majority opinion, after an unpersuasive attempt to show that a consensus against the penalty existed, in the end came down to this: "'[T]he Constitution contemplates that in the end our own judgment will be brought to bear on the question of the acceptability of the death penalty under the Eighth Amendment.'" Of course the Constitution contemplates no such thing; the proposed Eighth Amendment would have been laughed to scorn if it had read "no criminal penalty shall be imposed which the Supreme Court deems unacceptable." But that is what the majority opinion said, and there is no reason to believe that absence of a national consensus would provoke second thoughts.

While the new evidence of American opinion is ultimately irrelevant to the majority's decision, let there be no doubt that it utterly destroys the majority's claim to be discerning a national consensus and not just giving effect to the majority's own preference. As noted in the letter from Members of Congress, the bill providing the death penalty for child rape passed the Senate 95–0; it passed the House 374–41, with the votes of a majority of each State's delegation; and was signed by the President.

What would be gained, and what would be lost, if the Court dispensed with bringing its "own judgment . . . to bear on the question of the acceptability of the death penalty under the Eighth Amendment"? In the final analysis, who has the better of the arguments regarding the constitutionality of capital punishment for the rape of an adult (as in *Coker*) or for the rape of a child (as in *Kennedy*)? What about the ancillary policy arguments— that is, if the Eighth Amendment were interpreted to permit the death penalty for rape of an adult or a child, would it be advisable or prudent to enact authorizing legislation?

The Death Penalty for (the "Non-Trigger Person" in) Felony Murder

The Court's conclusion in *Coker v. Georgia* rested heavily on the premise that "in terms of moral depravity and of the injury to the person and to the public, [the crime of raping an adult] does not compare with murder, which does involve the unjustified taking of human life. . . . The murderer kills; the rapist, if no more than that, does not. . . . We have the abiding conviction that the death penalty, which 'is unique in its severity and irrevocability,' is an excessive penalty for the rapist who, as such, does not take human life."[16] Similarly, in *Kennedy v. Louisiana*, in rejecting capital punishment for the rape of a child, the Court emphasized, "As it relates to crimes against individuals, . . . the death penalty should not be expanded to instances where the victim's life was not taken."[17]

Do these statements imply that offenders convicted of murder, where human life has been taken, are precluded from arguing that punishment by death is constitutionally excessive? What if the offender has been found guilty of murder committed during the perpetration of a felony, where the evidence reveals that an accomplice was the "trigger person" who directly caused the victim's death? In many jurisdictions, a killing committed by one felon during the perpetration of inherently dangerous crimes such as armed robbery, rape, kidnapping, and arson, makes all of the participating co-felons guilty of murder. Murder liability typically attaches under such circumstances even for unintentional killings. Can it be argued that capital punishment is excessive for offenders found guilty under the felony murder rule when they did not personally kill the victim and evidence regarding their intent to kill is lacking?

Earl Enmund was the getaway car driver in a case arising in Florida where his two companions, Sampson and Jeanette Armstrong, entered the home of an elderly couple and shot and killed them while robbing them of valuables. Enmund remained in the car, parked some 200 yards away, while the killings took place. After the Armstrongs emerged from the victims' home they re-entered the car and fled the scene, with Enmund driving. They all were later apprehended. Enmund was indicted for first-degree murder predicated on Florida's felony-murder rule. The trial judge instructed the jury that:

> In order to sustain a conviction of first degree murder while engaging in the perpetra-
> tion . . . of the crime of robbery, the evidence must establish beyond a reasonable doubt that
> the defendant was actually present and was actively aiding and abetting the robbery . . . and
> that the unlawful killing occurred in the perpetration of . . . the robbery.[18]

The jury found Enmund guilty of first-degree murder and robbery. At the ensuing penalty hearing, the jury heard additional evidence and recommended that Enmund be sentenced to death. The trial judge accepted that recommendation and the Florida Supreme Court affirmed. The U.S. Supreme Court "granted Enmund's petition for certiorari, presenting the question whether death is a valid penalty under the Eighth and Fourteenth Amendments for one who neither took life, attempted to take life, nor intended to take life."[19] Justice White's opinion for the majority in a 5–4 ruling answered that question negatively.

Turning first to the objective prong of the proportionality analysis, Justice White noted that Florida was one of a distinct minority of jurisdictions that authorized capital punishment for felony murder absent proof that the offender personally committed the killing or intended the death of his victim. He further observed that juries typically had "rejected the death penalty in cases such as this one where the defendant did not commit the homicide, was not present when the killing took place, and did not participate in a plot or scheme to murder. . . ."[20] Among the nearly 800 offenders under sentence of death in 1981, the year before the Court's decision, available evidence suggested that only three, including Enmund, fit within that description. Then, embarking on the Court's independent analysis of the Eighth Amendment question, Justice White explained:

In *Gregg v. Georgia* the opinion announcing the judgment observed that "[t]he death penalty is said to serve two principal social purposes: retribution and deterrence of capital crimes by prospective offenders." 428 U.S. [153, 183 (1976)] (footnote omitted). Unless the death penalty when applied to those in Enmund's position measurably contributes to one or both of these goals, it "is nothing more than the purposeless and needless imposition of pain and suffering," and hence an unconstitutional punishment. *Coker v. Georgia,* 433 U.S. [584, 592 (1977)]. We are quite unconvinced, however, that the threat that the death penalty will be imposed for murder will measurably deter one who does not kill and has no intention or purpose that life will be taken. Instead, it seems likely that "capital punishment can serve as a deterrent only when murder is the result of premeditation and deliberation," *Fisher v. United States,* 328 U.S. 463, 484 (1946) (Frankfurter, J., dissenting), for if a person does not intend that life be taken or contemplate that lethal force will be employed by others, the possibility that the death penalty will be imposed for vicarious felony murder will not "enter into the cold calculus that precedes the decision to act." *Gregg v. Georgia,* 428 U.S., at 186 (footnote omitted).

It would be very different if the likelihood of a killing in the course of a robbery were so substantial that one should share the blame for the killing if he somehow participated in the felony. But competent observers have concluded that there is no basis in experience for the notion that death so frequently occurs in the course of a felony for which killing is not an essential ingredient that the death penalty should be considered as a justifiable deterrent to the felony itself. . . .

As for retribution as a justification for executing Enmund, we think this very much depends on the degree of Enmund's culpability—what Enmund's intentions, expectations, and actions were. American criminal law has long considered a defendant's intention—and therefore his moral guilt—to be critical to "the degree of [his] criminal culpability," *Mullaney v. Wilbur,* 421 U.S. 684, 698 (1975), and the Court has found criminal penalties to be unconstitutionally excessive in the absence of intentional wrongdoing. . . .

For purposes of imposing the death penalty, Enmund's criminal culpability must be limited to his participation in the robbery, and his punishment must be tailored to his personal responsibility and moral guilt. Putting Enmund to death to avenge two killings that he did not commit and had no intention of committing or causing does not measurably contribute to the retributive end of ensuring that the criminal gets his just deserts. This is the judgment of most of the legislatures that have recently addressed the matter, and we have no reason to disagree with that judgment for purposes of construing and applying the Eighth Amendment.

Justice O'Connor, joined by Chief Justice Burger and Justices Powell and Rehnquist, dissented from the holding, "not only because I believe that it is not supported by the analysis in our previous cases, but also because [it] interferes with state criteria for assessing legal guilt by recasting intent as a matter of federal constitutional law."[21] Just five years later, Justice O'Connor wrote for the majority in another 5–4 decision, carefully distinguishing the Court's ruling in *Enmund v. Florida* and upholding the constitutionality of the death penalty for a different subclass of offenders convicted of felony murder.

Tison v. Arizona, 481 U.S. 137, 107 S.Ct. 1676, 95 L.Ed.2d 127 (1987) arose in Justice O'Connor's home state, where she had been a member of the state senate and later a judge on the Arizona Court of Appeals. The case involved what Harvard Law School Professor Alan Dershowitz, who represented Ricky and Raymond Tison before the U.S. Supreme Court, called "the most publicized jailbreak, mass murder, and manhunt in Arizona history."[22] Along with their brother Donald, Ricky and Raymond Tison helped their father Gary, a convicted murderer then serving a life term sentence, escape from the Arizona State Prison. The brothers had concealed a cache of guns in an ice chest, which they smuggled into the prison. Gary Tison's cellmate, Randy Greenawalt, also a convicted murderer, escaped with the family. The five men fled by car into the desert, where two flat tires immobilized their vehicle. While the others hid, Raymond Tison flagged down a passing automobile driven by John Lyons, in which Lyons' wife, their 15-year-old niece, and their 2-year-old son were passengers. The family was quickly overpowered by the Tisons and Greenawalt, who commandeered their car and drove them deeper into the desert.[23]

Gary Tison instructed his sons to return to the roadside and get water while he and Greenawalt stood guard over the Lyons family. As the younger Tisons did so, they heard shots and turned to see their father and Greenawalt gunning down the four captives with repeated shotgun blasts. Several days later, while still on the run, the men encountered a police roadblock. Donald Tison was killed in the ensuing shootout. Gary Tison eluded capture but subsequently was found dead from exposure in the desert. Ricky and Raymond Tison and Greenawalt were taken into custody. At separate trials, the Tisons were convicted of felony-murder and each was sentenced to death (Greenawalt, who along with Gary Tison had fired the shots that killed the Lyons family, also was convicted of murder and sentenced to death).[24]

The U.S. Supreme Court granted certiorari to consider whether Ricky and Raymond Tisons' "participation in the events leading up to and following the murder of four members of a family makes the sentences of death imposed by the Arizona courts constitutionally permissible although neither petitioner specifically intended to kill the victims and neither inflicted the fatal gunshot wounds."[25] Justice O'Connor's opinion ultimately remanded the cases to the Arizona courts for further consideration, but in the process it distinguished and significantly limited the reach of the Court's ruling in *Enmund.*

Enmund explicitly dealt with two distinct subsets of all felony murders in assessing whether Enmund's sentence was disproportional under the Eighth Amendment. At one pole was Enmund himself: the minor actor in an armed robbery, not on the scene, who neither intended to kill nor was found to have had any culpable mental state. Only a small minority of States even authorized the death penalty in such circumstances and even within those jurisdictions the death penalty was almost never exacted for such a crime. The Court held that capital punishment was disproportional in these cases. *Enmund* also clearly dealt with the other polar case: the felony murderer who actually killed, attempted to kill, or intended to kill. The Court clearly held that the equally small minority of jurisdictions that limited the death penalty to these circumstances could continue to exact it in accordance with local law when the circumstances warranted. The Tison brothers' cases fall into neither of these neat categories.

Petitioners argue strenuously that they did not "intend to kill" as that concept has been generally understood in the common law. We accept this as true. Traditionally, "one intends certain consequences when he desires that his acts cause those consequences or knows that those consequences are substantially certain to result from his acts." W. LaFave & A. Scott, Criminal Law § 28, p. 196 (1972). As petitioners point out, there is no evidence that either Ricky or Raymond Tison took any act which he desired to, or was substantially certain would, cause death. . . .

On the other hand, it is equally clear that petitioners also fall outside the category of felony murderers for whom *Enmund* explicitly held the death penalty disproportional: their degree of participation in the crimes was major rather than minor, and the record would support a finding of the culpable mental state of reckless indifference to human life. . . .

Raymond Tison brought an arsenal of lethal weapons into the Arizona State Prison which he then handed over to two convicted murderers, one of whom he knew had killed a prison guard in the course of a previous escape attempt. By his own admission he was prepared to kill in furtherance of the prison break. He performed the crucial role of flagging down a passing car occupied by an innocent family whose fate was then entrusted to the known killers he had previously armed. He robbed these people at their direction and then guarded the victims at gunpoint while they considered what next to do. He stood by and watched the killing, making no effort to assist the victims before, during, or after the shooting. Instead, he chose to assist the killers in their continuing criminal endeavors, ending in a gun battle with the police in the final showdown.

Ricky Tison's behavior differs in slight details only. . . .

These facts not only indicate that the Tison brothers' participation in the crime was anything but minor; they also would clearly support a finding that they both subjectively appreciated that their acts were likely to result in the taking of innocent life. The issue raised by this case is whether the Eighth Amendment prohibits the death penalty in the intermediate case of the defendant whose participation is major and whose mental state is one of reckless indifference to the value of human life. *Enmund* does not specifically address this point. . . .

Like the *Enmund* Court, we find the state legislatures' judgment as to proportionality in these circumstances relevant to this constitutional inquiry. . . . This substantial and recent legislative authorization of the death penalty for the crime of felony murder regardless of the absence of a finding of an intent to kill powerfully suggests that our society does *not* reject the death penalty as grossly excessive under these circumstances. . . .

Against this backdrop, we now consider the proportionality of the death penalty in these midrange felony-murder cases for which the majority of American jurisdictions clearly authorize capital punishment and for which American courts have not been nearly so reluctant to impose death as they are in the case of felony murder *simpliciter*.

A critical facet of the individualized determination of culpability required in capital cases is the mental state with which the defendant commits the crime. Deeply ingrained in our legal tradition is the idea that the more purposeful is the criminal conduct, the more serious is the offense, and, therefore, the more severely it ought to be punished. . . .

A narrow focus on the question of whether or not a given defendant "intended to kill," however, is a highly unsatisfactory means of definitively distinguishing the most culpable and dangerous of murderers. Many who intend to, and do, kill are not criminally liable at all—those who act in self-defense or with other justification or excuse. Other intentional homicides, though criminal, are often felt undeserving of the death penalty—those that are the result of provocation. On the other hand, some nonintentional murderers may be among the most dangerous and inhumane of all—the person who tortures another not caring whether the victim lives or dies, or the robber who shoots someone in the course of the robbery, utterly indifferent to the fact that the desire to rob may have the unintended consequence of killing the victim as well as taking the victim's property. This reckless indifference to the value

of human life may be every bit as shocking to the moral sense as an "intent to kill." . . . [W]e hold that the reckless disregard for human life implicit in knowingly engaging in criminal activities known to carry a grave risk of death represents a highly culpable mental state, a mental state that may be taken into account in making a capital sentencing judgment when that conduct causes its natural, though also not inevitable, lethal result.

The petitioners' own personal involvement in the crimes was not minor, but rather, as specifically found by the trial court, "substantial." Far from merely sitting in a car away from the actual scene of the murders acting as the getaway driver to a robbery, each petitioner was actively involved in every element of the kidnaping-robbery and was physically present during the entire sequence of criminal activity culminating in the murder of the Lyons family and the subsequent flight. The Tisons' high level of participation in these crimes further implicates them in the resulting deaths. Accordingly, they fall well within the overlapping second intermediate position which focuses on the defendant's degree of participation in the felony.

. . . We will not attempt to precisely delineate the particular types of conduct and states of mind warranting imposition of the death penalty here. Rather, we simply hold that major participation in the felony committed, combined with reckless indifference to human life, is sufficient to satisfy the *Enmund* culpability requirement.[FN12] The Arizona courts have clearly found that the former exists; we now vacate the judgments below and remand for determination of the latter in further proceedings not inconsistent with this opinion.

FN12. Although we state these two requirements separately, they often overlap. For example, we do not doubt that there are some felonies as to which one could properly conclude that any major participant necessarily exhibits reckless indifference to the value of human life. Moreover, even in cases where the fact that the defendant was a major participant in a felony did not suffice to establish reckless indifference, that fact would still often provide significant support for such a finding.

Justice Brennan's dissenting opinion, which was joined by Justice Marshall and in relevant part by Justices Blackmun and Stevens, described the felony-murder doctrine as "a living fossil from a legal era in which all felonies were punishable by death; in those circumstances, the state of mind of the felon with respect to the murder was understandably superfluous, because he or she could be executed simply for intentionally committing the felony."[26] He continued:

[T]he basic flaw in today's decision is the Court's failure to conduct the sort of proportionality analysis that the Constitution and past cases require. Creation of a new category of culpability is not enough to distinguish this case from *Enmund*. The Court must also establish that death is a proportionate punishment for individuals in this category. In other words, the Court must demonstrate that major participation in a felony with a state of mind of reckless indifference to human life deserves the same punishment as intending to commit a murder or actually committing a murder. . . .

. . . [A]n exception to the requirement that only intentional murders be punished with death might be made for persons who actually commit an act of homicide; *Enmund*, by distinguishing from the accomplice case "those who kill," clearly reserved that question. But the constitutionality of the death penalty for those individuals is no more relevant to this case than it was to *Enmund*, because this case, like *Enmund*, involves accomplices *who did not kill*. Thus, although some of the "most culpable and dangerous of murderers" may be those who killed without specifically intending to kill, it is considerably more difficult to apply that rubric convincingly to those who not only did not intend to kill, but who also have not killed.

It is precisely in this context—where the defendant has not killed—that a finding that he or she nevertheless intended to kill seems indispensable to establishing capital culpability. It is important first to note that such a defendant has not committed an *act* for which he or she could be sentenced to death. The applicability of the death penalty therefore turns entirely on the defendant's mental state with regard to an act committed by another. Factors such as the defendant's major participation in the events surrounding the killing or the defendant's presence at the scene are relevant insofar as they illuminate the defendant's mental state with regard to the killings. They cannot serve, however, as independent grounds for imposing the death penalty.

Second, when evaluating such a defendant's mental state, a determination that the defendant acted with intent is qualitatively different from a determination that the defendant acted with reckless indifference to human life. The difference lies in the nature of the choice each has made. The reckless actor has not *chosen* to bring about the killing in the way the intentional actor has. The person who chooses to act recklessly and is indifferent to the possibility of fatal consequences often deserves serious punishment. But because that person has not chosen to kill, his or her moral and criminal culpability is of a different degree than that of one who killed or intended to kill. . . .

What makes this a difficult case is the challenge of giving substantive content to the concept of criminal culpability. Our Constitution demands that the sentencing decision itself, and not merely the procedures that produce it, respond to the reasonable goals of punishment. But the decision to execute these petitioners, . . . like other decisions to kill, appears responsive less to reason than to other, more visceral, demands. The urge to employ the felony-murder doctrine against accomplices is undoubtedly strong when the killings stir public passion and the actual murderer is beyond human grasp. And an intuition that sons and daughters must sometimes be punished for the sins of the father may be deeply rooted in our consciousness.[FN20] Yet punishment that conforms more closely to such retributive instincts than to the Eighth Amendment is tragicly [sic] anachronistic in a society governed by our Constitution.

FN20. The prophets warned Israel that theirs was "a jealous God, visiting the iniquity of the fathers upon the children unto the third and fourth generation of them that hate [Him]." Exodus, 20:5 (King James version). See, *e.g.,* Horace, Odes III, 6:1 (C. Bennett trans. 1939) ("Thy fathers' sins, O Roman, thou, though guiltless, shall expiate"); W. Shakespeare, The Merchant of Venice, Act III, scene 5, line 1 ("Yes, truly, for look you, the sins of the father are to be laid upon the children"); H. Ibsen, Ghosts (1881).

Is a convincing case made that the death penalty is justifiable for the Tisons but not for Enmund? Should the outcomes in the two cases have been the same—either that capital punishment is constitutionally permissible for both, or is permissible for neither—or were the actions and the mental states of the respective defendants sufficiently different that the different results are understandable?

Following remand of Ricky and Raymond Tisons' cases by the Supreme Court, an Arizona Superior Court judge ruled that the brothers' incriminating admissions to law enforcement authorities were obtained unlawfully and had to be suppressed from evidence. Without their statements, the prosecution was unable to establish that their participation in the murders rendered them eligible for the death penalty. Ricky Tison consequently was resentenced to consecutive terms of life imprisonment, and Raymond Tison was sentenced to life imprisonment without the possibility of parole for 50 years.[27]

Offenders Punishable by Death

The Supreme Court decisions discussed in the previous section strongly suggest that the Constitution forbids capital punishment for all interpersonal crimes (in contrast to crimes committed against the State) except aggravated murder. In this section we consider whether this necessary condition for imposing the death penalty also is sufficient. That is, are all offenders convicted of aggravated murder constitutionally eligible to be punished by death, or are some exempt from death-penalty eligibility even though they are guilty of committing heinous crimes? Our particular focus will be on juveniles and murderers who suffer from intellectual disability (mental retardation) and serious mental illness.

Juveniles

Children, even very young children, have been known to kill playmates, siblings, their parents, and strangers.[28] At common law, children younger than 14 were presumed to be incompetent, and thus immune from criminal conviction and punishment. This presumption, however, was rebuttable, allowing children as young as age 7 to be charged with and punished for crimes.[29] With criminal responsibility came the prospect of capital punishment. And young offenders sometimes were executed for their crimes, as explained by William Blackstone in his 18th-century treatise, *Commentaries on the Laws of England.*

> [U]nder fourteen, though an infant shall be *prima facie* adjudged to be *doli incapax*; yet if it appear to the court and jury, that he was *doli capax*, and could discern between good and evil, he may be convicted and suffer death. Thus a girl of thirteen has been burnt for killing her mistress: and one boy of ten, and another of nine years old, who had killed their companions, have been sentenced to death, and he of ten years actually hanged; because it appeared upon their trials, that the one hid himself, and the other hid the body he had killed; which hiding manifested a consciousness of guilt, and a discretion to discern between good and evil. And there was an instance in the last century, where a boy of eight years old was tried at Abingdon for firing two barns; and, it appearing that he had malice, revenge, and cunning, he was found guilty, condemned, and hanged accordingly. Thus also, in very modern times, a boy of ten years old was convicted on own confession of murdering his bedfellow; there appearing in his whole behavior plain tokens of a mischievous discretion: and, as the sparing this boy merely on account of his tender years might be of dangerous consequence to the public, by propagating a notion that children might commit such atrocious crimes with impunity, it was unanimously agreed by all the judges that he was a proper subject of capital punishment. But, in all such cases, the evidence of that malice, which to supply age, ought to be strong and clear beyond all doubt or contradiction.[30]

Nor has the execution of juvenile offenders been unheard of in this country's history. Records dating back to 1642, which are certainly incomplete, document at least 366 executions of offenders who committed their crimes before turning 18, including 22 executions carried out since 1985.[31] Two 19th-century executions, one in Louisiana in 1855 and one under federal authority in 1885, involved offenders who were just 10 years old at the time of their crimes.[32] Fortune Ferguson, Jr. appears to be the youngest person executed in the United States during the 20th century. A Black youth, Ferguson was convicted at age 13 of raping an 8-year-old White girl in Alachua County, Florida. He was hanged for that crime in 1927.[33] All but one of the juvenile offenders executed during the modern (post-*Furman*) era of capital punishment was 17 when he committed his crime. The lone exception was Sean Sellers, who was executed in Oklahoma in 1999 for a murder he committed at age 16.[34]

Are children who are old enough to commit crimes as serious as aggravated murder thereby old enough to be punished by death? Should a minimum age threshold be established so that all younger juveniles should categorically be ineligible for execution, or should death penalty decisions be made on a case-by-case basis depending on the individual child's maturity and the seriousness of his or her crimes? If a minimum age at time of offense is made a prerequisite to death-eligibility, where should the line be drawn: at age 7, as at common law? Or perhaps age 16, when youths in most states first qualify for a driver's license; or age 18, when voting and a number of other legal rights are first enjoyed; or perhaps 21, the legal drinking age? If a minimum age is set, should that decision be a legislative or a judicial one, and should it be based on policy considerations or an interpretation of the Constitution?

The Supreme Court first tackled such issues in 1988, in *Thompson v. Oklahoma.*[35] Along with three older perpetrators, 15-year-old William Wayne Thompson murdered his former brother-in-law—a man who had subjected Thompson's sister to repeat acts of domestic violence—and then disposed of his body in a river after weighing it down with chains and cinder blocks. Under Oklahoma law, Thompson's case could have been adjudicated in juvenile court, but following a hearing a judge ruled that Thompson should be tried as an adult. A jury convicted him of capital murder and sentenced him to death. The Oklahoma Court of Criminal Appeals affirmed his conviction and death sentence on appeal, and the U.S. Supreme Court granted certiorari "to consider whether a sentence of death is cruel and unusual punishment for a crime committed by a 15-year-old child. . . ."[36]

A fragmented Supreme Court concluded that the Eighth Amendment categorically bars capital punishment for crimes committed by offenders younger than 16. Justice Stevens' plurality opinion employed the same analytical framework used to determine whether death is an excessive or disproportional punishment for offenses other than aggravated murder. It initially considered objective indicia of societal standards of decency regarding punishing 15-year-old murderers with death. The opinion thus consulted authorizing legislation, sentencing practices, the views of professional organizations, and international law. It then invoked the justices' independent judgment, informed principally by examination of the death penalty's ability to promote retribution and deterrence when applied against such young offenders. Both analyses supported the plurality opinion's conclusion that the Eighth Amendment prohibits the capital punishment of juveniles, such as Thompson, who committed their crimes at age 15.

Justice O'Connor concurred only in the judgment. She found it decisive that in Oklahoma, as in many other states, there was no indication that the legislature had ever considered a minimum age of death-penalty eligibility. Absent such specification in the statute, she was unwilling to assume that the legislature intended to authorize the capital punishment of children younger than 16. She explained that, "[b]y leaving open for now the broader Eighth Amendment question that both the plurality and the dissent would resolve, the approach I take allows the ultimate moral issue at stake in the constitutional question to be addressed in the first instance by those best suited to do so, the people's elective representatives."[37]

Justice Kennedy did not participate in the case's consideration. Justice Scalia, joined by Chief Justice Rehnquist and Justice White, issued a lengthy dissent. He stated his core objection:

> The question . . . is whether there is a national consensus that no criminal so much as one day under 16, after individuated consideration of his circumstances, including the overcoming of a presumption that he should not be tried as an adult, can possibly be deemed mature enough to be punished with death for any crime. . . . [T]here seems to me no plausible basis for answering this . . . question in the affirmative.[38]

One year after deciding *Thompson*, the Court considered whether the death sentences imposed on 17-year-old Kevin Stanford and 16-year-old Heath Wilkins, for murders committed respectively in Kentucky and Missouri, were constitutionally excessive. The cases were decided jointly in *Stanford v. Kentucky*.[39] Another fractured ruling resulted, with five justices concluding that the offenders' youthful status presented no Eighth Amendment barrier to their execution. Justice Scalia's lead opinion was joined in full by three other members of the Court, and in part by Justice O'Connor. Four justices dissented through an opinion authored by Justice Brennan. So matters stood with respect to the constitutionality of capital punishment imposed on juvenile murderers until 2005, when the Supreme Court revisited the issue in a case from Missouri involving a death-sentenced 17-year-old murderer, *Roper v. Simmons*.[40]

Acting with a 15-year-old accomplice, Christopher Simmons, then seven months shy of his 18th birthday, entered the home of Mrs. Shirley Crook, bound Mrs. Crook, and drove her to a railroad trestle spanning a nearby river. There, the two adolescents tied her hands and feet more securely, wrapped her head in duct tape, and threw her into the water below, causing her to drown. Simmons had earlier assured his accomplice that "they could 'get away with it' because they were minors."[41] On being arrested, Simmons confessed and performed a videotaped reenactment of the crime. He was tried as an adult for first-degree murder, convicted, and sentenced to death. The Missouri Supreme Court affirmed his conviction and death sentence in 1997.[42]

In 2002, the U.S. Supreme Court ruled in *Atkins v. Virginia*[43] (a case we consider in this chapter's next section) that the Eighth Amendment forbids the execution of mentally retarded murderers. The following year, relying on the Supreme Court's reasoning in *Atkins*, the Missouri Supreme Court revisited Simmons' case and concluded that the U.S. Constitution also forbids the execution of juveniles. The state court consequently vacated Simmons' death sentence.[44] The U.S. Supreme Court granted certiorari to consider the continuing viability of *Stanford v. Kentucky* and "whether it is permissible under the Eighth and Fourteenth Amendments to the Constitution of the United States to execute a juvenile offender who was older than 15 but younger than 18 when he committed a capital crime."[45] Justice Kennedy authored the majority opinion in the Court's 5–4 decision.

As the Court explained in *Atkins*, the Eighth Amendment guarantees individuals the right not to be subjected to excessive sanctions. The right flows from the basic "'precept of justice that punishment for crime should be graduated and proportioned to [the] offense.'" 536 U.S.[304, 311 (2002)] (quoting *Weems v. United States*, 217 U.S. 349, 367 (1910)). By protecting even those convicted of heinous crimes, the Eighth Amendment reaffirms the duty of the government to respect the dignity of all persons.

The prohibition against "cruel and unusual punishments," like other expansive language in the Constitution, must be interpreted according to its text, by considering history, tradition, and precedent, and with due regard for its purpose and function in the constitutional design. To implement this framework we have established the propriety and affirmed the necessity of referring to "the evolving standards of decency that mark the progress of a maturing society" to determine which punishments are so disproportionate as to be cruel and unusual. *Trop v. Dulles*, 356 U.S. 86, 100–101 (1958) (plurality opinion). . . .

. . . [W]e now reconsider the issue decided in *Stanford*. The beginning point is a review of objective indicia of consensus, as expressed in particular by the enactments of legislatures that

have addressed the question. These data give us essential instruction. We then must determine, in the exercise of our own independent judgment, whether the death penalty is a disproportionate punishment for juveniles.

III

A

The evidence of national consensus against the death penalty for juveniles is similar, and in some respects parallel, to the evidence *Atkins* held sufficient to demonstrate a national consensus against the death penalty for the mentally retarded. When *Atkins* was decided, 30 States prohibited the death penalty for the mentally retarded. This number comprised 12 that had abandoned the death penalty altogether, and 18 that maintained it but excluded the mentally retarded from its reach. By a similar calculation in this case, 30 States prohibit the juvenile death penalty, comprising 12 that have rejected the death penalty altogether and 18 that maintain it but, by express provision or judicial interpretation, exclude juveniles from its reach. *Atkins* emphasized that even in the 20 States without formal prohibition, the practice of executing the mentally retarded was infrequent. . . . In the present case, too, even in the 20 States without a formal prohibition on executing juveniles, the practice is infrequent. Since *Stanford,* six States have executed prisoners for crimes committed as juveniles. In the past 10 years, only three have done so: Oklahoma, Texas, and Virginia. . . .

. . . Since *Stanford,* no State that previously prohibited capital punishment for juveniles has reinstated it. This fact, coupled with the trend toward abolition of the juvenile death penalty, carries special force in light of the general popularity of anticrime legislation, and in light of the particular trend in recent years toward cracking down on juvenile crime in other respects. . . .

As in *Atkins,* the objective indicia of consensus in this case—the rejection of the juvenile death penalty in the majority of States; the infrequency of its use even where it remains on the books; and the consistency in the trend toward abolition of the practice—provide sufficient evidence that today our society views juveniles, in the words *Atkins* used respecting the mentally retarded, as "categorically less culpable than the average criminal." 536 U.S., at 316.

B

A majority of States have rejected the imposition of the death penalty on juvenile offenders under 18, and we now hold this is required by the Eighth Amendment.

Because the death penalty is the most severe punishment, the Eighth Amendment applies to it with special force. Capital punishment must be limited to those offenders who commit "a narrow category of the most serious crimes" and whose extreme culpability makes them "the most deserving of execution." *Atkins,* at 319. . . .

Three general differences between juveniles under 18 and adults demonstrate that juvenile offenders cannot with reliability be classified among the worst offenders. First, as any parent knows and as the scientific and sociological studies . . . tend to confirm, "[a] lack of maturity and an underdeveloped sense of responsibility are found in youth more often than in adults and are more understandable among the young. These qualities often result in impetuous and ill-considered actions and decisions." *Johnson* [*v. Texas,* 509 U.S. 350, 367 (1993)]. . . . In recognition of the comparative immaturity and irresponsibility of juveniles, almost every State prohibits those under 18 years of age from voting, serving on juries, or marrying without parental consent.

The second area of difference is that juveniles are more vulnerable or susceptible to negative influences and outside pressures, including peer pressure. . . .

The third broad difference is that the character of a juvenile is not as well formed as that of an adult. The personality traits of juveniles are more transitory, less fixed.

These differences render suspect any conclusion that a juvenile falls among the worst offenders. The susceptibility of juveniles to immature and irresponsible behavior means "their irresponsible conduct is not as morally reprehensible as that of an adult." *Thompson, supra,* at 835 (plurality opinion). Their own vulnerability and comparative lack of control over their immediate surroundings mean juveniles have a greater claim than adults to be forgiven for failing to escape negative influences in their whole environment. The reality that juveniles still struggle to define their identity means it is less supportable to conclude that even a heinous crime committed by a juvenile is evidence of irretrievably depraved character. From a moral standpoint it would be misguided to equate the failings of a minor with those of an adult, for a greater possibility exists that a minor's character deficiencies will be reformed. . . .

Once the diminished culpability of juveniles is recognized, it is evident that the penological justifications for the death penalty apply to them with lesser force than to adults. . . . Whether viewed as an attempt to express the community's moral outrage or as an attempt to right the balance for the wrong to the victim, the case for retribution is not as strong with a minor as with an adult. Retribution is not proportional if the law's most severe penalty is imposed on one whose culpability or blameworthiness is diminished, to a substantial degree, by reason of youth and immaturity.

As for deterrence, it is unclear whether the death penalty has a significant or even measurable deterrent effect on juveniles. . . . [T]the same characteristics that render juveniles less culpable than adults suggest as well that juveniles will be less susceptible to deterrence. In particular, as the plurality observed in *Thompson*, "[t]he likelihood that the teenage offender has made the kind of cost-benefit analysis that attaches any weight to the possibility of execution is so remote as to be virtually nonexistent." 487 U.S., at 837. To the extent the juvenile death penalty might have residual deterrent effect, it is worth noting that the punishment of life imprisonment without the possibility of parole is itself a severe sanction, in particular for a young person.

In concluding that neither retribution nor deterrence provides adequate justification for imposing the death penalty on juvenile offenders, we cannot deny or overlook the brutal crimes too many juvenile offenders have committed. Certainly it can be argued, although we by no means concede the point, that a rare case might arise in which a juvenile offender has sufficient psychological maturity, and at the same time demonstrates sufficient depravity, to merit a sentence of death. . . . [P]etitioner and his *amici*. . . . assert that even assuming the truth of the observations we have made

about juveniles' diminished culpability in general, jurors nonetheless should be allowed to consider mitigating arguments related to youth on a case-by-case basis, and in some cases to impose the death penalty if justified. . . .

We disagree. The differences between juvenile and adult offenders are too marked and well understood to risk allowing a youthful person to receive the death penalty despite insufficient culpability. An unacceptable likelihood exists that the brutality or cold-blooded nature of any particular crime would overpower mitigating arguments based on youth as a matter of course, even where the juvenile offender's objective immaturity, vulnerability, and lack of true depravity should require a sentence less severe than death. In some cases a defendant's youth may even be counted against him. . . .

Drawing the line at 18 years of age is subject, of course, to the objections always raised against categorical rules. The qualities that distinguish juveniles from adults do n~~ ~~sap-pear when an individual t~~ ~~me token, some ~~ ~~l a level of matur~~ ~~h. For the reason~~ ~~line must be dr~~ ~~point where soci~~ ~~purposes between~~ ~~is, we conclude, the~~ ~~death eligibility ougl~~ ~~or

IV

Our determination that the death penalty is disproportionate punishment for offenders under 18 finds confirmation in the stark reality that the United States is the only country in the world that continues to give official sanction to the juvenile death penalty. . . .

It is proper that we acknowledge the overwhelming weight of international opinion against the juvenile death penalty, resting in large part on the understanding that the instability and emotional imbalance of young people may often be a factor in the crime. The opinion of the world community, while not controlling our outcome, does provide respected and significant confirmation for our own conclusions. . . .

The Eighth and Fourteenth Amendments forbid imposition of the death penalty on offenders who were under the age of 18 when their crimes were committed. The judgment of the Missouri Supreme Court setting aside the sentence of death imposed upon Christopher Simmons is affirmed.

Justice O'Connor issued a dissenting opinion, in which she reasoned, in part:

[T]he rule decreed by the Court rests, ultimately, on its independent moral judgment that death is a disproportionately severe punishment for any 17-year-old offender. I do not subscribe to this judgment. Adolescents *as a class* are undoubtedly less mature, and therefore less culpable for their misconduct, than adults. But the Court has adduced no evidence impeaching the seemingly reasonable conclusion reached by many state legislatures: that at least *some* 17-year-old murderers are sufficiently mature to deserve the death penalty in an appropriate case. Nor has it been shown that capital sentencing juries are incapable of accurately assessing a youthful defendant's maturity or of giving due weight to the mitigating characteristics associated with youth.

. . . I would not substitute our judgment about the moral propriety of capital punishment for 17-year-old murderers for the judgments of the Nation's legislatures. Rather, I would demand a clearer showing that our society truly has set its face against this practice before reading the Eighth Amendment categorically to forbid it. . . .

Justice Scalia also dissented, in an opinion joined by Chief Justice Rehnquist and Justice Thomas.

The Court reaches [its] implausible result by purporting to advert, not to the original meaning of the Eighth Amendment, but to "the evolving standards of decency," of our national society. It then finds, on the flimsiest of grounds, that a national consensus which could not be perceived in our people's laws barely 15 years ago now solidly exists. Worse still, the Court says in so many words that what our people's laws say about the issue does not, in the last analysis, matter: "[I]n the end our own judgment will be brought to bear on the question of the acceptability of the death penalty under the Eighth Amendment." The Court thus proclaims itself sole arbiter of our Nation's moral standards—and in the course of discharging that awesome responsibility purports to take guidance from the views of foreign courts and legislatures. Because I do not believe that the meaning of our Eighth Amendment, any more than the meaning of other provisions of our Constitution, should be determined by the subjective views of five Members of this Court and like-minded foreigners, I dissent.

I

In determining that capital punishment of offenders who committed murder before age 18 is "cruel and unusual" under the Eighth Amendment, the Court first considers, in accordance with our modern (though in my view mistaken) jurisprudence, whether there is a "national consensus" that laws allowing such executions contravene our modern "standards of decency." We have held that this determination should be based on "objective indicia that reflect the public attitude toward a given sanction"—namely, "statutes passed by society's elected representatives." *Stanford v. Kentucky,* 492 U.S. 361, 370 (1989). As in *Atkins v. Virginia,* 536 U.S. 304, 312 (2002), the Court dutifully recites this test and claims halfheartedly that a national consensus has emerged since our decision in *Stanford,* because 18 States—or 47% of States that permit capital punishment—now have legislation prohibiting the execution of offenders under 18, and because all of 4 States have adopted such legislation since *Stanford.*

Words have no meaning if the views of less than 50% of death penalty States can constitute a national consensus. . . .

The Court's reliance on the infrequency of executions for under–18 murderers, credits an argument that this Court considered and explicitly rejected in *Stanford.* That infrequency is explained, we accurately said, both by "the undisputed fact that a far smaller percentage of capital crimes are committed by persons under 18 than over 18," and by the fact that juries are required at sentencing to consider the

offender's youth as a mitigating factor. Thus, "it is not only possible, but overwhelmingly probable, that the very considerations which induce [respondent] and [his] supporters to believe that death should *never* be imposed on offenders under 18 cause prosecutors and juries to believe that it should *rarely* be imposed." *Stanford,* at 374. . . .

II

Of course, the real force driving today's decision is . . . the Court's "own judgment" that murderers younger than 18 can never be as morally culpable as older counterparts. . . . If the Eighth Amendment set forth an ordinary rule of law, it would indeed be the role of this Court to say what the law is. But the Court having pronounced that the Eighth Amendment is an ever-changing reflection of "the evolving standards of decency" of our society, it makes no sense for the Justices then to *prescribe* those standards rather than discern them from the practices of our people. On the evolving-standards hypothesis, the only legitimate function of this Court is to identify a moral consensus of the American people. By what conceivable warrant can nine lawyers presume to be the authoritative conscience of the Nation?

The reason for insistence on legislative primacy is obvious and fundamental: "'[I]n a democratic society legislatures, not courts, are constituted to respond to the will and consequently the moral values of the people.'" *Gregg v. Georgia,* 428 U.S. 153, 175–176 (1976) (quoting *Furman v. Georgia,* 408 U.S. 238, 383 (1972) (Burger, C.J., dissenting)). For a similar reason we have, in our determination of society's moral standards, consulted the practices of sentencing juries: Juries "'maintain a link

181

between contemporary community values and the penal system'" that this Court cannot claim for itself. *Gregg*, at 181 (quoting *Witherspoon v. Illinois*, 391 U.S. 510, 519, n. 15 (1968)). . . .

That "almost every State prohibits those under 18 years of age from voting, serving on juries, or marrying without parental consent," is patently irrelevant—and is yet another resurrection of an argument that this Court gave a decent burial in *Stanford*. . . . As we explained in *Stanford*, 492 U.S., at 374, it is "absurd to think that one must be mature enough to drive carefully, to drink responsibly, or to vote intelligently, in order to be mature enough to understand that murdering another human being is profoundly wrong, and to conform one's conduct to that most minimal of all civilized standards." Serving on a jury or entering into marriage also involve decisions far more sophisticated than the simple decision not to take another's life.

Moreover, the age statutes the Court lists "set the appropriate ages for the operation of a system that makes its determinations in gross, and that does not conduct individualized maturity tests." *Ibid.* The criminal justice system, by contrast, provides for individualized consideration of each defendant. In capital cases, this Court requires the sentencer to make an individualized determination, which includes weighing aggravating factors and mitigating factors, such as youth. . . .

The Court's contention that the goals of retribution and deterrence are not served by executing murderers under 18 is also transparently false. The argument that "[r]etribution is not proportional if the law's most severe penalty is imposed on one whose culpability or blameworthiness is diminished," is simply an extension of the earlier, false generalization that youth *always* defeats culpability. The Court claims that "juveniles will be less susceptible to deterrence," because "'[t]he likelihood that the teenage offender has made the kind of cost-benefit analysis that attaches any weight to the possibility of execution is so remote as to be virtually nonexistent.'" The Court unsurprisingly finds no support for this astounding proposition, save its own case law. . . .

III

Though the views of our own citizens are essentially irrelevant to the Court's decision today, the views of other countries and the so-called international community take center stage. . . .

. . . [T]he basic premise of the Court's argument—that American law should conform to the laws of the rest of the world—ought to be rejected out of hand.

If you were a legislator, how would you vote on a bill that proposed excluding juveniles younger than 18 who commit murder from death-penalty eligibility?

If you were a member of the Supreme Court, how would you vote in deciding whether the Constitution exempts juveniles younger than 18 who commit murder from death-penalty eligibility?

How would your reasoning differ in these different capacities?

If an offender's youthful age arguably is relevant to his or her suitability for the death penalty, which is the preferred way of taking it into account: drawing a bright line at a certain age (such as 18) so that all who are younger automatically are excluded from death-eligibility—the "categorical" approach—or, instead, allowing youth to be considered as one of several factors in the punishment decision on an individualized basis—the "case-by-case" approach? Do adolescents undergo such a magical transformation on the morning of their 18th birthdays that they awaken with a qualitatively different measure of maturity, experience, and sophistication compared to when they went to sleep the night before as 17-year-olds? This question arose in various forms during the oral argument of *Roper v. Simmons*. The first exchange reprinted below occurred between James Layton, the attorney representing Missouri, and Justice Scalia. The second exchange involved Mr. Layton and Justice Stevens.

Mr. Layton: . . . There is no study in anything that Mr. Simmons cites that . . . that justifies that particular day, 18.

They talk about adolescence.

They talk about young adolescence, old adolescence.

They talk about adolescence continuing until the mid-20's.

Nothing justifies the age of 18.

That makes it the kind of fact that a legislature ought to be evaluating, not a court.

Justice Scalia: Does adolescence as a scientific term . . . does it always occur on the same day for . . . for all individuals?

Mr. Layton: No. The . . . the studies point out that adolescence is . . . well, they don't agree on what adolescence means, and they don't . . . and they point out that it begins and ends on different times for different people.

Justice Stevens: Of course, one . . . one of the objections in . . . in *Atkins* was we needed a bright line test.

We'd have difficulty determining which ones are mentally retarded.

Here we don't have that problem at all.

I guess everybody knows whether or not the defendant is over or under 18.

Mr. Layton:—Well, if that's the bright line.

We don't know whether they're mature or immature, and we have to measure that somehow.

Justice Stevens: But the . . . but the purpose of a bright line test is to avoid litigation over the borderline cases, and you just have completely avoided that in this category.

Mr. Layton: Because the . . . having a bright line test means that the individual who murders at age 17, 364 days is treated differently than a more . . . a less mature individual who is 2 days older.

Justice Stevens: But it's an equally arbitrary line if it's 16, 17, or 15.

Mr. Layton: Yes, it is, and it's an arbitrary line that the legislatures have set because it's a legislative type determination based on . . . legislative facts.[46]

On the other hand, if youth is but one consideration in the capital sentencing process, is there a risk that other factors, such as the heinous nature of the crime, might be so dominant as to result in children being sentenced to death who, because of their immaturity, should not be classified among the worst of the worst offenders? Which type of error should be considered the more serious: to exclude some young offenders from death-eligibility even though their maturity is on par with that of adults, or to allow some children who lack a full measure of responsibility and culpability to suffer execution?[47]

Intellectually Disabled (Mentally Retarded) Offenders

Believing that the term "mentally retarded" had acquired a somewhat negative or stigmatizing connotation, the former American Association on Mental Retardation (AAMR) recently changed its name to the American Association on Intellectual and Developmental Disabilities (AAIDD) and endorsed using "intellectually disabled" as the preferred descriptive term.[48] When the broad contours of the debate relevant to capital punishment unfolded, mental health professionals, litigators, legislation, and court decisions consistently referred to "mental retardation," and hence that term's usage preponderates in this section. The central issue is whether, owing to their intellectual deficiencies and compromised behavioral adaptations, mentally retarded murderers should be exempt from suffering the ultimate punishment of death. Important ancillary questions include how mental retardation should be defined and what procedures should be used to determine whether offenders in individual cases fit within that classification.

As we have seen, the Supreme Court's 2005 ruling in *Roper v. Simmons*[49] that the Eighth Amendment prohibits the capital punishment of offenders younger than age 18 relied heavily on its decision three years earlier in *Atkins v. Virginia*,[50] which exempted mentally retarded offenders from death-penalty eligibility. And just as *Roper v. Simmons* repudiated the Court's 1989 decision in *Stanford v. Kentucky*[51] (which held that juveniles as young as 16 are constitutionally eligible for execution), *Atkins v. Virginia* overruled *Penry v. Lynaugh*,[52] a 1989 decision concluding that the Constitution is not offended by the capital punishment of mentally retarded offenders. Both sets of cases are a testament to the Court linking its interpretation of the Eighth Amendment's cruel and unusual punishments clause to society's continuously evolving "standards of decency," and to the justices' growing skepticism that capital punishment serves retributive or deterrence objectives when applied to exceptionally young and intellectually disabled offenders.

Although the Supreme Court's rulings regarding the death penalty for juveniles and mentally retarded offenders parallel one another in many respects, they differ in important particulars. One significant difference concerns how the respective classes of offenders are identified. Age is easily measured and documented. In contrast, what does it mean to be "mentally retarded"? Who should determine whether an individual is mentally retarded: a psychiatrist or psychologist? A trial judge? A jury? What procedures should govern this inquiry? Should the prosecution or the defense have the burden of persuasion when mental retardation is at issue? Substantively, what difference should it make if an individual who commits murder is mentally retarded in deciding whether he can or should be sentenced to death? Should legislatures be entitled to resolve this question as a matter of policy, or is the answer to be found through judicial interpretation of the Constitution?

In August 1996, 18-year-old Daryl Atkins and his 26-year-old companion William Jones abducted Eric Nesbitt, an airman in the U.S. Air Force, as Nesbitt made a withdrawal from an automatic teller machine in Hampton, Virginia. Holding Nesbitt at gunpoint, they took control of his truck and drove to an isolated spot in nearby York County, where Nesbitt's bullet-ridden body later was found. Atkins and Jones subsequently were arrested and charged with abduction, robbery, and murder. Each accused the other of firing the shots that killed Nesbitt. Jones pled guilty to murder in exchange for the prosecution's agreement not to seek the death penalty and testified against Atkins at the latter's capital murder trial. The jury found Atkins guilty, setting the stage for the trial's penalty phase.[53]

At the penalty hearing, the defense presented the testimony of a forensic psychologist, Dr. Evan Nelson, whose evaluation of Atkins included the results of a standard intelligence test indicating that Atkins' IQ was 59. Dr. Nelson concluded that Atkins was "mildly mentally retarded," a classification normally reserved for individuals whose IQ levels range between 50–55 and 70.[54] Mental retardation customarily is not determined simply by reference to IQ score. The following definition was used by the AAMR at the time of Atkins' trial:

> *Mental retardation* refers to substantial limitations in present functioning. It is characterized by significantly subaverage intellectual functioning, existing concurrently with related limitations in two or more of the following applicable adaptive skill areas: communication, self-care, home living, social skills, community use, self-direction, health and safety, functional academics, leisure, and work. Mental retardation manifests before age 18.[55]

A prosecution expert, Dr. Stanton Samenow, disagreed with Dr. Nelson's evaluation, and through rebuttal testimony offered the opinion that Atkins possessed at least average intelligence.[56] After considering the expert opinions and other evidence, the jury sentenced Atkins to death. Atkins' conviction and death sentence were affirmed on appeal to the Virginia Supreme Court. The U.S. Supreme Court granted certiorari "to revisit the issue that we first addressed in . . . *Penry* [*v. Lynaugh*, 492 U.S. 302 (1989)],"[57] *i.e.*, whether the capital punishment of mentally retarded offenders violates the Eighth Amendment's prohibition against cruel and unusual punishments. Explaining that "[m]uch has changed"[58] since *Penry* was decided, Justice Stevens' majority opinion in a 6–3 ruling answered that question affirmatively.

In 1989, when the Court considered the issue in *Penry*, only Georgia and Maryland among death-penalty states, and the federal government, exempted mentally retarded offenders from capital punishment through legislation. In contrast, when Atkins' case reached the justices in 2002, a total of 18 states had enacted statutory exclusions. The *Atkins* majority concluded:

It is not so much the number of these States that is significant, but the consistency of the direction of change. . . . And it appears that even among those States that regularly execute offenders and that have no prohibition with regard to the mentally retarded, only five have executed offenders possessing a known IQ less than 70 since we decided *Penry*. The practice, therefore, has become truly unusual, and it is fair to say that a national consensus has developed against it.[59]

Justice Stevens' opinion continued:

This consensus unquestionably reflects widespread judgment about the relative culpability of mentally retarded offenders, and the relationship between mental retardation and the penological purposes served by the death penalty. Additionally, it suggests that some characteristics of mental retardation undermine the strength of the procedural protections that our capital jurisprudence steadfastly guards.

. . . Mentally retarded persons frequently know the difference between right and wrong and are competent to stand trial. Because of their impairments, however, by definition they have diminished capacities to understand and process information, to communicate, to abstract from mistakes and learn from experience, to engage in logical reasoning, to control impulses, and to understand the reactions of others. There is no evidence that they are more likely to engage in criminal conduct than others, but there is abundant evidence that they often act on impulse rather than pursuant to a premeditated plan, and that in group settings they are followers rather than leaders. Their deficiencies do not warrant an exemption from criminal sanctions, but they do diminish their personal culpability.

In light of these deficiencies, our death penalty jurisprudence provides two reasons consistent with the legislative consensus that the mentally retarded should be categorically excluded from execution. First, there is a serious question as to whether either justification that we have recognized as a basis for the death penalty [retribution and deterrence] applies to mentally retarded offenders. . . .

With respect to retribution—the interest in seeing that the offender gets his "just deserts"—the severity of the appropriate punishment necessarily depends on the culpability of the offender. Since *Gregg*, our jurisprudence has consistently confined the imposition of the death penalty to a narrow category of the most serious crimes. . . . If the culpability of the average murderer is insufficient to justify the most extreme sanction available to the State, the lesser culpability of the mentally retarded offender surely does not merit that form of retribution. Thus, pursuant to our narrowing jurisprudence, which seeks to ensure that only the most deserving of execution are put to death, an exclusion for the mentally retarded is appropriate.

With respect to deterrence—the interest in preventing capital crimes by prospective offenders—"it seems likely that 'capital punishment can serve as a deterrent only when murder is the result of premeditation and deliberation,'" *Enmund* [*v. Florida*, 458 U.S. 782, 799 (1982)]. Exempting the mentally retarded from that punishment will not affect the "cold calculus that precedes the decision" of other potential murderers. *Gregg*, 428 U.S., at 186. Indeed, that sort of calculus is at the opposite end of the spectrum from behavior of mentally retarded offenders. The theory of deterrence in capital sentencing is predicated upon the notion that the increased severity of the punishment will inhibit criminal actors from carrying out murderous conduct. Yet it is the same cognitive and behavioral impairments that make these defendants less morally culpable—for example, the diminished ability to understand and process information, to learn from experience, to engage in logical reasoning, or to control impulses—that also make it less likely that they can process the information of the possibility of execution as a penalty and, as a result, control their conduct based upon that information. Nor will exempting the mentally retarded from execution lessen the deterrent effect of the death penalty with respect to offenders who are not mentally retarded. Such individuals are unprotected by the exemption and will continue to face the threat of execution. Thus, executing the mentally retarded will not measurably further the goal of deterrence.

The reduced capacity of mentally retarded offenders provides a second justification for a categorical rule making such offenders ineligible for the death penalty. The risk "that the death penalty will be imposed in spite of factors which may call for a less severe penalty," *Lockett v. Ohio,* 438 U.S. 586, 605 (1978), is enhanced, not only by the possibility of false confessions, but also by the lesser ability of mentally retarded defendants to make a persuasive showing of mitigation in the face of prosecutorial evidence of one or more aggravating factors. Mentally retarded defendants may be less able to give meaningful assistance to their counsel and are typically poor witnesses, and their demeanor may create an unwarranted impression of lack of remorse for their crimes. . . . [M]oreover, reliance on mental retardation as a mitigating factor can be a two-edged sword that may enhance the likelihood that the aggravating factor of future dangerousness will be found by the jury. Mentally retarded defendants in the aggregate face a special risk of wrongful execution.

Our independent evaluation of the issue reveals no reason to disagree with the judgment of "the legislatures that have recently addressed the matter" and concluded that death is not a suitable punishment for a mentally retarded criminal. We are not persuaded that the execution of mentally retarded criminals will measurably advance the deterrent or the retributive purpose of the death penalty. Construing and applying the Eighth Amendment in the light of our "evolving standards of decency," we therefore conclude that such punishment is excessive and that the Constitution "places a substantive restriction on the State's power to take the life" of a mentally retarded offender. *Ford* [*v. Wainwright,* 477 U.S. 399, 405 (1986)].

The judgment of the Virginia Supreme Court is reversed and the case is remanded for further proceedings not inconsistent with this opinion.

Chief Justice Rehnquist and Justices Scalia and Thomas dissented. The Chief Justice observed, in part:

The question presented by this case is whether a national consensus deprives Virginia of the constitutional power to impose the death penalty on capital murder defendants like petitioner, *i.e.,* those defendants who indisputably are competent to stand trial, aware of the punishment they are about to suffer and why, and whose mental retardation has been found an insufficiently compelling reason to lessen their individual responsibility for the crime. The Court pronounces the punishment cruel and unusual primarily because 18 States recently have passed laws limiting the death eligibility of certain defendants based on mental retardation alone, despite the fact that the laws of 19 other States besides Virginia continue to leave the question of proper punishment to the individuated consideration of sentencing judges or juries familiar with the particular offender and his or her crime.

. . . [T]he Court's assessment of the current legislative judgment regarding the execution of defendants like petitioner more resembles a *post hoc* rationalization for the majority's subjectively preferred result rather than any objective effort to ascertain the content of an evolving standard of decency.

Justice Scalia's dissent agreed with the Chief Justice's contention, and added additional objections.

Beyond the empty talk of a "national consensus," the Court gives us a brief glimpse of what really underlies today's decision: pretension to a power confined *neither* by the moral sentiments originally enshrined in the Eighth Amendment (its original meaning) *nor even* by the current moral sentiments of the American people. "'[T]he Constitution,' the Court says, 'contemplates that in the end *our own judgment* will be brought to bear on the question of the acceptability of the death penalty under the Eighth Amendment.'" . . . The arrogance of this assumption of power takes one's breath away. . . .

The genuinely operative portion of the opinion . . . is the Court's statement of the reasons why it agrees with the contrived consensus it has found, that the "diminished capacities" of the mentally retarded render the death penalty excessive. The Court's analysis rests on two fundamental assumptions: (1) that the Eighth Amendment prohibits excessive punishments, and (2) that sentencing juries or judges are unable to account properly for the "diminished capacities" of the retarded. The first assumption is wrong . . . The second assumption—inability

of judges or juries to take proper account of mental retardation—is not only unsubstantiated, but contradicts the immemorial belief . . . that they play an *indispensable* role in such matters. . . .

Proceeding from these faulty assumptions, the Court gives two reasons why the death penalty is an excessive punishment for all mentally retarded offenders. First, the "diminished capacities" of the mentally retarded raise a "serious question" whether their execution contributes to the "social purposes" of the death penalty, viz., retribution and deterrence. (The Court conveniently ignores a third "social purpose" of the death penalty—"incapacitation of dangerous criminals and the consequent prevention of crimes that they may otherwise commit in the future," *Gregg v. Georgia,* 428 U.S. 153, 183, n. 28 (1976) (joint opinion of Stewart, Powell, and Stevens, JJ.). But never mind; its discussion of even the other two does not bear analysis.) Retribution is not advanced, the argument goes, because the mentally retarded are *no more culpable* than the average murderer, whom we have already held lacks sufficient culpability to warrant the death penalty. Who says so? Is there an established correlation between mental acuity and the ability to conform one's conduct to the law in such a rudimentary matter as murder? Are the mentally retarded really more disposed (and hence more likely) to commit willfully cruel and serious crime than others? In my experience, the opposite is true: being childlike generally suggests innocence rather than brutality.

Assuming, however, that there is a direct connection between diminished intelligence and the inability to refrain from murder, what scientific analysis can possibly show that a mildly retarded individual who commits an exquisite torture-killing is "no more culpable" than the "average" murderer in a holdup-gone-wrong or a domestic dispute? Or a moderately retarded individual who commits a series of 20 exquisite torture-killings? Surely culpability, and deservedness of the most severe retribution, depends not merely (if at all) upon the mental capacity of the criminal (above the level where he is able to distinguish right from wrong) but also upon the depravity of the crime—which is precisely why this sort of question has traditionally been thought answerable not by a categorical rule of the sort the Court today imposes upon all trials, but rather by the sentencer's weighing of the circumstances (both degree of retardation and depravity of crime) in the particular case. The fact that juries continue to sentence mentally retarded offenders to death for extreme crimes shows that society's moral outrage sometimes demands execution of retarded offenders. By what principle of law, science, or logic can the Court pronounce that this is wrong? There is none. Once the Court admits (as it does) that mental retardation does not render the offender morally *blameless*, there is no basis for saying that the death penalty is *never* appropriate retribution, no matter *how* heinous the crime.

As long as a mentally retarded offender knows "the difference between right and wrong," only the sentencer can assess whether his retardation reduces his culpability enough to exempt him from the death penalty for the particular murder in question.

As for the other social purpose of the death penalty that the Court discusses, deterrence: That is not advanced, the Court tells us, because the mentally retarded are "less likely" than their non-retarded counterparts to "process the information of the possibility of execution as a penalty and . . . control their conduct based upon that information." . . . But surely the deterrent effect of a penalty is adequately vindicated if it successfully deters many, but not all, of the target class. . . . In other words, the supposed fact that *some* retarded criminals cannot fully appreciate the death penalty has nothing to do with the deterrence rationale, but is simply an echo of the arguments denying a retribution rationale. . . .

The Court throws one last factor into its grab bag of reasons why execution of the retarded is "excessive" in all cases: Mentally retarded offenders "face a special risk of wrongful execution" because they are less able "to make a persuasive showing of mitigation," "to give meaningful assistance to their counsel," and to be effective witnesses. "Special risk" is pretty flabby language (even flabbier than "less likely")—and I suppose a similar "special risk" could be said to exist for just plain stupid people, inarticulate people, even ugly people. If this unsupported claim has any substance to it (which I doubt), it might support a due process claim in all criminal prosecutions of the mentally retarded; but it is hard to see how it has anything to do with an *Eighth Amendment* claim that execution of the mentally retarded is cruel and unusual. We have never before held it to be cruel and unusual punishment to impose a sentence in violation of some *other* constitutional imperative.

Daryl Atkins' victory in the Supreme Court was short-lived. Following the remand of his case "for further proceedings not inconsistent with this opinion," a new hearing was ordered to resolve whether Atkins in fact was mentally retarded and hence ineligible for execution. A jury was convened in 2005 to make this determination in the Virginia trial court where Atkins originally was convicted and sentenced to death. New evidence was presented, including that Atkins' IQ was measured as high as 74 and 76 on tests administered in 2004. In addition, the prosecution's expert witness testified that Atkins "knew that Lincoln was president during the Civil War, that Michelangelo painted the Sistine chapel, that there were twelve months in a year, and that Rome was the capital of Italy. Atkins could associate Einstein with the theory of relativity and was only slightly inaccurate in identifying 3.15 as Pi. He correctly used sophisticated words, like 'déjà vu'. . . ."[60] The jury concluded that the defense had failed to demonstrate by a preponderance of the evidence that Atkins was mentally retarded. The trial judge thus reinstated the originally imposed death sentence and set an execution date.[61]

However, finding that errors had occurred at the hearing on Atkins' mental retardation, the Virginia Supreme Court vacated the judgment on appeal and ordered that yet another sentencing hearing be conducted. Atkins avoided execution when an unrelated issue surfaced in the new round of litigation, involving the prosecution's failure to disclose evidence that could have materially affected the jury's sentencing verdict. Atkins ultimately was resentenced to life imprisonment.[62]

The controversy surrounding whether Atkins qualified for the very exemption that was established, in principle, in his own case before the Supreme Court is not unusual. In the first place, the justices had pointedly declined to define "mental retardation," leaving that task to the states.

To the extent there is serious disagreement about the execution of mentally retarded offenders, it is in determining which offenders are in fact retarded. In this case, for instance, the Commonwealth of Virginia disputes that Atkins suffers from mental retardation. Not all people who claim to be mentally retarded will be so impaired as to fall within the range of mentally retarded offenders about whom there is a national consensus. As was our approach in *Ford v. Wainwright*, 477 U.S. 399 (1986), with regard to insanity, "we leave to the State[s] the task of developing appropriate ways to enforce the constitutional restriction upon [their] execution of sentences." *Id.*, at 405.[63]

In an accompanying footnote, the opinion explained that "the statutory definitions of mental retardation are not identical but generally conform to the clinical definitions"[64] used by the American Association on Mental Retardation[65] and the American Psychiatric Association.[66]

Once mental retardation is defined, it still must be decided whether a particular defendant does or does not merit that classification. As in Atkins' case, expert opinions can be expected to differ. Diagnostic tests designed to measure and detect "subaverage intellectual functioning" can be imprecise, inconsistent, and often lend themselves to different interpretation. The repeat administration of intelligence tests tends to produce artificially inflated scores, as does a phenomenon known as "the Flynn effect," which occurs when a dated IQ test is administered to a subject and the results are compared to norms from an earlier day rather than contemporary ones.[67] The uncertainties and accompanying room for disagreement are compounded because mental retardation traditionally is not defined exclusively in terms of significantly subaverage intelligence. It typically requires additional demonstrated deficits in "adaptive skill areas," embracing such vague constructs as conceptual, practical, and social adaptive skills.[68]

A Florida statute exempts "intellectually disabled" offenders from death-penalty eligibility as follows:

> As used in this section, the term "intellectually disabled" or "intellectual disability" means significantly subaverage general intellectual functioning existing concurrently with deficits in adaptive behavior and manifested during the period from conception to age 18. The term "significantly subaverage general intellectual functioning," for the purpose of this section, means performance that is two or more standard deviations from the mean score on a standardized intelligence test specified in the rules of the Agency for Persons with Disabilities. The term "adaptive behavior," for the purpose of this definition, means the effectiveness or degree with which an individual meets the standards of personal independence and social responsibility expected of his or her age, cultural group, and community. The Agency for Persons with Disabilities shall adopt rules to specify the standardized intelligence tests as provided in this subsection.[69]

The Florida Supreme Court has construed the statutory requirement that "significantly subaverage general intellectual functioning" be demonstrated by "performance that is two or more standard deviations from the mean score on a standardized intelligence test" to mean that only defendants who score 70 or lower on an IQ test can qualify. It has rejected claims that imposing a flat cut-off score at 70 is arbitrary and risks erroneously subjecting offenders to the death penalty who truly are intellectually disabled but score slightly higher on standardized IQ tests.[70] In October 2013, the U.S. Supreme Court granted certiorari in *Hall v. Florida*[71] to consider whether this strict definition of intellectual disability is constitutionally permissible. The defendant's IQ in *Hall* was variously measured as 71, 73, and 80 on standardized intelligence tests. He had been sentenced to death following his conviction for capital murder prior to the

Supreme Court's decision in *Atkins*. Although in 1991 the judge who sentenced Hall to death concluded that he was mentally retarded—then considered only a mitigating factor—the same judge in 2010, in reliance on the fact that Hall had scored above 70 on the administered IQ tests, rejected Hall's claim that he was intellectually disabled and hence ineligible for execution under *Atkins*.[72]

In addition to not offering a precise definition of mental retardation in *Atkins*, the Supreme Court did not specify what procedures must be used to determine whether a capital murder defendant is mentally retarded. The murky nature of this essentially factual issue underscores the significance of the procedures chosen for its determination. Jurisdictions differ in such important particulars as when the issue of the defendant's mental retardation should be litigated (prior to trial? prior to or as a part of penalty phase hearings if the defendant is found guilty?); who makes the determination (judge or jury?); who bears the burden of persuasion (defendant or prosecution?); and how weighty that burden is (preponderance of the evidence? clear and convincing evidence? beyond a reasonable doubt?).[73]

For instance, Georgia is alone among death-penalty jurisdictions in requiring a murder defendant to prove beyond a reasonable doubt that he is mentally retarded and thus must be excluded from death-penalty eligibility. A state trial judge found that Warren Hill, who was convicted of capital murder in 1991, had established his mental retardation by a preponderance of the evidence but that he did not meet the higher "proof beyond a reasonable doubt" standard. He consequently qualified for execution under Georgia law. Hill came within an hour of being executed in February 2013, when he won a stay upon alleging that three mental health experts who earlier had testified for the prosecution had reconsidered their diagnoses and presently were of the opinion that Hill was mentally retarded. The 11th Circuit Court of Appeals ruled (2–1) in April 2013 that Hill was procedurally barred from presenting this new evidence, again paving the way for his execution.[74] Hill subsequently requested the U.S. Supreme Court to intervene. His execution later was stayed by a state court judge pending resolution of litigation focusing on the drugs used for carrying out executions by lethal injection in Georgia.[75]

In light of the definitional, evidentiary, and procedural complexities, does a categorical ban on executing "mentally retarded" offenders appear to be a sound approach? Is it preferable to the position advocated by Justice Scalia, under which the sentencing authority would determine whether the offender should be punished by death or imprisonment after "weighing . . . the circumstances (both degree of retardation and depravity of crime) in the particular case"? What advantages might there be in adopting such a case-by-case approach? What drawbacks might there be?

A Note About Severely Mentally Ill Offenders

The Supreme Court's exclusion of juvenile and mentally retarded offenders from death-penalty eligibility—based in part on their compromised culpability (relevant to retribution) and their impulsivity and diminished capacity for rational planning (relevant to deterrence)—has led some to question whether offenders who suffer from serious mental illness likewise should be categorically exempt from execution.[76] Several professional organizations, including the American Bar Association, the American Psychiatric Association, the American Psychological Association, the National Alliance for the Mentally Ill, and the National Mental Health Association, have urged that severely mentally ill individuals who are convicted of murder should be excluded from the reach of capital punishment.[77] The constitutional grounding for such an exemption is questionable because, unlike trends regarding the capital punishment of juveniles and mentally retarded individuals, the "objective" prong of the Eighth Amendment analysis—which relies heavily on legislation and sentencing practices—provides little evidence that executing seriously mentally ill offenders violates contemporary societal standards of decency.[78] Several lower courts have declined to recognize a constitutional basis for excluding severely mental ill murderers from death-penalty eligibility.[79] In addition, "mental illness," a nebulous concept in itself, can wax and wane, in contrast to the stable traits of age and mental retardation.

Nevertheless, it can be argued that individuals whose conduct—even conduct as serious as homicide—springs not solely or primarily from a venal character or unfettered volition, but in part is rooted in severe mental illness, should not be considered fully blameworthy and hence should not be subject to capital punishment. This argument may be especially salient because (as the justices reasoned in *Atkins v. Virginia* with respect to mentally retarded individuals) mentally ill offenders may be at heightened risk of execution if jurors perceive in their demeanor a lack of remorse or consider mental illness to be an aggravating factor associated with future dangerousness rather than a mitigating consideration.[80]

In 2004, a Task Force formed by the American Bar Association Section of Individual Rights and Responsibilities adopted the following proposal:

> Defendants should not be executed or sentenced to death if, at the time of the offense, they had a severe mental disorder or disability that significantly impaired their capacity (a) to appreciate the nature, consequences, or wrongfulness of their conduct; (b) to exercise rational judgment in relation to conduct; or (c) to conform their conduct to the requirements of the law. A disorder manifested primarily by repeated criminal conduct or attributable solely to the acute effects of voluntary use of alcohol or other drugs does not, standing alone, constitute a mental disorder or disability for purposes of this provision.[81]

A bill introduced in the North Carolina General Assembly during its 2013 session included a similar proposal, although the measure was not enacted into law.[82] If called upon as a legislator, how would you have voted on such a bill?

Conclusion

At some point, it seems likely that everyone would agree that capital punishment, society's ultimate penalty, would be excessive if applied to certain offenses (for example, jaywalking) and some offenders (perhaps a 7-year-old child who shoots and kills a playmate with her father's gun), and consequently should never be available or imposed. As more serious crimes (such as rape and felony murder) and offenders (such as adolescents and intellectually impaired or mentally ill individuals) who arguably are more fully responsible than very young children are considered, it becomes increasingly important to be able to articulate precisely why categorical exclusions from death-penalty eligibility may be appropriate, and who (legislatures or the courts) should have the authority to recognize them. The divided views of Supreme Court justices on these issues should not be surprising. Their search for controlling principles pursuant to the Eighth Amendment's prohibition against cruel and unusual punishments has produced widespread disagreement, not only about the analytical framework to be employed, but also about how the identified governing premises should be applied to individual case decisions.

At a lower level of abstraction, even if it is agreed that certain crimes and offenders should be exempt from capital punishment, identifying them through the trial process presents challenges. For example, in the context of felony murder, what does it mean for an offender who does not actually kill the victim to be a "major participant" in the felony, or to act "with reckless indifference to human life"? And what is the meaning of "mental retardation" and how is that condition to be diagnosed and proven in a specific case?

At bottom, what does it mean to be "sufficiently culpable" or "fully blameworthy" so that the death penalty is appropriate retribution? What qualities determine whether a prospective offender might plausibly be deterred by the threat of capital punishment? How can society's "evolving standards of decency" be ascertained and applied to help answer these issues of death-penalty eligibility?

Is it any wonder that these questions defy easy resolution?

Endnotes

1. Adam J. Hirsch, *The Rise of the Penitentiary* 11–12, 55–68 (New Haven, CT: Yale University Press 1992).
2. James R. Acker & Charles S. Lanier, "Beyond Human Ability? The Rise and Fall of Death Penalty Legislation," in James R. Acker, Robert M. Bohm & Charles S. Lanier (eds.), *America's Experiment With Capital Punishment: Reflections on the Past, Present, and Future of the Ultimate Penal Sanction* 85, 89 (Durham, NC: Carolina Academic Press, 2d ed. 2003); David J. Rothman, *The Discovery of the Asylum: Social Order and Disorder in the New Republic* 48–56 (Boston: Little, Brown and Company 1971).
3. John D. Bessler, *Cruel & Unusual: The American Death Penalty and the Founders' Eighth Amendment* 79–91 (Boston: Northeastern University Press 2012); Edwin R. Keedy, "History of the Pennsylvania Statute Creating Degrees of Murder," 97 *University of Pennsylvania Law Review* 759 (1949); Matthew A. Pauley, "Murder by Premeditation," 36 *American Criminal Law Review* 427, 431–432 (1999).
4. *Furman v. Georgia*, 408 U.S. 238 (1972).
5. United States Bureau of Justice, *Sourcebook of Criminal Justice Statistics—1977*, 706–707, Table 6.101 (Washington, D.C.: U.S. Government Printing Office 1978).

6. Hugo A. Bedau, "Offenses Punishable by Death," in Hugo Adam Bedau (ed.), *The Death Penalty in America* 39, 46 (Garden City, NY: Anchor Books, rev. ed. 1967).

7. *Gregg v. Georgia,* 428 U.S. 153 (1976); *Proffitt v. Florida,* 428 U.S. 242 (1976); *Jurek v. Texas,* 428 U.S. 262 (1976); *Woodson v. North Carolina,* 428 U.S. 280 (1976); *Roberts v. Louisiana,* 428 U.S. 325 (1976).

8. *Gregg v. Georgia,* 428 U.S. 153, 187 & n. 35 (1976) (opinion of Stewart, Powell, and Stevens, J.J.).

9. United States Supreme Court, transcript of oral argument, *Coker v. Georgia,* retrieved May 23, 2013 from www.oyez.org/cases/1970-1979/1976/1976_75_5444.

10. Jeffrey J. Pokorak, "Rape as a Badge of Slavery: The Legal History of, and Remedies for, Prosecutorial Race-of-Victim Charging Discrepancies," 7 *Nevada Law Journal* 1, 31 (2006); Marvin E. Wolfgang & Marc Reidel, "Trends in the Use of Capital Punishment," 284 *Annals of the American Academy of Political and Social Science* 119, 123 (1973).

11. Dennis D. Dorin, "Two Different Worlds: Criminologists, Justices and Racial Discrimination in the Imposition of Capital Punishment in Rape Cases," 72 *Journal of Criminal Law & Criminology* 1667, 1669 (1981); Wofgang & Reidel, *supra* note 10.

12. *Kennedy v. Louisiana,* 554 U.S. 407, 413 (2008).

13. *Id.,* 554, U.S., at 437.

14. *Id.*

15. *Kennedy v. Louisiana,* 554 U.S. 945 (2008).

16. *Coker v. Georgia,* 433 U.S. 584, 598 (1977) (plurality opinion) (citation omitted).

17. *Kennedy v. Louisiana,* 554 U.S. 407, 437 (2008).

18. *Enmund v. Florida,* 458 U.S. 782, 785 (1982).

19. *Id.,* 458 U.S., at 787.

20. *Id.,* 458 U.S., at 795.

21. *Id.,* 458 U.S., at 801–802 (O'Connor, J., dissenting).

22. Alan M. Dershowitz, *The Best Defense* 290 (New York: Vintage Books 1983).

23. *Tison v. Arizona,* 481 U.S. 137, 139–140 (1987).

24. *Id.,* 481 U.S., at 141–143; Dershowitz, *supra* note 22, at 295–305.

25. *Tison v. Arizona,* 481 U.S. 137, 138 (1987).

26. *Id.,* 481 U.S., at 159 (Brennan, J., dissenting).

27. David McCord, "State Death Sentencing for Felony Murder Accomplices Under the *Enmund* and *Tison* Standards," 32 *Arizona State Law Journal* 843, 874 & nn. 166–168 (2000).

28. Kathleen M. Heide, *Young Killers: The Challenge of Juvenile Homicide* (Thousand Oaks, CA: Sage Publications 1999). *See generally Miller v. Alabama,* 132 S.Ct. 2455, 2479 n. 1 (2012) (Roberts, C.J., dissenting); *id.,* 132 S.Ct. at 2489 n. 1 (Alito, J., dissenting).

29. Andrew M. Carter, "Age Matters: The Case for a Constitutionalized Infancy Defense," 54 *University of Kansas Law Review* 687, 710 (2006).

30. William Blackstone, 4 *Commentaries on the Laws of England* *23-*24 (1765–1769), retrieved May 28, 2013 from http://avalon.law.yale.edu/18th_century/blackstone_bk4ch2.asp.

31. Victor L. Streib, *The Juvenile Death Penalty Today: Death Sentences and Executions for Juvenile Crimes, January 1, 1973-February 28, 2005,* p. 3 (issue #77, Oct. 7, 2005), retrieved May 28, 2013 from www.deathpenaltyinfo.org/documents/StreibJuvDP2005.pdf.

32. Victor L. Streib, *Death Penalty for Juveniles* 57 (Bloomington, IN: Indiana University Press 1987). James Arcene, a Native American who was executed by federal authorities for a murder and robbery he committed with an adult accomplice when he was 10, eluded apprehension for several years and was 23 years old when hanged. *Id.,* at 82–83.

33. *Id.,* at 93–94.

34. Streib, *supra* note 31, at 4–5.

35. 487 U.S. 815, 108 S.Ct. 2687, 101 L.Ed.2d 702 (1988).

36. *Id.*, 487 U.S., at 820.
37. *Id.*, 487 U.S., at 858–859 (O'Connor, J., concurring in the judgment).
38. *Id.*, 487 U.S., at 859 (Scalia, J., dissenting).
39. 492 U.S. 361, 109 S.Ct. 2969, 106 L.Ed.2d 306 (1989).
40. 543 U.S. 551, 125 S.Ct. 1183, 161 L.Ed.2d 1 (2005).
41. *Id.*, 543 U.S., at 556.
42. *State v. Simmons*, 944 S.W.2d 165 (Mo.) (en banc), *cert. denied*, 522 U.S. 953 (1997).
43. 536 U.S. 304, 122 S.Ct. 2242, 153 L.Ed.2d 335 (2002).
44. *Simmons v. Roper*, 112 S.W.3d 397 (Mo. 2003) (en banc).
45. *Roper v. Simmons*, 543 U.S. 551, 555–556 (2005).
46. Transcript of oral argument, *Roper v. Simmons*, retrieved May 30, 2013 from www.oyez.org/cases/2000–2009/2004/2004_03_633.
47. *See generally*, Joseph L. Hoffmann, "On the Perils of Line-Drawing: Juveniles and the Death Penalty," 40 *Hastings Law Journal* 229 (1989).
48. John H. Blume, Sheri Lynn Johnson & Christopher Seeds, "Mental Retardation and the Death Penalty Five Years After *Atkins*," in Charles S. Lanier, William J. Bowers & James R. Acker (eds.), *The Future of America's Death Penalty: An Agenda for the Next Generation of Capital Punishment Research* 241, 241 n. 1 (Durham, NC: Carolina Academic Press 2009).
49. 543 U.S. 551 (2005).
50. 536 U.S. 304 (2002).
51. 492 U.S. 361 (1989).
52. 492 U.S. 302 (1989).
53. *Atkins v. Virginia*, 536 U.S. 304, 307–308 (2002); Thomas G. Walker, *Eligible for Execution: The Story of the Daryl Atkins Case* 2–12, 37–43, 101–125 (Washington, DC: CQ Press 2009).
54. *Atkins v. Virginia*, 536 U.S. 304, 308–309 & n. 3 (2002).
55. *Id.*, 536 U.S., at 308 n. 3, *quoting* American Association on Mental Retardation, *Mental Retardation: Definition, Classification, and Systems of Supports* 5 (9th ed. 1992).
56. Dr. Samenow's testimony was offered at the second penalty-phase hearing in Atkins' case, which was conducted after the Virginia Supreme Court set aside the death sentence imposed at the original trial and ordered that a new penalty hearing take place. *Id.*, 536 U.S., at 309.
57. *Id.*, 536 U.S., at 310.
58. *Id.*, 536 U.S., at 314.
59. *Id.*, 536 U.S., at 315–316 (footnotes omitted).
60. Walker, *supra* note 53, at 255.
61. *Id.*, at 244–258.
62. *Id.*, at 258–278; *In re Commonwealth of Virginia*, 677 S.E.2d 236 (Va. 2009).
63. *Atkins v. Virginia*, 536 U.S. 304, 317 (2002) (footnote omitted).
64. *Id.*, 536 U.S., at 317 n. 22.
65. See text accompanying note 55, *supra*.
66. "The essential feature of Mental Retardation is significantly subaverage general intellectual functioning (Criterion A) that is accompanied by significant limitations in adaptive functioning in at least two of the following skill areas: communication, self-care, home living, social/interpersonal skills, use of community resources, self-direction, functional academic skills, work, leisure, health, and safety (Criterion B). The onset must occur before age 18 years (Criterion C). Mental Retardation has many different etiologies and may be seen as a final common pathway of various pathological processes that affect the functioning of the central nervous system." American Psychiatric Association, *Diagnostic and Statistical Manual of Mental Disorders* 41 (4th ed. 2000), *quoted in Atkins v. Virginia*, 536 U.S. 304, 308 n. 3 (2002).
67. Blume, Johnson & Seeds, *supra* note 48, at 243–246.
68. *Id.* at 246–249.
69. Florida Stat. Ann. § 921.137 (1) (2012).

70. *See Franqui v. State*, 59 So.3d 82 (Fla. 2011); *Nixon v. State*, 2 So.3d 137 (Fla. 2009); *Cherry v. State*, 959 So.2d 702 (Fla. 2007).

71. ___ S.Ct. ___, 2013 WL 3153535 (2013).

72. *Hall v. State*, 109 So.3d 704 (Fla. 2012).

73. *See* Blume, Johnson & Seeds, *supra* note 48, at 251–253; Carol S. Steiker & Jordan M. Steiker, "*Atkins v. Virginia*: Lessons From Substance and Procedure in the Constitutional Regulation of Capital Punishment," 57 *DePaul Law Review* 721 (2008); Peggy M. Tobolowsky, "*Atkins*' Aftermath: Identifying Mentally Retarded Offenders and Excluding Them From Execution," 30 *Journal of Legislation* 77 (2003).

74. *In re Hill*, 715 F.3d 284 (11th Cir. 2013). *See also Hill v. Humphrey*, 662 F.3d 1335 (11th Cir. 2011) (en banc), *cert. denied*, 132 S.Ct. 2727 (2012). *See generally* Nathaniel Koslov, "Insurmountable Hill: How Undue AEDPA Deference Has Undermined the *Atkins* Ban on Executing the Intellectually Disabled," 54 *Boston College Law Review E-Supplement* 189 (2013); Recent Case, "Federal Habeas Corpus—Death Penalty—Eleventh Circuit Rejects Challenge to Georgia's 'Beyond a Reasonable Doubt' Standard for Defendants' Mental Retardation Claims—*Hill v. Humphrey*, 662 F.3d 1335 (11th Cir. 2011) (en banc)," 125 *Harvard Law Review* 2185 (2012).

75. Death Penalty Information Center, "Intellectual Disability and the Death Penalty, Updates: The Case of Warren Hill in Georgia," retrieved August 15, 2013 from www.deathpenalty info.org/intellectual-disability-and-death-penalty.

76. *See* Christopher Slobogin, "Mental Disorder as an Exemption From the Death Penalty: The ABA-IRR Task Force Recommendations," 54 *Catholic University Law Review* 1133, 1139–41 (2005). *See generally* Jean Mattimoe, "The Death Penalty and the Mentally Ill: A Selected and Annotated Bibliography," 5 *the crit: a Critical Studies Journal* 1 (Summer 2012).

77. Ronald J. Tabak, "Overview of Task Force Proposal on Mental Disability and the Death Penalty," 54 *Catholic University Law Review* 1123 (2005).

78. *See* Pamela A. Wilkins, "Rethinking Categorical Prohibitions on Capital Punishment: How the Current Test Fails Mentally Ill Offenders and What to Do About It," 40 *University of Memphis Law Review* 423 (2009).

79. *See* Lyn Entzeroth, "The Challenge and Dilemma of Charting a Course to Constitutionally Protect the Severely Mentally Ill Capital Defendant From the Death Penalty," 44 *Akron Law Review* 529, 571–572 & nn. 217–221 (2011) (collecting cases).

80. *See* Bruce J. Winick, "The Supreme Court's Evolving Death Penalty Jurisprudence: Severe Mental Illness as the Next Frontier," 50 *Boston College Law Review* 785 (2009); Tabak, *supra* note 77, at 1128–29.

81. "Recommendations of the American Bar Association Section of Individual Rights and Responsibilities Task Force on Mental Disability and the Death Penalty," 54 *Catholic University Law Review* 1115, § 2 (2005).

82. General Assembly of North Carolina, House Bill 722 (2013), retrieved June 1, 2013 from http://ncleg.net/Sessions/2013/Bills/House/PDF/H722v0.pdf.

6

THE NEW DEATH-PENALTY LAWS IN APPLICATION

RACE DISCRIMINATION AND ARBITRARINESS

Introduction

The post-*Furman* era of capital punishment was introduced with the Supreme Court's approval of legislation that promised to harness sentencing discretion and hence minimize, if not eliminate, the attendant arbitrariness—invidious discrimination, freakishness, irregularity—that various justices had perceived as tainting the administration of the earlier death-penalty laws. The Court upheld the new "guided discretion" capital-sentencing statutes in 1976, shortly after their enactment. Having scant opportunity to examine actual sentencing practices under the revised laws, the justices' focus was confined almost exclusively to the text of the statutes. Yet the written laws revealed little more than how the novel sentencing procedures were *designed* to operate. It remained to be seen whether the "laws in practice," *i.e.*, how the capital-sentencing statutes actually were applied in the jurisdictions that had adopted them, conformed to the Court's expectations concerning the "laws on the books."

The ensuing years offered researchers, policymakers, and the justices the opportunity to gather and evaluate evidence pertaining to the new death-penalty laws' administration. This chapter investigates the extent to which modern era statutes appear to have succeeded in expunging racial discrimination from capital sentencing systems. It also briefly considers evidence regarding other potential sources of arbitrariness in capital case decisions, including gender-based and geographical disparities. Chapter 7 examines the performance of two sets of actors within criminal justice systems whose roles are vital to death-penalty statutes' fair administration: defense attorneys and trial jurors.

Race Discrimination

The death penalty in the United States historically has been intertwined with the nation's ignoble legacy of racial discrimination. Capital punishment was employed by Whites in several states as a harsh mechanism for repressing slaves in antebellum America. It was used to similar effect in Southern states that enacted "Black Codes" during the Reconstruction era—laws that reserved capital punishment for select crimes committed exclusively by the newly freed former slaves.[1] When the Fourteenth Amendment was ratified to guarantee all persons within states "the equal protection of the laws," thus prohibiting overt legal discrimination, racial prejudices were not so readily eliminated. Summary trials and executions of Blacks for crimes committed against Whites—real or imagined—were barren of all but the façade of due process and amounted to little more than legal lynching.[2] As we saw in chapter 5, evidence of race discrimination in the death penalty's application persisted deep into the pre-*Furman* 20th century, during which statistics revealed the wildly disproportionate use of capital punishment against Black men convicted of raping White women.[3] Indeed, the primary reason motivating the National Association for the Advancement of Colored People (NAACP) Legal Defense Fund (LDF) to mount its legal assault against capital punishment in the 1960s was the long-standing connection between the death penalty and race discrimination.[4]

Justice Douglas's opinion in *Furman* argued that laws allowing juries unfettered sentencing discretion, although neutral as written, unleashed systematic discrimination in the death penalty's use against Blacks, among other vulnerable groups.[5] Although the sufficiency of the evidence in support of this claim was disputed by some other members of the Court,[6] it was difficult to quarrel with his fundamental premise:

> A law that stated that anyone making more than $50,000 would be exempt from the death penalty would plainly fail, as would a law that in terms said that blacks, those who never went beyond the fifth grade in school, those who made less than $3,000 a year, or those who were unpopular or unstable should be the only people executed. A law which in the overall view reaches the same result in practice has no more sanctity than a law which in terms provides the same.[7]

In the years following the Court's approval of the post-*Furman* guided discretion capital-sentencing statutes in *Gregg v. Georgia*[8] and companion cases,[9] as the nation's death row populations swelled, researchers began to evaluate whether the revised laws—neutral on their faces and replete with checks on arbitrariness deemed satisfactory to withstand constitutional challenge as written—appeared to have purged the death penalty of the vestiges of racial discrimination in application. Studies conducted in several states during the first decade of the new laws' operation were not encouraging. Findings were regularly reported of persistent racial disparities in capital sentencing practices under the revised capital-sentencing statutes.[10]

The most comprehensive study was completed in Georgia, the very state whose death-penalty laws were at issue in both *Furman* and *Gregg*. The study, which centered on the operation of Georgia's post-*Furman* capital-punishment statute, was completed by University of Iowa College of Law Professor David Baldus and his colleagues. The results of the "the Baldus study," as it became known, would give rise to yet another landmark ruling, the Supreme Court's 1987 decision in *McCleskey v. Kemp*.[11]

The Baldus study identified nearly 2,500 criminal homicides committed in Georgia between 1973 (the first full year the state's post-*Furman* death-penalty law was effective) and 1979. As a preliminary step to explore possible racial disparities in the death-penalty law's application, the researchers simply compared the relative frequency with which Black and White defendants in murder cases were sentenced to death. Contrary to what might have been predicted, it appeared that White offenders were somewhat more likely than Black offenders to receive a death sentence: roughly "4% of the black defendants received the death penalty, as opposed to 7% of the white defendants."[12] However, further inspection of the cases revealed glaring death-sentencing discrepancies based on the race of homicide *victims*. "[D]efendants charged with killing white persons received the death penalty in 11% of the cases, but defendants charged with killing blacks received the death penalty in only 1% of the cases."[13]

> Baldus also divided the cases according to the combination of the race of the defendant and the race of the victim. He found that the death penalty was assessed in 22% of the cases involving black defendants and white victims; 8% of the cases involving white defendants and white victims; 1% of the cases involving black defendants and black victims; and 3% of the cases involving white defendants and black victims.[14]

These results were certainly suggestive of race-of-victim discrimination. White-victim cases appeared to be dealt with considerably more harshly than Black-victim cases. Moreover, Black defendants who killed White victims were especially likely to be sentenced to death. As pronounced as the different death-sentencing rates were in the various offender-victim categories, this level of analysis was far too simplistic to support the conclusion that race, and race alone, was the explanation. Too many factors other than race—for example, whether the offender had a serious prior record, whether a killing qualified as capital murder and, if so, what specific aggravating circumstance(s) were involved, whether a public defender or privately retained counsel represented the offender, among numerous other possibilities—could help account for the discrepancies.

The researchers thus made detailed examination of more than 1,000 of the homicides, including all death-penalty cases, a sample of the murder cases that ended with life prison sentences, and a sample of voluntary manslaughter cases. They combed court records to collect information on 230 different variables from the cases to develop comprehensive descriptions of how the offense was committed, offenders' characteristics, and processing details, such as whether the defendant pled guilty or was convicted following a trial, whether defense counsel was court-appointed or retained, and other relevant factors. They then used statistical techniques in an attempt to isolate the specific case characteristics that influenced capital charging and sentencing decisions. Race of victim remained a powerful factor. In otherwise similar cases, the odds of a defendant being sentenced to death were 4.3 times higher if a White victim was killed than if the victim was Black.[15] The study allowed the magnitude of the race-of-victim effect to be compared to other case factors. For example:

> A defendant's chances of receiving a death sentence increased by a factor of 4.3 if the victim is white, but only by 2.3 if the defendant was the prime mover behind the homicide.

A prior record of conviction for murder, armed robbery, rape, or kidnaping with bodily injury increases the chances of a defendant's receiving a death sentence by a factor of 4.9.[16]

Warren McCleskey, who was Black, was convicted of capital murder and sentenced to death in Fulton County (Atlanta), Georgia, in 1978. His victim was a White police officer, Frank Schlatt. The officer was shot and killed while responding to an armed robbery in an Atlanta furniture store. McCleskey admitted participating in the robbery with three other men but denied being the shooter. Prosecution evidence supported the claim that he was. McCleskey argued that the Baldus study demonstrated that race impermissibly tainted the administration of the death penalty under Georgia's post-*Furman* law, particularly in cases such as his, involving Black defendants and White victims. He challenged his death sentence in the U.S. Supreme Court in reliance on the Fourteenth Amendment's Equal Protection Clause and the Eighth Amendment's prohibition against cruel and unusual punishments. The justices rejected his claims, by vote of 5–4.

Justice Powell's majority opinion was willing to "assume the [Baldus] study is valid statistically. . . ."[17] The opinion elaborated:

> Our assumption that the Baldus study is statistically valid does not include the assumption that the study shows that racial considerations actually enter into any sentencing decisions in Georgia. Even a sophisticated multiple-regression analysis such as the Baldus study can only demonstrate a *risk* that the factor of race entered into some capital sentencing decisions and a necessarily lesser risk that race entered into any particular sentencing decision.[18]

The opinion concluded that McCleskey's reliance on the results of the Baldus study to support a claim that his equal protection rights had been violated was fundamentally flawed. The reasoning was straightforward. The study was based on an analysis of criminal homicides committed and brought to trial in counties throughout the state, involving scores of prosecutors and hundreds of juries over a six-year period. As such, the findings revealed nothing in particular about McCleskey's own trial and death sentence.

> Our analysis begins with the basic principle that a defendant who alleges an equal protection violation has the burden of proving "the existence of purposeful discrimination." *Whitus v. Georgia*, 385 U.S. 545, 550 (1967). . . . Thus, to prevail under the Equal Protection Clause, McCleskey must prove that the decisionmakers in *his* case acted with discriminatory purpose. He offers no evidence specific to his own case that would support an inference that racial considerations played a part in his sentence.[19]

In other contexts, such as employment and jury discrimination, broad-based statistical disparities in practices involving different racial groups have been deemed sufficient to create a *prima facie* case that purposeful discrimination is at work. Once the party alleging unlawful treatment establishes a *prima facie* case of purposeful discrimination, the burden shifts to the challenged party to come forward with legitimate, race-neutral reasons to explain the disparities and why an adverse decision was made in the case being litigated. Such a policy seems fair because otherwise, short of securing an admission, it would be virtually impossible for an individual to demonstrate that intentional racial discrimination motivated a decision in his or her case. The Court in *McCleskey* nevertheless was unwilling to apply this analysis, which would have required Georgia to account for the dramatic race-of-victim differences in capital sentencing revealed by the Baldus study. Justice Powell's opinion reasoned that decisions made in the death-penalty context are the product of too many diverse "entities" and considerations to allow the statewide pattern of racial disparities in capital sentencing outcomes to support an inference of purposeful discrimination in McCleskey's own case.

> [T]he nature of the capital sentencing decision, and the relationship of the statistics to that decision, are fundamentally different from the corresponding elements in [jury pool and employment discrimination] cases. Most importantly, each particular decision to impose the death penalty is made by a petit jury selected from a properly constituted venire. Each jury is unique in its composition, and the Constitution requires that its decision rest on consideration of innumerable factors that vary according to the characteristics of the individual defendant and the facts of the particular capital offense. Thus, the application of an inference drawn from the general statistics to a specific decision in a trial and sentencing simply is not comparable to the application of an inference drawn from general statistics to a specific [jury pool or employment discrimination] case. In those cases, the statistics relate to fewer entities, and fewer variables are relevant to the challenged decisions.[20]

Legitimate reasons clearly existed to support a death sentence in McCleskey's case: he was found guilty of murdering a police officer during an armed robbery. Discretion could lawfully be exercised to produce such a sentence, and "[b]ecause discretion is essential to the criminal justice process, we would demand exceptionally clear proof before we would infer that the discretion has been abused."[21] Nor was the fact that the state legislature presumably had knowledge of the racially disparate capital sentencing patterns and had allowed its death penalty law to remain in effect following enactment sufficient to demonstrate an equal protection violation. Having knowledge about an outcome is different from intending it, or acting with a purpose to accomplish it.

> For this claim to prevail, McCleskey would have to prove that the Georgia Legislature enacted or maintained the death penalty statute *because of* an anticipated racially discriminatory effect. In *Gregg v. Georgia,* this Court found that the Georgia capital sentencing system could operate in a fair and neutral manner. There was no evidence then, and there is none now, that the Georgia Legislature enacted the capital punishment statute to further a racially discriminatory purpose.[22]

The majority opinion was not any more receptive to the Eighth Amendment basis of McCleskey's challenge. The justices had relied on the Eighth Amendment to invalidate Georgia's death-penalty law in *Furman,* concluding that unfettered sentencing discretion created an unacceptable risk of arbitrariness in the law's administration. McCleskey maintained that even if the Baldus study could not show that race had influenced the sentencing decision in his own case, the researchers' carefully conducted statistical analyses demonstrated not only a risk, but the very existence of arbitrariness—in the pernicious guise of the influence of race—in the administration of the state's death-penalty law.

To evaluate McCleskey's challenge, we must examine exactly what the Baldus study may show. Even Professor Baldus does not contend that his statistics *prove* that race enters into any capital sentencing decisions or that race was a factor in McCleskey's particular case. Statistics at most may show only a likelihood that a particular factor entered into some decisions. There is, of course, some risk of racial prejudice influencing a jury's decision in a criminal case. There are similar risks that other kinds of prejudice will influence other criminal trials. The question "is at what point that risk becomes constitutionally unacceptable," *Turner v. Murray*, 476 U.S. 28, 36, n. 8 (1986). McCleskey asks us to accept the likelihood allegedly shown by the Baldus study as the constitutional measure of an unacceptable risk of racial prejudice influencing capital sentencing decisions. This we decline to do.

Because of the risk that the factor of race may enter the criminal justice process, we have engaged in "unceasing efforts" to eradicate racial prejudice from our criminal justice system. *Batson v. Kentucky*, 476 U.S. 79, 85 (1986). Our efforts have been guided by our recognition that "the inestimable privilege of trial by jury . . . is a vital principle, underlying the whole administration of criminal justice," *Ex parte Milligan*, 4 Wall. 2, 123 (1866). . . .

. . . The capital sentencing decision requires the individual jurors to focus their collective judgment on the unique characteristics of a particular criminal defendant. It is not surprising that such collective judgments often are difficult to explain. But the inherent lack of predictability of jury decisions does not justify their condemnation. On the contrary, it is the jury's function to make the difficult and uniquely human judgments that defy codification and that "buil[d] discretion, equity, and flexibility into a legal system." H. Kalven & H. Zeisel, The American Jury 498 (1966).

McCleskey's argument that the Constitution condemns the discretion allowed decisionmakers in the Georgia capital sentencing system is antithetical to the fundamental role of discretion in our criminal justice system. Discretion in the criminal justice system offers substantial benefits to the criminal defendant. Not only can a jury decline to impose the death sentence, it can decline to convict or choose to convict of a lesser offense. Whereas decisions against a defendant's interest may be reversed by the trial judge or on appeal, these discretionary exercises of leniency are final and unreviewable. Similarly, the capacity of prosecutorial discretion to provide individualized justice is "firmly entrenched in American law." 2 W. LaFave & D. Israel, Criminal Procedure § 13.2(a), p. 160 (1984). . . . [A] prosecutor can decline to charge, offer a plea bargain, or decline to seek a death sentence in any particular case. Of course, "the power to be lenient [also] is the power to discriminate," K. Davis, Discretionary Justice 170 (1973), but a capital punishment system that did not allow for discretionary acts of leniency "would be totally alien to our notions of criminal justice." *Gregg v. Georgia,* 428 U.S., at 200, n. 50.

At most, the Baldus study indicates a discrepancy that appears to correlate with race. Apparent disparities in sentencing are an inevitable part of our criminal justice system. The discrepancy indicated by the Baldus study is "a far cry from the major systemic defects identified in *Furman,*" *Pulley v. Harris,* 465 U.S. [37, 54 (1984)]. As this Court has recognized, any mode for determining guilt or punishment "has its weaknesses and the potential for misuse." *Singer v. United States,* 380 U.S. 24, 35 (1965). . . . Despite these imperfections, our consistent rule has been that constitutional guarantees are met when "the mode [for determining guilt or punishment] itself has been surrounded with safeguards to make it as fair as possible." *Singer v. United States,* 380 U.S., at 35. Where the discretion that is fundamental to our criminal process is involved, we decline to assume that what is unexplained is invidious. In light of the safeguards designed to minimize racial bias in the process, the fundamental value of jury trial in our criminal justice system, and the benefits that discretion provides to criminal defendants, we hold that the Baldus study does not demonstrate a constitutionally significant risk of racial bias affecting the Georgia capital sentencing process. . . .

Two additional concerns inform our decision in this case. First, McCleskey's claim, taken to its logical conclusion, throws into serious question the principles that underlie our entire criminal justice system. The Eighth Amendment is not limited in application to capital punishment, but applies to all penalties. Thus, if we accepted McCleskey's claim that racial bias has impermissibly tainted the capital sentencing decision, we could soon be faced with similar claims as to other types of penalty. Moreover, the claim that his sentence rests on the irrelevant factor of race easily could be extended to apply to claims based on unexplained discrepancies that correlate to membership in other minority groups, and even to gender. Similarly, since McCleskey's claim relates to the race of his victim, other claims could apply with equally logical force to statistical disparities that correlate with the race or sex of other actors in the criminal justice system, such as defense attorneys, or judges. Also, there is no logical reason that such a claim need be limited to racial or sexual bias. If arbitrary and capricious punishment is the touchstone under the Eighth Amendment, such a claim could—at least in theory—be based upon any arbitrary variable, such as the defendant's facial characteristics, or the physical attractiveness of the defendant or the victim, that some statistical study indicates may be influential in jury decisionmaking. As these examples illustrate, there is no limiting principle to the type of challenge brought by McCleskey. The Constitution does not require that a State eliminate any demonstrable disparity that correlates with a potentially irrelevant factor in order to operate a criminal justice system that includes capital punishment. As we have stated specifically in the context of capital punishment, the Constitution does not "plac[e] totally unrealistic conditions on its use." *Gregg v. Georgia,* 428 U.S., at 199, n. 50.

Second, McCleskey's arguments are best presented to the legislative bodies. It is not the responsibility—or indeed even the right—of this Court to determine the appropriate punishment for particular crimes. It is the legislatures, the elected representatives of the people, that are "constituted to respond to the will and consequently the moral values of the people." *Furman v. Georgia,* 408 U.S., at 383 (Burger,

C.J., dissenting). Legislatures also are better qualified to weigh and "evaluate the results of statistical studies in terms of their own local conditions and with a flexibility of approach that is not available to the courts," *Gregg v. Georgia*, 428 U.S., at 186. Capital punishment is now the law in more than two-thirds of our States. It is the ultimate duty of courts to determine on a case-by-case basis whether these laws are applied consistently with the Constitution. Despite McCleskey's wide-ranging arguments that basically challenge the validity of capital punishment in our multiracial society, the only question before us is whether in his case, the law of Georgia was properly applied. We agree with the District Court and the Court of Appeals for the Eleventh Circuit that this was carefully and correctly done in this case.

The Supreme Court's decisive rejection of McCleskey's claims "ended what [death penalty] opponents had called their last sweeping challenge to capital punishment."[23] The decision also elicited forceful dissenting opinions from Justices Brennan, Blackmun, and Stevens (Justice Marshall also dissented but did not write separately). Justice Brennan objected to the majority opinion's Eighth Amendment analysis.

Justice BRENNAN, with whom Justice MARSHALL joins, and with whom Justice BLACKMUN and Justice STEVENS join in all but Part I, dissenting. . . .

III

A

It is important to emphasize at the outset that the Court's observation that McCleskey cannot prove the influence of race on any particular sentencing decision is irrelevant in evaluating his Eighth Amendment claim. Since *Furman v. Georgia*, 408 U.S. 238 (1972), the Court has been concerned with the *risk* of the imposition of an arbitrary sentence, rather than the proven fact of one. . . .

B

The Baldus study indicates that, after taking into account some 230 nonracial factors that might legitimately influence a sentencer, the jury *more likely than not* would have spared McCleskey's life had his victim been black.

The study distinguishes between those cases in which (1) the jury exercises virtually no discretion because the strength or weakness of aggravating factors usually suggests that only one outcome is appropriate; and (2) cases reflecting an "intermediate" level of aggravation, in which the jury has considerable discretion in choosing a sentence. McCleskey's case falls into the intermediate range. In such cases, death is imposed in 34% of white-victim crimes and 14% of black-victim crimes, a difference of 139% in the rate of imposition of the death penalty. In other words, just under 59%—almost 6 in 10—defendants comparable to McCleskey would not have received the death penalty if their victims had been black. . . .

C

Evaluation of McCleskey's evidence cannot rest solely on the numbers themselves. We must also ask whether the conclusion suggested by those numbers is consonant with our understanding of history and human experience. Georgia's legacy of a race-conscious criminal justice system, as well as this Court's own recognition of the persistent danger that racial attitudes may affect criminal proceedings, indicates that McCleskey's claim is not a fanciful product of mere statistical artifice. . . .

History and its continuing legacy thus buttress the probative force of McCleskey's statistics. Formal dual criminal laws may no longer be in effect, and intentional discrimination may no longer be prominent. Nonetheless, as we acknowledged in *Turner* [*v. Murray*, 476 U.S. 28, 35 (1986)], "subtle, less consciously held racial attitudes" continue to be of concern, and the Georgia system gives such attitudes considerable room to operate. The conclusions drawn from McCleskey's statistical evidence are therefore consistent with the lessons of social experience.

IV

The Court cites four reasons for shrinking from the implications of McCleskey's evidence: the desirability of discretion for actors in the criminal justice system, the existence of statutory safeguards against abuse of that discretion, the potential consequences for broader challenges to criminal sentencing, and an understanding of the contours of the judicial role. While these concerns underscore the need for sober deliberation, they do not justify rejecting evidence as convincing as McCleskey has presented.

The Court maintains that petitioner's claim "is antithetical to the fundamental role of discretion in our criminal justice system." It states that "[w]here the discretion that is fundamental to our criminal process is involved, we decline to assume that what is unexplained is invidious."

Reliance on race in imposing capital punishment, however, is antithetical to the very rationale for granting sentencing discretion. Discretion is a means, not an end. . . .

The Court also declines to find McCleskey's evidence sufficient in view of "the safeguards designed to minimize racial bias in the [capital sentencing] process." *Gregg v. Georgia* upheld the Georgia capital sentencing statute against a facial challenge. . . . It is clear that *Gregg* bestowed no permanent approval on the Georgia system. It simply held that the State's statutory safeguards were assumed sufficient to channel discretion without evidence otherwise.

It has now been over 13 years since Georgia adopted the provisions upheld in *Gregg*. Professor Baldus and his colleagues have compiled data on almost 2,500 homicides committed during the period 1973–1979. They have taken into account the influence of 230 nonracial variables, using a multitude of data from the State itself, and have produced striking evidence that the odds of being sentenced to death are significantly greater than average if a defendant is black or his or her victim is white. The challenge to the Georgia system is not speculative or theoretical; it is empirical. As a result, the Court cannot rely on the statutory safeguards in discounting McCleskey's evidence, for it is the very effectiveness of those safeguards that such evidence calls into question. . . .

The Court next states that its unwillingness to regard petitioner's evidence as sufficient is based in part on the fear that recognition of McCleskey's claim would open the door to widespread challenges to all aspects of criminal sentencing. Taken on its face, such a statement seems to suggest a fear of too much justice. Yet surely the majority would acknowledge that if striking evidence indicated that other minority groups, or women, or even persons with blond hair, were disproportionately sentenced to death, such a state of affairs would be repugnant to deeply rooted conceptions of fairness. The prospect that there may be more widespread abuse than McCleskey documents may be dismaying, but it does not justify complete abdication of our judicial role. . . .

It hardly needs reiteration that this Court has consistently acknowledged the uniqueness of the punishment of death. . . .

Race is a consideration whose influence is expressly constitutionally proscribed. . . . That a decision to impose the death penalty could be influenced by *race* is thus a particularly repugnant prospect, and evidence that race may play even a modest role in levying a death sentence should be enough to characterize that sentence as "cruel and unusual." . . .

The Court's projection of apocalyptic consequences for criminal sentencing is thus greatly exaggerated. The Court can indulge in such speculation only by ignoring its own jurisprudence demanding the highest scrutiny on issues of death and race. As a result, it fails to do justice to a claim in which both those elements are intertwined—an occasion calling for the most sensitive inquiry a court can conduct. Despite its acceptance of the validity of Warren McCleskey's evidence, the Court is willing to let his death sentence stand because it fears that we cannot successfully define a different standard for lesser punishments. This fear is baseless.

Finally, the Court justifies its rejection of McCleskey's claim by cautioning against usurpation of the legislatures' role in devising and monitoring criminal punishment. . . . The judiciary's role in this society counts for little if the use of governmental power to extinguish life does not elicit close scrutiny. . . .

V

At the time our Constitution was framed 200 years ago this year, blacks "had for more than a century before been regarded as beings of an inferior order, and altogether unfit to associate with the white race, either in social or political relations; and so far inferior, that they had no rights which the white man was bound to respect." *Dred Scott v. Sandford,* 19 How. 393, 407 (1857). Only 130 years ago, this Court relied on these observations to deny American citizenship to blacks. *Ibid.* A mere three generations ago, this Court sanctioned racial segregation, stating that "[i]f one race be inferior to the other socially, the Constitution of the United States cannot put them upon the same plane." *Plessy v. Ferguson,* 163 U.S. 537, 552 (1896).

In more recent times, we have sought to free ourselves from the burden of this history. Yet it has been scarcely a generation since this Court's first decision striking down racial segregation, and barely two decades since the legislative prohibition of racial discrimination in major domains of national life. These have been honorable steps, but we cannot pretend that in three decades we have completely escaped the grip of a historical legacy spanning centuries. Warren McCleskey's evidence confronts us with the subtle and persistent influence of the past. His message is a disturbing one to a society that has formally repudiated racism, and a frustrating one to a Nation accustomed to regarding its destiny as the product of its own will. Nonetheless, we ignore him at our peril, for we remain imprisoned by the past as long as we deny its influence in the present.

Justice Blackmun's dissent took exception with the majority opinion's treatment of the equal protection claim. He pointed out that the decisions made by prosecutors about whether to pursue the death penalty in murder cases were immune to statutory or other formal regulation. Those decisions, both statewide and in Fulton County, where McCleskey was prosecuted, were the source of a substantial measure of the race-of-victim disparities revealed by the Baldus study.

Justice BLACKMUN, with whom Justice MARSHALL and Justice STEVENS join, and with whom Justice BRENNAN joins in all but Part IV-B, dissenting. . . .

McCleskey produced evidence concerning the role of racial factors at the various steps in the decisionmaking process, focusing on the prosecutor's decision as to which cases merit the death sentence. McCleskey established that the race of the victim is an especially significant factor at the point where the defendant has been convicted of murder and the prosecutor must choose whether to proceed to the penalty phase of the trial and create the possibility that a death sentence may be imposed or to accept the imposition of a sentence of life imprisonment. McCleskey demonstrated this effect at both the statewide level, and in Fulton County where he was tried and sentenced. The statewide statistics indicated that black-defendant/white-victim cases advanced to the penalty trial at nearly five times the rate of the black-defendant/black-victim cases (70% v. 15%), and over three times the rate of white-defendant/black-victim cases (70% v. 19%). The multiple-regression analysis demonstrated that racial factors had a readily identifiable effect at a statistically significant level. . . . .

Individualized evidence relating to the disposition of the Fulton County cases that were most comparable to McCleskey's case was consistent with the evidence of the race-of-victim effect as well. Of the 17 defendants, including McCleskey, who were arrested and charged with homicide of a police officer in Fulton County during the 1973–1979 period, McCleskey, alone, was sentenced to death. The only other defendant whose case even proceeded to the penalty phase received a sentence of life imprisonment. That defendant had been convicted of killing a black police officer.

. . . McCleskey showed that the process by which the State decided to seek a death penalty in his case and to pursue that sentence throughout the prosecution was susceptible to abuse. Petitioner submitted the deposition of Lewis R. Slaton, who, as of the date of the deposition, had been the District Attorney for 18 years in the county in which McCleskey was tried and sentenced. . . . [Mr. Slaton] testified that during his years in the office, there were no guidelines informing the Assistant District Attorneys who handled the cases how they should proceed at any particular stage of the prosecution. There were no guidelines as to when they should seek an indictment for murder as opposed to lesser charges; when they should recommend acceptance of a guilty plea to murder, acceptance of a guilty plea to a lesser charge, reduction of charges, or dismissal of charges at the postindictment-preconviction stage; or when they should seek the death penalty. Slaton testified that these decisions were left to the discretion of the individual attorneys who then informed Slaton of their decisions as they saw fit. . . .

The above-described evidence, considered in conjunction with the other record evidence . . . gives rise to an inference of discriminatory purpose. . . . McCleskey's showing is of sufficient magnitude that, absent evidence to the contrary, one must conclude that racial factors entered into the decisionmaking process that yielded McCleskey's death sentence.

The burden, therefore, shifts to the State to explain the racial selections. It must demonstrate that legitimate racially neutral criteria and procedures yielded this racially skewed result. . . .

III

. . . The Court's refusal to require that the prosecutor provide an explanation for his actions . . . is completely inconsistent with this Court's longstanding precedents. . . .

IV

A

One of the final concerns discussed by the Court may be the most disturbing aspect of its opinion. Granting relief to McCleskey in this case, it is said, could lead to further constitutional challenges. That, of course, is no reason to deny *McCleskey* his rights under the Equal Protection Clause. If a grant of relief to him were to lead to a closer examination of the effects of racial considerations throughout the criminal justice system, the system, and hence society, might benefit. Where no such factors come into play, the integrity of the system is enhanced. Where such considerations are shown to be significant, efforts can be made to eradicate their impermissible influence and to ensure an evenhanded application of criminal sanctions.

B

Like Justice STEVENS, I do not believe acceptance of McCleskey's claim would eliminate capital punishment in Georgia. Justice STEVENS points out that the evidence presented in this case indicates that in extremely aggravated murders the risk of discriminatory enforcement of the death penalty is minimized. I agree that narrowing the class of death-eligible defendants is not too high a price to pay for a death penalty system that does not discriminate on the basis of race. Moreover, the establishment of guidelines for Assistant District Attorneys as to the appropriate basis for exercising their discretion at the various steps in the prosecution of a case would provide at least a measure of consistency. The Court's emphasis on the procedural safeguards in the system ignores the fact that there are none whatsoever during the crucial process leading up to trial. As Justice WHITE stated for the plurality in *Turner v. Murray,* I find "the risk that racial prejudice may have infected petitioner's capital sentencing unacceptable in light of the ease with which that risk could have been minimized." 476 U.S., at 36. I dissent.

As alluded to by both Justices Brennan and Blackmun, the Baldus study classified murder cases into different "aggravation levels" in an attempt to get a more refined understanding of the capital charging and sentencing decisions made in Georgia. The researchers reasoned that certain types of cases were highly unlikely to be prosecuted capitally or result in a death sentence—regardless of the race of the victim or the offender—because the killings were accompanied by insufficient aggravating factors. They further reasoned that some killings were so highly aggravated that death sentences almost always would be sought and imposed—once again, regardless of racial considerations. Discretion would most likely be exercised, and was most susceptible to abuse, in "mid-range" aggravation cases. As Professor Baldus explained during his testimony in the U.S. District Court:

> "[W]hen the cases become tremendously aggravated so that everybody would agree that if we're going to have a death sentence, these are the cases that should get it, the race effects go away. It's only in the mid-range of cases where the decision makers have a real choice as to what to do. If there's room for the exercise of discretion, then the [racial] factors begin to play a role."[24]

Their analysis yielded that precise finding. No death sentences were imposed in homicides classified among the two lowest aggravation levels, regardless of race of victim or offender. Conversely, death sentences resulted in nearly 90% of the cases categorized as the most highly aggravated, and race effects were negligible. The "mid-range" cases involved the most variability in capital charging and sentencing decisions, and exhibited significant race-of-victim and race-of-offender disparities.[25] McCleskey's case, perhaps surprisingly, because he had been convicted of murdering a police officer during a robbery, was considered a mid-range case. As Justice Blackmun's opinion explained, among the 17 police officer killings in Fulton County, where McCleskey was prosecuted, McCleskey's was the only case resulting in a death sentence during the period studied. Justice Stevens seized upon this general finding of the Baldus study to suggest one way that Georgia's death-penalty system might continue to operate without the taint of racial discrimination.

Justice STEVENS, with whom Justice BLACKMUN joins, dissenting. . . .

In this case it is claimed—and the claim is supported by elaborate studies which the Court properly assumes to be valid—that the jury's sentencing process was likely distorted by racial prejudice. The studies demonstrate a strong probability that McCleskey's sentencing jury . . . was influenced by the fact that McCleskey is black and his victim was white, and that this same outrage would not have been generated if he had killed a member of his own race. This sort of disparity is constitutionally intolerable. It flagrantly violates the Court's prior "insistence that capital punishment be imposed fairly, and with reasonable consistency, or not at all." *Eddings v. Oklahoma*, 455 U.S. 104, 112 (1982).

The Court's decision appears to be based on a fear that the acceptance of McCleskey's claim would sound the death knell for capital punishment in Georgia. If society were indeed forced to choose between a racially discriminatory death penalty (one that provides heightened protection against murder "for whites only") and no death penalty at all, the choice mandated by the Constitution would be plain. But the Court's fear is unfounded. One of the lessons of the Baldus study is that there exist certain categories of extremely serious crimes for which prosecutors consistently seek, and juries consistently impose, the death penalty without regard to the race of the victim or the race of the offender. If Georgia were to narrow the class of death-eligible defendants to those categories, the danger of arbitrary and discriminatory imposition of the death penalty would be significantly decreased, if not eradicated. . . . [S]uch a restructuring of the sentencing scheme is surely not too high a price to pay.

The Baldus study was regarded by many as "among the best empirical studies on criminal sentencing ever conducted. . . ."[26] Although Justice Powell's majority opinion in *McCleskey* assumed that the study was "statistically valid,"[27] it stopped short of acknowledging that the research demonstrated that racial considerations actually influenced the administration of Georgia's death penalty. "Statistics at most may show only a likelihood that a particular factor entered into some decisions,"[28] the opinion cautioned. "At most, the Baldus study indicates a discrepancy that appears to correlate with race."[29] The opinion ultimately concluded that "we decline to assume that what is unexplained is invidious."[30]

This conclusion is at odds with the logic of the detailed, multivariate analysis the study employed.

> [T]he Baldus study examined hundreds of nonracial variables, and none of them, separately or in combination, accounted for the effects of race. If this study does not adequately 'explain' that these large racial "discrepancies" are in fact caused by race, then the task is meaningless.[31]

Professor Baldus and his colleagues disagreed with the majority opinion's interpretation of their findings:

> Justice Powell's dismissal of McCleskey's statistical evidence as sufficient proof of only a risk of discrimination is disingenuous. As proof of classwide discrimination, the persistence of a statistically significant racial disparity of the magnitude estimated in *McCleskey*—after adjusting for all plausible background variables that would be expected to be an influence in the system—is commonly accepted as proof that race is an influence in a highly discretionary selection-process and that race was the decisive factor in some decisions. . . .
>
> The clear implication . . . is that, for reasons unrelated to its probative force, the Court is simply unwilling to accept statistical proof of discrimination to support an Eighth Amendment claim in the death-penalty context. . . . Justice Powell's rejection of statistical evidence of discrimination in the death-sentencing context bespeaks an unwillingness to destabilize the capital-sentencing process in any fundamental respect, regardless of such evidence.[32]

Justice Powell retired from the Supreme Court in 1987, just a few months after he authored the majority opinion in *McCleskey v. Kemp*. Four years later:

> Powell was asked [by his biographer and former law clerk, John Jeffries, Jr.] whether he would change his vote in any case:
>
> > [Powell:] "Yes, *McCleskey v. Kemp*."
> > [Jeffries:] "Do you mean you would now accept the argument from statistics?"
> > "No, I would vote the other way in any capital case."
> > "In *any* capital case?"
> > "Yes."
> > "Even in *Furman v. Georgia*?"
> > "Yes. I have come to think that capital punishment should be abolished."[33]

The retired Justice explained that he believed that the death penalty "serves no useful purpose" and that the "seemingly endless litigation in every capital case" frustrated and brought "discredit on the whole legal system."[34] Warren McCleskey was executed in 1991, the same year that the retired Justice offered his remarks.

If the Baldus study is interpreted to support the inference that racial considerations did influence the administration of Georgia's post-*Furman* death-penalty law—and in particular, that White-victim murders were significantly more likely to result in a death sentence than comparable black-victim murders—what might explain this outcome? Justice Brennan suggested that the enactment of a law is insufficient to eradicate and ensure the transformation of pre-existing deep-seated social attitudes about race. He pointed to "Georgia's legacy of a race-conscious criminal justice system"[35] and argued that "it would be unrealistic to ignore the influence of history in assessing the plausible implications of McCleskey's evidence."[36] Justice Blackmun quoted approvingly from a study that explained:

> "Since death penalty prosecutions require large allocations of scarce prosecutorial resources, prosecutors must choose a small number of cases to receive this expensive treatment. In making these choices they may favor homicides that are visible and disturbing to the majority of the community, and these will tend to be white-victim homicides."[37]

Do either or both of these theories seem plausible? Do they appear to be related?

If the racial disparities exposed by the Baldus study are of concern, are any solutions apparent short of abolishing capital punishment? Would "the establishment of guidelines for Assistant District Attorneys . . . for exercising their discretion"[38] in potentially capital cases, as Justice Blackmun suggested, be a step in the right direction? The federal government uses a related check on prosecutorial discretion by requiring United States Attorneys throughout the country to forward potential death-penalty cases in their jurisdiction to Washington D.C. for review by a special screening committee overseen by the United States Attorney General. The committee solicits input from defense counsel and reviews the alleged case facts and the defendant's criminal history before approving or designating cases for capital prosecution.[39]

Justice Stevens suggested that only the most highly aggravated murder cases—which the study reported are largely unaffected by racial considerations—should be death-penalty eligible. Is this suggestion feasible? If it would be difficult to identify those cases in advance, could the death-eligible class of cases at least be narrowed by excluding some murders, such as those accompanied only by the "contemporaneous felony" aggravating circumstance? Some commentators and study commissions have recommended significantly limiting the types of murders eligible for capital punishment, thereby refining the search for the "worst of the worst" murders and murderers and simultaneously reducing the potential influence of race in charging and sentencing decisions.[40]

Would it be too demanding to require the prosecution in a case such as McCleskey's, involving a Black defendant and White victim, to come forward with legitimate, race-neutral reasons to explain statistical disparities of the sort revealed by the Baldus study and to rebut the inference that race influenced the death penalty decision in a specific case? The majority opinion in *McCleskey* declined to make either the Fulton County prosecutor or a state representative, such as the Attorney General, offer any explanation in response to the study's findings. Rather, the Court concluded that the normal equal protection framework for demonstrating purposeful discrimination simply did not apply in this context. The opinion stated that "McCleskey's arguments are best presented to the legislative bodies."[41]

In the aftermath of *McCleskey*, the House of Representatives twice voted to enact a Racial Justice Act that would have responded to the Court's invitation. The proposed legislation would have permitted death-sentenced offenders to create a rebuttable presumption that race discrimination tainted their individual cases by making a statistical showing of racially disparate capital sentencing patterns within their state. The Senate declined to approve the measures and they never became law.[42] Kentucky enacted a "quite weak"[43] state Racial Justice Act in 1993,[44] and North Carolina adopted a more comprehensive one in 2009[45]—only to repeal it four years later, in 2013.[46]

What is the relationship between the fair or equitable administration of the death penalty and fundamental justice? Warren McCleskey was convicted of murdering a police officer. If that is a legitimate basis for sentencing him to death, should it matter that other offenders in other cases—for example, those involving Black murder victims—are *not* sentenced to death? Consider the argument made by Ernest van den Haag:

> [I]f the death penalty is morally just, however discriminatorily applied to only some of the guilty, it remains just in each case in which it is applied.
>
>   The utilitarian (political) effects of unequal justice may well be detrimental to the social fabric because they outrage our passion for equality before the law. Unequal justice also is morally repellent. Nonetheless unequal justice is still justice. The guilty do not become innocent or less deserving of punishment because others escaped it. . . . Justice remains just, however unequal, while injustice remains unjust however equal. While both are desired, justice and equality are not identical. Equality before the law should be extended and enforced—but not at the expense of justice.[47]

Do you agree? Can a system that dispenses "justice" that is not evenhanded truly be considered just? Is it too much to expect both justice and equality; or that death-penalty systems dispatch, in the words chiseled into the marble front of the U.S. Supreme Court Building, "Equal Justice Under Law"?

McCleskey was sentenced to death in Georgia in 1978. The research used to challenge his death sentence relied on information from cases spanning the years 1973–1979. The Baldus study is limited accordingly. It tells us nothing in particular about possible race disparities in the administration of capital punishment in other states or at other times. However, many studies investigating race and the administration of capital punishment under post-*Furman* laws have been completed in other jurisdictions throughout the country. With discouraging regularity they report finding significant race-of-victim and/or race-of-offender disparities in capital charging and/or sentencing decisions. Studies reporting such results have been conducted in states as diverse as Florida, Illinois, California, Texas, North Carolina, South Carolina, Arizona, Kentucky, Indiana, Maryland, Connecticut, New Mexico, and Missouri.[48] More localized studies, including one conducted in Philadelphia,[49] and another in Almeida County, California,[50] also have found capital punishment decisions to be linked to race. Still other studies have reported finding significant racial disparities in the use of the death penalty by the federal government[51] and the U.S. Military.[52]

Recent Gallup polls indicate that 60% of Americans are "in favor of the death penalty for a person convicted of murder," while 52% believe that "the death penalty is applied fairly . . . in this country today" (October 2013 results). Among respondents who oppose the death penalty, just 4% cited its "unfair application" as a reason—tying it for last among the several reasons offered (May 2003 results).[53] A 2007 poll indicated that 70% of Whites favored the death penalty for a person convicted of murder while 26% opposed it. In contrast, 40% of Blacks reported favoring the death penalty for a convicted murderer and 56% opposed it.[54]

What is the relationship, if any, between public opinion about the death penalty and the research studies' findings concerning racial disparities in the death penalty's administration? What relevance, if any, might the public opinion results have with respect to the Supreme Court's decision in *McCleskey v. Kemp*? Is it plausible to suggest that a link exists between public opinion about the death penalty and legislative action (and inaction) regarding the issues raised in *McCleskey*?

Does the death penalty have a potentially deep, and perhaps subconscious, symbolic association with issues of race? David Garland has argued that it does. He has written that the NAACP Legal Defense Fund's litigation leading up to *Furman*:

> had represented the death penalty as a civil rights violation, a kind of legal lynching that ought to be abolished along with segregation and Southern racism. [In the aftermath of *Furman*, the death penalty] became a popular crime-fighting measure, an emblem of states' rights democracy and a symbolic battleground in the emerging culture wars. In the process, death penalty discourse became infused with powerful currents of race and class resentment and with white fears of black violence.[55]

How closely connected are race and the death penalty in contemporary America? What implications does the answer to this question have with respect to the death penalty's perpetuation and use? What are the implications with respect to contemporary American society?

Arbitrariness: Gender and Geography

Gender Disparities

If good reasons exist to be concerned about whether racial considerations influence capital punishment decisions, would similar concerns be raised by the suggestion that gender plays a role in the death penalty's administration?

Consider the following statistics compiled by Professor Victor Streib regarding women and capital punishment in this country, covering the period January 1, 1973, through December 31, 2012.

(1) Women account for about 10% of murder arrests annually;
(2) Women account for only 2.1% (178/8,375) of death sentences imposed at the trial level;
(3) Women account for only 1.9% (61/3,146) of persons presently on death row; and
(4) Women account for only 0.9% (12/1,320) of persons actually executed in this modern era.[56]

What might account for this progressive winnowing, and in particular the substantial gap between the proportion of murders committed by women (roughly 10%, using arrests as a proxy) and their representation on death row (roughly 2%)? Is "chivalry" at work—*i.e.*, a reluctance motivated by "gallantry," chauvinism, or sympathy to use the harsh punishment of death because of the offender's status as a woman?[57] Might the discrepancies exist because the kinds of killings committed by women—including a significant percentage involving domestic violence—are considerably less likely to qualify as capital murder?[58] Does the relative infrequency of women confronting imminent execution generate publicity and increase the pressure on governors and pardon boards to grant clemency?[59] Do stereotypes matter, so that women who are perceived as more feminine or attractive (for example, Karla Faye Tucker, a "born again" and physically attractive White woman who ultimately was executed in Texas amidst a wash of publicity and pleas for clemency[60]) are treated differently from women whose demeanor or physical attributes essentially deprive them of whatever mantle of protection femininity otherwise might provide?[61]

Studies in diverse jurisdictions also have found that the death penalty is more likely to be sought and imposed in cases where women are the victims of murder.[62] Are such killings more deserving of capital punishment because of women's perceived or actual vulnerability at the hands of a male offender? Are differences likely to be explained, in part, because murder committed in the perpetration of rape is a common capital crime or aggravating circumstance? A study of capital sentencing practices in California concluded that significant gender-of-victim disparities persisted, with female-victim cases being dealt with more harshly, even outside of the rape-murder context and after other case circumstances were considered. The authors also found significant differences involving male and female offenders, with females being treated more leniently. They concluded:

> The data reveals disparities in death sentencing by both the gender of the defendant and the gender of the victim, with the gender of the victim having an even greater impact on penalty outcomes than the gender of the defendant. . . . [T]hese disparities cannot be explained away by the nature of the murders. Treating women as less culpable and less to be feared when they murder and weaker and more in need of society's protection when they are victims is a clear expression of chivalric values.[63]

If these findings are accepted, are they morally and/or legally problematic? What, if anything, could or should be done in response to gender disparities in the death penalty's administration?

Geographic Disparities

In December 2013, 32 states, the federal government, and the United States Military had viable death-penalty laws. Great variation exists among these jurisdictions with respect to actually using their laws. Texas is far and away the leader in executions, having carried out 507 of the 1355 executions nationwide (37.4%) during the post-*Furman* era through December 1, 2013. The next closest state, Virginia, put 110 convicted murderers to death. At the same time, more than a dozen states have five or fewer executions to their credit during the modern era, and Kansas and New Hampshire have none at all.[64] Death row populations are similarly diverse. At the beginning of 2013, 727 prisoners were under sentence of death in California, representing nearly a quarter (23.3%) of the nation's total (3,125), while 413 awaited execution in Florida, as did 300 in Texas. In contrast, lone offenders inhabited the "death rows" of New Hampshire and Wyoming, and a dozen or fewer offenders were under a death sentence in ten other jurisdictions.[65]

While eye-opening, such differences arguably reflect "one of the happy incidents" of federalism,[66] under which diverse policies among the states on matters of crimes and punishments flourish.[67] But what if the focus shifts from variation *between* the states to differences *within* states in the use of capital-punishment laws? Would it be surprising to learn, for example, that as prominent as the State of Texas is in imposing and carrying out death sentences, not a single offender has been sentenced to death during the post-*Furman* period in more than half of the state's 254 counties?[68] Nationwide, between 1973 and 1995:

> [T]hirty-four states sentenced at least one person to death, yet fully 60% of the counties in those States did not impose a single sentence of death. . . .
>
> . . . More than half of the death sentences imposed nationwide over the twenty-three year . . . period originated in only sixty-six, or 2% of the nation's 3143 counties, parishes, and boroughs. Sixteen percent of the nation's counties (510 out of 3143) accounted for 90% of its death verdicts in the period.

. . . [T]hese numbers are not a result of the heavy use of the death penalty by a small number of densely populated counties. Between 1973 and 1995, the counties where only a fifth of all Americans lived imposed two-thirds of its death sentences. Counties with 10% of the nation's residents imposed 43% of its death sentences. Even considering only death-sentencing States, counties comprising around 10% of the population were responsible for over 38% of the death sentences.[69]

The skewed contribution made by relatively few counties to national death sentence totals appears to have widened more recently.

In 2009, Los Angeles County, California sentenced the same number of people to death as the State of Texas. Maricopa County, Arizona sentenced more people to death than the State of Alabama. This is not the exception to the rule; just 10% of counties in the United States account for all death sentences imposed from 2004 to 2009. Even within that 10% of counties, the divide between the most and least active jurisdictions is stark: only 4% of counties (121) in the United States sentenced more than one person to death in that time period. Those 4% of counties account for roughly 76% of the death sentences returned nationally. Twenty-nine counties—fewer than 1% of counties in the country—rendered death sentences at a rate of one or more new sentences per year. That 1% of counties accounts for roughly 44% of all death sentences. Fourteen counties sentenced ten or more individuals to death, which represents a return of almost two death sentences per year. Those fourteen counties account for roughly one-third of death sentences nationally from 2004 to 2009.[70]

A similar pattern of counties' uneven contributions to new death sentences emerges within states.

For example, in California [between 2004 and 2009], 64% of counties did not sentence anyone to death, and 90% returned no more than one death sentence. Just six counties returned death sentences at the rate of more than one sentence per year. Three counties— Los Angeles (33), Riverside (15), and Orange (14)—collectively account for more than half of all death sentences imposed in California from 2004 to 2009.

    California is not the only state where this trend exists. Fewer than half of the counties in Florida, for instance, did not sentence anyone to death from 2004 to 2009. Nearly three of every four Florida counties sentenced two or fewer people to death. Only three counties imposed death sentences at a rate of more than one new sentence per year: Duval (13), Broward (10), and Polk (8). Texas has 254 counties, of which 222 (88%) sentenced no one to death from 2004 to 2009. Of the thirty-two counties that did sentence someone to death, seventeen sentenced only one person to death. Just four counties imposed death sentences at a rate of more than one per year: Bexar (10), Dallas (8), Harris (21), and Tarrant (10).[71]

Individual counties similarly dominate in generating death sentences that result in an execution. Between 1977 and October 2010, just 14 counties were responsible for the death sentences that produced 29.8% of the nation's executions. Harris County, Texas (Houston) alone accounted for more than 9% (115) of the 1,229 individuals executed during this period. Only 454 of the country's 3,146 counties (14.4%) returned a death sentence that resulted in an execution during this 33-year interval.[72]

Although most crimes, and all murders, have individual victims, in the legal sense crimes are an offense against the state (a term used here to represent the government, including the federal jurisdiction). Punishments are prescribed by state law. Should the specific location within a state where a homicide was committed make a difference for capital punishment purposes? Is a killing more or less death-worthy depending on which side of a county line it occurs?

For instance, over the course of a decade (1988–1997) before Illinois repealed its death-penalty statute in 2011, researchers found that "the odds of receiving a death sentence for killing a victim(s) in Cook County [Chicago] are on average 83.6% lower than for killing a victim(s) in the rural county region of Illinois controlling for the other 26 variables in the analysis."[73] While Maryland retained the death penalty, "a death-eligible case in Baltimore County [was] twenty-three times more likely ultimately to result in a death sentence than a death-eligible case in Baltimore City."[74] Studies completed in several other states have reported that the odds that a murder will be prosecuted capitally or result in a death sentence vary markedly depending on the county or type of county (rural vs. urban) in which the killing occurred.[75] Federal capital prosecutions likewise are over- and underrepresented in different regions of the country.[76]

Are such findings evidence of arbitrariness in the application of death-penalty laws? Or are intrastate differences in capital charging and sentencing decisions not only inevitable but justifiable since crimes including murder can and do affect communities of different size and cohesiveness so differently? Are such differences a defensible product of criminal justice systems in which prosecutors are elected locally, manage budgets that are commonly rooted in county-level funding,[77] and presumably are responsive to the sentiments of their constituents?[78]

Perfect consistency in the administration of discretionary systems of justice is not possible, and may not be desirable, within states comprised of dense urban centers, sparsely populated rural communities, and counties of diverse size, character, and composition. On the other hand, is death sufficiently different from other criminal punishments that greater consistency within jurisdictions should be demanded in the application of capital-punishment statutes than in the enforcement of other criminal laws of statewide application? Or should variation in the death penalty's administration within jurisdictions be accepted as an altogether appropriate exercise of discretion by the elected officials and citizens most immediately affected by capital murder?

Conclusion

It is not surprising to find slippage, or an imperfect fit, between the law as written and the law as it is administered in practice. Death-penalty laws and their application are no exception. Crimes cannot be reconstructed with precision and humans, with all of their complexities and limitations, remain responsible for the investigation, prosecution, and adjudication of criminal offenses. When the Supreme Court gave its approval to the guided-discretion capital-sentencing laws enacted in the aftermath of *Furman*, the justices were willing to assume that the reform legislation would succeed in minimizing the arbitrariness that they perceived to reign under the pre-*Furman* laws. After all, the new laws were considerably more demanding than prior legislation. They limited death-penalty eligibility to a relatively narrow class of offenses, they incorporated legislative standards that identified especially aggravated killings, and they mandated appellate review of capital sentencing verdicts.

The ensuing years allowed information to be collected about how the new sentencing laws operated in practice. As we have seen, the evidence suggests that the justices' expectations were not realized in many respects. The exposed problems tend to be at the core rather than the periphery of the capital-punishment enterprise. They involve the death penalty's racially disparate application, differential use of the capital sanction that correlates with the gender of offenders and their victims, and inconsistent charging and sentencing practices within jurisdictions.

The question thus lingers whether the apparent discrepancies between the law as written and the law as practiced should be received with the same equanimity in the death-penalty context as in other applications. If the revealed problems do not rise to the level of constitutional significance, are there nevertheless reforms that could or should be implemented to respond to them legislatively or administratively? Or, do the research findings simply confirm that, in application, no laws can be free of imperfection?

When all is said and done, should the significant legislative and doctrinal reforms that characterize capital-sentencing laws in the post-*Furman* era be deemed successes or failures? Should they be considered constitutional or unconstitutional, fair or unfair, as they are administered within justice systems?

Endnotes

1. *See* Stuart Banner, *The Death Penalty: An American History* 8–9, 139–143 (Cambridge, MA: Harvard University Press 2002); Randall Kennedy, *Race, Crime, and the Law* 76–86 (New York: Vintage Books 1997); Ursula Bentele, "Race and Capital Punishment in the United States and Africa," 19 *Brooklyn Journal of International Law* 235, 253–256 (1993); Vada Berger, Nicole Walthou, Angela Dorn, Dan Lindsey, Pamela Thompson & Gretchen von Helms, "Too Much Justice: A Legislative Response to *McCleskey v. Kemp*, 24 *Harvard Civil Rights-Civil Liberties Law Review* 437, 439–447 (1989).
2. *See* David Garland, *Peculiar Institution: America's Death Penalty in an Age of Abolition* 124–125 (Cambridge, MA: The Belknap Press of Harvard University Press 2010); Margaret Vandiver, *Lethal Punishment: Lynchings and Legal Executions in the South* (New Brunswick, NJ: Rutgers University Press 2006); Franklin E. Zimring, *The Contradictions of American Capital Punishment* 89–98 (New York: Oxford University Press 2003).

3. Jeffrey J. Pokorak, "Rape as a Badge of Slavery: The Legal History of, and Remedies for, Prosecutorial Race-of-Victim Charging Disparities," 7 *Nevada Law Journal* 1, 28–34 (2006); Dennis D. Dorin, "Two Different Worlds: Criminologists, Justices and Racial Discrimination in the Imposition of Capital Punishment in Rape Cases," 72 *Journal of Criminal Law & Criminology* 1667 (1981).

4. Evan J. Mandery, *A Wild Justice: The Death and Resurrection of Capital Punishment in America* 48–53 (New York: W.W. Norton & Co. 2013); Michael Meltsner, *Cruel and Unusual: The Supreme Court and Capital Punishment* 3–19 (New York: Random House 1973).

5. *Furman v. Georgia,* 408 U.S. 238, 249–257 (1972) (concurring in the judgment).

6. *Id.,* 408 U.S., at 310 (Stewart, J., concurring in the judgment) ("My concurring Brothers [Justices Douglas and Marshall] have demonstrated that, if any basis can be discerned for the selection of these few to be sentenced to die, it is the constitutionally impermissible basis of race. But racial discrimination has not been proved, and I put it to one side."); *Id.,* 408 U.S., at 389 n. 12 (Burger, C.J., dissenting).

7. *Id.,* 408 U.S., at 256 (Douglas, J., concurring in the judgment).

8. 428 U.S. 153 (1976).

9. *Proffitt v. Florida,* 428 U.S. 242 (1976); *Jurek v. Texas,* 428 U.S. 262 (1976).

10. *See, e.g.,* Samuel R. Gross & Robert Mauro, *Death & Discrimination: Racial Disparities in Capital Sentencing* 20–117 (Boston: Northeastern University Press 1989); Raymond Paternoster & Anne Marie Kazyaka, "The Administration of the Death Penalty in South Carolina: Experiences Over the First Few Years," 39 *South Carolina Law Review* 245 (1988); David C. Baldus, Charles A. Pulaski, Jr. & George Woodworth, "Arbitrariness and Discrimination in the Administration of the Death Penalty: A Challenge to State Supreme Courts," 15 *Stetson Law Review* 133 (1986); Michael Radelet & Margaret Vandiver, "Race and Capital Punishment: An Overview of the Issues," 25 *Crime & Social Justice* 94 (1986); William J. Bowers & Glenn Pierce, "Arbitrariness and Discrimination Under Post-*Furman* Capital Statutes," 26 *Crime & Delinquency* 563 (1980).

11. 481 U.S. 279 (1987).

12. *McCleskey v. Kemp,* 481 U.S. 279, 286 (1987).

13. *Id.*

14. *Id.*

15. *Id.,* 481 U.S., at 287.

16. *Id.,* 481 U.S., at 355 nn. 9 & 10 (Blackmun, J., dissenting).

17. *Id.,* 481 U.S., at 291 n. 7.

18. *Id.*

19. *Id.,* 481 U.S., at 292–293 (footnote omitted) (emphasis in original).

20. *Id.,* 481 U.S., at 294–295 (footnotes omitted).

21. *Id.,* 481 U.S., at 297.

22. *Id.,* 481 U.S., at 298 (footnote omitted) (emphasis in original).

23. Stuart Taylor, Jr., "Court, 5–4, Rejects Racial Challenge to Death Penalty," *New York Times* A1 (Apr. 23, 1987).

24. *McCleskey v. Kemp,* 481 U.S. 279, 287 n. 5 (1987). *See id.,* 481 U.S., at 325 (Brennan, J., dissenting).

25. *Id. See also* David C. Baldus, George G. Woodworth & Charles A. Pulaski, Jr., *Equal Justice and the Death Penalty: A Legal and Empirical Analysis* 88–133 (Boston: Northeastern University Press 1990); James R. Acker, "Social Sciences and the Criminal Law: Capital Punishment by the Numbers—An Analysis of *McCleskey v. Kemp,*" 23 *Criminal Law Bulletin* 454, 461–464 (1987).

26. *Id.,* at 455 n. 8 (*quoting* Amicus Curiae Brief for Dr. Franklin Fisher *et al. McCleskey v. Kemp,* p. 3).

27. *McCleskey v. Kemp,* 481 U.S. 279, 291 n. 7 (1987). See text accompanying notes 17 & 18, *supra.*

28. *Id.*, 481 U.S., at 308.
29. *Id.*, 481 U.S., at 312.
30. *Id.*, 481 U.S., at 313.
31. Gross & Mauro, *supra* note 10, at 171.
32. Baldus, Woodworth & Pulaski, Jr., *supra* note 25, at 378–380.
33. John C. Jeffries, Jr., *Justice Lewis F. Powell, Jr.* 451 (New York: Charles Scribner's Sons 1994).
34. *Id.*, at 452.
35. *McCleskey v. Kemp*, 481 U.S. 279, 328 (1987) (Brennan, J., dissenting).
36. *Id.*, 481 U.S., at 332.
37. *Id.*, 481 U.S., at 360–361 n. 13 (Blackmun, J., dissenting), *quoting* Samuel R. Gross & Robert Mauro, "Patterns of Death: An Analysis of Racial Disparities in Capital Sentencing and Homicide Victimization," 37 *Stanford Law Review* 106–107 (1984).
38. *McCleskey v. Kemp*, 481 U.S. 279, 365 (1987) (Blackmun, J., dissenting).
39. *See* Rory K. Little, "The Federal Death Penalty: History and Some Thoughts About the Department of Justice's Role," 26 *Fordham Urban Law Journal* 347, 440–502 (1999). *See also* David C. Baldus & George Woodworth, "Race Discrimination and the Legitimacy of Capital Punishment: Reflections on the Interaction of Fact and Perception," 53 *DePaul Law Review* 1411, 1465–66 (2004); John Gleeson, "Supervising Federal Capital Punishment: Why the Attorney General Should Defer When U.S. Attorneys Recommend Against the Death Penalty," 89 *Virginia Law Review* 1697 (2003).
40. *See generally,* Andrew Welsh-Huggins, "Reform Would Limit Death Penalty to Worst Killers," *Columbus Dispatch* (June 28, 2013), retrieved July 3, 2013 from www.dispatch.com/content/stories/local/2013/06/27/death-penalty-reforms-proposed-ohio.html; Chelsea Creo Sharon, "The 'Most Deserving' of Death: The Narrowing Requirement and the Proliferation of Aggravating Factors in Capital Sentencing Statutes," 46 *Harvard Civil Rights-Civil Liberties Law Review* 223 (2011); David McCord, "Should Commission of a Contemporaneous Arson, Burglary, Kidnapping, Rape, or Robbery Be Sufficient to Make a Murderer Eligible for a Death Sentence?—An Empirical and Normative Analysis," 49 *Santa Clara Law Review* 1 (2009); Sara Dareshshori, Jeffrey L. Kirchmeier, Colleen Quinn Brady & Evan Mandery, "Empire State Injustice: Based Upon a Decade of New York Information, a Preliminary Evaluation of How New York's Death Penalty System Fails to Meet Standards for Accuracy and Fairness," 4 *Cardozo Public Law, Policy and Ethics Journal* 85, 109–111 (2006); Joseph L. Hoffmann, "Protecting the Innocent: The Massachusetts Governor's Council Report," 95 *Journal of Criminal Law & Criminology* 561, 569 (2005); Daniel Givelber, "The New Law of Murder," 69 *Indiana Law Journal* 375 (1994). Richard A Rosen, "Felony Murder and the Eighth Amendment Jurisprudence of Death," 31 *Boston College Law Review* 1103 (1990); Gross & Mauro, *supra* note 37.
41. *McCleskey v. Kemp*, 481 U.S. 279, 319 (1987).
42. *See* Racial Justice Act of 1990, H.R. 2466, 101st Cong. § 3(c) (1989); Racial Justice Act of 1994, H.R. 4017, 103d Cong. § 2921(e) (1994). *See also* Sandra L. Simpson, "Everyone Else Is Doing It, Why Can't We? A New Look at the Use of Statistical Data in Death Penalty Cases," 12 *Journal of Gender, Race and Justice* 509, 535–538 (2009); Erwin Chemerinsky, "Eliminating Discrimination in Administering the Death Penalty: The Need for the Racial Justice Act," 35 *Santa Clara Law Review* 519 (1995).
43. Simpson, *supra* note 42, at 539.
44. Ky. Rev. Stat. Ann. § 532.300 (1993).
45. N.C. Gen. Stat. Ann. §§ 15A-2010–2012 (2009) (repealed 2013). *See* Barbara O'Brien & Catherine Grosso, "Confronting Race: How a Confluence of Social Movements Convinced North Carolina to Go Where the *McCleskey* Court Wouldn't," 2011 *Michigan State Law Review* 463 (2011); Seth Kotch & Robert P. Mosteller, "The Racial Justice Act and the Long Struggle With Race and the Death Penalty in North Carolina," 88 *North Carolina Law Review* 2031 (2010).

46. Kim Severson, "North Carolina Repeals Law Allowing Racial Bias Claim in Death Penalty Challenges," *New York Times* A1 (June 6, 2013).

47. Ernest van den Haag, "In Defense of the Death Penalty: A Legal-Practical-Moral Analysis," 14 *Criminal Law Bulletin* 51, 56 (1978).

48. The studies and their results are discussed in David C. Baldus & George Woodworth, "Race Discrimination and the Death Penalty: An Empirical and Legal Overview," in James R. Acker, Robert M. Bohm & Charles S. Lanier (eds.), *America's Experiment With Capital Punishment: Reflections on the Past, Present, and Future of the Ultimate Penal Sanction* 501, 536–545 (Durham, NC: Carolina Academic Press, 2d ed. 2003); Steven F. Shatz & Terry Dalton, "Challenging the Death Penalty With Statistics: *Furman, McCleskey,* and a Single County Case Study," 34 *Cardozo Law Review* 1227, 1244–51 (2013); David C. Baldus, George Woodworth, Catherine M. Grosso & Aaron M. Christ, "Arbitrariness and Discrimination in the Administration of the Death Penalty: A Legal and Empirical Analysis of the Nebraska Experience (1973–1999)," 81 *Nebraska Law Review* 486, 499–501 (2002); Jules Epstein, "Death-Worthiness and Prosecutorial Discretion in Capital Case Charging," 19 *Temple Political & Civil Rights Law Review* 389, 408–410 (2010); Michael J. Songer & Isaac Unah, "The Effect of Race, Gender, and Location on Prosecutorial Decisions to Seek the Death Penalty in South Carolina," 58 *South Carolina Law Review* 161 (2006); Katherine Barnes, David Sloss & Stephen Thaman, "Place Matters (Most): An Empirical Study of Prosecutorial Decision-Making in Death-Eligible Cases," 51 *Arizona Law Review* 305 (2009); United States General Accounting Office, *Death Penalty Sentencing: Research Indicates Pattern of Racial Disparities* (GAO/GGD-90–57) (1990), retrieved June 26, 2013 from www.gao.gov/assets/220/212180.pdf.

49. David C. Baldus, George Woodworth, David Zuckerman, Neil Alan Weiner & Barbara Broffitt, "Racial Discrimination and the Death Penalty in the Post-*Furman* Era: An Empirical and Legal Overview, With Recent Findings From Philadelphia," 83 *Cornell Law Review* 1638 (1998).

50. Shatz & Dalton, *supra* note 48. *See generally* G. Ben Cohen, "*McCleskey's* Omission: The Racial Geography of Retribution," 10 *Ohio State Journal of Criminal Law* 65 (2012).

51. United States Dept. of Justice, *Survey of the Federal Death Penalty System (1988–2000)* (Washington, D.C. 2000).

52. David C. Baldus, Catherine M. Grosso, George Woodworth & Richard Newell, "Racial Discrimination in the Administration of the Death Penalty: The Experience of the United States Armed Forces (1984–2005)," 101 *Journal of Criminal Law & Criminology* 1227 (2011).

53. Gallup, "U.S. Death Penalty Support Lowest in More Than 40 Years," retrieved November 30, 2013 from www.gallup.com/poll/165626/death-penalty-support-lowest-years.aspx; Gallup, "Death Penalty," retrieved June 26, 2013 from www.gallup.com/poll/1606/death-penalty.aspx.

54. Lydia Saad, "Racial Disagreement Over Death Penalty Has Varied Historically," *Gallup News Service* (July 30, 2007), retrieved June 26, 2013 from www.gallup.com/poll/28243/racial-disagreement-over-death-penalty-has-varied-historically.aspx.

55. Garland, *supra* note 2, at 244.

56. Victor Streib, *Death Penalty for Female Offenders, January 1, 1973, Through December 31, 2012,* 3 (Feb. 20, 2013), retrieved July 3, 2013 from www.deathpenaltyinfo.org/documents/FemDeathDec2012.pdf.

57. *See* Steven F. Shatz & Naomi R. Shatz, "Chivalry Is Not Dead: Murder, Gender, and the Death Penalty," 27 *Berkeley Journal of Gender, Law & Justice* 64 (2012); Andrea Shapiro, "Unequal Before the Law: Men, Women and the Death Penalty," 8 *American University Journal of Gender, Social Policy and the Law* 427, 456–457 (2000).

58. *See* Elizabeth Rapaport, "Equality of the Damned: The Execution of Women on the Cusp of the 21st Century," 26 *Ohio Northern University Law Review* 581 (2000); Elizabeth Rapaport, "The Death Penalty and Gender Discrimination," 25 *Law & Society Review* 367 (1991).

59. *See* Michael Heise, "Mercy by the Numbers: An Empirical Analysis of Clemency and Its Structure," 89 *Virginia Law Review* 239, 277–278 (2003); Elizabeth Rapaport, "Staying Alive: Executive Clemency, Equal Protection, and the Politics of Gender in Women's Capital Cases," 4 *Buffalo Criminal Law Review* 967 (2001).

60. *See generally* Mary Sigler, "Mercy, Clemency, and the Case of Karla Faye Tucker," 4 *Ohio State Journal of Criminal Law* 455 (2007); Melynda J. Price, "Litigating Salvation: Race, Religion and Innocence in the Karla Faye Tucker and Gary Graham Cases," 15 *Southern California Review of Law & Social Justice* 267 (2006); Joan W. Howarth, "Executing White Masculinities: Learning From Karla Faye Tucker," 81 *Oregon Law Review* 183 (2002).

61. *See* Shapiro, *supra* note 57, at 458–459 (discussing the "evil woman" theory in explanation of why some women are more apt to be sentenced to death than others); Elizabeth Marie Reza, "Gender Bias in North Carolina's Death Penalty," 12 *Duke Journal of Gender Law & Policy* 179, 183–184 (2005) (same).

62. *See* Shatz & Dalton, *supra* note 48, at 1251–52; Shatz & Shatz, *supra* note 57.

63. Shatz & Shatz, *supra* note 57, at 109–110.

64. Death Penalty Information Center, "Number of Executions by State and Region Since 1976," retrieved November 30, 2013 from www.deathpenaltyinfo.org/number-executions-state-and-region-1976.

65. Death Penalty Information Center, "Death Row Inmates by State," retrieved July 4, 2013 from www.deathpenaltyinfo.org/death-row-inmates-state-and-size-death-row-year#state.

66. "It is one of the happy incidents of the federal system that a single courageous State may, if its citizens choose, serve as a laboratory; and try novel social and economic experiments without risk to the rest of the country." *New State Ice Co. v. Liebmann*, 285 U.S. 262, 311 (1932) (Brandeis, J., dissenting).

67. *See Harmelin v. Michigan*, 501 U.S. 957, 989–990 (1991) (plurality opinion).

68. Jennifer Lynn Owens, *Capital Punishment in the Lone Star State: A County-Level Analysis of Contextual Effects of Sentencing* 4, 139 (2013) (unpublished PhD dissertation, State University of New York at Albany); Texas Coalition to Abolish the Death Penalty, *Texas Death Penalty Developments in 2012: The Year in Review* 1–3, 15 (2013), retrieved July 4, 2013 from www.tcadp.org/TexasDeathPenaltyDevelopments2012.pdf; Texas Coalition to Abolish the Death Penalty, *Death Sentences by County: 1976–2012*, retrieved July 4, 2013 from http://tcadp.org/1976–2012-county-map/.

69. James S. Liebman & Peter Clarke, "Minority Practice, Majority's Burden: The Death Penalty Today," 9 *Ohio State Journal of Criminal Law* 255, 254–265 (2011) (footnotes omitted).

70. Robert J. Smith, "The Geography of the Death Penalty and Its Ramifications," 92 *Boston University Law Review* 227, 233–234 (2012) (footnotes omitted). *See also* Liebman & Clarke, *supra* note 69, at 331–332.

71. Smith, *supra* note 70, at 231–232 (footnotes omitted).

72. Frank R. Baumgartner, *The Geography of the Death Penalty* 3–5 (2010), retrieved July 4, 2013 from www.unc.edu/~fbaum/Innocence/NC/Baumgartner-geography-of-capital-punishment-oct-17–2010.pdf.

73. Glenn L. Pierce & Michael L. Radelet, "Race, Region, and Death Sentencing in Illinois, 1988–1997," 81 *Oregon Law Review* 39, 65 (2002).

74. Andrew Ditchfield, "Challenging the Intrastate Disparities in the Application of Capital Punishment Statutes," 95 *Georgetown Law Journal* 801, 809 (2007). *See* Raymond Paternoster *et al.*, *An Empirical Analysis of Maryland's Death Sentencing System With Respect to the Influence of Race and Legal Jurisdiction: Final Report* (2003), retrieved July 4, 2013 from www.newsdesk.umd.edu/pdf/finalrep.pdf.

75. *See* Songer & Unah, *supra* note 48 (South Carolina); Barnes, Sloss & Thaman, *supra* note 48 (Missouri); Stephanie Hindson, Hillary Potter & Michael L. Radelet, "Race, Gender, Region and Death Sentencing in Colorado, 1980–1999, 77 *University of Colorado Law Review* 549,

574–576 (2006) (Colorado); David C. Baldus, George Woodworth, Catherine M. Grosso & Aaron M. Christ, *supra* note 48 (Nebraska); Jennifer Adger & Christopher Weiss, "Why Place Matters: Exploring County-Level Variations in Death Sentencing in Alabama," 2011 *Michigan State Law Review* 659 (2011) (Alabama). *See generally* Shatz & Dalton, *supra* note 48, at 1253–55; Ditchfield, *supra* note 74, at 809–810; Charles S. Lanier & James R. Acker, "Capital Punishment, the Moratorium Movement, and Empirical Questions," 10 *Psychology, Public Policy, and Law* 577, 598–600 (2004).

76. G. Ben Cohen & Robert J. Smith, "The Racial Geography of the Federal Death Penalty," 85 *Washington Law Review* 425 (2010).

77. *See* Ashley Rupp, "Death Penalty Prosecutorial Charging Decisions and County Budgetary Restrictions: Is the Death Penalty Arbitrarily Applied Based on County Funding?," 71 *Fordham Law Review* 2735 (2003).

78. *See* Shatz & Dalton, *supra* note 48, at 1255 (discussing support offered for within-state variation in capital charging and sentencing practices in Maryland and California).

7

DEFENSE ATTORNEYS AND CAPITAL JURORS

Introduction

Contemporary guided-discretion death-penalty statutes are far more complex than the sentencing laws that prevailed during the pre-*Furman v. Georgia* (1972)[1] era of capital punishment. The new statutes approved by the justices in *Gregg v. Georgia* (1976)[2] and companion cases[3] narrowed the range of death-penalty eligible crimes, separated capital-murder trials into distinct guilt and penalty phases, defined criteria to guide sentencing decisions, and ensured appellate court review of cases resulting in a sentence of death. As with other laws, however, and as discussed in the preceding chapter, their success or failure ultimately would hinge not on their written form but on whether the contemplated reforms translated meaningfully into practice. In this regard it is difficult to overestimate the crucial functions of the lawyers charged with representing defendants in capital cases, and the jurors entrusted with making guilt and punishment decisions. This chapter examines the performance of defense attorneys and trial jurors in capital cases, two sets of actors within criminal justice systems who play critical roles in death-penalty statutes' implementation.

Capital Defense Attorneys

Prosecutors play a vital role in the death penalty's administration, particularly in their charging decisions and plea bargaining policies. The discretion they exercise in choosing cases for capital prosecution is largely unregulated. Their charging decisions have obvious ripple effects encompassing sentencing through execution. Prosecutors' decisions have been challenged in several jurisdictions as contributing to the racially disparate and otherwise arbitrary application of the death penalty.[4] Defense attorneys serve as the counterweight to prosecutors in adversarial systems of justice. Nowhere is there a more urgent need for them to function as vigorous and effective advocates for the accused than in capital cases, where their clients' lives are literally on the line.

It is no accident that one of the Supreme Court's earliest rulings that a criminal conviction imposed by a state court was constitutionally deficient involved the right to the effective representation of defense counsel in a capital trial. The Court's 1932 decision in *Powell v. Alabama*[5] was returned following its review of the convictions and death sentences in the famous "Scottsboro Boys" case. This case involved nine young African

Americans between the ages of 13 and 20 who were accused of raping two White women on a freight train that was making its way through northern Alabama. Word that the women had been raped preceded the train's arrival at its next scheduled stop, where the county sheriff and dozens of deputized, armed White men awaited. The boys were taken into custody at the Paint Rock train station and transported to the nearby town of Scottsboro. The Governor of Alabama dispatched National Guard troops to quell the risk of lynching after an angry mob gathered outside of the Scottsboro jail.[6]

The rapes allegedly occurred on March 25, 1931. Rape was then punishable by death in Alabama. The boys were arrested, indicted, arraigned, and brought to trial within a two-week period. Because they were charged with a capital offense, Alabama law entitled them to court-appointed counsel. Confusion reigned concerning the assignment of counsel. The judge had appointed "all members of the [Scottsboro] bar" to represent the boys at the time of their arraignment. When the trial opened the judge declared that he had "anticipated [the appointed lawyers] to continue to help them. . . ."[7] It soon became apparent that no lawyer had actually undertaken the boys' representation. Thus, not until the morning the trial commenced did an attorney specifically assume the role of defense counsel for the nine young men. The boys were convicted in four separate trials, which were completed within a period of three days. Eight of them were sentenced to death; the youngest was spared that fate after the jury was unable to agree about a sentencing verdict.[8] The convictions and death sentences were upheld by the Alabama Supreme Court.

The United States Supreme Court reversed. Justice Sutherland's opinion for the Court in *Powell v. Alabama*, 287 U.S. 45 (1932), concluded that the untimely appointment of defense counsel had violated the boys' due process rights.

The defendants, young, ignorant, illiterate, surrounded by hostile sentiment, haled back and forth under guard of soldiers, charged with an atrocious crime regarded with especial horror in the community where they were to be tried, were . . . put in peril of their lives within a few moments after counsel for the first time charged with any degree of responsibility began to represent them. . . .

It never has been doubted by this court, or any other so far as we know, that notice and hearing are preliminary steps essential to the passing of an enforceable judgment, and that they, together with a legally competent tribunal having jurisdiction of the case, constitute basic elements of the constitutional requirement of due process of law. . . .

What, then, does a hearing include? Historically and in practice, in our own country at least, it has always included the right to the aid of counsel when desired and provided by the party asserting the right. The right to be heard would be, in many cases, of little avail if it did not comprehend the right to be heard by counsel. Even the intelligent and educated layman has small and sometimes no skill in the science of law. If charged with crime, he is incapable, generally, of determining for himself whether the indictment is good or bad. He is unfamiliar with the rules of evidence. Left without the aid of counsel he may be put on trial without a proper charge, and convicted upon incompetent evidence, or evidence irrelevant to the issue or otherwise inadmissible. He lacks both the skill and knowledge adequately to prepare his defense, even though he have a perfect one. He requires the guiding hand of counsel at every step in the proceedings against him. Without it, though he be not guilty, he faces the danger of conviction because he does not know how to establish his innocence. If that be true of men of intelligence, how much more true is it of the ignorant and illiterate, or those of feeble intellect. If in any case, civil or criminal, a state or federal court were arbitrarily to refuse to hear a party by counsel, employed by and appearing for him, it reasonably may not be doubted that such a refusal would be a denial of a hearing, and, therefore, of due process in the constitutional sense. . . .

In the light of the facts outlined in the forepart of this opinion—the ignorance and illiteracy of the defendants, their youth, the circumstances of public hostility, the imprisonment and the close surveillance of the defendants by the military forces, the fact that their friends and families were all in other states and communication with them necessarily difficult, and above all that they stood in deadly peril of their lives—we think the failure of the trial court to give them reasonable time and opportunity to secure counsel was a clear denial of due process.

But passing that, and assuming their inability, even if opportunity had been given, to employ counsel, as the trial court evidently did assume, we are of opinion that, under the circumstances just stated, the necessity of counsel was so vital and imperative that the failure of the trial court to make an effective appointment of counsel was likewise a denial of due process within the meaning of the Fourteenth Amendment. Whether this would be so in other criminal prosecutions, or under other circumstances, we need not determine. All that it is necessary now to decide, as we do decide, is that in a capital case, where the defendant is unable to employ counsel, and is incapable adequately of making his own defense because of ignorance, feeble-mindedness, illiteracy, or the like, it is the duty of the court, whether requested or not, to assign counsel for him as a necessary requisite of due process of law; and that duty is not discharged by an assignment at such a time or under such circumstances as to preclude the giving of effective aid in the preparation and trial of the case. . . . In a case such as this, whatever may be the rule in other cases, the right to have counsel appointed, when necessary, is a logical corollary from the constitutional right to be heard by counsel. . . .

Let us suppose the extreme case of a prisoner charged with a capital offense, who is deaf and dumb, illiterate, and feeble-minded, unable to employ counsel, with the whole power of the state arrayed against him, prosecuted by counsel for the state without assignment of counsel for his defense, tried, convicted, and sentenced to death. Such a result, which, if carried into execution, would be little short of judicial murder, it cannot be doubted would be a gross violation of the guarantee of due process of law; and we venture to think that no appellate court, state or federal, would hesitate so to decide. The duty of the trial court to appoint counsel under such circumstances is clear, as it is clear under circumstances such as are disclosed by the record here; and its power to do so, even in the absence of a statute, can not be questioned.

Today, few would quarrel with the premise that a layperson on trial for his or her life, and facing an experienced prosecutor who is trained in the law and equipped with the vast resources of the state, requires the assistance of defense counsel as a matter of fundamental fairness and justice. The Scottsboro Boys were represented by court-appointed counsel at their trial. Yet the Supreme Court nevertheless invalidated their convictions, concluding, in essence, that the lawyer was incapable of serving as an effective advocate in light of his last-minute appointment and his consequent inability to investigate the charges and otherwise prepare for trial. It thus is clear that the Constitution requires more than the simple presence of an attorney at trial, or one capable of passing the "cloudy mirror" test: "If the defense lawyer breathes on a mirror and it clouds up, he was effective."[9] The quality of representation that is required to constitute minimally effective assistance of defense counsel in a criminal case is considerably less clear, although the Supreme Court has announced the governing constitutional standards.

In *Strickland v. Washington*, 466 U.S. 668 (1984), David Washington pled guilty to capital murder in Florida, waived his right to a sentencing hearing before an advisory jury, and was sentenced to death by a judge who found insufficient evidence to mitigate the sentence to life imprisonment. Washington later alleged that his court-appointed lawyer violated his right to the effective assistance of counsel as guaranteed by the Sixth and Fourteenth Amendments, in that he had failed to conduct an adequate investigation and call witnesses whose mitigation testimony could have helped produce a life sentence. The Supreme Court rejected his claims and Washington was executed two months later.[10] Justice O'Connor authored the majority opinion that set forth the constitutional test for ineffective assistance of defense counsel.

A convicted defendant's claim that counsel's assistance was so defective as to require reversal of a conviction or death sentence has two components. First, the defendant must show that counsel's performance was deficient. This requires showing that counsel made errors so serious that counsel was not functioning as the "counsel" guaranteed the defendant by the Sixth Amendment. Second, the defendant must show that the deficient performance prejudiced the defense. This requires showing that counsel's errors were so serious as to deprive the defendant of a fair trial, a trial whose result is reliable. Unless a defendant makes both showings, it cannot be said that the conviction or death sentence resulted from a breakdown in the adversary process that renders the result unreliable.

A

. . . [T]he proper standard for attorney performance is that of reasonably effective assistance. . . . When a convicted defendant complains of the ineffectiveness of counsel's assistance, the defendant must show that counsel's representation fell below an objective standard of reasonableness.

More specific guidelines are not appropriate. . . . The proper measure of attorney performance remains simply reasonableness under prevailing professional norms.

Representation of a criminal defendant entails certain basic duties. Counsel's function is to assist the defendant, and hence counsel owes the client a duty of loyalty, a duty to avoid conflicts of interest. From counsel's function as assistant to the defendant derive the overarching duty to advocate the defendant's cause and the more particular duties to consult with the defendant on important decisions and to keep the defendant informed of important developments in the course of the prosecution. Counsel also has a duty to bring to bear such skill and knowledge as will render the trial a reliable adversarial testing process.

These basic duties neither exhaustively define the obligations of counsel nor form a checklist for judicial evaluation of attorney performance. In any case presenting an ineffectiveness claim, the performance inquiry must be whether counsel's assistance was reasonable considering all the circumstances. Prevailing norms of practice as reflected in American Bar Association standards and the like, are guides to determining what is reasonable, but they are only guides. No particular set of detailed rules for counsel's conduct can satisfactorily take account of the variety of circumstances faced by defense counsel or the range of legitimate decisions regarding how best to represent a criminal defendant. Any such set of rules would interfere with the constitutionally protected independence of counsel and restrict the wide latitude counsel must have in making tactical decisions. . . . [T]he purpose of the effective assistance guarantee of the Sixth Amendment is not to improve the quality of legal representation, although that is a goal of considerable importance to the legal system. The purpose is simply to ensure that criminal defendants receive a fair trial.

Judicial scrutiny of counsel's performance must be highly deferential. It is all too tempting for a defendant to second-guess counsel's assistance after conviction or adverse sentence, and it is all too easy for a court, examining counsel's defense after it has proved unsuccessful, to conclude that a particular act or omission of counsel was unreasonable. A fair assessment of attorney performance requires that every effort be made to eliminate the distorting effects of hindsight, to reconstruct the circumstances of counsel's challenged conduct, and to evaluate the conduct from counsel's perspective at the time. Because of the difficulties inherent in making the evaluation, a court must indulge a strong presumption that counsel's conduct falls within the wide range of reasonable professional assistance; that is, the defendant must overcome the presumption that, under the circumstances, the challenged action "might be considered sound trial strategy." See Michel v. Louisiana, 350 U.S. [91, 101 (1955)]. There are countless ways to provide effective assistance in any given case. Even the best criminal defense attorneys would not defend a particular client in the same way. . . .

B

An error by counsel, even if professionally unreasonable, does not warrant setting aside the judgment of a criminal proceeding if the error had no effect on the judgment. The purpose of the Sixth Amendment guarantee of counsel is to ensure that a defendant has the assistance necessary to justify reliance on the outcome of the proceeding. Accordingly, any deficiencies in counsel's performance must be prejudicial to the defense in order to constitute ineffective assistance under the Constitution.

In certain Sixth Amendment contexts, prejudice is presumed. Actual or constructive denial of the assistance of counsel altogether is legally presumed to result in prejudice. So are various kinds of state interference with counsel's assistance. Prejudice in these circumstances is so likely that case-by-case inquiry into prejudice is not worth the cost. . . .

Conflict of interest claims aside, actual ineffectiveness claims alleging a deficiency in attorney performance are subject to a general requirement that the defendant affirmatively prove prejudice. . . . Even if a defendant shows that particular errors of counsel were unreasonable, . . . the defendant must show that they actually had an adverse effect on the defense. . . .

Accordingly, the appropriate test for prejudice finds its roots in the test for materiality of exculpatory information not disclosed to the defense by the prosecution, and in the test for materiality of testimony made unavailable to the defense by Government deportation of a witness. The defendant must show that there is a reasonable probability that, but for counsel's unprofessional errors, the result of the proceeding would have been different. A reasonable probability is a probability sufficient to undermine confidence in the outcome. . . .

. . . When a defendant challenges a conviction, the question is whether there is a reasonable probability that, absent the errors, the factfinder would have had a reasonable doubt respecting guilt. When a defendant challenges a death sentence such as the one at issue in this case, the question is whether there is a reasonable probability that, absent the errors, the sentencer . . . would have concluded that the balance of aggravating and mitigating circumstances did not warrant death.

In making this determination, a court hearing an ineffectiveness claim must consider the totality of the evidence before the judge or jury. . . . Taking the unaffected findings as a given, and taking due account of the effect of the errors on the remaining findings, a court making the prejudice inquiry must ask if the defendant has met the burden of showing that the decision reached would reasonably likely have been different absent the errors.

The *Strickland* test for constitutionally ineffective assistance of counsel, involving the two-part showing of deficient performance and resulting prejudice, is easily stated but not so easily applied. The test has been criticized as being both vague[11] and toothless,[12] and as affording defendants in capital cases inadequate protection from hopelessly incompetent and ill-prepared attorneys. Throughout the 1980s and 1990s, in particular, many cases arose supporting that dim assessment. For example, Calvin Burdine was convicted of capital murder and sentenced to death in Texas at a trial in which his court-appointed counsel repeatedly fell asleep during prosecution witnesses' testimony. Finding that Burdine had not been "prejudiced" as required by *Strickland,* the state courts and a panel of the Fifth Circuit Court of Appeals upheld his conviction and death sentence. Following a rehearing *en banc*, the Fifth Circuit ultimately agreed that a sleeping lawyer is not a constitutionally effective one and granted Burdine relief.[13]

In other cases, indigent defendants were convicted of murder, sentenced to death, and later executed after being represented by lawyers who were fresh out of law school with scant experience in criminal trials, or intoxicated, or ignorant of the governing law, or who made disparaging and racially insensitive remarks about their clients to the jury, or who had failed to investigate potentially viable defenses or secure mitigation evidence, yet whose performance nevertheless passed scrutiny under *Strickland's* standards.[14] Justice Blackmun lamented the all-too-common inadequacy of defense counsel in capital trials and state post-conviction proceedings, and the factors contributing to the deficient representation they provided, in his dissent from the Supreme Court's denial of *certiorari* in *McFarland v. Scott*, 512 U.S. 1256 (1994).

I . . . write to address the crisis in trial and state postconviction legal representation for capital defendants . . .

Without question, "the principal failings of the capital punishment review process today are the inadequacy and inadequate compensation of counsel at trial and the unavailability of counsel in state post-conviction proceedings." Robbins, Toward a More Just and Effective System of Review in State Death Penalty Cases, Report of the American Bar Association's Recommendations Concerning Death Penalty Habeas Corpus, 40 Am.U.L.Rev. 1, 16 (1990) (ABA Report). The unique, bifurcated nature of capital trials and the special investigation into a defendant's personal history and background that may be required, the complexity and fluidity of the law, and the high, emotional stakes involved all make capital cases more costly and difficult to litigate than ordinary criminal trials. Yet, the attorneys assigned to represent indigent capital defendants at times are less qualified than those appointed in ordinary criminal cases. See Coyle, et al., Fatal Defense, 12 Nat. L.J. 30, 44 (June 11, 1990) (Capital-defense attorneys in eight States were disbarred, suspended, or disciplined at rates 3 to 46 times higher than the general attorney-discipline rates).

Two factors contribute to the general unavailability of qualified attorneys to represent capital defendants. The absence of standards governing court-appointed capital-defense counsel means that unqualified lawyers often are appointed, and the absence of funds to compensate lawyers

prevents even qualified lawyers from being able to present an adequate defense. Many States that regularly impose the death penalty have few, if any, standards governing the qualifications required of court-appointed capital-defense counsel. . . . According to a 1990 survey by the National Law Journal, . . . Florida, Georgia, Mississippi, Texas, and California have no binding statewide qualification criteria for capital-defense counsel. See Coyle, 12 Nat.L.J., at 32. Capital-defense attorneys in Louisiana must have five years' experience practicing in some area of law, but are not required to have experience in capital defense or any form of criminal practice.

In addition to the lack of standards, compensation for attorneys representing indigent capital defendants often is perversely low. Although a properly conducted capital trial can involve hundreds of hours of investigation, preparation, and lengthy trial proceedings, many States severely limit the compensation paid for capital defense. Louisiana limits the compensation for court-appointed capital-defense counsel to $1,000 for *all* pretrial preparation and trial proceedings. Kentucky pays a maximum of $2,500 for the same services. Alabama limits reimbursement for out-of-court preparation in capital cases to a maximum of $1,000 each for the trial and penalty phases.

Court-awarded funds for the appointment of investigators and experts often are either unavailable, severely limited, or not provided by state courts. As a result, attorneys appointed to represent capital defendants at the trial level frequently are unable to recoup even their overhead costs and out-of-pocket expenses, and effectively may be required to work at minimum wage or below while funding from their own pockets their client's defense. A recent survey by the Mississippi Trial Lawyers' Association estimated that capital-defense attorneys in that State are compensated at an average rate of $11.75 per hour. See Coyle, 12 Nat. L.J., at 32. Compensation rates of $5 per hour or less are not uncommon. Strasser, $1,000 Fee Cap Makes Death Row's 'Justice' A Bargain for the State, 12 Nat. L.J. 33 (June 11, 1990).[FN1] The prospect that hours spent in trial preparation or funds expended hiring psychiatrists or ballistics experts will be uncompensated unquestionably chills even a qualified attorney's zealous representation of his client.

FN1. Recent improvements have been made, however. The Florida Supreme Court struck down the State's maximum fee of $3,500 as unconstitutional when applied in such a manner as to impinge on the right to effective counsel in capital cases. *White v. Board of County Comm'rs*, 537 So.2d 1376 (1989). The court found itself "hard pressed to find any capital case in which the circumstances would not warrant an award of attorneys' fees in excess of the [$3,500] fee cap." *Id.*, at 1378. South Carolina's Supreme Court also refused, on Sixth Amendment grounds, to enforce the State's $10 and $15 per hour and $5,000 maximum compensation levels in capital cases. *Bailey v. State*, 424 S.E.2d 503, 508 (1992). The Oklahoma and Arkansas Supreme Courts recently struck down their States' respective compensation caps of $3,200 and $1,000 as unconstitutional takings when applied to capital cases. See *State v. Lynch*, 796 P.2d 1150 (Okla.1990); *Arnold v. Kemp*, 813 S.W.2d 770 (Ark. 1991).

The practical costs of such ad hoc systems of attorney selection and compensation are well documented. Capital defendants have been sentenced to death when represented by counsel who never bothered to read the state death penalty statute, *e.g.*, *Smith v. State*, 581 So.2d 497 (Ala.Crim.App.1990), slept through or otherwise were not present during trial, or failed to investigate or present any mitigating evidence at the penalty phase, *Mitchell v. Kemp*, 483 U.S. 1026 (1987) (Marshall, J., dissenting from denial of certiorari). Other indigent defendants have been represented by attorneys who had been admitted to the bar only six months before and never had conducted a criminal trial. *E.g.*, *Paradis v. Arave*, 954 F.2d 1483, 1490–1491 (CA9 1992), vacated and remanded, 507 U.S. 1026 (1993), relief denied, 20 F.3d 950, 959 (1994). One Louisiana defendant was convicted of capital murder following a 1-day trial and 20-minute penalty phase proceeding, in which his counsel stipulated to the defendant's age at the time of the crime and rested. *State v. Messiah*, 538 So.2d 175, 187 (La.1988), cert. denied, 493 U.S. 1063 (1990). When asked to cite the criminal cases he knew, one defense attorney who failed to challenge his client's racially unrepresentative jury pool could name only two cases: *Miranda v. Arizona*, 384 U.S. 436 (1966), and *Dred Scott v. Sandford*, 15 L.Ed. 691 (1857).

The consequences of such poor trial representation for the capital defendant, of course, can be lethal. Evidence not presented at trial cannot later be discovered and introduced; arguments and objections not advanced are forever waived. Nor is a capital defendant likely to be able to demonstrate that his legal counsel was ineffective, given the low standard for acceptable attorney conduct and the high showing of prejudice required under *Strickland v. Washington*, 466 U.S. 668 (1984). Ten years after the articulation of that standard, practical experience establishes that the *Strickland* test, in application, has failed to protect a defendant's right to be represented by something more than "a person who happens to be a lawyer." *Id.,* at 685.

The impotence of the *Strickland* standard is perhaps best evidenced in the cases in which ineffective-assistance claims have been denied. John Young, for example, was represented in his capital trial by an attorney who was addicted to drugs and who a few weeks later was incarcerated on federal drug charges. The Court of Appeals for the Eleventh Circuit rejected Young's ineffective-assistance-of-counsel claim on federal habeas, *Young v. Zant,* 727 F.2d 1489 (1984), and this Court denied review, 470 U.S. 1009 (1985). Young was executed in 1985. John Smith and his codefendant Rebecca Machetti were sentenced to death by juries selected under the same Georgia statute. Machetti's attorneys successfully challenged the statute under a recent Supreme Court decision, *Taylor v. Louisiana,* 419 U.S. 522 (1975), winning Machetti a new trial and ultimately a life sentence. *Machetti v. Linahan,* 679 F.2d 236 (CA11 1982). Smith's counsel was unaware of the Supreme Court decision, however, and failed similarly to object at trial. *Smith v. Kemp,* 715 F.2d 1459 (CA11 1983). Smith was executed in 1983.

Jesus Romero's attorney failed to present any evidence at the penalty phase and delivered a closing argument totaling 29 words. Although the attorney later was suspended on unrelated grounds, Romero's ineffective-assistance claim was rejected by the Court of Appeals for the Fifth Circuit, *Romero v. Lynaugh,* 884 F.2d 871, 875 (1989), and this Court denied certiorari, 494 U.S. 1012 (1990). Romero was executed in 1992. Larry Heath was represented on direct appeal by counsel who filed a 6-page

brief before the Alabama Court of Criminal Appeals. The attorney failed to appear for oral argument before the Alabama Supreme Court and filed a brief in that court containing a 1-page argument and citing a single case. The Eleventh Circuit found no prejudice, *Heath v. Jones,* 941 F.2d 1126, 1131 (1991), and this Court denied review, 502 U.S. 1077 (1992). Heath was executed in Alabama in 1992.

James Messer, a mentally impaired capital defendant, was represented by an attorney who at the trial's guilt phase presented *no* defense, made no objections, and emphasized the horror of the capital crime in his closing statement. At the penalty phase, the attorney presented no evidence of mental impairment, failed to introduce other substantial mitigating evidence, and again repeatedly suggested in closing that death was the appropriate punishment. The Eleventh Circuit refused to grant relief, *Messer v. Kemp,* 760 F.2d 1080 (1985), and this Court denied certiorari, 474 U.S. 1088 (1986). Messer was executed in 1988. Even the attorney who could name only *Miranda* and *Dred Scott* twice has survived ineffective-assistance challenges.[FN2] None of these cases inspires confidence that the adversarial system functioned properly or "that the trial ca[n] be relied on as having produced a just result." *Strickland,* 466 U.S., at 686. Yet, in none of these cases was counsel's assistance found to be ineffective.

FN2. For further discussion of these and other examples of indigent capital defense representation, see, *e.g.,* Bright, Counsel for the Poor: The Death Sentence Not for the Worst Crime but for the Worst Lawyer, 103 Yale L.J. 1835 (1994).

Regardless of the quality of counsel, capital defendants constitutionally are entitled to have *some* "person who happens to be a lawyer . . . present at trial alongside the accused." *Id.,* at

685. The same cannot be said for state post-conviction review. State habeas corpus proceedings are a vital link in the capital review process, not the least because all federal habeas claims first must be adequately raised in state court. This Court thus far has declined to hold that indigent capital defendants have a right to counsel at this level, based on the assumption that capital defendants generally can obtain volunteer or other counsel to represent them in these state proceedings. *Murray v. Giarratano,* 492 U.S. 1, 14 (1989) (KENNEDY, J., concurring in judgment) (In "the case before us . . . no prisoner on death row in Virginia has been unable to obtain counsel to represent him in postconviction proceedings").

Though perhaps true for some jurisdictions, this assumption bears little resemblance to the realities confronting McFarland and other condemned inmates in Texas. A recent study of state postconviction capital representation in Texas sponsored by the State Bar of Texas concluded that the capital-defense situation in that State is "desperate." The Spangenberg Group, A Study of Representation in Capital Cases in Texas, ii (Mar. 1993). According to the Spangenberg Group, "Texas has already reached the crisis stage in capital representation and . . . the problem is substantially worse than that faced by any other state with the death penalty." *Id.,* at i.

Texas has the second largest death row in the country, with approximately 375 inmates currently facing execution. Since 1976, Texas has executed approximately one third of all the defendants put to death in the United States, and the pace of executions in Texas is increasing. In June 1993, this Court denied certiorari in an unprecedented 29 capital cases from Texas, including McFarland's. During the ensuing period between June 1 and October 21, 1993, Texas scheduled 39 executions

and actually executed 10 capital defendants. All told, the Lone Star State set more than 100 execution dates in 1993, at least 8 of which were set within 45 days of the close of direct review.

Finding qualified defense counsel capable of meeting this demand might be formidable even if an adequate pool of attorneys and adequate funds were available. Capital defendants in Texas, however, have no statutory right to counsel in state postconviction proceedings, receive little benefit from the State's skeletal public defender service, and are not provided even discretionary court-appointed counsel. Although the Texas Code of Criminal Procedure, Arts. 11.07, 26.04, 26.05, gives state courts discretion to appoint and compensate counsel for state habeas corpus proceedings, "this is almost never done." Spangenberg Group, at vii. Funds for experts and other expenses also "are almost never approved." *Ibid.* . . . Capital defendants in state postconviction proceedings must rely almost exclusively on volunteer private counsel—volunteers who are increasingly difficult to find. . . . The lack of attorney compensation and Texas' aggressive practice of "[d]ocket control by execution date," Jones, Death Penalty Procedures: A Proposal for Reform, 53 Tex.Bar J. 850, 851 (1990), have left an estimated 75 capital defendants in Texas who currently are facing execution dates without any legal representation.

The right to qualified legal counsel in federal habeas corpus proceedings bestowed by § 848(q)(4)(B) is triggered only after a capital defendant has completed his direct review and, generally, some form of state postconviction proceeding. The continuing importance of federal habeas corpus in correcting constitutional errors is well documented. Of the capital cases reviewed in federal habeas corpus proceedings between 1976 and 1991, nearly half (46%) were found to have constitutional error. Liebman, More than 'Slightly Retro:' The Rehnquist Court's Rout of Habeas Corpus Jurisdiction in *Teague v. Lane,* 18 N.Y.U.Rev.L. & Soc. Change 537, 541, n. 15 (1990–1991). The total reversal rate of capital cases at all stages of review during the same time period was estimated at 60% or more. *Id.,* at 541, n. 15. This Court itself frequently has granted capital defendants relief in federal habeas corpus proceedings.

The mere presence of "[s]uch a high incidence of uncorrected error" found in capital habeas corpus proceedings, *Murray v. Giarratano,* 492 U.S., at 24 (STEVENS, J., dissenting), testifies to the inadequacy of the legal representation afforded at the trial and state post-conviction stages. Yet the barriers to relief in federal habeas corpus proceedings are high. Even the best lawyers cannot rectify a meritorious constitutional claim that has been procedurally defaulted or waived by prior inadequate counsel. The accumulating and often byzantine restrictions this Court has imposed on federal habeas corpus review, make it even less likely that future capital defendants who receive qualified legal counsel in federal habeas actually will obtain relief. And it is the capital defendant who pays the price for the failings of counsel and this review process—generally with his life.

Our system of justice is adversarial and depends for its legitimacy on the fair and adequate representation of all parties at all levels of the judicial process. The trial is the main event in this system, where the prosecution and the defense do battle to reach a presumptively reliable result. When we execute a capital defendant in this country, we rely on the belief that the individual was guilty, and was convicted and sentenced after a fair trial, to justify the imposition of state-sponsored killing. And when this Court curtails federal oversight of state-court proceedings, it does so in reliance on the proposition that justice has been done at the trial level. My 24 years of overseeing the imposition of the death penalty from this Court have left me in grave doubt whether this reliance is justified and whether the constitutional requirement of competent legal counsel for capital defendants is being fulfilled. It is my hope and belief that this Nation soon will come to realize that capital punishment cannot morally or constitutionally be imposed. Until that time, however, we must have the courage to recognize the failings of our present system of capital representation and the conviction to do what is necessary to improve it.

The quality of defense counsel in capital cases is not always as low as in the cases cited by Justice Blackmun. Indeed, a number of skilled and dedicated lawyers have worked in highly professional organizations or publicly funded offices that represent indigent capital defendants, or have volunteered to provide their services in capital cases. More recently, there is reason to believe that defendants in capital cases have generally begun to receive improved representation. Beginning in 2000, the justices appeared to elevate their expectations for capital defense representation. With increasingly frequent reference to standards promulgated by the American Bar Association for the appointment and performance of defense counsel in capital cases,[15] the Court vacated the death sentences imposed in three separate cases because attorneys had made inadequate investigation and presentation of mitigation evidence.[16] Meanwhile, the capital defense bars in several states were becoming increasingly specialized.[17] In some jurisdictions, appointed counsel in capital cases were governed by considerably more demanding requirements for training and experience and were compensated at somewhat higher levels than court-appointed counsel in other serious cases, though such reforms seriously lagged elsewhere.[18] Although inconsistent between cases and jurisdictions, the overall quality of defense attorneys' performance in capital trials appears to have made a modest uptick coinciding with the Supreme Court toughening its application of the *Strickland* test.

Indigent defendants in capital and noncapital cases have a constitutional right to court-appointed counsel, but only for their trial and the initial appeal of their convictions.[19] Even in capital cases, there is no constitutional right to appointed counsel at later stages of judicial review, including petitioning a state court or the United States Supreme Court for certiorari,[20] making a collateral challenge to a conviction or sentence in state post-conviction proceedings,[21] or petitioning a federal court to issue a writ of habeas corpus. State post-conviction review normally is reserved for issues that could not have been raised on appeal, such as allegations of ineffective assistance of trial counsel, prosecutors' failure to disclose exculpatory evidence, and claims of newly discovered evidence of innocence. Evidentiary hearings before a judge typically are required to resolve such issues, creating extraordinary difficulties for incarcerated defendants who lack the assistance of counsel.[22] Moreover, unless such claims are raised in state court proceedings, they normally cannot be presented later to the federal courts.[23] Most states, but not all, provide a statutory right to court-appointed counsel in post-conviction proceedings for indigent death-sentenced defendants.[24]

Alabama is one of the few states that fails to provide a statutory right to court-appointed counsel for indigent criminal defendants seeking post-conviction review of their convictions or sentences. Cory Maples was found guilty of two counts of capital murder and sentenced to death in Alabama. The state courts affirmed the trial court's judgments on appeal in 1999.[25] Two volunteer lawyers from a large New York City law firm undertook Maples' representation to pursue relief in state post-conviction proceedings. The out-of-state lawyers were admitted to practice in Alabama in this limited capacity through a motion filed by an Alabama attorney, but they otherwise had exclusive responsibility for representing Maples. The court presiding over the post-conviction hearing rejected Maples' request for relief in 2003. Through a series of regrettable lapses, precipitated by the two volunteer lawyers leaving the firm with which they had been associated without notifying Maples or the Alabama courts of their inability to continue representing him, no appeal was made of the state court's denial of post-conviction relief. Later, other attorneys filed a petition for writ of habeas corpus in federal court on Maples' behalf. The U.S. District Court refused to consider the issues that had been raised at the state post-conviction hearing, ruling that the failure to appeal resulted in the issues being forfeited and thus unavailable for review on federal habeas corpus.[26]

In *Maples v. Thomas*, 132 S.Ct. 912 (2012), the U.S. Supreme Court ruled (7–2) that under these circumstances, the lawyers' failure to appeal would not bar Maples from presenting his claims on federal habeas corpus. The majority, concurring, and dissenting opinions in the case alternatively castigated Alabama for its laws and practices governing the appointment of counsel in capital cases, and dismissed the significance of the state's policies in this regard.

Justice GINSBURG delivered the opinion of the Court. . . .

I

A

Alabama sets low eligibility requirements for lawyers appointed to represent indigent capital defendants at trial. American Bar Association, Evaluating Fairness and Accuracy in State Death Penalty Systems: The Alabama Death Penalty Assessment Report 117–120 (June 2006) (hereinafter ABA Report). Appointed counsel need only be a member of the Alabama bar and have "five years' prior experience in the active practice of criminal law." Ala.Code § 13A–5–54 (2006). Experience with capital cases is not required. Nor does the State provide, or require appointed counsel to gain, any capital-case-specific professional education or training.

Appointed counsel in death penalty cases are also undercompensated. Until 1999, the State paid appointed capital defense attorneys just "$40.00 per hour for time expended in court and $20.00 per hour for time reasonably expended out of court in the preparation of [the defendant's] case." Ala. Code § 15–12–21(d) (1995). Although death penalty litigation is plainly time intensive,[FN1] the State capped at $1,000 fees recoverable by capital defense attorneys for out-of-court work.[FN2] Even today, court-appointed attorneys receive only $70 per hour.

FN1. One study of federal capital trials from 1990 to 1997 found that defense attorneys spent an average of 1,480 out-of-court hours preparing a defendant's case.

FN2. In 1999, the State removed the cap on fees for out-of-court work in capital cases. Ala. Code § 15–12–21(d) (2010 Cum. Supp.). Perhaps not coincidentally, 70% of the inmates on Alabama's death row in 2006, including Maples, had been convicted when the $1,000 cap was in effect.

Nearly alone among the States, Alabama does not guarantee representation to indigent capital defendants in postconviction proceedings. The State has elected, instead, "to rely on the efforts of typically well-funded [out-of-state] volunteers." Brief in Opposition in *Barbour v. Allen*, O.T.2006, No. 06–10605, p. 23. Thus, as of 2006, 86% of the attorneys representing Alabama's death row inmates in state collateral review proceedings "either worked for the Equal Justice Initiative (headed by NYU Law professor Bryan Stevenson), out-of-state public interest groups like the Innocence Project, or an out-of-state mega-firm." Brief in Opposition 16, n. 4. On occasion, some prisoners sentenced to death receive no postconviction representation at all. See ABA Report 112 ("[A]s of April 2006, approximately fifteen of Alabama's death row inmates in the final rounds of state appeals had no lawyer to represent them.").

B

This system was in place when, in 1997, Alabama charged Maples with two counts of capital murder. . . . Maples pleaded not guilty, and his case proceeded to trial, where he was represented by two court-appointed Alabama attorneys. Only one of them had earlier served in a capital case. Neither counsel had previously tried the penalty phase of a capital case. Compensation for each lawyer was capped at $1,000 for time spent out-of-court preparing Maples' case, and at $40 per hour for in-court services.

Finding Maples guilty on both counts, the jury recommended that he be sentenced to death. . . . Accepting the jury's recommendation, the trial court sentenced Maples to death. On direct appeal, the Alabama Court of Criminal Appeals and the Alabama Supreme Court affirmed the convictions and sentence.

Two out-of-state volunteers represented Maples in postconviction proceedings. . . .

With the aid of his *pro bono* counsel, Maples filed a petition for postconviction relief. . . . Among other claims, Maples asserted that his court-appointed attorneys provided constitutionally ineffective assistance during both guilt and penalty phases of his capital trial. He alleged, in this regard, that his inexperienced and underfunded attorneys failed to develop and raise an obvious intoxication defense, did not object to several egregious instances of prosecutorial misconduct, and woefully underprepared for the penalty phase of his trial. . . .

[As explained above, thereafter the trial court rejected Maples' petition for post-conviction relief, no appeal was taken because of the attorneys' lapses, and the lower federal courts refused to hear the non-appealed issues on Maples' petition for writ of habeas corpus.]

. . . Through no fault of his own, Maples lacked the assistance of any authorized attorney during the 42 days Alabama allows for noticing an appeal from a trial court's denial of postconviction relief. . . . [H]e had no reason to suspect that, in reality, he had been reduced to *pro se* status. Maples was disarmed by extraordinary circumstances quite beyond his control. He has shown ample cause, we hold, to excuse the procedural default into which he was trapped when counsel of record abandoned him without a word of warning. . . .

For the reasons stated, the judgment of the Court of Appeals for the Eleventh Circuit is reversed, and the case is remanded for further proceedings consistent with this opinion. . . .

Justice ALITO, concurring. . . .

In an effort to obtain relief for his client, petitioner's counsel in the case now before us cast blame for what occurred on Alabama's system of providing legal representation for capital defendants at trial and in state collateral proceedings. But whatever may be said about Alabama's system, I do not think that Alabama's system had much if anything to do with petitioner's misfortune. The quality of petitioner's representation at trial obviously played no role in the failure to meet the deadline for filing his notice of appeal from the denial of his state postconviction petition. Nor do I see any important connection between what happened in this case and Alabama's system for providing representation for prisoners who are sentenced to death and who wish to petition the state courts for collateral relief. Unlike other States, Alabama relies on attorneys who volunteer to represent these prisoners *pro bono*, and we are told that most of these volunteers work for large, out-of-state firms. Petitioner's brief states that the Alabama system had "a direct bearing on the events giving rise . . . to the procedural default at issue," but a similar combination of untoward events could have occurred if petitioner had been represented by Alabama attorneys who were appointed by the court and paid for with state funds. The firm whose lawyers represented petitioner *pro bono* is one of the country's most prestigious and expensive, and I have little doubt that the vast majority of criminal defendants would think that they had won the lottery if they were given the opportunity to be represented by attorneys from such a firm. . . .

What occurred here was not a predictable consequence of the Alabama system but a veritable perfect storm of misfortune, a most unlikely combination of events that, without notice, effectively deprived petitioner of legal representation. Under these unique circumstances, I agree that petitioner's procedural default is overcome.

Justice SCALIA, with whom Justice THOMAS joins, dissenting. . . .

One suspects that today's decision is motivated in large part by an understandable sense of frustration with the State's refusal to waive Maples' procedural default in the interest of fairness. Indeed, that frustration may well explain the Court's lengthy indictment of Alabama's general procedures for providing representation to capital defendants, a portion of the Court's opinion that is so disconnected from the rest of its analysis as to be otherwise inexplicable.

But if the interest of fairness justifies our excusing Maples' procedural default here, it does so whenever a defendant's procedural default is caused by his attorney. That is simply not the law—and cannot be, if the states are to have an orderly system of criminal litigation conducted by counsel. Our precedents allow a State to stand on its rights and enforce a habeas petitioner's procedural default even when counsel is to blame. Because a faithful application of those precedents leads to the conclusion that Maples has not demonstrated cause to excuse his procedural default; and because the reasoning by which the Court justifies the opposite conclusion invites future evisceration of the principle that defendants are responsible for the mistakes of their attorneys; I respectfully dissent.

Can a system of justice be considered fair if it denies indigent defendants under sentence of death the assistance of court-appointed counsel throughout the entire judicial review process?

Can appeals and later stages of judicial review in capital cases make up for less-than-exemplary trial representation?

Strategically, how should a lawyer conduct a defense in a capital murder trial? Is the best approach to contest guilt vigorously by denying that the defendant committed the murder and then, in the event of a conviction, try to present the defendant as a sympathetic and remorseful figure whose life should be spared? Should the focus instead be to avoid a death sentence, essentially using the guilt phase of the trial as prelude to the presentation of mitigation evidence and/or the defendant's acceptance of responsibility and expression of remorse at the sentencing hearing? Is it possible to do both, *i.e.*, vigorously contest guilt and then ask the jury to be understanding and spare the defendant's life at the penalty phase?

What would motivate a lawyer to represent a defendant who has been charged with capital murder? Should it matter if the lawyer knows that the defendant is guilty, *i.e.,* that his or her client has in fact committed an aggravated murder that qualifies for capital punishment? What toll—personal and professional—do you imagine is exacted on the lawyers who represent defendants in capital cases, burdened as they are with the knowledge that their efforts or their shortcomings could well make the difference between life and death for their clients?[27]

The Capital Jury

Defendants in criminal cases have a constitutional right to have their guilt or innocence determined by a jury.[28] Outside of the death-penalty context, in almost all of the states and in the federal courts, the jury's duties then are complete. In most jurisdictions, judges are given exclusive responsibility for sentencing. The practice is quite different in capital cases. Juries are entrusted with deciding whether a convicted capital offender should be sentenced to death in 30 of the 34 capital-punishment jurisdictions in this country. Montana stands alone in conferring capital case sentencing authority to judges without input from a jury.[29] In Alabama, Delaware, and Florida, judges make the final sentencing decision in capital cases after receiving a non-binding punishment recommendation from the jury.[30] The Supreme Court has ruled that juries must decide the critical facts needed to support punishment by death (such as the existence of statutory aggravating factors).[31] This fact-finding requirement has not been extended to deny judges the authority to make the ultimate decision of whether an offender should be sentenced to life imprisonment or death.[32]

What explains the anomaly of so many jurisdictions placing such extensive reliance on juries, rather than judges, to make capital sentencing decisions?

The Supreme Court approved Florida's post-*Furman* death-penalty statute in *Proffitt v. Florida* (1976)[33]—one of the companion cases to *Gregg v. Georgia.*[34] The Florida law gave final sentencing authority in capital cases to the trial judge, following the judge's consideration of the jury's non-binding recommendation. The jury in *Proffitt* had recommended a death sentence, and the trial judge concurred. In *Spaziano v. Florida* (1984),[35] the trial judge sentenced Joseph Spaziano to death notwithstanding the jury's recommendation that he receive a sentence of life imprisonment. The Court thus confronted an issue not squarely presented in *Proffitt*: whether "allowing a judge to override a jury's recommendation of life [imprisonment] violates the Eighth Amendment's proscription against 'cruel and unusual punishments.'"[36] Justice Blackmun's majority opinion concluded that the judicial override was not constitutionally objectionable. In the process, the Court rejected Spaziano's "fundamental premise . . . that the capital sentencing decision is one that, in all cases, should be made by a jury."[37]

> In light of the facts that the Sixth Amendment does not require jury sentencing, that the demands of fairness and reliability in capital cases do not require it, and that neither the

nature of, nor the purpose behind, the death penalty requires jury sentencing, we cannot conclude that placing responsibility on the trial judge to impose the sentence in a capital case is unconstitutional.[38]

Justice Stevens disagreed. His dissenting opinion, joined in relevant part by Justices Brennan and Marshall, explained why he believed that juries, and not judges, must serve as the sentencing authority in capital cases.

In the 12 years since *Furman v. Georgia*, 408 U.S. 238 (1972), every Member of this Court has written or joined at least one opinion endorsing the proposition that because of its severity and irrevocability, the death penalty is qualitatively different from any other punishment, and hence must be accompanied by unique safeguards to ensure that it is a justified response to a given offense. Because it is the one punishment that cannot be prescribed by a rule of law as judges normally understand such rules, but rather is ultimately understood only as an expression of the community's outrage—its sense that an individual has lost his moral entitlement to live—I am convinced that the danger of an excessive response can only be avoided if the decision to impose the death penalty is made by a jury rather than by a single governmental official. This conviction is consistent with the judgment of history and the current consensus of opinion that juries are better equipped than judges to make capital sentencing decisions. The basic explanation for that consensus lies in the fact that the question whether a sentence of death is excessive in the particular circumstances of any case is one that must be answered by the decisionmaker that is best able to "express the conscience of the community on the ultimate question of life or death." *Witherspoon v. Illinois*, 391 U.S. 510, 519 (1968). . . .

. . . [S]entencing has traditionally been a question with which the jury is not concerned.

Deciding upon the appropriate sentence for a person who has been convicted of a crime is the routine work of judges. By reason of this experience, as well as their training, judges presumably perform this function well. But, precisely because the death penalty is unique, the normal presumption that a judge is the appropriate sentencing authority does not apply in the capital context. . . .

. . . [I]n the final analysis, capital punishment rests on not a legal but an ethical judgment—an assessment of what we called in *Enmund* [*v. Florida*, 458 U.S. 782, 800–801 (1982)], the "moral guilt" of the defendant. And if the decision that capital punishment is the appropriate sanction in extreme cases is justified because it expresses the community's moral sensibility—its demand that a given affront to humanity requires retribution—it follows, I believe, that a representative cross section of the community must be given the responsibility for making that decision. In no other way can an unjustifiable risk of an excessive response be avoided.

The authors of our federal and state constitutional guarantees uniformly recognized the special function of the jury in any exercise of plenary power over the life and liberty of the citizen. In our jurisprudence, the jury has always played an essential role in legitimating the system of criminal justice.

"The guarantees of jury trial in the Federal and State Constitutions reflect a profound judgment about the way in which law should be enforced and justice administered. A right to jury trial is granted to criminal defendants in order to prevent oppression by the Government. Those who wrote our constitutions knew from history and experience that it was necessary to protect against unfounded criminal charges brought to eliminate enemies and against judges too responsive to the voice of higher authority. The framers of the constitutions strove to create an independent judiciary but insisted upon further protection against arbitrary action. Providing an accused with the right to be tried by a jury of his peers gave him an inestimable safeguard against the corrupt or overzealous prosecutor and against the compliant, biased, or eccentric judge. If the defendant preferred the common-sense judgment of a jury to the more tutored but perhaps less sympathetic reaction of the single judge, he was to have it. Beyond this, the jury trial provisions in the Federal and State Constitutions reflect a fundamental decision about the exercise of official power—a reluctance to entrust plenary powers over the life and liberty of the citizen to one judge or to a group of judges. Fear of unchecked power, so typical of our State and Federal Governments in other respects, found expression in the criminal law in this insistence upon community participation in the determination of guilt or innocence." *Duncan v. Louisiana*, 391 U.S. 145, 155–156 (1968). . . .

The same consideration that supports a constitutional entitlement to a trial by a jury rather than a judge at the guilt or innocence stage—the right to have an authentic representative of the community apply its lay perspective to the determination that must precede a deprivation of liberty—applies with special force to the determination that must precede a deprivation of life. . . . [T]he life-or-death decision in capital cases depends upon its link to community values for its moral and constitutional legitimacy. In *Witherspoon v. Illinois*, 391 U.S. 510

(1968), after observing that "a jury that must choose between life imprisonment and capital punishment can do little more—and must do nothing less—than express the conscience of the community on the ultimate question of life or death," *id.*, at 519, the Court added:

"[O]ne of the most important functions any jury can perform in making such a selection is to maintain a link between contemporary community values and the penal system—a line without which the determination of punishment could hardly reflect 'the evolving standards of decency that mark the progress of a maturing society.'" *Id.*, at 519, n. 15 (quoting *Trop v. Dulles*, 356 U.S. 86, 101 (1958) (plurality opinion)).

. . . [T]he lesson history teaches is that the jury—and in particular jury sentencing—has played a critical role in ensuring that capital punishment is imposed in a manner consistent with evolving standards of decency. This is a lesson of constitutional magnitude, and one that was forgotten during the enactment of the Florida statute. . . .

. . . Juries—comprised as they are of a fair cross section of the community—are more representative institutions than is the judiciary; they reflect more accurately the composition and experiences of the community as a whole, and inevitably make decisions based on community values more reliably, than can that segment of the community that is selected for service on the bench. . . . [T]he available empirical evidence indicates that judges and juries do make sentencing decisions in capital cases in significantly different ways, thus supporting the conclusion that entrusting the capital decision to a single judge creates an unacceptable risk that the decision will not be consistent with community values. . . .

History, tradition, and the basic structure and purpose of the jury system persuade me that jury sentencing is essential if the administration of capital punishment is to be governed by the community's evolving standards of decency. The constitutional legitimacy of capital punishment depends upon the extent to which the process is able to produce results which reflect the community's moral sensibilities. Judges simply cannot acceptably mirror those sensibilities—the very notion of a right to jury trial is premised on that realization. Judicial sentencing in capital cases cannot provide the type of community participation in the process upon which its legitimacy depends.

If the State wishes to execute a citizen, it must persuade a jury of his peers that death is an appropriate punishment for his offense. If it cannot do so, then I do not believe it can be said with an acceptable degree of assurance that imposition of the death penalty would be consistent with the community's sense of proportionality. Thus, in this case Florida has authorized the imposition of disproportionate punishment in violation of the Eighth and Fourteenth Amendments.

In the three states where judges are at liberty to depart from juries' sentencing recommendations, their authority can be exercised in both directions: overriding a life sentence recommendation and sentencing the offender to death, or rejecting a recommended death sentence and imposing a sentence of life imprisonment. Different patterns of judicial overrides have surfaced within jurisdictions, over time, and between jurisdictions.

In Florida, trial judges during the first two decades of the post-*Furman* law's implementation were far more likely to sentence offenders to death in disregard of a jury's life sentence recommendation than to impose a life sentence after a jury recommended death. Between 1973 and 1994, Florida judges overrode jury sentencing recommendations in 216 cases. They rejected life recommendations and imposed death sentences in 160 of those cases (74.1%), and made death-to-life sentence overrides in 56 of them (25.9%). One theory advanced in explanation of this pattern was that elected trial judges in a state in which the death penalty commands substantial popularity curry greater political favor with voters when their sentencing decisions favor capital punishment than when they favor life imprisonment.[39]

However, in ensuing years judicial overrides of juries' sentencing recommendations in Florida were increasingly infrequent and became skewed in the other direction. Between 1995 and 2010, Florida judges exercised their override authority in 41 cases, including just 6 (14.6%) in which they sentenced offenders to death after a jury's recommendation of life and 35 (85.4%) in which they imposed life sentences in disregard of a jury's recommendation of death. In no cases after 1999 did a judge override a jury's life sentence recommendation.[40] One reason explaining this turnaround was certainly the Florida Supreme Court's propensity to reverse death sentences on appeal when trial judges overrode juries' advisory verdicts favoring life imprisonment.[41]

In Delaware, trial judges overrode juries' death penalty recommendations and imposed life sentences in 17 cases between 1991 and 2011. Just one judge made a life-to-death override, doing so twice in the same case: first, at the original trial, and again after the Delaware Supreme Court vacated the sentence and ordered a new sentencing hearing. The Delaware Supreme Court vacated the second death sentence, as well, and ordered the defendant sentenced to life imprisonment.[42]

Judge overrides of jury sentencing recommendations are decidedly one-sided in favor of death in Alabama. Between 1981 and 2011, Alabama trial judges sentenced 93 offenders to death after juries recommended life imprisonment, while overriding recommendations of death and imposing life sentences in just 9 cases.[43] Contrary to the practice in both Florida and Delaware, no standards have been articulated in Alabama to govern when it is appropriate for trial judges to deviate from a jury's sentencing recommendation in capital cases. The absence of legal standards was the basis for the defendant's claim in *Harris v. Alabama* (1995)[44] that the state's judicial override policies in capital cases were arbitrary and hence violated the Eighth Amendment. With Justice Stevens the lone dissenter, the Supreme Court disagreed, finding no constitutional infirmity in the state's procedures. In 2013, Justice Sotomayor sharply criticized Alabama's continuing reliance on its standardless judicial override procedure and the penchant for judges there to reject juries' life sentence recommendations in favor of imposing sentences of death. She was joined by Justice Breyer in dissenting from the denial of certiorari in *Woodward v. Alabama*.[45]

What could explain Alabama judges' distinctive proclivity for imposing death sentences in cases where a jury has already rejected that penalty? There is no evidence that criminal activity is more heinous in Alabama than in other States, or that Alabama juries are particularly lenient in weighing aggravating and mitigating circumstances. The only answer that is supported by empirical evidence is one that, in my view, casts a cloud of illegitimacy over the criminal justice system: Alabama judges, who are elected in partisan proceedings, appear to have succumbed to electoral pressures. One Alabama judge, who has overridden jury verdicts to impose the death penalty on six occasions, campaigned by running several advertisements voicing his support for capital punishment. One of these ads boasted that he had "'presided over more than 9,000 cases, including some of the most heinous murder trials in our history,'" and expressly named some of the defendants whom he had sentenced to death, in at least one case over a jury's contrary judgment. With admirable candor, another judge, who has overridden one jury verdict to impose death, admitted that voter reaction does "'have some impact, especially in high-profile cases.'" Velasco, More Judges Issue Death Despite Jury, Birmingham News, July 17, 2011, p. 11A. "'Let's face it,'" the judge said, "'we're human beings. I'm sure it affects some more than others.'" *Id.*, at 12A. Alabama judges, it seems, have "ben[t] to political pressures when pronouncing sentence in highly publicized capital cases." *Harris* [*v. Alabama*, 513 U.S. 504, 520 (1995) (Stevens, J., dissenting)].

By permitting a single trial judge's view to displace that of a jury representing a cross-section of the community, Alabama's sentencing scheme has led to curious and potentially arbitrary outcomes. For example, Alabama judges frequently override jury life-without-parole verdicts even in cases where the jury was unanimous in that verdict. In many cases, judges have done so without offering a meaningful explanation for the decision to disregard the jury's verdict. In sentencing a defendant with an IQ of 65, for example, one judge concluded that "'[t]he sociological literature suggests Gypsies intentionally test low on standard IQ tests.'" Another judge, who was facing reelection at the time he sentenced a 19–year–old defendant, refused to consider certain mitigating circumstances found by the jury, which had voted to recommend a life-without-parole sentence. He explained his sensitivity to public perception as follows: "'If I had not imposed the death sentence, I would have sentenced three black people to death and no white people.'" These results do not seem to square with our Eighth Amendment jurisprudence, and they raise important concerns that are worthy of this Court's review. . . .

There is a second reason why Alabama's sentencing scheme deserves our review. Since our decisions in *Spaziano* [*v. Florida*, 468 U.S. 447 (1984)] and *Harris*, our Sixth Amendment jurisprudence has developed significantly. Five years after we decided *Harris*, we held in *Apprendi v. New Jersey*, 530 U.S. 466 (2000), that the Sixth Amendment does not permit a defendant to be "expose[d] . . . to a penalty exceeding the maximum he would receive if punished according to the facts reflected in the jury verdict alone." *Id.*, at 483 (emphasis deleted). When "a State makes an increase in a defendant's authorized punishment contingent on the finding of fact," we explained, "that fact—no matter how the State labels it—must be found by a jury beyond a reasonable doubt." *Ring* [*v. Arizona*, 536 U.S. 584, 602 (2002)]. . . .

The statutorily required finding that the aggravating factors of a defendant's crime outweigh the mitigating factors is . . . necessary to impose the death penalty [in Alabama]. It is clear, then, that this factual finding exposes the defendant to a greater punishment than he would otherwise receive: death, as opposed to life without parole. Under *Apprendi* and *Ring*, a finding that has such an effect must be made by a jury. . . .

Eighteen years have passed since we last considered Alabama's capital sentencing scheme, and much has changed since then. Today, Alabama stands alone: No other State condemns prisoners to death despite the considered judgment rendered by a cross-section of its citizens that the defendant ought to live. And *Apprendi* and its progeny have made clear the sanctity of the jury's role in our system of criminal justice. Given these developments, we owe the validity of Alabama's system a fresh look. I therefore respectfully dissent from the denial of certiorari.

Which sentencing authority—jury or judge—has the greater claim to competency in deciding whether an individual convicted of capital murder should live or die? Which has the greater claim to legitimacy? Do the combined life experiences of twelve laypeople, their independence from government office, and their collective ability to represent the greater community compensate for their relative unfamiliarity with the law and their presumed inexperience in making decisions of such moment? Does a judge, who is learned in the law, experienced in making sentencing decisions, and who is formally obligated to serve as a neutral and impartial decision-maker, seem better suited to the task? Should efforts be made to capitalize on the respective strengths of both juries and judges, by allowing juries to hear evidence in aggravation and mitigation of punishment and recommend a sentence, with final sentencing authority residing with the judge? Do other possible sentencing models come to mind?

As we have seen, the great majority of jurisdictions rely exclusively on juries to make the sentencing decision in capital cases. The membership of juries in capital murder trials thus can be expected to be critically important. The composition of capital juries is determined in part by legal standards that govern who is and who is not qualified to serve, and thereafter by the procedures used to select the panel of twelve individuals who will hear evidence and render guilt-innocence and sentencing verdicts in specific trials. Another important facet of death-penalty laws' implementation, particularly in light of the Supreme Court's assumptions that the legislation enacted in the aftermath of *Furman* would substantially reduce the risk of arbitrary capital sentencing, is whether jurors faithfully apply the criteria and follow the procedures specified in the new laws.

A juror's oath includes a commitment to render a verdict based on the evidence presented in court and pursuant to the governing law. Anyone who is unable or unwilling to do so—for example, an individual who already has concluded prior to a trial that the accused is guilty based on media reports, or someone who disagrees with a rule of law and therefore would refuse to apply it in a trial—is disqualified by operation of law from serving as a juror. In capital trials, potential jurors' strongly held personal opinions about the death penalty can be in conflict with the law, which demands a willingness to at least consider sentencing a convicted offender to death or life imprisonment depending on the weight of the evidence and pursuant to the statutory procedures and criteria. Individuals whose opposition to capital punishment would significantly compromise their willingness to impose a death sentence or would prevent them from doing so are not "death qualified" and consequently are ineligible for jury service in capital trials. Individuals who so strongly believe in "eye-for-an-eye" retributive justice that they would be unwilling to impose a sentence other than death if a defendant is convicted of capital murder, irrespective of the comparative weight of aggravating and mitigating evidence, are not "life qualified." They, too, are excluded by operation of law from service as jurors in capital trials.

The Supreme Court first addressed the legal criteria that justify excusing prospective jurors "for cause"—*i.e.*, by operation of law—from serving in a capital trial because of their death-penalty attitudes in *Witherspoon v. Illinois*, 391 U.S. 510 (1968). Witherspoon was convicted of murdering a Chicago police officer and was sentenced to death in 1960. An Illinois statute then in effect provided:

> In trials for murder it shall be a cause for challenge of any juror who shall, on being examined, state that he has conscientious scruples against capital punishment, or that he is opposed to the same.[46]

Applying this statute, the trial judge dismissed 47 of the 95 individuals who made up the venire that reported for jury service.[47] Most of the dismissed jurors had indicated that they "did not believe in" or had "qualms" or "reservations" about the death penalty; only five stated that they would be unwilling to impose a death sentence under any circumstances.[48] The Supreme Court ruled that Illinois' death-qualification standard, as it was applied at Witherspoon's trial, was far too broad. Justice Stewart's majority opinion explained that an individual "who opposes the death penalty, no less than one who favors it, can make the discretionary [sentencing] judgment entrusted to him by the State and can thus obey the oath he takes as a juror."[49] "[A] sentence of death cannot be carried out if the jury that imposed or recommended it was chosen by excluding veniremen for cause simply because they voiced general objections to the death penalty or expressed conscientious or religious scruples against its infliction."[50]

> The most that can be demanded of a venireman . . . is that he be willing to consider all of the penalties provided by state law, and that he not be irrevocably committed, before the trial has begun, to vote against the penalty of death regardless of the facts and circumstances that might emerge in the course of the proceedings. . . .
>
> [H]owever, . . . nothing we say today bears upon the power of a State to execute a defendant sentenced to death by a jury from which the only veniremen who were in fact excluded for cause were those who made unmistakably clear (1) that they would automatically vote against the imposition of capital punishment without regard to any evidence that might be developed at the trial of the case before them, or (2) that their attitude toward the death penalty would prevent them from making an impartial decision as to the defendant's guilt.[51]

Witherspoon's trial and the Supreme Court's decision in his case predated *Furman*. Consequently, in addition to being shaped by Illinois' overly broad death-qualification statute, the jury that sentenced him to death was unguided by legislative standards and it was not privy to relevant sentencing information that might have been introduced at a separate penalty hearing. In *Wainwright v. Witt*, 469 U.S. 412 (1985), the Court considerably softened *Witherspoon's* demanding death-qualification test, ruling that in the era of guided-discretion capital-sentencing legislation:

> [T]he proper standard for determining when a prospective juror may be excluded for cause because of his or her views on capital punishment . . . is whether the juror's views would "prevent or substantially impair the performance of his duties as a juror in accordance with his instructions and his oath." . . . [I]n addition to dispensing with *Witherspoon's* reference to "automatic" decisionmaking, this standard likewise does not require that a juror's bias be proved with "unmistakable clarity." . . . [M]any veniremen simply cannot be asked enough questions to reach the point where their bias has been made "unmistakably clear"; these veniremen may not know how they will react when faced with imposing the death sentence, or may be unable to articulate, or may wish to hide their true feelings. . . . [T]here will be situations where the trial judge is left with the definite impression that a prospective juror

would be unable to faithfully and impartially apply the law. . . . [Accordingly,] deference must be paid to the trial judge who sees and hears the juror.[52]

In *Morgan v. Illinois,* 504 U.S. 719 (1992), the justices ruled that just as prospective jurors who are not "death qualified" can be excused for cause from serving in capital trials, those who are not "life qualified" must similarly be excluded.

> A juror who will automatically vote for the death penalty in every case will fail in good faith to consider the evidence of aggravating and mitigating circumstances as the instructions require him to do. Indeed, because such a juror has already formed an opinion on the merits, the presence or absence of either aggravating or mitigating circumstances is entirely irrelevant to such a juror. Therefore, based on the requirement of impartiality embodied in the Due Process Clause of the Fourteenth Amendment, a capital defendant may challenge for cause any prospective juror who maintains such views.[53]

Research studies suggest that individuals otherwise eligible for jury service who are not death qualified significantly outnumber those who are not life qualified. It is difficult for academic researchers to simulate the intensive questioning by prosecutors and defense attorneys that prospective jurors undergo in capital cases as their attitudes about the death penalty and their willingness to follow the law are explored. With this limitation in mind, the results of a 1981 California survey suggested that 8.1% of the respondents held such strong views against capital punishment that they could not be impartial in deciding guilt or innocence in a capital murder trial, while an additional 11.6% indicated that they could decide guilt or innocence impartially but would be unwilling to consider sentencing a convicted defendant to death. In contrast, a national survey completed that same year revealed that just 1% of respondents would not be life qualified and hence would be excluded from jury service in capital trials because of their "automatic death penalty" attitudes.[54] On the other hand, some researchers have pointed to the difficulty of fleshing out the attitudes of "automatic death penalty" jurors and have estimated that they are a sizable group, perhaps representing as much as 30% of otherwise eligible jurors in some jurisdictions.[55]

At the time of Witherspoon's trial (1960) and the Supreme Court's decision (1968), public opinion polls reflected considerable opposition to capital punishment. Justice Stewart noted in his majority opinion that "in 1966, approximately 42% of the American public favored capital punishment for convicted murderers, while 47% opposed it and 11% were undecided. In 1960, the comparable figures were 51% in favor, 36% opposed, and 13% undecided."[56] If we were to indulge the (erroneous) assumption that these figures translate neatly into the percentage of prospective jurors who were not death qualified (as in *Witherspoon,* where the trial judge's expansive application of Illinois' death qualification statute excluded almost precisely half (47 of 95) of the jury venire from service), we would discern the tension between two fundamental assumptions underlying criminal trial juries: that they be impartial and that they be drawn from a representative cross-section of the community.

In a court of law, it seems almost self-evident that both the accused and the prosecution should be entitled to a trial by jurors who are willing to follow the law. A juror who refuses to be bound by the law is not an *impartial* juror. On the other hand, if the quest for impartial jurors—meaning, in the death-qualification context, individuals who are willing to consider sentencing a convicted offender to death if the evidence satisfies the statutory criteria—results in the exclusion of a sizeable portion of the population from jury service in capital trials, the corollary imperative of a trial by a jury of one's peers, or one drawn from a *representative cross-section of the community*, appears to be at risk. Of relevance to the fair cross-section principle, the *Witherspoon* Court explicitly noted that "a jury that must choose between life imprisonment and capital punishment can do little more—and must do nothing less—than express the conscience of the community on the ultimate question of life or death."[57]

Justice Douglas was alone in *Witherspoon* in objecting to Illinois' death qualification of capital trial jurors because the practice undermined the "representative cross-section of the community" requirement.

The constitutional question is whether the jury must be 'impartially drawn from a cross-section of the community,' or whether it can be drawn with systematic and intentional exclusion of some qualified groups . . .

A fair cross-section of the community may produce a jury almost certain to impose the death penalty if guilt were found; or it may produce a jury almost certain not to impose it. The conscience of the community is subject to many variables, one of which is the attitude toward the death sentence. If a particular community were overwhelmingly opposed to capital punishment, it would not be able to exercise a discretion to impose or not impose the death sentence. . . .

In such instance, why should not an accused have the benefit of that controlling principle of mercy in the community? Why should his fate be entrusted exclusively to a jury that was either enthusiastic about capital punishment or so undecided that it could exercise a discretion to impose it or not, depending on how it felt about the particular case?

I see no constitutional basis for excluding those who are so opposed to capital punishment that they would never inflict it on a defendant. Exclusion of them means the selection of jurors who are either protagonists of the death penalty or neutral concerning it. That results in a systematic exclusion of qualified groups, and the deprivation to the accused of a cross-section of the community for decision on both his guilt and his punishment.

Years later, in *Lockhart v. McCree*, 476 U.S. 162 (1986), the death-qualification issues first presented to the Supreme Court in *Witherspoon* were reprised. Ardia McCree was charged with capital murder in Arkansas and was brought to trial in 1978. The prosecution sought the death penalty and eight prospective trial jurors were excused for cause because they were not death qualified. The resulting death-qualified jury convicted McCree of capital murder but sentenced him to life imprisonment. McCree claimed that the death-qualification process deprived him of an impartial jury at the guilt-innocence phase of his trial, and also violated his right to trial by a jury drawn from a fair cross-section of the community. The state courts rejected his arguments, but after receiving evidence supporting the claims, a federal district court granted McCree relief.[58] The Eighth Circuit Court of Appeals affirmed.[59] The Supreme Court granted certiorari to

> address the question left open by our decision nearly 18 years ago in *Witherspoon v. Illinois*: Does the Constitution prohibit the removal for cause, prior to the guilt phase of a bifurcated capital trial, of prospective jurors whose opposition to the death penalty is so strong that it would prevent or substantially impair the performance of their duties as jurors at the sentencing phase of the trial?[60]

In addition to challenging the impartiality of his jury with respect to its sentencing function, Witherspoon had argued that the wholesale exclusion of potential jurors who were not death qualified violated his right to an impartial jury to determine his guilt or innocence. He contended that individuals who opposed the death penalty were especially likely to hold attitudes associated with a "due process" model of criminal justice[61]—such as maintaining a relatively high threshold definition of "proof beyond a reasonable doubt," not inferring guilt based on a defendant's failure to testify at trial, being receptive to the insanity defense, and a willingness to carefully scrutinize the testimony of law enforcement officers rather than reflexively crediting it. Because death-qualified juries were systematically purged of individuals likely to hold such attitudes, Witherspoon maintained, they were significantly more likely than a non-death-qualified jury to find a defendant guilty as charged. He called the justices' attention to research evidence in support of his argument that death-qualified juries are "conviction prone," rather than impartial in determining guilt or innocence.[62]

Although the majority opinion considered it "self-evident that, in its role as arbiter of the punishment to be imposed, [Witherspoon's] jury fell woefully short of that impartiality to which the petitioner was entitled,"[63] it declined to extend its holding to the guilt phase of the trial. The studies on which Witherspoon relied were considered

> too tentative and fragmentary to establish that jurors not opposed to the death penalty tend to favor the prosecution in the determination of guilt. We simply cannot conclude, either on the basis of the record now before us or as a matter of judicial notice, that the exclusion of jurors opposed to capital punishment . . . substantially increases the risk of conviction.[64]

Taking this and other language in the opinion[65] as an invitation to produce additional evidence on the issue, researchers continued their investigation of death-qualified juries and their relative propensity to return guilty verdicts following the Court's decision in *Witherspoon*. With great consistency, the later studies replicated the findings of the earlier "tentative and fragmentary" ones: Death-qualified juries are more likely to find defendants guilty, and guilty of more serious charges (for example, first-degree murder rather than second-degree murder or manslaughter) than non-death-qualified juries. The studies were presented and subjected to adversarial testing in an exhaustive hearing conducted by the federal district court judge considering McCree's claims.[66]

Two basic reasons helped account for the studies' findings concerning the relative conviction-proneness of death-qualified juries. The first mirrored Witherspoon's claim regarding the greater "due process" orientation of individuals who strongly oppose the death penalty and the consequences of excluding those moderating views from juries comprised exclusively of death-qualified individuals.[67] The second reason implicated the death-qualification *process*. Extensive questioning of prospective jurors about their willingness to impose a death sentence subtly helps create a presumption of guilt, conveying the impression that a trial's most serious question does not concern the defendant's guilt or innocence, but rather his or her punishment.[68] Moreover, the trial judge's disqualification of prospective jurors from service in a capital trial based on their expressed opposition to the death penalty is sometimes interpreted by retained jurors as official condemnation of those anti-death penalty sentiments, and as a corresponding endorsement of the prosecution's case.[69]

The post-*Witherspoon* studies were greeted with skepticism in Justice Rehnquist's majority opinion in *Lockhart v. McCree*. The Court rejected the claim that the death-qualified jurors in McCree's trial were not impartial in determining his guilt. Parsing the "15 social science studies in support of [McCree's] constitutional claims," Justice Rehnquist first "point[ed] out what we believe to be several serious flaws in the evidence upon which the courts below reached the conclusion that 'death qualification' produces 'conviction-prone' juries."[70] After criticizing the research studies' methodologies and findings, the Court decisively foreclosed further pursuit of the issue. It did so by addressing and then dismissing McCree's arguments after begrudgingly "assum[ing] for purposes of this opinion that the studies are both methodologically valid and adequate to establish that 'death qualification' in fact produces juries somewhat more 'conviction-prone' than 'non-death-qualified' juries."[71] The nub of the reasoning for rejecting the claim involved the majority opinion's distinction between impartial "jurors" (all individuals on McCree's jury were deemed to fit that definition because of their willingness to return a verdict on guilt or innocence based on the evidence and the law) and an impartial "jury."

McCree's "impartiality" argument apparently is based on the theory that, because all individual jurors are to some extent predisposed towards one result or another, a constitutionally impartial *jury* can be constructed only by "balancing" the various predispositions of the individual *jurors*. Thus, according to McCree, when the State "tips the scales" by excluding prospective jurors with a particular viewpoint, an impermissibly partial jury results. We have consistently rejected this view of jury impartiality, including as recently as last Term when we squarely held that an impartial *jury* consists of nothing more than "*jurors* who will conscientiously apply the law and find the facts." *Wainwright v. Witt*, 469 U.S. 412, 423 (1985) (emphasis added).

The view of jury impartiality urged upon us by McCree is both illogical and hopelessly impractical. McCree characterizes the jury that convicted him as "slanted" by the process of "death qualification." But McCree admits that exactly the same 12 individuals could have ended up on his jury through the "luck of the draw," without in any way violating the constitutional guarantee of impartiality. Even accepting McCree's position that we should focus on the *jury* rather than the individual *jurors*, it is hard for us to understand the logic of the argument that a given jury is unconstitutionally partial when it results from a state-ordained process, yet impartial when exactly the same jury results from mere chance. On a more practical level, if it were true that the Constitution required a certain mix of individual viewpoints on the jury, then trial judges would be required to undertake the Sisyphean task of "balancing" juries, making sure that each contains the proper number of Democrats and Republicans, young persons and old persons, white-collar executives and blue-collar laborers, and so on.

McCree's argument that the death-qualification of jurors at his trial violated his right to a jury chosen from a "representative cross-section" of the community fared no better before the Supreme Court. Based on the research evidence presented, the lower courts had agreed with McCree's claims regarding this issue. The district court found "that the [*Witherspoon* excludable] group is of substantial size both nationally and within the state of Arkansas, ranging between 11% and 17% of those eligible for jury service."[72] Moreover, the exclusion of non-death-qualified jurors disproportionally affected the representation of Blacks and women on juries. The results of an Arkansas survey revealed that "29% of the blacks would never impose the death penalty compared to 9% of the whites. And, whereas only 8% of Arkansas men would be *Witherspoon* Excludables . . . , 13% of Arkansas women would fall into that classification."[73] The Supreme Court's analysis of the fair-cross-section claim rendered these findings irrelevant.

We have never invoked the fair-cross-section principle to invalidate the use of either for-cause or peremptory challenges to prospective jurors, or to require petit juries, as opposed to jury panels or venires, to reflect the composition of the community at large. See *Duren v. Missouri*, 439 U.S. 357 (1979); *Taylor v. Louisiana*, 419 U.S. 522, 538 (1975) ("[W]e impose no requirement that petit juries actually chosen must mirror the community and reflect the various distinctive groups in the population"). The limited scope of the fair-cross-section requirement is a direct and inevitable consequence of the practical impossibility of providing each criminal defendant with a truly "representative" petit jury. . . . We remain convinced that an extension of the fair-cross-section requirement to petit juries would be unworkable and unsound, and we decline McCree's invitation to adopt such an extension.

But even if we were willing to extend the fair-cross-section requirement to petit juries, we would still reject the . . . conclusion that "death qualification" violates that requirement. The essence of a "fair-cross-section" claim is the systematic exclusion of "a 'distinctive' group in the community." *Duren*, 439 U.S., at 364. In our view, groups defined solely in terms of shared attitudes that would prevent or substantially impair members of the group from performing one of their duties as jurors, such as the "*Witherspoon*-excludables" at issue here, are not "distinctive groups" for fair-cross-section purposes. . . .

Our prior jury-representativeness cases, whether based on the fair-cross-section component of the Sixth Amendment or the Equal Protection Clause of the Fourteenth Amendment, have involved such groups as blacks, women, and Mexican-Americans. . . . Because these groups were excluded for reasons completely unrelated to the ability of members of the group to serve as jurors in a particular case, the exclusion raised at least the possibility that the composition of juries would be arbitrarily skewed in such a way as to deny criminal defendants the benefit of the common-sense judgment of the community. In addition, the exclusion from jury service of large groups of individuals not on the basis of their inability to serve as jurors, but on the basis of some immutable characteristic such as race, gender, or ethnic background, undeniably gave rise to an "appearance of unfairness." Finally, such exclusion improperly deprived members of these often historically disadvantaged groups of their right as citizens to serve on juries in criminal cases.

The group of "*Witherspoon*-excludables" involved in the case at bar differs significantly from the groups we have previously recognized as "distinctive." "Death qualification," unlike the wholesale exclusion of blacks, women, or Mexican-Americans from jury service, is carefully designed to serve the State's concededly legitimate interest in obtaining a single jury that can properly and impartially apply the law to the facts of the case at both the guilt and sentencing phases of a capital trial. There is very little danger, therefore, and McCree does not even argue, that "death qualification" was

instituted as a means for the State to arbitrarily skew the composition of capital-case juries.

Furthermore, unlike blacks, women, and Mexican-Americans, "*Witherspoon*-excludables" are singled out for exclusion in capital cases on the basis of an attribute that is within the individual's control. It is important to remember that not all who oppose the death penalty are subject to removal for cause in capital cases; those who firmly believe that the death penalty is unjust may nevertheless serve as jurors in capital cases so long as they state clearly that they are willing to temporarily set aside their own beliefs in deference to the rule of law. Because the group of "*Witherspoon*-excludables" includes only those who cannot and will not conscientiously obey the law with respect to one of the issues in a capital case, "death qualification" hardly can be said to create an "appearance of unfairness."

Finally, the removal for cause of "*Witherspoon*-excludables" in capital cases does not prevent them from serving as jurors in other criminal cases, and thus leads to no substantial deprivation of their basic rights of citizenship. They are treated no differently than any juror who expresses the view that he would be unable to follow the law in a particular case.

In sum, "*Witherspoon*-excludables," or for that matter any other group defined solely in terms of shared attitudes that render members of the group unable to serve as jurors in a particular case, may be excluded from jury service without contravening any of the basic objectives of the fair-cross-section requirement. It is for this reason that we conclude that "*Witherspoon*-excludables" do not constitute a "distinctive group" for fair-cross-section purposes, and hold that "death qualification" does not violate the fair-cross-section requirement.

Does the limitation of the "fair cross-section" requirement to the jury venire (*i.e.,* to the entire pool of jurors summoned to court)—rather than its applying to the much smaller (typically, 12-member) trial or "petit" juries that sit in individual cases—seem defensible based on "the practical impossibility of providing each criminal defendant with a truly representative petit jury"? On the other hand, what should be made of the rejoinder included in Justice Marshall's dissenting opinion?

> The right to have a particular group represented on venires is of absolutely no value if every member of that group will automatically be excluded from service as soon as he is found to be a member of that group. Whether a violation of the fair-cross-section requirement has occurred can hardly turn on *when* the wholesale exclusion of a group takes place. If, for example, blacks were systematically struck from petit juries pursuant to state law, the effect—and the infringement of a defendant's Sixth Amendment rights—would be the same as if they had never been included on venires in the first place.[74]

Recall that McCree was convicted of capital murder by a death-qualified jury but then was sentenced to life imprisonment. He did not claim that death-qualifying a jury at the *penalty* phase of a capital trial would be constitutionally objectionable. If McCree had prevailed and secured a ruling that a jury cannot be death-qualified at the *guilt* phase of a capital trial, how would a jurisdiction be able to conduct such trials? Would it have to impanel two juries: one (which would not be death-qualified) to determine guilt or innocence, and another (which would be death-qualified) to determine sentence if a capital murder conviction resulted? Could it choose instead to rely on judge sentencing? Would such solutions tend to undermine what the majority opinion in *Lockhart v. McCree* recognized as "the State's concededly legitimate interest in obtaining a single jury that can properly and impartially apply the law to the facts of the case at both the guilt and sentencing phases of a capital trial"? Justice Marshall did not believe so. He quoted approvingly from a law review article in explanation of his conclusion.

> First, capital cases constitute a relatively small number of criminal trials. Moreover, the number of these cases in which a penalty determination will be necessary is even smaller. A penalty determination will occur only where a verdict on guilt has been returned that authorizes the possible imposition of capital punishment, and only where the prosecutor decides that a death sentence should be sought. Even in cases in which a penalty determination will occur, the impaneling of a new penalty jury may not always be necessary. In some cases, it may be possible to have alternate jurors replace any 'automatic life imprisonment' jurors who served at the guilt determination trial.[75]

Justice Marshall conceded the propriety of excluding individuals from jury service during the guilt phase of capital trials if their strong opposition to the death penalty precluded them from impartially deciding guilt or innocence (such persons make up the class called "nullifiers"). He then commented on the ease with which nullifiers could be identified before trial without any extended focus on how jurors would conduct themselves at a capital sentencing proceeding. Potential jurors could be asked, for example, "if there be any reason why any of them could not fairly and impartially try the issue of defendant's guilt in accordance with the evidence presented at the trial and the court's instructions as to the law."[76]

Do you agree? How effective would such a general question likely be in exposing "nullifiers," whose views in opposition to capital punishment would prevent them from being impartial at the guilt phase of a capital murder trial?

The death-qualification process involves challenging prospective jurors "for cause" because they do not meet the legal requirement for impartiality. There is no limit to the number of "cause" challenges the parties can make in a trial. All jurisdictions additionally permit both the prosecution and the defense to use a limited number of peremptory challenges in criminal trials. Peremptory challenges allow the parties to excuse prospective jurors from service who are not excludable for cause. The prosecutor and defense counsel normally can excuse jurors peremptorily for virtually any reason and without explanation. The exception is that peremptory challenges cannot be used because of a prospective juror's race, ethnicity, or gender.[77] More peremptory challenges typically are allotted the parties in capital cases (usually in the range of 8 to 20 or more) than in non-capital trials.[78]

Peremptory challenges traditionally have been considered important to help ensure that fair-minded jurors are impaneled, in recognition of the reality that not all individuals who are qualified by law to render judgment in a trial are well suited to do so in fact. Allowing the parties a limited opportunity to excuse prospective jurors who they would prefer not participate additionally helps reinforce the litigants' perceptions that they are being treated fairly.[79] At the same time, peremptory challenges can be abused: constitutionally impermissible grounds for exercising them are easily concealed and can be almost impossible to expose.

For example, the prosecutor in Thomas Miller-El's capital murder trial in Dallas, Texas, used peremptory challenges to strike 10 of the 11 Black prospective jurors who remained in the venire following the "cause" challenges. Miller-El, a Black man, was convicted and sentenced to death by a jury that included a single Black member. The state courts and the lower federal courts that considered Miller-El's case found no evidence that the peremptory challenges were racially motivated. Not until the case reached the Supreme Court was the prosecutor's use of peremptory challenges condemned, by vote of 6–3, as being constitutionally infirm.[80] The ease with which peremptory challenges, which are not constitutionally required, can be abused has led two Supreme Court justices to call for their elimination.[81]

Prospective jurors who express support or opposition for capital punishment during *voir dire* yet maintain that they would not let those views interfere with their application of the law are obvious targets for the parties' exercise of peremptory challenges in capital murder trials. Predictably, prosecutors use peremptory strikes to excuse individuals who voice reservations about the death penalty, while defense attorneys use their strikes to eliminate prospective jurors who admit to favoring or supporting capital punishment.[82] When prosecutors exercise their peremptory challenges against anti-death penalty prospective jurors who survive "cause" challenges, the skewed composition of the petit jury that results from the death-qualification process is magnified. One consequence is further reducing the representation of individuals whose attitudes align with "due process" values. Another is the likely further erosion of Blacks on the jury panel because Blacks, more than Whites, tend to disfavor the death penalty.[83] Indeed, the prosecutor in *Miller-El v. Dretke* attributed many of the peremptory strikes he used against Blacks to the prospective jurors' attitudes about the death penalty.[84]

On balance, do the availability and exercise of peremptory challenges tend to enhance or diminish the goal of achieving justice in capital cases?

If you were on trial for your life, or if you were representing someone who was, would you want to be able to excuse some prospective jurors peremptorily? Would you be comfortable with the first 12 individuals called to the jury box who survived "cause" challenges?

If you were the prosecutor representing the government in a capital murder trial, what would your response be to these same questions?

If the principal problem with peremptory challenges lies in their potential to be abused on racial or other constitutionally impermissible grounds, can you envision effective ways of guarding against this danger?

The Supreme Court approved the post-*Furman* guided discretion capital-sentencing statutes because they incorporated safeguards that were designed to prevent the death penalty's arbitrary application. Accordingly, another vitally important question relevant to capital juries is whether the laws are understood and implemented by jurors in the intended manner. Legislative reforms that are not realized in practice would be hollow, accomplishing change that is cosmetic rather than meaningful.

> The trial judge's charge to the jury is the law's mechanism for bridging the gap between abstract doctrine and the rules governing the resolution of specific cases. The legitimacy of the trial system rests on the "crucial assumption . . . that juries will follow the instructions given them by the trial judge."[85]

Trial judges go to great lengths to instruct jurors about what the law requires. Their instructions typically are administered orally and at the very end of a trial, immediately before the jurors begin their verdict deliberations. They can be long and laden with the sometimes arcane language of the law. Consider, for example, the following instructions administered to jurors during the penalty phase of an Illinois capital trial, prior to that state repealing its death-penalty law:[86]

If, from your consideration of the evidence and after your due deliberation, there is at least one of you who finds that there is at least one mitigating factor sufficient to preclude the imposition of the death sentence then you should return a verdict that the Defendant be sentenced to imprisonment. On the other hand, if from your consideration of the evidence and after your due deliberation you unanimously find that there are no mitigating factors sufficient to preclude the imposition of the death sentence then you should return a verdict that the Defendant be sentenced to death. . . .

If you unanimously find from your consideration of all the evidence that there are no mitigating factors sufficient to preclude the imposition of a sentence of death then you should return a verdict imposing a sentence of death. If, on the other hand, you do not unanimously find that there are no mitigating factors sufficient to preclude the imposition of a sentence of death then you should return a verdict that the sentence of death should not be imposed.

Imagine hearing these instructions (rather than reading them), and hearing them delivered just once, embedded in a far lengthier recital that ranges over numerous other topics. What measure of confidence would you have in your ability to comprehend and follow them? Although the instructions were criticized by linguists[87] and challenged by defense counsel as being virtually unintelligible, including usage of a "quadruple negative,"[88] they were upheld as constitutionally permissible by the state and federal courts.[89]

Even when trial judges' instructions about the laws that govern capital sentencing decisions are less obtuse, questions linger about their effectiveness in guiding jurors' deliberations. Researchers with the Capital Jury Project (CJP) conducted extensive interviews with some 1,200 individuals who had served as jurors in more than 350 capital trials conducted in 14 different states. The interviews were designed to explore how the former jurors had arrived at their sentencing decisions.[90] The interviews revealed profound gaps between the sentencing laws' design and the jurors' application of them. Among the numerous discrepancies were:

- "*Premature punishment decision-making: deciding on punishment at the guilt trial.*"[91] Nearly half (49.2%) of the former jurors reported forming an opinion, and frequently being "absolutely convinced" about what sentence the defendant should receive at the conclusion of the trial's guilt phase, *i.e.*, before evidence had even been presented at the trial's penalty phase.
- "*Misguided punishment decision-making: misunderstanding the standards for considering mitigation.*"[92] Almost half of the former jurors believed that the defendant was obligated to prove the existence of mitigating factors "beyond a reasonable doubt," and more than half believed that the jury was required to be unanimous in finding that one or more mitigating factors existed before they could be taken into account. Neither understanding is correct.

- *"Mistakenly believing a death sentence is required."*[93] Large numbers of the inter-
  viewees reported believing that the death penalty was mandatory once the prosecution established that a murder was "heinous, vile or depraved" (43.9%) or that
  the offender "would be dangerous in the future" (37.0%).
- *"Race Linked Punishment Decision-Making."*[94] The interviews suggested that the
  race of the jurors, the defendants, and murder victims interacted to affect perceptions of offenders' future dangerousness, jurors' receptivity to mitigation evidence,
  and the dynamics of sentencing deliberations. In general, White jurors were more
  likely to favor death sentences than Black jurors and death sentences were especially likely to result when at least five White males served on the same jury.

If the interview results and descriptive statistics reported by the Capital Jury Project
accurately reflect how jurors in capital trials understand and apply "guided discretion"
death-penalty laws, how successful have those laws been in practice? William Bowers,
the director of the CJP, has argued that the study's "findings raise the fundamental
question of whether making the life or death sentencing decision free of the arbitrariness forbidden in *Furman* is simply beyond human capabilities. . . ."[95]

Conclusion

"Death, in its finality, differs more from life imprisonment than a 100-year prison term
differs from one of only a year or two. Because of that qualitative difference, there is a
corresponding difference in the need for reliability in the determination that death is
the appropriate punishment in a specific case."[96] More than any other guiding principle, this fundamental and oft-repeated premise explains the Supreme Court's intensive, decades-long scrutiny of capital-punishment laws and their administration. The
postulate that "death is different" is largely responsible for the complex and prolix constitutional jurisprudence that the justices have fashioned in their capital case decisions.
The lawyers who represent the individuals whose lives are at stake in death-penalty
trials, and the jurors who sit in judgment of them, directly leave their imprint on the
proceedings that are reflected in the cold case records that underlie the justices' doctrinal pronouncements. And in turn, it is through the critical work performed by defense
counsel and trial jurors, conducted amid the ambiguities and raw emotions inherent
in capital murder proceedings, that the abstract principles of law announced by the
Supreme Court are translated into practice.

Unless defense lawyers and jurors carry out their expected constitutional functions,
the formal rules of law constructed to govern capital proceedings will serve as little
more than empty promises. In some death-penalty cases, the gulf between the written
law and the law as practiced unfortunately has been substantial. Justice has been subverted in capital trials through ineffective representation provided by defense counsel,
whose performance frequently is handicapped by inadequate funding and the absence

of other necessary resources. Jurors, as well, may be compromised in their willingness or ability to discharge their solemn duties as contemplated by law. In other cases, just as clearly, defense attorneys and trial juries have been indispensable in helping ensure that justice is served. Perhaps in these respects, capital cases—depending as they must on human actors and the systems of justice in which they operate to give substance and meaning to abstract rules of law—are not demonstrably different from others.

Endnotes

1. 408 U.S. 238 (1972).
2. 428 U.S. 153 (1976).
3. *Proffitt v. Florida,* 428 U.S. 242 (1976); *Jurek v. Texas,* 428 U.S. 262 (1976).
4. See the discussion in Chapter 6.
5. 287 U.S. 45, 53 (1932).
6. *See* James R. Acker, *Scottsboro and Its Legacy: The Cases That Challenged American Legal and Social Justice* 1–4 (Westport, CT: Praeger 2008). *See generally* James Goodman, *Stories of Scottsboro* (New York: Vintage Books 1994); Dan T. Carter, *Scottsboro: A Tragedy of the American South* (Baton Rouge, LA: Louisiana State University Press, rev. ed. 1979).
7. *Powell v. Alabama,* 287 U.S. 45, 53 (1932).
8. *See* Acker, *supra* note 6, at 19–34.
9. Gary Hengstler, "Attorneys for the Damned," *American Bar Association Journal* 56, 60 (Jan. 1, 1987), *quoting* David Bruck, an experienced capital defense lawyer. *See* Charles S. Lanier & James R. Acker, "Capital Punishment, the Moratorium Movement, and Empirical Questions," 10 *Psychology, Public Policy, and Law* 577, 589 (2004).
10. Death Penalty Information Center, *Searchable Execution Database,* retrieved July 5, 2013 from www.deathpenaltyinfo.org/views-executions?exec_name_1=david+washington&sex=All&sex_1=All&federal=All&foreigner=All&juvenile=All&volunteer=All.
11. Jenny Roberts, "Why Misdemeanors Matter: Defining Effective Advocacy in Lower Criminal Courts," 45 *U.C. Davis Law Review* 277, 336 (2011); Gregory J. O'Meara, "'You Can't Get There From Here?': Ineffective Assistance Claims in Federal Circuit Courts After AEDPA," 93 *Marquette Law Review* 545, 568–569 (2009).
12. Cara H. Drinan, "Getting Real About *Gideon*: The Next Fifty Years of Enforcing the Right to Counsel," 70 *Washington & Lee Law Review* 1309, 1318 & n. 48 (2013); Vivian Chang, "Where Do We Go From Here: Plea Colloquy Warnings and Immigration Consequences Post-*Padilla*," 45 *University of Michigan Journal of Law Reform* 189, 203–204 & n. 82 (2011); Robert R. Rigg, "The T-Rex Without Teeth: Evolving *Strickland v. Washington* and the Test for Ineffective Assistance of Counsel," 35 *Pepperdine Law Review* 77 (2007).
13. *Burdine v. Johnson,* 262 F.3d 336 (5th Cir. 2001) (en banc), *cert. denied,* 535 U.S. 1120 (2002).
14. *See* Adam Lamparello, "Establishing Guidelines for Attorney Representation of Criminal Defendants at the Sentencing Phase of Capital Trials," 62 *Maine Law Review* 97, 98–100 (2010); Jeffrey L. Kirchmeier, "Drink, Drugs, and Drowsiness: The Constitutional Right to Effective Assistance of Counsel and the *Strickland* Prejudice Requirement," 75 *Nebraska Law Review* 425 (1996); Stephen B. Bright, "Counsel for the Poor: The Death Sentence Not for the Worst Crime But for the Worst Lawyer," 103 *Yale Law Journal* 1835 (1994); Note, "The Eighth Amendment and Ineffective Assistance of Counsel in Capital Trials," 107 *Harvard Law Review* 1923 (1994); Bruce A. Green, "Lethal Fiction: The Meaning of 'Counsel' in the Sixth Amendment," 78 *Iowa Law Review* 433 (1993); Marcia Coyle, Fred Strasser & Marianne Lavelle, "Fatal Defense: Trial and Error in the Nation's Death Belt," *National Law Journal* 30 (June 11, 1990).

15. *See* "American Bar Association Guidelines for the Appointment and Performance of Counsel in Death Penalty Cases," 31 *Hofstra Law Review* 913 (2003); "Supplementary Guidelines for the Mitigation Function of Defense Teams in Death Penalty Cases," 36 *Hofstra Law Review* 677 (2008).

16. *Williams v. Taylor,* 529 U.S. 362 (2000); *Wiggins v. Smith,* 539 U.S. 510 (2003); *Rompilla v. Beard,* 545 U.S. 374 (2005). *See generally* J. Richard Broughton, "Capital Prejudice," 43 *University of Memphis Law Review* 135 (2012); Stephen F. Smith, "Taking *Strickland* Claims Seriously," 93 *Marquette Law Review* 515 (2009); John H. Blume & Stacey D. Neumann, "'It's Like Déjà Vu All Over Again': *Williams v. Taylor, Wiggins v. Smith, Rompilla v. Beard* and a (Partial) Return to the Guidelines Approach to Effective Assistance of Counsel," 34 *American Journal of Criminal Law* 127 (2005).

17. *See* Alexa Woodward, "It Takes a Village to Save a Life: A Statewide Model for Indigent Capital Defense," 11 *New York City Law Review* 159 (2007); Carol S. Steiker & Jordan M. Steiker, "Should Abolitionists Support Legislative 'Reform' of the Death Penalty?," 63 *Ohio State Law Journal* 417, 426–427 (2002).

18. *See* Cory Isaacson, "How Resource Disparity Makes the Death Penalty Unconstitutional: An Eighth Amendment Argument Against Structurally Imbalanced Capital Trials," 12 *Berkeley Journal of Criminal Law* 297 (2012); Kenneth Williams, "Ensuring the Capital Defendant's Right to Competent Counsel: It's Time for Some Standards!," 51 *Wayne Law Review* 129 (2005); James S. Liebman, "Opting for Real Death Penalty Reform," 63 *Ohio State Law Journal* 315 (2002).

19. The constitutional right to court-appointed trial counsel in criminal cases is limited to felonies and misdemeanors that result in incarceration or a suspended jail or prison sentence. *See Gideon v. Wainwright,* 372 U.S. 335 (1963); *Argersinger v. Hamlin,* 407 U.S. 25 (1972); *Scott v. Illinois,* 440 U.S. 367 (1979). *See also Alabama v. Shelton,* 535 U.S. 654 (2002) (prohibiting activation of a suspended jail sentence when indigent defendant was not provided court-appointed counsel at trial). The Court recognized that indigents have a right to court-appointed counsel on appeal in *Douglas v. California,* 372 U.S. 353 (1963).

20. *Ross v. Moffitt,* 417 U.S. 600 (1974).

21. *Murray v. Giarratano,* 492 U.S. 1 (1989) (capital case); *Pennsylvania v. Finley,* 481 U.S. 551 (1987).

22. *See* Emily Garcia Uhrig, "A Case for a Constitutional Right to Counsel in Habeas Corpus," 60 *Hastings Law Journal* 541 (2009); Sarah L. Thomas, "A Legislative Challenge: A Proposed Model Statute to Provide for the Appointment of Counsel in State Habeas Corpus Proceedings for Indigent Petitioners," 54 *Emory Law Journal* 1139 (2005).

23. The Supreme Court recently has recognized limited exceptions in cases where state prisoners seeking federal habeas corpus have not received adequate representation by counsel during state post-conviction proceedings. *See Trevino v. Thaler,* 133 S.Ct. 1911 (2013); *Martinez v. Ryan,* 132 S.Ct. 1309 (2012); *Maples v. Thomas,* 132 S.Ct. 912 (2012). *See generally* Wendy Zorana Zupac, "Mere Negligence or Abandonment? Evaluating Claims of Attorney Misconduct After *Maples v. Thomas,*" 122 *Yale Law Journal* 1328 (2013).

24. Celestine Richards McConville, "The Meaninglessness of Delayed Appointments and Discretionary Grants of Capital Postconviction Counsel," 42 *Tulsa Law Review* 253, 253 n. 1 (2006); Celestine Richards McConville, "The Right to Effective Assistance of Capital Postconviction Counsel: Constitutional Implications of Statutory Grants of Capital Counsel," 2003 *Wisconsin Law Review* 31, 63–66 (2003).

25. *Maples v. State,* 758 So.2d 1 (Ala. Crim. App.), *aff'd, Ex parte Maples,* 758 So.2d 81 (Ala. 1999).

26. *Maples v. Thomas,* 132 S.Ct. 912 (2012).

27. *See* Susannah Sheffer, *Fighting for Their Lives: Inside the Experience of Capital Defense Attorneys* (Nashville: Vanderbilt University Press 2013).

28. The Sixth Amendment right to trial by jury applies to the States through the Fourteenth Amendment and is available in trials for all "non-petty" offenses, which typically means crimes punishable by more than six months of incarceration. *Duncan v. Louisiana*, 391 U.S. 145 (1968); *Baldwin v. New York*, 399 U.S. 66 (1970).

29. Mont. Code §§ 46–18–301, 46–18–305 (2013). *See Woodward v. Alabama*, 2013 WL 6050109, p. 2 (U.S. Supreme Court 2013) (Sotomayor, J., dissenting from denial of certiorari).

30. *See* Shannon Heery, "If It's Constitutional, Then What's the Problem?: The Use of Judicial Override in Alabama Death Sentencing," 34 *Washington University Journal of Law and Policy* 347 (2010); Michael L. Radelet, "Overriding Jury Sentencing Recommendations in Florida Capital Cases: An Update and Possible Half-Requiem," 2011 *Michigan State Law Review* 793 (2011); Sheri Lynn Johnson, John H. Blume, Theodore Eisenberg, Valerie P. Hans & Martin T. Wells, "The Delaware Death Penalty: An Empirical Study," 97 *Iowa Law Review* 1925 (2012). In Delaware, the jury formally does not make a sentencing recommendation to the judge, although it does report whether it has found that the proven aggravating factors outweigh the mitigating circumstances in the case. Del. Code Ann. Tit. 11 § 4209 (c)(3)(a) (2) (2013). "The jury's recommendation concerning whether the aggravating circumstances found to exist outweigh the mitigating circumstances found to exist shall be given such consideration as deemed appropriate by the Court. . . . The jury's recommendation shall not be binding on the Court." *Id.*, at § 4209 (d)(1).

31. *Ring v. Arizona*, 536 U.S. 584 (2002).

32. *Id.*, 536 U.S., at 612–613 (Scalia, J., concurring); *Harris v. Alabama*, 513 U.S. 504 (1995); *Spaziano v. Florida*, 468 U.S. 447 (1984). *But see Woodward v. Alabama*, 2013 WL 6050109, pp. 4–6 (U.S. Supreme Court 2013) (Sotomayor, J., dissenting from denial of certiorari).

33. 428 U.S. 242 (1976).

34. 428 U.S. 153 (1976).

35. 468 U.S. 447 (1984).

36. *Spaziano v. Florida*, 468 U.S. 447, 457 (1984).

37. *Id.*, 468 U.S., at 458.

38. *Id.*, 468 U.S., at 464.

39. *See* Michael L. Radelet & Michael Mello, "Death-to-Life Overrides: Saving the Resources of the Florida Supreme Court," 20 *Florida State University Law Review* 195 (1992); Radelet, *supra* note 30, at 819–820; Fred B. Burnside, "Dying to Get Elected: A Challenge to the Jury Override," 1999 *Wisconsin Law Review* 1017 (1999).

40. Radelet, *supra* note 30, at 809, 819–820.

41. *Id.*, at 810; Michael Mello, "The Jurisdiction to Do Justice: Florida's Jury Override and the State Constitution," 18 *Florida State University Law Review* 923, 937 (1991); Scott E. Erlich, "The Jury Override: A Blend of Politics and Death," 45 *American University Law Review* 1432 (1996). In *Tedder v. State*, 322 So.2d 908, 910 (Fla. 1975), the Florida Supreme Court held that "[i]n order to sustain a sentence of death following a jury recommendation of life, the facts suggesting a sentence of death should be so clear and convincing that virtually no reasonable person could differ."

42. Radelet, *supra* note 30, at 798–799.

43. *Id.*, at 802–803.

44. 513 U.S. 504 (1995).

45. ___ S.Ct., ___, 2013 WL 6050109 (2013).

46. *Witherspoon v. Illinois*, 391 U.S. 510, 512 (1968), *quoting* Ill. Rev. Stat., c. 38, § 743 (1959).

47. *Id.*, 391 U.S., at 530 n. 12 (opinion of Douglas, J.).

48. *Id.*, 391 U.S., at 513–515, 518.

49. *Id.*, 391 U.S., at 519.

50. *Id.*, 391 U.S., at 522 (footnote omitted).

51. *Id.,* 391 U.S., at 522 n. 21.

52. *Wainwright v. Witt,* 469 U.S. 412, 425–426 (1985) (footnotes omitted), *quoting Adams v. Texas,* 448 U.S. 38, 45 (1980).

53. *Morgan v. Illinois,* 504 U.S. 719, 729 (1992).

54. Joseph B. Kadane, "After *Hovey:* A Note on Taking Account of the Automatic Death Penalty Jurors," 8 *Law and Human Behavior* 115, 116 (1984) (citing studies).

55. *See* Marla Sandys & Scott McClelland, "Stacking the Deck for Guilt and Death: The Failure of Death Qualification to Ensure Impartiality," in James R. Acker, Robert M. Bohm & Charles S. Lanier (eds.), *America's Experiment With Capital Punishment: Reflections on the Past, Present, and Future of the Ultimate Penal Sanction* 385, 394 (Durham, NC: Carolina Academic Press, 2d ed. 2003); John H. Blume, Sheri Lynn Johnson & A. Brian Threlkeld, "Probing 'Life Qualification' Through Expanded Voir Dire," 29 *Hofstra Law Review* 1209, 1220–24 (2001); Ronald C. Dillehay & Marla R. Sandys, "Life Under *Wainwright v. Witt*: Juror Dispositions and Death Qualification, 20 *Law and Human Behavior* (1996).

56. *Witherspoon v. Illinois,* 391 U.S. 510, 520 n. 16 (1968) (citations omitted).

57. *Id.,* 391 U.S., at 519 (footnote omitted).

58. *Grigsby v. Mabry,* 569 F. Supp. 1273 (E.D. Ark. 1983).

59. *Grigsby v. Mabry,* 758 F.2d 226 (8th Cir. 1985) (en banc). The district court had ruled in favor of McCree on both of his arguments, *i.e.,* that death qualification results in an impartial jury for determining guilt-innocence, and also violates the requirement that a jury be drawn from a representative cross-section of the community. The Court of Appeals reached only the "representative cross-section" argument, finding it unnecessary to address the claimed violation of the "impartial jury" requirement.

60. *Lockhart v. McCree,* 476 U.S. 162, 165 (1986).

61. *See generally,* Herbert L. Packer, *The Limits of the Criminal Sanction* 149–173 (Stanford, CA: Stanford University Press 1968).

62. *Witherspoon v. Illinois,* 391 U.S. 510, 517 n. 10 (1968).

63. *Id.,* 391 U.S., at 518.

64. *Id.,* 391 U.S., at 517–518.

65. "[A] defendant convicted by [a death-qualified] jury in some further [sic] case might still attempt to establish that the jury was less than neutral with respect to guilt. . . ." *Id.,* 391 U.S., at 520 n. 18.

66. *Grigsby v. Mabry,* 569 F. Supp. 1273 (E.D. Ark. 1983).

67. *See* Robert Fitzgerald & Phoebe C. Ellsworth, "Due Process vs. Crime Control: Death Qualification and Jury Attitudes," 8 *Law and Human Behavior* 31 (1984); Claudia L. Cowan, William C. Thompson & Phoebe C. Ellsworth, "The Effects of Death Qualification on Jurors' Predisposition to Convict and on the Quality of Deliberation," 8 *Law and Human Behavior* 53 (1984); Phoebe C. Ellsworth, Raymond M. Bukaty, Claudia L. Cowan & William C. Thompson, "The Death-Qualified Jury and the Defense of Insanity," 8 *Law and Human Behavior* 81 (1984); William C. Thompson, Claudia L. Cowan, Phoebe C. Ellsworth & Joan C. Harrington, "Death Penalty Attitudes and Conviction Proneness: The Translation of Attitudes Into Verdicts," 8 *Law and Human Behavior* 95 (1984).

68. *See* Craig Haney, "Examining Death Qualification: Further Analysis of the Process Effect," 8 *Law and Human Behavior* 133 (1984).

69. Craig Haney, "On the Selection of Capital Juries: The Biasing Effects of the Death-Qualification Process," 8 *Law and Human Behavior* 121 (1984).

70. *Lockhart v. McCree,* 476 U.S. 162, 169, 168 (1986).

71. *Id.,* 476 U.S., at 173. One of the researchers whose studies were under consideration described the majority opinion as follows: "The actual decision was worse than disappointing; it was lamentable. Justice Rehnquist, writing for the majority, first attacked the research in ways that suggested that the majority Justices had either not understood it or not read it, or that they just didn't care. He then declared that it didn't matter how compelling the

data might be, because it is constitutionally permissible to try capital cases before juries that are biased toward guilty verdicts. In short, 'we don't believe the data, but if we did it wouldn't matter.'" Phoebe C. Ellsworth, "Unpleasant Facts: The Supreme Court's Response to Empirical Research Evidence on Capital Punishment," in Kenneth C. Haas & James A. Inciardi (eds.), *Challenging Capital Punishment: Legal and Social Science Approaches* 177, 193 (Newbury Park, CA: Sage Publications 1988).

72. *Grigsby v. Mabry*, 758 F.2d 226, 231 (8th Cir. 1985) (en banc), *quoting* 569 F. Supp. 1273, 1285 (E.D. Ark. 1983).
73. *Grigsby v. Mabry*, 569 F. Supp. 1273, 1294 (E.D. Ark. 1983).
74. *Lockhart v. McCree*, 476 U.S. 162, 193 n. 16 (1986) (Marshall, J., dissenting).
75. *Id.*, 476 U.S., at 204, *quoting* Bruce J. Winick, "Prosecutorial Peremptory Challenge Practices in Capital Cases: An Empirical Study and a Constitutional Analysis," 81 *Michigan Law Review* 1, 57 (1982).
76. *Lockhart v. McCree*, 476 U.S. 162, 203 (1986) (Marshall, J., dissenting), *quoting Grigsby v. Mabry*, 569 F. Supp. 1273, 1310 (E.D. Ark. 1983).
77. *J.E.B. v. Alabama*, 511 U.S. 127 (1994) (gender); *Hernandez v. New York*, 500 U.S. 352 (1991) (ethnicity); *Batson v. Kentucky*, 476 U.S. 79 (1986) (race).
78. *See* James R. Acker & Charles S. Lanier, "Law, Discretion, and the Capital Jury: Death Penalty Statutes and Proposals for Reform," 32 *Criminal Law Bulletin* 134, 160–165 (1996).
79. *Batson v. Kentucky*, 476 U.S. 79, 120–121 (1986) (Burger, C.J., dissenting); *Swain v. Alabama*, 380 U.S. 202, 219 (1965), *overruled in part, Batson v. Kentucky, supra*; Barbara Allen Babcock, "Voir Dire: Preserving 'Its Wonderful Power,'" 27 *Stanford Law Review* 545, 549–550 (1975).
80. *Miller-El v. Dretke*, 545 U.S. 231 (2005).
81. *Batson v. Kentucky*, 476 U.S. 79, 107–108 (1986) (Marshall, J., concurring); *Miller-El v. Dretke*, 545 U.S. 231, 266–273 (2005) (Breyer, J., concurring).
82. *See Gray v. Mississippi*, 481 U.S. 648, 667, 678 n. 19 (1987) (plurality opinion); David C. Baldus, George Woodworth, David Zuckerman, Neil Alan Weiner & Barbara Broffitt, "The Use of Peremptory Challenges in Capital Murder Trials: A Legal and Empirical Analysis," 3 *University of Pennsylvania Journal of Constitutional Law* 3 (2001); Winick, note 75, *supra*.
83. *See* note 141 and accompanying text, *supra*; Baldus *et al.*, *supra* note 82; Winick, *supra* note 75; Melynda J. Price, "Performing Discretion or Performing Discrimination: Race, Ritual, and Peremptory Challenges in Capital Jury Selection," 15 *Michigan Journal of Race and Law* 57 (2009).
84. 545 U.S., at 242–252.
85. Acker & Lanier, *supra* note 78, at 173–174, *quoting Parker v. Randolph*, 442 U.S. 62, 73 (1979).
86. *Free v. Peters*, 19 F.3d 389, 390 (7th Cir.), *cert. denied*, 513 U.S. 967 (1994) (Rovner, J., dissenting from denial of rehearing en banc).
87. Acker & Lanier, *supra* note 78, at 175–176 n. 187 (citing cases and studies).
88. *Id.*, citing *Gacy v. Welborne*, 994 F.2d 305, 314 (7th Cir.), *cert. denied*, 510 U.S. 899 (1993).
89. *Free v. Peters*, 12 F.3d 700 (7th Cir. 1993), *cert. denied*, 513 U.S. 967 (1994); *Gacy v. Welborne*, 994 F.2d 305, 314 (7th Cir.), *cert. denied*, 510 U.S. 899 (1993).
90. *See* William J. Bowers, "The Capital Jury Project: Rationale, Design, and Preview of Early Findings," 70 *Indiana Law Journal* 1043 (1995).
91. William J. Bowers, Benjamin D. Fleury-Steiner & Michael E. Antonio, "The Capital Sentencing Decision: Guided Discretion, Reasoned Moral Judgment, or Legal Fiction," in James R. Acker, Robert M. Bohm & Charles S. Lanier (eds.), *America's Experiment With Capital Punishment: Reflections on the Past, Present, and Future of the Ultimate Penal Sanction* 413, 425 (Durham, NC: Carolina Academic Press, 2d ed. 2003).
92. *Id.*, at 436.
93. *Id.*, at 439.

94. *Id.,* at 449. *See also* William J. Bowers, Benjamin D. Steiner & Marla Sandys, "Death Sentencing in Black and White: An Empirical Analysis of the Role of Jurors' Race and Jury Racial Composition," 3 *University of Pennsylvania Journal of Constitutional Law* 171 (2001).
95. William J. Bowers, "A Tribute to David Baldus, a Determined and Relentless Champion of Doing Justice," 97 *Iowa Law Review* 1879, 1899 (2012).
96. *Woodson v. North Carolina,* 428 U.S. 280, 305 (1976) (plurality opinion).

III

POST-CONVICTION

8

CAPITAL ERRORS

PROCEDURAL ISSUES AND ACTUAL INNOCENCE

Introduction

While denying a motion filed by criminal defendants to inspect the minutes of the grand jury proceedings in their case, United States District Court Judge Learned Hand professed unqualified confidence in the legal protections afforded individuals accused of crimes. He dismissed as fanciful the notion that amidst those layers of protection there lurked the risk of error.

> Under our criminal procedure the accused has every advantage. While the prosecution is held rigidly to the charge, he need not disclose the barest outline of his defense. He is immune from question or comment on his silence; he cannot be convicted when there is the least fair doubt in the minds of any of the twelve [jurors]. Why in addition he should in advance have the whole evidence against him to pick over at his leisure, and make his defense, fairly or foully, I have never been able to see. No doubt grand juries err and indictments are calamities to honest men, but we must work with human beings and we can correct such errors only at too large a price. Our dangers do not lie in too little tenderness to the accused. Our procedure has been always haunted by the ghost of the innocent man convicted. It is an unreal dream. What we need to fear is the archaic formalism and the watery sentiment that obstructs, delays, and defeats the prosecution of crime.[1]

Judge Hand expressed those sentiments in an opinion issued in 1923. Although his contributions to the nation's jurisprudence were numerous and widely heralded,[2] the passage of time and accumulation of cases in which errors are known to have subverted the law's protections suggest that even distinguished jurists sometimes get it wrong. Criminal cases are not immune from error. This is true even for capital cases—and, surprisingly, perhaps *especially* for capital cases, where the consequences of error are particularly profound.

This chapter surveys two categories of error that have infected capital trials. The first concerns procedural irregularities that require reversal of either the defendant's capital murder conviction or the ensuing death sentence. The second involves the wrongful conviction and sentencing to death of innocent persons, *i.e.*, individuals who flatly did not commit the crimes for which they were arrested, prosecuted, and sent to death row. The two types of error are not tightly compartmentalized. Errors that traditionally are classified as procedural in nature—for example, violations of the defendant's right to the effective assistance of counsel, prosecutors' failure to divulge exculpatory evidence, the denial of confrontation rights, allowing expert witnesses to offer unfounded testimony—can undermine the reliability of a verdict and hence help produce a wrongful conviction. Nevertheless, serious procedural errors also require reversals in cases involving defendants who are not or may not be factually innocent. They consequently will be considered here as a separate set of reasons for upsetting a guilt or sentencing verdict in a capital case.

Procedural Error

In early American history, executions followed closely on the heels of the defendant's conviction. They sometimes occurred within days of the trial's conclusion, although typically at least a few weeks passed, a long enough time to give the offender the opportunity to repent, the community to receive notice of the sentence, and for the authorities to arrange for the accompanying public rituals.[3] Although various mechanisms were available to allow further judicial review of trial court judgments, no right of appeal was provided in capital (or other criminal) cases. The absence of a right of appeal endured well into the 20th century in many jurisdictions, particularly for defendants too poor to afford to pursue review of their cases in a higher court.[4]

Times have changed. Between 1930 and 1967 (the year of the last execution in the pre-*Furman v. Georgia*[5] era), the average time lapse between the imposition of a death sentence and the offender's execution was slightly more than 36 months.[6] By 1984, that interval more than doubled, to 74 months. It doubled again, to 147 months, for offenders executed in 2005. The 43 individuals executed in 2011 were sentenced to death an average of 198 months (16 ½ years) earlier, *i.e.*, in trials completed in 1994 or 1995.[7]

Appeals of capital convictions and sentences now not only are available as of right, but they are mandatory in almost all jurisdictions, even if the defendant does not want to pursue one.[8] The appeal marks only the first step in a multi-stage process of state and federal judicial review that is available and generally utilized in capital cases.[9] Following the appeal, which typically bypasses courts of intermediate jurisdiction and is filed directly in a state's highest court,[10] federal constitutional challenges to the conviction or sentence can be raised by petition for writ of certiorari in the U.S. Supreme Court. The Supreme Court has great discretion over its docket and is under no obligation to hear such cases. Only rarely do the justices grant certiorari and agree to review a lower court's decision.

Barring relief via these "direct" avenues of review, collateral challenges to the conviction and sentence can be pursued. State post-conviction proceedings are available to resolve issues that could not be presented on appeal, typically including claims of ineffective assistance of trial counsel, prosecutorial misconduct, or newly discovered evidence. An appeal to an intermediate state court, a petition for discretionary review filed in the state supreme court, and another petition for writ of certiorari to the U.S. Supreme Court then can follow.

On failing to secure relief in the state courts, defendants are in a position to ask U.S. District Courts to vacate their convictions and/or sentences by filing petitions for writs of habeas corpus. Habeas corpus review is available for state defendants exclusively to resolve whether their federal constitutional rights were violated in the state court proceedings. With narrow exceptions, only issues first presented in the state courts and rejected by them can be raised. Although not automatic,[11] leave for appeal commonly is granted to allow a defendant under sentence of death to have a district court's denial of habeas relief reviewed in a U.S. Court of Appeal.[12] Cases are decided in the U.S. Courts of Appeal by three-judge panels, but the losing party can request a rehearing *en banc,* or by a larger complement of judges. Thereafter, another petition for writ of certiorari can be filed in the U.S. Supreme Court. A decision adverse to the defendant by the Supreme Court would be the final step in the judicial review process, although last-minute requests for a stay of execution to resolve other issues might be filed and litigated as well.

Capital cases have traditionally occasioned rigorous appellate and post-conviction judicial review. Long before the Supreme Court's jurisprudence explicitly recognized that "death is different," various justices acknowledged in their capital case decisions the importance of knowing that the defendant's life hung in the balance.[13] Justice Harlan expressed this sentiment in his concurring opinion in *Reid v. Covert*, 354 U.S. 1 (1957).

> So far as capital cases are concerned, I think they stand on quite a different footing than
> other offenses. In such cases the law is especially sensitive to demands for . . . procedural
> fairness. . . . I do not concede that whatever process is "due" an offender faced with a fine or
> a prison sentence necessarily satisfies the requirements of the Constitution in a capital case.
> The distinction is by no means novel, . . . nor is it negligible, being literally that between
> life and death.[14]

In 2000, James Liebman, Jeffrey Fagan, and Valerie West published a groundbreaking study of appellate and federal court reversals in state cases that resulted in a death sentence over the period 1973 to 1995. The following were among the key findings in the study, *A Broken System: Error Rates in Capital Cases, 1973–1995*:

- "Nationally, during the 23-year study period, the overall rate of prejudicial error in the American capital punishment system was *68%.* In other words, courts found serious, reversible error in nearly 7 of every 10 of the thousands of capital sentences that were fully reviewed during the period."
- "[S]tate courts threw out 47% of death sentences due to serious flaws, [and] a later federal review found 'serious error'—error undermining the reliability of the outcome—in 40% of the *remaining* sentences."
- "The most common errors—prompting a majority of reversals at the state post-conviction stage—are (1) egregiously incompetent defense lawyers who didn't even look for—*and demonstrably missed*—important evidence that the defendant was innocent or did not deserve to die; and (2) police or prosecutors who *did* discover that kind of evidence but *suppressed* it, again keeping it from the jury."

- "High error rates put many individuals at risk of wrongful execution: *82%* of the people whose capital judgments were overturned by state post-conviction courts due to serious error were found to deserve a sentence less than death when the errors were cured on retrial; *7% were found to be innocent of the capital crime.*"
- "High error rates persist over time. More than 50% of all cases reviewed were found seriously flawed in 20 of the 23 study years, including 17 of the last 19. In half the years, including the most recent one, the error rate was over 60%."
- "Catching so much error takes time—a national average of 9 years from death sentence to the last inspection and execution. By the end of the study period, that average had risen to 10.6 years. In *most* cases, death row inmates wait for years for the lengthy review procedures needed to uncover all this error. Then, their death sentences are *reversed.*"[15]

By any standards, a reversal rate of 68%—or in two out of three cases that result in a death sentence—is striking. It far exceeds the reversal rate in non-capital criminal cases, where an estimated 10% or less of appeals result in overturned judgments. State post-conviction and federal habeas corpus reversals are rarer still.[16] "Whatever one thinks of the death penalty, [these findings] are disturbing. Any system generating two or more duds for every keeper—and requiring more than a decade to find it—is irrational and cries out for explanation."[17]

Definitive explanations for the high rate of reversals in capital cases are elusive. Different possibilities exist. In the first place, capital trials involve two separate hearings, a guilt phase and a penalty phase, which naturally amplifies the likelihood that errors will be committed. Capital trials also are governed by complex and—especially during the first decade of the death penalty's modern era—unsettled legal doctrine that attorneys and trial judges might find obscure. They additionally require rulings on issues, such as the death-qualification of jurors, which never or only rarely are confronted in noncapital cases. Cost-cutting measures that influence the quality of defense counsel or the provision of court-appointed investigators and expert witnesses may play a role in the reversal rate. The high stakes and publicity associated with capital trials might tempt law enforcement authorities or prosecutors to withhold exculpatory evidence or otherwise break or bend rules.[18] Another possibility is that judges greatly intensify their scrutiny of death-penalty cases on post-conviction review, homing in on issues and finding error where they might not in their review of non-capital cases. In all probability, some combination of these factors—the complexities of the law, the protracted and high-stakes nature of the proceedings, and the judicial mindset in reviewing capital cases for error—is responsible for the conspicuously high reversal rate.

Other systemic, political, and social factors also could be at work. In a follow-up analysis to *A Broken System*, Professor Liebman and colleagues found that the highest reversal rates in death-penalty cases were associated with the states and counties that imposed death sentences at the highest rates. Reversals were all the more likely in cases that were not highly aggravated. Relying on these factors, they identified the "overproduction of death penalty verdicts" as a principal cause of capital case error.[19] They additionally found that racial and political considerations correlated with high capital case error rates. A comparatively high representation of African Americans and relatively high rates of White-victim homicides within a state were associated with high reversal rates. Another link was found between high error rates and trial court judges' securing office as a result of partisan popular elections.[20]

> Our main finding indicates that if we are going to have the death penalty, it should be reserved for the worst of the worst. Heavy and indiscriminate use of the death penalty creates a high risk that mistakes will occur. The more often officials use the death penalty, the wider the range of crimes to which it is applied, and the more it is imposed for offenses that are not highly aggravated, the greater the risk that capital convictions and sentences will be seriously flawed.
>
> Most disturbing of all, we find that the conditions evidently pressuring counties and states to overuse the death penalty and thus increase the risk of unreliability and error include *race, politics* and *poorly performing law enforcement systems.* Error also is linked to overburdened and underfunded state courts.[21]

Detecting and correcting error in capital cases requires time and resources. Judicial review of capital convictions and sentences is essential to determine whether error has been committed, yet it also is the main reason for the substantial delays that commonly ensue between the imposition of sentence and execution in cases that survive the review process. Criticisms often are directed at the slow pace of justice in capital proceedings. Others object that the review process must be deliberate to ensure that justice—both procedural and substantive—has not been compromised. Disagreement reigns about whether appeals and post-conviction review of capital convictions and sentences can be expedited without sacrificing fairness or accuracy.

In busy death-penalty jurisdictions such as California and Florida, capital cases can account for 25% or more of the appellate docket.[22] Their bulk, complexity, and importance cause them to exert disproportionate demands on attorneys' and judges' time and energies.[23] Appellate delays are attributable in part to the voluminous trial records in capital cases, which must first be transcribed, and then studied by the lawyers representing the defense and prosecution so they can prepare and file briefs in the state supreme court. The appellate judges then must comb the record and briefs, hear oral argument, deliberate, conduct their own research, and write opinions in support of their decisions.[24]

In California, where more than 730 defendants are under sentence of death and qualified appellate attorneys are scarce, more than five years can lapse before a lawyer is appointed to represent a death-sentenced offender on appeal. It is not unusual for a decade to separate the conclusion of a capital trial and the California Supreme Court's decision of an appeal.[25] Nationally, "about five years lapse[d] between [imposition of a death] sentence and the first direct appeal"[26] in trials concluded between 1973 and 1995. A study of the length of the direct appeals process in 14 states involving capital cases decided between 1992 and 2002 found that the median time between notice of appeal and decision was approximately 2½ years, with considerable variation (a low of 295 days in Virginia, to more than 3½ years, in Ohio).[27]

The direct appeal is only the first step in what is usually a much longer process if the defendant is not granted relief at that stage. Requests for discretionary review, state post-conviction proceedings, and rounds of federal habeas corpus litigation follow and require resolution.[28] Delays are compounded when reversible error is detected and new trials or new sentencing hearings are conducted. In a case involving a Florida prisoner who was still contesting his case after spending 23 years on death row, Justice Breyer noted that the defendant "has experienced that delay because of the State's own faulty procedures. . . . His three successful appeals account for 18 of the 23 years of delay. A fourth appeal accounts for the remaining five years. . . ."[29]

Concerned about protracted post-conviction proceedings in capital cases, Congress imposed limits on the federal courts' review of state prisoners' claims on habeas corpus when it enacted the Antiterrorism and Effective Death Penalty Act of 1996 (AEDPA).[30]

> [T]he legislation sought to speed up habeas proceedings in two basic ways: directly, by setting time limits on various procedural steps, and indirectly, by providing that the federal courts should not grant the writ unless the state proceedings "resulted in a decision that was contrary to, or involved an unreasonable application of, clearly established federal law as determined by the Supreme Court of the United States."[31]

One provision of AEDPA requires petitions for a writ of habeas corpus to be filed within a year of a state court's judgment becoming final.[32] In addition, state prisoners must comply with numerous and sometimes daunting procedural requirements or risk forfeiting the opportunity to have their claims reviewed on federal habeas corpus, no matter how meritorious.[33] The forfeiture policies are subject to strictly enforced exceptions, including one available when a strong showing is made of the petitioner's actual innocence.[34]

Some states have joined in taking steps to try to shorten capital case processing time. For example, Florida's "Timely Justice Act," enacted in 2013, imposes strict time limits on attorneys, the courts, and the governor for taking action in death-penalty cases in an attempt to speed up the post-conviction stages.[35] A number of states have adopted "unitary review systems" in which post-conviction relief must be sought shortly after a capital trial's conclusion, before the appeal is perfected. If relief is denied, the post-conviction issues must be joined with those raised in the appeal to streamline the review process.[36]

While there is little agreement about what procedures offer the best blend of timeliness, fairness, and finality in providing for the judicial review of capital convictions and sentences, many agree that current practices disserve multiple interests. It has been urged that if more highly qualified and better-funded defense lawyers were involved earlier in capital cases, particularly in providing trial representation, fewer errors would be committed, and hence fewer matters would require correction on appeal and in later stages of review.[37] Such "up front" investments thus not only would be cost effective, but also would help promote fairness.

Innocence

As controversial and contentious as many issues surrounding capital punishment can be, no one disputes the utter wrongfulness of executing an innocent person. There is less agreement about closely related matters, including what it means to be "innocent" of a capital crime, whether (and how many) innocent people have been wrongfully convicted of capital offenses and/or executed, and what legal and policy implications, if any, should follow if it is acknowledged that the death penalty exposes innocent persons to the risk of execution.

A person found guilty of a capital crime would certainly be considered "innocent" if: (a) the crime really did not occur; or (b) the crime occurred but somebody else committed it.

An instance of the former, "no crime" situation would be a case where the defendant was convicted of murder but the ostensible victim was actually quite alive. Such occurrences are not unknown.[38] For example, in Manchester, Vermont, in 1819, brothers Jesse and Stephen Boorn were convicted of murdering their brother-in-law, Russell Colvin, who had disappeared years earlier without explanation amid widespread knowledge that bad blood existed among the three of them. Neighborhood gossip, a relative's vivid dream, and recently uncovered evidence combined to suggest that Colvin had met with foul play. A renewed investigation resulted in both brothers admitting to having killed Colvin, although Jesse later recanted his confession. Both of the Boorns were convicted of Colvin's murder and sentenced to death. Jesse's sentence was commuted to life imprisonment, but Stephen was scheduled to be executed. Three weeks before Stephen was to be hanged, Colvin was located, alive and well in New Jersey. When Colvin was tricked into returning to Vermont, Stephen was spared and both brothers' murder convictions were vacated.[39]

A more recent and somewhat less dramatic "no crime" case involved Sabrina Butler, who was sentenced to death in Mississippi in 1990 following her conviction for murdering her 9-month-old son. The child had suffered extensive internal injuries and his body was badly bruised. Butler maintained that her son, who suffered from asthma, had stopped breathing and that the injuries were inflicted when she performed cardiopulmonary resuscitation (CPR) in an attempt to revive him. The prosecution contended that the child's injured body evidenced aggravated physical abuse, which was the cause of death. The Mississippi Supreme Court reversed Butler's conviction on appeal, finding that procedural error had occurred during her trial.[40] Butler was acquitted following retrial in 1995 after the medical examiner who testified at her original trial admitted that he had made mistakes and other experts opined that the child's death likely resulted from Sudden Infant Death Syndrome or kidney disease.[41]

Far more common than "no crime" cases in producing wrongful convictions are "wrong person" cases, in which a criminal offense was committed but by somebody other than the individual who was charged with and convicted of it.[42] Numerous factors can contribute to the erroneous conviction of factually innocent people. Chief among the sources of error are mistaken eyewitness identifications; flawed forensic analysis and testimony; false confessions; misplaced reliance on statements secured from "incentivized" witnesses such as jailhouse informants; the misconduct and lapses of police, prosecutors, and defense counsel; witness perjury; and simple bad luck and mistakes made by fallible humans.[43]

In addition to the "no crime" and "wrong person" cases, which involve fairly straightforward notions of innocence, other types of cases present more challenging definitional questions. For example, what classification should be given to a defendant who killed another and was convicted of capital murder but who "in fact" acted in justifiable self defense; or who "in fact" was severely mentally ill and came within the legal definition of insanity; or who "in fact" committed an unlawful killing but lacked the *mens rea* required for capital murder (such as premeditation or intent to kill) and thus should not have been convicted of a death penalty–eligible crime? Should any or all of those cases be considered as producing the conviction of a person who is "innocent" of capital murder?

Although a persuasive case might be made that some or all of the above examples would represent the conviction of a person who is innocent of capital murder, more conservative, traditional definitions tend to confine the concept of innocence narrowly, as applying only to individuals who did not commit the necessary acts associated with an offense.[44] Convictions following the failure to credit a legitimate affirmative defense, such as self defense or insanity, or when the actor lacked the required *mens rea*, thus would not qualify.

More is required than reaching conceptual agreement about the meaning of innocence to determine whether innocent people have been erroneously convicted of capital crimes and/or executed. An "operational definition" also is needed, one that provides the objective, observable criteria for identifying a case as involving the conviction of an innocent person. Not all cases are as clear cut as those of Jesse and Stephen Boorn, whose "victim" appeared, very much alive, following their conviction for murder.[45] And despite the potential value of DNA in helping to identify "wrong person" cases, no DNA evidence exists in the vast majority of cases.[46] When it is available, a DNA exclusion—for example, where post-conviction analysis determines that semen or blood found at the crime scene belongs to someone other than the defendant—does not necessarily mean that the defendant did not participate in the crime.[47]

There is no perfect solution to this problem. The Death Penalty Information Center (DPIC), which was asked by Representative Don Edwards, the Chair of the House Subcommittee on Civil and Constitutional Rights, to compile a list of the innocent persons who had been erroneously convicted and sentenced to death during the modern capital punishment era, relies on official determinations. DPIC's "Innocence List" is limited to death-sentenced individuals who subsequently had:

- Been acquitted of all charges related to the crime that placed them on death row; or
- Had all charges related to the crime that placed them on death row dismissed by the prosecution; or
- Been granted a complete pardon based on evidence of innocence.[48]

One virtue of this approach is its objectivity. Another is its reliance "only [on] the decisions rendered by the justice system, as it applied its traditional procedures and criteria for determining guilt or innocence. . . ."[49] Yet using such official indicators as proxies for innocence invites other problems. One concern is the substantial gap between a "not guilty" verdict—as contemplated by the criterion of being "acquitted [on retrial] of all charges related to the crime that placed [the individual] on death row"—and unambiguous "innocence." A not guilty verdict signifies only that the prosecution failed to prove the accused's guilt beyond a reasonable doubt. While certainly appropriate in a case of factual innocence, such a verdict could stem from any number of other reasons including the unavailability of a crucial witness or a missing item of evidence. The same reasons might induce a prosecutor to dismiss charges rather than pursue a futile retrial.

Another drawback of making a determination of innocence that depends on official action, such as a jury verdict, a prosecutor's dismissal of charges, or a governor's pardon, is the considerable risk that many deserving cases will never come to light. Indeed, there is some irony in relying on the same system of justice that allegedly caused an innocent person to be convicted in the first place to determine that very issue when the question is revisited. The "failure by the authorities to acknowledge error is not very convincing evidence that errors have not occurred."[50] Thus, Hugo Adam Bedau and Michael Radelet used an alternative approach to compile a list of 350 erroneous convictions in capital and potentially capital cases between 1900 and 1985. They included cases "in which we believe a majority of neutral observers, given the evidence at our disposal, would judge the defendant in question to be innocent."[51] While avoiding overdependence on official recognition of "innocence," the subjectivity inherent in this approach invites its own problems.[52]

As of December 2013, the Death Penalty Information Center had identified 143 innocent people, using the criteria identified above, who had been convicted of capital murder and sentenced to death since 1973. Post-conviction DNA evidence helped clear 18 of the wrongfully convicted capital defendants. On average, those on DPIC's innocence list had spent slightly more than a decade (10.1 years) on death row before being released.[53] Some came within hours or days of scheduled execution dates.[54] Computing the ratio of post-conviction exonerations in death-penalty cases to the total number of death sentences imposed, and making adjustments for the normal time lag between conviction and exoneration, researchers have estimated that 2.3% of cases resulting in a death sentence during the modern capital punishment era, and as many as 3.3% to 5% of death sentences for capital rape-murder, have involved innocent persons.[55]

If these estimates are at all close to being accurate, what are their implications? Would an error rate of 2.3%, representing the proportion of the nation's death row population who are factually innocent, be shockingly high? Or should it be considered acceptably low, since perfection can hardly be expected in any human undertaking, including the administration of justice? If applied to the national death row population as of January 1, 2013,[56] this error rate would mean that 72 of the 3125 prisoners awaiting execution are innocent.

None of the identified cases of wrongful conviction resulted in an innocent person's execution. Should the detection of error prior to execution be taken as evidence that "the system works"? Or would that conclusion be offensive to an innocent person who was wrongfully convicted, sentenced to death, and then incarcerated on death row under the threat of execution for a decade or more before being exonerated? Would it matter how the error was uncovered—e.g., through the regular process of judicial review and with the cooperation of government officials, or instead through the investigative efforts of journalists and private organizations while government attorneys argued strenuously to uphold a conviction and against delaying an execution?

Controversy persists over whether innocent persons have in fact been executed. Using their largely subjective criterion for determining innocence, as explained above,[57] Bedau and Radelet identified 23 cases in which innocent people were executed during the 20th century. All but two of the executions occurred between 1905 and 1945; one took place in 1960, and one in 1974.[58] More recently, serious concerns have been raised that Cameron Todd Willingham, who was executed in Texas in 2004 for murdering his children by setting his house afire, was innocent. Willingham consistently maintained his innocence and scientists who reassessed the forensic evidence supporting the expert opinion offered at Willingham's 1992 trial that the fire was intentionally set concluded that the analysis was wholly unreliable.[59] In another case from Texas, an extensive investigation led by Professor James Liebman concluded that Carlos DeLuna, who was executed in 1989, also was innocent. The investigation produced evidence suggesting that another man named Carlos, who bore a striking physical resemblance to DeLuna, was the actual murderer.[60]

The risk that innocent people would be executed led former Illinois Governor George Ryan to place a moratorium on executions in 2000 and then to commute the death sentences of all 167 prisoners on that state's death row to life imprisonment when he left office in 2003. At the time Ryan acted, Illinois had executed 12 convicted murderers under its post-*Furman* capital-punishment statute, while 13 death-sentenced individuals had been exonerated.[61] This dramatic clearing of Illinois' death row, coupled with a spate of highly publicized DNA-based exonerations that left no doubt that wrongful convictions happen, helped thrust innocence-related concerns into prominence in debates about capital punishment.[62]

Various advisory and legislative bodies responded. Study commissions in Illinois,[63] California,[64] and elsewhere[65] recommended that legislative reforms be enacted to guard against wrongful capital convictions and executions. Concluding that the risk of executing innocent persons was unavoidable, and identifying other problems with capital punishment's administration, the study commission appointed in New Jersey recommended that the state's death-penalty law be repealed.[66] The legislature took that step and the governor signed the abolition bill in 2007.[67] Concerns about executing the innocent also were front and center in New Mexico's abolition of capital punishment in 2009,[68] and when death-penalty laws were repealed in Illinois (2011),[69] Connecticut (2012),[70] and Maryland (2013).[71]

Short of abolition, reforms designed to minimize if not eliminate the threat of wrongful executions have been suggested that would still enable capital-punishment laws to remain in effect. Before its death-penalty provisions were rescinded as incapable of harnessing capital sentencing discretion,[72] the Model Penal Code (MPC) included a requirement for a heightened standard of proof to support a death sentence. A section of the Code directed trial judges to sentence a capital offender to prison, rather than death, on being "satisfied that . . . although the evidence suffices to sustain the verdict, it does not foreclose all doubt respecting the defendant's guilt."[73] Although the Model Penal Code was highly influential with respect to many other provisions that found their way into modern capital-punishment statutes,[74] this provision of the MPC was roundly ignored.[75]

Proposals much more ambitious than the one originally incorporated in the MPC have been advanced in an attempt to safeguard the innocent from the risk of execution. In 2003, former Massachusetts Governor Mitt Romney charged a special committee "to recommend the legal and forensic safeguards that would be necessary before a fair death penalty statute could be considered in Massachusetts."[76] He stressed that a priority was "to ensure—as much as humanly possible—that no innocent person will ever wrongly be condemned to death."[77] The following year the committee issued its report. Its ten recommendations included significantly restricting the categories of murder punishable by death; adopting guidelines and procedures to constrain prosecutors' charging discretion; ensuring that only highly qualified defense attorneys participate in capital trials; providing for different juries to decide guilt and sentence, at the defendant's request; delivering cautionary jury instructions regarding the potential unreliability of various types of evidence; requiring the jury to find that "conclusive scientific evidence" connects the defendant to the crime and corroborates guilt; instructing the jury that it must find "that there is 'no doubt' about the defendant's guilt" before a death sentence can be imposed; requiring independent scientific review and confirmation of the reliability of scientific evidence introduced in capital trials; investing both the trial courts and appellate courts with broad authority to set aside death sentences; and creation of a death-penalty review commission to investigate claims of substantive error and recommend that judicial action be taken to consider and correct error in appropriate cases.[78]

The committee's recommendations stirred more academic interest than legislative. Massachusetts had not had a viable death-penalty statute since the state's high court invalidated legislative enactments in the 1970s and 1980s. No one had been executed in the state since 1947. The Massachusetts General Assembly showed little interest in reinstating the death penalty, whether or not authorizing legislation included safeguards against executing innocent persons.[79]

Events unfolded differently in Maryland. In 2008 the General Assembly appointed a study commission to examine and make recommendations concerning the administration of capital punishment in the state. The commission issued a lengthy report later that year and, by majority vote, recommended that Maryland's death-penalty law be repealed.[80] One of the report's findings was that "[d]espite the advance of forensic sciences, particularly DNA testing, the risk of execution of an innocent person is a real possibility."[81] One member of the study commission, Kirk Bloodsworth, could speak directly to that conclusion. Bloodsworth was convicted of raping and murdering a nine-year-old child and was sentenced to death in Maryland in 1985. He remained incarcerated for almost nine years, when DNA testing excluded him as the source of the semen found in the child's body. The true perpetrator later was identified through a DNA match and was convicted for the crimes and sentenced to life in prison.[82]

In 2009, the Maryland legislature considered abolishing the death penalty but did not go so far. It instead enacted compromise legislation, which incorporated distinctive limitations designed to curtail the risk of executing the innocent.[83] The new law specifically provided:

A defendant found guilty of murder in the first degree may be sentenced to death only if: . . .
    (3) the state presents the court or jury with:

   (i) biological evidence or DNA evidence that links the defendant to the act of murder;
   (ii) a videotaped, voluntary interrogation and confession of the defendant to the murder;
      or
   (iii) a video recording that conclusively links the defendant to the murder.[84]

Those provisions remained in effect only until 2013, when Maryland abolished capital punishment altogether. The short-lived reforms nevertheless illustrate another approach available to jurisdictions that seek to retain the death penalty yet also guard against it being applied to innocent people. While the evidentiary limitations embedded in Maryland's reform legislation undoubtedly would reduce the risk of erroneous executions, is the Maryland model a promising one that should be considered for adoption elsewhere?

In the first place, how ironclad do the safeguards appear to be? For instance, what sorts of "biological evidence" might qualify, and what does it mean to "link[ ]" a defendant to the charged murder? Where, precisely, is the line between a "voluntary" and an "involuntary" confession, and could a confession nevertheless be false even if it is voluntary and captured on videotape? Would a video-recording of a criminal homicide be able to resolve such questions as defendant's *mens rea* or his or her possible insanity or mental retardation?[85]

Additional vexing issues arise with respect to whether the statute's evidentiary prerequisites for death-penalty eligibility can be squared with capital punishment's primary objectives. Proof through the specific forms of evidence required by the law will be absent in untold numbers of murder cases, some of which might cry out for the death penalty on grounds of retribution, general deterrence, or incapacitation.

> Maryland Attorney General Douglas Gansler pinpointed the problems created by the statutory scheme. First invoking Osama bin Laden and Timothy McVeigh as among the "[h]einous criminals who commit certain crimes [and hence] forfeit their right to live," he continued:
>
> Consider this: A hundred people observe and take photographs of a convicted serial killer pumping bullets into another man while shouting, "I am killing this man on purpose to steal his money and I have deliberated for weeks before doing so." There likely would be no DNA, videotape of the shooting or video-taped confession. Thus, the case would be ineligible for the death penalty.[86]

While study commissions and legislatures have wrestled with concerns that the death penalty exposes innocent people to the risk of execution, the courts also have confronted this issue. In 2002, U.S. District Court Judge Jed Rakoff declared the Federal Death Penalty Act of 1994 unconstitutional for that very reason. Although his decision was quickly overturned on appeal,[87] Judge Rakoff's opinion merits consideration.

United States v. Quinones, 205 F.Supp.2d 256 (S.D.N.Y. 2002)

RAKOFF, District Judge.

In its Opinion dated April 25, 2002, the Court, upon review of the parties' written submissions and oral arguments, declared its tentative decision to grant defendants' motion to dismiss the death penalty aspects of this case on the ground that the Federal Death Penalty Act, 18 U.S.C. §§ 3591–3598, is unconstitutional. *United States v. Quinones,* 196 F.Supp.2d 416, 420 (S.D.N.Y. 2002). . . . [A]fter careful

consideration, the Court adheres to its prior view and declares the Federal Death Penalty Act unconstitutional. . . .

. . . [T]he Government argues that the evidence on which the Court premises its legal conclusions is either unreliable, irrelevant, or both. . . .

Regarding the DNA testing that has exonerated at least 12 death row inmates since 1993, the Government argues that, since such testing is now available prior to trial in many cases, its effect, going forward, will actually be to reduce the risk of mistaken convictions. This completely misses the point. What DNA testing has proved, beyond cavil, is the remarkable degree of fallibility in the basic fact-finding processes on which we rely in criminal cases. In each of the 12 cases of DNA-exoneration of death row inmates referenced in *Quinones*, the defendant had been found guilty by a unanimous jury that concluded there was proof of his guilt beyond a reasonable doubt; and in each of the 12 cases the conviction had been affirmed on appeal, and collateral challenges rejected, by numerous courts that had carefully scrutinized the evidence and the manner of conviction. Yet, for all this alleged "due process," the result, in each and every one of these cases, was the conviction of an innocent person who, because of the death penalty, would shortly have been executed (some came within days of being so) were it not for the fortuitous development of a new scientific technique that happened to be applicable to their particular cases.

DNA testing may help prevent some such near-tragedies in the future; but it can only be used in that minority of cases involving recoverable, and relevant, DNA samples. Other scientific techniques may also emerge in the future that will likewise expose past mistakes and help prevent future ones, and in still other cases, such as those referenced below, exoneration may be the result of less scientific and more case-specific developments, such as witness recantations or discovery of new evidence. But there is no way to know whether such exoneration will come prior to (or during) trial or, conversely, long after conviction. What is certain is that, for the foreseeable future, traditional trial methods and appellate review will not prevent the conviction of numerous innocent people. . . .

While the DNA evidence alone is sufficient to establish this basic point, the Court, in its Opinion of April 25, also relied on the even larger number of death row inmates who have been exonerated over the past decade by investigations that, while inspired by the DNA testing, used more conventional methods. Although, as the Government notes in its Memorandum and as the Court itself noted in its prior Opinion, the website of the Death Penalty Information Center ("DPIC") that lists these cases may be over-inclusive, the Court, upon review of the underlying case summaries, conservatively concluded that at least 20 such defendants released from death row over the past decade for reasons unrelated to DNA testing were factually innocent. *Quinones* at 418. These included people like Joseph Burrows, who was released after 5 years on death row only after the state's chief witness against him confessed to the murder; Anthony Porter, who spent no less than 16 years on death row until prosecutors decided they had made a mistake (upon which determination they then brought murder charges against a different suspect, who confessed); and Gary Drinkard, whose 1995 conviction and death sentence were overturned in 2001 only after an entire team of lawyers and investigators uncovered conclusive proof that he was at home at the time of the murder for which he was charged. . . . [T]hese additional 20 innocent convicts served an average of 10 years in prison before their innocence was established.

The Government does not deny that an increasing number of death row defendants have been released from prison in recent years for reasons other than DNA testing. Nor does the Government, despite its quibbles with the DPIC website, directly contest the Court's conservative conclusion that at least 20 of these non-DNA exonerations likely involved the capital convictions of innocent persons. Instead, the Government argues that both the DNA and non-DNA exonerations are irrelevant to consideration of the Federal Death Penalty Act because the exonerated defendants were all state convicts, rather than federal. This, moreover, is no accident, argues the Government, but is rather the result of the allegedly greater protections that federal procedure generally, and the Federal Death Penalty Act in particular, afford defendants.

Upon analysis, however, the Government's distinction proves ephemeral, for several reasons. To begin with, while it true that none of the 31 persons so far sentenced to death under the Federal Death Penalty Act has been subsequently exonerated (though five of the sentences have already been reversed), the sample is too small, and the convictions too recent, to draw any conclusions therefrom. The 32 exonerated death row inmates identified by the Court in its prior Opinion, are part of a relevant pool of anywhere from around 800 to around 3,700 death row inmates, depending on how you look at it. As previously noted, moreover, the time-lag between conviction and exoneration for the 32 exonerated inmates averaged somewhere in the range of 7 to 10 years after conviction. Consequently, if federal practices were equally as vulnerable to wrongful capital convictions as state practices, still, on any reasonable statistical analysis, one would not expect any exonerations to have yet emerged with respect to a sample as small as 31 federal capital convicts, none of whom was sentenced before 1995.[FN13]

FN13. It may also be noted that, as the Government concedes, at least one of the 31 federal death row inmates, David Ronald Chandler, had a colorable claim of actual innocence, but his sentence was commuted by President Clinton. However, although the commutation was seemingly prompted by serious doubts about Chandler's guilt, it should also be noted that Chandler was not granted a full pardon. More generally, as noted in the Court's prior Opinion, the use of executive clemency to rectify wrongful death penalty convictions, always a haphazard remedy at best, has significantly diminished in recent years, notwithstanding the greater number of cases of proven innocence. Clemency, moreover, cannot address the problem of the mistakenly convicted defendant who is executed before he can prove his innocence.

More fundamentally, there is no logical reason to suppose that practices and procedures under the Federal Death Penalty Act will be materially more successful in preventing mistaken convictions than the deficient state procedures that have already been shown to be wanting. . . .

If anything, certain federal practices present a greater risk of wrongful capital convictions than parallel state practices. For example, federal practice, in contrast to that of many states that allow the death penalty, permits conviction on the uncorroborated testimony of an accomplice. Similarly, federal practice treats circumstantial evidence identically to direct evidence and permits conviction based solely on such evidence, whereas many states that allow the death penalty permit a conviction based solely on circumstantial evidence only if such evidence excludes to a moral certainty every other reasonable inference except guilt.

Even more fundamentally, it appears reasonably well established that the single most common cause of mistaken convictions is inaccurate eye-witness testimony. . . . The federal rules of evidence are no less receptive to such eye-witness testimony than state rules, and federal courts, at both the trial and appellate levels, apply, even more than state courts, highly deferential standards to jury findings premised on such testimony. . . .

In its Opinion of April 25, the Court also supported its overall conclusions by reference to the unusually high rate of legal error (68%) detected in appeals (both state and federal) from death penalty convictions, as shown by the comprehensive study of those appeals released in 2000 by Professor James Liebman and his colleagues. While legal error is not a direct measure of factual error, Liebman's study was concerned with errors that the appellate courts had determined were not harmless and that therefore could be outcome-determinative. *See* James S. Liebman, et al., *A Broken System: Error Rates In Capital Cases, 1973–1995* (2000) at 32. That such errors could infect nearly 7 out of every 10 capital cases strongly suggests that, at a minimum, the trial process appears to operate with less reliability in the context of capital cases than elsewhere. Moreover, Liebman and his colleagues conclude,

in a recently-released follow-up analysis of their data, that the 68% error rate if anything understates the extent of the problem so far as factually mistaken capital convictions are concerned. *See* James S. Liebman, et al., *A Broken System*, Part II: *Why There Is So Much Error in Capital Cases, and What Can Be Done About It* (2002), at 25. . . .

. . . [N]o judge has a monopoly on reason, and the Court fully expects its analysis to be critically scrutinized. Still, to this Court, the unacceptably high rate at which innocent persons are convicted of capital crimes, when coupled with the frequently prolonged delays before such errors are detected (and then often only fortuitously or by application of newly-developed techniques), compels the conclusion that execution under the Federal Death Penalty Act, by cutting off the opportunity for exoneration, denies due process and, indeed, is tantamount to foreseeable, state-sponsored murder of innocent human beings.

Accordingly, the Court grants defendant's motion to strike all death penalty aspects from this case, on the ground that the Federal Death Penalty Act is unconstitutional. . . .

The Second Circuit Court of Appeals reversed Judge Rakoff's decision less than six months after it was issued.

United States v. Quinones, 313 F.3d 49 (2d Cir. 2002), *rehearing denied*, 317 F.3d 96 (2d Cir. 2003)

JOSÉ A. CABRANES, Circuit Judge:

. . . Even before the founding of our country, European nations from which we derived our laws recognized that capital punishment inherently entails a risk that innocent people will be executed. In the mid-1770s, the British scholar Jeremy Bentham argued that capital punishment differs from all other punishments

because "[f]or death, there is no remedy." Jeremy Bentham, *The Rationale of Punishment* 186 (Robert Heward ed., 1830) (circa 1775). Bentham recognized that there could be no "system of penal procedure which could insure the Judge from being misled by false evidence or the fallibility of his own judgment," *id.* at 187, and he argued that execution prevents "the oppressed [from meeting] with some fortunate event by which his innocence may be proved," *id.* at 189.

In the United States, opponents of capital punishment "began to argue that innocent people were often executed by mistake" as early as the mid-Nineteenth Century. Stuart Banner, *The Death Penalty: An American History* 121 (2002). These abolitionists maintained that "[the] government ought to abandon capital punishment in general because so many innocent people were going to their deaths on the gallows." Since that time, there has been a prodigious scholarly debate over whether the likelihood that innocent people will be executed justifies abolition of the death penalty. *See, e.g.,* Edwin M. Borchard, *Convicting the Innocent: Errors of Criminal Justice* Intro., *passim* (1932) (chronicling sixty-five prosecutions and convictions of "completely innocent people," *id.* at xiii, and noting that, although exactly "[h]ow many wrongfully convicted persons have actually been executed . . . is impossible to say . . . these cases offer a convincing argument for the abolition of the death penalty," *id.* at xix); E. Roy Calvert, *Capital Punishment in the Twentieth Century* 123–134 (5th red. Patterson Smith 1973) (1936) (arguing that "no human tribunal is ever competent to impose an irrevocable penalty," *id.* at 123, and noting that "it is surprising how many cases are actually known of the execution of the innocent" given that, "[b]y the infliction of the capital penalty the person primarily concerned is prevented from urging his claim," *id.* at 125–26); George R. Scott, *The History of Capital Punishment* 248–63 (1950) (chronicling cases in which innocent persons have been executed and insisting that "we have no means of knowing whether or not other persons have been wrongly convicted and executed [because]. . . . [t]he accused is dead and,

therefore, unable to supply information and evidence which may be necessary [for his or her exoneration,]" *id.* at 251–52); Jerome & Barbara Frank, *Not Guilty* 248–49 (1957) (noting "the intolerably monstrous nature of any death sentence . . . [because] [i]t cannot be undone" and insisting that "[n]o one knows how many innocent men, erroneously convicted of murder, have been put to death by American governments [because] . . . once a convicted man is dead, all interest in vindicating him usually evaporates"); Charles L. Black, Jr., *Capital Punishment: The Inevitability of Caprice and Mistake passim* (1974) (arguing that the death penalty, no matter how it is administered, inherently encounters the possibility of mistake in its application); Hugo Adam Bedau & Michael L. Radelet, *Miscarriages of Justice in Potentially Capital Cases,* 40 Stan. L.Rev. 21 (1987) (citing their own study for the proposition that, from 1900 through 1985, at least 139 innocent persons were sentenced to death and at least 23 innocent persons were executed).[FN12]

FN12. The study by Bedau and Radelet has sparked a significant amount of scholarly controversy over the extent to which innocent persons are executed. *See, e.g.,* Stephen J. Markman & Paul G. Cassell, *Protecting the Innocent: A Response to the Bedau-Radelet Study,* 41 Stan. L.Rev. 121 (1988).

Further, prior to the FDPA's enactment, Congress had been presented with extensive evidence in support of the argument that innocent individuals might be executed. . . . While not determinative, it is noteworthy that Congress enacted the FDPA against the backdrop of repeated assertions by some members that innocent people have been executed. This informed, deliberative legislative action itself casts doubt on the assertion that the right to a continued opportunity for exoneration throughout the course of one's natural life is "rooted in the . . . conscience of our people."

Most importantly, the Supreme Court has upheld state and federal statutes providing for capital punishment for over two hundred years, and it has done so despite a clear recognition of the possibility that, because our judicial system—indeed, any judicial system—is fallible, innocent people might be executed and, therefore, lose any opportunity for exoneration. . . .

The Supreme Court first expressly acknowledged the argument pressed here—namely, that capital punishment might deprive innocent persons of the ability to exonerate themselves—in *Furman v. Georgia*, 408 U.S. 238 (1972). . . .

. . . Justice Marshall expressly recognized that "there is evidence that innocent people have been executed before their innocence can be proved." 408 U.S. at 364 (Marshall, J., concurring):

> Just as Americans know little about who is executed and why, they are unaware of the potential dangers of executing an innocent man. Our 'beyond a reasonable doubt' burden of proof in criminal cases is intended to protect the innocent, but we know it is not foolproof. Various studies have shown that people whose innocence is later convincingly established are convicted and sentenced to death. . . .
>
> No matter how careful courts are, the possibility of perjured testimony, mistaken honest testimony, and human error remain all too real. We have no way of judging how many innocent persons have been executed but we can be certain that there were some. *Id.* at 366–68 (footnotes omitted).

Justice Brennan took the argument one step further, expressly acknowledging that execution deprives innocent persons of the opportunity for exoneration:

> . . . A prisoner remains a member of the human family. Moreover, *he retains the right of access to the courts. His punishment is not irrevocable.* Apart from *the common charge, grounded upon the recognition of human fallibility, that the punishment of death must inevitably be inflicted upon innocent men,* we know that death has been the lot of men whose convictions were unconstitutionally secured in view of later, retroactively applied, holdings of this Court. The punishment itself may have been unconstitutionally inflicted, yet *the finality of death precludes relief. An executed person has indeed 'lost the right to have rights.'* 408 U.S. at 290 (internal citation omitted) (emphasis added).

These excerpts demonstrate beyond any possible doubt that the basic thesis of the District Court's opinion—that capital punishment is unconstitutional because it denies individuals the opportunity for exoneration—is not a new one. . . .

More importantly, just four years after *Furman,* the Court expressly held in *Gregg v. Georgia* that capital punishment does not constitute a *per se* violation of the Eighth Amendment. The Court reached this conclusion despite the petitioner's argument that the death penalty "entail[s] both mistake and caprice," and that "some people will be killed wrongly," Br. for Petitioner in *Gregg* at 10a. . . . The *Gregg* Court was therefore keenly aware of the argument asserted here, that execution terminates any asserted right to the opportunity for exoneration during one's natural life. Despite this awareness, the Court rejected the proposition that capital punishment is unconstitutional *per se.*

More recently, in *Herrera v. Collins,* 506 U.S. 390 (1993), the Supreme Court affirmed the denial of a petition for a writ of habeas corpus in which the petitioner claimed that his execution would violate both the Due Process Clause and the Eighth Amendment because new evidence could prove his "actual innocence." . . . The Court . . . declined to hold that "execution of a person who is innocent of the crime for which he was convicted" amounts to an independent violation of either the Eighth Amendment *or* the Due Process Clause. *Id.* at 398. . . .

. . . *Herrera* prevents us from finding capital punishment unconstitutional based solely on a statistical or theoretical possibility that a defendant might be innocent. . . . Accordingly, in light of *Herrera,* the District Court erred in recognizing a "[fundamental] right of an innocent person not to be deprived, by execution, of the opportunity to demonstrate his innocence," and we likewise would err if we were to ignore or reject the jurisprudence of the Supreme Court on this subject.

In sum, if the well-settled law on this issue is to change, that is a change that only the Supreme Court or Congress is authorized to make. . . .

In invalidating the Federal Death Penalty Act because it places innocent persons at risk of being deprived of life without due process of law, the District Court's opinion in *Quinones* relied extensively on the number of cases of exonerated death-sentenced prisoners during the post-*Furman* era. The Court of Appeals' opinion concluded that the recent cases of exoneration are not highly relevant because the possibility that capital-punishment laws will produce erroneous executions has been understood for centuries, including by Congress when it enacted the Federal Death Penalty Act in 1994 and by the Supreme Court when it approved modern death-penalty laws in *Gregg v. Georgia* and later cases. Which court's reasoning do you find more persuasive? To what extent do innocence-related concerns with the death penalty present *constitutional* issues as opposed to *policy* issues?

The Court of Appeals relied heavily on the Supreme Court's decision in *Herrera v. Collins,* 506 U.S. 390 (1993) in overturning the District Court's decision in *Quinones.* Leonel Herrera was sentenced to death in Texas in 1982 for murdering a police officer, Enrique Carrisalez. Evidence presented at the trial suggested that Herrera shot and killed Carrisalez after the officer pulled his car over for speeding. The evidence further suggested that shortly before Herrera encountered Officer Carrisalez, he had killed another police officer, David Rucker. After he was convicted and sentenced to death for killing Officer Carrisalez, Herrera pled guilty to murdering Officer Rucker. He was sentenced to life imprisonment for the latter offense. The state courts affirmed Herrera's conviction and death sentence for Officer Carrisalez's murder, as did the federal courts in rejecting Herrera's petition for a writ of habeas corpus. The Supreme Court denied certiorari in 1990.

The following year, Herrera returned to state court, claiming to have newly discovered evidence to support his claim that he was innocent of murdering both police officers. His allegations were backed by sworn statements submitted by several witnesses. One statement was provided by an attorney who had represented Herrera's brother, Raul, who had died in 1994 (thus freeing the lawyer from the attorney-client confidentiality privilege). The attorney revealed that Raul had confessed to him that he (Raul) had killed both Officer Rucker and Officer Carrisalez. A former prison cellmate of Raul's provided a statement to that same effect, as did a family friend. In addition, Raul's son swore that when he was 9 years old and was in a car being driven by his father, he witnessed Raul shoot and kill both of the police officers. Texas law provided that the state courts lack jurisdiction to consider newly discovered evidence of innocence unless such evidence was presented within 30 days of the entry of final judgment in a case. Because Leonel Herrera sought to present his new evidence of innocence several years after his conviction and death sentence had become final, the state courts refused to hear it.

Herrera thus filed a second habeas corpus petition in 1992 in federal court, alleging "that he is innocent of the murders of Rucker and Carrisalez, and that his execution would thus violate the Eighth and Fourteenth Amendments." The lower federal courts declined to grant Herrera relief on his habeas petition. In dismissing Herrera's appeal from the denial of his habeas petition, the Fifth Circuit Court of Appeals also vacated the stay of execution that the district court had granted. The United States Supreme Court then granted certiorari to consider the case—action which requires the affirmative vote of four justices. After agreeing to review Herrera's claims, the Supreme Court inscrutably refused to grant Herrera a stay of execution—action which requires the affirmative vote of five justices.[88] The Texas Court of Criminal Appeals reluctantly intervened and entered a stay of execution nearly two months later. Using classic understatement, the state court explained that "we find under the present circumstances it would be improper for this Court to allow applicant's execution to be carried out before his petition for writ of certiorari is fully reviewed by the Supreme Court."[89] The Supreme Court thus confronted the question of whether Herrera's newly discovered evidence of innocence entitled him to relief on federal habeas corpus.

Herrera v. Collins, 506 U.S. 390, 113 S.Ct. 853, 122 L.Ed.2d 203 (1993)

Chief Justice REHNQUIST delivered the opinion of the Court. . . .

Petitioner asserts that the Eighth and Fourteenth Amendments to the United States Constitution prohibit the execution of a person who is innocent of the crime for which he was convicted. This proposition has an elemental appeal, as would the similar proposition that the Constitution prohibits the imprisonment of one who is innocent of the crime for which he was convicted. After all, the central purpose of any system of criminal justice is to convict the guilty and free the innocent. But the evidence upon which petitioner's claim of innocence rests was not produced at his trial, but rather eight years later. In any system of criminal justice, "innocence" or "guilt" must be determined in some sort of a judicial proceeding. Petitioner's showing of innocence, and indeed his constitutional claim for relief based upon that showing, must be evaluated in the light of the previous proceedings in this case, which have stretched over a span of 10 years.

A person when first charged with a crime is entitled to a presumption of innocence, and may insist that his guilt be established beyond a reasonable doubt. Other constitutional provisions also have the effect of ensuring against the risk of convicting an innocent person. In capital cases, we have required additional protections because of the nature of the penalty at stake. . . . But we have also observed that "[d]ue process does not require that every conceivable step be taken, at whatever cost, to eliminate the possibility of convicting an innocent person." *Patterson v. New York*, 432 U.S. 197, 208 (1977). To conclude otherwise would all but paralyze our system for enforcement of the criminal law.

Once a defendant has been afforded a fair trial and convicted of the offense for which he was charged, the presumption of innocence disappears. Here, it is not disputed that the State met its burden of proving at trial that petitioner was guilty of the capital murder of Officer Carrisalez beyond a reasonable doubt. Thus, in the eyes of the law, petitioner does not come before the Court as one who is "innocent," but, on the contrary, as one who has been convicted by due process of law of two brutal murders.

Based on affidavits here filed, petitioner claims that evidence never presented to the trial court proves him innocent notwithstanding the verdict reached at his trial. Such a claim is not cognizable in the state courts of Texas. For to obtain a new trial based on newly discovered evidence, a defendant must file a motion within 30 days after imposition or suspension of sentence. . . .

Claims of actual innocence based on newly discovered evidence have never been held to state a ground for federal habeas relief absent an independent constitutional violation occurring in the underlying state criminal proceeding. . . .

This rule is grounded in the principle that federal habeas courts sit to ensure that individuals are not imprisoned in violation of the Constitution—not to correct errors of fact. . . . Few rulings would be more disruptive of our federal system than to provide for federal habeas review of freestanding claims of actual innocence. . . .

Petitioner is understandably imprecise in describing the sort of federal relief to which a suitable showing of actual innocence would entitle him. In his brief he states that the federal habeas court should have "an important initial opportunity to hear the evidence and resolve the merits of Petitioner's claim." Acceptance of this view would presumably require the habeas court to hear testimony from the witnesses who testified at trial as well as those who made the statements in the affidavits which petitioner has presented, and to determine anew whether or not petitioner is guilty of the murder of Officer Carrisalez. . . .

Yet there is no guarantee that the guilt or innocence determination would be any more exact. To the contrary, the passage of time only diminishes the reliability of criminal adjudications. . . .

This is not to say that our habeas jurisprudence casts a blind eye toward innocence. In a series of cases culminating with *Sawyer v. Whitley*, 505 U.S. 333 (1992), . . . we have held that a petitioner otherwise subject to defenses of abusive or successive use of the writ may have his federal constitutional claim considered on the merits if he makes a proper showing of actual innocence. . . . But this body of our habeas jurisprudence makes clear that a claim of "actual innocence" is not itself a constitutional claim, but instead a gateway through which a habeas petitioner must pass to have his otherwise barred constitutional claim considered on the merits. . . .

Petitioner asserts that this case is different because he has been sentenced to death. . . . We have, of course, held that the Eighth Amendment requires increased reliability of the process by which capital punishment may be imposed. But petitioner's claim does not fit well into the doctrine of these cases, since, as we have pointed out, it is far from clear that a second trial 10 years after the first trial would produce a more reliable result.

Perhaps mindful of this, petitioner urges not that he necessarily receive a new trial, but that his death sentence simply be vacated if a federal habeas court deems that a satisfactory showing of "actual innocence" has been made. But such a result is scarcely logical; petitioner's claim is not that some error was made in imposing a capital sentence upon him, but that a fundamental error was made in finding him guilty of the underlying murder in the first place. It would be a rather strange jurisprudence, in these circumstances, which held that under our Constitution he could not be executed, but that he could spend the rest of his life in prison. . . .

Alternatively, petitioner invokes the Fourteenth Amendment's guarantee of due process of law in support of his claim that his showing of actual innocence entitles him to a new trial, or at least to a vacation of his death sentence. . . . [W]e have found criminal process lacking only where it "'offends some principle of justice so rooted in the traditions and conscience of our people as to be ranked as fundamental.'" "Historical practice is probative of whether a procedural rule can be characterized as fundamental." . . .

[The opinion reviewed historical and contemporary practices regarding time limitations placed on submitting newly discovered evidence in support of a request for a new trial, and concluded that Texas's rule barring the presentation of such evidence later than 30 days after the entry of final judgment was not unduly restrictive.]

In light of the historical availability of new trials, our own [rules], and the contemporary practice in the States, we cannot say that Texas' refusal to entertain petitioner's newly discovered evidence eight years after his conviction transgresses a principle of fundamental fairness "rooted in the traditions and conscience of our people." *Patterson v. New York*, 432 U.S., at 202. This is not to say, however, that petitioner is left without a forum to raise his actual innocence claim. For under Texas law, petitioner may file a request for executive clemency. Clemency is deeply rooted in our Anglo-American tradition of law, and is the historic remedy for preventing miscarriages of justice where judicial process has been exhausted. . . .

Executive clemency has provided the "fail safe" in our criminal justice system. It is an unalterable fact that our judicial system, like the human beings who administer it, is fallible. But history is replete with examples of wrongfully convicted persons who have been pardoned in the wake of after-discovered evidence establishing their innocence. . . .

We may assume, for the sake of argument in deciding this case, that in a capital case a truly persuasive demonstration of "actual innocence" made after trial would render the execution of a defendant unconstitutional, and warrant federal habeas relief if there were no state avenue open to process such a claim. But because of the very disruptive effect that entertaining claims of actual innocence would have on the need for finality in capital cases, and the enormous burden that having to retry cases based on often stale evidence would place on the States, the threshold showing for such an assumed right would necessarily be extraordinarily high. The showing made by petitioner in this case falls far short of any such threshold. . . .

The affidavits filed in this habeas proceeding were given over eight years after petitioner's trial. No satisfactory explanation has been given as to why the affiants waited until the 11th hour—and, indeed, until after the alleged perpetrator of the murders himself was dead—to make their statements. Equally troubling, no explanation has been offered as to why petitioner, by hypothesis an innocent man, pleaded guilty to the murder of Rucker.

Moreover, the affidavits themselves contain inconsistencies, and therefore fail to provide a convincing account of what took place on the night Officers Rucker and Carrisalez were killed. For instance, the affidavit of Raul, Junior, who was nine years old at the time, indicates that there were three people in the speeding car from which the murderer emerged, whereas Hector Villarreal attested that Raul, Senior, told him that there were two people in the car that night. Of course, [Officer] Hernandez testified at petitioner's trial that the murderer was the only occupant of the car. The affidavits also conflict as to the direction in which the vehicle was heading when the murders took place and petitioner's whereabouts on the night of the killings.

Finally, the affidavits must be considered in light of the proof of petitioner's guilt at trial—proof which included two eyewitness identifications, numerous pieces of circumstantial evidence, and a handwritten letter in which petitioner apologized for killing the officers and offered to turn himself in under certain conditions. That proof, even when considered alongside petitioner's belated affidavits, points strongly to petitioner's guilt.

This is not to say that petitioner's affidavits are without probative value. Had this sort of testimony been offered at trial, it could have been weighed by the jury, along with the evidence offered by the State and petitioner, in deliberating upon its verdict. Since the statements in the affidavits contradict the evidence received at trial, the jury would have had to decide important issues of credibility. But coming 10 years after petitioner's trial, this showing of innocence falls far short of that which would have to be made in order to trigger the sort of constitutional claim which we have assumed, *arguendo*, to exist.

The judgment of the Court of Appeals is *Affirmed.*

Justice O'CONNOR, with whom Justice KENNEDY joins, concurring.

I cannot disagree with the fundamental legal principle that executing the innocent is inconsistent with the Constitution. Regardless of the verbal formula employed—"contrary to contemporary standards of decency," "shocking to the conscience," or offensive to a "principle of justice so rooted in the traditions and conscience of our people as to be ranked as fundamental,"—the execution of a legally and factually innocent person would be a constitutionally intolerable event. Dispositive to this case, however, is an equally fundamental fact: Petitioner is not innocent, in any sense of the word.

. . . [P]etitioner is not innocent in the eyes of the law because . . . [h]e was tried before a jury of his peers, with the full panoply of protections that our Constitution affords criminal defendants. At the conclusion of that trial, the jury found petitioner guilty beyond a reasonable doubt. . . .

[In addition, the] record makes it abundantly clear that petitioner is . . . the established perpetrator of two brutal and tragic [murders]. . . .

. . . At some point in time, the State's interest in finality must outweigh the prisoner's interest in yet another round of litigation . . . Unless federal proceedings and relief—if they are to be had at all—are reserved for "extraordinarily high" and "truly persuasive demonstration[s] of 'actual innocence'" that cannot be presented to state authorities, the federal courts will be deluged with frivolous claims of actual innocence. . . .

Justice SCALIA, with whom Justice THOMAS joins, concurring.

We granted certiorari on the question whether it violates due process or constitutes cruel and unusual punishment for a State to execute a person who, having been convicted of murder after a full and fair trial, later alleges that newly discovered evidence shows him to be "actually innocent." I would have preferred to decide that question, particularly since, as the Court's discussion shows, it is perfectly clear what the answer is: There is no basis in text, tradition, or even in contemporary practice (if that were enough) for finding in the Constitution a right to demand judicial consideration of newly discovered evidence of innocence brought forward after conviction. . . .

. . . I can understand, or at least am accustomed to, the reluctance of the present Court to admit publicly that Our Perfect Constitution lets stand any injustice, much less the execution of an innocent man who has received, though to no avail, all the process that our society has traditionally deemed adequate. With any luck, we shall avoid ever having to face this embarrassing question again, since it is improbable that evidence of innocence as convincing as today's opinion requires would fail to produce an executive pardon. . . .

Justice WHITE, concurring in the judgment.

In voting to affirm, I assume that a persuasive showing of "actual innocence" made after trial, even though made after the expiration of the time provided by law for the presentation of newly discovered evidence, would render unconstitutional the execution of petitioner in this case. To be entitled to relief, however, petitioner would at the very least be required to show that based on proffered newly discovered evidence and the entire record before the jury that convicted him, "no rational trier of fact could [find] proof of guilt beyond a reasonable doubt." *Jackson v. Virginia*, 443 U.S. 307, 324 (1979). . . . [P]etitioner's showing falls far short of satisfying even that standard, and I therefore concur in the judgment.

Justice BLACKMUN, with whom Justice STEVENS and Justice SOUTER join with respect to Parts I-IV, dissenting.

Nothing could be more contrary to contemporary standards of decency, or more shocking to the conscience, than to execute a person who is actually innocent.

. . . [T]he Court assumes, "for the sake of argument in deciding this case, that in a capital case a truly persuasive demonstration of 'actual innocence' made after trial would render the execution of a defendant unconstitutional." Without articulating the standard it is applying, however, the Court then decides that this petitioner has not made a sufficiently persuasive case. Because I believe that in the first instance the District Court should decide whether petitioner is entitled to a hearing and whether he is entitled to relief on the merits of his claim, I would reverse the order of the Court of Appeals and remand this case for further proceedings in the District Court.

I

The Court's enumeration of the constitutional rights of criminal defendants surely is entirely beside the point. These protections sometimes fail. We really are being asked to decide whether the Constitution forbids the execution of a person who has been validly convicted and sentenced but who, nonetheless, can prove his innocence with newly discovered evidence. Despite the State of Texas' astonishing protestation to the contrary, I do not see how the answer can be anything but "yes."

A

The Eighth Amendment prohibits "cruel and unusual punishments." This proscription is not static but rather reflects evolving standards of decency. I think it is crystal clear that the execution of an innocent person is "at odds with contemporary standards of fairness and decency." Indeed, it is at odds with any standard of decency that I can imagine. . . .

The Court . . . suggests that allowing petitioner to raise his claim of innocence would not serve society's interest in the reliable imposition of the death penalty because it might require a new trial that would be less accurate than the first. This suggestion misses the point entirely. The question is not whether a second trial would be more reliable than the first but whether, in light of new evidence, the result of the first trial is sufficiently reliable for the State to carry out a death sentence. . . .

B

Execution of the innocent is equally offensive to the Due Process Clause of the Fourteenth Amendment. . . .

. . . The Due Process Clause of the Fifth Amendment provides that "No person shall . . . be deprived of life, liberty, or property, without due process of law. . . ." . . . So-called "substantive due process" prevents the government from engaging in conduct that "shocks the conscience," *Rochin v. California,* 342 U.S. 165,

172 (1952), or interferes with rights "implicit in the concept of ordered liberty," *Palko v. Connecticut,* 302 U.S. 319, 325–326 (1937). . . .

. . . Execution of an innocent person is . . . an imposition from which one never recovers and for which one can never be compensated. Thus, I . . . believe that petitioner may raise a substantive due process challenge to his punishment on the ground that he is actually innocent. . . .

II

The majority's discussion of petitioner's constitutional claims is even more perverse when viewed in the light of this Court's recent habeas jurisprudence. . . .

Having adopted an "actual-innocence" requirement for review of abusive, successive, or defaulted claims, . . . the majority would now take the position that "a claim of 'actual innocence' is not itself a constitutional claim, but instead a gateway through which a habeas petitioner must pass to have his otherwise barred constitutional claim considered on the merits." In other words, having held that a prisoner who is incarcerated in violation of the Constitution must show he is actually innocent to obtain relief, the majority would now hold that a prisoner who is actually innocent must show a constitutional violation to obtain relief. The only principle that would appear to reconcile these two positions is the principle that habeas relief should be denied whenever possible.

III

. . . Whatever procedures a State might adopt to hear actual-innocence claims, one thing is certain: The possibility of executive clemency is *not* sufficient to satisfy the requirements of the Eighth and Fourteenth Amendments. . . . The vindication of rights guaranteed by the Constitution has never been made to turn on the unreviewable discretion of an executive official or administrative tribunal. . . . The possibility of executive clemency "exists in every case in which a defendant challenges his sentence under the Eighth Amendment. Recognition of such a bare possibility would make judicial review under the Eighth Amendment meaningless." . . .

The question that remains is what showing should be required to obtain relief on the merits of an Eighth or Fourteenth Amendment claim of actual innocence. . . .

. . . I would hold that, to obtain relief on a claim of actual innocence, the petitioner must show that he probably is innocent. . . .

[T]he court charged with deciding such a claim should make a case-by-case determination about the reliability of the newly discovered evidence under the circumstances. The court then should weigh the evidence in favor of the prisoner against the evidence of his guilt. Obviously, the stronger the evidence of the prisoner's guilt, the more persuasive the newly discovered evidence of innocence must be. . . .

V

I have voiced disappointment over this Court's obvious eagerness to do away with any restriction on the States' power to execute whomever and however they please. I have also expressed doubts about whether, in the absence of such restrictions, capital punishment remains constitutional at all. Of one thing, however, I am certain. Just as an execution without adequate safeguards is unacceptable, so too is an execution when the condemned prisoner can prove that he is innocent. The execution of a person who can show that he is innocent comes perilously close to simple murder.

———

The Supreme Court rendered its decision in *Herrera v. Collins* on January 25, 1993. Leonel Herrera was executed May 12, 1993.[90]

Is a rule defensible that bars courts from considering newly discovered evidence of innocence unless that evidence is offered within a certain time interval—such as 30 days of the judgment of guilt becoming final, as observed by Texas? Would a somewhat longer opportunity to present newly discovered evidence be preferable? Should any time limit at all be placed on a defendant's ability to offer new evidence of innocence to challenge a capital murder conviction that results in a death sentence?

If the state courts are closed to newly discovered evidence in a case such as Leonel Herrera's, should the federal courts be open so they can consider the new evidence and, if appropriate, vacate a state prisoner's conviction and/or death sentence? Should the federal courts routinely consider state prisoners' claims of innocence? What federal constitutional right(s) would be at issue in such cases? What interests are at stake from the State's perspective? How persuasive should a prisoner's new evidence of innocence have to be before a federal court should consider it and possibly order a new trial?

In *In re Davis*, 557 U.S. 952 (2009), the Supreme Court ordered a federal district court to "receive testimony and make findings of fact as to whether evidence that could not have been obtained at the time of trial clearly establishes petitioner's innocence."

Troy Davis had been convicted and sentenced to death in a Georgia state court in 1991 for murdering a police officer, Mark MacPhail. By 2007, several of the witnesses who had testified for the prosecution at Davis's trial had recanted their testimony. Additional evidence surfaced that pointed to another man's guilt. The state courts had refused to consider the new evidence and the lower federal courts likewise declined to grant a hearing to consider the new evidence. Justice Scalia, joined by Justice Thomas, dissented from the Court's order directing the district court to consider the claim.

Justice SCALIA, with whom Justice THOMAS joins, dissenting.

Today this Court takes the extraordinary step—one not taken in nearly 50 years—of instructing a district court to adjudicate a state prisoner's petition for an original writ of habeas corpus. The Court proceeds down this path even though every judicial and executive body that has examined petitioner's stale claim of innocence has been unpersuaded, and (to make matters worst) even though it would be impossible for the District Court to grant any relief. Far from demonstrating . . . "exceptional circumstances" that "warrant the exercise of the Court's discretionary powers," petitioner's claim is a sure loser. Transferring his petition to the District Court is a confusing exercise that can serve no purpose except to delay the State's execution of its lawful criminal judgment. . . .

Eighteen years ago, after a trial untainted by constitutional defect, a unanimous jury found petitioner Troy Anthony Davis guilty of the murder of Mark Allen MacPhail. The evidence showed that MacPhail, an off-duty police officer, was shot multiple times after responding to the beating of a homeless man in a restaurant parking lot. Davis admits that he was present during the beating of the homeless man, but he maintains that it was one of his companions who shot Officer MacPhail. It is this claim of "actual innocence"—the same defense Davis raised at trial but now allegedly supported by new corroborating affidavits—that Davis raises

as grounds for relief. And (presumably) it is this claim that the Court wants the District Court to adjudicate once the petition is transferred. . . .

The Georgia Supreme Court rejected petitioner's "actual-innocence" claim on the merits, denying his extraordinary motion for a new trial. Davis can obtain relief only if that determination was contrary to, or an unreasonable application of, "clearly established Federal law, as determined by the Supreme Court of the United States." It most assuredly was not. This Court has *never* held that the Constitution forbids the execution of a convicted defendant who has had a full and fair trial but is later able to convince a habeas court that he is "actually" innocent. Quite to the contrary, we have repeatedly left that question unresolved, while expressing considerable doubt that any claim based on alleged "actual innocence" is constitutionally cognizable. See *Herrera v. Collins,* 506 U.S. 390 (1993). . . .

Today, without explanation and without any meaningful guidance, this Court sends the District Court for the Southern District of Georgia on a fool's errand. That court is directed to consider evidence of actual innocence which has been reviewed and rejected at least three times, and which, even if adequate to persuade the District Court, cannot (as far as anyone knows) form the basis for any relief. I truly do not see how the District Court can discern what is expected of it. If this Court thinks it possible that capital convictions obtained in full compliance with law can never be final, but are always subject to being set aside by federal courts for the reason of "actual innocence," it should set this case on our own docket so that we can (if necessary) resolve that question. Sending it to a district court that "might" be authorized to provide relief, but then again "might" be reversed if it did so, is not a sensible way to proceed.

After hearing witnesses at the proceeding ordered by the Supreme Court, the U.S. District Court ruled that the evidence was not sufficiently strong to substantiate Davis's claim of innocence. The Supreme Court declined further review of the case.[91] Davis was executed in Georgia on September 21, 2011.[92]

One of the lengthiest exchanges among Supreme Court justices about innocence and capital punishment occurred in a case that had little direct relevance to those issues. The question presented for decision in *Kansas v. Marsh*, 548 U.S. 163 (2006) involved a procedural aspect of Kansas's capital-sentencing statute: specifically, whether the law's requirement that a death sentence be imposed unless the jury found that mitigating factors outweighed the aggravating factors—or, as the Court put it, even when the "aggravating evidence and mitigating evidence are in equipoise"[93]—violates the Eighth Amendment. Justice Thomas's opinion in a 5–4 ruling concluded that the sentencing provision was constitutional. Justice Souter's dissent addressed not only the sentencing procedure, but spoke to the risks the death penalty poses to the factually innocent. Justice Thomas offered a brief rejoinder, while Justice Scalia responded at much greater length.

Kansas v. Marsh, 548 U.S. 163, 126 S.Ct. 2516, 165 L.Ed.2d 429 (2006)

Justice THOMAS delivered the opinion of the Court. . . .

Justice SOUTER (hereinafter dissent) argues that the advent of DNA testing has resulted in the "exoneratio[n]" of "innocent" persons "in numbers never imagined before the development of DNA tests." Based upon this "new empirical argument about how 'death is different,'" the dissent concludes that Kansas' sentencing system permits the imposition of the death penalty in the absence of reasoned moral judgment.

But the availability of DNA testing, and the questions it might raise about the accuracy of guilt-phase determinations in capital cases, is simply irrelevant to the question before the Court today, namely, the constitutionality of Kansas' capital *sentencing* system. Accordingly, the accuracy of the dissent's factual claim that DNA testing has established the "innocence" of numerous convicted persons under death sentences—and the incendiary debate it invokes—is beyond the scope of this opinion.[FN7]

> FN7. But see The Penalty of Death, in Debating the Death Penalty: Should America Have Capital Punishment? The Experts on Both Sides Make Their Best Case 117, 127–132, 134 (H. Bedau & P. Cassell eds. 2004). See also Markman & Cassell, Protecting the Innocent: A Response to the Bedau-Radelet Study, 41 Stan. L. Rev. 121, 126–145 (1988) (examining accuracy in use of the

term "innocent" in death penalty studies and literature); Marquis, The Myth of Innocence, 95 J.Crim. L. & C. 501, 508 (2005) ("Words like 'innocence' convey enormous moral authority and are intended to drive the public debate by appealing to a deep and universal revulsion at the idea that someone who is genuinely blameless could wrongly suffer for a crime in which he had no involvement"); *People v. Smith*, 708 N.E.2d 365, 371 (Ill. 1999) ("While a not guilty finding is sometimes equated with a finding of innocence, that conclusion is erroneous. . . . Rather, [a reversal of conviction] indicates simply that the prosecution has failed to meet its burden of proof").

. . . The logical consequence of the dissent's argument is that the death penalty can only be just in a system that does not permit error. Because the criminal justice system does not operate perfectly, abolition of the death penalty is the only answer to the moral dilemma the dissent poses. This Court, however, does not sit as a moral authority. Our precedents do not prohibit the States from authorizing the death penalty, even in our imperfect system. And those precedents do not empower this Court to chip away at the States' prerogatives to do so on the grounds the dissent invokes today. . . .

Justice SCALIA, concurring. . . .

. . . I must say a few words (indeed, more than a few) in response to Part III of Justice SOUTER's dissent. This contains the disclaimer that the dissenters are not *(yet)* ready to "generaliz[e] about the soundness of capital sentencing across the country," but that is in fact precisely what they do. The dissent essentially argues that capital punishment is such an undesirable institution—it results in the condemnation of such a large number of innocents—that any

legal rule which eliminates its pronouncement, including the one favored by the dissenters in the present case, should be embraced.

As a general rule, I do not think it appropriate for judges to heap either praise or censure upon a legislative measure that comes before them, lest it be thought that their validation, invalidation, or interpretation of it is driven by their desire to expand or constrict what they personally approve or disapprove as a matter of policy. In the present case, for example, people might leap to the conclusion that the dissenters' views on whether Kansas's equipoise rule is constitutional are determined by their personal disapproval of an institution that has been democratically adopted by 38 States and the United States. But of course that requires no leap; just a willingness to take the dissenters at their word. . . . [T]he dissenters' very argument is that imposition of the death penalty should be minimized by invalidation of the equipoise rule because it is a bad, "risk[y]," and "hazard[ous]" idea. A broader conclusion that people should derive, however (and I would not consider this much of a leap either), is that the dissenters' encumbering of the death penalty in *other* cases, with unwarranted restrictions neither contained in the text of the Constitution nor reflected in two centuries of practice under it, will be the product of their policy views— views not shared by the vast majority of the American people. The dissenters' proclamation of their policy agenda in the present case is especially striking because it is nailed to the door of the wrong church—that is, set forth in a case litigating a rule that has nothing to do with the evaluation of guilt or innocence. . . .

There exists in some parts of the world sanctimonious criticism of America's death penalty, as somehow unworthy of a civilized society. (I say sanctimonious, because most of the countries to which these finger-waggers belong had the death penalty themselves until recently—and indeed, many of them would still have it if the democratic will prevailed.[FN3]) It is a certainty that the opinion of a near-majority of the United States Supreme Court to the effect that our system condemns many innocent defendants to death will be trumpeted abroad as vindication of these criticisms. For that reason, I take the trouble to point out that the dissenting opinion has nothing substantial to support it.

> FN3. It is commonly recognized that "[m]any European countries . . . abolished the death penalty in spite of public opinion rather than because of it." Bibas, Transparency and Participation in Criminal Procedure, 81 N.Y.U.L.Rev. 911, 931–932 (2006). Abolishing the death penalty has been made a condition of joining the Council of Europe, which is in turn a condition of obtaining the economic benefits of joining the European Union. . . .

It should be noted at the outset that the dissent does not discuss a single case—not one—in which it is clear that a person was executed for a crime he did not commit. If such an event had occurred in recent years, we would not have to hunt for it; the innocent's name would be shouted from the rooftops by the abolition lobby. The dissent makes much of the new-found capacity of DNA testing to establish innocence. But in every case of an executed defendant of which I am aware, that technology has *confirmed* guilt.

This happened, for instance, only a few months ago in the case of Roger Coleman. Coleman was convicted of the gruesome rape and murder of his sister-in-law, but he persuaded many that he was actually innocent and became the posterchild for the abolitionist lobby. Around the time of his eventual execution, his picture was on the cover of Time magazine ('This Man Might Be Innocent. This Man Is Due to Die'). He was interviewed from death row on 'Larry King Live,' the 'Today' show, 'Primetime Live,' 'Good Morning America' and 'The Phil Donahue Show.' Even one Justice of this Court, in an opinion filed shortly before the execution, cautioned that "Coleman has now produced substantial evidence that he may be innocent of the crime for which he was sentenced to die." *Coleman v. Thompson,* 504 U.S. 188, 189 (1992) (Blackmun, J., dissenting). Coleman ultimately failed a lie-detector test offered by the Governor of Virginia as a condition of a possible stay; he was executed on May 20, 1992.

In the years since then, Coleman's case became a rallying point for abolitionists, who hoped it would offer what they consider the "Holy Grail: proof from a test tube that an innocent person had been executed." But earlier this year, a DNA test ordered by a later Governor of Virginia proved that Coleman was guilty, even though his defense team had "proved" his innocence and had even identified "'the real killer'" (with whom they eventually settled a defamation suit). And Coleman's case is not unique. See Truth and Consequences: The Penalty of Death, in Debating the Death Penalty: Should America Have Capital Punishment? The Experts on Both Sides Make Their Best Case 117, 128–129 (H. Bedau & P. Cassell eds. 2004) (discussing the cases of supposed innocents Rick McGinn and Derek Barnabei, whose guilt was also confirmed by DNA tests).

Instead of identifying and discussing any particular case or cases of mistaken execution, the dissent simply cites a handful of studies that bemoan the alleged prevalence of wrongful death sentences. One study (by Lanier and Acker) is quoted by the dissent as claiming that "'more than 110' death row prisoners have been released since 1973 upon findings that they were innocent of the crimes charged, and 'hundreds of additional wrongful convictions in potentially capital cases have been documented over the past century.'" (opinion of SOUTER, J.). For the first point, Lanier and Acker cite the work of the Death Penalty Information Center (more about that below) and an article in a law review jointly authored by Radelet, Lofquist, and Bedau (two professors of sociology and a professor of philosophy). For the second point, they cite only a 1987 article by Bedau and Radelet. See Miscarriages of Justice in Potentially Capital Cases, 40 Stan. L. Rev. 21. In the very same paragraph which the dissent quotes, Lanier and Acker also refer to that 1987 article as "hav[ing] identified 23 individuals who, in their judgment, were convicted and executed in this country during the 20th century notwithstanding their innocence." Lanier & Acker, Capital Punishment, the Moratorium Movement, and Empirical Questions, 10 Psychology, Public Policy & Law 577, 593 (2004). This 1987 article has been highly influential in the abolitionist world. Hundreds of academic articles, including those relied on by today's dissent, have cited it. It also makes its appearance in judicial decisions—cited recently in a six-judge dissent in *House v. Bell*, 386 F.3d 668, 708 (C.A.6 2004) (en banc) (Merritt, J., dissenting), for the proposition that "the system is allowing some innocent defendants to be executed." The article therefore warrants some further observations.

The 1987 article's obsolescence began at the moment of publication. The most recent executions it considered were in 1984, 1964, and 1951; the rest predate the Allied victory in World War II. (Two of the supposed innocents are Sacco and Vanzetti.) Even if the innocence claims made in this study were true, all except (perhaps) the 1984 example would cast no light upon the functioning of our current system of capital adjudication. The legal community's general attitude toward criminal defendants, the legal protections States afford, the constitutional guarantees this Court enforces, and the scope of federal habeas review are all vastly different from what they were in 1961. So are the scientific means of establishing guilt, and hence innocence—which are now so striking in their operation and effect that they are the subject of more than one popular TV series. (One of these new means, of course, is DNA testing—which the dissent seems to think is primarily a way to identify defendants erroneously convicted, rather than a highly effective way to avoid conviction of the innocent.)

But their current relevance aside, this study's conclusions are unverified. And if the support for its most significant conclusion—the execution of 23 innocents in the 20th century—is any indication of its accuracy, neither it, nor any study so careless as to rely upon it, is worthy of credence. The only execution of an innocent man it alleges to have occurred after the restoration of the death penalty in 1976—the Florida execution of James Adams in 1984—is the easiest case to verify. As evidence of Adams' innocence, it describes a hair that could not have been his as being "clutched in the victim's hand," Bedau & Radelet, *supra*, at 91. The hair was *not* in the victim's hand; "[i]t was a remnant of a sweeping of the ambulance and so could have come from another source." Markman & Cassell, Protecting the Innocent: A Response to the Bedau-Radelet Study, 41 Stan. L.Rev.

121, 131 (1988). The study also claims that a witness who "heard a voice inside the victim's home at the time of the crime" testified that the "voice was a woman's," Bedau & Radelet, *supra,* at 91. The witness's actual testimony was that the voice, which said "'"In the name of God, don't do it"'" (and was hence unlikely to have been the voice of anyone but the male victim), "'sounded "kind of like a woman's voice, kind of like strangling or something. . . ."'" Markman & Cassell, 41 Stan. L. Rev., at 130. Bedau and Radelet failed to mention that upon arrest on the afternoon of the murder Adams was found with some $200 in his pocket—one bill of which "was stained with type O blood. When Adams was asked about the blood on the money, he said that it came from a cut on his finger. His blood was type AB, however, while the victim's was type O." *Id.,* at 132. Among the other unmentioned, incriminating details: that the victim's *eyeglasses* were found in Adams' car, along with jewelry belonging to the victim, and clothing of Adams' stained with type O blood. This is just a sample of the evidence arrayed against this "innocent."

Critics have questioned the study's findings with regard to all its other cases of execution of alleged innocents for which "appellate opinions . . . set forth the facts proved at trial in detail sufficient to permit a neutral observer to assess the validity of the authors' conclusions." *Id.,* at 134. (For the rest, there was not "a reasonably complete account of the facts . . . readily available," *id.,* at 145.) As to those cases, the only readily verifiable ones, the authors of the 1987 study later acknowledged, "We agree with our critics that we have not 'proved' these executed defendants to be innocent; we never claimed that we had." Bedau & Radelet, The Myth of Infallibility: A Reply to Markman

and Cassell, 41 Stan. L.Rev. 161, 164 (1988). One would have hoped that this disclaimer of the study's most striking conclusion, if not the study's dubious methodology, would have prevented it from being cited as authority in the pages of the United States Reports. But alas, it is too late for that. . . .

Remarkably avoiding any claim of erroneous executions, the dissent focuses on the large numbers of *non*-executed "exonerees" paraded by various professors. It speaks as though exoneration came about through the operation of some outside force to correct the mistakes of our legal system, rather than *as a consequence of the functioning of our legal system.* Reversal of an erroneous conviction on appeal or on habeas, or the pardoning of an innocent condemnee through executive clemency, demonstrates not the failure of the system but its success. Those devices are part and parcel of the multiple assurances that are applied before a death sentence is carried out.

Of course even in identifying exonerees, the dissent is willing to accept anybody's say-so. It engages in no critical review, but merely parrots articles or reports that support its attack on the American criminal justice system. The dissent places significant weight, for instance, on the Illinois Report (compiled by the appointees of an Illinois Governor who had declared a moratorium upon the death penalty and who eventually commuted all death sentences in the State, which it claims shows that "false verdicts" are "remarkable in number." (opinion of SOUTER, J.). The dissent claims that this report identifies 13 inmates released from death row after they were determined to be innocent. To take one of these cases, discussed by the dissent as an example of a judgment "as close to innocence as any judgments courts normally render," *post,* at n. 2: In *People v. Smith,* 708 N.E.2d 365 (Ill.

1999), the defendant was twice convicted of murder. After his first trial, the Supreme Court of Illinois "reversed [his] conviction based upon certain evidentiary errors" and remanded his case for a new trial. *Id.*, at 366. The second jury convicted Smith again. The Supreme Court of Illinois again reversed the conviction because it found that the evidence was insufficient to establish guilt beyond a reasonable doubt. The court explained:

> "While a not guilty finding is sometimes equated with a finding of innocence, that conclusion is erroneous. Courts do not find people guilty or innocent. . . . A not guilty verdict expresses no view as to a defendant's innocence. Rather, [a reversal of conviction] indicates simply that the prosecution has failed to meet its burden of proof." *Id.*, at 371.

This case alone suffices to refute the dissent's claim that the Illinois Report distinguishes between "exoneration of a convict because of actual innocence, and reversal of a judgment because of legal error affecting conviction or sentence but not inconsistent with guilt in fact," *post*, at n. 2. The broader point, however, is that it is utterly impossible to regard "exoneration"—however casually defined—as a failure of the capital justice system, rather than as a vindication of its effectiveness in releasing not only defendants who are innocent, but those whose guilt has not been established beyond a reasonable doubt.

Another of the dissent's leading authorities on exoneration of the innocent is Gross, Jacoby, Matheson, Montgomery, & Patil, Exonerations in the United States 1989 Through 2003, 95 J. Crim. L. & C. 523 (2005) (hereinafter Gross). The dissent quotes that study's self-congratulatory "criteria" of exoneration seemingly so rigorous that no one could doubt the study's reliability. See *post*, at n. 3 (opinion of SOUTER, J.). But in fact that article, like the others cited, is notable not for its rigorous investigation and analysis, but for the fervor of its belief that the American justice system is condemning the innocent "in numbers," as the dissent puts it, "never imagined before the development of DNA tests." *Post*, (opinion of SOUTER, J.). Among the article's list of 74 "exonerees," is Jay Smith of Pennsylvania. Smith—a school principal—earned three death sentences for slaying one of his teachers and her two young children. See *Smith v. Holtz*, 210 F.3d 186, 188 (C.A.3 2000). His retrial for triple murder was barred on double-jeopardy grounds because of prosecutorial misconduct during the first trial. But Smith could not leave well enough alone. He had the gall to sue, under 42 U.S.C. § 1983, for false imprisonment. The Court of Appeals for the Third Circuit affirmed the jury verdict for the defendants, observing along the way that "our confidence in Smith's convictions is not diminished in the least. We remain firmly convinced of the integrity of those guilty verdicts." 210 F.3d, at 198.

Another "exonerated" murderer in the Gross study is Jeremy Sheets, convicted in Nebraska. His accomplice in the rape and murder of a girl had been secretly tape recorded; he "admitted that he drove the car used in the murder . . . , and implicated Sheets in the murder." *Sheets v. Butera*, 389 F.3d 772, 775 (C.A.8 2004). The accomplice was arrested and eventually described the murder in greater detail, after which a plea agreement was arranged, conditioned on the accomplice's full cooperation. The resulting taped confession, which implicated Sheets, was "[t]he crucial portion of the State's case," *State v. Sheets*, 618 N.W.2d 117, 122 (Neb. 2000). But the accomplice committed suicide in jail, depriving Sheets of the opportunity to cross-examine him. This, the Nebraska Supreme Court held, rendered the evidence inadmissible under the Sixth Amendment. After the central evidence was excluded, the State did not retry Sheets. Sheets brought a § 1983 claim; the U.S. Court of Appeals for the Eighth Circuit affirmed the District Court's grant of summary judgment against him. Sheets also sought the $1,000 he had been required to pay to the Nebraska Victim's Compensation Fund; the State Attorney General—far from concluding that Sheets had been "exonerated" and was entitled to the money—refused to return it. The court action left open the possibility that Sheets could be retried, and the Attorney General did "not believe the reversal on the ground of improper admission of evidence . . . is a favorable disposition of charges."

In its inflation of the word "exoneration," the Gross article hardly stands alone; mischaracterization of reversible error as actual innocence is endemic in abolitionist rhetoric, and other prominent catalogues of "innocence" in the death-penalty context suffer from the same defect. Perhaps the best known of them is the List of Those Freed From Death Row, maintained by the Death Penalty Information Center. See http://www.deathpenaltyinfo.org/article.php?scid=6&did=110. This includes the cases from the Gross article described above, but also enters some dubious candidates of its own. Delbert Tibbs is one of them. We considered his case in *Tibbs v. Florida*, 457 U.S. 31 (1982), concluding that the Double Jeopardy Clause does not bar a retrial when a conviction is "revers[ed] based on the weight, rather than the sufficiency, of the evidence," *id.*, at 32. The case involved a man and a woman hitchhiking together in Florida. A driver who picked them

up sodomized and raped the woman, and killed her boyfriend. She eventually escaped and positively identified Tibbs. The Florida Supreme Court reversed the conviction on a 4-to-3 vote. *Tibbs v. State*, 337 So.2d 788 (Fla.1976). The Florida courts then grappled with whether Tibbs could be retried without violating the Double Jeopardy Clause. The Florida Supreme Court determined not only that there was no double-jeopardy problem, but that the *very basis on which it had reversed the conviction was no longer valid law*, and that its action in "reweigh[ing] the evidence" in Tibbs' case had been "clearly improper." After we affirmed the Florida Supreme Court, however, the State felt compelled to drop the charges. The state attorney explained this to the Florida Commission on Capital Cases: "'By the time of the retrial, [the] witness/victim . . . had progressed from a marijuana smoker to a crack user and I could not put her up on the stand, so I declined to prosecute. Tibbs, in my opinion, was never an innocent man wrongfully accused. He was a lucky human being. He was guilty, he was lucky and now he is free. His 1974 conviction was not a miscarriage of justice.'" Florida Commission on Capital Cases, Case Histories: A Review of 24 Individuals Released From Death Row 136–137 (rev. Sept. 10, 2002), http://www.floridacapitalcases.state.fl.us/Publications/innocentsproject.pdf. Other state officials involved made similar points.

Of course, even with its distorted concept of what constitutes "exoneration," the claims of the Gross article are fairly modest: Between 1989 and 2003, the authors identify 340 "exonerations" *nationwide*—not just for capital cases, mind you, nor even just for murder convictions, but for various felonies. Joshua Marquis, a district attorney in Oregon, recently responded to this article as follows:

"[L]et's give the professor the benefit of the doubt: let's assume that he understated the number of innocents by roughly a factor of 10, that instead of 340 there were 4,000 people in prison who weren't involved in the crime in any way. During that same 15 years, there were more than 15 million felony convictions across the country. That would make the error rate .027 percent—or, to put it another way, a success rate of 99.973 percent." The Innocent and the Shammed, N.Y. Times, Jan. 26, 2006, p. A23.

The dissent's suggestion that capital defendants are *especially* liable to suffer from the lack of 100% perfection in our criminal justice system is implausible. Capital cases are given especially close scrutiny at every level, which is why in most cases many years elapse before the sentence is executed. And of course capital cases receive special attention in the application of executive clemency. Indeed, one of the arguments made by abolitionists is that the process of finally completing all the appeals and reexaminations of capital sentences is so lengthy, and thus so expensive for the State, that the game is not worth the candle. The proof of the pudding, of course, is that as far as anyone can determine (and many are looking), *none* of the cases included in the .027% error rate for American verdicts involved a capital defendant erroneously executed.

Since 1976 there have been approximately a half million murders in the United States. In that time, 7,000 murderers have been sentenced to death; about 950 of them have been executed; and about 3,700 inmates are currently on death row. See Marquis, The Myth of Innocence, 95 J. Crim. L. & C. 501, 518 (2005). As a consequence of the sensitivity of the criminal justice system to the due-process rights of defendants sentenced to death, almost two-thirds of all death sentences are overturned. "Virtually none" of these reversals, however, are attributable to a defendant's "'actual innocence.'" Most are based on legal errors that have little or nothing to do with guilt. See *id.,* at 519–520. The studies cited by the dissent demonstrate nothing more.

Like other human institutions, courts and juries are not perfect. One cannot have a system of criminal punishment without accepting the possibility that someone will be punished mistakenly. That is a truism, not a revelation. But with regard to the punishment of death in the current American system, that possibility has been reduced to an insignificant minimum. This explains why those ideologically driven to ferret out and proclaim a mistaken modern execution have not a single verifiable case to point to, whereas it is easy as pie to identify plainly guilty murderers who have been set free. The American people have determined that the good to be derived from capital punishment—in deterrence, and perhaps most of all in the meting out of condign justice for horrible crimes—outweighs the risk of error. It is no proper part of the business of this Court, or of its Justices, to second-guess that judgment, much less to impugn it before the world, and less still to frustrate it by imposing judicially invented obstacles to its execution. . . .

Justice SOUTER, with whom Justice STEVENS, Justice GINSBURG, and Justice BREYER join, dissenting. . . .

[The Court's relevant] precedent, demanding reasoned moral judgment, developed in response to facts that could not be ignored, the kaleidoscope of life and death verdicts that made no sense in fact or morality in the random sentencing before *Furman* [*v. Georgia,* 408 U.S. 238] was decided in 1972. Today, a new body of fact must be accounted for in deciding what, in practical terms, the Eighth Amendment guarantees should tolerate, for the period starting in 1989 has seen repeated exonerations of convicts under death sentences, in numbers never imagined before the development of DNA tests. We cannot face up to these facts and still hold that the guarantee of morally justifiable sentencing is hollow enough to allow maximizing death sentences, by requiring them when juries fail to find the worst degree of culpability: when, by a State's own standards and a State's own characterization, the case for death is "doubtful."

A few numbers from a growing literature will give a sense of the reality that must be addressed. When the Governor of Illinois imposed a moratorium on executions in 2000, 13 prisoners under death sentences had been released since 1977 after a number of them were shown to be innocent, as described in a report which used their examples to illustrate a theme common to all 13, of "relatively little solid evidence connecting the charged defendants to the crimes." State of Illinois, G. Ryan, Governor, Report of the Governor's Commission on Capital Punishment: Recommendations Only 7 (Apr. 2002) (hereinafter Report). During the same period, 12 condemned convicts had been executed. Subsequently the Governor determined that four more death row inmates were innocent.[FN2] Illinois had thus wrongly convicted and condemned even more capital defendants than it had executed, but it may well not have been otherwise unique; one recent study reports that between 1989 and 2003, 74 American prisoners condemned to death were exonerated, Gross, Jacoby, Matheson, Montgomery, & Patil, Exonerations in the United States 1989 Through 2003, 95 J. Crim. L. & C. 523, 531 (2006) (hereinafter Gross), many of them cleared by DNA evidence.[FN3]

Another report states that "more than 110" death row prisoners have been released since 1973 upon findings that they were innocent of the crimes charged, and "[h]undreds of additional wrongful convictions in potentially capital cases have been documented over the past century." Lanier & Acker, Capital Punishment, the Moratorium Movement, and Empirical Questions, 10 Psychology, Public Policy & Law 577, 593 (2004). Most of these wrongful convictions and sentences resulted from eyewitness misidentification, false confession, and (most frequently) perjury, Gross 544, 551–552, and the total shows that among all prosecutions homicide cases suffer an unusually high incidence of false conviction, probably owing to the combined difficulty of investigating without help from the victim, intense pressure to get convictions in homicide cases, and the corresponding incentive for the guilty to frame the innocent, id., at 532.

FN2. The Illinois Report emphasizes the difference between exoneration of a convict because of actual innocence, and reversal of a judgment because of legal error affecting conviction or sentence but not inconsistent with guilt in fact. See Report 9 (noting that, apart from the 13 released men, a "broader review" discloses that more than half of the State's death penalty cases "were reversed at some point in the process"). More importantly, it takes only a cursory reading of the Report to recognize that it describes men released who were demonstrably innocent or convicted on grossly unreliable evidence. Of one, the Report notes "two other persons were subsequently convicted in Wisconsin of" the murders. Id., at 8. Of two others, the Report states that they were released after "DNA tests revealed that none of them were the source of the semen found in the victim. That same year, two other men confessed to the crime, pleaded guilty and were sentenced to life in prison, and a third was tried and convicted for the crime." *Ibid.* Of yet another, the Report says that "another man subsequently confessed to the crime for which [the released man] was convicted. He entered a plea of guilty and is currently serving a prison term for that crime." *Id.,* at 9.

A number were subject to judgments as close to innocence as any judgments courts normally render. In the case of one of the released men, the Supreme Court of Illinois found the evidence insufficient to support his conviction. See *People v. Smith,* 708 N.E.2d 365 (Ill. 1999). Several others obtained acquittals, and still more simply had the charges against them dropped, after receiving orders for new trials.

At least 2 of the 13 were released at the initiative of the executive. We can reasonably assume that a State under no obligation to do so would not release into the public a person against whom it had a valid conviction and sentence unless it were certain beyond all doubt that the person in custody was not the perpetrator of the crime. The reason that the State would forgo even a judicial forum in which defendants would demonstrate grounds for vacating their convictions is a matter of common sense: evidence going to innocence was conclusive.

FN3. The authors state the criteria for their study: "As we use the term, 'exoneration' is an official act declaring a defendant not guilty of a crime for which he or she had previously been convicted. The exonerations we have studied occurred in four ways: (1) In forty-two cases governors (or other appropriate executive officers) issued pardons based on evidence of the defendants' innocence. (2) In 263 cases criminal charges were dismissed by courts after new evidence of innocence emerged, such as DNA. (3) In thirty-one cases the defendants were acquitted at a retrial on the basis of evidence that they had no role in the crimes for which they were originally convicted. (4) In four cases, states posthumously acknowledged the innocence of defendants who had already died in prison. . . ." Gross 524 (footnote omitted). The authors exclude from their list of exonerations "any case in which a dismissal or an acquittal appears to have been based on a decision that while the defendant was not guilty of the charges in the original conviction, he did play a role in the crime and may be guilty of some lesser crime that is based on the same conduct. For our purposes, a defendant who is acquitted of murder on retrial, but convicted of involuntary manslaughter, has not been exonerated. We have also excluded any case in which a dismissal was entered in the absence of strong evidence of factual innocence, or in which—despite such evidence—there was unexplained physical evidence of the defendant's guilt." *Id.,* at 524, n. 4.

We are thus in a period of new empirical argument about how "death is different," *Gregg,* 428 U.S., at 188 (joint opinion of STEWART, POWELL, and STEVENS, JJ.): not only would these false verdicts defy correction after the fatal moment, the Illinois experience shows them to be remarkable in number, and they are probably disproportionately high in capital cases. While it is far too soon for any generalization about the soundness of capital sentencing across the country, the cautionary lesson of recent experience addresses the tie-breaking potential of the Kansas statute: the same risks of falsity that infect proof of guilt raise questions about sentences, when the circumstances of the crime are aggravating factors and bear on predictions of future dangerousness.

In the face of evidence of the hazards of capital prosecution, maintaining a sentencing system mandating death when the sentencer finds the evidence pro and con to be in equipoise is obtuse by any moral or social measure. And unless application of the Eighth Amendment no longer calls for reasoned moral judgment in substance as well as form, the Kansas law is unconstitutional.

At what point does the risk of executing innocent people become too large to tolerate, from either a constitutional perspective or a policy perspective? Justice Thomas suggests that "the logical consequence of the dissent's argument is that the death penalty can only be just in a system that does not permit error." Consequently, "abolition of the death penalty is the only answer to the moral dilemma the dissent poses." Does the debate about innocence and the death penalty reduce to these extremes—that unless "a system . . . does not permit error" the death penalty's "abolition . . . is the only answer"? Are more moderate positions possible regarding either the acceptable error rate or about the implications of acknowledging that mistakes occur? Or is Justice Thomas correct: that is, if it is stipulated that the risk of executing innocents cannot be eliminated, the necessary response must be to halt all executions?

Justice Scalia appears less inclined to engage the debate in all-or-nothing terms, but rather to define it as involving a benefit-cost analysis of the death penalty as an instrument of social policy. Conceding that "[o]ne cannot have a system of criminal punishment without accepting the possibility that someone will be punished mistakenly," he infers that "[t]he American people have determined that the good to be derived from capital punishment . . . outweighs the risk of error." The envisioned calculus requires balancing the benefits ascribed to the death penalty—"in deterrence, and perhaps most of all in the meting out of condign justice for horrible crimes"—against the costs associated with executing an unknown number of innocent persons. Is this a better way of framing the essential controversy? Are "[t]he American people," rather than judges whose obligation is limited to interpreting and applying constitutional commands, best situated to carry out the postulated balancing process?

Is Justice Souter correct that the frequency of "exonerations of convicts under death sentences, in numbers never imagined before the development of DNA tests," bears directly on what "the Eighth Amendment guarantees should tolerate" concerning capital punishment? Precisely what do those exonerations prove? How many involve incontrovertibly innocent persons? If exonerations result in the release of death-sentenced individuals before their execution, do they, as Justice Scalia argues, "demonstrate[] not the failure of the system but its success"?

Justice Scalia further argues that

the dissent does not discuss a single case—not one—in which it is clear that a person was executed for a crime he did not commit. If such an event had occurred in recent years, we would not have to hunt for it; the innocent's name would be shouted from the rooftops by the abolition lobby.

How important would identifying a recent, clear-cut case of an innocent person's execution be to deciding either the legal issues or social policy questions concerning capital punishment?[94] Would it be likely to change Justice Scalia's views?

Absent documented proof that an innocent person has been executed, should we assume that no such cases exist? Given the number of wrongful capital convictions that have come to light during the modern death-penalty era, is it plausible, if not likely, that one or more individuals erroneously convicted of capital murder have "slip[ped] through the cracks"[95] and were executed? If so, what might the likelihood be that an innocent person has been executed in recent years? Examining the number of death sentences imposed, capital case exonerations, and executions in Texas during the post-*Furman* era, researchers have used statistical formulas to estimate that "[t]here is a 99% probability that Texas has executed an innocent person" since 1982.[96]

In a study discussed by both Justice Souter and Justice Scalia in *Kansas v. Marsh*, Professor Samuel Gross and colleagues reported uncovering 340 exonerations between 1989 and 2003 of individuals who had been wrongfully convicted of crimes in this country[97] (the researchers' definition of "exoneration" is noted in footnote 3 of Justice Souter's opinion). As quoted in Justice Scalia's opinion in *Kansas v. Marsh*, Oregon prosecutor Joshua Marquis made his own foray into statistical probabilities in downplaying the significance of Gross's findings. After "giv[ing] the professor the benefit of the doubt" and assuming that "he underestimated the number of innocents by roughly a factor of 10," thus boosting the 340 exoneration cases to 4,000, Marquis observed that "more than 15 million felony convictions" were returned nationally between 1989 and 2003. "That would make the error rate .027 percent—or to put it another way, a success rate of 99.973 percent."[98] Following this interpretation of his study and its apparent endorsement by Justice Scalia, Professor Gross responded:

> If false convictions were vanishingly rare—0.027% or some other absurd figure—they would not be much of a problem. That estimate, and other similar ones, are based on some version of dividing the number of known false convictions—exonerations—by the total of all convictions, ignoring the fact that almost all of these exonerations occurred in a few narrow categories of crime (primarily murder and rape) and that even within those categories many false convictions remain unknown, perhaps the great majority. By this logic we could estimate the proportion of baseball players who have used steroids by dividing the number of major league players who have been caught by the total of all baseball players at all levels: major league, minor leagues, semipro, college, and Little League—and maybe throwing in football and basketball players as well.

. . . For capital murder, we can now estimate that at least 2.3% of death sentences are based on false convictions.[99]

Building on his original investigation, Gross and others have documented more than 1,250 cases of exonerations (including 105 involving a conviction for capital murder and death sentence) from 1989 through late 2013.[100]

Conclusion

Criminal trials rely on overlapping evidentiary and constitutional rules to govern the guilt-determination process. As with other human endeavors, trials are prone to error. Procedural errors cause reversals in disproportionately high numbers of capital cases. Their occurrence additionally may undermine confidence in the reliability of verdicts. Costs and delays inevitably are incurred in all cases when a conviction or death sentence is vacated on procedural grounds. A considerable psychological toll also is taken on murder victims' family members, the accused, and others in the justice system.

Other errors—the wrongful conviction of individuals who are innocent of crimes— strike at the very heart of justice. The precise number of innocent persons convicted of capital crimes and sentenced to death is unknown and perhaps unknowable. The number of wrongfully convicted persons who have been executed is similarly unknown. Some cases of wrongful capital convictions almost certainly remain undiscovered. Although disagreement exists about whether some exonerated defendants are actually innocent, in other cases there is no doubt that individuals were convicted and sentenced to death for crimes they simply did not commit. Some argue that exonerations are a testament to the justice system's ultimate efficiency in detecting error. Others vigorously dispute that exposure of a wrongful conviction for capital murder, resulting in an individual's release from confinement after spending years on death row, can possibly be evidence that "the system works." They maintain that exonerations commonly occur despite, rather than because of, the justice system's workings.

While the definitional and empirical questions that surround the risk of error in capital cases are controversial, even more complicated is reaching agreement about their moral significance and their legal and policy implications. Concerns that innocent people are at risk of execution have contributed to the repeal of death-penalty legislation in several states in recent years. The same concerns continue to surface in public opinion polls as a primary reason for many individuals' opposition to the death penalty. Most jurisdictions within the United States nevertheless retain and make use of capital punishment. Many individuals and policymakers downplay the magnitude of the risk of executing innocent persons or simply believe that the risk of error is unavoidable in the administration of criminal justice and is insufficient reason to stop administering capital punishment. There are few signs that the centuries-old debates surrounding innocence and the death penalty will soon abate.

Endnotes

1. *United States v. Garsson,* 291 F. 646, 649 (S.D.N.Y. 1923).
2. *See, e.g.,* Gerald Gunther, *Learned Hand: The Man and the Judge* (New York: Alfred A. Knopf 1994).
3. *See* Stuart Banner, *The Death Penalty: An American History* 16–18 (Cambridge, MA: Harvard University Press 2002); Rudolph J. Gerber, "Economic and Historical Implications for Capital Punishment Deterrence," 18 *Notre Dame Journal of Law, Ethics & Public Policy* 437, 441 (2004); Dwight Aarons, "Can Inordinate Delay Between a Death Sentence and Execution Constitute Cruel and Unusual Punishment?," 29 *Seton Hall Law Review* 147, 179–181 (1998).
4. *See* Peter D. Marshall, "A Comparative Analysis of the Right to Appeal," 22 *Duke Journal of Comparative & International Law* 1 (2011); Mark M. Arkin, "Rethinking the Constitutional Right to a Criminal Appeal," 39 *UCLA Law Review* 503 (1992).
5. 408 U.S. 238 (1972).
6. Aarons, *supra* note 3, at 181–182.
7. Tracy L. Snell, *Capital Punishment, 2011—Statistical Tables* 14 (Table 10) (Washington, D.C.: U.S. Dept. of Justice, Bureau of Justice Statistics, July 2013), retrieved July 24, 2013 from www.bjs.gov/content/pub/pdf/cp11st.pdf.
8. James R. Acker & Charles S. Lanier, "Statutory Measures for More Effective Appellate Review of Capital Cases," 31 *Criminal Law Bulletin* 211, 226–229 (1995).
9. For a general overview, *see* Eric M. Freedman, "Federal Habeas Corpus in Capital Cases," in James R. Acker, Robert M. Bohm & Charles S. Lanier (eds.), *America's Experiment With Capital Punishment: Reflections on the Past, Present, and Future of the Ultimate Penal Sanction* 553, 553–554 (Durham, NC: Carolina Academic Press, 2d ed. 2003).
10. Acker & Lanier, *supra* note 8, at 231–232.
11. *See* Jonah J. Horwitz, "Certifiable: Certificates of Appealability, Habeas Corpus, and the Perils of Self-Judging," 17 *Roger Williams University Law Review* 695 (2012); Christopher Q. Cutler, "Friendly Habeas Reform—Reconsidering a District Court's Threshold Role in the Appellate Habeas Process," 43 *Willamette Law Review* 281 (2007).
12. David R. Dow & Eric M. Freedman, "The Effects of AEDPA on Justice," in Charles S. Lanier, William J. Bowers & James R. Acker (eds.), *The Future of America's Death Penalty: An Agenda for the Next Generation of Capital Punishment Research* 261, 267 (Durham, NC: Carolina Academic Press 2009).
13. *See* James R. Acker, "Actual Innocence: Is Death Different?," 27 *Behavioral Sciences and the Law* 297, 301 (2009).
14. *Reid v. Covert,* 354 U.S. 1, 77 (1957) (Harlan, J., concurring in the result).
15. James S. Liebman, Jeffrey Fagan & Valerie West, *A Broken System: Error Rates in Capital Cases, 1973–1995,* pp. i–iii (emphasis in original), retrieved July 25, 2013 from www2.law.columbia.edu/instructionalservices/liebman/liebman_final.pdf.
16. James S. Liebman, "The Overproduction of Death," 100 *Columbia Law Review* 2030, 2053 n. 90 (2000) (citing studies and concluding that "the noncapital direct appeal reversal rate . . . is certainly less than 15% and probably far less than 10%."). Moreover, "[t]he noncapital reversal rate on state post-conviction is close to zero. On habeas corpus, it is almost certainly less than five percent." *Id.* (citations omitted).
17. *Id.,* at 2058 (2000) (footnote omitted).
18. *See* Samuel R. Gross, "The Risks of Death: Why Erroneous Convictions Are Common in Capital Cases," 44 *Buffalo Law Review* 469, 478–479 (1996).
19. James S. Liebman, Jeffrey Fagan, Andrew Gelman, Valerie West, Garth Davies & Alexander Kiss, *A Broken System, Part II: Why There Is So Much Error in Capital Cases, and What Can Be Done About It* pp. ii–iii (2002), retrieved July 25, 2013 from www2.law.columbia.edu/brokensystem2/report.pdf. *See also* Liebman, *supra* note 16.

20. Liebman *et al, supra* note 19, at p. iii.
21. *Id.,* at p. i (emphasis in original).
22. Arthur L. Alarcon & Paula M. Mitchell, "Executing the Will of the Voters? A Roadmap to Mend or End the California Legislature's Multi-Billion-Dollar Death Penalty Debacle," 44 *Loyola of Los Angeles Law Review* S41, S85 n. 154 (2011); Acker & Lanier, *supra* note 8, at 232–233.
23. James N.G. Cauthen & Barry Latzer, "Why So Long? Explaining Processing Time in Capital Appeals," 29 *Justice System Journal* 298, 299 (2008).
24. *See* Jeremy Root, "Cruel and Unusual Punishment: A Reconsideration of the *Lackey* Claim," 27 *New York University Review of Law and Social Change* 281, 294–295 (2001–2002).
25. Alarcon & Mitchell, *supra* note 22, at S80-S82.
26. James S. Liebman, Jeffrey Fagan, Valerie West & Jonathan Lloyd, "Capital Attrition: Error Rates in Capital Cases, 1973–1995," 78 *Texas Law Review* 1839, 1862 n. 68 (2000).
27. Cauthen & Latzer, *supra* note 23, at 303–304.
28. *See* Root, *supra* note 24, at 295–298.
29. *Elledge v. Florida,* 525 U.S. 944 (1998) (dissenting from denial of certiorari).
30. Pub. L. 104–132 (codified as amended at 28 U.S.C. §§ 2244, 2253–2255, 2261–2266).
31. Freedman, *supra* note 9, at 568, *quoting* 28 U.S.C. § 2254 (d).
32. 28 U.S.C. § 2244 (d)(1). *See* Marni von Wilpert, "*Holland v. Florida*: A Prisoner's Last Chance, Attorney Error, and the Antiterrorism and Effective Death Penalty Act's One-Year Statute of Limitations Period for Federal Habeas Corpus Review," 79 *Fordham Law Review* 1429 (2010).
33. *See, e.g.,* Lee Kovarsky, "AEDPA's Wrecks: Comity, Finality, and Federalism," 82 *Tulane Law Review* 443 (2007); Brent E. Newton, "A Primer on Post-Conviction Habeas Corpus Review," 29 *Champion* 16 (June 2005); Andrew Hammel, "Diabolical Federalism: A Functional Critique and Proposed Reconstruction of Death Penalty Federal Habeas," 39 *American Criminal Law Review* 1 (2002); Bryan A. Stevenson, "The Politics of Fear and Death: Successive Problems in Capital Federal Habeas Corpus Cases," 77 *New York University Law Review* 699 (2002).
34. *See, e.g., McQuiggin v. Perkins,* 133 S.Ct. 1924 (2013); *House v. Bell,* 547 U.S. 518 (2006); *Schlup v. Delo,* 513 U.S. 298 (1995); *Sawyer v. Whitley,* 505 U.S. 333 (1992). *See generally,* Lee Kovarsky, "Death Ineligibility and Habeas Corpus," 95 *Cornell Law Review* 329 (2010).
35. Florida House Bill No. 7083. The measure became effective July 1, 2013, following its signature by Governor Rick Scott. *See* Mary Ellen Klas, "Gov. Rick Scott Signs Bill Speeding Up Executions in Florida," *Miami Herald* (June 14, 2013), retrieved July 26, 2013 from www.miamiherald.com/2013/06/14/v-print/3451849/gov-rick-scott-signs-bill-to-speed.html.
36. *See* Dwight H. Sullivan, "Killing Time: Two Decades of Military Capital Litigation," 189 *Military Law Review* 1, 24–26 & n. 89 (2006); Joan M. Fisher, "Expedited Review of Capital Post-Conviction Claims: Idaho's Flawed Process," 2 *Journal of Appellate Practice and Procedure* 85 (2000).
37. *See generally,* James S. Liebman, "Opting for Real Death Penalty Reform," 63 *Ohio State Law Journal* 315, 327–332 (2002).
38. *See* Samuel R. Gross, "Convicting the Innocent," 4 *Annual Review of Law & Social Science* 173, 182–184 (2008); Hugo Adam Bedau & Michael L. Radelet, "Miscarriages of Justice in Potentially Capital Cases," 40 *Stanford Law Review* 21, 64–65 (1987).
39. *See* Gerald M. McFarland, *The Counterfeit Man: The True Story of the Boorn-Colvin Murder* (Amherst, MA: University of Massachusetts Press 1990); Rob Warden, *First Wrongful Conviction,* retrieved July 29, 2013 from www.law.northwestern.edu/legalclinic/wrongfulconvictions/exonerations/vt/boorn-brothers.html.
40. *Butler v. State,* 608 So.2d 314 (Miss. 1992).
41. *See* Death Penalty Information Center, "Innocence Cases: Sabrina Butler," retrieved December 3, 2013 from www.deathpenaltyinfo.org/node/4900#59; Angela J. Davis, "Film Review:

'Mississippi Innocence and the Prosecutor's Guilt,'" 25 *Georgetown Journal of Legal Ethics* 689, 1006 (2012); Michelle Oberman, "Mothers Who Kill: Coming to Terms With Modern American Infanticide," 8 *DePaul Journal of Health Care Law* 3, 55–56 (2004). I thank Margaret Vandiver for her suggestion of including mention of this case.

42. *See, e.g.,* Keith A. Findley, "Defining Innocence," 74 *Albany Law Review* 1157, 1159–60 (2010–2011); Marvin Zalman, "An Integrated Model of Wrongful Convictions," 74 *Albany Law Review* 1465, 1470 (2010–2011).

43. *See* The Innocence Project, *Understanding the Causes,* retrieved July 29, 2013 from www. innocenceproject.org/understand/; Brandon L. Garrett, *Convicting the Innocent: Where Criminal Prosecutions Go Wrong* (Cambridge, MA: Harvard University Press 2011).

44. *See* James R. Acker & Catherine L. Bonventre, "Protecting the Innocent in New York: Moving Beyond Changing Only Their Names," 73 *Albany Law Review* 1245, 1250 (2010).

45. See text accompanying note 39, *supra.*

46. *See* Brandon L. Garrett, "Claiming Innocence," 92 *Minnesota Law Review* 1629, 1681 n. 240 (2008); Daniel S. Medwed, "Innocentrism," 2008 *University of Illinois Law Review* 1549, 1570–71 (2008).

47. *See* James S. Liebman, "The New Death Penalty Debate: What's DNA Got to Do With It?," 33 *Columbia Human Rights Law Review* 527, 543 (2002) ("[P]rosecutors have become more sophisticated about hypothesizing the existence of 'unindicted co-ejaculators' (to borrow Peter Neufeld's phrase) to explain how the defendant can still be guilty, though another man's semen is found on the rape-murder victim."). *See also* Hilary S. Ritter, "It's the Prosecution's Story, but They're Not Sticking to It: Applying Harmless Error and Judicial Estoppel to Exculpatory Post-Conviction DNA Testing Cases," 74 *Fordham Law Review* 825, 843–844 (2005).

48. Richard C. Dieter, "The Future of Innocence," in Charles S. Lanier, William J. Bowers & James R. Acker, *The Future of America's Death Penalty: An Agenda for the Next Generation of Capital Punishment Research* 225, 229 (Durham, NC: Carolina Academic Press 2009).

49. *Id.*

50. Bedau & Radelet, note 38 *supra,* at 25.

51. *Id.,* at 47.

52. *See* Stephen J. Markman & Paul G. Cassell, "Protecting the Innocent: A Response to the Bedau-Radelet Study," 41 *Stanford Law Review* 121 (1988). *But see* Hugo Adam Bedau & Michael L. Radelet, "The Myth of Infallibility: A Reply to Markman and Cassell," 41 *Stanford Law Review* 161 (1988).

53. Death Penalty Information Center, *Innocence: List of Those Freed From Death Row,* retrieved December 3, 2013 from www.deathpenaltyinfo.org/innocence-list-those-freed-death-row.

54. *See* David Horan, "The Innocence Commission: An Independent Review Board for Wrongful Convictions," 20 *Northern Illinois University Law Review* 91, 172 n. 445 (2000) (discussing case of Anthony Porter, who was wrongfully convicted of capital murder and sentenced to death in Illinois, whose scheduled execution was stayed 48 hours before it was to be carried out); Michael Mello, "Outlaw Executive: 'Crazy Joe,' the Hypnotized Witness, and the Mirage of Clemency in Florida," 23 *Journal of Contemporary Law* 1, 41 (1997) (identifying several cases in which death-sentenced individuals who subsequently were determined to be innocent came within hours or days of a scheduled execution).

55. Samuel R. Gross and Barbara O'Brien, "Frequency and Predictors of False Conviction: Why We Know So Little, and New Data on Capital Cases," 4 *Journal of Empirical Legal Studies* 927 (2008) (estimating 2.3% error rate for cases in which death sentences were imposed between 1973 and 2004); Michael D. Risinger, "Innocents Convicted: An Empirically Justified Factual Wrongful Conviction Rate," 97 *Journal of Criminal Law & Criminology* 761 (2007) (estimating 3.3% to 5% rate of convicting innocent persons of capital rape murder based on analysis of cases tried between 1982 and 1987).

56. Death Penalty Information Center, "Death Row Inmates by State and Size of Death Row by Year," retrieved August 6, 2013 from www.deathpenaltyinfo.org/death-row-inmates-state-and-size-death-row-year#state.

57. See text accompanying notes 51–52, *supra*.

58. Bedau & Radelet, *supra* note 38, at 72.

59. *See* David Grann, "Trial by Fire: Did Texas Execute an Innocent Man?," *The New Yorker* (Sept. 7, 2009), retrieved July 30, 2013 from www.newyorker.com/reporting/2009/09/07/090907fa_fact_grann?printable=true&currentPage=all; Jessica Dwyer-Moss, "Flawed Forensics and the Death Penalty: Junk Science and Potentially Wrongful Executions," 11 *Seattle Journal for Social Justice* 757, 783–787 (2013); Meghan J. Ryan, "Remedying Wrongful Executions," 45 *University of Michigan Journal of Law Reform* 261, 264–273 (2012).

60. James S. Liebman, Shawn Crowley, Andrew Markquart, Lauren Rosenberg, Lauren Gallo White & Daniel Zharkovsky, "Los Tocayos Carlos," 43 *Columbia Human Rights Law Review* 711 (2012).

61. Rob Warden, "Illinois Death Penalty Reform: How It Happened, What It Promises," 95 *Journal of Criminal Law & Criminology* 381, 382 (2005); Austin Sarat, "Putting a Square Peg in a Round Hole: Victims, Retribution, and George Ryan's Clemency," 82 *North Carolina Law Review* 1345 (2004).

62. *See* Frank Baumgartner, Suzanna L. De Boef & Amber E. Boydstun, *The Decline of the Death Penalty and the Discovery of Innocence* (New York: Cambridge University Press 2008).

63. Illinois Governor's Commission on Capital Punishment, *Report of the Governor's Commission on Capital Punishment* (2002), retrieved July 31, 2013 from http://illinoismurderindictments.law.northwestern.edu/docs/Illinois_Moratorium_Commission_complete-report.pdf. *See* Barbara J. Hayler, "Moratorium and Reform: Illinois's Efforts to Make the Death Penalty Process 'Fair, Just, and Accurate,'" 29 *Justice System Journal* 21 (2008); Thomas P. Sullivan, "Repair or Repeal—Report of the Illinois Governor's Commission on Capital Punishment," 49 *Federal Lawyer* 40 (Sept. 2002). No legislative action was taken on many of the recommended reforms. *See* Leigh B. Bienen, "Capital Punishment in Illinois in the Aftermath of the Ryan Commutations: Reforms, Economic Realities, and a New Saliency for Issues of Cost," 100 *Journal of Criminal Law & Criminology* 1301 (2010).

64. California Commission on the Fair Administration of Justice, *Report and Recommendations on the Administration of the Death Penalty in California* (2008), retrieved July 31, 2013 from www.ccfaj.org/documents/reports/dp/official/FINAL%20REPORT%20DEATH%20PENALTY.pdf. *See* Sarah Rose Weinman, "The Potential and Limits of Death Penalty Commissions as Tools for Reform: Applying Lessons From Illinois and New Jersey to Understand the California Experience," 14 *Berkeley Journal of Criminal Law* 303 (2009).

65. James R. Acker, "Scrutinizing the Death Penalty: State Death Penalty Study Commissions and Their Recommendations," in Robert M. Bohm (ed.), *The Death Penalty Today* 29 (Boca Raton, FL: CRC Press 2008); Charles S. Lanier & James R. Acker, "Capital Punishment, the Moratorium Movement, and Empirical Questions: Looking Beyond Innocence, Race, and Bad Lawyering in Death Penalty Cases," 10 *Psychology, Public Policy, and Law* 577 (2004).

66. New Jersey Death Penalty Study Commission, *New Jersey Death Penalty Study Commission Report* (2007), retrieved July 31, 2013 from www.njleg.state.nj.us/committees/dpsc_final.pdf.

67. *See* Robert J. Martin, "Killing Capital Punishment in New Jersey: The First State in Modern History to Repeal Its Death Penalty Statute," 41 *University of Toledo Law Review* 485 (2010); James B. Johnson, "Executing Capital Punishment via Case Study: A Socratic Chat About New Jersey's Abolition of the Death Penalty and Convincing Other States to Follow Suit," 34 *Journal of Legislation* 1 (2008); George W. Conk, "Herald of Change? New Jersey's Repeal of the Death Penalty," 33 *Seton Hall Legislative Journal* 21 (2008).

68. Aliza B. Kaplan, "Oregon's Death Penalty: The Practical Reality," 17 *Lewis & Clark Law Review* 1, 30 (2013). *See generally* Vincent R. Jones & Bruce Wilson, "Innocence and Its

Impact on the Reassessment of the Utility of Capital Punishment: Has the Time Come to Abolish the Ultimate Sanction?," 67 *University of Miami Law Review* 459 (2013).

69. Rob Warden, "How and Why Illinois Abolished the Death Penalty," 30 *Law & Inequality* 245 (2012).

70. Kaplan, *supra* note 68, at 31.

71. "Maryland Governor Signs Repeal of the Death Penalty," *New York Times* (May 2, 2013), retrieved July 31, 2013 from www.nytimes.com/2013/05/03/us/maryland-governor-signs-repeal-of-the-death-penalty.html?pagewanted=print; "Movement on the Death Penalty," *New York Times* (May 2, 2013), retrieved July 31, 2013 from www.nytimes.com/2013/05/03/opinion/death-penalty-news.html?pagewanted=print.

72. *See* Carol S. Steiker & Jordan M. Steiker, "No More Tinkering: The American Law Institute and the Death Penalty Provisions of the Model Penal Code," 89 *Texas Law Review* 353 (2010); Carol S. Steiker & Jordan M. Steiker, "Part II: Report to the ALI Concerning Capital Punishment," 89 *Texas Law Review* 367 (2010).

73. Model Penal Code and Commentaries § 210.6 (1)(f) (1980).

74. *See* Franklin E. Zimring, "The Unexamined Death Penalty: Capital Punishment and Reform of the Model Penal Code," 105 *Columbia Law Review* 1396 (2005); Russell Dean Covey, "Exorcizing Wechsler's Ghost: The Influence of the Model Penal Code on Death Penalty Sentencing Jurisprudence," 31 *Hastings Constitutional Law Quarterly* 189 (2004).

75. *See* Margaret Malkin Koosed, "Averting Mistaken Executions by Adopting the Model Penal Code's Exclusion of Death in the Presence of Lingering Doubt," 21 *Northern Illinois University Law Review* 41 (2001).

76. Massachusetts Governor's Council on Capital Punishment, *Final Report* 3 (2004), retrieved July 31, 2013 from www.lawlib.state.ma.us/docs/5-3-04governorsreportcapitalpunishment.pdf. *See generally* Joseph L. Hoffmann, "Protecting the Innocent: The Massachusetts Governor's Council Report," 95 *Journal of Criminal Law & Criminology* 561 (2005).

77. Massachusetts Governor's Council on Capital Punishment, *supra* note 76, at 4.

78. *Id.*, at 6–29.

79. *See* Russell G. Murphy, "Execution Watch: Mitt Romney's 'Foolproof' Death Penalty Act and the Politics of Capital Punishment," 45 *Suffolk University Law Review* 1 (2011). *See generally* Brian Hauck, Cara Hendrickson & Zena Yoslov, "Capital Punishment Legislation in Massachusetts," 36 *Harvard Journal on Legislation* 479 (1999).

80. Maryland Commission on Capital Punishment, *Final Report to the General Assembly* (2008), retrieved July 31, 2013 from www.goccp.maryland.gov/capital-punishment/documents/death-penalty-commission-final-report.pdf.

81. *Id.*, at 18.

82. *See* Tim Junkin, *Bloodsworth: The True Story of the First Death Row Inmate Exonerated by DNA* (Chapel Hill, NC: Algonquin Books of Chapel Hill 2004); Mid-Atlantic Innocence Project, "Kirk Bloodsworth," retrieved July 31, 2013 from www.exonerate.org/other-local-victories/kirk-bloodsworth/.

83. Maryland Code, Criminal Law § 202 (2009). *See* Michael Millemann, "Limiting Maryland's New Death Penalty Law," 70 *Maryland Law Review* 272 (2010).

84. Maryland Code, Criminal Law § 202 (a)(3) (2009).

85. *See* James R. Acker & Rose Bellandi, "Firmament or Folly? Protecting the Innocent, Promoting Capital Punishment, and the Paradoxes of Reconciliation," 29 *Justice Quarterly* 287, 298–299 (2012).

86. *Id.*, at 293, *quoting* Douglas F. Gansler, "A Worthy Compromise? Rethinking Maryland's Death Penalty—No: It Goes Too Far in Restricting Eligibility," *Baltimore Sun* (March 19, 2009).

87. *United States v. Quinones*, 313 F.3d 49 (2d Cir. 2002), *rehearing denied*, 317 F.3d 86 (2d Cir. 2003).

88. *Herrera v. Collins*, 502 U.S. 1085 (1992) ("The . . . petition for writ of certiorari [is] granted. The order of this day denying the application for stay of execution of sentence of death is to remain in effect.").

89. *Ex parte Herrera,* 828 S.W.2d 8, 9 (Tex. Crim. App. 1992).

90. Death Penalty Information Center, "Leonel Herrera," retrieved August 3, 2013 from www. deathpenaltyinfo.org/leonel-herrera.

91. *In re Davis,* 2010 WL 3385081 (S.D. Ga.), *appeal dismissed,* 625 F.3d 716 (11th Cir. 2010), *cert. denied,* 131 S.Ct. 1787 (2011).

92. Death Penalty Information Center, "Troy Davis," retrieved August 3, 2013 from www. deathpenaltyinfo.org/troy-davis.

93. *Kansas v. Marsh,* 548 U.S. 163, 166 (2006).

94. *See* Jeffrey L. Kirchmeier, "Dead Innocent: The Death Penalty Abolitionist Search for a Wrongful Execution," 42 *Tulsa Law Review* 403 (2006).

95. Franklin E. Zimring, *The Contradictions of American Capital Punishment* 167 (New York: Oxford University Press 2003).

96. Daniel H. Benson, Hans Hansen & Peter Westfall, "Executing the Innocent," 3 *Alabama Civil Rights & Civil Liberties Law Review* 1, 12 (2013).

97. Samuel R. Gross, Kristen Jacoby, Daniel J. Matheson, Nicholas Montgomery & Sujata Patil, "Exonerations in the United States 1989 Through 1973," 95 *Journal of Criminal Law & Criminology* 523 (2005).

98. Joshua Marquis, "The Innocent and the Shammed," *New York Times* A23 (Jan. 26, 2006), *quoted in Kansas v. Marsh,* 548 U.S. 163, 197–198 (2006) (Scalia, J., concurring).

99. Gross, *supra* note 38, at 176.

100. *See* The National Registry of Exonerations, "Summary View," retrieved December 5, 2013 from www.law.umich.edu/special/exoneration/Pages/browse.aspx (listing 1252 exonerations); *id.,* exonerations sorted by sentence imposed, "death sentence"), retrieved December 5, 2013 from www.law.umich.edu/special/exoneration/Pages/detaillist.aspx?View={faf6eddb-5a68-4f8f-8a52-2c61f5bf9ea7}&FilterField1=Crime&FilterValue1=8_Murder&&Sort-Field=Sentence&SortDir=Asc&FilterField2=Sentence&FilterValue2=Death.

9

THE FINAL STAGES
DEATH ROW, CLEMENCY, AND EXECUTION

Introduction

Carried out to its intended conclusion, the capital-punishment process culminates in the execution of offenders who have been duly convicted of aggravated murder, have been sentenced to death, and have exhausted their appeals. In the interval between sentence and execution, condemned prisoners will face confinement under conditions of heightened security. They typically spend more than a decade of incarceration on death row, with an execution date looming progressively nearer. The mental health of some of the condemned, which may already have been compromised well in advance of their confinement, deteriorates to the point that they may not understand why they have been incarcerated and what fate awaits them. Shortly before their scheduled execution, most offenders under sentence of death will ask the governor or another authority within the executive branch of government to spare them from execution by granting clemency. Those securing no relief will die pursuant to the court-ordered judgment in their case.

This chapter examines the final stages of the capital-punishment process. It begins by considering prisoners' lives under sentence of death, including their conditions of confinement, the choices made by "volunteers" who forgo full judicial review of their capital convictions and sentences in order to expedite their executions, and psychological and legal issues involving their competency for execution. It next focuses on executive clemency, including its purposes, procedures, and how frequently governors and pardon boards have granted clemency in capital cases. It concludes by reviewing methods of execution that have been used to carry out death sentences during different periods of American history and the constitutional challenges that have been leveled against them.

Life Under Sentence of Death

Death Row Confinement

Prisoners under sentence of death are presumed to be both "desperate and . . . dangerous,"[1] and hence represent heightened security risks. In the words of one prison administrator, "These are people who have been convicted of especially heinous murders and who have nothing to lose by attacking each other, themselves or, worse, our staff."[2] Their conditions of confinement have traditionally been restricted accordingly.

With dramatic discrepancies in the sizes of the death-sentenced population in the nation's capital-punishment jurisdictions—California had 727 prisoners under sentence of death as of January 1, 2013, while New Hampshire and Wyoming each had one[3]—it is not surprising that the restrictions imposed on condemned prisoners and conditions for housing them are far from uniform.[4]

In Missouri, for example, most death-sentenced prisoners are "mainstreamed" into the general inmate population rather than confined to a special unit. They thus share cells, recreation, programming opportunities, meals, and other aspects of institutional life with other prisoners in the maximum security Potosi Correctional Center.[5] Missouri is atypical. Prisoners under sentence of death in most other jurisdictions are segregated from other inmates, are subject to more restrictive conditions of confinement, and have far more limited privileges. A recent investigation concluded that states with comparatively high execution rates tend to confine death-sentenced prisoners under especially rigorous regimens, with the following characteristics:

1. Death row inmates are celled alone;
2. Death row inmates eat their meals alone in their cells;
3. Death row inmates spend on average 22 or 23 hours a day alone in their cells, and may spend 24 hours a day alone in their cells on weekends and holidays;
4. Death row inmates take recreation under close supervision, often in an indoor or outdoor cage that resembles a dog run or kennel, usually but not always alone;
5. Death row inmates have limited access to visits and are, as a practical matter, if not a matter of policy, denied contact visits;
6. Death row inmates have limited access to television (if they can afford one), and in some cases, notably Texas, no access to television at all;
7. Death row inmates are accompanied by one or more security officers, and are restrained with handcuffs and sometimes leg irons, and frequently strip-searched when physically removed from their cells (for example, for visits);
8. Death row inmates, with the rare exception of the menial job of tier cleaner, have no access to work;
9. Death row inmates have little or no access to education or correctional programming.[6]

Prisoners in several jurisdictions have challenged their death-row confinement as being sufficiently oppressive so as to violate their constitutional rights.[7] Ruling on such a claim in 1985, which had been brought by Tennessee death-row prisoners, a federal district court agreed. The judge ruled that "the totality of conditions in Unit VI [of the Tennessee State Penitentiary, which housed prisoners under sentence of death] violates the Eighth Amendment's prohibition against cruel and unusual punishment."[8] The court described the conditions that then existed on Tennessee's death row in its opinion, below.

Groseclose v. Dutton, 609 F. Supp. 1432 (M.D. Tenn. 1985).

I. FINDINGS OF FACT

A. *Unit VI*

Unit VI is a compound located within the confines of the Tennessee State Penitentiary. There are two visitation rooms at the front of the building. There are four walks, two outside walks that permit natural light through translucent glass and two inside walks with no natural light. Each walk contains fluorescent lighting that remains on twenty-four hours a day. Many inmates have fashioned cardboard shades in order to block the light while sleeping. There are two death watch cells that are separate from the walks and immediately adjacent to the death chamber. In order to enter the cellblock area, it is necessary to pass through one locked door and then through the locked door for each walk. Each cell is also individually locked. Outside the walks, but inside the cellblock, is a small room known as the law library. The defendants acknowledge that the room is merely a meeting room with some old law books in it. Between the walks are ventilation chambers, which also contain some of the plumbing for the cells. Immediately behind the facility is a small exercise yard with a steel mesh sheet overhead. The yard is approximately twenty feet in width and sixty feet in length. At one end of the yard is a covered passageway leading to a larger exercise yard, which contains basketball facilities. The large exercise yard is shared with Unit I.

B. *The Cells*

Nine cells in Unit VI are approximately thirty-five square feet, and the remaining thirty-nine cells are approximately forty-four square feet. Although only one inmate is housed in each cell, each cell contains a double bunk. With the space taken up by the bunk, an inmate has enough room to take approximately three paces, turn around and take three paces back. Each cell contains a combination toilet and wash basin, and some cells have old-fashioned concrete toilets. Although replacement commodes made of stainless metal have been available for two years, they have not been installed in all cells. Homemade repairs, such as cardboard lids, are used to try to reduce the odor associated with the toilets. The cells do not contain windows. Ventilation and odors have been a serious problem in Unit VI. Often the stale air, laden with cigarette smoke, malodorous emissions from toilets, and paint fumes, make existence in the cells extremely uncomfortable. Insect infestation is a problem for the inmates. Defendants acknowledge that some inmates do not use bug spray in their cells because of the added odor from the insecticides.

There is no natural light on walks 2 and 3 and minimal sunlight on walks 1 and 4. The State provides a single low wattage light bulb that renders reading difficult if not impossible for any prolonged period. Dr. Dorothy O. Lewis, a Professor of Psychiatry at New York University, Bellevue Medical Center, and a clinical Professor of Psychiatry at Yale University Child Study Center, testified that both the cells and the walk on which Mr. Harries was housed were very dark. Dr. Seymour Leon Halleck, a Professor of Psychiatry at the University of North Carolina Medical School and Adjunct Professor of Law at the University of North Carolina Law School with extensive experience in criminology, described the walks on Unit VI as giving one a sense of being entombed. The lack of natural lighting has had an adverse impact on the sleep cycle of many, if not all, inmates. Many inmates remain in their bunks twenty hours a day or more.

Inability to regulate indoor temperatures in the summer and winter also presents significant problems for the inmates. The evidence indicates that in the summer temperatures in the mid-eighties and higher are common. Inmates sometimes must remove their clothing because of high temperatures. Dr. Halleck testified that after he spent part of a rainy, cold day inside Unit VI, he left the facility "shivering."

Dr. Lewis testified that, based on her tours of death rows in several states, Tennessee had the worst death row that she had seen. She compared it to cages in a zoo. Dr. Halleck testified that of the death rows of which he was aware, it was the worst in the nation in terms of the deprivations, lack of exercise, and lack of human contact. Dr. Harold Jordan, former Commissioner of Mental Health for the State of Tennessee, described the conditions as inhumane, deplorable, and completely lacking any stimuli. Reverend Joe Ingle concluded, based upon his experience as Director of the Southern Coalition on Jails and Prisons, his numerous publications about death rows and death penalty cases, and his visits to every death row in the South, that because of the "extraordinarily long hours that the men are locked down in their cells, the overwhelming idleness of the men . . . and the lack of programs available for the men and the absence of diagnostic and classification procedures to identify their respective personalities, traits, and problems[,] . . . the conditions and circumstances under which condemned men are confined on the Tennessee death row fail to afford even minimal levels

of basic human decency. . . ." Ingle considered only the Louisiana death row worse because of its lack of electricity and "dog runs" for exercising the inmates.

C. *Classification*

The defendants use no system of classification for the inmates housed in Unit VI. All death sentenced inmates are considered the same in terms of security risk and needs. The only classification they go through is completion of a one page personal data information sheet. Individuals are assigned to Unit VI based entirely on their sentences and, rather than undergoing normal classification procedure, they are automatically assigned the most restrictive classification, "mandatory segregation." That classification is changed to a less restrictive classification only if the sentence of death is lifted. Ronald Bishop, Deputy Commissioner of Corrections, testified that the officials do not normally conduct any psychological or personality testing of the inmates sentenced to death. Although some death sentenced inmates have been classified, that classification has had no impact on their treatment while confined to Unit VI.

All other inmates in the Tennessee penal system are routinely classified by administration of psychological testing, personality testing, aptitude tests, medical and dental examinations, initial entry counseling, and similar methods. The classification system mandated by state law is used to determine what level of security is required for the inmate and what the needs of the inmate are. Classification enables the institution to identify violent tendencies and escape risks from those with minimal escape tendencies.

The plaintiff class is composed of individuals who have been convicted of murder with aggravating circumstances. For this reason the prison administration has determined that these individuals must be segregated from the general prison population. From the evidence presented at trial, it is clear that there is disagreement among professional correctional authorities as to whether segregation of death sentenced inmates is necessary.

D. *Out of Cell Time*

The evidence indicates that the inmates typically spend more than twenty-two hours per day locked in their cells. The inmates may leave their cells for one hour of outdoor exercise daily in the small exercise yard. This yard contains weights, a bench, and a punching bag. The small yard is completely enclosed, including the steel mesh "roof" through which officers view the inmates while they are in the yard. Once every four days the inmates use the large exercise yard, which is shared with Unit I. No inmates from Unit I are in the larger yard when the Unit VI inmates are using it. Inmates are permitted to shower immediately after their exercise as part of their one hour exercise period.

Within the building in which the cells are located are two visitation rooms and one room known as the law library. The visitation rooms are used only for inmate contact with the outside world. The "law library" is a small room used by individual inmates or by small groups of inmates. Inmates must sign up to use the law library, and the typical waiting period is three days.

Inmates also may receive out of cell time by acting as "rockman." One man from each walk may volunteer and serve as a rockman, and the positions are rotated daily. The designated rockman cleans the walk, collects trays, and talks with the other inmates on the walk. Five inmates rotate as rockman for the area on the crosswalks in Unit VI.

Death row inmates are not permitted access to the commissary, although they may order items from it. They have no access to the gymnasium, nor do they have access to work programs. The inmates may not visit the prison's law library, although they may order books from it. With the exception of the ceremony pursuant to this Court's Order of December 18, 1984, inmates are not allowed congregate religious ceremonies, although they may meet with ministers in the visitation rooms. The inmates are not allowed to have formal educational classes. Inmates have no access to a dining area and must eat their meals alone in their cells. The defendants maintain that all of these restrictions have been imposed for valid security reasons.

E. *In Cell Time*

There are prolonged periods of idleness in Unit VI because the institutional policy is one of "deadlock," which means that the death sentenced inmates are to be locked down twenty-four hours a day, except when exercising, showering, or receiving a visitor. As Warden Dutton admitted, this means that inmates are confined to their cells more than twenty-two hours each day. Defendants do little to alleviate the boredom, and the inmates are largely powerless to take any steps to relieve the tedium.

The extremely cluttered and crowded conditions in the cells preclude exercise opportunities within the cells. Religious counseling in the inmates' cells is no longer available. There are no in cell work programs. The State does not pay for correspondence courses. Especially in the summer, the heat and poor ventilation combine to inflict even more lethargy and idleness upon the inmates. Although radios and televisions are not provided by the State, many inmates possess them and thereby while away their in cell hours. Although radios and televisions may be necessities to the inmates, their collective blare only adds to the overall sense of defeat that prevails in Unit VI.

The prison counselor visits inmates in the cells for short periods of time and, considering the proximity of the cells, private conversations with him are impossible. Only one counselor is assigned for all forty-four inmates on death row, and that person is also the sole counselor for Unit I, which has over eighty inmates. As Dr. Halleck testified, "[t]he absence of any kind of work, the absence of any kind of education, the absence of any kind of group meeting and primarily the absence of any opportunity to talk to anybody except by screaming across the cells, that kind of inactivity . . . makes for depression and lethargy."

F. *Necessities*

There is no evidence before the Court to indicate that the food provided the inmates on Unit VI is not nutritious. However, all meals must be eaten in the cells, often near a malodorous cement commode. Medical services regarding physical ailments appear to be adequate. Sick call occurs daily, and there is no indication that inmates who have emergency medical needs are ignored. The most evident medical problem of a physical nature is the lack of out of cell opportunities and consequent deterioration of physical health.

The emotional needs of the inmates are another matter. The Court finds that the evidence is overwhelming that the defendants have not provided the inmates with adequate psychological and psychiatric assistance necessary for one confined and sentenced to death. Dr. Halleck testified that inmates facing a sentence of death have emotional problems that are different from those of other inmates. Virtually all witnesses who testified as to conditions at Unit VI supported the idea that emotionally the inmates housed there were different from the remainder of the inmate population. The only effort by defendants to deal with these problems is to make available the counselor, George Keeling, who meets with the inmates at their cells without benefit of privacy for a total of one to two hours per week for the entire Unit VI population.

G. *Fire Safety*

The defendants' policies require that fire evacuation training and a fire drill be conducted every three months. Warden Dutton admits that this policy has never been followed in regard to Unit VI. In the event of a fire in Unit VI, evacuation of the inmates housed there would be extremely difficult. First, the two outside doors would have to be unlocked. Then each cell must be unlocked individually. There have been no walk-through fire drills with the inmates in Unit VI and consequently the risk of injury and death to the inmates in the event of a fire is substantial. In the event of a serious fire, the gate from the small exercise yard to the large exercise yard presumably would also have to be unlocked to find safety for the inmates. In order to alert the guards to a fire, the inmates must shout through the doors, and there have been situations when it was extremely difficult to get the attention of a correctional officer. Several fires have occurred in Unit VI.

H. *Access to the Courts*

All of the inmates on death row have attorneys. Furthermore, they may request books from the prison's library and may request meetings with an inmate law clerk.

I. *Contact with the Outside World*

Inmates in Unit VI may meet with their attorneys at reasonable hours without restriction in the visitation rooms. In addition, personal visitation is permitted in the visitation rooms. Inmates are limited to two visitors per week for one or two hours for each visit depending on the distance that the visitor must travel. There are often lengthy waits of two to three hours for visitors. There are two telephones available to the inmates daily for a total of two hours per walk. Those telephones can be used to make collect calls only. In addition, a pay telephone is available in the big exercise yard, which the inmates may visit for approximately one hour every four days.

J. *Officer Training*

The correctional officers assigned to Unit VI have received training at either the Tennessee Corrections Institute or the Tennessee Corrections Academy. They have no special training for working on death row.

What would it be like to spend the night, or a few days, in a facility like the Tennessee State Penitentiary's Unit VI? How might that experience be altered by the knowledge that the confinement was designed to last for years, in order to secure the inhabitant in contemplation of his or her execution? In earlier periods in American history, executions followed within days, weeks, months, or at most a few years of sentencing.[9] Nowadays, as discussed in chapter 8, condemned prisoners commonly spend at least a decade and sometimes as much as three decades or more under confinement as they await execution. Some members of the Supreme Court have been troubled by these circumstances, although others have dismissed their constitutional significance. Justice Stevens identified his concerns in a memorandum respecting the Court's denial of certiorari in *Lackey v. Texas*, 514 U.S. 1045 (1995). Later cases involving the consequences of prisoners' lengthy death row confinement thus have been referred to as presenting "*Lackey* claims."

Lackey v. Texas, 514 U.S. 1045, 115 S.Ct. 1421, 131 L.Ed.2d 304 (1995)

Memorandum of Justice STEVENS, respecting the denial of certiorari.

Petitioner raises the question whether executing a prisoner who has already spent some 17 years on death row violates the Eighth Amendment's prohibition against cruel and unusual punishment. Though the importance and novelty of the question presented by this certiorari petition are sufficient to warrant review by this Court, those factors also provide a principled basis for postponing consideration of the issue until after it has been addressed by other courts.

Though novel, petitioner's claim is not without foundation. In *Gregg v. Georgia*, 428 U.S. 153 (1976), this Court held that the Eighth Amendment does not prohibit capital punishment. Our decision rested in large part on the grounds that (1) the death penalty was considered permissible by the Framers, and (2) the death penalty might serve "two principal social purposes: retribution and deterrence," *id.*, at 183.

It is arguable that neither ground retains any force for prisoners who have spent some 17 years under a sentence of death. Such a delay, if it ever occurred, certainly would have been rare in 1789, and thus the practice of the Framers would not justify a denial of petitioner's claim. Moreover, after such an extended time, the acceptable state interest in retribution has arguably been satisfied by the severe punishment already inflicted. Over a century ago, this Court recognized that "when a prisoner sentenced by a court to death is confined in the penitentiary awaiting the execution of the sentence, one of the most horrible feelings to which he can be subjected during that time is the uncertainty during the whole of it." *In re Medley,* 134 U.S. 160, 172 (1890). If the Court accurately described the effect of uncertainty in *Medley,* which involved a period of four weeks, that description should apply with even greater force in the case of delays that last for many years.[FN*] Finally, the additional deterrent effect from an actual execution now, on the one hand, as compared to 17 years on death row followed by the prisoner's continued incarceration for life, on the other, seems minimal. As Justice White noted, when the death penalty "ceases realistically to further these purposes, . . . its imposition would then be the pointless and needless extinction of life with only marginal contributions to any discernible social or public purposes. A penalty with such negligible returns to the State would be patently excessive and cruel and unusual punishment violative of the Eighth Amendment." *Furman v. Georgia,* 408 U.S. 238, 312 (1972) (opinion concurring in judgment); see also *Gregg v. Georgia,* 428 U.S., at 183 ("[T]he sanction imposed cannot be so totally without penological justification that it results in the gratuitous infliction of suffering").

FN* See also *People v. Anderson,* 493 P.2d 880, 894 (Cal. 1972) ("The cruelty of capital punishment lies not only in the execution itself and the pain incident thereto, but also in the dehumanizing effects of the lengthy imprisonment prior to execution during which the judicial and administrative procedures essential to due process of law are carried out. Penologists and medical experts agree that the process of carrying out a verdict of death is often so degrading and brutalizing to the human spirit as to constitute psychological torture"); *Furman v. Georgia,* 408 U.S. 238, 288–289 (1972) (Brennan, J., concurring) ("[T]he prospect of pending execution exacts a frightful toll during the inevitable long wait between the imposition of sentence and the actual infliction of death"); *Solesbee v. Balkcom,* 339 U.S. 9, 14 (1950) (Frankfurter, J., dissenting) ("In the history of murder, the onset of insanity while awaiting execution of a death sentence is not a rare phenomenon"); *Suffolk County District Attorney v. Watson,* 411 N.E.2d 1274, 1287 (Mass. 1980) (Braucher, J., concurring) (death penalty is unconstitutional under State Constitution in part because "[i]t will be carried out only after agonizing months and years of uncertainty"); *id.,* at 1289–1295 (Liacos, J., concurring).

Petitioner's argument draws further strength from conclusions by English jurists that "execution after inordinate delay would have infringed the prohibition against cruel and unusual punishments to be found in section 10 of the Bill of Rights 1689." *Riley v. Attorney General of Jamaica,* [1983] 3 All E.R. 469, 478 (P.C.1983) (Lord Scarman, dissenting, joined by Lord Brightman). As we have previously recognized, that section is undoubtedly the precursor of our own Eighth Amendment.

Finally, as petitioner notes, the highest courts in other countries have found arguments such as petitioner's to be persuasive. See *Pratt v. Attorney General of Jamaica*, [1994] 4 All E.R. 769 (P.C.1993) (en banc); *id.*, at 785–786 (collecting cases).

Closely related to the basic question presented by the petition is a question concerning the portion of the 17-year delay that should be considered in the analysis. There may well be constitutional significance to the reasons for the various delays that have occurred in petitioner's case. It may be appropriate to distinguish, for example, among delays resulting from (a) a petitioner's abuse of the judicial system by escape or repetitive, frivolous filings; (b) a petitioner's legitimate exercise of his right to review; and (c) negligence or deliberate action by the State. Thus, though English cases indicate that the prisoner should not be held responsible for delays occurring in the latter two categories, it is at least arguable that some portion of the time that has elapsed since this petitioner was first sentenced to death in 1978 should be excluded from the calculus.

. . . [T]he Court's denial of certiorari does not constitute a ruling on the merits. Often, a denial of certiorari on a novel issue will permit the state and federal courts to "serve as laboratories in which the issue receives further study before it is addressed by this Court." *McCray v. New York*, 461 U.S. [961, 963 (1983) (Stevens, J., respecting denial of *certiorari*)]. Petitioner's claim, with its legal complexity and its potential for far-reaching consequences, seems an ideal example of one which would benefit from such further study.

Justice BREYER agrees with Justice STEVENS that the issue is an important undecided one.

Justice Breyer elaborated on his belief about the importance of the *Lackey* issue in his dissent from the Court's denial of certiorari in *Knight v. Florida*, 528 U.S. 990 (1999) and *Moore v. Nebraska* (*id.*). In these cases, the petitioners had been imprisoned for more than 24 years and more than 19 years, respectively, since their death sentences originally were imposed. Justice Breyer's opinion prompted Justice Thomas to register his contrary views, as follows.

Knight v. Florida, Moore v. Nebraska, 528 U.S. 990, 120 S.Ct. 459, 145 L.Ed.2d 370 (1999)

Justice THOMAS, concurring [in the denial of *certiorari*].

I write only to point out that I am unaware of any support in the American constitutional tradition or in this Court's precedent for the proposition that a defendant can avail himself of the panoply of appellate and collateral procedures and then complain when his execution is delayed. Indeed, were there any such support in our own jurisprudence, it would be unnecessary for proponents of the claim to rely on the European Court of Human Rights, the Supreme Court of Zimbabwe, the Supreme Court of India, or the Privy Council.

It is worth noting, in addition, that, in most cases raising this novel claim, the delay in carrying out the prisoner's execution stems from this Court's Byzantine death penalty jurisprudence. . . . In that sense, Justice BREYER is unmistakably correct when he notes that one cannot "justify lengthy delays [between conviction and sentence] by reference to [our] constitutional tradition." *Post*, at 463. Consistency would seem to demand that those who accept our death penalty jurisprudence as a given also accept the lengthy delay between sentencing and execution as a necessary consequence. It is incongruous to arm capital defendants with an arsenal of "constitutional" claims with which they may delay their executions, and simultaneously to complain when executions are inevitably delayed.

Ironically, the neoteric Eighth Amendment claim proposed by Justice BREYER would further prolong collateral review by giving virtually every capital prisoner yet another ground on which to challenge and delay his execution. The claim might, in addition, provide reviewing courts a perverse incentive to give short shrift to a capital defendant's legitimate claims so as to avoid violating the Eighth Amendment right suggested by Justice BREYER.

Five years ago, Justice STEVENS issued an invitation to state and lower courts to serve as "laboratories" in which the viability of this claim could receive further study. *Lackey v. Texas*, 514 U.S. 1045 (1995) (memorandum respecting denial of certiorari). These courts have resoundingly rejected the claim as meritless. . . . I submit that the Court should consider the experiment concluded.

The Supreme Court has yet to give full consideration to a death-sentenced prisoner's *Lackey* claim. Justice Breyer has continued to urge his colleagues to address the issue.[10]

As noted in the justices' opinions in *Lackey* and *Knight/Moore*, several courts outside of the United States have disapproved of the lengthy confinement of prisoners who have been sentenced to death. Those rulings frequently have arisen in the context of the courts' considering whether a decision to honor an extradition request to deliver an individual to this country to face a capital murder trial and possible death sentence would expose the person to inhumane or cruel punishment and hence violate international law or the home country's own governing legal principles.[11]

What significance, if any, should attach to the fact that prisoners' lengthy death-row incarceration may in large part owe to the extensive litigation they initiate to secure judicial review of their convictions and sentences? Should it matter that, when error is found and a new trial or new sentencing hearing is required, the government—and not the prisoner—can fairly be held accountable for the delay? In assessing the merits of a *Lackey* claim, should the conditions of confinement to which the prisoner has been subjected make a difference? Should the specific toll taken on the prisoner's physical or mental health be considered?[12]

Not all death-sentenced prisoners choose to fight against their execution. Indeed, the first execution in the post-*Furman* era involved a so-called "volunteer," Gary Gilmore, who waived his appeal to the Utah Supreme Court as well as all other judicial review of his capital murder convictions and death sentence.[13] Gilmore died by firing squad in Utah on January 17, 1977, less than three months after his trial and a scant five months after committing his murders. His last words were, "Let's do it."[14]

Although an initial appeal is required in capital cases in most jurisdictions whether or not the defendant requests one,[15] condemned prisoners need not continue to challenge their conviction and death sentence if the appeal is denied. They can forgo further judicial review of their cases upon making a knowing, intelligent, and voluntary waiver of their right to pursue such review.[16] A significant number of death-sentenced prisoners choose to do so. Beginning with Gilmore, approximately one out of every 10 persons executed under modern death-penalty laws has opted at some juncture not to pursue available legal challenges.[17]

It has been argued that prisoners who choose to be executed instead of seeking relief in the courts have been so psychologically debilitated by their bleak existence on death row that their attempts to waive further review should be rejected as not being fully intelligent and voluntary. This asserted "death row syndrome"[18] was at issue, for example, when Michael Ross sought execution in Connecticut instead of continuing to contest his death sentences for committing multiple murders. Ross had first been sentenced to death in 1984. Twenty years later, in 2004, Ross's lawyers advised the state court trial judge that Ross wanted to waive further legal challenges and have an execution date set. Following a competency hearing, at which psychiatric testimony was received, the trial court granted Ross's request. Ross was executed amid continuing controversy in 2005.[19]

Prisoners who volunteer for execution present challenging ethical issues for defense lawyers. While many defense attorneys strongly oppose the death penalty, they have a professional obligation to advocate in support of their clients' interests. Respecting their clients' decision-making autonomy thus may conflict with lawyers' deep-seated personal and professional opposition to capital punishment.[20] This dilemma is at least partly averted when attorneys believe that their death-sentenced client's competency to make a decision about what truly is in his or her best interests has been compromised.[21] The attorneys who sought to challenge Ross's competency to waive further review of his death sentences were not allowed do so because the courts ruled that they lacked standing to intervene.[22]

Competency for Execution

"In the history of murder, the onset of insanity while awaiting execution of a death sentence is not a rare phenomenon."[23] If this observation was accurate when Justice Frankfurter offered it in 1950, there is all the more reason to credit it today, when prisoners languish under sentence of death many years longer than they did then. Many capital offenders enter death row already suffering from mental illness and moderate to severe emotional and intellectual disabilities.[24] Lengthy confinement under the harsh conditions that confront most death-sentenced prisoners obviously has the potential to exacerbate pre-existing mental illness as well as undermine the psychological well-being of inmates who previously had none.[25] At some point, prisoners awaiting execution may become so acutely psychotic that the legal and moral foundation for carrying out their sentences is called into question.

Consider the case of Andre Thomas, who was sentenced to death in Texas in 2005 for murdering his estranged wife, their four-year-old son, and his wife's 13-month-old daughter. Thomas had a long history of alcohol and drug abuse. Several of his family members suffered from mental illness. Thomas's behavior had become "increasingly 'bizarre,'"[26] in the weeks and months prior to the killings.

> He put duct tape over his mouth and refused to speak; he talked about how the dollar bill contains the meaning of life; he stated that he was experiencing *déjà vu* and reliving events time and again; he had a religious fixation and heard the voice of God. . . . [He] was heard by others talking about his auditory and visual hallucinations of God and demons.[27]

On March 25, 2004, Thomas consumed a large amount of vodka, took several tablets of Coricidin (a euphoria-inducing drug) and stabbed himself. When taken to the hospital, he "explained that he was a 'fallen angel' who could 'open the gates of Heaven' by . . . stabbing himself in the heart. Although the wound was not life-threatening, he did not understand why he did not die and therefore concluded that he was 'immortal.'"[28] Two days later, the day of the killings, Thomas reported receiving a command from God "to stab and kill his wife and the children using three different knives so as not to 'cross contaminate' their blood and 'allow the demons inside them to live.'"[29]

> He burst into the apartment, then stabbed and killed [his wife] Laura and the two children. He used a different knife on each one of the victims, and then he carved out the children's hearts and stuffed them into his pockets. He mistakenly cut out part of Laura's lung, instead of her heart, and put that into his pocket. He then stabbed himself in the heart which, he thought, would assure the death of the demons that had inhabited his wife and children. But he did not die, so he walked home, changed his clothes, and put the hearts into a paper bag and threw them in the trash. He walked to his father's house with the intention of calling Laura, whom he had just killed. He called Laura's parents instead.[30]

Thomas subsequently was driven to the police station and told the police what he had done and why. He received treatment at a hospital for his chest wound and then was taken to jail. "Five days after the killings, [Thomas] was in his cell with his Bible. After reading a Bible verse to the effect that, 'If the right eye offends thee, pluck it out,' [Thomas] gouged out his right eye."[31]

Three psychologists examined Thomas. Each diagnosed him as suffering from schizophrenia. Thomas initially was found to be incompetent to stand trial but following weeks of treatment, including the administration of strong anti-psychotic medication, he was deemed competent. He pled not guilty by reason of insanity. The jury rejected the insanity defense, found Thomas guilty of capital murder, and sentenced him to death in March 2005.[32]

Thomas was sent to death row "where, like the rest of the condemned, he would spend 23 hours a day alone in a 6-by-10 cell. There, Thomas' mental illness seemed to worsen."[33] Having previously clawed out his right eye while in jail awaiting trial, "[o]n Dec. 9, 2008, Thomas jammed his fingers behind his left eyeball and pulled it from the socket. He ate it whole."[34]

In 2009, the Texas Court of Criminal Appeals reviewed several trial-related issues raised by Thomas's lawyers in a habeas corpus application, rejecting each of them. In a concurring opinion, one of the judges concluded: "This is a sad case. [Thomas] is clearly 'crazy,' but he is also 'sane' under Texas law."[35]

A defendant's mental illness can be relevant at different stages of the criminal justice process. In 2005, Thomas was found to be competent to stand trial, meaning that a court determined that he possessed "'sufficient present ability to consult with his lawyer with a reasonable degree of rational understanding' and has 'a rational as well as factual understanding of the proceedings against him.'"[36] Evidence presented at the trial centered on Thomas's plea of not guilty by reason of insanity. The focus thus turned to his mental state in March 2004, when he killed his wife and the two children. To prevail on a defense of insanity under Texas law, the defendant must prove by a preponderance of the evidence "that, at the time of the conduct charged, . . . as a result of severe mental disease or defect, [he] did not know that his conduct was wrong."[37] Thomas, of course, lost on his bid to be found not guilty by reason of insanity and was convicted of capital murder. Then, applying Texas law, the jury concluded that Thomas posed a threat of future dangerousness and that neither his mental illness nor other circumstances were sufficiently mitigating to spare his life. It thus sentenced him to death. As of February 2013, he remained under sentence of death, confined in a psychiatric prison.[38]

Should this be the end of the law's interest in Thomas's mental health? As long as he was competent to be tried and adjudged guilty of committing murder, is his state of mind of any continuing relevance to his scheduled execution? Even if the now blinded-at-his-own-hands Thomas continues to suffer from schizophrenia and believes that he regularly "hear[s] the voice of God" and that he is "immortal," would any reason exist to scuttle his date with the executioner?

In some respects, Thomas's case resembles that of Alvin Ford, who was convicted of murder in Florida in 1974 and sentenced to death. Confined on death row, by 1982 Ford's mental health had deteriorated. He came to believe that he was at the center of a conspiracy and that prison guards had begun taking several of his family members as well as various government officials hostage. In a letter to the state attorney general, Ford announced that he had fired those responsible for fostering the hostage crisis. Referring to himself as Pope John Paul, III, he declared that he had appointed nine new justices to the Florida Supreme Court and that he could no longer be executed because of the landmark case he had won. His communications with his lawyers eventually digressed to the point where he was "speaking only in a code characterized by intermittent use of the word 'one,' making statements such as 'Hands one, face one. Mafia one. God one, father one, Pope one. Pope one. Leader one.'"[39]

Ford's lawyers sought to halt his execution because of his mental condition. A panel of three psychiatrists appointed by the governor examined him. Two of them concluded that Ford was psychotic and the third found that he had a "severe adaptational disorder," but all agreed that he was not so impaired that he lacked understanding of his death sentence and his impending execution. In 1984, after receiving the psychiatrists' reports, the governor signed a death warrant authorizing Ford's execution. Ford's attorneys sought a hearing in federal district court in an attempt to block the execution, but the court rejected their request. After the court of appeals affirmed this ruling, the Supreme Court granted certiorari "in order to resolve the important issue whether the Eighth Amendment prohibits the execution of the insane and, if so, whether the District Court should have held a hearing on [Ford's] claim."[40]

Ford v. Wainwright, 477 U.S. 399, 106 S.Ct. 2595, 91 L.Ed.2d 335 (1986)

Justice MARSHALL announced the judgment of the Court and delivered the opinion of the Court with respect to Parts I and II and an opinion with respect to Parts III, IV, and V, in which Justice BRENNAN, Justice BLACKMUN, and Justice STEVENS join.

For centuries no jurisdiction has countenanced the execution of the insane, yet this Court has never decided whether the Constitution forbids the practice. Today we keep faith with our common-law heritage in holding that it does. . . .

II

. . . The bar against executing a prisoner who has lost his sanity bears impressive historical credentials; the practice consistently has been branded "savage and inhuman." 4 W. Blackstone, Commentaries * 24–* 25 (hereinafter Blackstone). . . .

Sir Edward Coke had earlier expressed the same view of the common law of England: "[B]y intendment of Law the execution of the offender is for example, . . . but so it is not when a mad man is executed, but should be a miserable spectacle, both against Law, and of extream inhumanity and cruelty, and can be no

example to others." 3 E. Coke, Institutes 6 (6th ed. 1680). Other recorders of the common law concurred.

As is often true of common-law principles, the reasons for the rule are less sure and less uniform than the rule itself. One explanation is that the execution of an insane person simply offends humanity, another, that it provides no example to others and thus contributes nothing to whatever deterrence value is intended to be served by capital punishment. Other commentators postulate religious underpinnings: that it is uncharitable to dispatch an offender "into another world, when he is not of a capacity to fit himself for it," Hawles [Remarks on the Trial of Mr. Charles Bateman, 11 How.St.Tr. 474, 477 (1685)]. It is also said that execution serves no purpose in these cases because madness is its own punishment: *furiosus solo furore punitur.* Blackstone * 395. More recent commentators opine that the community's quest for "retribution"—the need to offset a criminal act by a punishment of equivalent "moral quality"—is not served by execution of an insane person, which has a "lesser value" than that of the crime for which he is to be punished. Hazard & Louisell, Death, the State, and the Insane: Stay of Execution, 9 UCLA L.Rev. 381, 387 (1962).

Unanimity of rationale, therefore, we do not find. "But whatever the reason of the law is, it is plain the law is so." Hawles 477. We know of virtually no authority condoning the execution of the insane at English common law. . . .

This ancestral legacy has not outlived its time. Today, no State in the Union permits the execution of the insane. It is clear that the ancient and humane limitation upon the State's ability to execute its sentences has as firm a hold upon the jurisprudence of today as it had centuries ago in England. The various reasons put forth in support of the common-law restriction have no less logical, moral, and practical force than they did when first voiced. For today, no less than before, we may seriously question the retributive value of executing a person who has no comprehension of why he has been singled out and stripped of his fundamental right to life. Similarly, the natural abhorrence civilized societies feel at killing one who has no capacity to come to grips with his own conscience or deity is still vivid today. And the intuition that such an execution simply offends humanity is evidently shared across this Nation. Faced with such widespread evidence of a restriction upon sovereign power, this Court is compelled to conclude that the Eighth Amendment prohibits a State from carrying out a sentence of death upon a prisoner who is insane. Whether its aim be to protect the condemned from fear and pain without comfort of understanding, or to protect the dignity of society itself from the barbarity of exacting mindless vengeance, the restriction finds enforcement in the Eighth Amendment.

Having confirmed the constitutional prohibition against executing "insane" prisoners—those who are not "competent to be executed"—Justice Marshall then explained in a plurality opinion (joined only by three other justices) why the procedures used by the state were inadequate to resolve the competency issue in Ford's case. The fact-finding process provided no opportunity for Ford to offer evidence bearing on his mental state, allowed him no opportunity to challenge the state-appointed psychiatrists' opinions, and entrusted the ultimate decision about Ford's competency to the governor—a member of the executive branch of government and "[t]he commander of the State's corps of prosecutors [who] cannot be said to have the neutrality that is necessary for reliability in the factfinding proceeding."[41]

Having identified various failings of the Florida scheme, we must conclude that the State's procedures for determining sanity are inadequate to preclude federal redetermination of the constitutional issue. We do not here suggest that only a full trial on the issue of sanity will suffice to protect the federal interests; we leave to the State the task of developing appropriate ways to enforce the constitutional restriction upon its execution of sentences. It may be that some high threshold showing on behalf of the prisoner will be found a necessary means to control the number of nonmeritorious or repetitive claims of insanity. Other legitimate pragmatic considerations may also supply the boundaries of the procedural safeguards that feasibly can be provided.

Yet the lodestar of any effort to devise a procedure must be the overriding dual imperative of providing redress for those with substantial claims and of encouraging accuracy in the factfinding determination. The stakes are high, and the "evidence" will always be imprecise. It is all the more important that the adversary presentation of relevant information be as unrestricted as possible. Also essential is that the manner of selecting and using the experts responsible for producing that "evidence" be conducive to the formation of neutral, sound, and professional judgments as to the prisoner's ability to comprehend the nature of the penalty. Fidelity to these principles is the solemn obligation of a civilized society.

Justice Powell concurred in the judgment but declined to join portions of Justice Marshall's opinion. He elaborated about two issues: "(i) the meaning of insanity in this context, and (ii) the procedures States must follow" to satisfy constitutional requirements.[42]

I

The Court holds today that the Eighth Amendment bars execution of a category of defendants defined by their mental state. The bounds of that category are necessarily governed by federal constitutional law. I therefore turn to the same sources that give rise to the substantive right to determine its precise definition: chiefly, our common-law heritage and the modern practices of the States, which are indicative of our "evolving standards of decency." *Trop v. Dulles*, 356 U.S. 86, 101 (1958) (plurality opinion).

A

. . . [T]he ancient prohibition on execution of the insane rested on differing theories. Those theories do not provide a common answer when it comes to defining the mental awareness required by the Eighth Amendment as a prerequisite to a defendant's execution. On the one hand, some authorities contended that the prohibition against executing the insane was justified as a way of preserving the defendant's ability to make arguments on his own behalf. See 1 M. Hale, Pleas of the Crown 35 (1736) ("if after judgment he become of *non sane memory*, his execution shall be spared; for were he of sound memory he might allege somewhat in stay of judgment or execution"). Other authorities suggest, however, that the prohibition derives from more straightforward humanitarian concerns. Coke expressed the view that execution was intended to be an "example" to the living, but that the execution of "a mad man" was such "a miserable spectacle . . . of extream inhumanity and cruelty" that it "can be no example to others." 3 E. Coke, Institutes 6 (—-th ed. 1794). Hawles added that it is "against christian charity to send a great offender quick . . . into another world, when he is not of a capacity to fit himself for it." Hawles, Remarks on the Trial of Mr. Charles Bateman, 11 How.St.Tr. 474, 477 (1685).

The first of these justifications has slight merit today. Modern practice provides far more extensive review of convictions and sentences than did the common law, including not only direct appeal but ordinarily both state and federal collateral review. Throughout this process, the defendant has access to counsel, by constitutional right at trial, and by employment or appointment at other stages of the process whenever the defendant raises substantial claims. . . . These guarantees are far broader than those enjoyed by criminal defendants at common law. It is thus unlikely indeed that a defendant today could go to his death with knowledge of undiscovered trial error that might set him free.

In addition, in cases tried at common law execution often followed fairly quickly after trial, so that incompetence at the time of execution was linked as a practical matter with incompetence at the trial itself. Our decisions already recognize, however, that a defendant must be competent to stand trial, and thus the notion that a defendant must be able to assist in his defense is largely provided for.

B

The more general concern of the common law—that executions of the insane are simply cruel—retains its vitality. It is as true today as when Coke lived that most men and women value the opportunity to prepare, mentally and spiritually, for their death. Moreover, today as at common law, one of the death penalty's critical justifications, its retributive force, depends on the defendant's awareness of the penalty's existence and purpose. Thus, it remains true that executions of the insane both impose a uniquely cruel penalty and are inconsistent with one of the chief purposes of executions generally. For precisely these reasons, Florida requires the Governor to stay executions of those who "d[o] not have the mental capacity to understand the nature of the death penalty and why it was imposed" on them. Fla.Stat. § 922.07 (1985). A number of States have more rigorous standards,[FN3] but none disputes the need to require that those who are executed know the fact of their impending execution and the reason for it.

FN3. A number of States have remained faithful to Blackstone's view that a defendant

cannot be executed unless he is able to assist in his own defense. . . . I find no sound basis for constitutionalizing the broader definition of insanity, with its requirement that the defendant be able to assist in his own defense. States are obviously free to adopt a more expansive view of sanity in this context than the one the Eighth Amendment imposes as a constitutional minimum.

Such a standard appropriately defines the kind of mental deficiency that should trigger the Eighth Amendment prohibition. If the defendant perceives the connection between his crime and his punishment, the retributive goal of the criminal law is satisfied. And only if the defendant is aware that his death is approaching can he prepare himself for his passing. Accordingly, I would hold that the Eighth Amendment forbids the execution only of those who are unaware of the punishment they are about to suffer and why they are to suffer it. . . .

Petitioner's claim of insanity plainly fits within this standard. . . . Thus, the question is whether petitioner's evidence entitles him to a hearing in Federal District Court on his claim.

III

While the procedures followed by Florida in this case do not comport with basic fairness, I would not require the kind of full-scale "sanity trial" that Justice MARSHALL appears to find necessary. . . .

We need not determine the precise limits that due process imposes in this area. In general, however, . . . [t]he State should provide an impartial officer or board that can receive evidence and argument from the prisoner's counsel, including expert psychiatric evidence that may differ from the State's own psychiatric examination. Beyond these basic requirements, the States should have substantial leeway to determine what process best balances the various interests at stake. As long as basic fairness is observed, I would find due process satisfied.

Having prevailed in the U.S. Supreme Court, Ford earned a federal court hearing on the issue of his competency for execution. The hearing was conducted in 1988 and included testimony from multiple mental health experts called by both Ford's lawyers and the state. In 1989 the district court judge concluded that Ford was malingering; that he was not seriously mentally ill and that he was competent to be executed. Ford's attorneys appealed to the 11th Circuit Court of Appeals, which heard oral argument in 1990. On February 28, 1991, before the Court of Appeals issued a decision, Alvin Ford died. He was 37 years old. He had spent 16 years on Florida's death row. The cause of death was listed as "acute respiratory distress syndrome associated with fulminant acute pancreatitis."[43]

The Supreme Court revisited the issue of incompetency for execution in *Panetti v. Quarterman*, 551 U.S. 930, 127 S.Ct. 2842, 168 L.Ed.2d 662 (2007), a case originating in Texas in 1992 when Scott Panetti shot and killed his mother-in-law and his father-in-law. Panetti had a documented history of mental illness dating back at least as far as 1981. He nevertheless served as his own attorney at his capital murder trial in 1995, where he pled not guilty by reason of insanity. His trial behavior, described by his standby counsel as "bizarre,"[44] included dressing in a purple cowboy suit and identifying John F. Kennedy and Jesus Christ among his intended witnesses.[45] The jury convicted him of capital murder and sentenced him to death. After the state courts set a 2003 execution date for Panetti, his lawyers challenged his competency for execution. He was denied relief in the state courts and thereafter in the federal district court and the Fifth Circuit Court of Appeals. The Supreme Court reversed in a 5–4 decision. While also addressing several procedural issues, Justice Kennedy's majority opinion elaborated on the appropriate definition of competency for execution.

The Court of Appeals stated that competency is determined by whether a prisoner is aware "'that he [is] going to be executed and why he [is] going to be executed.'" To this end, the Court of Appeals identified the relevant District Court findings as follows: First, petitioner is aware that he committed the murders; second, he is aware that he will be executed; and, third, he is aware that the reason the State has given for the execution is his commission of the crimes in question. Under Circuit precedent this ends the analysis as a matter of law; for the Court of Appeals regards these three factual findings as necessarily demonstrating that a prisoner is aware of the reason for his execution.

The Court of Appeals concluded that its standard foreclosed petitioner from establishing incompetency by the means he now seeks to employ: a showing that his mental illness obstructs a rational understanding of the State's reason for his execution. As the court explained, "[b]ecause we hold that 'awareness,' as that term is used in *Ford*, is not necessarily synonymous with 'rational understanding,' as argued by [petitioner,] we conclude that the district court's findings are sufficient to establish that [petitioner] is competent to be executed."

In our view the Court of Appeals' standard is too restrictive to afford a prisoner the protections granted by the Eighth Amendment. . . .

The Court of Appeals' standard treats a prisoner's delusional belief system as irrelevant if the prisoner knows that the State has identified his crimes as the reason for his execution. Yet the *Ford* opinions nowhere indicate that delusions are irrelevant to "comprehen[sion]" or "aware[ness]" if they so impair the prisoner's concept of reality that he cannot reach a rational understanding of the reason for the execution. If anything, the *Ford* majority suggests the opposite.

Explaining the prohibition against executing a prisoner who has lost his sanity, Justice Marshall in the controlling portion of his opinion set forth various rationales, including recognition that "the execution of an insane person simply offends humanity;" that it "provides no example to others;" that "it is uncharitable to dispatch an offender into another world, when he is not of a capacity to fit himself for it;" that "madness is its own punishment;" and that executing an insane person serves no retributive purpose.

Considering the last—whether retribution is served—it might be said that capital punishment is imposed because it has the potential to make the offender recognize at last the gravity of his crime and to allow the community as a whole, including the surviving family and friends of the victim, to affirm its own judgment that the culpability of the prisoner is so serious that the ultimate penalty must be sought and imposed. The potential for a prisoner's recognition of the severity of the offense and the objective of community vindication are called in question, however, if the prisoner's mental state is so distorted by a mental illness that his awareness of the crime and punishment has little or no relation to the understanding of those concepts shared by the community as a whole. This problem is not necessarily overcome once the test set forth by the Court of Appeals is met. And under a similar logic the other rationales set forth by *Ford* fail to align with the distinctions drawn by the Court of Appeals.

Whether *Ford's* inquiry into competency is formulated as a question of the prisoner's ability to "comprehen[d] the reasons" for his punishment or as a determination into whether he is "unaware of . . . why [he is] to suffer it," then, the approach taken by the Court of Appeals is inconsistent with *Ford*. The principles set forth in *Ford* are put at risk by a rule that deems delusions relevant only with respect to the State's announced reason for a punishment or the fact of an imminent execution, as opposed to the real interests the State seeks to vindicate. We likewise find no support elsewhere in *Ford*, including in its discussions of the common law and the state standards, for the proposition that a prisoner is automatically foreclosed from demonstrating incompetency once a court has found he can identify the stated reason for his execution. A prisoner's awareness of the State's rationale for an execution is not the same as a rational understanding of it. *Ford* does not foreclose inquiry into the latter.

This is not to deny the fact that a concept like rational understanding is difficult to define. And we must not ignore the concern that some prisoners, whose cases are not implicated by this decision, will fail to understand why they are to be punished on account of reasons other than those stemming from a severe mental illness. The mental state requisite for competence to suffer capital punishment neither presumes nor requires a person who would be considered "normal," or even "rational," in a layperson's understanding of those terms. Someone who is condemned to death for an atrocious murder may be so callous as to be unrepentant; so self-centered and devoid of compassion as to lack all sense of guilt; so adept in transferring blame to others as to be considered, at least in the colloquial sense, to be out of touch with reality. Those states of mind, even if extreme compared to the criminal population at large, are not what petitioner contends lie at the threshold of a competence inquiry. The beginning of doubt about competence in a case like petitioner's is not a misanthropic personality or an amoral character. It is a psychotic disorder.

Petitioner's submission is that he suffers from a severe, documented mental illness that is the source of gross delusions preventing him from comprehending the meaning and purpose of the punishment to which he has been sentenced. This argument, we hold, should have been considered.

. . . Gross delusions stemming from a severe mental disorder may put an awareness of a link between a crime and its punishment in a context so far removed from reality that the punishment can serve no proper purpose. It is therefore error to derive from *Ford*, and the substantive standard for incompetency its opinions broadly identify, a strict test for competency that treats delusional beliefs as irrelevant once the prisoner is aware the State has identified the link between his crime and the punishment to be inflicted. . . .

What should be done with a prisoner who is found incompetent to be executed? Consider the wry observations offered in 1935 by Thurman Arnold:

> Over ten years ago a criminal was convicted of murder in the State of New York. Shortly before he was to hang he got into that state of mind which is commonly called insanity. . . . It was clear that this made it morally, logically, and legally impossible to hang him because he could not know what he was being hanged for. Thus, it could not be a lesson to him. . . .
>
> What is to be done with him? . . . Sickness rationally demands curative treatment. Therefore he goes to a hospital. . . .
>
> He is kept in the hospital for ten years. Thousands of dollars are spent on him. Finally by a miracle of psychiatric skill he is pronounced cured. Obviously we must now hang him.[46]

If this outcome seems ironic, consider the dilemma confronting a psychiatrist or psychologist who is asked to treat a prisoner who is so seriously mentally ill that he is incompetent for execution. If the mental illness is successfully treated, and competency for execution thus restored, has the mental health professional acted in his or her patient's best interests? Such intervention sometimes is referred to as "the cure that kills."[47] Yet can a mental health professional stand idly by and tender no help knowing that the prisoner is consigned to a life of daily suffering in the throes of severe psychosis? There is no easy ethical solution to this problem.[48] When Maryland's death penalty was still in effect, prisoners ruled incompetent for execution were permanently removed from death row and resentenced to life imprisonment. Although consistent with the English tradition, Maryland's practice was exceptional in this country. In almost all other states, "prisoners who are adjudged incompetent to be executed perpetually linger under sentence of death, and face execution if and when they regain competency."[49]

Is the government's interest in carrying out a lawfully ordered execution sufficiently strong that prison officials should be authorized to administer psychotropic medication to the inmate, without first securing his or her consent, in an attempt to restore competency for execution? The United States Supreme Court was poised to answer this question in 1990, in *Perry v. Louisiana,* but ultimately remanded the case to the state courts for reconsideration in light of a recent related Supreme Court ruling.[50] Following that action, the Louisiana Supreme Court relied on its state constitution to rebuff the state's attempt to involuntarily administer drugs to Perry and then execute him.

> For centuries no jurisdiction has approved the execution of the insane. The state's attempt to circumvent this well-settled prohibition by forcibly medicating an insane prisoner with antipsychotic drugs violates his rights under our state constitution. First, it violates his right to privacy or personhood. Such involuntary medication requires the unjustified invasion of his brain and body with discomforting, potentially dangerous and painful drugs, the seizure of control of his mind and thoughts, and the usurpation of his right to make decisions regarding his health or medical treatment. Furthermore, implementation of the state's plan to medicate forcibly and execute the insane prisoner would constitute cruel, excessive and unusual punishment. This particular application of the death penalty fails to measurably contribute to the social goals of capital punishment. Carrying out this punitive scheme would add severity and indignity to the prisoner's punishment beyond that required for the mere extinguishment of life. This type of punitive treatment system is not accepted anywhere in contemporary society and is apt to be administered erroneously, arbitrarily or capriciously.[51]

In 2003, the Eighth Circuit Court of Appeals considered the case of a mentally ill Arkansas prisoner, Charles Singleton, whose competency for execution was at issue and who was involuntarily administered medication after it was determined that he was dangerous in his untreated condition and that the treatment was in his medical interest. In *Washington v. Harper,* 494 U.S. 210 (1990), the Supreme Court had approved of the forcible administration of medication to prisoners who posed a danger to themselves or others if the treatment was medically appropriate and was authorized through appropriate procedures. As a consequence of the involuntarily administered medication, Singleton's competency for execution was restored. He argued that the involuntary medication was unconstitutional because it left him at risk of execution and therefore was not in his medical interest.[52]

Sitting *en banc,* a majority of the Eighth Circuit Court of Appeals ruled that since the medication was authorized under the *Washington v. Harper* standard, Singleton's constitutional rights were not violated even if the medication had the incidental effect of rendering him competent for execution.[53] In dissent, Judge Heaney argued that the drugs simply "masked" the symptoms of Singleton's psychosis, rather than "treating" the underlying illness. In his opinion, "to execute a man who is severely deranged without treatment, and arguably incompetent when treated, is the pinnacle of what Justice Marshall [in *Ford v. Wainwright*, 477 U.S. 399, 410 (1986)] called 'the barbarity of exacting mindless vengeance.'"[54]

The Supreme Court has not ruled on whether forcibly medicating a prisoner for the purpose of restoring competency for execution would violate the Eighth Amendment, offend due process, or otherwise breach federal constitutional rights.

Executive Clemency

When the extended judicial review process has wound its course and a capital murder conviction and death sentence are left undisturbed, all that typically separates condemned prisoners from the executioner (with the exception of last gasp applications to the courts for a stay of execution) is an executive clemency decision. Inmates confronting execution need not seek clemency, although most do. Clemency can take the form of a *pardon,* which forgives or nullifies a criminal conviction; a *commutation* of sentence, which reduces the severity of a punishment; or a *reprieve,* which temporarily postpones infliction of the punishment, usually to permit further deliberation about a related issue.[55] For the most part, condemned prisoners seek a commutation of their death sentences to life imprisonment when they petition for clemency.

Consistent with the constitutional wisdom underlying the separation of governmental powers, clemency authority lies outside of the judicial system that has adjudged guilt and imposed sentence. The clemency power resides in the executive branch of government. In federal cases, the Constitution confers clemency authority exclusively to the president. The states follow different models. In some, the governor has sole decision-making authority, sometimes acting only after a pardon board or analogous body has issued a nonbinding clemency recommendation. In other states, the governor can grant clemency (but is not required to do so) only if a pardon board first has made a positive recommendation. In a few states, a pardon board, rather than the governor, makes clemency decisions.[56]

Clemency decisions are discretionary and, short of being patently arbitrary (Justice O'Connor has suggested that "[j]udicial intervention might, for example, be warranted [if] . . . a state official flipped a coin to determine whether to grant clemency"[57]), are immune from judicial review. Decisions to grant clemency can be grounded on diverse considerations.[58] Chief among them is the executive's "benign prerogative of mercy,"[59] compassion, or sympathy for an offender in recognition of the frailties of the human condition.[60] Clemency also can be used to temper laws that are unduly harsh or inflexible as written or applied, or make allowances for procedural unfairness or irregularities, and thus to approximate justice more closely in individual cases.[61] The most extreme justice-related reason for exercising clemency is to provide the "fail safe"[62] envisioned by the Supreme Court in *Herrera v. Collins*, 506 U.S. 390 (1993) (a case we considered in chapter 8) against the wrongful execution of an innocent person. Because they are influenced by so many considerations, often lack formal fact-finding procedures,[63] and are largely immune from judicial review,[64] clemency decisions are far from foolproof as a safety net to catch cases of innocence.[65]

When the Supreme Court reviewed and upheld the states' post-*Furman* guided-discretion capital-sentencing statutes in 1976, the lead opinion in *Gregg v. Georgia* observed that death-penalty systems that failed to allow for the exercise of executive clemency "would be totally alien to our notions of criminal justice."[66] Indeed, in England during the late 18th and early 19th centuries, when numerous felonies carried mandatory capital sentences, the Crown used its clemency powers to spare the majority of offenders sentenced to death.[67] During the pre-*Furman* era in this country, governors and pardon boards in several states commuted capital sentences to terms of imprisonment with some regularity. For example, 641 offenders were executed in New York between 1900 and 1963, while governors commuted the death sentences of 175 others, or in 21% of capital cases.[68] In Texas, 461 offenders were executed between 1923 and 1967, while 100 (17%) had their death sentences commuted.[69] California exhibited a similar pattern: 501 executions were carried out between 1893 and 1967, and governors commuted 105 death sentences (17%).[70] Other states had even higher incidences of commutations in pre-*Furman* capital cases, including North Carolina (40%) between 1903 and 1963, Maryland (36%) between 1935 and 1961, and Massachusetts (36%) between 1900 and 1958.[71]

Aside from the blanket commutations issued by Governors Pat Quinn of Illinois in 2011 (commuting the death sentences of 15 offenders following repeal of the state's death-penalty law), Jon Corzine of New Jersey in 2007 (commuting eight death sentences after legislative repeal of the state's death-penalty statute), George Ryan of Illinois in 2003 (commuting death sentences in 167 cases on leaving office), and Toney Anaya of New Mexico in 1986 (commuting five offenders' death sentences on leaving office),[72] capital case commutations have been considerably rarer during the post-*Furman* era.[73] Nationally, 1342 executions were carried out between 1977 and August 1, 2013.[74] If the death-row-clearing commutations of Governors Quinn, Corzine, Ryan, and Anaya are included, that same period saw 273 commutation decisions sparing prisoners from execution for "humanitarian reasons"—*i.e.*, for reasons other than responding to court decisions such as those invalidating mandatory capital sentences.[75] Thus, roughly 17% of the total of 1615 cases (273 commutations + 1342 executions) resulted in death sentences being commuted. However, without those large scale commutations factored in, executive authorities commuted just 78 death sentences for humanitarian reasons during this period, a much smaller proportion (5.5%) of the 1420 cases (78 commutations + 1342 executions) that reached the executioner's doorstep.

The politically charged nature of capital punishment and the risk that a governor's or pardon board's decision to spare the life of a condemned prisoner will be perceived as being soft on crime are commonly cited reasons explaining this trend.[76] Many more factors also help account for the more prevalent use of clemency authority historically. Changes in the modern death penalty era that almost certainly have contributed to the reduction of commutations include the elimination of mandatory capital punishment, the bifurcation of capital trials to allow for consideration of relevant sentencing information, the exclusion of juveniles and mentally retarded offenders from death-penalty eligibility, and the greater availability of judicial review of capital convictions and sentences.[77]

Still, there is no denying that capital case commutation decisions and political considerations are closely intertwined. A case in point is Rickey Ray Rector, a severely brain-damaged inmate on Arkansas' death row who had fired a bullet into his own head after murdering a police officer. Rector's execution was scheduled for January 1992, when then-Governor Bill Clinton was campaigning in New Hampshire before the state's presidential primary election. In the preceding presidential election, Democratic candidate Michael Dukakis, who opposed the death penalty, had fumbled badly in response to a question during his debate with George H.W. Bush about how he would react in the event that his wife was raped and murdered. Clinton not only declined to commute Rector's death sentence, he made a much publicized return to Arkansas to be present in the state for the execution. Rector, who had declared his intention to vote for Clinton for President, left the piece of pie that was served with his last meal in his cell prior to being taken to the execution chamber. He reportedly did so in order to be able to eat it after his execution was carried out.[78]

In Missouri, triple murderer Darrell Mease had much better timing. His execution had been scheduled to coincide with Pope John Paul II's visit to St. Louis in late January 1999. The Pope asked Governor Mel Carnahan to spare Mease's life. After having allowed the 26 previously scheduled executions to go forward, the governor commuted Mease's death sentence to life imprisonment without the possibility of parole. He based his decision on "the extraordinary circumstance of the Pontiff's direct and personal appeal for mercy and because of the deep and abiding respect I have for him and all that he represents. . . ."[79] The next offenders in line for execution in Missouri during 1999 were not as fortunate. Following the Pope's departure, eight executions were carried out that year in the state.[80]

Clemency decisions frequently present a complex blend of competing principles. Backward-looking precepts of retributive justice may conflict with mercy's pull, and with the offender's substantial reformation in the years between the crime and the scheduled execution.

One such case confronted California Governor Arnold Schwarzenegger, who was asked in 2005 to commute the death sentences imposed 24 years earlier on Stanley "Tookie" Williams. Williams grew up in Los Angeles and was the co-founder of the Crips, a street gang known for violence and drug-dealing that would gain footholds across the country. He was convicted of four murders in 1981 and sentenced to death. He consistently maintained that he was not guilty of the killings. While on death row, he spent six years in solitary confinement, reading voraciously. He emerged with a very different philosophy than had led to his involvement with and leadership of the Crips. He dedicated himself to ending gang violence and reaching out to young people through writing books. He was nominated for the Nobel Peace Prize in 2001 for his efforts to preempt illegal gang activities, and he also was nominated for the Nobel Prize in Literature. A made-for-television movie about his life, called *Redemption*, starred Jamie Foxx and aired in 2004.[81]

The clemency petition filed on his behalf trumpeted the theme of redemption.

This is a petition which seeks to spare the life of one man who has lifted himself up from the furthest depths, and whose redemption is a beacon of hope to others. Yet, because that man is Stanley Williams, and because he is a man with a unique voice who is using that voice to send a message of education, self-discipline and peace to the most disadvantaged of Americans, this is a petition which raises other considerations which cannot be ignored.

It is about the very nature of clemency. . . .

It is about the message that will be sent to the parents, teachers, gang members, prisoners and children who have found hope for their own lives in Stanley Williams' redemption and message.

It is about the purpose of the prison system as a whole, and whether rehabilitation is just another word. . . .

It is about the opportunity for you, as Governor, to send the message that hope lives even in the most difficult circumstances, that striving for good is important, that purpose can be found, and that lives can be changed.[82]

How would you rule on Stanley Williams' request for clemency if you had the power to spare his life?

In *The Federalist Papers*, Alexander Hamilton had argued for placing constitutional clemency authority solely with the President, rather than allocating it to a body where responsibility was diffused among multiple parties. He reasoned that,

As the sense of responsibility is always strongest in proportion as it is undivided, it may be inferred that a single man would be most ready to attend to those motives which might plead for mitigation of the rigor of the law, and least apt to yield to considerations which were calculated to shelter a fit object of its vengeance. . . . [O]ne man appears to be a more eligible dispenser of the mercy of the government than a body of men.[83]

Governor Schwarzenegger was entrusted with clemency authority and this sense of responsibility in California. His decision in Stanley Williams' case was foreshadowed in the initial sentence of his statement in explanation of it.

Stanley Williams has been convicted of brutally murdering four people during two separate armed robberies in February and March 1979. . . .

But Williams claims that he is particularly deserving of clemency because he has reformed and been redeemed for his violent past. Williams' claim of redemption triggers an inquiry into his atonement for all his transgressions. Williams protests that he has no reason to apologize for these murders because he did not commit them. But he is guilty and a close look at Williams' post-arrest and post-conviction conduct tells a story that is different from redemption.

[The statement then noted Williams' conspiring to escape from prison shortly after his incarceration, the role he played in founding the Crips, "a notorious street gang that has contributed to and continues to contribute to predatory and exploitative violence," and that he dedicated one of his books to several individuals, including Mumia Abu-Jamal and George Jackson, who "have violent pasts and some have been convicted of committing heinous murders, including the killing of law enforcement."]

Is Williams' redemption complete and sincere, or is it just a hollow promise? Stanley Williams insists he is innocent, and that he will not and should not apologize or otherwise atone for the murders of the four victims in this case. Without an apology and atonement for these senseless and brutal killings there can be no redemption. . . .

Clemency decisions are always difficult and this one is no exception. After reviewing and weighing the showing Williams has made in support of his clemency request, there is nothing that compels me to nullify the jury's decision of guilt and sentence. . . .

Therefore, based on the totality of circumstances in this case, Williams' request for clemency is *denied*.[84]

Stanley Williams was executed at San Quentin Prison on December 13, 2005, the day after Governor Schwarzenegger made his decision denying Williams' petition for clemency.[85]

Execution

As with other Bill of Rights safeguards, the Eighth Amendment's prohibition against cruel and unusual punishments was embraced by a generation of Americans keenly aware of the history of governmental abuses perpetuated under British rule. Capital punishment was commonly employed in England and in the American colonies and the early United States. But various methods of execution that prevailed in England and endured there into the 19th century, well after the U.S. Constitution and its Bill of Rights were ratified,[86] were considered by Americans to be cruelly excessive and hence forbidden by the Eighth Amendment. In *Wilkerson v. Utah*, 99 U.S. 130 (1879), when it first addressed the meaning of the constitutional prohibition against cruel and unusual punishments, the Supreme Court recognized that although "[d]ifficulty would attend the effort to define with exactness" its full scope, "it is safe to affirm that punishments of torture . . . and all others in the same line of unnecessary cruelty are forbidden. . . ."[87] Among the examples cited were cases "where the prisoner was drawn or dragged to the place of execution, . . . or where he was emboweled alive, beheaded, and quartered," as well as "public dissection . . . and burning [the offender] alive. . . ."[88]

In *Wilkerson,* a case arising when Utah was a territory and not yet a state, the Court determined that the Eighth Amendment posed no barrier to execution by firing squad. Hanging was the more common mode of carrying out executions in 19th-century America. Conducted properly, with careful attention given to the condemned prisoner's weight, the length of drop, and placement of the rope and knot, hangings broke the neck of the prisoner and thus caused death rapidly. However, mishaps occurred with some regularity. Prisoners sometimes dangled for seemingly interminable minutes at the end of the rope, gasping for breath and eventually strangling to death. Other cases resulted in decapitation.[89]

Problems with hangings inspired New York Governor David Hill in 1885 to press the state legislature to seek alternative execution methods. "The present mode of executing criminals by hanging has come down to us from the dark ages," said the governor, "and it may well be questioned whether the science of the present day cannot provide a means for taking the life of such as are condemned to die in a less barbarous manner."[90] The New York legislature responded, appointing "a commission to investigate and report 'the most humane and practical method known to modern science of carrying into effect the sentence of death in capital cases.'"[91] The commission did its work, identifying some 34 ways of executing people known over the course of history throughout the world, ranging alphabetically from "*auto da fe*" (public burnings during the Spanish inquisition) through "suffocation."[92] The commission endorsed causing death by electric current, a recommendation that precipitated an unseemly public tiff between industrial titans Thomas Edison and George Westinghouse (inspired by Edison's plan for bringing electricity to households by direct current, while Westinghouse promoted alternating current[93]). The commission's recommendation ultimately resulted in the birth of the electric chair. Through legislation enacted in 1888, New York became the first state to provide for electrocution as the means for carrying out death sentences.[94]

The following year, William Kemmler was convicted in Buffalo of murdering his common law wife Tillie Ziegler, striking her repeatedly with a hatchet.[95] He would become the first person to die in New York's electric chair, although not until after the Supreme Court considered and rejected his challenge to this novel method of execution. Expressly declining to consider Kemmler's claim under the Eighth Amendment (not until 1962 did the Supreme Court rule that the cruel and unusual punishments clause applies to the states, as opposed to only actions of the federal government[96]), the justices discerned no reason under due process principles to invalidate the law, which provided: "The punishment of death must, in every case, be inflicted by causing to pass through the body of the convict a current of electricity of sufficient intensity to cause death, and the application of such current must be continued until such convict is dead."[97] Although intimating that a state would run afoul of due process if it prescribed punishments that were "manifestly cruel and unusual as burning at the stake, crucifixion, breaking on the wheel, or the like,"[98] the *Kemmler* Court perceived no such qualities in death caused by electric current.

> Punishments are cruel when they involve torture or a lingering death; but the punishment of death is not cruel within the meaning of that word as used in the constitution. It implies there something inhuman and barbarous—something more than the mere extinguishment of life.[99]

Regrettably, "something more than the mere extinguishment of life" befell William Kemmler after he was strapped into the electric chair at Auburn Prison on August 6, 1890. He appeared to have died following the initial 17-second administration of electric current. However, a half minute later his body twitched and he resumed breathing. Officials administered another round of electricity, this one lasting 70 seconds. "The stench of burning hair and flesh filled the room."[100] Witnesses vomited. Newspapers reported that Kemmler "slowly roasted to death," and characterized the electrocution as "death by torture" and a "disgrace to civilization."[101] Harkening back to the controversy sparked by the electric chair's development, one headline read, "Kemmler Westinghoused."[102] George Westinghouse said, "They could have done better with an axe."[103]

Kemmler's death in the electric chair was the first, but would not be the last one, to diminish confidence in this method of execution. In May 1946, Willie Francis, who had been sentenced to death for a murder he committed at age 15, was strapped into the portable electric chair used throughout the state of Louisiana to carry out executions in parish jails. Electricity was supplied from a generator located in the back of a pickup truck parked outside of the St. Martin Parish jail.[104] A witness described what happened:

> I saw the electrocutioner [sic] turn on the switch and I saw [Francis'] lips puff out and swell, his body tensed and stretched. I heard the one in charge yell to the man outside for more juice when he saw that Willie Francis was not dying and the one on the outside yelled back he was giving him all he had. Then Willie Francis cried out "Take it off. Let me breath [sic]." Then they took the hood from his eyes and unstrapped him.[105]

The officials were unable to correct the malfunctioning apparatus. Francis was returned to his jail cell, very much alive. His father secured a lawyer, who maintained that a second attempt to execute Francis would be unconstitutional, representing double jeopardy, cruel and unusual punishment, and a violation of due process. The case made its way to the U.S. Supreme Court which, by vote of 5–4, authorized the State to carry out Francis's death sentence. Justice Reed's plurality opinion reasoned:

> The cruelty against which the Constitution protects a convicted man is cruelty inherent in the method of punishment, not the necessary suffering involved in any method employed to extinguish life humanely. The fact that an unforeseeable accident prevented the prompt consummation of the sentence cannot, it seems to us, add an element of cruelty to a subsequent execution.[106]

Justice Frankfurter concurred that executing Francis after the "innocent misadventure"[107] that caused the initial attempt to be aborted would not offend the fundamental principles of justice comprising due process. Protesting the cruelty of "death by installments,"[108] Justice Burton disagreed in his dissenting opinion.

If the state officials deliberately and intentionally had placed [Francis] in the electric chair five times and, each time, had applied electric current to his body in a manner not sufficient, until the final time, to kill him, such a form of torture would rival that of burning at the stake. Although the failure of the first attempt, in the present case, was unintended, the reapplication of the electric current will be intentional. How many deliberate and intentional reapplications of electric current does it take to produce a cruel, unusual and unconstitutional punishment? While five applications would be more cruel and unusual than one, the uniqueness of the present case demonstrates that, today, two separated applications are sufficiently 'cruel and unusual' to be prohibited. If five attempts would be 'cruel and unusual,' it would be difficult to draw the line between two, three, four and five. It is not difficult, however, as we here contend, to draw the line between the one continuous application prescribed by statute and any other application of the current.

Lack of intent that the first application be less than fatal is not material. The intent of the executioner cannot lessen the torture or excuse the result. It was the statutory duty of the state officials to make sure that there was no failure.

Following the adverse Supreme Court decision, the Louisiana Pardons Board recommended against commuting Francis's death sentence to life imprisonment.[109] On May 9, 1947, Willie Francis again was strapped into Louisiana's electric chair. This time there was no malfunction.[110]

Nearly four decades later, dissenting from the Court's denial of certiorari in another Louisiana case in which a murderer faced electrocution, Justice Brennan argued that the continued use of the electric chair violated the Eighth Amendment's prohibition against cruel and unusual punishments.

Glass v. Louisiana, 471 U.S. 1080, 105 S.Ct. 2159, 85 L.Ed.2d 514 (1985)

Justice BRENNAN, with whom Justice MARSHALL joins, dissenting from denial of certiorari.

The petitioner Jimmy L. Glass has been condemned to death by electrocution—"that is, causing to pass through the body of the person convicted a current of electricity of sufficient intensity to cause death, and the application and continuance of such current through the body of the person convicted until such person is dead." La.Rev.Stat.Ann. § 15:569 (West 1981). Glass contends that "electrocution causes the gratuitous infliction of unnecessary pain and suffering and does not comport with evolving standards of human dignity," and that this method of officially sponsored execution therefore violates the Eighth and Fourteenth Amendments....

State and federal courts recurrently cite to [*In re Kemmler*, 136 U.S. 436 (1890)] as having conclusively resolved that electrocution is a constitutional method of extinguishing life, and accordingly that further factual and legal consideration of the issue is unnecessary. But *Kemmler* clearly is antiquated authority. It is now well established that the Eighth Amendment applies to the States through the Fourteenth Amendment. . . .

What are the objective factors by which courts should evaluate the constitutionality of a challenged method of punishment? First and foremost, the Eighth Amendment prohibits "the unnecessary and wanton infliction of pain." *Gregg v. Georgia,* 428 U.S. [153, 173 (1976)]. The Court has *never* accepted the proposition that notions of deterrence or retribution might legitimately be served through the infliction of pain beyond that which is minimally necessary to terminate an individual's life. Thus in explaining the obvious unconstitutionality of such ancient practices as disembowelling while alive, drawing and quartering, public dissection, burning alive at the stake, crucifixion, and breaking at the wheel, the Court has emphasized that the Eighth Amendment forbids "inhuman and barbarous" methods of execution that go at all beyond "the mere extinguishment of life" and cause "torture or a lingering death." *In re Kemmler,* 136 U.S., at 447. It is beyond debate that the Amendment proscribes all forms of "unnecessary cruelty" that cause gratuitous "terror, pain, or disgrace." *Wilkerson v. Utah,* 99 U.S. 130, 135–136 (1879).

The Eighth Amendment's protection of "the dignity of man," *Trop v. Dulles,* 356 U.S. [86, 100 (1958) (plurality opinion)], extends beyond prohibiting the unnecessary infliction of pain when extinguishing life. Civilized standards, for example, require a minimization of physical violence during execution irrespective of the pain that such violence might inflict on the condemned. See, *e.g.,* Royal Commission on Capital Punishment, 1949–1953 Report ¶ 732, p. 255 (1953) (hereinafter Royal Commission Report). Similarly, basic notions of human dignity command that the State minimize "mutilation" and "distortion" of the condemned prisoner's body. These principles explain the Eighth Amendment's prohibition of such barbaric practices as drawing and quartering.

In evaluating the constitutionality of a challenged method of capital punishment, courts must determine whether the factors discussed above—unnecessary pain, violence, and mutilation—are "*inherent* in the method of punishment." *Louisiana ex rel. Francis v. Resweber,* 329 U.S. [459, 464 (1947)] (emphasis added). A single, unforeseeable accident in carrying out an execution does not establish that the method of execution itself is unconstitutional. . . .

A different case would be presented, however, if the Court were confronted with "a series of abortive attempts." *Id.,* at 471. This is because the Eighth Amendment requires that, as much as humanly possible, a chosen method of execution minimize the risk of unnecessary pain, violence, and mutilation. If a method of execution does not satisfy these criteria—if it causes "torture or a lingering death" in a significant number of cases, *In re Kemmler,* 136 U.S., at 447—then unnecessary cruelty inheres in that method of execution and the method violates the Cruel and Unusual Punishments Clause.

II

Because contemporary courts have summarily rejected constitutional challenges to electrocution, the evidence respecting this method of killing people has not been tested through the adversarial truthfinding process. There is considerable empirical evidence and eyewit-ness testimony, however, which if correct would appear to demonstrate that electrocution vio-lates every one of the principles set forth above. This evidence suggests that death by electrical current is extremely violent and inflicts pain and indignities far beyond the "mere extin-guishment of life." Witnesses routinely report that, when the switch is thrown, the con-demned prisoner "cringes," "leaps," and "'fights the straps with amazing strength.'" "The hands turn red, then white, and the cords of the neck stand out like steel bands." The prisoner's limbs, fingers, toes, and face are severely contorted. The force of the electrical current is so powerful that the prisoner's eyeballs sometimes pop out and "rest on [his] cheeks." The prisoner often defecates, urinates, and vomits blood and drool.

"The body turns bright red as its tempera-ture rises," and the prisoner's "flesh swells and his skin stretches to the point of breaking." Sometimes the prisoner catches on fire, partic-ularly "if [he] perspires excessively." Witnesses hear a loud and sustained sound "like bacon frying," and "the sickly sweet smell of burn-ing flesh" permeates the chamber. . . . In the meantime, the prisoner almost literally boils: "the temperature in the brain itself approaches the boiling point of water," and when the post-electrocution autopsy is performed "the liver is so hot that doctors have said that it cannot be touched by the human hand." The body fre-quently is badly burned and disfigured.

The violence of killing prisoners through electrical current is frequently explained away by the assumption that death in these cir-cumstances is instantaneous and painless. This assumption, however, in fact "is open to serious question" and is "a matter of sharp conflict of expert opinion." Throughout the 20th century a number of distinguished electrical scientists

and medical doctors have argued that the avail-able evidence strongly suggests that electrocu-tion causes unspeakable pain and suffering. Because "'[t]he current flows along a restricted path into the body, and destroys all the tissue confronted in this path . . . [i]n the meantime the vital organs may be preserved; and pain, too great for us to imagine, is induced. . . . For the sufferer, time stands still; and this excruciating torture seems to last for an eternity.'" . . .

Although it is an open question whether and to what extent an individual feels pain upon electrocution, there can be no serious dis-pute that in numerous cases death is far from instantaneous. Whether because of shoddy technology and poorly trained personnel, or because of the inherent differences in the "physiological resistance" of condemned pris-oners to electrical current, it is an inescapable fact that the 95-year history of electrocution in this country has been characterized by repeated failures swiftly to execute and the resulting need to send recurrent charges into condemned prisoners to ensure their deaths. . . .

This pattern of "death by installments" is by no means confined to bygone decades. Here is one eyewitness account of Alabama's electrocution of John Louis Evans on April 22, 1983:

"At 8:30 p.m. the first jolt of 1900 volts of electricity passed through Mr. Evans' body. It lasted thirty seconds. Sparks and flames erupted from the electrode tied to Mr. Evans' left leg. His body slammed against the straps holding him in the electric chair and his fist clenched permanently. The electrode appar-ently burst from the strap holding it in place. A large puff of greyish smoke and sparks poured out from under the hood that covered Mr. Evans' face. An overpowering stench of burnt flesh and clothing began pervading the witness room. Two doctors examined Mr. Evans and declared that he was not dead.

"The electrode on the left leg was refastened. At 8:30 p.m. [*sic*] Mr. Evans was administered a second thirty second jolt of electricity. The stench of burning flesh was nauseating. More smoke emanated from his leg and head. Again, the doctors examined Mr. Evans. The doctors reported that his heart was still beating, and that he was still alive.

"At that time, I asked the prison commissioner, who was communicating on an open telephone line to Governor George Wallace to grant clemency on the grounds that Mr. Evans was being subjected to cruel and unusual punishment. The request for clemency was denied.

"At 8:40 p.m., a third charge of electricity, thirty seconds in duration, was passed through Mr. Evans' body. At 8:44, the doctors pronounced him dead. The execution of John Evans took fourteen minutes." [FN35]

FN35. Affidavit of Russell F. Canan (June 22, 1983), attached to Pet. for Cert.

. . . Thus there is considerable evidence suggesting—at the very least—that death by electrocution causes far more than the "mere extinguishment of life." *In re Kemmler*, 136 U.S., at 447. . . .

. . . Several state legislatures have abandoned electrocution in favor of lethal injection for these very reasons. . . . Other States have rejected electrocution in favor of the use of lethal gas.

For me, arguments about the "humanity" and "dignity" of *any* method of officially sponsored executions are a constitutional contradiction in terms. . . . But having concluded that the death penalty in the abstract is consistent with the "evolving standards of decency that mark the progress of a maturing society," *Trop v. Dulles*, 356 U.S., at 101 (plurality opinion), courts cannot now avoid the Eighth Amendment's proscription of "the unnecessary and wanton infliction of pain" in carrying out that penalty simply by relying on 19th-century precedents that appear to have rested on inaccurate factual assumptions and that no longer embody the meaning of the Amendment. For the reasons set forth above, there is an evermore urgent question whether electrocution in fact is a "humane" method for extinguishing human life or is, instead, nothing less than the contemporary technological equivalent of burning people at the stake.

As problems recurred in states' use of the electric chair and lethal injection emerged as an alternative method of carrying out executions, the Georgia Supreme Court (in 2001)[111] and the Nebraska Supreme Court (in 2008)[112] ruled that their respective state constitutions barred further executions by electrocution.

Lethal gas was introduced in 1921 in Nevada as an alternative to the electric chair for executing condemned prisoners. Ten other states turned to lethal gas as an execution method prior to *Furman* and several continued to rely on it for modern era executions.[113] The original Nevada legislation envisioned that gas would be released into the prisoner's cell while he slept, overcoming him and causing death without his awakening. It quickly became obvious that logistic difficulties—the wafting of the deadly fumes throughout the prison—precluded that approach.[114]

The tightly sealed gas chamber thus was developed to contain the released hydrogen cyanide, a poisonous gas that prohibits the transfer of oxygen to blood cells. Unconsciousness typically follows quickly on inhalation of the deadly gas, preventing the prisoner from experiencing "cellular suffocation," the rough equivalent of drowning or being strangled.[115] That, at least, was the assumption. In 1983, dissenting from the Supreme Court's denial of certiorari in a Mississippi case involving a scheduled gas-chamber execution, Justice Brennan chronicled very different accounts of prisoners dying by that method.[116] Years later, Justice Stevens called for more thorough consideration of a California prisoner's claim that execution by lethal gas is a cruel and unusual punishment.

Gomez v. United States District Court for the Northern District of California, 503 U.S. 653, 112 S.Ct. 1652, 118 L.Ed.2d 293 (1992)

PER CURIAM

[Robert Alton] Harris claims that execution by lethal gas is cruel and unusual in violation of the Eighth Amendment. . . .

. . . This claim could have been brought more than a decade ago. There is no good reason for this abusive delay, which has been compounded by last-minute attempts to manipulate the judicial process. . . .

The application to vacate the stay of execution of death is granted, and it is ordered that the orders staying the execution of Robert Alton Harris entered by the United States Court of Appeals for the Ninth Circuit . . . on April 20, 1992, are vacated.

Justice STEVENS, with whom Justice BLACKMUN joins, dissenting.

In a time when the Court's jurisprudence concerning the imposition of the death penalty grows ever more complicated, Robert Alton Harris brings a simple claim. He argues that California's method of execution—exposure to cyanide gas—constitutes cruel and unusual punishment and therefore violates the Eighth and Fourteenth Amendments. In light of all that we know today about the extreme and unnecessary pain inflicted by execution by cyanide gas, and in light of the availability of more humane and less violent methods of execution, Harris' claim has merit. I would deny the State's application to vacate the stay imposed by the Court of Appeals and allow the courts below to hear and rule on Harris' claim.

Execution by cyanide gas is "in essence asphyxiation by suffocation or strangulation." As dozens of uncontroverted expert statements filed in this case illustrate, execution by cyanide gas is extremely and unnecessarily painful.

"Following inhalation of cyanide gas, a person will first experience hypoxia, a condition defined as a lack of oxygen in the body. The hypoxic state can continue for several minutes after the cyanide gas is released in the execution chamber. During this time, a person will remain conscious and immediately may suffer extreme pain throughout his arms, shoulders, back, and chest. The sensation may be similar to pain felt by a person during a massive heart attack."

"Execution by gas. . . . produces prolonged seizures, incontinence of stool and urine, salivation, vomiting, retching, ballistic writhing, flailing, twitching of extremities, [and] grimacing." This suffering lasts for 8 to 10 minutes, or longer.

Eyewitness descriptions of executions by cyanide gas lend depth to these clinical accounts. On April 6, 1992, Arizona executed Don Eugene Harding.

"When the fumes enveloped Don's head he took a quick breath. A few seconds later he again looked in my direction. His face was red and contorted as if he were attempting to fight through tremendous pain. His mouth was pursed shut and his jaw was clenched tight. Don then took several more quick gulps of the fumes.

"At this point Don's body started convulsing violently. . . . His face and body turned a deep red and the veins in his temple and neck began to bulge until I thought they might explode.

"After about a minute Don's face leaned partially forward, but he was still conscious. Every few seconds he continued to gulp in. He was shuddering uncontrollably and his body was racked with spasms. His head continued to snap back. His hands were clenched.

"After several more minutes, the most violent of the convulsions subsided. At this time the muscles along Don's left arm and back began twitching in a wavelike motion under his skin. Spittle drooled from his mouth. . . .

"Don did not stop moving for approximately eight minutes, and after that he continued to twitch and jerk for another minute. Approximately two minutes later, we were told by a prison official that the execution was complete.

"Don Harding took ten minutes and thirty one seconds to die."

The unnecessary cruelty of this method of execution convinced Arizona's Attorney General that that State should abandon execution by gas in favor of execution by lethal injection. His conclusion coincides with that of numerous medical, legal, and ethical experts.

. . . When the California statute requiring execution by cyanide gas was enacted in 1937, the gas chamber was considered a humane method of execution. Fifty-five years of history and moral development have superseded that judgment. The barbaric use of cyanide gas in the Holocaust, the development of cyanide agents as chemical weapons, our contemporary understanding of execution by lethal gas, and the development of less cruel methods of execution all demonstrate that execution by cyanide gas is unnecessarily cruel. . . .

Nowhere is this moral progress better demonstrated than in the decisions of the state legislatures. Of the 20 or so States to adopt new methods of execution since our ruling in *Gregg v. Georgia*, 428 U.S. 153 (1976), not a single State has chosen execution by lethal gas. Ten years ago, 10 States mandated execution by lethal gas; one by one, those States have abandoned that method as inhumane and torturous. Only California, Maryland, and Arizona currently mandate execution by gas. Of the 168 persons executed in the United States since 1977, only 6 have been executed by lethal gas. We have frequently emphasized that "[t]he clearest and most reliable objective evidence of contemporary values is the legislation enacted by the country's legislatures." *Penry v. Lynaugh*, 492 U.S. 302, 331 (1989). These "objective indicia that reflect the public attitude" toward execution by lethal gas, *Stanford v. Kentucky*, 492 U.S. [361, 370 (1989)], clearly exhibit a nearly universal rejection of that means of execution. All of this leads me to conclude that execution by cyanide gas is both cruel and unusual, and that it violates contemporary standards of human decency. . . .

The State contends that Harris should have brought his claim earlier. This is not reason enough to upset the stay issued by the Court of Appeals. . . .

[I]f execution by cyanide gas is in fact unconstitutional, then the State lacks the *power* to impose such punishment. Harris' delay, even if unjustified, cannot endow the State with the authority to violate the Constitution. . . .

Accordingly, I dissent.

In 1996, the Ninth Circuit Court of Appeals agreed with the detailed opinion issued by the United States District Court for the Northern District of California and ruled that California's continued use of the gas chamber violated the Eighth Amendment's prohibition against cruel and unusual punishments.[117] The Supreme Court vacated that decision and directed the Court of Appeals to reconsider it in light of California's enactment of a statute providing for executions to be carried out by lethal injection.[118] The statute allowed prisoners sentenced to death when lethal gas was the sole method of execution "the opportunity to elect to have the punishment imposed by lethal gas or lethal injection."[119]

Lethal injection now is the exclusive or primary method of execution in all death-penalty jurisdictions in the United States.[120] Oklahoma was the first state to authorize execution by lethal injection, through legislation enacted in 1977. Texas carried out the first execution using lethal drugs five years later.[121] Lethal injection marked the next step in the nation's continuing quest to minimize the pain and risk of error in executions. Like euthanizing a pet, the concept seems familiar and relatively uncomplicated. In 1973, while still governor of California, Ronald Reagan put it this way:

> Being a former farmer and horse raiser, I know what it's like to try to eliminate an injured horse by shooting him. Now you call the veterinarian and the vet gives it a shot and the horse goes to sleep—that's it. I myself have wondered if maybe this isn't part of our problem [with capital punishment], if maybe we should review and see if there aren't even more humane methods now—the simple shot or tranquilizer.[122]

As with other execution methods, causing death by lethal injection is not always so straightforward. To the contrary, problems with lethal injection including "personnel, training, drugs, architecture, drug administration apparatuses, monitoring, recordkeeping, and contingency plans,"[123] not to mention the unavailability of essential chemicals, have confounded specific executions and paralyzed entire systems of capital punishment.[124] Among the most distressing concerns is one associated with the three-drug protocol used for lethal injections in several jurisdictions. Prisoners on the lethal injection gurney are intended to be rendered unconscious, under the effects of a sedative, while immobilized by a second drug that inhibits movement. When the procedure goes awry, the sedative will have worn off before the third drug, which induces cardiac arrest, takes effect and causes death. Under such circumstances the condemned prisoner would be fully awake and experiencing excruciating pain, though entirely unable to move, with all signs of suffering masked.[125]

In *Baze v. Rees*, 553 U.S. 35 (2008), the Supreme Court considered whether Kentucky's reliance on a three-drug protocol to carry out executions by lethal injection violated the Eighth Amendment's prohibition against cruel and unusual punishments. Chief Justice Roberts' plurality opinion, joined by Justices Kennedy and Alito, concluded that it did not. Four justices concurred in the judgment and Justices Ginsburg and Souter dissented. The Chief Justice's opinion explained the plurality's reasoning.

Baze v. Rees, 553 U.S. 35, 128 S.Ct. 1520, 170 L.Ed.2d 420 (2008)

Chief Justice ROBERTS announced the judgment of the Court and delivered an opinion, in which Justice KENNEDY and Justice ALITO join.

. . . Petitioners in this case—each convicted of double homicide—acknowledge that [Kentucky's] lethal injection procedure, if applied as intended, will result in a humane death. They nevertheless contend that the lethal injection protocol is unconstitutional under the Eighth Amendment's ban on "cruel and unusual punishments," because of the risk that the protocol's terms might not be properly followed, resulting in significant pain. They propose an alternative protocol, one that they concede has not been adopted by any State and has never been tried.

. . . [P]etitioners have not carried their burden of showing that the risk of pain from maladministration of a concededly humane lethal injection protocol, and the failure to adopt untried and untested alternatives, constitute cruel and unusual punishment. . . .

I

. . . A total of 36 States have now adopted lethal injection as the exclusive or primary means of implementing the death penalty, making it by far the most prevalent method of execution in the United States. It is also the method used by the Federal Government.

Of these 36 States, at least 30 (including Kentucky) use the same combination of three drugs in their lethal injection protocols. The first drug, sodium thiopental (also known as Pentothol), is a fast-acting barbiturate sedative that induces a deep, comalike unconsciousness when given in the amounts used for lethal injection. The second drug, pancuronium bromide (also known as Pavulon), is a paralytic agent that inhibits all muscular-skeletal movements and, by paralyzing the diaphragm, stops respiration. Potassium chloride, the third drug, interferes with the electrical signals that stimulate the contractions of the heart, inducing cardiac arrest. The proper administration of the first drug ensures that the prisoner does not experience any pain associated with the paralysis and cardiac arrest caused by the second and third drugs. . . .

II

. . . We begin with the principle . . . that capital punishment is constitutional. It necessarily follows that there must be a means of carrying it out. Some risk of pain is inherent in any method of execution—no matter how humane—if only from the prospect of error in following the required procedure. It is clear, then, that the Constitution does not demand the avoidance of all risk of pain in carrying out executions.

Petitioners . . . contend that the Eighth Amendment prohibits procedures that create an "unnecessary risk" of pain. Specifically, they argue that courts must evaluate "(a) the severity of pain risked, (b) the likelihood of that pain occurring, and (c) the extent to which alternative means are feasible, either by modifying existing execution procedures or adopting alternative procedures." . . .

. . . [P]etitioners claim that there is a significant risk that the procedures will *not* be properly followed—in particular, that the sodium thiopental will not be properly administered to achieve its intended effect—resulting in severe pain when the other chemicals are administered. Our cases recognize that subjecting individuals to a risk of future harm—not simply actually inflicting pain—can qualify as cruel and unusual punishment. . . . We have explained that to prevail on such a claim there must be a "substantial risk of serious harm," an "objectively intolerable risk of harm" that prevents prison officials from pleading that they were "subjectively blameless for purposes of the Eighth Amendment." *Farmer v. Brennan*, 511 U.S. 825, 842, 846, and n. 9 (1994).

Simply because an execution method may result in pain, either by accident or as an inescapable consequence of death, does not establish the sort of "objectively intolerable risk of harm" that qualifies as cruel and unusual. . . .

Much of petitioners' case rests on the contention that they have identified a significant risk of harm that can be eliminated by adopting alternative procedures, such as a one-drug

protocol that dispenses with the use of pancuronium and potassium chloride, and additional monitoring by trained personnel to ensure that the first dose of sodium thiopental has been adequately delivered. Given what our cases have said about the nature of the risk of harm that is actionable under the Eighth Amendment, a condemned prisoner cannot successfully challenge a State's method of execution merely by showing a slightly or marginally safer alternative.

Permitting an Eighth Amendment violation to be established on such a showing would threaten to transform courts into boards of inquiry charged with determining "best practices" for executions, with each ruling supplanted by another round of litigation touting a new and improved methodology. . . .

Instead, the proffered alternatives must effectively address a "substantial risk of serious harm." *Farmer, supra,* at 842. To qualify, the alternative procedure must be feasible, readily implemented, and in fact significantly reduce a substantial risk of severe pain. If a State refuses to adopt such an alternative in the face of these documented advantages, without a legitimate penological justification for adhering to its current method of execution, then a State's refusal to change its method can be viewed as "cruel and unusual" under the Eighth Amendment.

III

. . . In order to meet their "heavy burden" of showing that Kentucky's procedure is "cruelly inhumane," petitioners point to numerous aspects of the protocol that they contend create opportunities for error. Their claim hinges on the improper administration of the first drug, sodium thiopental. It is uncontested that, failing a proper dose of sodium thiopental that would render the prisoner unconscious, there is a substantial, constitutionally unacceptable risk of suffocation from the administration of pancuronium bromide and pain from the injection of potassium chloride. . . . [H]owever, that petitioners have not shown that the risk of an inadequate dose of the first drug is substantial. And we reject the argument that the Eighth Amendment requires Kentucky to adopt the untested alternative procedures petitioners have identified.

A

Petitioners contend that there is a risk of improper administration of thiopental because the doses are difficult to mix into solution form and load into syringes; because the protocol fails to establish a rate of injection, which could lead to a failure of the IV; because it is possible that the IV catheters will infiltrate into surrounding tissue, causing an inadequate dose to be delivered to the vein; because of inadequate facilities and training; and because Kentucky has no reliable means of monitoring the anesthetic depth of the prisoner after the sodium thiopental has been administered. . . .

. . . [T]he asserted problems . . . do not establish a sufficiently substantial risk of harm to meet the requirements of the Eighth Amendment. . . .

In any event, the Commonwealth's continued use of the three-drug protocol cannot be viewed as posing an "objectively intolerable risk" when no other State has adopted the one-drug method and petitioners proffered no study showing that it is an equally effective manner of imposing a death sentence. . . . We need not endorse the accuracy of those conclusions to note simply that the comparative efficacy of a one-drug method of execution is not so well established that Kentucky's failure to adopt it constitutes a violation of the Eighth Amendment.

Petitioners also contend that Kentucky should omit the second drug, pancuronium bromide, because it serves no therapeutic purpose while suppressing muscle movements that could reveal an inadequate administration of the first drug. The state trial court, however, specifically found that pancuronium serves two purposes. First, it prevents involuntary physical movements during unconsciousness that may accompany the injection of potassium chloride. The Commonwealth has an interest in preserving the dignity of the procedure, especially where convulsions or seizures could be misperceived as signs of consciousness or distress. Second, pancuronium stops respiration, hastening death. Kentucky's decision to include the drug does not offend the Eighth Amendment. . . .

. . . A stay of execution may not be granted on grounds such as those asserted here unless the condemned prisoner establishes that the State's lethal injection protocol creates a demonstrated risk of severe pain. He must show that the risk is substantial when compared to the known and available alternatives. A State with a lethal injection protocol substantially similar to the protocol we uphold today would not create a risk that meets this standard.

* * *

Reasonable people of good faith disagree on the morality and efficacy of capital punishment, and for many who oppose it, no method of execution would ever be acceptable. . . .

Throughout our history, whenever a method of execution has been challenged in this Court as cruel and unusual, the Court has rejected the challenge. Our society has nonetheless steadily moved to more humane methods of carrying out capital punishment. The firing squad, hanging, the electric chair, and the gas chamber have each in turn given way to more humane methods, culminating in today's consensus on lethal injection. The broad framework of the Eighth Amendment has accommodated this progress toward more humane methods of execution, and our approval of a particular method in the past has not precluded legislatures from taking the steps they deem appropriate, in light of new developments, to ensure humane capital punishment. There is no reason to suppose that today's decision will be any different.

The judgment below concluding that Kentucky's procedure is consistent with the Eighth Amendment is, accordingly, affirmed.

As Chief Justice Roberts' opinion forecast, in keeping with the country's historical progression "toward more humane methods of execution," jurisdictions have continued "taking the steps they deem appropriate, in light of new developments" to alter their means of carrying out executions. Contrary to the practices existing in 2008, some states, beginning with Ohio in 2009, now have abandoned the three-drug sequence at issue in *Baze v. Rees* and instead have relied on a single drug (a lethal dose of a sedative) to cause death.[126] Kentucky, where *Baze v. Rees* arose, switched to a single-drug protocol in 2012.[127]

The Chief Justice noted that one of the justifications for using more than a single drug to carry out executions, and specifically the use of pancuronium bromide, the paralytic substance, is that "it prevents involuntary physical movements during unconsciousness that may accompany the injection of potassium chloride. The Commonwealth has an interest in preserving the dignity of the procedure, especially where convulsions or seizures could be misperceived as signs of consciousness or distress." What is the more particular state interest in "preserving the dignity of the procedure" and how is that interest implicated in this context? Consider the following argument advanced by Albert Camus, in *Reflections on the Guillotine.*

> [M]y father, who was especially aroused by the murder of the children [among the family the killer had slain] . . . wanted to witness the [man's] execution. . . . What he saw that morning he never told anyone. My mother relates merely that he came rushing home, his face distorted, refused to talk, lay down for a moment on the bed, and suddenly began to vomit. He had just discovered the reality hidden under the noble phrases with which it was masked. Instead of the slaughtered children, he could think of nothing but that quivering body that had just been dropped onto a board to have its head cut off. . . .
>
> . . . [I]f people are shown the machine, made to touch the wood and steel and to hear the sound of a head falling, then public imagination, suddenly awakened, will repudiate both the vocabulary and the penalty [of death].[128]

Justice Stevens expressed his conviction in *Baze v. Rees* "that this case will generate debate not only about the constitutionality of the three-drug protocol [for lethal injection], . . . but also about the justification for the death penalty itself."[129] He then wrote at length explaining that although he felt bound by precedent to concur in the Court's judgment, and in 1976 had joined the lead opinion in *Gregg v. Georgia* upholding the post-*Furman* guided discretion capital punishment legislation, his experience serving on the Supreme Court since then had led him to alter his views.

> I have . . . [reached] the conclusion that the imposition of the death penalty represents "the pointless and needless extinction of life with only marginal contributions to any discernible social or public purposes. A penalty with such negligible returns to the State [is] patently excessive and cruel and unusual punishment violative of the Eighth Amendment."[130]

Conclusion

This chapter has focused on the ultimate stages of the death-penalty process: the conditions and consequences of death row incarceration in anticipation of condemned offenders' executions; available forms of executive clemency, the reasons justifying this traditional avenue of relief from punishment, and the frequency with which clemency has been and currently is granted to offenders under sentence of death; and the different methods of execution that have been used historically and are used currently to carry out lawfully imposed death sentences.

These topics, like the gruesome crimes that occasion punishment by death, are not uplifting. Yet they are vital aspects of the law and practice of capital punishment and, as with the many other issues associated with the death penalty, are accompanied by a host of difficult and compelling ethical questions and policy implications. Considering the end stages of the death-penalty process is necessary to help complete the circle to its beginnings. Among the issues implicated are the retributive, deterrence, and incapacitation functions of capital punishment, the procedures used to determine the crimes and offenders selected for punishment by death, and the gulf that sometimes separates principle and practice in the operation of law. The ending stages of death-penalty cases must inevitably loop back to the antecedent objectives and machinations of systems of capital punishment.

Endnotes

1. Robert Johnson & Harmony Davies, "Life Under Sentence of Death: Historical and Contemporary Perspectives," in James R. Acker, Robert M. Bohm & Charles S. Lanier (eds.), *America's Experiment With Capital Punishment: Reflections on the Past, Present, and Future of the Ultimate Penal Sanction* (Durham, NC: Carolina Academic Press, 3d ed. forthcoming).
2. William Glaberson, "On a Reinvented Death Row, the Prisoners Can Only Wait," *New York Times* A1 (June 4, 2002), *quoting* James Flateau, Spokesperson for the New York State Department of Correctional Services (*quoted in* Andrea D. Lyon & Mark D. Cunningham, "'Reason Not the Need': Does the Lack of Compelling State Interest in Maintaining a Separate Death Row Make It Unlawful?," 33 *American Journal of Criminal Law* 1, 2 n. 2 [2005]).
3. Death Penalty Information Center, "Death Row Inmates by State," retrieved August 7, 2013 from www.deathpenaltyinfo.org/death-row-inmates-state-and-size-death-row-year#state.
4. *See* Death Penalty Information Center, "Death Row Conditions" (last updated June 2008), retrieved August 7, 2013 from www.deathpenaltyinfo.org/death-row.

5. Lyon & Cunningham, *supra* note 2, at 3.

6. Johnson & Davies, *supra* note 1.

7. *See, e.g., Gates v. Cook,* 376 F.3d 323 (5th Cir. 2004) (upholding several aspects of district court findings that conditions on Mississippi's death row violated the inmates' Eighth Amendment rights); *Peterkin v. Jeffes,* 855 F.2d 1021 (3d Cir. 1988) (rejecting claims by death-sentenced prisoners in Pennsylvania that conditions of confinement violated their Eighth Amendment rights).

8. *Groseclose v. Dutton,* 609 F.Supp. 1432, 1446 (M.D. Tenn. 1985), *appeal dismissed,* 788 F.2d 356 (6th Cir. 1986), *vacated on other grounds,* 829 F.2d 581 (6th Cir. 1987).

9. *See* Dwight Aarons, "Can Inordinate Delay Between a Death Sentence and Execution Constitute Cruel and Unusual Punishment?," 29 *Seton Hall Law Review* 147, 181 (1998).

10. *See, e.g., Valle v. Florida,* 132 S.Ct. 1, 180 L.Ed.2d 940 (2011) (Breyer, J., dissenting from denial of certiorari and denial of stay of execution).

11. *See, e.g., Minister of Justice v. Burns,* 2001 SCC 7 (Canada 2001); *Soering v. United Kingdom,* 11 Eur. H.R. Rep. 439 (1989).

12. *See generally* Kara Sharkey, "Delay in Considering the Constitutionality of Inordinate Delay: The Death Row Phenomenon and the Eighth Amendment," 161 *University of Pennsylvania Law Review* 861 (2013); Erin Simmons, "Challenging an Execution After Prolonged Confinement on Death Row [*Lackey* Revisited]," 59 *Case Western Reserve Law Review* 1249 (2009); David A. Sadoff, "International Law and the Mortal Precipice: A Legal Policy Critique of the Death Row Phenomenon," 17 *Tulane Journal of International and Comparative Law* 77, 98–107 (2008); Kate McMahon, "Dead Man Waiting: Death Row Delays, the Eighth Amendment, and What Courts and Legislatures Can Do," 25 *Buffalo Public Interest Law Journal* 43 (2006–2007); Aarons, *supra* note 9.

13. *See Gilmore v. Utah,* 429 U.S. 1012 (1976).

14. *See* Matthew T. Norman, "Standards and Procedures for Determining Whether a Defendant Is Competent to Make the Ultimate Choice—Death; Ohio's New Precedent for Death Row 'Volunteers,'" 13 *Journal of Law and Health* 103, 112–113 (1998–1999); Welsh S. White, "Defendants Who Elect Execution," 48 *University of Pittsburgh Law Review* 853, 872 (1987). *See generally,* Norman Mailer, *The Executioner's Song* (Boston: Little, Brown & Company 1979).

15. James R. Acker & Charles S. Lanier, "Statutory Measures for More Effective Appellate Review of Capital Cases," 31 *Criminal Law Bulletin* 211, 226–229 (1995).

16. *Whitmore v. Arkansas,* 495 U.S. 149 (1990) (rejecting claim that third party had standing to challenge the defendant's [Ronald Simmons] waiver of the appeal of his capital murder conviction and death sentence); *Gilmore v. Utah,* 429 U.S. 1012 (1976) (same).

17. Death Penalty Information Center, "Information on Defendants Who Were Executed Since 1976 and Designated as 'Volunteers,'" (identifying, as of July 29, 2013, 141 individuals who were executed after "waiv[ing] at least part of their ordinary appeals" among the 1343 persons executed during the post-*Furman* era, or 10.5%), retrieved August 8, 2013 from www.deathpenaltyinfo.org/information-defendants-who-were-executed-1976-and-designated-volunteers). *See also* Margaret Vandiver, David J. Giacopassi & K.B. Turner, "'Let's Do It!': An Analysis of Consensual Executions," in Robert M. Bohm (ed.), *The Death Penalty Today* 187 (Boca Raton, FL: CRC Press 2008); John H. Blume, "Killing the Willing: 'Volunteers,' Suicide and Competency," 103 *Michigan Law Review* 939 (2005).

18. *See* Patricia Cooper, "Competency of Death Row Inmates to Waive the Right to Appeal: A Proposal to Scrutinize the Motivations of Death Row Volunteers and to Consider the Impact of Death Row Syndrome in Determining Competency," 28 *Developments in Mental Health Law* 105 (2009); Amy Smith, "Not 'Waiving' but Drowning: The Anatomy of Death Row Syndrome and Volunteering for Execution," 17 *Boston University Public Interest Law Journal* 237 (2008).

19. Stephen Blank, "Killing Time: The Process of Waiving Appeal—The Michael Ross Death Penalty Cases," 14 *Journal of Law & Policy* 735 (2006). *See also State v. Ross,* 863 A.2d 654 (Conn. 2005).

20. Avi Brisman, "'Docile Bodies' or Rebellious Spirits?: Issues of Time and Power in the Waiver and Withdrawal of Death Penalty Appeals," 43 *Valparaiso University Law Review* 459 (2009); Julie Levinsohn Milner, "Dignity or Death Row: Are Death Row Rights to Die Diminished? A Comparison of the Right to Die for the Terminally Ill and the Terminally Sentenced," 24 *New England Journal on Criminal and Civil Confinement* 279 (1998); John R. Mitchell, "Attorneys Representing Death Row Clients: Client Autonomy Over Personal Opinions," 25 *Capital University Law Review* 643 (1996).

21. Brisman, *supra* note 20, at 465–466; Richard Bonnie, "The Dignity of the Condemned," 74 *Virginia Law Review* 1363, 1367 (1988).

22. *State v. Ross,* 863 A.2d 654 (Conn. 2005).

23. *Solesbee v. Balkcom,* 339 U.S. 9, 14 (1950) (Frankfurter, J., dissenting).

24. Brisman, *supra* note 20, at 468–471.

25. "[A]lthough hard statistics would be difficult to compile, it has been estimated that five to ten percent of people on death row have a 'serious mental illness.'" Lauren E. Perry, "Hiding Behind Precedent: Why *Panetti v. Quarterman* Will Create Confusion for Incompetent Death Row Inmates," 86 *North Carolina Law Review* 1068, 1075 (2008), *quoting* ACLU, "Mental Illness and the Death Penalty in the United States" (Jan. 31, 2005), www.aclu.org/capital/mentalillness/10617pub20050131.html. The quoted ACLU report apparently has been reissued and updated. *See* ACLU, "Mental Illness and the Death Penalty" (May 5, 2009), at p. 1, retrieved August 8, 2013 from www.aclu.org/files/pdfs/capital/mental_illness_may2009.pdf. *See also* Hannah Robertson Miller, "'A Meaningless Ritual': How the Lack of a Postconviction Competency Standard Deprives the Mentally Ill of Effective Habeas Review in Texas," 87 *Texas Law Review* 267, 270–272 (2008) ("Prisons and jails have become the largest providers of psychiatric services in the United States, and the proportion of prisoners suffering from major mental disorders has climbed to five times that of the general population. Today, there are a greater number of severely mentally ill persons confined in prisons and jails than treated in all mental-health facilities nationwide. Estimates suggest that around 64% of prison inmates reported mental-health problems in 2006, and more than 300,000 American prisoners are in need of intensive psychiatric services. . . . Even those who enter prison with no prior history of psychiatric disorders may experience the onset of mental illness due to the trauma of incarceration. Nowhere is this phenomenon more pronounced than on America's death rows. . . . It has been estimated that half of all death row inhabitants in the United States are suffering from serious psychiatric disorders.") (footnotes omitted).

26. *Ex parte Thomas,* 2009 WL 693606, at p. 1 (Tex. Crim. App. 2009) (Cochran, J., concurring in denial of application for writ of habeas corpus).

27. *Id.*

28. *Id.,* at 2 n. 6.

29. *Id.,* at 2.

30. *Id.*

31. *Id.,* at 3.

32. *Id.*

33. Brandi Grissom, "Andre Thomas: Mental Health, Criminal Justice Collide," *Texas Tribune* (Feb. 20, 2013), retrieved August 9, 2013 from www.texastribune.org/2013/02/20/andre-thomas-mental-health-and-criminal-justice-co/.

34. *Id.*

35. *Ex parte Thomas,* 2009 WL 693606, at p. 6 (Tex. Crim. App. 2009) (Cochran, J., concurring in denial of application for writ of habeas corpus).

36. *Godinez v. Martinez,* 509 U.S. 389, 396 (1993), *quoting Dusky v. United States,* 362 U.S. 402 (1960) (per curiam).

37. Texas Penal Code Annotated § 8.01(a) (Vernon 2012). *See Ruffin v. State,* 270 S.W.3d 586 (Tex. Crim. App. 2008); *Bigby v. State,* 892 S.W.2d 864 (Tex. Crim. App. 1994).
38. Brandi Grissom, "Andre Thomas: Questions of Competence," *Texas Tribune* (Feb. 26, 2013), retrieved August 9, 2013 from www.texastribune.org/2013/02/26/andre-thomas-questions-competency/.
39. *Ford v. Wainwright,* 477 U.S. 399, 403 (1986). *See id.,* 477 U.S. at 401–403.
40. *Id.,* 477 U.S., at 405. *See id.,* 477 U.S., at 403–405.
41. *Id.,* 477 U.S., at 416. *See id.,* 477 U.S., at 413–416.
42. *Id.,* 477 U.S., at 418 (Powell J., concurring in part and concurring in the judgment).
43. Kent S. Miller & Michael L. Radelet, *Executing the Mentally Ill: The Criminal Justice System and the Case of Alvin Ford* 159 (Newbury Park, CA: Sage Publications 1993). *See id.* at 146–160.
44. *Panetti v. Quarterman,* 551 U.S. 930, 936 (2007).
45. Grissom, *supra* note 38.
46. Thurman W. Arnold, *The Symbols of Government* 10–11 (New Haven, CT: Yale University Press 1935), *quoted in* Joseph Goldstein, Alan M. Dershowitz & Richard D. Schwartz, *Criminal Law: Theory and Process* 351 (New York: The Free Press 1974). *See also* James R. Acker & Charles S. Lanier, "Unfit to Live, Unfit to Die: Incompetency for Execution Under Modern Death Penalty Legislation," 33 *Criminal Law Bulletin* 107 (1997).
47. *See, e.g.,* Kristen Wenstrup Crosby, "*State v. Perry*: Louisiana's Cure-to-Kill Scheme Forces Death-Row Inmates to Choose Between a Life Sentence of Untreated Insanity and Execution," 77 *Minnesota Law Review* 1193 (1993); Nancy S. Horton, "Restoration of Competency for Execution: *Furioso Solo Furore Punitur,*" 44 *Southwestern Law Journal* 1191, 1214 (1990).
48. *See, e.g.,* Michaela P. Sewall, "Pushing Execution Over the Constitutional Line: Forcible Medication of Condemned Inmates and the Eighth and Fourteenth Amendments," 51 *Boston College Law Review* 1279 (2010); Kursten B. Hensl, "Restored to Health to Be Put to Death: Reconciling the Legal and Ethical Dilemmas of Medicating to Execute in *Singleton v. Norris,*" 49 *Villanova Law Review* 291 (2004); Charles Patrick Ewing, "'Above All, Do No Harm': The Role of Health and Mental Health Professionals in the Capital Punishment Process," in James R. Acker, Robert M. Bohm & Charles S. Lanier (eds.), *America's Experiment With Capital Punishment: Reflections on the Past, Present, and Future of the Ultimate Penal Sanction* 597, 605–607 (Durham, NC: Carolina Academic Press, 2d ed. 2003).
49. Acker & Lanier, *supra* note 46, at 142.
50. *Perry v. Louisiana,* 498 U.S. 38 (1990), vacating lower court judgment and remanding for reconsideration in light of *Washington v. Harper,* 494 U.S. 210 (1990).
51. *State v. Perry,* 610 So.2d 746, 747–748 (La. 1992).
52. *Singleton v. Norris,* 319 F.3d 1018 (8th Cir.) (en banc), *cert. denied,* 540 U.S. 832 (2003).
53. *Id.*
54. *Id.,* 319 F.3d, at 1030 (Heaney, J., dissenting).
55. *See* Kathleen Dean Moore, *Pardons: Justice, Mercy, and the Public Interest* 4–5 (New York: Oxford University Press 1989).
56. *See* Michael Heise, "Mercy by the Numbers: An Empirical Analysis of Clemency and Its Structure," 89 *Virginia Law Review* 239, 254–259 (2003); James R. Acker & Charles S. Lanier, "May God—or the Governor—Have Mercy: Executive Clemency and Executions in Modern Death-Penalty Systems," 36 *Criminal Law Bulletin* 200, 216–220 (2000).
57. *Ohio Adult Parole Authority v. Woodard,* 523 U.S. 272, 289 (1998) (O'Connor, J., concurring in part and concurring in the judgment).
58. *See* James R. Acker, Talia Harmon & Craig Rivera, "Merciful Justice: Lessons From 50 Years of New York Death Penalty Commutations," 35 *Criminal Justice Review* 183, 185–186 (2010).
59. *Ex parte Garland,* 71 U.S. (4 Wall.) 333, 380 (1866).

60. *See, e.g.,* Paul W. Cobb, Jr., "Reviving Mercy in the Structure of Capital Punishment," 99 *Yale Law Journal* 389 (1989).

61. *See* Dan Markel, "Against Mercy," 88 *Minnesota Law Review* 1421 (2004); Bruce Ledewitz & Scott Staples, "The Role of Executive Clemency in Modern Death Penalty Cases," 27 *University of Richmond Law Review* 227, 234–236 (1993).

62. *Herrera v. Collins,* 506 U.S. 390, 415 (1993).

63. *See* Molly Clayton, "Forgiving the Unforgivable: Reinvigorating the Use of Executive Clemency in Capital Cases," 54 *Boston College Law Review* 751 (2013); Daniel T. Kobil, "The Evolving Role of Clemency in Capital Cases," in James R. Acker, Robert M. Bohm & Charles S. Lanier (eds.), *America's Experiment With Capital Punishment: Reflections on the Past, Present, and Future of the Ultimate Penal Sanction* 673 (Durham, NC: Carolina Academic Press, 2d ed. 2003).

64. *Ohio Adult Parole Authority v. Woodard,* 523 U.S. 272 (1998). *See* Daniel T. Kobil, "Compelling Mercy: Judicial Review and the Clemency Power," 9 *University of St. Thomas Law Journal* 698 (2012).

65. *See* Elizabeth R. Jungman, "Beyond All Doubt," 91 *Georgetown Law Journal* 1065, 1079–80 (2003); Alyson Dinsmore, "Clemency in Capital Cases: The Need to Ensure Meaningful Review," 49 *UCLA Law Review* 1825 (2002).

66. *Gregg v. Georgia,* 428 U.S. 153, 199 n. 50 (1976) (opinion of Stewart, Powell, and Stevens, JJ.).

67. Acker & Lanier, *supra* note 56, at 211–212.

68. Talia Roitberg Harmon, James R. Acker & Craig Rivera, "The Power to Be Lenient: Examining New York Governors' Capital Case Clemency Decisions," 27 *Justice Quarterly* 742, 749 (2010). Governor Nelson Rockefeller commuted the sentences of 16 additional offenders on death row after New York's last execution occurred in 1963. *Id.*

69. Acker & Lanier, *supra* note 56, at 213.

70. Mary-Beth Moylan & Linda E. Carter, "Clemency in California Capital Cases," 14 *Berkeley Journal of Criminal Law* 37, 45–45 (2009).

71. Acker & Lanier, *supra* note 56, at 212–213.

72. Death Penalty Information Center, "Clemency," retrieved August 10, 2013 from www.deathpenaltyinfo.org/clemency.

73. *See* Acker, Harmon & Rivera, *supra* note 58, at 186–187.

74. Death Penalty Information Center, "Execution List 2013," retrieved August 12, 2013 from www.deathpenaltyinfo.org/execution-list-2013.

75. Death Penalty Information Center, "Clemency," retrieved August 12, 2013 from www.deathpenaltyinfo.org/clemency. *See* Michael L. Radelet & Barbara A. Zsembik, "Executive Clemency in Post-*Furman* Capital Cases," 27 *University of Richmond Law Review* 289, 292–293 (1993) (differentiating between clemency decisions based on "judicial expediency" and "humanitarian reasons" in post-*Furman* capital cases).

76. *See* Stephen F. Smith, "The Supreme Court and the Politics of Death," 94 *Virginia Law Review* 283, 317–327 (2008); Cathleen Burnett, "The Failed Failsafe: The Politics of Executive Clemency," 8 *Texas Journal on Civil Liberties and Civil Rights,* 191 (2003); Acker & Lanier, *supra* note 56, at 210–211 & nn. 53 & 55.

77. *See* Acker, Harmon & Rivera, *supra* note 58; Harmon, Acker & Rivera, *supra* note 68.

78. Stephen B. Bright, "The Politics of Capital Punishment: The Sacrifice of Fairness for Executions," in James R. Acker, Robert M. Bohm & Charles S. Lanier (eds.), *America's Experiment With Capital Punishment: Reflections on the Past, Present, and Future of the Ultimate Penal Sanction* 127, 130 (Durham, NC: Carolina Academic Press, 2d ed. 2003); Acker & Lanier, *supra* note 56, at 200–201.

79. *Quoted in* Cathleen Burnett, *Justice Denied: Clemency Appeals in Death Penalty Cases* 174 (Boston: Northeastern University Press 2002).

80. Death Penalty Information Center, "Executions in the United States, Searchable Execution Database, Missouri, 1999," retrieved August 11, 2013 from www.deathpenaltyinfo.org/views-executions?exec_name_1=&exec_year=1999&sex=All&state=MO&sex_1=All&federal=All&foreigner=All&juvenile=All&volunteer=All. *See* Acker & Lanier, *supra* note 56, at 201.

81. *Petition for Executive Clemency on behalf of Stanley Tookie Williams* (Nov. 8, 2005). *See also People v. Williams*, 751 P.2d 901 (Cal. 1988); Adam Liptak, "After 24 Years on Death Row, Clemency Is Killer's Final Appeal," *New York Times* (Dec. 2, 2005), retrieved August 11, 2013 from www.nytimes.com/2005/12/02/national/02prison.html.

82. *Petition for Executive Clemency on behalf of Stanley Tookie Williams* 11 (Nov. 8, 2005).

83. *The Federalist* No. 74, at 447–448 (Alexander Hamilton) (Clinton Rossiter ed. 1961).

84. Governor Arnold Schwarzenegger, *Statement of Decision: Request for Clemency by Stanley Williams* (Dec. 12, 2005), retrieved August 11, 2013 from http://graphics8.nytimes.com/packages/pdf/national/Williams_Clemency_Decision.pdf.

85. Sarah Kershaw, "Stanley Tookie Williams, Crips Gang Co-Founder, Is Executed," *New York Times* (Dec. 13, 2005), retrieved August 11, 2013 from www.nytimes.com/2005/12/13/national/13cnd-tookie.html?pagewanted=all.

86. *See* Anthony F. Granucci, "'Nor Cruel and Unusual Punishments Inflicted': The Original Meaning," 57 *California Law Review* 839, 855–856 (1969).

87. *Wilkerson v. Utah*, 99 U.S. 130, 135–136 (1879).

88. *Id.*, 99 U.S., at 135.

89. *See* Austin Sarat, Aubrey Jones, Madeline Sprung-Keyser, Katherine Blumstein, Heather Richard & Robert Weaver, "Gruesome Spectacles: The Cultural Reception of Botched Executions in America," 1 *British Journal of American Legal Studies* 1 (2012); David T. Johnson, "Japan's Secretive Death Penalty Policy: Contours, Origins, Justifications, and Meanings," 7 *Asian-Pacific Law and Policy Journal* 62, & n. 178 (2006) ("Between 1622 and 2002, at least 170 legal hangings were 'botched' in the United States. . . ."); Pamela S. Nagy, "Hang by the Neck Until Dead: The Resurgence of Cruel and Unusual Punishment in the 1990s," 26 *Pacific Law Journal* 85, 87–88 (1994).

90. *In re Kemmler*, 136 U.S. 436, 444 (1890), *quoting* the "annual message of the governor of the state of New York, transmitted to the legislature January 6, 1885. . . ."

91. *Id.*, 136 U.S., at 444.

92. *See* Deborah W. Denno, "Is Electrocution an Unconstitutional Method of Execution? The Engineering of Death Over the Century," 35 *William and Mary Law Review* 551, 567 n. 87 (1994).

93. *Id.*, at 566–607. *See also* Mark Essig, *Edison & The Electric Chair: A Story of Light and Death* (New York: Walker & Co. 2003); Richard Moran, *Executioner's Current: Thomas Edison, George Westinghouse, and the Invention of the Electric Chair* (New York: Alfred A. Knopf 2002).

94. James R. Acker, "New York's Proposed Death Penalty Legislation: Constitutional and Policy Perspectives," 54 *Albany Law Review* 515, 517 n. 12 (1990).

95. *See* Essig, *supra* note 93, at 163–165; Moran, *supra* note 93, at 119–122.

96. *Robinson v. California*, 370 U.S. 660 (1962).

97. N.Y. Code Crim. Proc. § 505 (1888), *quoted in In re Kemmler*, 136 U.S. 436, 444 (1890).

98. *In re Kemmler*, 136 U.S. 436, 446 (1890).

99. *Id.*, 136 U.S., at 447.

100. Essig, *supra* note 93, at 253. *See also* Denno, *supra* note 92, at 600–601; Moran, *supra* note 93, at xix–xx.

101. Denno, *supra* note 92, at 603. *See also* Essig, *supra* note 93, at 254.

102. Moran, *supra* note 93, at xx.

103. Denno, *supra* note 92, at 603–604.

104. *See* Arthur S. Miller & Jeffrey H. Bowman, *Death by Installments: The Ordeal of Willie Francis* 1–9 (New York: Greenwood Press 1988).

105. *Louisiana ex rel. Francis v. Resweber,* 329 U.S. 459, 480 n. 2 (1947) (Burton, J., dissenting) (*quoting* affidavit of official witness Ignace Doucet).

106. *Id.,* 329 U.S., at 464.

107. *Id.,* 329 U.S., at 470 (Frankfurter, J., concurring in the judgment).

108. *Id.,* 329 U.S., at 474 (Burton, J., dissenting).

109. Miller & Bowman, *supra* note 104, at 134.

110. *Id.,* at 140–141.

111. *Dawson v. State,* 554 S.E.2d 137 (Ga. 2001).

112. *State v. Mata,* 745 N.W.2d 229 (Neb. 2008).

113. William J. Bowers, *Legal Homicide: Death as Punishment in America, 1864–1982,* 12–13 (Boston: Northeastern University Press 1984).

114. Hugo Adam Bedau (ed.), *The Death Penalty in America* 16 (New York: Oxford University Press, 3d ed. 1982); Jonathan S. Abernethy, "The Methodology of Death: Reexamining the Deterrence Rationale," 27 *Columbia Human Rights Law Review* 379, 403–404 (1996).

115. Allen Huang, "Hanging, Cyanide Gas, and the Evolving Standards of Decency: The Ninth Circuit's Misapplication of the Cruel and Unusual Clause of the Eighth Amendment," 74 *Oregon Law Review* 995, 1004–05 (1995).

116. *Gray v. Lucas,* 463 U.S. 1237 (1983) (Brennan, J., dissenting from denial of certiorari).

117. *Fierro v. Gomez,* 77 F.3d 301 (9th Cir. 1996).

118. *Gomez v. Fierro,* 519 U.S. 918 (1996).

119. Cal. Penal Code § 3604 (b) (1996).

120. Death Penalty Information Center, "Lethal Injection," retrieved August 13, 2013 from www.deathpenaltyinfo.org/lethal-injection-moratorium-executions-ends-after-supreme-court-decision.

121. Acker & Lanier, *supra* note 56, at 230.

122. Franklin E. Zimring & Gordon Hawkins, *Capital Punishment and the American Agenda* 110 (New York: Cambridge University Press 1986), *quoting* Schwarzschild, "Homicide by Injection," *New York Times* A15 (Dec. 23, 1982).

123. Eric Berger, "Lethal Injection and the Problem of Constitutional Remedies," 27 *Yale Law and Policy Review* 259, 298 (2009).

124. *See, e.g.,* Death Penalty Information Center, "Lethal Injection," *supra* note 120; Deborah W. Denno, "The Future of Execution Methods," in Charles S. Lanier, William J. Bowers & James R. Acker (eds.), *The Future of America's Death Penalty: An Agenda for the Next Generation of Capital Punishment Research* 483 (Durham, NC: Carolina Academic Press 2009); Richard C. Dieter, "Methods of Execution and Their Effect on the Use of the Death Penalty in the United States," 35 *Fordham Urban Law Journal* 789 (2008); Deborah W. Denno, "The Lethal Injection Quandary: How Medicine Has Dismantled the Death Penalty," 76 *Fordham Law Review* 49 (2007).

125. *See, e.g., Morales v. Tilton,* 465 F. Supp.2d 972 (N.D. Cal. 2006); Denno, *supra* note 124; Ellen Kreitzberg & David Richter, "But Can It Be Fixed? A Look at Constitutional Challenges to Lethal Injection Executions," 47 *Santa Clara Law Review* 445 (2007); Jason D. Hughes, "The Tri-Chemical Cocktail: Serene Brutality," 72 *Albany Law Review* 527 (2009); Matthew E. Feinberg, "The Crime, the Case, the Killer Cocktail: Why Maryland's Capital Punishment Procedure Constitutes Cruel and Unusual Punishment," 37 *University of Baltimore Law Review* 79, 104–105 (2007).

126. Death Penalty Information Center, "State by State Lethal Injection," retrieved August 14, 2013 from www.deathpenaltyinfo.org/state-lethal-injection. *See also* Elliot Garvey, "A Needle in the Haystack: Finding a Solution to Ohio's Lethal Injection Problems," 38 *Capital University Law Review* 609 (2010).

127. *Id. See also* John D. Bessler, "Tinkering Around the Edges: The Supreme Court's Death Penalty Jurisprudence," 49 *American Criminal Law Review* 1913, 1917 n. 42 (2012).

128. Albert Camus, "Reflections on the Guillotine," in *Resistance, Rebellion, and Death* 131–132 (New York: Modern Library 1960).

129. *Baze v. Rees,* 553 U.S. 35, 71 (2009) (Stevens, J., concurring in the judgment).

130. *Id.,* 553 U.S., at 86, *quoting Furman v. Georgia,* 408 U.S. 238, 312 (1972) (White, J., concurring in the judgment).

Bibliography

Books

Acker, James R. (2008) *Scottsboro and Its Legacy: The Cases That Challenged American Legal and Social Justice* (Westport, CT: Praeger)

American Association on Mental Retardation (1992) *Mental Retardation: Definition, Classification, and Systems of Supports* (Washington, DC: Author, 9th ed.)

American Law Institute (1962) *Model Penal Code* (Proposed Official Draft)

American Psychiatric Association (2000) *Diagnostic and Statistical Manual of Mental Disorders* (Washington, DC: Author, 4th ed.)

Arnold, Thurman W. (1935) *The Symbols of Government* (New Haven, CT: Yale University Press)

Baldus, David C., George G. Woodworth & Charles S. Pulaski, Jr. (1990) *Equal Justice and the Death Penalty: A Legal and Empirical Analysis* (Boston: Northeastern University Press)

Banner, Stuart (2002) *The Death Penalty: An American History* (Cambridge, MA: Harvard University Press)

Baumgartner, Frank, Suzanna L. De Boef & Amber E. Boydstun (2008) *The Decline of the Death Penalty and the Discovery of Innocence* (New York: Cambridge University Press)

Beccaria, Cesare (1963/1764) *On Crimes and Punishments* (Henry Paolucci, trans., Indianapolis: Bobbs-Merrill Co.)

Bedau, Hugo Adam (1982) (ed.), *The Death Penalty in America* (New York: Oxford University Press, 3d ed.)

Bentham, Jeremy (1789/1948) *An Introduction to the Principles of Morals and Legislation* (New York: Hafner Publishing Co.)

Berns, Walter (1991) *For Capital Punishment: Crime and the Morality of the Death Penalty* (Lanham, MD: University Press of America)

Bessler, John D. (2012) *Cruel & Unusual: The American Death Penalty and the Founders' Eighth Amendment* (Boston: Northeastern University Press)

Black, Charles L., Jr. (1974) *Capital Punishment: The Inevitability of Caprice and Mistake* (New York: W.W. Norton & Co.)

Bowers, William J. (1984) *Legal Homicide: Death as Punishment in America, 1864–1982* (Boston: Northeastern University Press)

Burnett, Cathleen (2002) *Justice Denied: Clemency Appeals in Death Penalty Cases* (Boston: Northeastern University Press)

Carter, Dan T. (1979) *Scottsboro: A Tragedy of the American South* (Baton Rouge, LA: Louisiana State University Press, rev. ed.)

Cushing, Renny R. & Susannah Sheffer (2002) *Dignity Denied: The Experience of Murder Victims' Family Members Who Oppose the Death Penalty* (Cambridge, MA: Murder Victims' Families for Reconciliation)

Dershowitz, Alan M. (1983) *The Best Defense* (New York: Vintage Books)

Durkheim, Emile (1984/1893) *The Division of Labor in Society* (W.D. Hall trans., New York: Free Press)

Essig, Mark (2003) *Edison & The Electric Chair: A Story of Light and Death* (New York: Walker & Co.)

Exodus 21:23–24

The Federalist No. 74 (Alexander Hamilton) (Clinton Rossiter ed. 1961)

Garland, David (2010) *Peculiar Institution: America's Death Penalty in an Age of Abolition* (Cambridge, MA: Belknap Press of Harvard University Press)

Garrett, Brandon L. (2011) *Convicting the Innocent: Where Criminal Prosecutions Go Wrong* (Cambridge, MA: Harvard University Press)

Gibbs, Jack P. (1975) *Crime, Punishment, and Deterrence* 80 (New York: Elsevier Scientific Publishing Co.)

Goldstein, Joseph, Alan M. Dershowitz & Richard D. Schwartz (1974) *Criminal Law: Theory and Process* (New York: The Free Press)

Goodman, James (1994) *Stories of Scottsboro* (New York: Vintage Books)

Gross, Samuel R. & Robert Mauro (1989) *Death & Discrimination: Racial Disparities in Capital Sentencing* (Boston: Northeastern University Press)

Gunther, Gerald (1994) *Learned Hand: The Man and the Judge* (New York: Alfred A. Knopf)

Hamilton, Luther, ed. (1854) *Memoirs, Speeches, and Writings of Robert Rantoul, Jr.* (Boston: John P. Jewett)

Heide, Kathleen M. (1999) *Young Killers: The Challenge of Juvenile Homicide* (Thousand Oaks, CA: Sage Publications)

Hirsch, Adam J. (1992) *The Rise of the Penitentiary* (New Haven, CT: Yale University Press)

Jeffries, John C., Jr. (1994) *Justice Lewis F. Powell, Jr.* (New York: Charles Scribner's Sons)

Junkin, Tim (2004) *Bloodsworth: The True Story of the First Death Row Inmate Exonerated by DNA* (Chapel Hill, NC: Algonquin Books of Chapel Hill)

Kennedy, Randall (1997) *Race, Crime, and the Law* (New York: Vintage Books)

King, Rachel (2003) *Don't Kill in Our Names: Families of Murder Victims Speak Out Against the Death Penalty* (Newark, NJ: Rutgers University Press)

Madeira, Jody Lynee (2012) *Killing McVeigh: The Death Penalty and the Myth of Closure* (New York: New York University Press)

Mailer, Norman (1979) *The Executioner's Song* (Boston: Little, Brown & Company)

Mandery, Evan J. (2013) *A Wild Justice: The Death and Resurrection of Capital Punishment in America* (New York: W.W. Norton & Co.)

McFarland, Gerald M. (1990) *The Counterfeit Man: The True Story of the Boorn-Colvin Murder* (Amherst, MA: University of Massachusetts Press)

Meltsner, Michael (1973) *Cruel and Unusual: The Supreme Court and Capital Punishment* (New York: Random House)

Miller, Arthur S. & Jeffrey H. Bowman (1988) *Death by Installments: The Ordeal of Willie Francis* (New York: Greenwood Press)

Miller, Kent S. & Michael L. Radelet (1993) *Executing the Mentally Ill: The Criminal Justice System and the Case of Alvin Ford* (Newbury Park, CA: Sage Publications)

Moore, Kathleen Dean (1989) *Pardons: Justice, Mercy, and the Public Interest* (New York: Oxford University Press)

Moran, Richard (2002) *Executioner's Current: Thomas Edison, George Westinghouse, and the Invention of the Electric Chair* (New York: Alfred A. Knopf)

Nozick, Robert (1981) *Philosophical Explanations* (Cambridge, MA: Harvard University Press)

Redmond, L.M. (1989) *Surviving: When Someone You Love Was Murdered* (Clearwater, FL: Psychological Consultation and Educational Services, Inc.).

Rothman, David J. (1971) *The Discovery of the Asylum: Social Order and Disorder in the New Republic* (Boston: Little, Brown and Company)

Sarat, Austin (2001) *When the State Kills: Capital Punishment and the American Condition* (Princeton, NJ: Princeton University Press)

Sheffer, Susannah (2013) *Fighting for Their Lives: Inside the Experience of Capital Defense Attorneys* (Nashville: Vanderbilt University Press)

Stephen, Sir James Fitzjames (1863) *A General View of the Criminal Law of England* (London: Macmillan)

Streib, Victor L. (1987) *Death Penalty for Juveniles* (Bloomington, IN: Indiana University Press)

United States Bureau of Justice (1978) *Sourcebook of Criminal Justice Statistics—1977* (Washington, D.C.: U.S. Government Printing Office)

United States Dept. of Justice (2000) *Survey of the Federal Death Penalty System (1988–2000)* (Washington, D.C.: U.S. Government Printing Office)

Vandiver, Margaret (2006) *Lethal Punishment: Lynchings and Legal Executions in the South* (New Brunswick, NJ: Rutgers University Press)

von Hirsch, Andrew (1976) *Doing Justice: The Choice of Punishments* (New York: Hill and Wang)

Walker, Thomas G. (2009) *Eligible for Execution: The Story of the Daryl Atkins Case* (Washington, DC: CQ Press)

Zimring, Franklin E. (2003) *The Contradictions of American Capital Punishment* (New York: Oxford University Press)

Zimring, Franklin E. & Gordon Hawkins (1986) *Capital Punishment and the American Agenda* (New York: Cambridge University Press)

Articles and Book Chapters

Aarons, Dwight (1998) "Can Inordinate Delay Between a Death Sentence and Execution Constitute Cruel and Unusual Punishment?," 29 *Seton Hall Law Review* 147

Abernethy, Jonathan S. (1996) "The Methodology of Death: Reexamining the Deterrence Rationale," 27 *Columbia Human Rights Law Review* 379

Acker, James R. (1987) "Social Sciences and the Criminal Law: Capital Punishment by the Numbers—An Analysis of *McCleskey v. Kemp*," 23 *Criminal Law Bulletin* 454

Acker, James R. (1990) "New York's Proposed Death Penalty Legislation: Constitutional and Policy Perspectives," 54 *Albany Law Review* 515

Acker, James R. (1993) "A Different Agenda: The Supreme Court, Empirical Research Evidence, and Capital Punishment Decisions, 1986–1989," 27 *Law & Society Review* 65

Acker, James R. (2003) "The Death Penalty: An American History," 6 *Contemporary Justice Review* 169

Acker, James R. (2008) "Be Careful What You Ask For: Lessons From New York's Recent Experiment With Capital Punishment," 32 *Vermont Law Review* 683

Acker, James R. (2008) "Scrutinizing the Death Penalty: State Death Penalty Study Commissions and Their Recommendations," in Robert M. Bohm (ed.), *The Death Penalty Today* 29 (Boca Raton, FL: CRC Press)

Acker, James R. (2009) "Actual Innocence: Is Death Different?," 27 *Behavioral Sciences and the Law* 297

Acker, James R. (2009) "The Flow and Ebb of American Capital Punishment," in Marvin D. Krohn, Alan J. Lizotte & Gina Penly Hall (eds.), *Handbook on Crime and Deviance* 297 (New York: Springer)

Acker, James R. (2013) "The Myth of Closure and Capital Punishment," in Robert M. Bohm & Jeffery T. Walker (eds.), *Demystifying Crime and Criminal Justice* 254 (New York: Oxford University Press, 2d ed.)

Acker, James R. (2013) "Your Money and Your Life: How Cost Nearly Killed California's Death Penalty," 24 *Correctional Law Reporter* 69

Acker, James R. & Rose Bellandi (2012) "Firmament or Folly? Protecting the Innocent, Promoting Capital Punishment, and the Paradoxes of Reconciliation," 29 *Justice Quarterly* 287

Acker, James R. & Catherine L. Bonventre (2010) "Protecting the Innocent in New York: Moving Beyond Changing Only Their Names," 73 *Albany Law Review* 1245

Acker, James R., Talia Harmon & Craig Rivera (2010) "Merciful Justice: Lessons From 50 Years of New York Death Penalty Commutations," 35 *Criminal Justice Review* 183

Acker, James R. & C.S. Lanier (1993) "Capital Murder From Benefit of Clergy to Bifurcated Trials: Narrowing the Class of Offenses Punishable by Death," 29 *Criminal Law Bulletin* 291

Acker, James R. & C.S. Lanier (1994) "'Parsing This Lexicon of Death': Aggravating Factors in Capital Sentencing Statutes," 30 *Criminal Law Bulletin* 107

Acker, James R. & Charles S. Lanier (1995) "Matters of Life or Death: The Sentencing Provisions in Capital Punishment Statutes," 31 *Criminal Law Bulletin* 19

Acker, James R. & Charles S. Lanier (1995) "Statutory Measures for More Effective Appellate Review of Capital Cases," 31 *Criminal Law Bulletin* 211

Acker, James R. & Charles S. Lanier (1996) "Law, Discretion, and the Capital Jury: Death Penalty Statutes and Proposals for Reform," 32 *Criminal Law Bulletin* 134

Acker, James R. & Charles S. Lanier (1997) "Unfit to Live, Unfit to Die: Incompetency for Execution Under Modern Death Penalty Legislation," 33 *Criminal Law Bulletin* 107

Acker, James R. & Charles S. Lanier (2000) "May God—or the Governor—Have Mercy: Executive Clemency and Executions in Modern Death-Penalty Systems," 36 *Criminal Law Bulletin* 200

Acker, James R. & Charles S. Lanier (2003) "Beyond Human Ability? The Rise and Fall of Death Penalty Legislation," in James R. Acker, Robert M. Bohm & Charles S. Lanier (eds.), *America's Experiment With Capital Punishment: Reflections on the Past, Present, and Future of the Ultimate Penal Sanction* 85 (Durham, NC: Carolina Academic Press, 2d ed.)

Adger, Jennifer & Christopher Weiss (2011) "Why Place Matters: Exploring County-Level Variations in Death Sentencing in Alabama," 2011 *Michigan State Law Review* 659

Alarcon, Arthur L. & Paula M. Mitchell (2011) "Executing the Will of the Voters?: A Roadmap to Mend or End the California Legislature's Multi-Billion Dollar Death Penalty Debacle," 44 *Loyola of Los Angeles Law Review* S41

Alschuler, Albert W. (2009) "Plea Bargaining and the Death Penalty," 58 *DePaul Law Review* 671

"American Bar Association Guidelines for the Appointment and Performance of Counsel in Death Penalty Cases" (2003) 31 *Hofstra Law Review* 913

Amick-McMullan, A., D.G. Kilpatrick & H.S. Resnick (1991) "Homicide as a Risk Factor for PTSD Among Surviving Family Members," 15 *Behavior Modification* 545

Amsterdam, Anthony (1982) "Capital Punishment," in Hugo Adam Bedau, ed., *The Death Penalty in America* 346 (New York: Oxford University Press, 3d ed.)

Arkin, Mark M. (1992) "Rethinking the Constitutional Right to a Criminal Appeal," 39 *UCLA Law Review* 503

Armour, Marilyn Peterson & Mark S. Umbreit (2012) "Assessing the Impact of the Ultimate Penal Sanction on Homicide Survivors: A Two State Comparison," 96 *Marquette Law Review* 1

Babcock, Barbara Allen (1975) "Voir Dire: Preserving 'Its Wonderful Power,'" 27 *Stanford Law Review* 545

Bailey, William C. (1998) "Deterrence, Brutalization, and the Death Penalty: Another Examination of Oklahoma's Return to Capital Punishment," 36 *Criminology* 711

Baldus, David C., Catherine M. Grosso, George Woodworth & Richard Newell (2011) "Racial Discrimination in the Administration of the Death Penalty: The Experience of the United States Armed Forces (1984–2005)," 101 *Journal of Criminal Law & Criminology* 1227

Baldus, David C., Charles A. Pulaski, Jr. & George Woodworth (1986) "Arbitrariness and Discrimination in the Administration of the Death Penalty: A Challenge to State Supreme Courts," 15 *Stetson Law Review* 133

Baldus, David C. & George Woodworth (2003) "Race Discrimination and the Death Penalty: An Empirical and Legal Overview," in James R. Acker, Robert M. Bohm & Charles S. Lanier (eds.), *America's Experiment With Capital Punishment: Reflections on the Past, Present, and Future of the Ultimate Penal Sanction* 501 (Durham, NC: Carolina Academic Press, 2d ed.)

Baldus, David C. & George Woodworth (2004) "Race Discrimination and the Legitimacy of Capital Punishment: Reflections on the Interaction of Fact and Perception," 53 *DePaul Law Review* 1411

Baldus, David C., George Woodworth, Catherine M. Grosso & Aaron M. Christ (2002) "Arbitrariness and Discrimination in the Administration of the Death Penalty: A Legal and Empirical Analysis of the Nebraska Experience (1973–1999)," 81 *Nebraska Law Review* 486

Baldus, David C., George Woodworth, David Zuckerman, Neil Alan Weiner & Barbara Broffitt (1998) "Racial Discrimination and the Death Penalty in the Post-*Furman* Era: An Empirical and Legal Overview, With Recent Findings From Philadelphia," 83 *Cornell Law Review* 1638

Baldus, David C., George Woodworth, David Zuckerman, Neil Alan Weiner & Barbara Broffitt (2001) "The Use of Peremptory Challenges in Capital Murder Trials: A Legal and Empirical Analysis," 3 *University of Pennsylvania Journal of Constitutional Law* 3

Bandes, Susan A. (2009) "Victims, 'Closure,' and the Sociology of Emotion," 72 *Law & Contemporary Problems* 1 (Spring)

Barnes, Katherine, David Sloss & Stephen Thaman (2009) "Place Matters (Most): An Empirical Study of Prosecutorial Decision-Making in Death-Eligible Cases," 51 *Arizona Law Review* 305

Bedau, Hugo A. (1967) "Offenses Punishable by Death," in Hugo Adam Bedau (ed.), *The Death Penalty in America* 39 (Garden City, NY: Anchor Books, rev. ed.)

Bedau, Hugo Adam (1983) "Bentham's Utilitarian Critique of the Death Penalty," 74 *Journal of Criminal Law & Criminology* 1033

Bedau, Hugo Adam (1997) "A Reply to van den Haag," in Hugo Adam Bedau (ed.), *The Death Penalty in America: Current Controversies* 457 (New York: Oxford University Press)

Bedau, Hugo Adam & Michael L. Radelet (1987) "Miscarriages of Justice in Potentially Capital Cases," 40 *Stanford Law Review* 21

Bedau, Hugo Adam & Michael L. Radelet (1988) "The Myth of Infallibility: A Reply to Markman and Cassell," 41 *Stanford Law Review* 161

Benson, Daniel H., Hans Hansen & Peter Westfall (2013) "Executing the Innocent," 3 *Alabama Civil Rights & Civil Liberties Law Review* 1 (2013)

Bentele, Ursula (1993) "Race and Capital Punishment in the United States and Africa," 19 *Brooklyn Journal of International Law* 235

Berger, Eric (2009) "Lethal Injection and the Problem of Constitutional Remedies," 27 *Yale Law and Policy Review* 259

Berger, Vada, Nicole Walthou, Angela Dorn, Dan Lindsey, Pamela Thompson & Gretchen von Helms (1989) "Too Much Justice: A Legislative Response to *McCleskey v. Kemp*, 24 *Harvard Civil Rights-Civil Liberties Law Review* 437

Berry, William W. III (2010) "Ending Death by Dangerousness: A Path to the De Facto Abolition of the Death Penalty," 52 *Arizona Law Review* 889

Bessler, John D. (2012) "Tinkering Around the Edges: The Supreme Court's Death Penalty Jurisprudence," 49 *American Criminal Law Review* 1913 (2012)

Bienen, Leigh B. (2010) "Capital Punishment in Illinois in the Aftermath of the Ryan Commutations: Reforms, Economic Realities, and a New Saliency for Issues of Cost," 100 *Journal of Criminal Law & Criminology* 1301

Bilionis, Louis D. (1991) "Moral Appropriateness, Capital Punishment, and the *Lockett* Doctrine," 82 *Journal of Criminal Law & Criminology* 283

Blair, Danya W. (1994) "A Matter of Life and Death: Why Life Without Parole Should Be a Sentencing Option in Texas," 22 *American Journal of Criminal Law* 191

Blank, Stephen (2006) "Killing Time: The Process of Waiving Appeal—The Michael Ross Death Penalty Cases," 14 *Journal of Law & Policy* 735

Blecker, Robert (2003) "Roots," in James R. Acker, Robert M. Bohm & Charles S. Lanier (eds.), *America's Experiment With Capital Punishment: Reflections on the Past, Present, and Future of the Ultimate Penal Sanction* 169 (Durham, NC: Carolina Academic Press, 2d ed.)

Blecker, Robert (2007) "But Did They Listen? The New Jersey Death Penalty Commission's Exercise in Abolitionism: A Reply," 5 *Rutgers Journal of Law & Public Policy* 9

Blecker, Robert (2008) "The Road Not Considered: Revising New Jersey's Death Penalty Statute," 32 *Seton Hall Legislative Journal* 241

Blume, John H. (2005) "Killing the Willing: 'Volunteers,' Suicide and Competency," 103 *Michigan Law Review* 939

Blume, John H., Stephen P. Garvey & Sheri Lynn Johnson (2001) "Future Dangerousness in Capital Cases: Always 'At Issue'," 86 *Cornell Law Review* 397

Blume, John H., Sheri Lynn Johnson & Christopher Seeds (2009) "Mental Retardation and the Death Penalty Five Years After *Atkins*," in Charles S. Lanier, William J. Bowers & James R. Acker (eds.), *The Future of America's Death Penalty: An Agenda for the Next Generation of Capital Punishment Research* 241 (Durham, NC: Carolina Academic Press)

Blume, John H., Sheri Lynn Johnson & A. Brian Threlkeld (2001) "Probing 'Life Qualification' Through Expanded Voir Dire," 29 *Hofstra Law Review* 1209

Blume, John H. & Stacey D. Neumann (2005) "'It's Like Déjà Vu All Over Again': *Williams v. Taylor, Wiggins v. Smith, Rompilla v. Beard* and a (Partial) Return to the Guidelines Approach to Effective Assistance of Counsel," 34 *American Journal of Criminal Law* 127

Bohm, Robert M. (2003) "The Economic Costs of Capital Punishment: Past, Present, and Future," in James R. Acker, Robert M. Bohm & Charles S. Lanier, eds., *America's Experiment With Capital Punishment: Reflections on the Past, Present, and Future of the Ultimate Penal Sanction* 573 (Durham, NC: Carolina Academic Press, 2d ed.)

Bonnie, Richard (1988) "The Dignity of the Condemned," 74 *Virginia Law Review* 1363

Borgmann, Caitlin E. (2009) "Rethinking Judicial Deference to Legislative Fact-Finding," 84 *Indiana Law Journal* 1

Borteck, Daina (2004) "Pleas for DNA Testing: Why Lawmakers Should Amend State Post-Conviction DNA Testing Statutes to Apply to Prisoners Who Pled Guilty," 25 *Cardozo Law Review* 1429

Bowers, William J. (1995) "The Capital Jury Project: Rationale, Design, and Preview of Early Findings," 70 *Indiana Law Journal* 1043

Bowers, William J. (2012) "A Tribute to David Baldus, A Determined and Relentless Champion of Doing Justice," 97 *Iowa Law Review* 1879

Bowers, William J., Benjamin D. Fleury-Steiner & Michael E. Antonio (2003) "The Capital Sentencing Decision: Guided Discretion, Reasoned Moral Judgment, or Legal Fiction," in James R. Acker, Robert M. Bohm & Charles S. Lanier (eds.), *America's Experiment With Capital Punishment: Reflections on the Past, Present, and Future of the Ultimate Penal Sanction* 413 (Durham, NC: Carolina Academic Press, 2d ed.)

Bowers, William J. & Glenn Pierce (1980) "Arbitrariness and Discrimination Under Post-*Furman* Capital Statutes," 26 *Crime & Delinquency* 563

Bowers, William J. & Glenn L. Pierce (1980) "Deterrence or Brutalization: What Is the Effect of Executions?" 26 *Crime & Delinquency* 453

Bowers, William J., Benjamin D. Steiner & Marla Sandys (2001) "Death Sentencing in Black and White: An Empirical Analysis of the Role of Jurors' Race and Jury Racial Composition," 3 *University of Pennsylvania Journal of Constitutional Law* 171

Bright, Stephen B. (1994) "Counsel for the Poor: The Death Sentence Not for the Worst Crime But for the Worst Lawyer," 103 *Yale Law Journal* 1835

Bright, Stephen B. (2003) "The Politics of Capital Punishment: The Sacrifice of Fairness for Executions," in James R. Acker, Robert M. Bohm & Charles S. Lanier (eds.), *America's Experiment With Capital Punishment: Reflections on the Past, Present, and Future of the Ultimate Penal Sanction* 127 (Durham, NC: Carolina Academic Press, 2d ed.)

Brisman, Avi (2009) "'Docile Bodies' or Rebellious Spirits?: Issues of Time and Power in the Waiver and Withdrawal of Death Penalty Appeals," 43 *Valparaiso University Law Review* 459

Broughton, J. Richard (2012) "Capital Prejudice," 43 *University of Memphis Law Review* 135

Burnett, Cathleen (2003) "The Failed Failsafe: The Politics of Executive Clemency," 8 *Texas Journal on Civil Liberties and Civil Rights* 191

Burnside, Fred B. (1999) "Dying to Get Elected: A Challenge to the Jury Override," 1999 *Wisconsin Law Review* 1017

Camus, Albert (1960) "Reflections on the Guillotine," in *Resistance, Rebellion, and Death* 131 (New York: Modern Library)

Carter, Andrew M. (2006) "Age Matters: The Case for a Constitutionalized Infancy Defense," 54 *University of Kansas Law Review* 687

Cassell, Paul (2008) "In Defense of the Death Penalty," 42 *Prosecutor* 10 (Dec.)

Cauthen, James N.G. & Barry Latzer (2008) "Why So Long? Explaining Processing Time in Capital Appeals," 29 *Justice System Journal* 298

Chang, Vivian (2011) "Where Do We Go From Here: Plea Colloquy Warnings and Immigration Consequences Post-*Padilla*," 45 *University of Michigan Journal of Law Reform* 189

Chemerinsky, Erwin (1995) "Eliminating Discrimination in Administering the Death Penalty: The Need for the Racial Justice Act," 35 *Santa Clara Law Review* 519

Clayton, Molly (2013) "Forgiving the Unforgivable: Reinvigorating the Use of Executive Clemency in Capital Cases," 54 *Boston College Law Review* 751

Cobb, Paul W., Jr. (1989) "Reviving Mercy in the Structure of Capital Punishment," 99 *Yale Law Journal* 389

Cochran, John K. & Mitchell B. Chamlin (2000) "Deterrence and Brutalization: The Dual Effects of Executions," 17 *Justice Quarterly* 685

Cochran, John K., Mitchell B. Chamlin & Mark Seith (1994) "Deterrence or Brutalization? An Impact Assessment of Oklahoma's Return to Capital Punishment," 32 *Criminology* 107

Cohen, G. Ben (2012) "*McCleskey's* Omission: The Racial Geography of Retribution," 10 *Ohio State Journal of Criminal Law* 65

Cohen, G. Ben & Robert J. Smith (2010) "The Racial Geography of the Federal Death Penalty," 85 *Washington Law Review* 425

Conk, George W. (2008) "Herald of Change? New Jersey's Repeal of the Death Penalty," 33 *Seton Hall Legislative Journal* 21

Cook, Philip J. (2009) "Potential Savings From Abolition of the Death Penalty in North Carolina," 11 *American Law and Economics Review* 498

Cooper, Patricia (2009) "Competency of Death Row Inmates to Waive the Right to Appeal: A Proposal to Scrutinize the Motivations of Death Row Volunteers and to Consider the Impact of Death Row Syndrome in Determining Competency," 28 *Developments in Mental Health Law* 105

Covey, Russell D. (2008) "Fixed Justice: Reforming Plea Bargaining With Plea-Based Ceilings," 82 *Tulane Law Review* 1237

Covey, Russell Dean (2004) "Exorcizing Wechsler's Ghost: The Influence of the Model Penal Code on Death Penalty Sentencing Jurisprudence," 31 *Hastings Constitutional Law Quarterly* 189

Cowan, Claudia L., William C. Thompson & Phoebe C. Ellsworth (1984) "The Effects of Death Qualification on Jurors' Predisposition to Convict and on the Quality of Deliberation," 8 *Law and Human Behavior* 53

Coyle, Marcia, Fred Strasser & Marianne Lavelle (1990) "Fatal Defense: Trial and Error in the Nation's Death Belt," *National Law Journal* 30 (June 11)

Crocker, Phyllis L. (1997) "Concepts of Culpability and Deathworthiness: Differentiating Between Guilt and Punishment in Death Penalty Cases," 66 *Fordham Law Review* 21

Crosby, Kristen Wenstrup (1993) "*State v. Perry*: Louisiana's Cure-to-Kill Scheme Forces Death-Row Inmates to Choose Between a Life Sentence of Untreated Insanity and Execution," 77 *Minnesota Law Review* 1193

Cunningham, Mark Douglas & Jon R. Sorensen (2007) "Capital Offenders in Texas Prisons: Rates, Correlates, and an Actuarial Analysis of Violent Misconduct," 31 *Law & Human Behavior* 553

Cunningham, Mark D., Jon R. Sorensen & Thomas J. Reidy (2009) "Capital Jury Decision-Making: The Limitations of Predictions of Future Violence," 15 *Psychology, Public Policy, and Law* 223

Cutler, Christopher Q. (2007) "Friendly Habeas Reform—Reconsidering a District Court's Threshold Role in the Appellate Habeas Process," 43 *Willamette Law Review* 281

Darehshori, Sara, Jeffrey L. Kirchmeier, Colleen Quinn Brady & Evan Mandery (2006) "Empire State Injustice: Based Upon a Decade of New York Information, a Preliminary Evaluation of How New York's Death Penalty System Fails to Meet Standards for Accuracy and Fairness," 4 *Cardozo Public Law, Policy and Ethics Journal* 85

Davis, Angela J. (2012) "Film Review: 'Mississippi Innocence and the Prosecutor's Guilt,'" 25 *Georgetown Journal of Legal Ethics* 689

Deise, Jerome & Raymond Paternoster (2013) "More Than a 'Quick Glimpse of the Life': The Relationship Between Victim Impact Evidence and Death Sentencing," 40 *Hastings Constitutional Law Quarterly* 611

Denno, Deborah W. (1994) "Is Electrocution an Unconstitutional Method of Execution? The Engineering of Death Over the Century," 35 *William and Mary Law Review* 551

Denno, Deborah W. (2007) "The Lethal Injection Quandary: How Medicine Has Dismantled the Death Penalty," 76 *Fordham Law Review* 49

Denno, Deborah W. (2009) "The Future of Execution Methods," in Charles S. Lanier, William J. Bowers & James R. Acker (eds.), *The Future of America's Death Penalty: An Agenda for the Next Generation of Capital Punishment Research* 483 (Durham, NC: Carolina Academic Press)

Dervan, Lucian E. (2012) "Bargained Justice: Plea-Bargaining's Innocence Problem and the *Brady* Safety-Valve," 2012 *Utah Law Review* 51

Dezhbakhsh, Hasham, Paul H. Rubin & Joanna M. Shepherd (2003) "Does Capital Punishment Have a Deterrent Effect? New Evidence From Postmoratorium Panel Data," 5 *American Law and Economics Review* 344

Dezhbakhsh, Hashem & Joanna M. Shepherd (2006) "The Deterrent Effect of Capital Punishment: Evidence From a 'Judicial Experiment,'" 44 *Economic Inquiry* 512

Diamond, Bernard L. (1975) "Murder and the Death Penalty: A Case Report," 45 *American Journal of Orthopsychiatry* 712

Dieter, Richard C. (2008) "Methods of Execution and Their Effect on the Use of the Death Penalty in the United States," 35 *Fordham Urban Law Journal* 789

Dieter, Richard C. (2009) "The Future of Innocence," in Charles S. Lanier, William J. Bowers & James R. Acker, *The Future of America's Death Penalty: An Agenda for the Next Generation of Capital Punishment Research* 225 (Durham, NC: Carolina Academic Press)

Dillehay, Ronald C. & Marla R. Sandys (1996) "Life Under *Wainwright v. Witt*: Juror Dispositions and Death Qualification, 20 *Law and Human Behavior* 147

Dinsmore, Alyson (2002) "Clemency in Capital Cases: The Need to Ensure Meaningful Review," 49 *UCLA Law Review* 1825

Ditchfield, Andrew (2007) "Challenging the Intrastate Disparities in the Application of Capital Punishment Statutes," 95 *Georgetown Law Journal* 801

Donohue, John J. & Justin Wolfers (2006) "Uses and Abuses of Empirical Evidence in the Death Penalty Debate," 58 *Stanford Law Review* 791

Dorin, Dennis D. (1981) "Two Different Worlds: Criminologists, Justices and Racial Discrimination in the Imposition of Capital Punishment in Rape Cases," 72 *Journal of Criminal Law & Criminology* 1667

Dorland, Mitzi & Daniel Krauss (2005) "The Danger of Dangerousness in Capital Sentencing: Exacerbating the Problem of Arbitrary and Capricious Decision-Making," 29 *Law & Psychology Review* 63

Dow, David R. & Eric M. Freedman (2009) "The Effects of AEDPA on Justice," in Charles S. Lanier, William J. Bowers & James R. Acker (eds.), *The Future of America's Death Penalty: An Agenda for the Next Generation of Capital Punishment Research* 261 (Durham, NC: Carolina Academic Press)

Drinan, Cara H. (2013) "Getting Real About *Gideon*: The Next Fifty Years of Enforcing the Right to Counsel," 70 *Washington & Lee Law Review* 1309

Dwyer-Moss, Jessica (2013) "Flawed Forensics and the Death Penalty: Junk Science and Potentially Wrongful Executions," 11 *Seattle Journal for Social Justice* 757

Ehrhard, Susan (2008) "Plea Bargaining and the Death Penalty: An Exploratory Study," 29 *Justice System Journal* 313

Ehrlich, Isaac (1975) "The Deterrent Effect of Capital Punishment: A Question of Life and Death," 65 *American Economic Review* 397

Ellsworth, Phoebe C. (1988) "Unpleasant Facts: The Supreme Court's Response to Empirical Research Evidence on Capital Punishment," in Kenneth C. Haas & James A. Inciardi (eds.), *Challenging Capital Punishment: Legal and Social Science Approaches* 177 (Newbury Park, CA: Sage Publications)

Ellsworth, Phoebe C., Raymond M. Bukaty, Claudia L. Cowan & William C. Thompson (1984) "The Death-Qualified Jury and the Defense of Insanity," 8 *Law and Human Behavior* 81

Entzeroth, Lyn (2011) "The Challenge and Dilemma of Charting a Course to Constitutionally Protect the Severely Mentally Ill Capital Defendant From the Death Penalty," 44 *Akron Law Review* 529

Entzeroth, Lyn (2012) "The End of the Beginning: The Politics of Death and the American Death Penalty Regime in the Twenty-First Century," 90 *Oregon Law Review* 797

Epstein, Jules (2010) "Death-Worthiness and Prosecutorial Discretion in Capital Case Charging," 19 *Temple Political & Civil Rights Law Review* 389

Erlich, Scott E. (1996) "The Jury Override: A Blend of Politics and Death," 45 *American University Law Review* 1432

Ewing, Charles Patrick (2003) "'Above All, Do No Harm': The Role of Health and Mental Health Professionals in the Capital Punishment Process," in James R. Acker, Robert M. Bohm & Charles S. Lanier (eds.), *America's Experiment With Capital Punishment: Reflections on the Past, Present, and Future of the Ultimate Penal Sanction* 597 (Durham, NC: Carolina Academic Press, 2d ed.)

Fagan, Jeffrey (2006) "Death and Deterrence Redux: Science, Law and Causal Reasoning on Capital Punishment," 4 *Ohio State Journal of Criminal Law* 255

Feinberg, Matthew E. (2007) "The Crime, the Case, the Killer Cocktail: Why Maryland's Capital Punishment Procedure Constitutes Cruel and Unusual Punishment," 37 *University of Baltimore Law Review* 79

Findley, Keith A. (2010–2011) "Defining Innocence," 74 *Albany Law Review* 1157

Fisher, Joan M. (2000) "Expedited Review of Capital Post-Conviction Claims: Idaho's Flawed Process," 2 *Journal of Appellate Practice and Procedure* 85

Fitzgerald, Robert & Phoebe C. Ellsworth (1984) "Due Process vs. Crime Control: Death Qualification and Jury Attitudes," 8 *Law and Human Behavior* 31

Freedman, Eric M. (2003) "Federal Habeas Corpus in Capital Cases," in James R. Acker, Robert M. Bohm & Charles S. Lanier (eds.), *America's Experiment With Capital Punishment: Reflections on the Past, Present, and Future of the Ultimate Penal Sanction* 553 (Durham, NC: Carolina Academic Press, 2d ed.)

Gansler, Douglas F. (2009) "A Worthy Compromise? Rethinking Maryland's Death Penalty—No: It Goes Too Far in Restricting Eligibility," *Baltimore Sun* (March 19)

Garey, Margot (1985) "The Cost of Taking a Life: Dollars and Sense of the Death Penalty," 18 *U.C. Davis Law Review* 1221

Garrett, Brandon L. (2008) "Claiming Innocence," 92 *Minnesota Law Review* 1629

Garvey, Elliot (2010) "A Needle in the Haystack: Finding a Solution to Ohio's Lethal Injection Problems," 38 *Capital University Law Review* 609

Gerber, Rudolph J. (2004) "Economic and Historical Implications for Capital Punishment Deterrence," 18 *Notre Dame Journal of Law, Ethics, & Public Policy* 437

Gey, Steven G. (1992) "Justice Scalia's Death Penalty," 20 *Florida State University Law Review* 67

Gibbs, Jack P. (1978) "Preventive Effects of Capital Punishment Other Than Deterrence," 14 *Criminal Law Bulletin* 34

Givelber, Daniel (1994) "The New Law of Murder," 69 *Indiana Law Journal* 375

Glaberson, William (2002) "On a Reinvented Death Row, the Prisoners Can Only Wait," *New York Times* A1 (June 4)

Gleeson, John (2003) "Supervising Federal Capital Punishment: Why the Attorney General Should Defer When U.S. Attorneys Recommend Against the Death Penalty," 89 *Virginia Law Review* 1697

Goldberg, Guy & Gena Bunn (2000) "Balancing Fairness and Finality: A Comprehensive Review of the Texas Death Penalty," 5 *Texas Review of Law and Politics* 49

Gottschalk, Marie (2006) "Dismantling the Carceral State: The Future of Penal Policy Reform," 84 *Texas Law Review* 1693

Gradess, Jonathan E. & Andrew L.B. Davies (2009) "The Cost of the Death Penalty in America: Directions for Future Research," in Charles S. Lanier, William J. Bowers & James R. Acker, eds., *The Future of America's Death Penalty: An Agenda for the Next Generation of Capital Punishment Research* 397 (Durham, NC: Carolina Academic Press)

Granucci, Anthony F. (1969) "'Nor Cruel and Unusual Punishments Inflicted': The Original Meaning," 57 *California Law Review* 839

Green, Bruce A. (1993) "Lethal Fiction: The Meaning of 'Counsel' in the Sixth Amendment," 78 *Iowa Law Review* 433

Gross, Samuel R. (1996) "The Risks of Death: Why Erroneous Convictions Are Common in Capital Cases," 44 *Buffalo Law Review* 469

Gross, Samuel R. (2008) "Convicting the Innocent," 4 *Annual Review of Law & Social Science* 173

Gross, Samuel R., Kristen Jacoby, Daniel J. Matheson, Nicholas Montgomery & Sujata Patil (2005) "Exonerations in the United States 1989 Through 1973," 95 *Journal of Criminal Law & Criminology* 523

Gross, Samuel R. & Daniel J. Matheson (2003) "What They Say at the End: Capital Victims' Families and the Press," 88 *Cornell Law Review* 486

Gross, Samuel R. & Robert Mauro (1984) "Patterns of Death: An Analysis of Racial Disparities in Capital Sentencing and Homicide Victimization," 37 *Stanford Law Review* 27

Gross, Samuel R. & Barbara O'Brien (2008) "Frequency and Predictors of False Conviction: Why We Know So Little, and New Data on Capital Cases," 4 *Journal of Empirical Legal Studies* 927

Hammel, Andrew (2002) "Diabolical Federalism: A Functional Critique and Proposed Reconstruction of Death Penalty Federal Habeas," 39 *American Criminal Law Review* 1

Haney, Craig (1984) "Examining Death Qualification: Further Analysis of the Process Effect," 8 *Law and Human Behavior* 133

Haney, Craig (1984) "On the Selection of Capital Juries: The Biasing Effects of the Death-Qualification Process," 8 *Law and Human Behavior* 121

Harden, Alicia N. (2010–2011) "Drawing the Line at Pushing 'Play': Barring Video Montages as Victim Impact Evidence at Capital Sentencing Trials," 99 *Kentucky Law Journal* 845

Harmon, Talia Roitberg, James R. Acker & Craig Rivera (2010) "The Power to Be Lenient: Examining New York Governors' Capital Case Clemency Decisions," 27 *Justice Quarterly* 742

Hauck, Brian, Cara Hendrickson & Zena Yoslov (1999) "Capital Punishment Legislation in Massachusetts," 36 *Harvard Journal on Legislation* 479

Hayler, Barbara J. (2008) "Moratorium and Reform: Illinois's Efforts to Make the Death Penalty Process 'Fair, Just, and Accurate,'" 29 *Justice System Journal* 21

Heery, Shannon (2010) "If It's Constitutional, Then What's the Problem?: The Use of Judicial Override in Alabama Death Sentencing," 34 *Washington University Journal of Law and Policy* 347

Heise, Michael (2003) "Mercy by the Numbers: An Empirical Analysis of Clemency and Its Structure," 89 *Virginia Law Review* 239

Henderson, Lynne (1998) "Co-opting Compassion: The Federal Victim's Rights Amendment," 10 *St. Thomas Law Review* 579

Hengstler, Gary (1987) "Attorneys for the Damned," *American Bar Association Journal* 56 (Jan. 1)

Hensl, Kursten B. (2004) "Restored to Health to Be Put to Death: Reconciling the Legal and Ethical Dilemmas of Medicating to Execute in *Singleton v. Norris*," 49 *Villanova Law Review* 291

Hindson, Stephanie, Hillary Potter & Michael L. Radelet (2006) "Race, Gender, Region and Death Sentencing in Colorado, 1980–1999," 77 *University of Colorado Law Review* 549

Hoffmann, Joseph L. (1989) "On the Perils of Line-Drawing: Juveniles and the Death Penalty," 40 *Hastings Law Journal* 229

Hoffmann, Joseph L. (2005) "Protecting the Innocent: The Massachusetts Governor's Council Report," 95 *Journal of Criminal Law & Criminology* 561

Holland, Emily (2012) "Moving Pictures . . . Maintaining Justice? Clarifying the Right Role for Victim Impact Videos in the Capital Context," 17 *Berkeley Journal of Criminal Law* 147

Horan, David (2000) "The Innocence Commission: An Independent Review Board for Wrongful Convictions," 20 *Northern Illinois University Law Review* 91

Horton, Nancy S. (1990) "Restoration of Competency for Execution: *Furioso Solo Furore Punitur*," 44 *Southwestern Law Journal* 1191

Horwitz, Jonah J. (2012) "Certifiable: Certificates of Appealability, Habeas Corpus, and the Perils of Self-Judging," 17 *Roger Williams University Law Review* 695

Howarth, Joan W. (2002) "Executing White Masculinities: Learning From Karla Faye Tucker," 81 *Oregon Law Review* 183

Howe, Scott W. (1992) "Resolving the Conflict in the Capital Sentencing Cases: A Desert-Oriented Theory of Regulation," 26 *Georgia Law Review* 323

Huang, Allen (1995) "Hanging, Cyanide Gas, and the Evolving Standards of Decency: The Ninth Circuit's Misapplication of the Cruel and Unusual Clause of the Eighth Amendment," 74 *Oregon Law Review* 995

Hughes, Jason D. (2009) "The Tri-Chemical Cocktail: Serene Brutality," 72 *Albany Law Review* 527

Isaacson, Cory (2012) "How Resource Disparity Makes the Death Penalty Unconstitutional: An Eighth Amendment Argument Against Structurally Imbalanced Capital Trials," 12 *Berkeley Journal of Criminal Law* 297

Johnson, David T. (2006) "Japan's Secretive Death Penalty Policy: Contours, Origins, Justifications, and Meanings," 7 *Asian-Pacific Law and Policy Journal* 62

Johnson, James B. (2008) "Executing Capital Punishment Via Case Study: A Socratic Chat About New Jersey's Abolition of the Death Penalty and Convincing Other States to Follow Suit," 34 *Journal of Legislation* 1

Johnson, Robert & Harmony Davies (forthcoming) "Life Under Sentence of Death: Historical and Contemporary Perspectives," in James R. Acker, Robert M. Bohm & Charles S. Lanier (eds.), *America's Experiment With Capital Punishment: Reflections on the Past, Present, and Future of the Ultimate Penal Sanction* (Durham, NC: Carolina Academic Press, 3d ed.)

Johnson, Sheri Lynn, John H. Blume, Theodore Eisenberg, Valerie P. Hans & Martin T. Wells (2012) "The Delaware Death Penalty: An Empirical Study," 97 *Iowa Law Review* 1925

Jones, Vincent R. & Bruce Wilson (2013) "Innocence and Its Impact on the Reassessment of the Utility of Capital Punishment: Has the Time Come to Abolish the Ultimate Sanction?," 67 *University of Miami Law Review* 459

Jungman, Elizabeth R. (2003) "Beyond All Doubt," 91 *Georgetown Law Journal* 1065

Kadane, Joseph B. (1984) "After *Hovey*: A Note on Taking Account of the Automatic Death Penalty Jurors," 8 *Law and Human Behavior* 115

Kahan, Dan M. & Martha C. Nussbaum (1996) "Two Conceptions of Emotion in Criminal Law," 96 *Columbia Law Review* 269

Kaplan, Aliza B. (2013) "Oregon's Death Penalty: The Practical Reality," 17 *Lewis & Clark Law Review* 1

Keedy, Edwin R. (1949) "History of the Pennsylvania Statute Creating Degrees of Murder," 97 *University of Pennsylvania Law Review* 759

Kimble, Marsha (2006) "My Journey and the Riddle," in James R. Acker & David R. Karp (eds.), *Wounds That Do Not Bind: Victim-Based Perspectives on the Death Penalty* 127 (Durham, NC: Carolina Academic Press)

Kirchmeier, Jeffrey L. (1996) "Drink, Drugs, and Drowsiness: The Constitutional Right to Effective Assistance of Counsel and the *Strickland* Prejudice Requirement," 75 *Nebraska Law Review* 425

Kirchmeier, Jeffrey L. (2006) "Dead Innocent: The Death Penalty Abolitionist Search for a Wrongful Execution," 42 *Tulsa Law Review* 403

Klein, Lawrence R., Brian Forst & Victor Filatov (1978) "The Deterrent Effect of Capital Punishment: An Assessment of the Estimates," in Alfred Blumstein, Jacqueline Cohen & Daniel Nagin (eds.), *Deterrence and Incapacitation: Estimating the Effects of Criminal Sanctions on Crime Rates* 336 (Washington, D.C.: National Academy of Sciences)

Kobil, Daniel T. (2003) "The Evolving Role of Clemency in Capital Cases," in James R. Acker, Robert M. Bohm & Charles S. Lanier (eds.), *America's Experiment With Capital Punishment: Reflections on the Past, Present, and Future of the Ultimate Penal Sanction* 673 (Durham, NC: Carolina Academic Press, 2d ed.)

Kobil, Daniel T. (2012) "Compelling Mercy: Judicial Review and the Clemency Power," 9 *University of St. Thomas Law Journal* 698

Koosed, Margaret Malkin (2001) "Averting Mistaken Executions by Adopting the Model Penal Code's Exclusion of Death in the Presence of Lingering Doubt," 21 *Northern Illinois University Law Review* 41

Koslov, Nathaniel (2013) "Insurmountable Hill: How Undue AEDPA Deference Has Undermined the *Atkins* Ban on Executing the Intellectually Disabled," 54 *Boston College Law Review E-Supplement* 189

Kotch, Seth & Robert P. Mosteller (2010) "The Racial Justice Act and the Long Struggle With Race and the Death Penalty in North Carolina," 88 *North Carolina Law Review* 2031

Kovandzic, Tomislav V., Lynne M. Vieraitis & Denise Paquette Boots (2009) "Does the Death Penalty Save Lives? New Evidence From State Panel Data, 1977 to 2006," 8 *Criminology & Public Policy* 803

Kovarsky, Lee (2007) "AEDPA's Wrecks: Comity, Finality, and Federalism," 82 *Tulane Law Review* 443

Kovarsky, Lee (2010) "Death Ineligibility and Habeas Corpus," 95 *Cornell Law Review* 329

Krause, Tammy (2006) "Reaching Out to the Other Side: Defense-Based Victim Outreach in Capital Cases," in James R. Acker & David R. Karp (eds.), *Wounds That Do Not Bind: Victim-Based Perspectives on the Death Penalty* 379 (Durham, NC: Carolina Academic Press)

Kreitzberg, Ellen & David Richter (2007) "But Can It Be Fixed? A Look at Constitutional Challenges to Lethal Injection Executions," 47 *Santa Clara Law Review* 445

Kuziemko, Ilyana (2006) "Does the Threat of the Death Penalty Affect Plea Bargaining in Murder Cases? Evidence From New York's 1995 Reinstatement of Capital Punishment," 8 *American Law and Economics Review* 116

Lamparello, Adam (2010) "Establishing Guidelines for Attorney Representation of Criminal Defendants at the Sentencing Phase of Capital Trials," 62 *Maine Law Review* 97

Land, Kenneth C., Raymond H.C. Teske, Jr. & Hui Zheng (2009) "The Short-Term Effects of Executions on Homicides: Deterrence, Displacement, or Both?," 47 *Criminology* 1009

Langbein, John H. (1983) "Shaping the Eighteenth-Century Criminal Trial: A View From the Ryder Sources," 50 *University of Chicago Law Review* 1

Lanier, Charles S. & James R. Acker (2004) "Capital Punishment, the Moratorium Movement, and Empirical Questions," 10 *Psychology, Public Policy, and Law* 577

Lash, Steve (2000) "Texas Death Case Set Aside," *Houston Chronicle* 1A (June 6)

Ledewitz, Bruce & Scott Staples (1993) "The Role of Executive Clemency in Modern Death Penalty Cases," 27 *University of Richmond Law Review* 227

Liebman, James S. (2000) "The Overproduction of Death," 100 *Columbia Law Review* 2030

Liebman, James S. (2002) "The New Death Penalty Debate: What's DNA Got to Do With It?," 33 *Columbia Human Rights Law Review* 527

Liebman, James S. (2002) "Opting for Real Death Penalty Reform," 63 *Ohio State Law Journal* 315

Liebman, James S. & Peter Clarke (2011) "Minority Practice, Majority's Burden: The Death Penalty Today," 9 *Ohio State Journal of Criminal Law* 255

Liebman, James S., Shawn Crowley, Andrew Markquart, Lauren Rosenberg, Lauren Gallo White & Daniel Zharkovsky (2012) "Los Tocayos Carlos," 43 *Columbia Human Rights Law Review* 711

Liebman, James S., Jeffrey Fagan, Valerie West & Jonathan Lloyd (2000) "Capital Attrition: Error Rates in Capital Cases, 1973–1995," 78 *Texas Law Review* 1839

Little, Rory K. (1999) "The Federal Death Penalty: History and Some Thoughts About the Department of Justice's Role," 26 *Fordham Urban Law Journal* 347

Logan, Wayne A. (2002) "Casting New Light on an Old Subject: Death Penalty Abolitionism for a New Millennium," 100 *Michigan Law Review* 1336

Long, Walter C. (1999) "Karla Faye Tucker: A Case for Restorative Justice," 27 *American Journal of Criminal Law* 117

Lyon, Andrea D. & Mark D. Cunningham (2005) "'Reason Not the Need': Does the Lack of Compelling State Interest in Maintaining a Separate Death Row Make It Unlawful?," 33 *American Journal of Criminal Law* 1

Mackey, Philip English (1974) "The Inutility of Mandatory Capital Punishment: An Historical Note," 54 *Boston University Law Review* 32

Markel, Dan (2004) "Against Mercy," 88 *Minnesota Law Review* 1421

Markman, Stephen J. & Paul G. Cassell (1988) "Protecting the Innocent: A Response to the Bedau-Radelet Study," 41 *Stanford Law Review* 121

Marquart, James W., Sheldon Ekland-Olson & Jonathan R. Sorensen (1989) "Gazing Into the Crystal Ball: Can Jurors Accurately Predict Dangerousness in Capital Cases?," 23 *Law & Society Review* 449

Marquart, James W. & Jonathan R. Sorensen (1989) "A National Study of the *Furman*-Commuted Inmates: Assessing the Threat to Society From Capital Offenders," 23 *Loyola of Los Angeles Law Review* 5

Marquis, Joshua (2006) "The Innocent and the Shammed," *New York Times* A23 (Jan. 26)

Marshall, Peter D. (2011) "A Comparative Analysis of the Right to Appeal," 22 *Duke Journal of Comparative & International Law* 1

Martin, Robert J. (2010) "Killing Capital Punishment in New Jersey: The First State in Modern History to Repeal Its Death Penalty Statute," 41 *University of Toledo Law Review* 485

Mattimoe, Jean (2012) "The Death Penalty and the Mentally Ill: A Selected and Annotated Bibliography," 5 *the crit: a Critical Studies Journal* 1 (Summer)

McConville, Celestine Richards (2003) "The Right to Effective Assistance of Capital Postconviction Counsel: Constitutional Implications of Statutory Grants of Capital Counsel," 2003 *Wisconsin Law Review* 31

McConville, Celestine Richards (2006) "The Meaninglessness of Delayed Appointments and Discretionary Grants of Capital Postconviction Counsel," 42 *Tulsa Law Review* 253

McCord, David (2000) "State Death Sentencing for Felony Murder Accomplices Under the *Enmund* and *Tison* Standards," 32 *Arizona State Law Journal* 843

McCord, David (2009) "Should Commission of a Contemporaneous Arson, Burglary, Kidnapping, Rape, or Robbery Be Sufficient to Make a Murderer Eligible for a Death Sentence?—An Empirical and Normative Analysis," 49 *Santa Clara Law Review* 1

McMahon, Kate (2006–2007) "Dead Man Waiting: Death Row Delays, the Eighth Amendment, and What Courts and Legislatures Can Do," 25 *Buffalo Public Interest Law Journal* 43

Medwed, Daniel S. (2008) "Innocentrism," 2008 *University of Illinois Law Review* 1549

Mello, Michael (1991) "The Jurisdiction to Do Justice: Florida's Jury Override and the State Constitution," 18 *Florida State University Law Review* 923

Mello, Michael (1997) "Outlaw Executive: 'Crazy Joe,' the Hypnotized Witness, and the Mirage of Clemency in Florida," 23 *Journal of Contemporary Law* 1

Millemann, Michael (2010) "Limiting Maryland's New Death Penalty Law," 70 *Maryland Law Review* 272

Miller, Hannah Robertson (2008) "'A Meaningless Ritual': How the Lack of a Postconviction Competency Standard Deprives the Mentally Ill of Effective Habeas Review in Texas," 87 *Texas Law Review* 267

Milner, Julie Levinsohn (1998) "Dignity or Death Row: Are Death Row Rights to Die Diminished? A Comparison of the Right to Die for the Terminally Ill and the Terminally Sentenced," 24 *New England Journal on Criminal and Civil Confinement* 279

Mitchell, John R. (1996) "Attorneys Representing Death Row Clients: Client Autonomy Over Personal Opinions," 25 *Capital University Law Review* 643

Monahan, John (2006) "A Jurisprudence of Risk Assessment: Forecasting Harm Among Prisoners, Predators, and Patients," 92 *Virginia Law Review* 391

Monahan, John & David Wexler (1978) "A Definite Maybe: Proof and Probability in Civil Commitment," 2 *Law & Human Behavior* 37

Moylan, Mary-Beth & Linda E. Carter (2009) "Clemency in California Capital Cases," 14 *Berkeley Journal of Criminal Law* 37

Murphy, Russell G. (2011) "Execution Watch: Mitt Romney's 'Foolproof' Death Penalty Act and the Politics of Capital Punishment," 45 *Suffolk University Law Review* 1

Nagy, Pamela S. (1994) "Hang by the Neck Until Dead: The Resurgence of Cruel and Unusual Punishment in the 1990s," 26 *Pacific Law Journal* 85

National Research Council of the National Academies, Committee on Deterrence and the Death Penalty (2012) *Deterrence and the Death Penalty* (Washington, DC: The National Academies Press)

Newton, Brent E. (2005) "A Primer on Post-Conviction Habeas Corpus Review," 29 *Champion* 16 (June)

Norman, Matthew T. (1998–1999) "Standards and Procedures for Determining Whether a Defendant Is Competent to Make the Ultimate Choice—Death; Ohio's New Precedent for Death Row 'Volunteers,'" 13 *Journal of Law and Health* 103

Note (1994) "The Eighth Amendment and Ineffective Assistance of Counsel in Capital Trials," 107 *Harvard Law Review* 1923

O'Brien, Barbara & Catherine Grosso (2011) "Confronting Race: How a Confluence of Social Movements Convinced North Carolina to Go Where the *McCleskey* Court Wouldn't," 2011 *Michigan State Law Review* 463

O'Meara, Gregory J. (2009) "'You Can't Get There From Here?': Ineffective Assistance Claims in Federal Circuit Courts After AEDPA," 93 *Marquette Law Review* 545

Oberman, Michelle (2004) "Mothers Who Kill: Coming to Terms With Modern American Infanticide," 8 *DePaul Journal of Health Care Law* 3

Owens, Jennifer Lynn (2013) *Capital Punishment in the Lone Star State: A County-Level Analysis of Contextual Effects of Sentencing* (unpublished PhD dissertation, State University of New York at Albany)

Paternoster, Raymond (2010) "How Much Do We Really Know About Criminal Deterrence?" 100 *Journal of Criminal Law & Criminology* 765

Paternoster, Raymond & Anne Marie Kazyaka (1988) "The Administration of the Death Penalty in South Carolina: Experiences Over the First Few Years," 39 *South Carolina Law Review* 245

Pauley, Matthew A. (1999) "Murder by Premeditation," 36 *American Criminal Law Review* 427

Perry, Lauren E. (2008) "Hiding Behind Precedent: Why *Panetti v. Quarterman* Will Create Confusion for Incompetent Death Row Inmates," 86 *North Carolina Law Review* 1068

Peterson, Ruth D. & William C. Bailey (2003) "Is Capital Punishment an Effective Deterrent for Murder? An Examination of Social Science Research," in James R. Acker, Robert M. Bohm & Charles S. Lanier (eds.), *America's Experiment With Capital Punishment: Reflections on the Past, Present, and Future of the Ultimate Penal Sanction* 251 (Durham, NC: Carolina Academic Press, 2d ed.)

Petition for Executive Clemency on behalf of Stanley Tookie Williams (2005) (Nov. 8)

Pierce, Glenn L. & Michael L. Radelet (2002) "Race, Region, and Death Sentencing in Illinois, 1988–1997," 81 *Oregon Law Review* 39

Pogarsky, Greg (2002) "Identifying 'Deterrable' Offenders: Implications for Research on Deterrence," 19 *Justice Quarterly* 431

Pogarsky, Greg, Alex R. Piquero & Ray Paternoster (2004) "Modeling Change in Perceptions About Sanction Threats: The Neglected Linkage in Deterrence Theory," 20 *Journal of Quantitative Criminology* 343

Pokorak, Jeffrey J. (2006) "Rape as a Badge of Slavery: The Legal History of, and Remedies for, Prosecutorial Race-of-Victim Charging Discrepancies," 7 *Nevada Law Journal* 1

Poulos, John W. (1986) "The Supreme Court, Capital Punishment, and the Substantive Criminal Law: The Rise and Fall of Mandatory Capital Punishment," 28 *Arizona Law Review* 143

Price, Melynda J. (2006) "Litigating Salvation: Race, Religion and Innocence in the Karla Faye Tucker and Gary Graham Cases," 15 *Southern California Review of Law & Social Justice* 267

Price, Melynda J. (2009) "Performing Discretion or Performing Discrimination: Race, Ritual, and Peremptory Challenges in Capital Jury Selection," 15 *Michigan Journal of Race and Law* 57

Radelet, Michael L. (2011) "Overriding Jury Sentencing Recommendations in Florida Capital Cases: An Update and Possible Half-Requiem," 2011 *Michigan State Law Review* 793

Radelet, Michael L. & Marian J. Borg (2000) "The Changing Nature of Death Penalty Debates," 26 *Annual Review of Sociology* 43

Radelet, Michael L. & Michael Mello (1992) "Death-to-Life Overrides: Saving the Resources of the Florida Supreme Court," 20 *Florida State University Law Review* 195

Radelet, Michael L. & Dawn Stanley (2006) "Learning From Homicide Co-Victims: A University-Based Project," in James R. Acker & David R. Karp, eds., *Wounds That Do Not Bind: Victim-Based Perspectives on the Death Penalty* 397 (Durham, NC: Carolina Academic Press)

Radelet, Michael & Margaret Vandiver (1986) "Race and Capital Punishment: An Overview of the Issues," 25 *Crime & Social Justice* 94

Radelet, Michael L. & Barbara A. Zsembik (1993) "Executive Clemency in Post-*Furman* Capital Cases," 27 *University of Richmond Law Review* 289

Rapaport, Elizabeth (1991) "The Death Penalty and Gender Discrimination," 25 *Law & Society Review* 367

Rapaport, Elizabeth (2000) "Equality of the Damned: The Execution of Women on the Cusp of the 21st Century," 26 *Ohio Northern University Law Review* 581

Rapaport, Elizabeth (2001) "Staying Alive: Executive Clemency, Equal Protection, and the Politics of Gender in Women's Capital Cases," 4 *Buffalo Criminal Law Review* 967

Rapaport, Elizabeth (2012) "A Modest Proposal: The Aged of Death Row Should Be Deemed Too Old to Execute," 77 *Brooklyn Law Review* 1089

Recent Case (2012) "Federal Habeas Corpus—Death Penalty—Eleventh Circuit Rejects Challenge to Georgia's 'Beyond a Reasonable Doubt' Standard for Defendants' Mental Retardation Claims—*Hill v. Humphrey*, 662 F.3d 1335 (11th Cir. 2011) (en banc)," 125 *Harvard Law Review* 2185

"Recommendations of the American Bar Association Section of Individual Rights and Responsibilities Task Force on Mental Disability and the Death Penalty" (2005) 54 *Catholic University Law Review* 1115

Reed, Mark D. & Brenda Simms Blackwell (2006) "Secondary Victimization Among Families of Homicide Victims: The Impact of the Justice Process on Co-Victims' Psychological Adjustment and Service Utilization," in James R. Acker & David R. Karp (eds.), *Wounds That Do Not Bind: Victim-Based Perspectives on the Death Penalty* 253 (Durham, NC: Carolina Academic Press)

Reza, Elizabeth Marie (2005) "Gender Bias in North Carolina's Death Penalty," 12 *Duke Journal of Gender Law & Policy* 179

Rigg, Robert R. (2007) "The T-Rex Without Teeth: Evolving *Strickland v. Washington* and the Test for Ineffective Assistance of Counsel," 35 *Pepperdine Law Review* 77

Risinger, Michael D. (2007) "Innocents Convicted: An Empirically Justified Factual Wrongful Conviction Rate," 97 *Journal of Criminal Law & Criminology* 761

Ritter, Hilary S. (2005) "It's the Prosecution's Story, but They're Not Sticking to It: Applying Harmless Error and Judicial Estoppel to Exculpatory Post-Conviction DNA Testing Cases," 74 *Fordham Law Review* 825

Roberts, Jenny (2011) "Why Misdemeanors Matter: Defining Effective Advocacy in Lower Criminal Courts," 45 *U.C. Davis Law Review* 277

Robson, Ruthann (2013) "Beyond Sumptuary: Constitutionalism, Clothes, and Bodies in Anglo-American Law," 2 *British Journal of American Legal Studies* 477

Roman, John K., Aaron J. Chalfin & Carly L. Knight (2009) "Reassessing the Cost of the Death Penalty Using Quasi-Experimental Methods: Evidence From Maryland," 11 *American Law and Economics Review* 530

Root, Jeremy (2001–2002) "Cruel and Unusual Punishment: A Reconsideration of the *Lackey* Claim," 27 *New York University Review of Law and Social Change* 281

Rosen, Richard A. (1990) "Felony Murder and the Eighth Amendment Jurisprudence of Death," 31 *Boston College Law Review* 1103

Rosenbaum, Ron (1990) "Travels with Dr. Death," *Vanity Fair* 141 (May)

Rosenbluth, Stanley & Phyllis Rosenbluth (2006) "Accidental Death Is Fate, Murder Is Pure Evil," in James R. Acker & David R. Karp (eds.), *Wounds That Do Not Bind: Victim-Based Perspectives on the Death Penalty* 103 (Durham, NC: Carolina Academic Press)

Rupp, Ashley (2003) "Death Penalty Prosecutorial Charging Decisions and County Budgetary Restrictions: Is the Death Penalty Arbitrarily Applied Based on County Funding?," 71 *Fordham Law Review* 2735

Ryan, Meghan J. (2012) "Remedying Wrongful Executions," 45 *University of Michigan Journal of Law Reform* 261

Sadoff, David A. (2008) "International Law and the Mortal Precipice: A Legal Policy Critique of the Death Row Phenomenon," 17 *Tulane Journal of International and Comparative Law* 77

Sandys, Marla & Scott McClelland (2003) "Stacking the Deck for Guilt and Death: The Failure of Death Qualification to Ensure Impartiality," in James R. Acker, Robert M. Bohm & Charles S. Lanier (eds.), *America's Experiment With Capital Punishment: Reflections on the Past, Present, and Future of the Ultimate Penal Sanction* 385 (Durham, NC: Carolina Academic Press, 2d ed.)

Sarat, Austin (2004) "Putting a Square Peg in a Round Hole: Victims, Retribution, and George Ryan's Clemency," 82 *North Carolina Law Review* 1345

Sarat, Austin, Aubrey Jones, Madeline Sprung-Keyser, Katherine Blumstein, Heather Richard & Robert Weaver (2012) "Gruesome Spectacles: The Cultural Reception of Botched Executions in America," 1 *British Journal of American Legal Studies* 1

Schwarzschild, Henry (1982) "Homicide by Injection," *New York Times* A15 (Dec. 23)

Sellin, Thorsten (1967) "Death and Imprisonment as Deterrents to Murder," in Hugo Adam Bedau (ed.), *The Death Penalty in America* 274 (Garden City, NY: Anchor Books, rev. ed.)

Sellin, Thorsten (1967) "Homicide in Retentionist and Abolitionist States," in Thorsten Sellin (ed.), *Capital Punishment* 135 (New York: Harper & Row)

Severson, Kim (2013) "North Carolina Repeals Law Allowing Racial Bias Claim in Death Penalty Challenges," *New York Times* A1 (June 6)

Sewall, Michaela P. (2010) "Pushing Execution Over the Constitutional Line: Forcible Medication of Condemned Inmates and the Eighth and Fourteenth Amendments," 51 *Boston College Law Review* 1279

Shapiro, Andrea (2000) "Unequal Before the Law: Men, Women and the Death Penalty," 8 *American University Journal of Gender, Social Policy and the Law* 427

Shapiro, Meghan (2008) "An Overdose of Dangerousness: How 'Future Dangerousness' Catches the Least Culpable Capital Defendants and Undermines the Rationale for the Executions It Supports," 35 *American Journal of Criminal Law* 145

Sharkey, Kara (2013) "Delay in Considering the Constitutionality of Inordinate Delay: The Death Row Phenomenon and the Eighth Amendment," 161 *University of Pennsylvania Law Review* 861

Sharon, Chelsea Creo (2011) "The 'Most Deserving' of Death: The Narrowing Requirement and the Proliferation of Aggravating Factors in Capital Sentencing Statutes," 46 *Harvard Civil Rights-Civil Liberties Law Review* 223

Shatz, Steven F. & Terry Dalton (2013) "Challenging the Death Penalty With Statistics: *Furman*, *McCleskey*, and a Single County Case Study," 34 *Cardozo Law Review* 1227

Shatz, Steven F. & Naomi R. Shatz (2012) "Chivalry Is Not Dead: Murder, Gender, and the Death Penalty," 27 *Berkeley Journal of Gender, Law & Justice* 64

Shepherd, Joanna M. (2005) "Deterrence Versus Brutalization: Capital Punishment's Differing Impacts Among States," 104 *Michigan Law Review* 203

Sidhu, Dawinder S. (2009) "On Appeal: Reviewing the Case Against the Death Penalty," 111 *West Virginia Law Review* 453

Sigler, Mary (2007) "Mercy, Clemency, and the Case of Karla Faye Tucker," 4 *Ohio State Journal of Criminal Law* 455

Simmons, Erin (2009) "Challenging an Execution After Prolonged Confinement on Death Row [*Lackey* Revisited]," 59 *Case Western Reserve Law Review* 1249

Simpson, Sandra L. (2009) "Everyone Else Is Doing It, Why Can't We? A New Look at the Use of Statistical Data in Death Penalty Cases," 12 *Journal of Gender, Race and Justice* 509

Slobogin, Christopher (2005) "Mental Disorder as an Exemption From the Death Penalty: The ABA-IRR Task Force Recommendations," 54 *Catholic University Law Review* 1133

Smith, Amy (2008) "Not 'Waiving' but Drowning: The Anatomy of Death Row Syndrome and Volunteering for Execution," 17 *Boston University Public Interest Law Journal* 237

Smith, Robert J. (2012) "The Geography of the Death Penalty and Its Ramifications," 92 *Boston University Law Review* 227

Smith, Stephen F. (2008) "The Supreme Court and the Politics of Death," 94 *Virginia Law Review* 283

Smith, Stephen F. (2009) "Taking *Strickland* Claims Seriously," 93 *Marquette Law Review* 515

Songer, Michael J. & Isaac Unah (2006) "The Effect of Race, Gender, and Location on Prosecutorial Decisions to Seek the Death Penalty in South Carolina," 58 *South Carolina Law Review* 161

Sorensen, Jon (2009) "Researching Future Dangerousness," in Charles S. Lanier, William J. Bowers & James R. Acker, eds., *The Future of America's Death Penalty: An Agenda for the Next Generation of Capital Punishment Research* 359 (Durham, NC: Carolina Academic Press)

Sorensen, Jon & James Marquart (2003) "Future Dangerousness and Incapacitation," in James R. Acker, Robert M. Bohm & Charles S. Lanier (eds.), *America's Experiment With Capital Punishment: Reflections on the Past, Present, and Future of the Ultimate Penal Sanction* 283 (Durham, NC: Carolina Academic Press, 2d ed.)

Sorensen, Jonathan R. & Rocky L. Pilgrim (2000) "An Actuarial Risk Assessment of Violence Posed by Capital Murder Defendants," 90 *Journal of Criminal Law & Criminology* 1251

Spangenberg, Robert L. & Elizabeth R. Walsh (1989) "Capital Punishment or Life Imprisonment? Some Cost Considerations," 23 *Loyola of Los Angeles Law Review* 45

Spector, Phillip M. (2002) "The Sentencing Rule of Lenity," 33 *University of Toledo Law Review* 511

Steiker, Carol S. (2005) "No, Capital Punishment Is Not Morally Required: Deterrence, Deontology, and the Death Penalty," 58 *Stanford Law Review* 751

Steiker, Carol S. & Jordan M. Steiker (1992) "Review Essay: Let God Sort Them Out? Refining the Individualization Requirement in Capital Sentencing," 102 *Yale Law Journal* 835

Steiker, Carol S. & Jordan M. Steiker (2002) "Should Abolitionists Support Legislative 'Reform' of the Death Penalty?," 63 *Ohio State Law Journal* 417

Steiker, Carol S. & Jordan M. Steiker (2008) "*Atkins v. Virginia*: Lessons From Substance and Procedure in the Constitutional Regulation of Capital Punishment," 57 *DePaul Law Review* 721

Steiker, Carol S. & Jordan M. Steiker (2010) "No More Tinkering: The American Law Institute and the Death Penalty Provisions of the Model Penal Code," 89 *Texas Law Review* 353

Steiker, Carol S. & Jordan M. Steiker (2010) "Part II: Report to the ALI Concerning Capital Punishment," 89 *Texas Law Review* 367

Stevenson, Bryan A. (2002) "The Politics of Fear and Death: Successive Problems in Capital Federal Habeas Corpus Cases," 77 *New York University Law Review* 699

Sullivan, Dwight H. (2006) "Killing Time: Two Decades of Military Capital Litigation," 189 *Military Law Review* 1

Sullivan, Thomas P. (2002) "Repair or Repeal—Report of the Illinois Governor's Commission on Capital Punishment," 49 *Federal Lawyer* 40 (Sept.)

Sunstein, Cass R. & Adrian Vermeule (2005) "Is Capital Punishment Morally Required? Acts, Omissions, and Life-Life Tradeoffs," 58 *Stanford Law Review* 703

"Supplementary Guidelines for the Mitigation Function of Defense Teams in Death Penalty Cases" (2008) 36 *Hofstra Law Review* 677

Tabak, Ronald J. (2005) "Overview of Task Force Proposal on Mental Disability and the Death Penalty," 54 *Catholic University Law Review* 1123

Taylor, Stuart, Jr. (1987) "Court, 5–4, Rejects Racial Challenge to Death Penalty," *New York Times* A1 (Apr. 23)

Thaxton, Sherod (2013) "Leveraging Death," 103 *Journal of Criminal Law & Criminology* 475

Thomas, George C., III (2005) "Colonial Criminal Law and Procedure: The Royal Colony of New Jersey 1449–57," 1 *N.Y.U. Journal of Law & Liberty* 671

Thomas, Sarah L. (2005) "A Legislative Challenge: A Proposed Model Statute to Provide for the Appointment of Counsel in State Habeas Corpus Proceedings for Indigent Petitioners," 54 *Emory Law Journal* 1139

Thompson, William C., Claudia L. Cowan, Phoebe C. Ellsworth & Joan C. Harrington (1984) "Death Penalty Attitudes and Conviction Proneness: The Translation of Attitudes into Verdicts," 8 *Law and Human Behavior* 95

Tobolowsky, Peggy M. (2003) "*Atkins*' Aftermath: Identifying Mentally Retarded Offenders and Excluding Them From Execution," 30 *Journal of Legislation* 77

Uhrig, Emily Garcia (2009) "A Case for a Constitutional Right to Counsel in Habeas Corpus," 60 *Hastings Law Journal* 541

van den Haag, Ernest (1978) "In Defense of the Death Penalty: A Legal-Practical-Moral Analysis," 14 *Criminal Law Bulletin* 51

van den Haag, Ernest (1997) "The Death Penalty Once More," in Hugo Adam Bedau (ed.), *The Death Penalty in America: Current Controversies* 445 (New York: Oxford University Press)

van den Haag, Ernest (2003) "Justice, Deterrence and the Death Penalty," in James R. Acker, Robert M. Bohm & Charles S. Lanier (eds.), *America's Experiment With Capital Punishment: Reflections on the Past, Present, and Future of the Ultimate Penal Sanction* 233 (Durham, NC: Carolina Academic Press, 2d ed.)

Vandiver, Margaret (2003) "The Impact of the Death Penalty on the Families of Homicide Victims and of Condemned Prisoners," in James R. Acker, Robert M. Bohm & Charles S. Lanier (eds.), *America's Experiment With Capital Punishment: Reflections on the Past, Present, and Future of the Ultimate Penal Sanction* 613 (Durham, NC: Carolina Academic Press, 2d ed.)

Vandiver, Margaret, David J. Giacopassi & K.B. Turner (2008) "'Let's Do It!': An Analysis of Consensual Executions," in Robert M. Bohm (ed.), *The Death Penalty Today* 187 (Boca Raton, FL: CRC Press)

von Wilpert, Marni (2010) "*Holland v. Florida*: A Prisoner's Last Chance, Attorney Error, and the Antiterrorism and Effective Death Penalty Act's One-Year Statute of Limitations Period for Federal Habeas Corpus Review," 79 *Fordham Law Review* 1429

Warden, Rob (2005) "Illinois Death Penalty Reform: How It Happened, What It Promises," 95 *Journal of Criminal Law & Criminology* 381

Warden, Rob (2012) "How and Why Illinois Abolished the Death Penalty," 30 *Law & Inequality* 245

Weinman, Sarah Rose (2009) "The Potential and Limits of Death Penalty Commissions as Tools for Reform: Applying Lessons From Illinois and New Jersey to Understand the California Experience," 14 *Berkeley Journal of Criminal Law* 303

Weisberg, Robert (1983) "Deregulating Death," 1983 *Supreme Court Review* 305

White, Welsh S. (1987) "Defendants Who Elect Execution," 48 *University of Pittsburgh Law Review* 853

White, Welsh S. (2003) "Confessions in Capital Cases," 2003 *Illinois Law Review* 979

Wilkins, Pamela A. (2009) "Rethinking Categorical Prohibitions on Capital Punishment: How the Current Test Fails Mentally Ill Offenders and What to Do About It," 40 *University of Memphis Law Review* 423

Williams, Kenneth (2005) "Ensuring the Capital Defendant's Right to Competent Counsel: It's Time for Some Standards!," 51 *Wayne Law Review* 129

Winick, Bruce J. (1982) "Prosecutorial Peremptory Challenge Practices in Capital Cases: An Empirical Study and a Constitutional Analysis," 81 *Michigan Law Review* 1

Winick, Bruce J. (2009) "The Supreme Court's Evolving Death Penalty Jurisprudence: Severe Mental Illness as the Next Frontier," 50 *Boston College Law Review* 785

Wolfgang, Marvin E. & Marc Reidel (1973) "Trends in the Use of Capital Punishment," 284 *Annals of the American Academy of Political and Social Science* 119

Woodward, Alexa (2007) "It Takes a Village to Save a Life: A Statewide Model for Indigent Capital Defense," 11 *New York City Law Review* 159

Zalman, Marvin (2010–2011) "An Integrated Model of Wrongful Convictions," 74 *Albany Law Review* 1465

Zimring, Franklin E. (2005) "The Unexamined Death Penalty: Capital Punishment and Reform of the Model Penal Code," 105 *Columbia Law Review* 1396

Zinzow, Heide M. et al. (2009) "Losing a Loved One to Homicide: Prevalence and Mental Health Correlates in a National Sample of Young Adults," 22 *Journal of Traumatic Stress* 20

Zupac, Wendy Zorana (2013) "Mere Negligence or Abandonment? Evaluating Claims of Attorney Misconduct After *Maples v. Thomas*," 122 *Yale Law Journal* 1328

Online Sources

ACLU, "Mental Illness and the Death Penalty in the United States" (Jan. 31, 2005), www.aclu.org/capital/mentalillness/10617pub20050131.html

ACLU, "Mental Illness and the Death Penalty" (May 5, 2009), retrieved August 8, 2013 from www.aclu.org/files/pdfs/capital/mental_illness_may2009.pdf

American Law Institute, *Report of the Council to the Membership of The American Law Institute on the Matter of the Death Penalty* (Apr. 15, 2009), retrieved June 15, 2013 from www.ali.org/doc/Capital%20Punishment_web.pdf

Baumgartner, Frank R., *The Geography of the Death Penalty* (2010), retrieved July 4, 2013 from www.unc.edu/~fbaum/Innocence/NC/Baumgartner-geography-of-capital-punishment-oct-17-2010.pdf

Blackstone, William, *Commentaries on the Laws of England* (1765–1769), Volume 4, retrieved May 28, 2013 from http://avalon.law.yale.edu/18th_century/blackstone_bk4ch2.asp

Bolinger, Josh, "Smigiel: Death Penalty Bill Was 'One of the Hardest Votes,'" *Cecil Daily* (March 18, 2013), retrieved March 30, 2013 from www.cecildaily.com/news/local_news/article_af2bd1f4-8f72-11e2-8c8c-001a4bcf887a.html

Brauchler, George H., "Death Penalty Is a Tool of Justice," *Denver Post* (March 31, 2013), retrieved April 12, 2013 from www.denverpost.com/opinion/ci_22895409/death-penalty-is-tool-justice

Calhoun, Caleb, "Local Residents Share Thoughts on Md. Death Penalty," *Herald-Mail.com* (Feb. 15, 2013), retrieved March 22, 2013 from http://articles.herald-mail.com/2013-02-15/news/37125225_1_death-penalty-capital-punishment-innocent-person

California Commission on the Fair Administration of Justice, *Final Report* (2008), retrieved March 23, 2013 from www.ccfaj.org/documents/CCFAJFinalReport.pdf

California Commission on the Fair Administration of Justice, *Report and Recommendations on the Administration of the Death Penalty in California* (2008), retrieved July 31, 2013 from www.ccfaj.org/documents/reports/dp/official/FINAL%20REPORT%20DEATH%20PENALTY.pdf

Colorado HB09-1274 (2009), Summary of Legislation, retrieved April 13, 2013 from www.leg.state.co.us/clics/clics2009a/csl.nsf/fsbillcont3/3D3051B266D2F5CA87257537001A3D75?Open&file=HB1274_00.pdf

Death Penalty Information Center, "Clemency," retrieved August 12, 2013 from www.deathpenaltyinfo.org/clemency

Death Penalty Information Center, *The Death Penalty in 2012: Year End Report* 1 (Dec. 2012), retrieved November 15, 2013 from http://deathpenaltyinfo.org/documents/2012Year End.pdf

Death Penalty Information Center, "Death Row Conditions" (last updated June 2008), retrieved August 7, 2013 from www.deathpenaltyinfo.org/death-row

Death Penalty Information Center, "Death Row Inmates by State," retrieved November 15, 2013 from www.deathpenaltyinfo.org/death-row-inmates-state-and-size-death-row-year#state

Death Penalty Information Center, "Death Sentences in the United States From 1977 by State and by Year," retrieved January 25, 2013 from www.deathpenaltyinfo.org/death-sentences-united-states-1977-2008

Death Penalty Information Center, "Deterrence: States Without the Death Penalty Have Consistently Lower Murder Rates," retrieved February 8, 2013 from www.deathpenaltyinfo.org/deterrence-states-without-death-penalty-have-had-consistently-lower-murder-rates#stateswithvwithout

Death Penalty Information Center, "Executions by Year," retrieved December 6, 2013 from www.deathpenaltyinfo.org/executions-year

Death Penalty Information Center, "Executions by Year Since 1976," retrieved January 25, 2013 from www.deathpenaltyinfo.org/executions-year

Death Penalty Information Center, "Executions in the United States, Searchable Execution Database, Missouri, 1999," retrieved August 11, 2013 from www.deathpenaltyinfo.org/views-executions?exec_name_1=&exec_year=1999&sex=All&state=MO&sex_1=All&federal=All&foreigner=All&juvenile=All&volunteer=All

Death Penalty Information Center, "Execution List 2013," retrieved August 12, 2013 from www.deathpenaltyinfo.org/execution-list-2013

Death Penalty Information Center, "Federal Death Penalty," retrieved March 30, 2013 from www.deathpenaltyinfo.org/federal-death-penalty#statutes

Death Penalty Information Center, "Information on Defendants Who Were Executed Since 1976 and Designated as 'Volunteers,'" retrieved August 8, 2013 from www.deathpenalty info.org/information-defendants-who-were-executed-1976-and-designated-volunteers

Death Penalty Information Center, "Innocence Cases: Sabrina Butler," retrieved December 3, 2013 from www.deathpenaltyinfo.org/node/4900#59

Death Penalty Information Center, *Innocence: List of Those Freed From Death Row*, retrieved December 3, 2013 from www.deathpenaltyinfo.org/innocence-list-those-freed-death-row

Death Penalty Information Center, "Intellectual Disability and the Death Penalty, Updates: The Case of Warren Hill in Georgia," retrieved August 15, 2013 from www.deathpenaltyinfo. org/intellectual-disability-and-death-penalty

Death Penalty Information Center, "Leonel Herrera," retrieved August 3, 2013 from www.death penaltyinfo.org/leonel-herrera

Death Penalty Information Center, "Lethal Injection," retrieved August 13, 2013 from www. deathpenaltyinfo.org/lethal-injection-moratorium-executions-ends-after-supreme-court-decision

Death Penalty Information Center, "Murder Rates Nationally and by State," retrieved February 8, 2013 from www.deathpenaltyinfo.org/murder-rates-nationally-and-state#MRalpha

Death Penalty Information Center, "Number of Executions by State and Region Since 1976," retrieved November 30, 2013 from www.deathpenaltyinfo.org/number-executions-state-and-region-1976

Death Penalty Information Center, "Searchable Execution Database." Retrieved July 5, 2013 from www.deathpenaltyinfo.org/views-executions?exec_name_1=david+washington&sex=All& sex_1=All&federal=All&foreigner=All&juvenile=All&volunteer=All

Death Penalty Information Center, "State by State Lethal Injection," retrieved August 14, 2013 from www.deathpenaltyinfo.org/state-lethal-injection

Death Penalty Information Center, "States With and Without the Death Penalty," retrieved November 15, 2013, from wwwwww.deathpenaltyinfo.org/states-and-without-death-penalty.

Death Penalty Information Center, "Time on Death Row," retrieved January 26, 2013 from wwwwww.deathpenaltyinfo.org/time-death-row

Death Penalty Information Center, "Troy Davis," retrieved August 3, 2013 from www.deathpen altyinfo.org/troy-davis

Fender, Jessica & Lynn Bartels, "Bid to Repeal Death Penalty Fails in Senate," *Denver Post* (May 6, 2009), retrieved April 13, 2013 from www.denverpost.com/politics/ci_12307296

Gallup, "Death Penalty," retrieved November 15, 2013 from www.gallup.com/poll/1606/death-penalty.aspx

Gallup, "U.S. Death Penalty Support Lowest in More Than 40 Years," retrieved November 30, 2013 from www.gallup.com/poll/165626/death-penalty-support-lowest-years.aspx

Gallup.com, "Death Penalty," retrieved January 12, 2013 from www.gallup.com/poll/1606/death-penalty.aspx

Grann, David, "Trial by Fire: Did Texas Execute an Innocent Man?," *The New Yorker* (Sept. 7, 2009), retrieved July 30, 2013 from www.newyorker.com/reporting/2009/09/07/090907fa_fact_grann?printable=true&currentPage=all

Grissom, Brandi, "Andre Thomas: Mental Health, Criminal Justice Collide," *Texas Tribune* (Feb. 20, 2013), retrieved August 9, 2013 from www.texastribune.org/2013/02/20/andre-thomas-mental-health-and-criminal-justice-co/

Grissom, Brandi, "Andre Thomas: Questions of Competence," *Texas Tribune* (Feb. 26, 2013), retrieved August 9, 2013 from www.texastribune.org/2013/02/26/andre-thomas-ques tions-competency/

Hegarty, Stephanie, "Iran Acid Attack: Ameneh Bahrami's Quest for Justice," *BBC News Middle East* (June 1, 2011), retrieved October 2, 2012 from www.bbc.co.uk/news/world-middle-east-13578731

Illinois Governor's Commission on Capital Punishment, *Report of the Governor's Commission on Capital Punishment* (2002), retrieved July 31, 2013 from http://illinoismurderindictments.law.northwestern.edu/docs/Illinois_Moratorium_Commission_complete-report.pdf

Innocence Project, The, "Understanding the Causes," retrieved July 29, 2013 from www.innocenceproject.org/understand/

"Iranian Man Who Blinded Student Saved From 'Eye for an Eye' Justice," *Telegraph* (July 31, 2011), retrieved October 2, 2012 from www.telegraph.co.uk/news/worldnews/middleeast/iran/8673476/Iranian-man-who-blinded-student-saved-from-eye-for-an-eye-justice.html

Kershaw, Sarah, "Stanley Tookie Williams, Crips Gang Co-Founder, Is Executed," *New York Times* (Dec. 13, 2005), retrieved August 11, 2013 from www.nytimes.com/2005/12/13/national/13cnd-tookie.html?pagewanted=all

Klas, Mary Ellen, "Gov. Rick Scott Signs Bill Speeding Up Executions in Florida," *Miami Herald* (June 14, 2013), retrieved July 26, 2013 from www.miamiherald.com/2013/06/14/v-print/3451849/gov-rick-scott-signs-bill-to-speed.html

Liebman, James S., Jeffrey Fagan, Andrew Gelman, Valerie West, Garth Davies & Alexander Kiss, *A Broken System, Part II: Why There Is So Much Error in Capital Cases, and What Can Be Done About It* (2002), retrieved July 25, 2013 from www2.law.columbia.edu/brokensystem2/report.pdf

Liebman, James S., Jeffrey Fagan & Valerie West, *A Broken System: Error Rates in Capital Cases, 1973–1995*, retrieved July 25, 2013 from www2.law.columbia.edu/instructionalservices/liebman/liebman_final.pdf

Liptak, Adam, "After 24 Years on Death Row, Clemency Is Killer's Final Appeal," *New York Times* (Dec. 2, 2005), retrieved August 11, 2013 from www.nytimes.com/2005/12/02/national/02prison.html

Maryland Commission on Capital Punishment, *Final Report to the General Assembly* (2008), retrieved July 31, 2013 from www.goccp.maryland.gov/capital-punishment/documents/death-penalty-commission-final-report.pdf

"Maryland Governor Signs Repeal of the Death Penalty," *New York Times* (May 2, 2013), retrieved July 31, 2013 from www.nytimes.com/2013/05/03/us/maryland-governor-signs-repeal-of-the-death-penalty.html?pagewanted=print

Massachusetts Governor's Council on Capital Punishment, *Final Report* 3 (2004), retrieved July 31, 2013 from www.lawlib.state.ma.us/docs/5-3-04governorsreportcapitalpunishment.pdf

"Message From ALI Director Lance Liebman," retrieved June 15, 2013 from www.ali.org/_news/10232009.htm

Mid-Atlantic Innocence Project, "Kirk Bloodsworth," retrieved July 31, 2013 from www.exonerate.org/other-local-victories/kirk-bloodsworth/

Mintz, Howard "The Cost of California's Death Penalty," *San Jose Mercury News* (May 16, 2012), retrieved April 13, 2013 from www.mercurynews.com/crime-courts/ci_20497754/cost-californias-death-penalty?

"Movement on the Death Penalty," *New York Times* (May 2, 2013), retrieved July 31, 2013 from www.nytimes.com/2013/05/03/opinion/death-penalty-news.html?pagewanted=print

National Registry of Exonerations, The, "Exonerations Sorted by Sentence Imposed, Death Sentence"), retrieved December 5, 2013 from www.law.umich.edu/special/exoneration/Pages/detaillist.aspx?View={faf6eddb-5a68-4f8f-8a52-2c61f5bf9ea7}&FilterField1=Crime&FilterValue1=8_Murder&&SortField=Sentence&SortDir=Asc&FilterField2=Sentence&FilterValue2=Death

National Registry of Exonerations, The, "Summary View," retrieved December 5, 2013 from www.law.umich.edu/special/exoneration/Pages/browse.aspx (listing 1252 exonerations)

New Jersey Death Penalty Study Commission, *New Jersey Death Penalty Study Commission Report* (2007), retrieved July 31, 2013 from www.njleg.state.nj.us/committees/dpsc_final.pdf

Newport, Frank, "In U.S., 64% Support Death Penalty in Cases of Murder," (Nov. 8, 2010), retrieved August 15, 2013 from www.gallup.com/poll/144284/support-death-penalty-cases-murder.aspx.

O'Malley, Martin, "Repealing Maryland's Death Penalty," *Politico* (March 18, 2013), retrieved March 22, 2013 from www.politico.com/story/2013/03/martin-omalley-repealing-mary lands-death-penalty-88972.html

Paternoster, Raymond et al., *An Empirical Analysis of Maryland's Death Sentencing System With Respect to the Influence of Race and Legal Jurisdiction: Final Report* (2003), retrieved July 4, 2013 from www.newsdesk.umd.edu/pdf/finalrep.pdf

Professor Robert Blecker's Statement to Accompany Testimony Before the New Jersey Death Penalty Study Commission 10/11/06 (Supplemented), retrieved October 6, 2012 from www.google.com/url?sa=t&rct=j&q=&esrc=s&source=web&cd=2&ved=0CCsQFjAB& url=http%3A%2F%2Fwww.cjlf.org%2Ffiles%2FNJDP_BleckerStatement.doc&ei= kohwUIKQJvSH0QHcwIGAAg&usg=AFQjCNH4h6kXpEIobDSkQ-m2ityhO8Vt7g

Proposition 34, Proposed Law, The SAFE California Act, § 3 (2), (3) (2012), retrieved April 13, 2013 from http://vig.cdn.sos.ca.gov/2012/general/pdf/text-proposed-laws-v2.pdf#named dest=prop34

Roman, John, Aaron Chalfin, Aaron Sundquist, Carly Knight & Askar Darmenov, *The Cost of the Death Penalty in Maryland*, Abstract (Urban Institute 2008), retrieved March 23, 2013 from www.urban.org/publications/411625.html

Saad, Lydia, "Racial Disagreement Over Death Penalty Has Varied Historically," *Gallup News Service* (July 30, 2007), retrieved June 26, 2013 from www.gallup.com/poll/28243/racial-disagreement-over-death-penalty-has-varied-historically.aspx

Scheidegger, Kent S., "The Death Penalty and Plea Bargaining to Life Sentences," Working Paper 09–01 (2009) (Sacramento, CA: Criminal Justice Legal Foundation), retrieved March 30, 2013 from www.cjlf.org/publications/papers/wpaper09–01.pdf

Schwarzenegger, Governor Arnold, *Statement of Decision: Request for Clemency by Stanley Williams* (Dec. 12, 2005), retrieved August 11, 2013 from http://graphics8.nytimes.com/packages/ pdf/national/Williams_Clemency_Decision.pdf

Snell, Tracy L., *Capital Punishment, 2011—Statistical Tables* 14 (Table 10) (Washington, DC: U.S. Dept. of Justice, Bureau of Justice Statistics, July 2013), retrieved July 24, 2013 from www. bjs.gov/content/pub/pdf/cp11st.pdf

Stephan, James J., *State Prison Expenditures, 2001* (Washington, DC: U.S. Dept. of Justice, Bureau of Justice Statistics 2004), retrieved March 30, 2013 from http://bjs.gov/content/pub/pdf/ spe01.pdf

Streib, Victor, *Death Penalty for Female Offenders, January 1, 1973, Through December 31, 2012* (Feb. 20, 2013), retrieved July 3, 2013 from www.deathpenaltyinfo.org/documents/Fem DeathDec2012.pdf

Streib, Victor L., *The Juvenile Death Penalty Today: Death Sentences and Executions for Juvenile Crimes, January 1, 1973-February 28, 2005*, p. 3 (issue #77, Oct. 7, 2005), retrieved May 28, 2013 from www.deathpenaltyinfo.org/documents/StreibJuvDP2005.pdf

Texas Coalition to Abolish the Death Penalty, *Death Sentences by County: 1976–2012*, retrieved July 4, 2013 from http://tcadp.org/1976–2012-county-map/

Texas Coalition to Abolish the Death Penalty, *Texas Death Penalty Developments in 2012: The Year in Review* (2013), retrieved July 4, 2013 from www.tcadp.org/TexasDeathPenaltyDevelop ments2012.pdf

Transcript of oral argument, *Furman v. Georgia*, 408 U.S. 238 (1972), retrieved October 8, 2012 from www.oyez.org/cases/1970-1979/1971/1971_69_5003

Transcript of oral argument, *Roper v. Simmons*, retrieved May 30, 2013 from www.oyez.org/ cases/2000-2009/2004/2004_03_633

Transcript of oral argument, *Woodson v. North Carolina,* 428 U.S. 280 (1976), retrieved October 8, 2012 from www.oyez.org/cases/1970-1979/1975/1975_75_5491

U.S. Dept. of Justice, Bureau of Justice Statistics, *Capital Punishment, 2010—Statistical Tables* (Dec. 2011), retrieved January 26, 2013 from http://bjs.ojp.usdoj.gov/content/pub/pdf/cp10st.pdf

U.S. Dept. of Justice, Bureau of Justice Statistics, *Capital Punishment, 2011—Statistical Tables* 5, Table 1 (July 2013), retrieved August 15, 2013 from www.deathpenaltyinfo.org/documents/cp11st.pdf

U.S. Dept. of Justice, Bureau of Justice Statistics, *Homicide Trends in the United States, 1980–2008* (Nov. 2011), retrieved January 25, 2013 from http://bjs.ojp.usdoj.gov/content/pub/pdf/htus8008.pdf

U.S. Dept. of Justice, Bureau of Justice Statistics, *Homicide Trends in the United States,* "Long Term Trends" (2010), retrieved January 25, 2013 from http://bjs.ojp.usdoj.gov/content/pub/pdf/htius.pdf

United States General Accounting Office, *Death Penalty Sentencing: Research Indicates Pattern of Racial Disparities* (GAO/GGD-90–57) (1990), retrieved June 26, 2013 from www.gao.gov/assets/220/212180.pdf

United States Supreme Court, transcript of oral argument, *Coker v. Georgia,* retrieved May 23, 2013 from www.oyez.org/cases/1970-1979/1976/1976_75_5444

Warden, Rob, *First Wrongful Conviction,* retrieved July 29, 2013 from www.law.northwestern.edu/legalclinic/wrongfulconvictions/exonerations/vt/boorn-brothers.html

Welsh-Huggins, Andrew, "Reform Would Limit Death Penalty to Worst Killers," *Columbus Dispatch* (June 28, 2013), retrieved July 3, 2013 from www.dispatch.com/content/stories/local/2013/06/27/death-penalty-reforms-proposed-ohio.html

Judicial Decisions

Abdul-Kabir v. Quarterman, 550 U.S. 233 (2007)

Adams v. Texas, 448 U.S. 38 (1980)

Addington v. Texas, 441 U.S. 418 (1979)

Alabama v. Shelton, 535 U.S. 654 (2002)

Allen v. Ornoski, 435 F.3d 946 (9th Cir.), *cert. den.,* 546 U.S. 1136 (2006)

Arave v. Creech, 507 U.S. 463 (1993)

Argersinger v. Hamlin, 407 U.S. 25 (1972)

Atkins v. Virginia, 536 U.S. 304 (2002)

Baldwin v. New York, 399 U.S. 66 (1970)

Barefoot v. Estelle, 463 U.S. 880 (1983)

Barefoot v. State, 596 S.W.2d 875 (Tex. Crim. App. 1980)

Batson v. Kentucky, 476 U.S. 79 (1986)

Baze v. Rees, 553 U.S. 35 (2008)

Bell v. Cone, 543 U.S. 447 (2005)

Bigby v. State, 892 S.W.2d 864 (Tex. Crim. App. 1994)

Blystone v. Pennsylvania, 494 U.S. 299 (1990)

Booth v. Maryland, 482 U.S. 496 (1987)

Brady v. United States, 397 U.S. 742 (1970)

Burdine v. Johnson, 262 F.3d 336 (5th Cir. 2001) (en banc), *cert. denied,* 535 U.S. 1120 (2002)

Butler v. State, 608 So.2d 314 (Miss. 1992)

California v. Brown, 538 U.S. 545 (1987)

Callins v. Collins, 510 U.S. 1141 (1994)

Cherry v. State, 959 So.2d 702 (Fla. 2007)

Coble v. State, 330 S.W.3d 253 (Tex. Crim. App. 2010), *cert. denied*, 131 S.Ct. 3030 (2011)
Coker v. Georgia, 433 U.S. 584 (1977)
Dawson v. State, 554 S.E.2d 137 (Ga. 2001)
Douglas v. California, 372 U.S. 353 (1963)
Druery v. State, 225 S.W.3d 491, 506–507 (Tex. Crim. App.), *cert. denied*, 552 U.S. 1028 (2007)
Duncan v. Louisiana, 391 U.S. 145 (1968)
Dusky v. United States, 362 U.S. 402 (1960)
Elledge v. Florida, 525 U.S. 944 (1998)
Enmund v. Florida, 458 U.S. 782 (1982)
Estelle v. Smith, 451 U.S. 454 (1981)
Estrada v. State, 313 S.W.3d 274 (Tex. Crim. App. 2010), *cert. denied*, 131 S.Ct. 905 (2011)
Evans v. Muncy, 498 U.S. 927 (1990)
Ewing v. California, 538 U.S. 11 (2003)
Ex parte Garland, 71 U.S. (4 Wall.) 333 (1866)
Ex parte Herrera, 828 S.W.2d 8 (Tex. Crim. App. 1992)
Ex parte Thomas, 2009 WL 693606 (Tex. Crim. App. 2009)
Ex parte Thomas, 2010 WL 1795738 (Tex. Crim. App. 2010)
Fierro v. Gomez, 77 F.3d 301 (9th Cir. 1996)
Ford v. Wainwright, 477 U.S. 399 (1986)
Franklin v. Lynaugh, 487 U.S. 164 (1988)
Franqui v. State, 59 So.3d 82 (Fla. 2011)
Free v. Peters, 12 F.3d 700 (7th Cir. 1993), *cert. denied*, 513 U.S. 967 (1994)
Free v. Peters, 19 F.3d 389 (7th Cir.), *cert. denied*, 513 U.S. 967 (1994)
Furman v. Georgia, 408 U.S. 238 (1972)
Gacy v. Welborne, 994 F.2d 305 (7th Cir.), *cert. denied*, 510 U.S. 899 (1993)
Gates v. Cook, 376 F.3d 323 (5th Cir. 2004)
Gideon v. Wainwright, 372 U.S. 335 (1963)
Gilmore v. Utah, 429 U.S. 1012 (1976)
Glass v. Louisiana, 471 U.S. 1080 (1985)
Godfrey v. Georgia, 446 U.S. 420 (1980)
Godinez v. Martinez, 509 U.S. 389 (1993)
Gomez v. Fierro, 519 U.S. 918 (1996)
Gomez v. United States District Court for the Northern District of California, 503 U.S. 653 (1992)
Gray v. Lucas, 463 U.S. 1237 (1983)
Gray v. Mississippi, 481 U.S. 648 (1987)
Gregg v. Georgia, 428 U.S. 153 (1976)
Gregg v. State, 210 S.E.2d 659 (Ga. 1974)
Grigsby v. Mabry, 569 F. Supp. 1273 (E.D. Ark. 1983)
Grigsby v. Mabry, 758 F.2d 226 (8th Cir. 1985) (en banc)
Groseclose v. Dutton, 609 F.Supp. 1432 (M.D. Tenn. 1985), *appeal dismissed*, 788 F.2d 356 (6th Cir. 1986), *vacated on other grounds*, 829 F.2d 581 (6th Cir. 1987)
Hall v. Florida, ___ S.Ct. ___, 2013 WL 3153535 (2013)
Hall v. State, 109 So.3d 704 (Fla. 2012)
Harmelin v. Michigan, 501 U.S. 957 (1991)
Harris v. Alabama, 513 U.S. 504 (1995)
Hernandez v. New York, 500 U.S. 352 (1991)
Herrera v. Collins, 502 U.S. 1085 (1992)
Herrera v. Collins, 506 U.S. 390 (1993)
Hill v. Humphrey, 662 F.3d 1335 (11th Cir. 2011) (en banc), *cert. denied*, 132 S.Ct. 2727 (2012)
Hitchcock v. Dugger, 481 U.S. 393 (1987)
House v. Bell, 547 U.S. 518 (2006)

In re Commonwealth of Virginia, 677 S.E.2d 236 (Va. 2009)

In re Davis, 557 U.S. 952 (2009)

In re Davis, 2010 WL 3385081 (S.D. Ga.), *appeal dismissed*, 625 F.3d 716 (11th Cir. 2010), *cert. denied*, 131 S.Ct. 1787 (2011)

In re Hill, 715 F.3d 284 (11th Cir. 2013)

In re Kemmler, 136 U.S. 436 (1890)

In re Winship, 397 U.S. 358 (1970)

J.E.B. v. Alabama, 511 U.S. 127 (1994)

Joubert v. State, 124 S.W.2d 368 (Tex. Crim. App. 1938)

Jurek v. State, 522 S.W.2d 934, 945 (Tex. Crim. App. 1975)

Jurek v. Texas, 428 U.S. 262 (1976)

Kansas v. Marsh, 548 U.S. 163 (2006)

Kelly v. California, 555 U.S. 1020 (2008)

Kennedy v. Louisiana, 554 U.S. 407 (2008)

Kennedy v. Louisiana, 554 U.S. 945 (2008)

King v. State, 553 S.W.2d 105 (Tex. Crim. App. 1977), *cert. denied*, 434 U.S. 1088 (1978)

Knight v. Florida, Moore v. Nebraska, 528 U.S. 990 (1999)

Lackey v. State, 819 S.W.2d 111, 132 (Tex. Crim. App 1989), *abrogated, Tennard v. Dretke*, 542 U.S. 274 (2004)

Lackey v. Texas, 514 U.S. 1045 (1995)

Lockett v. Ohio, 438 U.S. 586 (1978)

Lockhart v. McCree, 476 U.S. 162 (1986)

Louisiana ex rel. Francis v. Resweber, 329 U.S. 459 (1947)

Lowenfield v. Phelps, 484 U.S. 231 (1988)

Maples v. State, 758 So.2d 1 (Ala. Crim. App.), *aff'd, Ex parte Maples*, 758 So.2d 81 (Ala. 1999)

Maples v. Thomas, 132 S.Ct. 912 (2012)

Martinez v. Ryan, 132 S.Ct. 1309 (2012)

McCleskey v. Kemp, 481 U.S. 279 (1987)

McDuff v. State, 939 S.W.2d 607 (Tex. Crim. App.), *cert. denied*, 522 U.S. 944 (1997)

McFarland v. Scott, 512 U.S. 1256 (1994)

McGautha v. California, 402 U.S. 183 (1971)

McKoy v. North Carolina, 494 U.S. 433 (1990)

McQuiggin v. Perkins, 133 S.Ct. 1924 (2013)

Miller v. Alabama, 132 S.Ct. 2455 (2012)

Miller-El v. Dretke, 545 U.S. 231 (2005)

Mills v. Maryland, 486 U.S. 367 (1988)

Minister of Justice v. Burns, 2001 SCC 7 (Canada 2001)

Morales v. Tilton, 465 F. Supp.2d 972 (N.D. Cal. 2006)

Morgan v. Illinois, 504 U.S. 719 (1992)

Murphy v. State, 112 S.W.3d 592 (Tex. Crim. App. 2003) *cert. denied*, 541 U.S. 940 (2004)

Murray v. Giarratano, 492 U.S. 1 (1989)

New State Ice Co. v. Liebmann, 285 U.S. 262 (1932)

Nixon v. State, 2 So.3d 137 (Fla. 2009)

North Carolina v. Alford, 400 U.S. 25 (1970)

Ohio Adult Parole Authority v. Woodard, 523 U.S. 272 (1998)

Panetti v. Quarterman, 551 U.S. 930 (2007)

Parker v. Randolph, 442 U.S. 62 (1979)

Payne v. Tennessee, 501 U.S. 808 (1991)

Pennsylvania v. Finley, 481 U.S. 551 (1987)

Penry v. Lynaugh, 492 U.S. 302 (1989)

People v. Anderson, 493 P.2d 880 (Cal. 1972)

People v. LaValle, 817 N.E.2d 341 (N.Y. 2004)
People v. Taylor, 878 N.E.2d 969 (N.Y. 2007)
People v. Williams, 751 P.2d 901 (Cal. 1988)
Perry v. Louisiana, 498 U.S. 38 (1990)
Peterkin v. Jeffes, 855 F.2d 1021 (3d Cir. 1988)
Powell v. Alabama, 287 U.S. 45 (1932)
Proffitt v. Florida, 428 U.S. 242 (1976)
Pulley v. Harris, 465 U.S. 37 (1984)
Reid v. Covert, 354 U.S. 1 (1957)
Ring v. Arizona, 536 U.S. 584 (2002)
Roberts (Harry) v. Louisiana, 431 U.S. 633 (1977)
Roberts (Stanislaus) v. Louisiana, 428 U.S. 325 (1976)
Robinson v. California, 370 U.S. 660 (1962)
Rompilla v. Beard, 545 U.S. 374 (2005)
Roper v. Simmons, 543 U.S. 551 (2005)
Ross v. Moffitt, 417 U.S. 600 (1974)
Ruffin v. State, 270 S.W.3d 586 (Tex. Crim. App. 2008)
Rummel v. Estelle, 445 U.S. 263, 288 (1980)
Saldano v. State, 232 S.W.3d 77 (Tex. Crim. App. 2007)
Saldano v. Texas, 530 U.S. 1212 (2000)
Sawyer v. Whitley, 505 U.S. 333 (1992)
Schlup v. Delo, 513 U.S. 298 (1995)
Scott v. Illinois, 440 U.S. 367 (1979)
Simmons v. Roper, 112 S.W.3d 397 (Mo. 2003) (en banc)
Singleton v. Norris, 319 F.3d 1018 (8th Cir.) (en banc), *cert. denied*, 540 U.S. 832 (2003)
Soering v. United Kingdom, 11 Eur. H.R. Rep. 439 (1989)
Solesbee v. Balkcom, 339 U.S. 9 (1950)
Spaziano v. Florida, 468 U.S. 447 (1984)
Stanford v. Kentucky, 492 U.S. 361 (1989)
State v. Mata, 745 N.W.2d 229 (Neb. 2008)
State v. Perry, 610 So.2d 746 (La. 1992)
State v. Ross, 863 A.2d 654 (Conn. 2005)
State v. Simmons, 944 S.W.2d 165 (Mo.) (en banc), *cert. denied*, 522 U.S. 953 (1997)
Strickland v. Washington, 466 U.S. 668 (1984)
Sumner v. Shuman, 483 U.S. 66 (1987)
Swain v. Alabama, 380 U.S. 202 (1965)
Tedder v. State, 322 So.2d 908 (Fla. 1975)
Thomas v. State, 2008 WL 4531976 (Tex. Crim. App. 2008)
Thompson v. Oklahoma, 487 U.S. 815 (1988)
Tison v. Arizona, 481 U.S. 137 (1987)
Trevino v. Thaler, 133 S.Ct. 1911 (2013)
Tuilaepa v. California, 512 U.S. 967 (1994)
United States v. Garsson, 291 F. 646 (S.D.N.Y. 1923)
United States v. McVeigh, 153 F.3d 1166 (10th Cir. 1998), *cert. denied*, 526 U.S. 1007 (1999)
United States v. Quinones, 205 F.Supp.2d 256 (S.D.N.Y. 2002)
United States v. Quinones, 313 F.3d 49 (2d Cir. 2002), *rehearing denied*, 317 F.3d 86 (2d Cir. 2003)
Valle v. Florida, 132 S.Ct. 1 (2011)
Wainwright v. Witt, 469 U.S. 412 (1985)
Walton v. Arizona, 497 U.S. 639 (1990)
Washington v. Harper, 494 U.S. 210 (1990)
Whitmore v. Arkansas, 495 U.S. 149 (1990)

Wiggins v. Smith, 539 U.S. 510 (2003)
Wilkerson v. Utah, 99 U.S. 130 (1879)
Williams v. Taylor, 529 U.S. 362 (2000)
Witherspoon v. Illinois, 391 U.S. 510 (1968)
Woodson v. North Carolina, 428 U.S. 280 (1976)
Woodward v. Alabama, ___ S.Ct. ___, 2013 WL 6050109 (2013)
Zant v. Stephens, 297 S.E.2d 1 (Ga. 1982)
Zant v. Stephens, 462 U.S. 862 (1983)

Index